Building Cyberstores

Installation, Transaction Processing, and Management

Martin Nemzow

McGraw-Hill

New York   San Francisco   Washington, D.C.   Auckland   Bogotá
Caracas   Lisbon   London   Madrid   Mexico City   Milan
Montreal   New Delhi   San Juan   Singapore
Sydney   Tokyo   Toronto

Library of Congress Cataloging-in-Publication Data

Nemzow, Martin A. W.
    Building cyberstores : installation, transaction processing, and
management / Martin Nemzow.
        p.   cm.
    Includes bibliographical references and index.
    ISBN 0-07-913090-9 (pbk.)
    1. Electronic commerce—United States—Case studies.   2. Internet
marketing—United States—Case studies.   3. Web sites—Design and
construction.   I. Title.
    HF5548.325.U6N45   1997
    658.8'00285'4678—dc21

                                                97-2163
                                                CIP

McGraw-Hill

*A Division of The **McGraw·Hill** Companies*

Copyright © 1997 by The McGraw-Hill Companies, Inc. All rights reserved. Printed in the United States of America. Except as permitted under the United States Copyright Act of 1976, no part of this publication may be reproduced or distributed in any form or by any means, or stored in a data base or retrieval system, without the prior written permission of the publisher.

1 2 3 4 5 6 7 8 9 0   DOC/DOC   9 0 2 1 0 9 8 7

P/N 046388-3
PART OF
ISBN 0-07-913090-9

The sponsoring editor for this book was Steve M. Elliot and the production supervisor was Suzanne W. B. Rapcavage. It was set in Century Schoolbook by Graphic World, Inc.

Printed and bound by R. R. Donnelley & Sons Company.

 This book was printed on recycled, acid-free paper containing a minimum of 50% recycled de-inked fiber.

McGraw-Hill books are available at special quantity discounts to use as premiums and sales promotions, or for use in corporate training programs. For more information, please write to the Director of Special Sales, McGraw-Hill, Inc. 11 West 19th Street, New York, NY 10011. Or contact your local bookstore.

Contents

Preface

Introduction

The cyberstore is about lowering the cost for distributing a message. It is about cutting the cost for processing transactions. The *cyberstore* or *cybershop* is aimed at corporations, not-for-profit operations, and governmental agencies needing a 24-hour-per-day, 7-day-per-week sales and support presence. A cyberstore is an Internet-based point-of-sale presence. The *cybermall* is a central web presence providing commercial services to a range of retail and wholesale vendors. Although the strategy for different types of organizations is indeed distinct, the fundamental paradigm for "doing business" on the Internet is the same everywhere and is still evolving.

However, recognize that organizations do "commerce" differently so that this Internet-enablement paradigm will not work for every organization. The organization must be willing to integrate the Internet into workflow and perhaps modify the workflow to successfully include the Internet as a business communication sales and marketing channel. The technical complexity in establishing a cyberstore is not in the construction of the transactional website, but rather in the complex integration of a new point-of-sales (POS) channel into the workflow of an organization.

While I think that the Internet and the World Wide Web (WWW) are here to stay, the current trend for haphazard exploration will soon wear out in favor of more routine and industrial applications. The WWW is a file distribution platform and transactional processing metaphor on the Internet. WWW files can be data, images, sound, video, data, database records or transactions, or more complex compound documents. The WWW browser is really about a common graphical user interface that transcends platforms, operating systems, and even written language. It provides uniform access to documents and anything else that can be displayed as a "document." This industrial workflow makes it useful for transaction processing, low-cost virtual malls, cheaper mass marketing, on-line magazines, documentation, and product or service demonstrations. Because the Internet has more information on it than all the libraries in the world, and because even libraries are now adding their unique collections to the Internet, it provides a universal communications access medium that can support text, images, sounds, virtual reality, and video phone teleconferencing in real time. It represents the integration of mass-market communication technologies and distribution methods.

Nevertheless, any website or cyberstore is not a stand-alone entity but rather an addition to existing organizational activities that should integrate into existing infrastructures of host mainframes, local area networks (LANs), and computer telephone integration (CTI) services. Although it seems trendy, few websites can stand alone without content and purpose driven by external real-world activities. The organization workflows can now be integrated into a website. For best business practices, the new workflow should mesh with existing real-world practices and activities. While the concept of the cyberstore might seem new, it is really just an extension of preexisting services over a *new* distribution channel. Internet-enablement is an extension of catalogs on disks and CD-ROMs now updated constantly and with transaction processing capabilities.

I attribute the current disparity for these low-tech computer transactions as the prevalent disparity between the demographic composition of a catalog shopper and the average Internet user. That will change soon, though, as business-to-business electronic commerce begins to drive the electronic commerce integration technology. In other words, cyberstore activity must work within existing workflows as an adjunct to, not as a prototype for, organizational change. For practical website development, this means technical integration and tool selection should mesh with business strategies rather than challenge it. You can select the best of each technical solution described in this book to create a cyberstore that will fail quickly and waste a lot of money. Instead, *integrate* carefully, using products that will interoperate, implementing with trained people, clear objectives, and obvious systems to track the customers, the sales, and the cyberstore site hits, and where all the money goes.

Building Cyberstores

Time is of the essence for success, but technology is both the enabler and the disabler. I am aware of many programming tools that make almost anything possible on the Internet, from migration of client/server applications to complicated web interfaces with automation, multimedia extravaganzas that represent a slow torture to analog modem users, to the detailed marketing research possible with WWW hypertext forms and complex enabling scripts. If you use all these tools, you increase the development time for a website, complicate long-term site management, add risks for project completion, and raise the costs for upgrades and makeovers. Building a website is like baking a cake—you can select all good ingredients, the finest cookware, and use a new oven and you get results that range from exceptional to something that is not pretty, doesn't taste good, and no one will touch. With all the platforms, servers, development tools, and functional components necessary for cyberstores, you could also devise an integration goulash that will be unappealing (even if you use the best flour, sugar, chocolate, eggs, raspberries, and . . . black pepper, salmon, eggplant, cayenne, rice, potatoes, carrots, and parsnip). When you mix strategies, designs, marketing information, techniques, and tools without an appropriate plan, you create a foul looking, foul smelling, upsetting casserole.

In fact, using tools outside your normal expertise, familiarity, and ongoing experience is detrimental to website success. Pick tools that do things you currently cannot do and need to do, but recall that you have an installed base of transaction processing workflows. You also risk creating a trendy site that requires constant makeovers to remain stylish and desirable, or risks becoming dated and unfashionable. You also risk emphasizing image over substance. Consider the tensions between style, presentation, and content and the commensurate implementation costs for each.

Technology alone may not be your answer, nor even a significant part of it. Furthermore, the successful websites I have seen avoid the high-tech novelties (including complex frames, sound, movies, applets, garish color schemes, dense graphical content, and animated graphics) and focus on content, service, and presentation of relevant information. The best sites employ a simple visual interface that may seem primitive but is not necessarily technically or executionally primitive.

Simple tends to be efficient and effective. The best websites include tables of contents, indexes, keyword searches, and rapid access to information, solutions and answers, currency and relevance, and the commercial acquisition of products or services. They are consistent and provide clear information about the structure of the site and a client's relative position or path through the site. Realize that newspapers, paperback novels, and printed catalogs thrive in spite of radio, TV, and the newest media explosion, the Internet website. Remember that reality and plan your site within the scope of what the Internet does best, namely, site search capabilities, graphical display, lower cost access to information, and lowered costs for transaction processing.

Simple tends to be inexpensive and efficient. The returns on multimillion dollar websites are likely to be less than stellar; they tend to represent gaudy, interactive or dynamic sites that exceed the needs of a true cyberstore. Start simple and expand from there. Some sites are effective revenue generators, providing returns that average $0.15 for every $1.00 in revenue and $1.00 invested in site design, development, and maintenance. This is not a great stand-alone business, but one that can be combined and can augment existing channels.

I have seen thousands of sites that confuse me, turn me off, aggravate me, and leave a poor impression. I call them for information, and they ask me increduously, "Didn't you see our website?" My answer is that I did see their website, and that is why I want information from a human (typically because the site did not address fundamental questions). Some sites contain lost pointers and broken links to locations long since moved; lack basic contact information so I can call for help, send electronic mail (E-mail), or just talk to a person who can walk me through their maze of disorganized pages; or contain pages and topics written in techno-babble, suggesting everything but confirming or describing nothing. Can you imagine pages missing from a magazine or an article continuation to a page that simply doesn't exist or pointers to forthcoming events and articles that never appear? Most people cannot tolerate that in print, much less in the Internet where alternatives exist in multiplicity.

Some of the vendors apologize for their lack of home pages, effective home pages, or quality implementations. They state the excuse of the "shoemaker's children" syndrome—the situation where the shoemaker is so busy making shoes for everybody else he has no time to make shoes for his own children. I do not accept that argument, and find it spurious. A vendor site represents a significant sales and marketing opportunity that should not be squandered. It also represents a learning experience (not on a customer's time) to try new techniques and test cyberstore integration.

Thoughts for Readers

There are three thoughts to consider as you read this book; explore web presentation technology; integrate site hit trackers, site management tools, database and form engines; and think about the viability of some remarkable web development and migration tools. The tools really are exceptional, even though they are just the first generation of web and Internet tools and represent repackaging and redeployment of existing tools. Although the tools are first generation, you really can implement anything you can imagine. But, will you want to? Many of the marketing people for these tools are striving to get press notice and developer "mindshare" for products that are "me too" or better served by less flexible but more integral middleware solutions. For example, Java is an interesting development tool, but not always the best one for the cyberstore and all the functions required for a fully integrated workflow. Likewise, ActiveX is a client-side Windows-only solution, while Perl and Common Gateway Interface (CGI) applets represent unique process threads and a significant aggregate performance overhead.

The first thought to consider is how to get your message through the noisy din of the tens of thousands of websites, thousands of commercial sites, and the flourishing web-based catalog sales stores and virtual malls. Only a few sites of each type will survive and thrive. Perhaps only one or two. The handful of survivors will control an entire niche within just a few years based on price, quality, convenience, integrity, or service issues. Think about this assertion: a website is already a commodity item where duplicates are ridiculous. Although the Internet is cheaper as a mass-marketing medium, there is competition comparable to any U.S. Route 1 with strip malls lining both sides of the street for miles on end. If you get junk mail, you are likely to receive two pounds per day, which is the U.S. national average; message density is inversely proportional to message delivery cost. Just as some metropolitan areas are either over- or undersaturated with retail stores and wholesalers, you need to assess your message and how it fills a viable niche to get through that noisy din.

The second thought is about the relationship of the cyberstore to other existing sales channels and promotional techniques. The cyberstore is not too different from any other ordinary retail point-of-purchase procedures and requires the same point-of-sales transaction processing systems to track and control operations. In addition, back office flow requires financial discipline, reconciliation, asset control, investment planning, inventory tracking, and all the same sales lead generation and marketing management as any other retail or wholesale distribution operation. Although some technical, physical, and workflow differences set the cyberstore apart from retail sales, reseller support, and even telephone catalog sales, it is still a business that requires extensive integration into standard financial control systems.

The third thought relates to site content and how the website is really a derivative of magazines, catalogs, TV shows, movies, fads, and lifestyles. The library stacks are littered with defunct magazines (remember literary mainstays such as *Saturday Review* and *Look*?), Ronco with its glib presentations of kitchen gadgets you never knew you needed and I guess people never really needed, TV serials like "M*A*S*H" that became redundant episode after episode after a few years, and products such as hoola hoops, Rubix Cubes, Cabbage Patch dolls, and pet rocks that eventually grew stale and doomed the vendor to oblivion or at least quiet business solitude. Ambience and character originiate initial appeal and uniqueness that does not replace or transcend content.

Content is more important than the technology or imagery used to build a site. The accumulation of the best of everything to make a website is unlikely to yield the best website. With all the whiz-bang technology like interactive TV, surround-sound movies, CD-ROM games, and personal websites, shock-jock Howard Stern succeeds with old-fashioned talk radio and Dave Barry remakes the ancient art of the newspaper editorial. These are old technologies remade by charismatic content, consistency, and personal character and integrity. After these two people had succeeded within an initial medium, "common" TV and paperbacks extended their successes. Their success is not generated by advancing technology or using new technology but rather by basic application of old tools and desirable content. Thus, your site needs a purpose, a thesis, a niche, and an ongoing reason for existing. The website, even the cyberstore, is content driven. Everything you do to build your cyberstore must fundamentally relate to a focused purpose to pierce the noisy din of the tens of thousands of existing websites.

Martin Nemzow

Building Cyberstores

Overview

Introduction

Building Cyberstores: Installation, Transaction Processing, and Management shows you how to build a functional commercial site and Internet-enable an organization for automated transaction processing and round-the-clock information distribution and technical support. The book is technical and covers the detailed mechanics of integrating databases, the Internet, sales and marketing, organizational workflow, presentations, media content, and advertising. This book defines server-side techniques for building useful websites and addresses client (user) browser and activity issues only as it relates to site construction techniques and process limitations. Threads of business information and strategy are woven throughout the book to balance the technicalities and address the cohesion that must exist between a cauldron of complex components and corporate culture.

Just as there are many ways to make money on the Internet, there are also many more ways to lose money. Commercial websites, kiosks, and round-the-clock support facilities are complex integration projects of websites, support tools, databases, financial transaction systems, and designs that attract and appeal to the diverse community on the Internet. *Building Cyberstores* shows how and why the Internet represents a new communications conduit for doing business and the technical implementations to succeed at the task. The Internet provides a fantastic opportunity to extend a local organization to a global presence with minimal capital, no physical global presence, and limited inventory assets. For example, a small manufacturer or specialty retailer can reach out beyond the indigenous territorial market and sell to customers anywhere.

If you are planning a website or extending a simple site to encompass transaction processing, there are many tools, Internet sources, and examples on the Internet to follow step by step . . . from the cyberstore built for under $10,000 and thirty hours of work to the commercial sites supporting electronic commerce costing a minimum of $1 million. IDC Research estimates that the average commercial site requires an initial investment of $1.3 million while Forrester Research pegs minimum development costs at $3.4 million. Holiday Inn worldwide spent $300,000 for its reservation booking system and has spent another $560,000 for upgrades and maintenance. In contrast to these high costs, Holiday Inn and others estimate that it costs $2 on the web to generate each sales lead versus $9 to $24 for direct mail and cold calling.

However, realize that the downside to the Internet is that there is an explosion of information and application techniques that are not pertinent to you. A salesperson can make a customer feel comfortable about making a purchase in the first place, and real technical or server support people can resolve problems likely to become public relations nightmares if mishandled. If you think that the Internet and cyberstores represent a better mousetrap shown in Figure 1.1, but do not have a clue as to why you need a mousetrap and for that matter, why you need yet a better one, this book is certainly a place to start. If you do not understand how to implement the cyberstore, this book shows you how to make certain that the bait you set will attract your existing customers or the customers you want to attract and will work on these demographic groups, and that the trap will work to transact real business and is the appropriate size for the customer demographics. If the trap is too small, the customer is stung; if the trap is too big, the customer slips through the marketing strategy.

So many software companies, one of the first groups to implement on-line sales on the Internet, are experiencing an average of 100,000 downloads of demos per month and sales to that same group of only 0.0017 percent. If the margin for that software is $100 per unit, the cyberstore is generating $1700 a month. Does that income cover the setup costs and ongoing maintenance, and make it worthwhile to upgrade the site with more products

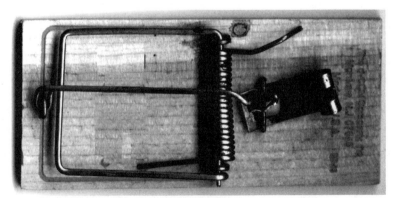

Figure 1.1 Make sure you have customers before setting the trap.

and better marketing techniques? Part of the success strategy for the cyber-store requires bait for the trap, which means marketing position, product, price, and placement. If that sounds like Marketing 101, it is, and not just Website Design 101 or Database/Web Hypertext Connectivity 101. These "technologies" go hand in hand to compromise and sustain each other in the successful website.

The Internet and on-line shopping will draw you in, mesmerize you, and waste your precious time. If you doubt this truth, create a plan for your cyber-store and what you think it should do. Commit that plan to paper so that you will have an accounting of your initial plans to contrast with the supplements you will add as you learn more. Allocate an hour surfing the Internet and note how many solutions you locate for the features you desire. The odds are you will be dazzled by technology you might never have imagined and each one becomes another path to explore and upgrade for your initial web plan. The search and the implementation process become exponentially larger as you drill into the technology. You will find multiple solutions for each feature you want to imple-ment and will add at least as many new functions to your cyberstore as you ini-tially had envisioned. This book focuses on the core business issues and on the technology needed to achieve the goal of creating a functional transaction pro-cessing website in a realistic time frame. The task is not all that difficult, as de-tailed in the six chapters of this book and the companion CD-ROM.

Purpose of the Book

Building Cyberstores: Installation, Transaction Processing, and Management presents practical information about website design, planning, installation, service, usage, utility, and troubleshooting. This book details the technology for implementation—usually not the simple technology tricks for program-ming websites, but the more complex integration mastery topics. However, this book does detail the interconnection of database technology with web pages and transaction processing for web-enabled interactive pages for sur-veying, remote database queries, and collection of data for order entry, credit card processing, and allied Internet financial transactions.

Cyberstores are about process, function, integrity, workflow, performance, and the images that create site and sales activity. In the tradition of this book and the cyberstore concept, Figure 1.2 positions the cyberstore as a box of laundry detergent.

The soapbox metaphor is uniquely appropriate because it reduces the cyberstore to a plain commodity (which it really is) and it recalls the insignif-icant differences that make product branding over content so important in many consumer markets. I use the word "consumer" as a generic label for any person buying information, product, or services of all types from a website. A consumer can refer to a mass-market consumer, an industrial buyer, or a reader who is looking at websites for information about legal services, web

Figure 1.2 *Building Cyberstores* shows you everything you need; just add components that match your plan and platform.

tools, website construction techniques, and also to "users" and "surfers" only browsing websites to see what is there. Everybody is a consumer.

A cyberstore and the tools that create it are not that far removed from other simple consumer products. If there is technology that defines the successful cyberstore, it seems to be similar to the differences between one brand of detergent and another. Just as success with some detergents is dependent on the mineral hardness of the wash water, the type of washing machine, loading characteristics, and temperature, success with your cyberstore may come down to design, integrity, message, and integration with existing resources. The book shows how a cyberstore is not a simple product or solution but rather a complex integration activity.

Building Cyberstores defines the *cyberstore* as an on-line place to conduct business for corporations, not-for-profit agencies, and governmental organizations. The *cybershop* is a small cyberstore with a minimum number of products, limited process integration, and virtually no need for a financial tracking system integrated into that process. The *cybermall* is a front for multiple entities, and is analogous to shopping malls. Two varieties exist. The simplest cybermall is a marketing mechanism to attract customers to a website that contains links to all the mall participants. The second and more complex cybermall consists of an organization building, managing, and processing all aspects of cybershopping, including advertising, marketing, product positioning, transaction processing, and even fulfillment. Some people might narrowly define the cyberstore as an on-line electronic retail showroom or sales catalog; however, this demotes the complete value of the Internet website for interactive transaction processing. A cyberstore provides some or all of these functions:

- A 24-hour per day, 7-day per week intelligent access point
- A presence comparable (equal) to any other Internet site
- Complete product or service line presentation
- Complete product or service descriptions and pricing
- On-line samples and demonstrations
- Delivery of multimedia (real-time streaming or runtime files)
- Complex presale computer-based training
- Ordering information
- Order taking (forms fill-in)
- Order processing
- Shipping details and pricing
- Transactional payments (credit card, virtual cash, EDI, drafts, ECH)
- Ordering fulfillment
- Order delivery (information, reports, and software)
- Order status and delivery tracking information
- Customer or constituent survey
- Phrase or keyword searching
- Context or text searching (random text search)
- Database lookup
- Service processing with remote/local software
- Client/server processing
- On-line help desk
- Fax back of documents to fulfill requests or provide feedback of orders

- Complex computer-based training and help videos
- Emergency response (E-mail, beeper, pager, call-back, Internet phone, Internet video phone, fax back, or download of documents, patches, and bug fixes)

There are many detriments to a cyberstore, not the least of which is the setup costs, maintenance costs, and resources required to make it run well. Many cyberstores suck resources and attention from other more important and lucrative organizational activities. Even not-for-profit enterprises have strategies and goals that can be diverted by resources flowing into a cyberstore. Keep those issues in perspective and your eye on your strategies as you read through this book. Some of the negatives include:

- Valuable information source for competitors
- A possible security and financial resource leak
- Possible loose access to Intranet information
- A technical hurdle
- Maintenance nightmare
- Management diversion
- Process flow disaster
- Technical support drain
- A pink elephant with limited economic value
- A financial drain
- No net return

Building Cyberstores is designed primarily to answer some serious business and technical questions you may not have considered yet. Much of the material in this book relates to cyberstore plumbing, database integration, middleware tools, platform limitations and choices, and how to actually build pages, make them interactive, and get paid by credit card and other cash substitutes. Some of the material may seem very business-oriented and below the threshold of a technical book; however, a cyberstore, whatever its category, is a business endeavor and should balance the business needs of available, reliable, and practical technical solutions with logical scripts and workflows so that a typical user can use the site, wants to use it, and returns again and again. You do not want to create a *cybersore* that confuses, confounds, and repels users after you have spent at least $100,000 building that website.

Intended audience

The primary audience of this book is people at any organization seeking to lower its costs for interorganization financial transactions. The Internet provides a less costly route to distribute and process nearly every type of transaction. Appropriate audiences include commercial organizations trying to move business out to the Internet, create a high-tech presence, and provide 24-hour-per-day sales and service every day of the week. The audience also includes workers at governmental agencies, overloaded with phone calls and faxes, and constituents seeking the same answers and the same materials easily provided by a data-driven interactive website. This book speaks to the people in nonprofit and not-for-profit groups needing a forum to educate and distribute information, solicit donations, and help keep people connected and in touch.

Building Cyberstores is aimed at people who work from home, telecommuters, MIS directors, industry consultants, network managers, workgroup managers, application developers building client/server and distributed networking applications, support technicians, and computer professionals. It is for anyone who uses the Internet for communication, to provide site-to-site or multisite connectivity and transaction processing, or who wants to learn about creating a fully functional cyberstore. This book is also a useful teaching tool; it covers many practical aspects of establishing a website, building a website hosted by a service provider, designing attractive and practical commercial sites, and bypassing the many security and legal hurdles of doing business on the Internet.

Book content

The content of *Building Cyberstores* is straightforward. This book walks you through the process of creating a functional website for on-line transaction processing, database integration, graphics design, help desks, and electronic payment; it helps you pick the tools that work and match strategic goals with realistic implementation. The Preface stated that you can do almost anything with a website; this needs to be tempered by budget, time, risk assessment, and your ability to withstand a complex tool, platform, and code integration project.

This book includes many website screen shots. Some show interesting or significant sites, others demonstrate the best or the worst in site design, and still other shots include my annotations to call your attention to important attributes, functionality, and results from certain development tools or skills. Although the new releases of the Microsoft and Netscape browsers condense the size of the tool bars and frame borders and hide more features in drop-down menus or floating toolbars, the screen shots in this book frequently show Netscape Navigator so as to include the text of the URL (universal resource location); indeed, you might want to go there yourself. Just note that IP (Internet protocol) addresses (of the form 999:999:999:999) and even the friendlier URLs (of the form http://www.company.com) are both addresses to websites. These addresses change over time as sites generate flexible IP addresses and organizations change service providers or just change names. An address of the form file://p:/netware/volume3/data/ indicates a file resource on a local disk drive, or as defined in this expressed example, a network file server volume. The form ftp://company.com indicates an Internet file archive site. If the location of a site has changed, use a search engine to relocate it, or see Chapter 4 for finding specific resources for faulty or incorrect URLs. The book site (at http://www.networkperf.com/cyberstores) is maintained with functional linkages to many sites.

Structure of the book

This preface presents the organization of *Building Cyberstores*. As an acknowledgment of the reader's valuable time and the many layers of building cybershops, cyberstores, and cybermalls, Figure 1.3 illustrates the design and flow of the knowledge contained within this book.

This chapter provides a general overview of the book, explaining the purpose, audience, book content, and structure.

Chapter 2 presents the business and technical fundamentals of Internet sites and the use of databases for *interactive* queries and *dynamic* world wide web (WWW) pages. This chapter explains the purpose and fundamental technical details to integrate search dialogs, surveys, E-mail, and database transaction processing into a website. It details how to establish merchant accounts for virtual cash payments, electronic data interchange (EDI) used mostly by large retailers and manufacturers, bank transfers, and credit card payments.

Chapter 3 shows the effects of different platforms on the cyberstore both in terms of design and development and operation. Issues include performance, security, cost per transaction, upsize potential, integration with existing workflows and processes, and a diverse range of transaction software and hardware. Several sections discuss how to hurdle some of the interconnectivity problems with Firewalls, routers, web servers, Intranets, local networks, and host mainframes.

Chapter 4 details the steps required to build a functional cyberstore. This chapter shows how to establish a server; build pages with interactive connections into databases, E-mail, and queries; and how to get paid with credit cards, EDI, cybercash, and other electronic equivalents to money.

Chapter 5 presents real case studies of Internet sites—where they are, why they were made, and how the site works for its owner. This chapter includes a lot of the nitty-gritty information behind the site, the rationale for decisions in the look and feel of the site, and how technology, marketing, and product advertising defined the development process and the thoughts for future enhancements. This chapter is a practical look at what works and what doesn't.

Chapter 6 describes the content of the companion CD-ROM, and the installation process of the applications, demonstrations, and various support docu-

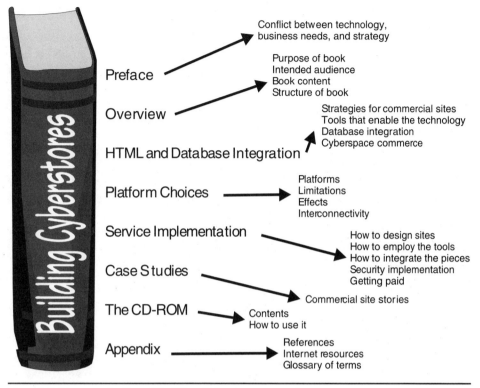

Figure 1.3   The organization of *Building Cyberstores*.

mentation. Although there are literally thousands of sites on the Internet about building websites; home pages; setting up commerce servers; and getting paid for products, software, and information with virtual money, bank transfers, and by credit card, there is just so much information it is not worth wasting your time when the CD-ROM includes the high points of the web as well as new information.

The appendix includes useful Internet and website sources, news groups, and some other technical documents about domain registration, security, design, and networking in general. It includes reference to cited materials and sources for statistics, models, software, notes, standards, photographs, and addresses to useful cyberstore-related Internet sites.

There is also a glossary with terms specific to the Internet, data networking, and WWW applications, which are defined and cross-referenced by the common acronyms. There are many terms in the glossary not directly defined in this book but that are referenced by tool vendors, service providers, and in the general design and implementation process when building cyberstores.

Contents of the CD-ROM

The companion CD-ROM includes a hypertext version of this book in Windows on-line help format and a hyperlinked format compatible with most web browsers. These formats are included so you can research the book for tools and techniques appropriate to solve an urgent problem or locate better methods for implementing your own cyberstore. The CD-ROM also includes website editing tools, multimedia demonstrations of techniques and tools, and actual working demonstration software of web development tools. This includes site mapping tools, text editing tools, graphic design and animation editors, and specialized rapid website development toolkits. In addition, the CD-ROM includes text and format from various web sources to show you how to register domain names, and protect text and images with copyrights, trademarks, and patents, and not infringe on others' legal rights. The companion disc also includes a text version of the *Building Cyberstores* information home page, as defined in the next section. The details of every file on the disc are described in detail in Chapter 6.

Contents of the Book's Information Home Page

The home page for this book, *Building Cyberstores,* is located at http://www. networkperf.com/cyberstores and provides informational site links to sites specifically referenced in this book. The site includes links to web pages that provide useful supplemental information and formal specifications for website markup, Cookies-based event-state tracking files, the website protocols, security, and encryption. The hypertext links include websites with shareware in the form of text, graphics, and tools. Some of the sites are interesting as templates, as ideas of what might work, and as *counterexamples* of effective web design or workflows at cyberstores. Please heed my warning that many sites represent a Pandora's box that will open more doors than you have time for and provide more information than you can absorb. The web represents a black hole that will suck your time and lead you down many false trails. Many sites duplicate material already organized within this book and at other sites. Nevertheless, these places are included as a reference in case you need the additional amplification.

2

HTML and Database Integration

Introduction

The cyberstore, cybermall, or cybershop represents the integration of Internet graphical web pages and transaction processing. Although several cited websites, samples of code, and other references in this chapter and Chapter 4 show how to implement transaction processing over the Internet without a database using only hypertext markup language (HTML) and common gateway interface (CGI) applications, the reality is that cyberstore financial accounting requirements necessitate linkages between web transactions, payment systems, and standard business accounting. Financial accounting is going to be driven by a database system, either a flat computerized record system as found in Quicken or Quickbooks, or a more robust relational database management system (DBMS) as typified in Solomon Software, Great Plains client/server financial systems, SAP R/3 Enterprise Resource Planning, Oracle Financials, and many other commercial or in-house proprietary systems.

The cyberstore is business at every level. It is a point-of-sales system (POS) comparable to any other credit card-based, catalog sales, or retail operation. The cyberstore requires a POS financial tracking system as a fundamental component to its success. If you believe that financial tracking is irrelevant and unnecessary, consider that sales through the Internet, with payment by credit card, and delivery by United States mail or even other interstate or international courier represent a significant potential for creating international or federal fraud. Nondelivery of merchandise (whether data, information, reports, physical product, or services) represents fraud or negligence. You must be capable of tracking orders, processing payment, and shipment of those orders to confirm completion of your sales transaction responsibility. In addition, how will management know if the cyberstore is performing if you cannot generate sales reports, return reports, or reports on shipping and inventory status, gross sales volumes, profit margins, and turnover? Information transposed from a credit card and electronic payment system (EPS) into the computerized business books by manual entry is likely to be delayed, if ever entered, and to exhibit data entry errors on the order of 30 percent. This is an enormous and ultimately costly error rate that can be overcome in the first place by integrating the business process with the business tracking systems as you design the cyber business.

The emphasis placed on analyzing hitcounts of Internet advertising and the accuracy and lack of distortion denotes the complexity with only a simple one-value posting of the hitcount. Consider how complex this can be with transaction processing. It is not only a posting but also an inbound collection operation. Although accounting seems dry and boring, the reality of the successful cyberstore depends on clear, useful, and concise financial reports. The cyberstore will not survive if buyers do not understand what product turnover is and why customers are buying certain products. Furthermore, do you really want to discover after the credit card posting period has closed that the $399.00 payment for a product with a charge of $8.25 for next day courier delivery has been automatically billed as $12.24 ($3.99 + $8.25)? If you make too many mistakes like that, the cyberstore will be out of business. The integration is a financial check on the integrity of cyberstore operations.

Although these financial systems may be called decision support systems (DSS) or executive information systems (EIS), the reality is that the financial tracking information is important at all levels of the cyberstore, including the design level. You want to feed the financial results back into the cyberstore design cycle so that it works better. For example, suppose you choose to design a cyberstore with a dozen products and base the implementation on the CGI/Perl (Practical Extraction and Reporting Language) code profiled later in this book. When it is financially and operationally successful, management says to you, the website designer, add to the site the other products that the company manufactures. If you do not realize that the company sells 37,842 additional products, the upgrade will not go well. You will not understand the need to make a set change from hand-coding to database integration and it's unlikely you can roll out and maintain such a vast cyberstore in real time despite a pool of programmers. You will need that DBMS and the decision-making systems.

The cyberstore decision is not "Let's all jump on the bandwagon and make big money." The National Association of Realtors (NAR) tried to reinvent the website and spent $12,900,000 before falling victim to overly ambitious goals, free-spending development efforts, unexpected technical changes (mainly from text presentation to graphics), and a problem attracting its primary customers—the real estate agents and its membership. Organizations need to apply the same financial discipline as they do with any other marketing discipline. The value, let's use return on investment (ROI), from a cyberstore or commercial website is not necessarily as straightforward as other sales channels because the website is not only providing direct sales channels, it is also likely representing an advertising effort, information collection, lead generation, customer research, technical maintenance, and customer support. Quantifying the value or the return on support functions is typically very difficult, but even more so with websites. Nevertheless, these issues need clarification at the beginning.

Dollar value for website development is likely to require $50,000 to $150,000 for hardware, with software and development and deployment costs around $150,000. Commercial site hosting typically costs about $300 to $500 per month. Some sites require investments of $500,000 to $750,000. Forrester Research cites the development costs for a promotional site at $200,000, a content-only site at $1,300,000, and transactional sites at $3,300,000. Contrast this with expenses to create the typical print-media advertisement (a single page) at $78,000 and add in the cost of placement at $7,000 to $35,000 per page per issue. A good product introduction easily costs $500,000 in print and $1,500,000 with television. TV placements can run from $250 per view to several hundred thousand dollars. Nevertheless, the systems and hit ratios are well established for print and TV media, and clearly not for web advertising and the secondary results from websites. Clarify the equity flows beforehand and exhibit some hard-headed fiscal controls and responsibility.

Mitch Ruud, Internet Products Manager at Great Plains Software, makes an important set of points about the cyberstore and Internet enablement. First, it is easier to plug the organization into the Internet, not necessarily plug the Internet into the workflow and policies of the business. Second, a cyberstore is a basic catalog sales adventure that provides new communication channels for an organization, but at its core, the cyberstore remains a merchandising operation typically controlled by seasoned entrepreneurial personalities and driven by "management by walking around" and complex sales reports.

Cyberstore activity and control will have to mesh with that hands-on mentality. If the cyberstore can provide effective activity reports, it must mesh with what management wants, and the management must be willing to look at the data. Management at many organizations is unwilling to adapt to this new channel. Third, Mr. Ruud suggests that there is a great difference between consumer and wholesale channels. He states that the transaction process is different too, that most Internet sales markets and cyberstores were based on the catalog sales to consumers concept. I reserve my judgment until Chapter 4. Business data related to cyberstore transactions and sales activity must be tracked, stored, retrieved, counted, and subjected to subsequent evaluations; these transactions predicated a complex and typically complicated system driven by a DBMS.

The choice of the DBMS is predicated by any existing financial systems. It is unwise to create a new system or a system in parallel. The only counterexample worth mentioning is when the current system represents technology unsuitable to support the current business and unlikely to support business growth. Most large-scale databases, which include Oracle, Sybase, Progress, Informix, and DB2, are accessible to open database connectivity (ODBC) drivers. This means that almost any web transaction can be converted and mapped into a format suitable for adding to the financial system.

Note that order entry usually represents a process with multiple steps that must maintain the relationship integrity of the financial database. This means that an order entry may generate a new customer entry or revised one; a validation of inventory availability for the order; shipment pricing based on weight, distance, and delivery time; the actual order list for picking and shipping; payment tracking; and the status of the order as a transactional entity. This implies a complex integration, or rather a process that mimics the order entry system to replicate the processes, workflows, and record creation within an existing financial system. In other words, the web transaction has to look functionally like it was created inside the existing financial system.

That means website developers need an available product that directly "interfaces" between a website and the database or financial system. Few of these exist yet. The next alternative is so-called *middleware,* a tool that provides the interface between the database or a financial system and the commercial web server. The least pleasant, most risky, and most expensive option is to mimic the operation of the existing financial system with ODBC calls, program code, component software (OLE, OCX, DLL, and VBX modules) and various database front-end tools. These option are depicted in Figure 2.1.

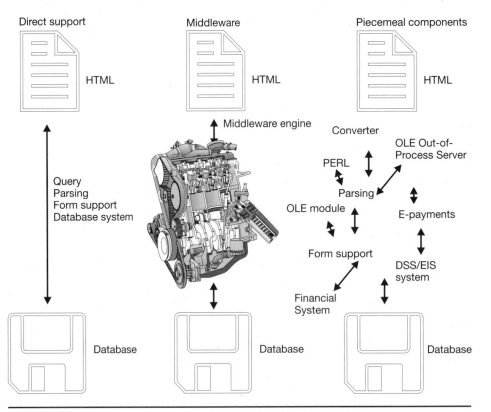

Figure 2.1 You need a range of tools for web page and database integration.

Further, as John Nilsson of WebMate Technologies states, "There is not much hope for most cyberstore developers to implement the various credit and electronic payment systems into their site from the incompatible and different specifications." There are SET, SSL, SHTTP, ACH, wire transfer, DigiCash, and NetCash, CyberCash, PGP, and other secure or encryption standards that become relevant in implementing the transaction payment. SET is an acronym for the Visa and MasterCard standard for Secure Electronic Transactions. SSL is a Netscape protocol for the Secure Sockets Layer, a CGI implementation of server to browser transaction encryption. SHTTP is secured web protocol that runs on top of the HyperText Transaction Protocol. ACH is an acronym for the automated clearing house banks you use to electronically wire funds between branches, among banks in different Federal Reserve regions, or internationally. PGP stands for pretty good privacy, a software application set that uses a two-part public/private key encryption system. And of course, every payment system requires a different processing engine, connection to another clearinghouse, and a method to account for credits and debits from transactions. Payment for intellectual property gets more interesting with micropayments by micromoney and systems of electronic payment after delivery rather than before, as with the IBM Cryptolopes® concept. The Cryptolopes concept (defined in Chapter 4) is a compound document that contains a descriptive header; some details about the contents, which may be advertising, a demonstration, or a partial view of the main contents; the securely-encrypted main contents; and a payment system that, when activated, will unlock the securely-encrypted contents. This is a useful mechanism for delivering information or software from a cyberstore to a customer over the Internet.

If you think that is the end of the system, realize that any noncurrency denomination, or a cyber currency that is not guaranteed to maintain a U.S. dollar, deutsche mark, or other standard currency will fluctuate in value. You will need a conversion method to handle discount rates, transaction fee costs, chargebacks, rolling reserves and consolidation of various international and cyber currencies into a net present value (NPV). The solution, in part, is available from vendors.

Realistically, this means that the middleware must be a tool to convert database information and flat file transactions into HTML, and HTML information back into the database or into the formats required for processes requiring flat files (such as a credit verification). The middleware must transform payment information and confirmations for insertion into the financial system. The process is more complex than that because formats differ (based on merchant clearing house or type of EPS) and interpretation must be provided. A quick example is the coding typically used to explain a transaction; the transaction type of "23" for example is not commonly understood to mean that the transaction is a third-party Medicare payment. Workers in the organization are not likely to remember all the codes, and you really do not want them to. Does a transaction number from one VISA clearinghouse mean that the payment has been accepted, or is it a phone number to process that card by voice? A raw

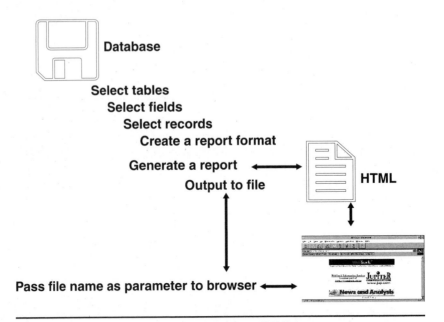

Figure 2.2 Steps for conversion of data for realistic HTML interpretation.

dump of database information into an HTML page is unlikely to be meaningful. Similarly, a raw dump of captured entry data (even the parsed HTML field data) into the database is unlikely to match required field formats, codes, or referential database integrity. These detailed operation steps are illustrated in Figure 2.2.

Cyberstore processing is also not just a single order and pay transaction. Nor is it just a return and credit charge process. There are other events that complicate the process. Consider whether an order/pay transaction represents just one event during the day when that event also must be consolidated and confirmed in the end-of-day batch close? A single transaction is part of the credit batch close process, the supplement rolling credit withholding for the merchant, the fee per transaction rates, and the per transaction discounts. Figure 2.3 illustrates an ICVerify ASCII transaction file (single transaction and batch close). You might note that this file is very small, very simple, and easily imported (with an ASCII, comma-delimited filter) into a DBMS.

```
 Notepad - ICVERIFC.410
File   Edit   Search   Help
"C1","FG Stone, IDI","Phone order
rush","433245427503","3411","254.00","","","","","","","0.00","","","","","",
"","","","",
"10-28-1994","11:50:02","0000000 APPROVED  009358","A","","000001"
"ST","254.00","1","0001","0.00","","","","","","","","","","","","","","","","
"","",
"10-28-1994","11:51:49","0050020 CLOSE    254.00 000001","S","","000001"
```

Figure 2.3 ICVerify submittal record, approval record, and end-of-day batch close transactions for merchant VISA payment.

In other words, if a cyberstore performs a single order paid by credit transaction during a batch day, that transaction may include the ticket amount, the fixed transaction fee, the discount fee for the transaction, the close batch fee, funds actually transferred by wire to the cyberstore's bank account, and funds withheld by the clearinghouse for a rolling reserve, in case of problems. Additional cyberstore credit costs include debits (chargebacks), chargeback fees, and chargebacks from unresolved consumer complaints forced on the cyberstore. The same policy will be necessary for CyberCash and other electronic payment systems because customers will be unhappy with products or service, will have received the wrong product, or the product may have been damaged in shipment and is no longer available.

As you can see, even a cashless payment process is by no means simple. If these steps are not implemented correctly and automated, the secondary burden of entering cyberstore transactions manually into an accounting system can reinstate that $100 that it costs most organizations to process an order. In addition, if order volume builds, as everyone hopes and expects, it may be impossible to withstand the load and recover if the organization gets too far behind. That is a good problem to actually have, but organizations that cannot sustain growth well and adjust to initial volume overloads within a reasonably short period do not typically thrive. If the volume is a trickle, something is very wrong with the cyberstore, the concept as implemented, marketing and promotion, and the value of your competitive niche. The cyberstore should anticipate a fairly extensive service volume.

Many conversion tools can convert between formats. The Help-to-HTML converter, HTML Transit, Web.Data, and Perl programs are explored in Chapter 4 and actually simplify the process. However, these tools are one-way, one-time tools. They are not interactive and are not middleware. A more complex class of tools includes WebDBC, WebDynamics, Star/Web, Marco Polo, WebOLAP, and DSS Server. Some of these tools are platform-specific, while others are available for many different platforms and provide multiplatform interconnectivity and scalability. These are important issues because many financial systems are not often linked into the local area network, have no interface to a web server, and represent a tightly controlled upper management resource. If upper management is unwilling to support this tactical linkage, other solutions are available, but you need to understand the ramifications. For example, another solution is operating a separate set of books (in reality, a duplicate financial system) strictly for the cyberstore that can be imported on a regular basis into the other system for consolidation.

Websites are collections of ASCII documents and sometimes other types of informational files and executable files. These may include sound bits (.AU, .WAV, and MIDI files), animated images (.GIF, .SCR, .MOV, and .AVI), and multimedia presentations built by tools from many different vendors and often incompatible with each other and identifiable by another file extent. The predominant documents are text files and possess hypertext markup, which means that keywords on each document enable jumps to other documents or connections to the files.

The reality is that hypertext markup language is a *primitive* ASCII tagging code for text processing that recalls the Wordstar, Waterloo text, and TROFF of ages past. Although the text markup in text processing is often hidden as control codes or a stored separate layer of the file not normally seen by the user, this is not always true for site developers or browser users. While there have been substantial efforts to create a universal tagging system for text, HTML is strictly a subset of the standard generalized markup language (SGML) which is used for optical character recognition (OCR), legal documents, word processing, indexing, and eventually web pages. There are multiple versions of HTML—version 1.0 and version 2.0, which are standardized; HTML+; version 3.0, which is under review and will not be universally released by the World Wide Web Consortium (W3C) due to distribution and support concerns; and a recently approved version 3.2, which defines some of the latest features common to the leading browsers. The complexity does not end there as many vendors, including Microsoft, Oracle, and Netscape have defined unique HTML extensions, many of which are important for transaction processing in cyberstores.

Because the cyberstore is a transactional processing environment that links HTML to databases and to flat file data sets, and activates or initiates secondary processing, the end result is that all presentations of graphical or textual information from a database must be translated into the HTML formats supported by the typical user's browser. HTML is the presentation medium supported by the current generation of HTML browsers. Although many companies are showing advanced browser front ends that support HTML, native file, and database formats, those extensions are not standardized yet. Therefore, all queries, all data input forms, and all complex reports and responses must be converted into HTML for universal access by most users.

Similarly, HTML inputs into forms with fields, check boxes, buttons, and list boxes must be extracted from the HTML form, parsed into string, parsed into identifiable fields, converted into a data format compatible with the database, and then the individual data elements must be added to or updated with the actual database. It is important to recognize, for example, that a radio button represents a multiple choice selection with one unique and at least default selection. The return value is typical of the index value of the selected button; radio buttons for a color selection of either red, green, blue, and yellow map to values 0, 1, 2, and 3. The database may capture this as raw information, as the actual color name, or more likely in the hard-pressed cyberstore environment, as the actual product codes for order pickers. This is often the UPC code. Other industries and markets have codes and bar codes specific to them. The book industry uses the ISBN code and many manufacturers are beginning to use dense, two-dimensional bar code systems. Since the UPC code for a green pair of pants is different from the UPC code for a matching green top, every item may contain a code to convert ordering selections into the expected database format.

In addition, an ordering selection is not simply stuffing data into a new or revised record. You need to match workflow and functionality with management needs. For example, the data probably needs to be checked against inventory balances for availability. After all, a key component of the cyberstore is immediacy. A shopper doesn't have to leave a chair, go to a store, and walk down the aisles. A catalog shopper hunting through a catalog calls a number and asks for availability and shipping information. The cyberstore should be readily accessible and equally convenient. It condenses marketing, design, workflow, and integration of transaction processing at the cyberstore server.

Marketing

Whether your website provides information about your charitable organization or is a round-the-clock automated catalog sales center, no matter how you want to look at it, the site is a promotional institution—an advertisement for your organization. Foremost, you want to get customers to pay attention and spend a lot of money for your products or services. You want constituents to use the website before they use other, more expensive communication channels. You want customers to look beyond the empirical product or service and feel the emotions of the website message. The rich potential of the web poses new obstacles because of its very success. You will need to position your cyberstore to draw people to it, compel them to use it, and above all, make it more entertaining (if appropriate and possible) and useful than other media.

You want to hit people over the head with information, you want to streamline the workflow for donations or taking credit cards for products, and you want to engender confidence and safety in the process. Avoid layers of mazelike pages that might confuse users. Avoid verbose introductions. Just because the Internet and web pages may be new to you and your organization, you cannot assume novelty for any customer coming to your page.

Assume that the web user is trained, motivated, and has limited time. Just as advertisers and product marketing managers assert that print media and packaging provides just 15 seconds to make an impression, you have just 15 seconds to grab and retain someone's attention. Surfers will avoid sites that look complex, redundant, or unsophisticated. Sites slow to load violate that principle. Furthermore, you must make the site inviting, attractive, and friendly.

Consider creating a newsletter on the website that is updated with some regularity. This can be hosted as a selection from the home page. Also, you can E-mail the newsletter to those people who request this option. Listservers are easy to set up and they provide effective direct marketing even when a customer forgets about your organization, your products, or the website, the E-mailed magazine provides that address again. If you can persuade readers to add content, you reinforce the importance and currency of the newsletter. This stratagem leverages the value of the newsletter itself because the names and organizations are listed in it. This technique also leverages the power of the cyberstore and keeps customers coming back because of the periodic brochures, newsletters, and E-mail you have permission to send to the customers. You refresh the cyberstore image and its address in the browsers' consciousness.

The website address is called the Uniform Resource Locator, or URL, as it is commonly referenced. The website address can be a character-based domain name, an agglomeration of domain name and actual file path to a file or web page, or an Internet Address (IP) based on a 16-byte numerical address or on the new 256-byte IPv6 numerical address. The next screen image (Figure 2.4) demonstrates a savvy technique from the vendor of the NetDynamics product. Spider Technologies captured the demo registration information to send out a low-keyed E-mail message about a week after my website demo download.

It is a nice reminder for people who download files and forget about them, and a nice follow up for people who may like the product but remain uncertain about actually using it. In contrast, overt advertising through bulk E-mail is called *spamming*. Because of the time required to view unsolicited mail messages, most Internet users are averse to spamming and respond with a flood of nasty messages, called *flames,* which usually work to inform advertisers that this technique is not effective. An advertiser who distributed 10,000 unsolicited messages to a group mail list is likely to receive 80,000 cease and desist replies. The density of these replies frequently overloads the source site and hosting web servers, and is quite effective at limiting future Internet abuses. Most advertising on the Internet is therefore passive and is posted on pages at a known website like a school bulletin board, not distributed like junk mail.

David Reske, president of Direct Choice, stated to me that "advertising on the web is like posting newspaper ads in the middle of the forest." It is an apt metaphor to classify the web as a deep, dark forest with advertising billboards on some of the trees. Some trees have WAIS, ARCHIE, and E-mail gateways, but no information for the average user. There is a lot of information available, but without a means to target what a customer can locate. The customer does

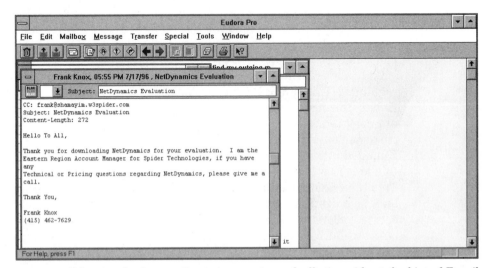

Figure 2.4 Cyberstore lead generation is inexpensive and effective without the hint of E-mail *Spam* broadcasting.

not know which trees have advertising and where the useful products are. In fact, the forest includes duplicates of everything dispersed randomly and chaotically, and concentrated in groves in some places where some organization has made a clear effort to provide content that cuts through the noisy din of the Internet forest. Figure 2.5 illustrates this web metaphor.

Figure 2.5 Who notices your site in the big web forest?

If you host a website in the big timberland of websites, who is going to visit your site? Who is going to notice your site on the Internet? How are they going to get there? Why are they going to want to stay there? Why will they notch a tree to create a trail marker (a URL bookmark) and come back again? These are fundamental questions that require management answers before technical implementation. You need to understand the *script,* the process of how potential customers locate your cyberstore, what they expect to find, how they hope to navigate through it, and what special information or ambience will encourage them to return again. This user surfing script should be a pattern for designing the cyberstore website.

This backwoods country can seem to be dark, damp, scary, noisy, and chaotic. It can be dangerous, too. Whatever you do on a website, your competitors will certainly analyze it for weaknesses and for competitive ideas; pirates may try to fake, steal, ruin, or disrupt the content at your site. When there is a potential for diverting cash flows, ACH bank-to-bank transfers, EDI flows, or credit payments, there are additional incentives. There are many hidden dangers, pitfalls, loose stones, and decaying trees ready to topple over and mar your site. Expect active dangers hunting for you, as Figure 2.6 shows.

The main point I want to make about the cybermall, the cybershop, and the cyberstore is that using the best host and the best tools does not mean people will get through, use your site, and make purchases. You need to promote your site with appropriate listings in commercial index services like

Figure 2.6 Many dangers are hunting for you as you hunt for web exposure.

Alta Vista, Yahoo, or Lycos. Furthermore, you want to check and update your topics, indexes, and listings with regularity. Think of these items as a trail of crumbs dropped in the forest leading to your site. Just as Hansel and Gretel were defeated by the birds, your site pointer crumbs get eaten up, making it essential to refresh the trail to your site in the forest, as shown in Figure 2.7.

Websites are a product. Bad websites are bad products, like the "cockroach in the hamburger," according to Sheldon Laube, a principal at USWeb whose organization is building and hosting them. Realize the purpose of the site, what it does best, and how it can improve traditional sales techniques, supplement existing sales channels, and augment customer communication and support. For example, a website cannot provide the speed and simplicity of a magazine advertisement, the immediacy of a phone call to a sales department, or the comprehensive product line catalog. However, it does provide an ever-increasing density of synchronized information 24 hours per day, 7 days per week including customer information, product literature, automated sales, and immediate beeper or callback responses. Perhaps most importantly for smaller business and cybershops with minimal staffing, the website can be available around the clock as Figure 2.8 shows.

Figure 2.7 Keep the trail fresh and clear to your website with topics, indexes, listings, references in E-mail, list servers, and even links to and from other sites.

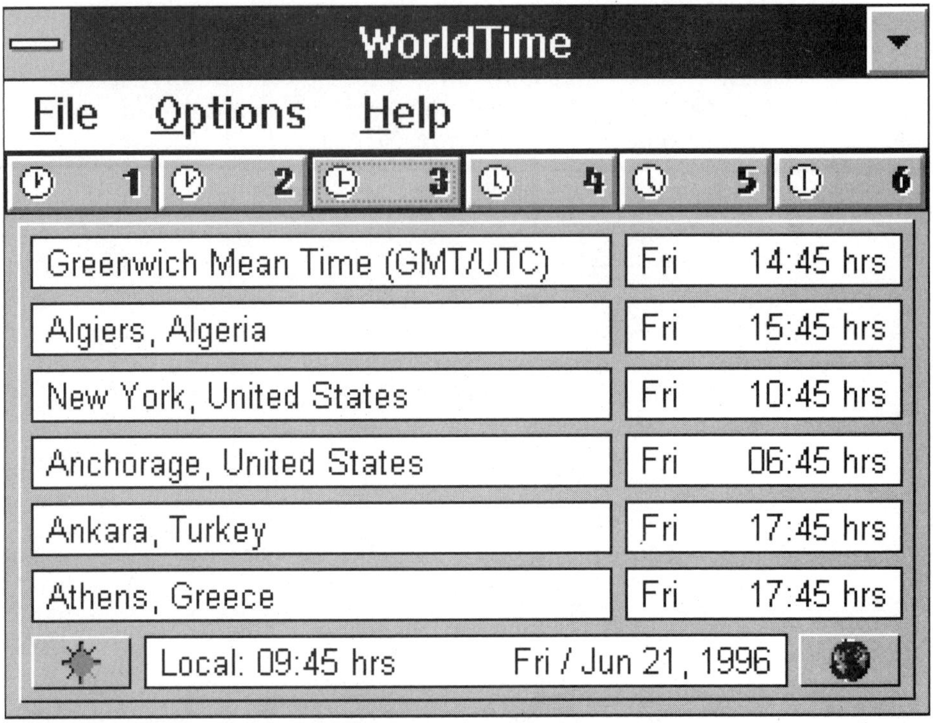

Figure 2.8 When it is time for you to go home, customers in some parts of the world are just waking up, getting product specifications, and placing orders.

Figure 2.9 shows the Softline World Clock, which shows graphically the time zone differences around the world. Because there are three shifts in a perpetual organization, a telemarketing organization comparable to a cyberstore would require at least three shifts of people to handle incoming requests and orders. In addition, a cyberstore can provide a first line or information requests around the clock to lower the workload for a telemarketing organization. Because the cost for a cyberstore transaction can be as low as $5 versus the $125 cost of manual ordering and supplemental accounting, this 7×24 service is cost efficient.

If your organization is operational from 6 a.m. Eastern Standard Time to 9 p.m. Eastern Standard Time, consider creating an applet to generate a local time for a customer to call your organization and find the appropriate department staffed and running. This can be a simple time computation, a database lookup (even connecting into an organization that is in calendar), or a series of images showing that the office is dark. Alternatively—and this is really simpler—you can create a sequence of 24 image files of a world clock or a metaphor for office operations that are loaded based on the local organizational time. They might even be screen shots showing different times of day captured from a utility like the world clock.

Site strategy

Building a commercial website, a cybershop, or the fully-automated and integrated cyberstore in order to fulfill market expectations, customer comfort levels, competitive pressures, or to be part of the great press for increased web presence has about the same cachet as running with a pack of lemmings. Life expectancy for the herded organization is significantly decreased in resource-limited niches and locations, and perhaps even less for visionless designers and implementations. A strategy for building a commercial website, a cybershop, or the fully-automated and integrated cyberstore should be represented by a clear statement of purpose. There are three basic categories of commercial websites according to Forrester Research:

- Promotional
- Content-only
- Transactional

I might add that commercial websites can include help desk and customer support as well, and even for governmental or service-oriented sites, the dispute-resolution arbitrator. U.S. Government agencies pursuing a secure commerce and transaction conduit include the U.S. Postal Service, the Department of the Treasury, the National Security Agency (NSA), and the National Institute of Standards and Technology (NIST). Agencies that provide welfare, social security, veteran's benefits, and agricultural subsidies are also

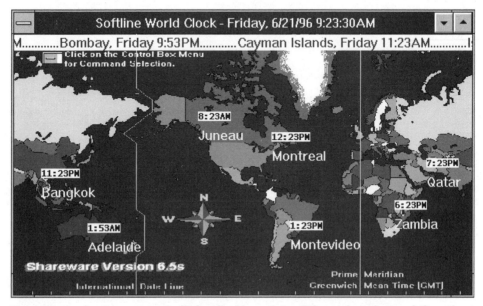

Figure 2.9 A cyberstore automatically handles the activity of three telemarketing shifts without the cost of the people.

interested in alternate delivery of funds to increase security and cut costs. The cyberstore is not only about customer-to-business transactions, but also business-to-business events and interagency transfer of information. The cyberstore embodies transaction processing and maybe one or more of the commercial website categories, too. Whatever the type of site or its purpose, make that purpose very clear. Some examples of a strategic mission statement for a commerce website include:

- Make it easier for our customers to do business with us.
- Provide more timely and accurate services information.
- Lower transaction processing costs.
- Lower bad collection debts and collection expenses.
- Provide 7×24 customer support.
- Present our product line in a better light than provided by print or TV.
- Provide access to information despite limited staff budgets.

Obviously, every organization will have a different charter, and hence, a different website strategy. The strategy for the website needs to mesh with that concept. Some manufacturers of consumer goods are trying to establish a new market outlet and channel to bypass the mass merchandisers for several important financial objectives. These retailers, such as Wal-Mart, Tandy, K-Mart, and Federated are squeezing profit margins because of the global market competition for processed goods, and secondarily because the retailers are forcing manufacturers to take back goods unsold at the end of each retailing season. No longer can manufacturers assume that a good "sold" to a retailer stays sold and doesn't come back as old excess inventory. The excesses get dumped on clearance and close-out vendors at significant losses and at the cannibalization of next season's merchandising efforts.

The manufacturers are therefore trying to bypass the retail channels with the Internet channel and do so without completely angering the retailers. Small businesses, particularly those in the Far East that are serviced by international delivery services such as UPS and Federal Express, are trying to market their wares in the U.S., Europe, and South America. In addition, the "cheap" suits of Hong Kong can be fitted, sold, and delivered by the Internet, challenging many primary clothing channels and the business concept that monogrammed and fitted products are wholly a local industry.

For examples of how organizations are extending new channels for credit card and catalog sales, L. L. Bean and Lands' End (profiled in Chapter 5) market high-quality products at a high markup based on image, name branding, and exceptional customer service. Their websites reflect those charters and merely extend the sales and marketing channel without detracting from the ambience of these vendors. On the other hand, Travelocity (also profiled in Chapter 5) caters to executives and corporate people who have traditionally been excluded from the travel market by travel agencies, the 15 percent fare discounts, and a lack of access to information systems. By providing extensive lists of services, providers, package deals, and a search engine for low-cost fares, Travelocity creates a totally new service based on the strategy of price and information. Riva Yamaha, profiled in Chapter 5, increases consumer access to parts, supplies, and performance accessories that jet ski and motorcycle owners typically do not know are available through a new channel and through combined channel advertising.

Demographics

So you think your cyberstore will do a booming business on the Internet. Get real. Get some numbers. Look at the demographics. Figure out who the average Internet user is and if that person is at all interested in your site. There are new surveys weekly, some on Internet websites, some listed in periodicals, and some that are available as pricey research reports costing from $1500 to $50,000 with breakdowns of usage by gender, time of day for access, core demographics, mean income, mean household expenses, Internet population, access by modem speeds, and other descriptive clusters. Here are some "average" Internet numbers from Forrester and IDG research services:

- 24 million North American Internet users (11% of population)
- 89 million worldwide Internet users (0.014% of population)
- 3.1 million Internet users have purchased products using the web
- Mean Internet user income is $62,000
- Mean Internet user education level is grade 17 (college + 1)
- 34% of all users access Internet daily

  66% of users are from work

  44% of users are from home

  8% of users are from school

- Internet users average 6.7 hours per week for WWW
- Internet users average 21 hours on-line (other services)
- 60% of Internet users subscribe to commercial services
- Only 8% of Internet users use commercial services for Internet access

Whether you believe the statistics is immaterial. There is some basis to their accuracy, and even if they are in error by a given magnitude, the implications are clear. Internet users are twice as educated as the average person and have 2.6 times greater income (30 times worldwide). They are more likely to access the Internet from work than from home or school, and the Internet web represents less than 33 percent of on-line access. The web is not the primary information source (Lexis, Nexis, AOL, Prodigy, CompuServe, and other services in aggregate are greater), and is only one of many sales and marketing channels. Cyberstore ventures will face significant channel competition from these other on-line information sources.

Website design is a socio-economic issue that must be considered in the design and deployment process so as to match expectations with reality. Failure to recognize product, sales, and audience limitations results in poor sales volume and the eventual failure of the cyberstore. Currently the audience is well-educated and well-paid, way above the norm, so that websites catering to almost any socio-economic group must include products and services of appeal.

Furthermore, cyberstore products and services need to mesh with the Internet user demographics. For example, I would suspect that these products would not appeal to the audience: Spam, Velveeta, bias-ply tires, collateralized credit cards, burial insurance, consignment clothing, chicken heads and gizzards, and used pickup trucks. By the way, the term for mass E-mailing as *spamming* speaks to the generic dislike of unsolicited E-mail.

While some products sell at higher volumes to more affluent market segments, some products, called economic *Giffin* goods, are bought in lower quantities or not at all as consumer income rises. Of course, some products have a loyalty based on culture and custom. In fact, some products or services may succeed because they have become so scarce and hard to find, with the result that Internet keyword search provides a special opportunity to reach a diverse and avid audience. In fact, the largest advertisement medium for collectibles (baseball cards, antiques, and dolls) is the Internet, not special magazines, auction brochures, or newsletters.

In general, though, the Internet audience might be attracted to power tools, computer equipment, building supplies, 4×4 leather-interior sport utility vehicles and minivans, cruises, package vacations, personal fitness training, vacation homes, accessories, financial services, credit card rebate programs, lease vehicle deals, boats, motorhomes, motorcycles, jet skis, gourmet foods, and new lines of clothing. The products do not necessarily need to be computer-related. Good prices or the lowest prices, a clever pitch, and integrity can attract the available audience. However, you will not reach that audience without site design and positioning consistent with the demographics. You will not reach a demographic audience lacking computers, without Internet access, and bereft of the finances or responsibility to purchase your products and services advertised only on a cyberstore.

Promotion

Fierce competitors have been known to sign up for a domain name that matches the business name of the competitor. They use that domain to point to their own website and divert business to their own cyberstore. This is perfectly legal as long as a domain name does not infringe on state or federal trademarks and international copyright laws. A competitor can also send mail to a search engine so that references to your products and services point to their own site instead of yours. It is perfectly legal, perfectly unfair, but within the real spirit of free competition. If a competitor cites your products and compares or contrasts the competitor's products with your own, the references are reasonable and may stand any formal challenge. However, slanderous, malicious, or libelous misstatements are beyond the limits of the law as is described in Chapter 4. Nevertheless, you want to make certain that site and cyberstore promotion for your specific products or services, a generic description of your products or services, and specific references to your organizational name are added to the databases of the Internet website search engines, which is shown in Figure 2.10.

The Liquid Image URL submission site creates database entries for about 20 search engines when you complete a single HTML form with information specific to your organization. This site formats the submission to each site to match the expected parameters and variances in URL formats, and sends the information off to the appropriate search engine information pages. This is shown by Figure 2.11. Some search engines expect a complete path in the form "http://www.company.com" whereas others suffice with company.com. Unusual addresses in the form of, for example, "shttp://arcade.games.downloads.com" may need careful submission to each engine one at a time to prevent the search engine from rejecting the entry and sending a rejection notice by E-mail.

If I said it only once, the point would not be said enough times—you need advertising for your site. Post keywords, concepts, the name of the organization, and special charm or the purpose of the site on every publicly-

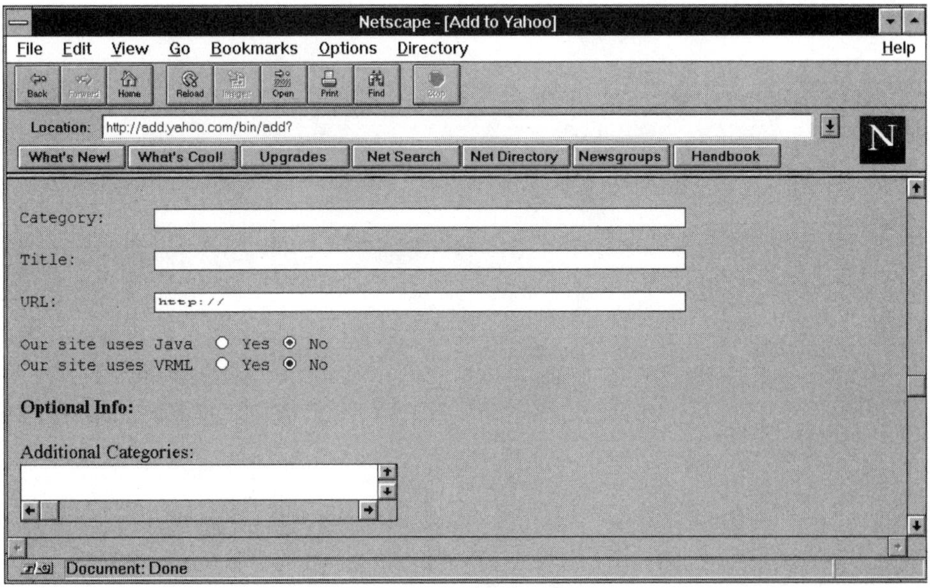

Figure 2.10 Adding your site URL to the search engine databases is de rigueur. Checking the search engines frequently is advisable.

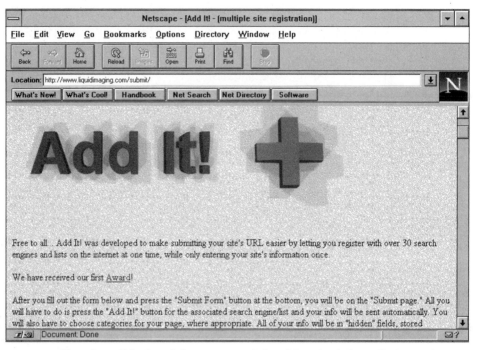

Figure 2.11 Keep the trail fresh and clear to your website with topics, indexes, listings, references in E-mail, list servers, and even links to and from other sites.

Figure 2.12 PostMaster is another search engine announcement tool.

accessible search engine as in Figure 2.12. I expect you will want to attract the indexing spiders to your cyberstore, and thus you should focus on the following four points. First, pick a subject for your site or page within a site and concentrate on making that single point. Second, choose the first several lines of text on your page carefully so that the spiders will index the important words and points. Third, use the optional page title (meta-) and heading tags so that the index spiders will get content from your page. Assign useful information (from a perspective of a search index) to these tags. Use other meta tags that might be captured by search engines. Fourth, concentrate on designing pages with useful and focused content that have a unique value to readers of your page and customers to your website.

I remember innocently saying in business school marketing class 101, "If a company builds a better product, consumers will buy it" only to get chastised by the teacher for how wrong I was. The company needs to educate consumers about the need for its product and the reasons why it is a better decision than something else. Nobody bothered with Vaseline or 3-M Post-It notes as products until the need for them was clearly positioned in the market. Some techniques that promote your cyberstore comprise:

- Include organization E-mail and cyberstore address on all print literature, stationary, display advertising, promotional merchandise, and products
- Include your cyberstore as part of larger malls and other sites
- Get active in USENET groups and mailing lists (but do not spam!)
- Advertise your store and products on the search engines
- Include your URL in the search engines
- Get referenced on industry-specific web pages
- Give customers a good reason to come
- Buy web advertising
- Buy print advertising and include the E-mail and URL

If you build a better web commercial site, a super cyberstore, or an easier to use and friendlier on-line catalog, how will anyone know about it? For new websites, you need to position them in the market, educate consumers about their existence, and post the URLs everywhere. Figure 2.13 shows standard magazine showcase advertising augmented with website addresses.

Customer base and sales volume is about mind share and taking business from the competition. The mechanism is similar to the strip malls on U.S. Highway Route 1 where retailers need to cut through the constant din of competition by positioning, pricing, placement, and product offerings. This problem is (and will become) even more acute on the Internet because access is uniform, as the full-page advertisement in a mainstream magazine for Lycos exemplifies in Figure 2.14.

Figure 2.13 Magazine showcase advertising bolstered with website addresses.

Some products do not sell through magazines, the Internet (per se), catalogs, or even television advertising. Some products represent one-time purchases in which the selling cycle is so infrequent with so much time between purchases that it is difficult to make consumers aware of the product and its special attraction. Yamaha Riva jet skis and the racing line of accessories provide a good example. But look at the racing logos in Figure 2.15 showing a prominent URL mixed in with the logos of the oil companies, clothing manufacturers, and cycle vendors.

If you have an odd URL, or one that has an unusual spelling and you are committed to it and want to retain it, consider adding corruptions of that path to the referring domain registrations. For example, if the site is wiener.com, register for weiner.com, winer.com, winner.com, whiner.com and even weaner.com. All these names map into the same logical website home page. I hit many sites because I mistype a complex URL and sometimes do not even realize my mistake until I check the content. In addition, consider plugging those same permutations into the various search engines—it is free and may yield more benefits than the extra domain names.

URL advertising and name dropping is all well and good, but sometimes marketing requires capturing users' attention and diverting them from the immediate purpose. The question is whether the banner advertising can convert users into customers by luring them from work (in this case, searching about eShop on Yahoo) to playing games based on Gummi Savers candies shown in Figure 2.16. The effectiveness is probably driven by the universality of the message and the timing. After lunch time and late afternoon are probably good sugar pickup times and likely times to lure people away from other tasks.

A serious inability to make money on the Internet stems from poor sales technique to inability to move the products. For example, look at all the software sites with demo software, shareware, and examples of what a customer can get. With purchase to download rates running about 0.017 percent, the issue is not that the software, the service, or the sample product is poor or defective, but that manufacturers, vendors, and buyers seem to have forgotten that the product must be sold. This may entail proactive reseller pro-

Figure 2.14   Even big names want to become bigger names and create a larger customer base.

Figure 2.15   URLs create recognition even on advertisements . . . or on jet skis.

grams, merchandising operations, cooperative advertising, and an analytical matchup with demographics and stocking decisions and product design.

Also, it is imperative that you are aware of the limiting and filtering technology that can disrupt, subvert, or transform your promotional message. There are a number of techniques and tools that can identify the type of site, steps on survey or Cookies collection, and kill the advertisements. For example, Fast Forward annotated in Figure 2.17, shows how it can filter your cyberstore. Tools like this one are likely to proliferate just as E-mail filters and automated flames and spam splatters help overloaded Internet junkies deal with the loads of unsolicited junk mail. Nevertheless, building the cyberstore proceeds from the server side and you need to be aware of these filters so that you can defeat them. You might try to ascertain if a site is using them, and compensate accordingly. The key is understanding how these filters work and what the possible setting preferences are, as shown in Figure 2.18.

When all is said and done, you need to examine your media plan and how it synthesizes with the website. More advertisements and more prominent dis-

Figure 2.16 Banner advertising has a window of opportunity of only 1 second to lure users to your site.

plays of URLs are not always better. You want to match the promotional efforts with the demographics. Test which ads work. An organization can have more than one URL that maps to a website or different parts of a website. You can create multiple website home pages accessible from different URLs (promoted in different places) and count hits and access to each of those sites. These statistics show the relative effectiveness of the various promotions.

Advertising placement does not have a defined cost. The number of consumer and general publications have decreased in the past several years because of rising paper and production costs and alternative channels for advertising. Agencies, brokers, and publishers are fighting hard for advertising dollars, so you might cut better deals and get even more statistical information about distribution demographics for more space. Watch the production costs because color separation, studio time, and creative costs can add up—these are

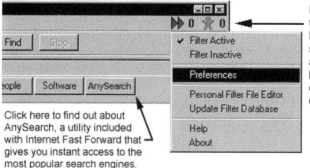

Figure 2.17 Fast Forward provides mute and VCR fast forward functions for websites.

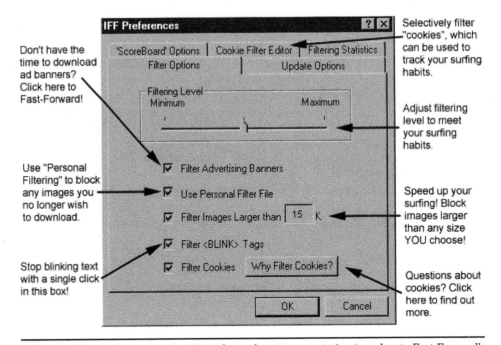

Figure 2.18 The preference settings (note the explanatory annotations) are key to Fast Forward's effectiveness.

not pertinent directly to website ROI. Create a unique ad that stands out, and do not vary its size, shape, or color scheme. That creates consistency and impact, and keeps those ad production costs in line.

Finally, reuse your customers. Develop a direct mail program or join a cooperative effort (like card decks under a magazine banner) that provides economies of scale. The best customers are your existing customers (unless you are doing something wrong) and they are most receptive to promotional efforts. If you want to reach customers on the Internet with E-mail, locate a new and current phone number for them, and even locate their physical position based on address; many people—the high-powered decision-makers—you want to reach have business phones, company address, and E-mail addresses, as shown in Figure 2.19. Understand that some method may be invasive, so use your discretion on tracking people.

Design

Internet design appears to be a free commodity because anybody who creates a web page invents a design. However, reality is very different; there is good website design and bad website design. The differences become accentuated with cyberstores because the site is not simply a repository of stale, invariant files. The cyberstore is also an automated attendant that provides product and

Figure 2.19 Internet tools for tracking existing customers.

pricing information, tries to guide a customer to high-margin items or sales discounts, and then gathers sufficient personal information to ship and receive payment for the order. This is an involved script that must be reflected in good and unmistakable design.

Design can be very costly, in terms of paying professional artists to create masterful work, creating supplemental studio art for print media, or in the loss of opportunity associated with a sleepy or ugly website. No matter what perception you and your organization are trying to create, the overall design is the first impression web surfers get when they find your home page or any page that is linked into other sites. Although Caere Omnipage, Xerox TextBridge, or HTML Transit can convert reams of paper and computer documents into web pages with minimal user input, the effective web format is very different from marketing literature—at a minimum. Figure 2.20 shows the annotated screen. The outer bracket shows the actual screen, the middle annotated bracket shows the window for a browser, and the inner annotation brackets show the actual window into the HTML page.

While the format for most printed presentations is vertical or fold-out with multipage brochures, the monitor typically permits a horizontal form. Also, note that the display in the last figure was 1024×768 pixels. This represents a high-resolution by MS Windows standards. Sun, AS/400, OS/2, Macintosh, and other platforms are different, usually less. The standard Windows platform for most corporate users is 640×480, smaller by almost 75 percent, and is a common size for laptop and home systems. Even when the browser is resized to the full desktop, most users (except those with

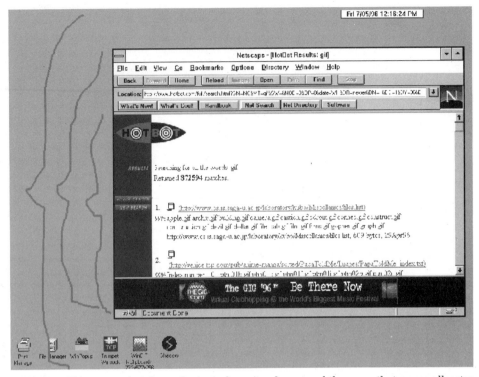

Figure 2.20 This screen shot shows the typical monitor format and the space that a user allocates to web surfing. The browser is not the entire desktop.

Radius monitors) are limited to this flag-shaped format. Although scrolling windows let a user see more of a vertical presentation and even multiple browsers let a user mix different pages or sites, the basic format limitation is the horizontal computer screen. This is a fundamental technical limitation that should constrain all website development. Figure 2.21 shows how the screen and browser space limitations can be overcome with good site organization.

Many commercial sites and even crafted cyberstores have the look and feel of ad hoc design and development. They lack ambience, character, and a clear declaration of the site's or organization's culture. Many sites manifest the technical Information Systems (IS) department's sensibilities over sales and promotion targets with a sterile information core-dump style. While character is a tenuous trait that cannot be taught or successfully copied, some aspects of design can be. For example, one of the overwhelming features that I have seen at many professionally-built (constructed by advertising or graphic agencies) sites is a distinct lack of consistency. For example, the home page will have one theme not at all reflected by subsequent pages. The layout will

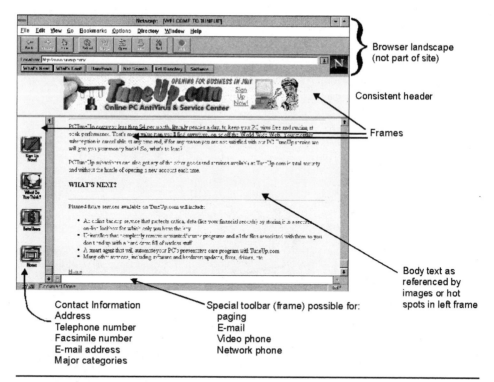

Browser landscape (not part of site)

Consistent header

Frames

Body text as referenced by images or hot spots in left frame

Contact Information
Address
Telephone number
Facsimile number
E-mail address
Major categories

Special toolbar (frame) possible for:
paging
E-mail
Video phone
Network phone

Figure 2.21 Screen and browser space limitations overcome with good site organization using frames or tables and concise message focus.

differ, the page shapes will differ from small thumbnails to pages that scroll off the window to the left and bottom, and backgrounds that compete, oppose, and convey the abhorrent message that the page belongs to someone else's site. The user will resize the browser for almost every page and scroll through some pages and not others. This total lack of consistency is illustrated by the flow in Figure 2.22.

A site with a good "page-onality" has consistency among pages. The page shape, background, type, and sizing, are uniform. If a home page contains a frame with navigational buttons to special sections, other pages should echo this format. I understand that top and side frames may waste space on supplemental pages, but the rule of consistency is that the supplemental pages should mirror the home page structure. Create a standard template and propagate it throughout the site. Even when you integrate databases and forms for the cyberstore transaction processing, retain the template, as shown in Figure 2.23.

Newspapers, reports, and magazines often have several page layout designs used on different pages or sections, but nevertheless repeated from issue to issue and often based on an overall fundamental principle. For

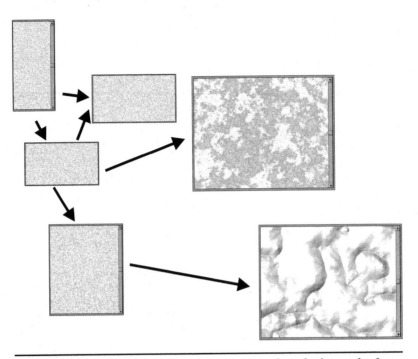

Figure 2.22 A lack of page design consistency extends to backgrounds, frame shapes, and layouts.

example, there might be a front page design, an inside design, full page spreads, call outs and sidebars. Multiple designs can work for the cyberstore if they mesh with a fundamental design principle. The key to various front and inside page designs is congruity among these designs. The consistency could be frame usage (of the same size and shape), identical size pages, and a consistency of frame backgrounds. If you want to color code pages by topic or purpose, echo these color codes in hyperlink buttons and include the buttons on every page. Architects Frank Lloyd Wright and I. M. Pei have demonstrated that new technology does work with simple design and a thematic consistency between elements. Ambience and character are important traits to a website because I suspect the sterile high-tech look will work as poorly in a website as it does in a mass-market retail outlet. The high-tech style is not necessarily ad hoc, but it may not be functionally acceptable.

The most successful text and image presentation styles are obvious in newspapers and magazines. These include multicolumn layouts, wrap-around text, sidebars, and call outs. Some website designs use HTML version 3.2 tables and frames of new style sheets to create a look similar to a *Cosmopolitan* or *Time* magazine. This clearly is the direction that web design will take over the next several years. Multicolumn layouts, wrap-around text, sidebars, and call outs represent difficult layouts because web pages can be displayed by so many dif-

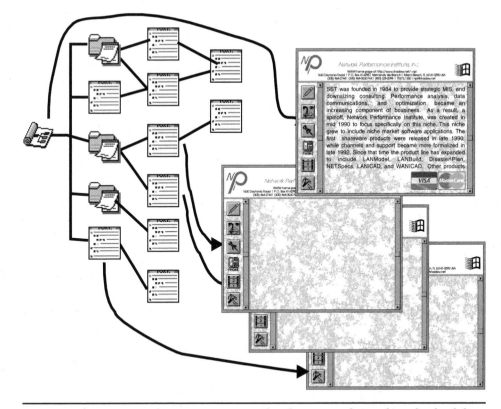

Figure 2.23 Site page template consistency provides character and a good comfort level for a customer.

ferent browsers, display resolutions, and other limitations. These technical limitations will most likely be addressed by new HTML specifications and more advanced browsers. Already, Adobe has released a Postscript Definition Format (PDF) development and display tool that integrates with websites and browsers.

Different tools enable different functions and features in a website. This can have a profound effect on initial template design and on the ultimate ease of navigation through the site. Cross-platform development leads to integration and reliability issues, not only to differing results. None of the current generation of web-development tools is great, perfect, or the unique solution to your site development needs. This is because the HTML language is amorphous and vendors are adding proprietary extensions at a frantic pace, and also because the metaphor for the actual process for developing a site and defining what a good site is are in flux. Several sections in this book show the process of using different tools; sometimes you will see screenshots with multiple tools running at the same time because each does something better, faster, or is the only one that does it (and others do not). Figure 2.24 shows a waterfall for web development and the relationship of tool choices.

The web development waterfall is also a trade-off of design issues, strategy requirements, site inclusions (sound, images, video), and the ambience of the site. Notice that the three main themes of a website—performance, consistency, and design—as shown in Figure 2.25 interrelate to create a multidimensional range of designs. Some of them are consistent with each other, whereas some design choices are mutually exclusive. For example, you cannot create a novel and charismatic site (such as MkzdK) without abdicating from consistency.

Page strategy

Every web page and all home pages and supplemental pages should have a strategy and clear message. The page in Figure 2.26 (from a site that is not yet live at the time I made this screen shot) is just a placeholder. It should not be available.

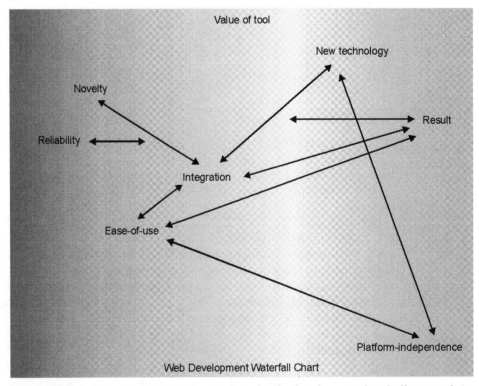

Figure 2.24 The choice of web development tools and technology has a profound effect on website characteristics.

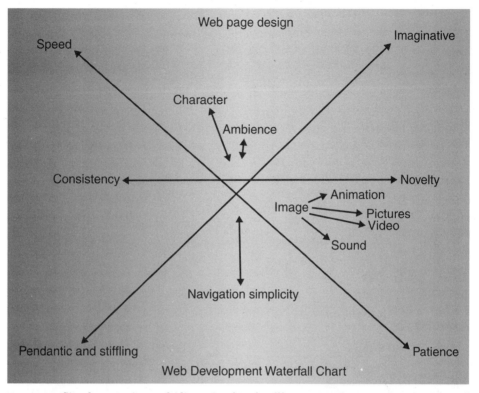

Figure 2.25 Site character is a multidimensional trade-off between performance, imagination, and design choices.

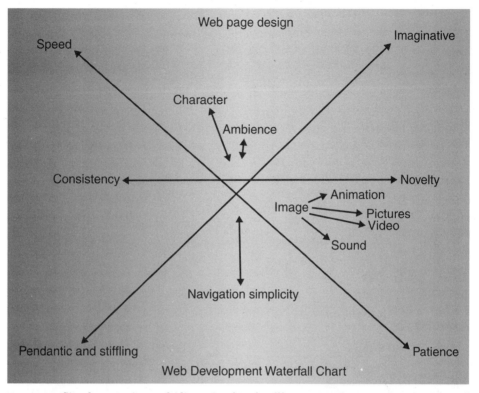

Figure 2.26 This site for personal watercraft has animated (GIF) images of a person digging with text, reinforcing the message that this page is not ready to be seen.

Furthermore, a lot of work went into this placeholder that could have been applied to getting a small but functional site operational. Look at the page. This wave or splash logo on a very muddy background might be related to jet skis. Your guess is as good as mine. The logo and background are clearly tiled, but convey no purpose to this official welcome page. The image is not clear enough, and the overall message is as muddy on that image. Although there are active hyperlinks, the first inference remains "go away, we are not ready."

Another page message error is to play on the words of the "World Wide Web." This is the reason so many products and tools have "web," "spider," "world," or navigation terms in the names or use pictures of webs, spiders, or planetary imagery. In most cases, these names have little relationship to the products or services offered at a cyberstore or commercial site. Use of this articulation is hackneyed and a waste of valuable store space. Can you tell what L5.com is promoting in this static home page, shown in Figure 2.27? It is similar to the pretty but misplaced Platinum splash screen shown later (Figure 2.33).

Deadly design sins

Web design is in flux. It is not clear to me what is best and will work best in the cyberstore, cybershop, or the information kiosk, but it is clear that some

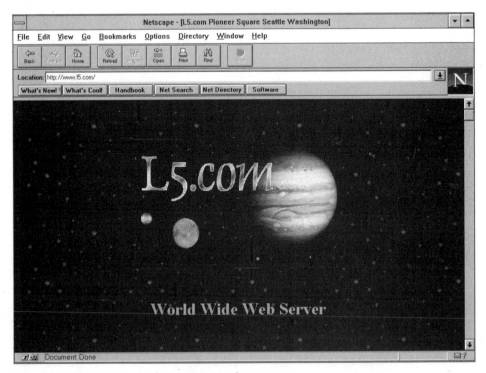

Figure 2.27 A banal message that wastes storefront space.

designs represent the worst in organization and consistency, lack a useful ambience or character, and fail to achieve the objects of the website. The complexity of transaction processing workflows in a cyberstore merely add confusion to sites with design problems. Potential customers see a website as a public representation of an organization. You want a glowing endorsement of that organization. Sore sites containing any of the following thirteen deadly sins of website design form the impression of an organization lacking quality and commitment:

1. Illegible pages

2. Graphic- or add-in-intensive sites

3. Dysfunctional links and controls

4. Under construction messages

5. Feature and function abuse

6. Anything insubstantial

7. Image over substance

8. Recycled sources

9. Lack of structure

10. Lack of focus

11. Maze mentality

12. Access limits

13. Untested, unchecked, unlinked pages

Be careful that websites do not reflect your overexcitement and need for self-expression that exceeds your natural gifts. You have a message to disseminate that needs to be clear, simple, and appealing. The message is broadcast with aesthetic design, informational content, technical balance, and an orchestration of design that is integral to the overall transaction process of a cyberstore. These sins are explored in greater depth in the next thirteen sections, each one reflecting an item in the design sin list.

Illegible pages. Illegible pages are a combination of text over obscuring graphics, use of colors that are not complementary or contrasting (in color, grayscale, or monochrome black & white), setting text font size too small or assigning awkward fonts (such as script, Olde English, and other stylized designs), and columnar designs that overfill or overwrite the browser window. Often, just plain vanilla is a good flavor, given the other complexities of a commercial website.

Graphic- or add-in-intensive sites. Graphic-intensive sites are torture to load. Use small images, and tile backgrounds if possible. Avoid large image maps and realize that an image that looks great on a development station may not scale correctly or fit on browser windows in smaller monitors. Colors may bleed, dither, or be replaced with unsuitable substitutes. Animated images can convey valuable information or draw attention to things otherwise unimportant, but too much motion is distracting and slow. Similarly, add-ins that may include sound, MIDI, ActiveX, VBScripts, and Java torture users with slow modems and connection through overloaded access sites.

Dysfunctional links and controls.   Controls and hyperlinks that do nothing are irritating and suggest that a site, the service it represents, and its products are not much better than the web page itself. Web pages are truly reflective of the organization—like spelling and technical errors in sales literature. What is worse, because the web lacks complete soundness, users are often uncertain about the source of dysfunctional links and controls, whether it is the browser, connection, or hosting site causing these lapses.

Under construction messages.   If a site is under construction, why call attention to that? Your organization would not publish a printed brochure with images missing or a message that the brochure is not yet ready. If a site is under construction, who wants to watch it change? That takes too long in the accelerated world of *hyper*text. If the site does not say anything at all, it has no value, and it doesn't matter whether it is under construction or is complete. If a site has value, why dishonor it with any suggestion that it really isn't good enough to view yet? Since most sites evolve over time to reflect browser, software, commercial processes, design and presentation upgrades, it is only natural that sites are always under construction. Commercial sites need to instill confidence, integrity, and stability; a text message or any of the frivolous signs shown in Figure 2.28 are detrimental to that message.

Figure 2.28 A medley of idiotic signs showing instability, lack of integrity, and a scarcity of confidence.

One site visited used the entire screen showed in Figure 2.29 as a place-holder for the missing page. Placeholders are both a good idea during development and a bad idea, too. They do show the structure, depth, and connectivity of a site, but they also falsely suggest that the site is complete when a web link tool is used to check the continuity and structure of a site. Consider including inactive hyperlinks as a reminder of placeholders or hyperlinks to missing pages.

It is more optimistic to post notification that something is new, fixed, updated, improved, released, hot, or exciting. In fact, the most important words on product packaging include:

- New!
- Improved!
- More!
- Bigger!
- Free!
- Contest!
- Giveaway
- Now . . .

When these terms are accentuated with colorful graphics, it doesn't matter if your site is literally under construction. You can also create a hole and ask surfers to guess what is coming soon or create an image that changes on a daily basis—which isn't a big task. Make it fun and games if your site can in-

Figure 2.29 A placeholder creates a false impression of site completion . . . to the developers.

dulge that attitude. Some leisure or lifestyle products reach out to children or adults after work hours. Consider how LifeSavers® promotes the Gummi candy with a flashy website and links to games in Figure 2.30.

When you consider that website development costs run upwards of $130,000, with maintenance costs equal to or greater than that, and that advertisement placement in trade or specialized consumer magazines can cost $7,500 per page per issue, giving away a PC ($1,500) or laptop ($4,000) is less costly promotion, as shown in Figure 2.31. However, you still need to get the message out that you have a contest or giveaway. That may require print advertising nevertheless. However, use the search engines to your site's best publicity and add URLs for contest, giveaway, challenge, lottery, or other similar terms. By the way, review the municipal and legal requirements in the geographical point-of-presence or where you do business for rules and requirements so that you do not create a legal predicament. It doesn't cost users much (just time) to fill out a form and register, but if you generate a mailing list, some interest in your site, hopefully create some solid sales leads, and perhaps even some on-line sales, then it is worthwhile.

Even if the site is somber, an image of the "missing pilot" formation or an empty place at a table can provide an effective message about the sorrow of a major loss or the need for that user or customer as a key donor. The user is attracted to visual highlights. Metaphors, allusions, allegory, and symbolism are powerful additions to an otherwise purely textual message. Use striking and attention-grabbing star bursts. Did your eyes go directly to the graphics in Figure 2.32 when you turned to this page?

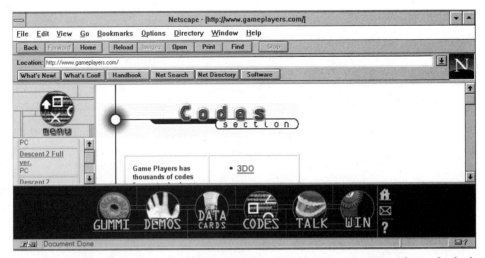

Figure 2.30 Interest in some products can be broadened with a game or tie-in with standard advertising practices, a web with glitz, and contest as with LifeSavers® Gummi candy.

Figure 2.31 The free giveaway is useful to attract users. It has elements of a lottery and actually represents a reasonable return on investment.

Feature and function abuse. It is not my suggestion or recommendation to imbed multimedia videos and audio stories (such as .WAV, .AVI, MIDI, and QuickTime) interactive transactions (through Java applets, Cookies, or VBScripts and ActiveX controls), various streaming presentation formats, remote window control, paging, and videoconferencing into a web page just because it is possible. Just as it is uncomfortable to listen to one person talk over a large and noisy crowd, it is jarring to see and hear competing messages. Avoid HTML, Java, and imbedded applet feature and function abuse unless it reinforces the strategic site message or simplifies site navigation. Use the technology to accentuate the message, not confuse it.

Anything insubstantial. Do you think your cyberstore will benefit from posting material that is weak, immaterial, scatterbrained, unintelligible, muddled, jumbled, incoherent, or confused? If you are posting material only to get a site established as a mere foothold, post a clear message. Do not overload the

Figure 2.32 These signs alerted you to the importance of the site.

site with lots of material because it is available or easy to convert with HTML Transit, Web.Data, or an optical character recognition (OCR) tool. General Motors created a huge site (1309 HTML pages) that is unwieldy, not searchable, and mostly noisy messages.

Instead, explain the purpose of the site, the nature of the organization, and highlight what is available at the site. If you are building a cyberstore and have nothing to say, at least imbed an E-mail or *Listserv* function so that you can gather potential customers' names on an E-mail mailing list or a bulk rate list for sending out postcards or brochures. That is a very good marketing use for a commercial website. Do not waste users' time with random thoughts. On the other hand, some sites are designed as puzzles or include puzzles to captivate a user. That purpose, let me assure you, is very calculated and very coherent, not scatterbrained or insubstantial.

Another pet peeve is the use of spurious images, video, sounds, and text to dress up a web page. Consider the *splash* image for Platinum Technology's home page as shown in Figure 2.33. Although this company makes very good products for integrating host mainframe databases for dynamic and interactive web pages (notably CICS and DB2 platforms), the logo has been expanded with these very irrelevant and insubstantial metaphors. This visual goulash seems to suggest that the lion, giraffe, and zebra can coexist in some messianic high-tech solar system. Although colorful and nicely executed, the splash screen sends no clear message and merely dampens my enthusiasm.

Image over substance. Although too many images irritate a user, images for the sake of prettiness over substance do not work at most cyberstores and do not lend themselves to providing a focused message. Stunning images that you think will knock customers over and get them to fight for your products or services instead show a fatal presumption that image is the only powerful selling tool. Image over substance is likely to repel the busiest and most powerful customers who have the true decision-making authority.

Figure 2.33 Insubstantial splash screen. Are they selling exotic "beef"?

However, Zen-like imagery does work for products and services that lack a clear quality, including luxurious travel, jewelry, and other lifestyle products. Images are effective to describe and define physical products in a catalog, but not when the images overwhelm descriptive documentation and the message. Images add to the detail in a substantial way, but do not substitute for price, quality, reliability, and delivery details, as shown in Figure 2.34.

Recycled sources. A website is meant to augment standard sales and marketing procedures. A business built on the cyberstore concept with no other outlets is unlikely to thrive. If you post product specification sheets, marketing brochures, and repeat print advertisements through the technology of format conversion and OCR, the website is just another slower and less convenient way to get the information. Recycled sources have little innate value. Instead, categorize the material and cross-index it so that it is easier to find; animate a salient point; or even make it interactive. Honda Motors does this very effectively with the Accord Sedan page, as shown in Figure 2.35.

This is a simple trick, as you can see, that requires no Java, no fancy animation, no applets, and no code, but is nonetheless very effective. It works because the most salient point of a car (for each make and model) to a buyer is its color (and its price). When you click on the different color paint chips, an entirely different HTML page is loaded. All seven pages are identical except that the image for the car in the center is a different file that shows a

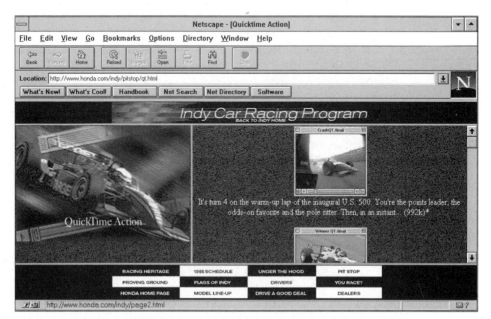

Figure 2.34 Lots of speed and flash, but where is the message as it relates to a car manufacturer and dealership chain?

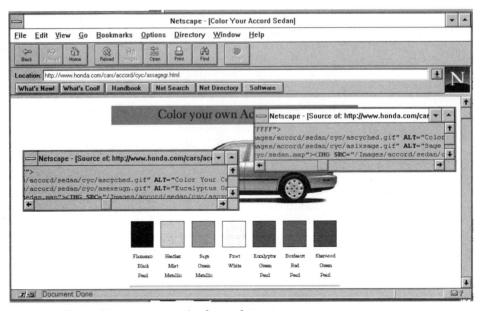

Figure 2.35 Interactive pages are as simple as a hotspot.

car of a different color. It is so simple a concept, let me repeat the process. The paint chips are standard web image files. Click on the paint chip to request a page that is a duplicate, except for the imbedded image file. If you still do not get how the "animation" is accomplished, go to the Honda site. Although this information is lifted directly from the brochure, the hook is the simple interactivity.

Honda could use the same technique with HTML list boxes enabling options (such as moon roof, air conditioning, and leather interior) to create a secondary pricing form. This is demonstrated elsewhere in the book for real estate and other complex products. The price with desired options is the other important buyer differentiation. It is part of the marketing concept called *targeted advertising* and is aimed at a select group or even an identified person. Honda also uses this site to gather marketing leads for mailing out brochures or connecting a buyer with the closest local dealer. A lot of this site's information is published in the brochures, but the little interactive hook and coordination of buyer with vendor raises this site from the lowly recycled bin of glossy print brochures.

Lack of structure. A novel has a structure; it is linear from start to finish. Newspapers have structure; there is a front page with lead-in stories and other sections also with lead-in news. TV news shows have a structure defined to the second to cover major events, weather, sports, and traffic, and allow room for contracted advertisements. "Fast-breaking" events are the "new" and "improved" hook to retain viewers. Websites require a comparable structure that is clear not only to the site developers, but more importantly, also to the user. You want to know where things are and how to find what you want. Maps help. Organization of topics into chapters and sections is important. Special attention-getting graphics are the hooks to topics the site designers are hoping you will notice. Structure makes a website cohesive, whereas the lack of comprehensive structure reflects badly on the quality, commitment, and integrity of the sponsoring organization.

Lack of focus.   A lack of focus confuses users. It hides, muddies, and distorts the point of a website. Having a focal point does not mean that a cyberstore does only one thing, but rather that the site represents a communication channel between vendor and user. For example, a focused website might include a framed introductory home page, icons to various sections and functions, and a map of the layout. The sections might include company contact information, mailing list subscription, product specifications, product descriptions, on-line ordering, hypertext on-line, technical support, and a complaint department. Think about the physical organization; it has a structure with subgroups usually defined by function, product, or purpose. Confused organizations do not work well and succeed. Confused websites do not succeed either.

Maze mentality.   Some sites create mazes as part of the ambience and character of the site. MkzdK is one of those labyrinth sites. However, a cyberstore requires a different script. Compare the process of shopping in a department store. You expect separate men's, women's, and children's departments. You expect a wide hallway and elevators to navigate between sections. You expect to pay within each department or take all the accumulated merchandise in a shopping cart to a register at a checkout. The shopping cart metaphor is very common with cyberstores and the tools to build them. If you need credit help, there is a department just for that. If you need a bathroom, you expect men's and women's to be near each other or located in the corresponding departments.

Store designers route you past end caps (highlighted and prominent displays) with merchandise the vendor wants to sell quickly, past specific sales or high-margin displays, and even through winding aisles or a series of constricted boutiques. It seems like a maze, and it is designed to lengthen the time a shopper browses. Nevertheless, the physical store is navigable and you can map it. And there are clerks to help you locate what you need. A customer gets very frustrated, even angry, when the store clerks are not around and the customer is endlessly lost. Customers do get angry in superstores (compare the "superfailure" of superstore Incredible Universe) when clerks mistakenly route them from one corner of the store back and forth looking for a product that is not stocked, out of stock, or somewhere else in the very big building.

Do not have a maze mentality when you design your website unless you have "cyber clerks" to route lost customers to products and services. You want to create a script for the website that includes sections, elevators, floor maps, and an alternative to clerks at counters to help you find a particular department. This alternative includes a table of contents, indexing, a consistent map of hyperlinks on every page, and a search engine that addresses questions not found in the road maps and basic department and feature signage. If you want to keep customers browsing at cyber end caps, virtual boutiques, and running through a maze of sale merchandise, you might want to create a maze through particular passages. Mark it well. Light it well. Map it well. Explain it clearly.

Nevertheless, make certain the site itself is navigable and can be mapped. Server side WebMapper and the CyberPilot Pro client-side tools create site maps that can be posted with a site so that surfers can get an overview of your cyberstore quickly without decoding your maze or trying to decipher your navigation maps. The CyberPilot approach standardizes the map, as shown with a NetCarta public library of site maps in Figure 2.36.

Access limits.   Not every user has the newest browser with all the add-ins, security features, and functional support of frames, columns, animation, and video-conferencing. In fact, some users disable graphics support *on purpose*. Design your site with a plain vanilla HTML interface so that its access is unrestricted to all users. Supplement graphics that play an integral part of communicating the site message with text for users with a browser that does not support graphics or for the user who has specifically disabled graphics. Create a text-only page and subordinate text-only pages to overcome access limitations as Excite does with their site as pictured in Figure 2.37. Web.Designer creates text replacements for nonshowing images automatically; just fill the form fields with useful text.

The mechanism is simply another tree of HTML pages accessible only from this low-bandwidth option. It contains all the information of the other track, but with replacements for images, sounds, and other byte-intensive add-ins.

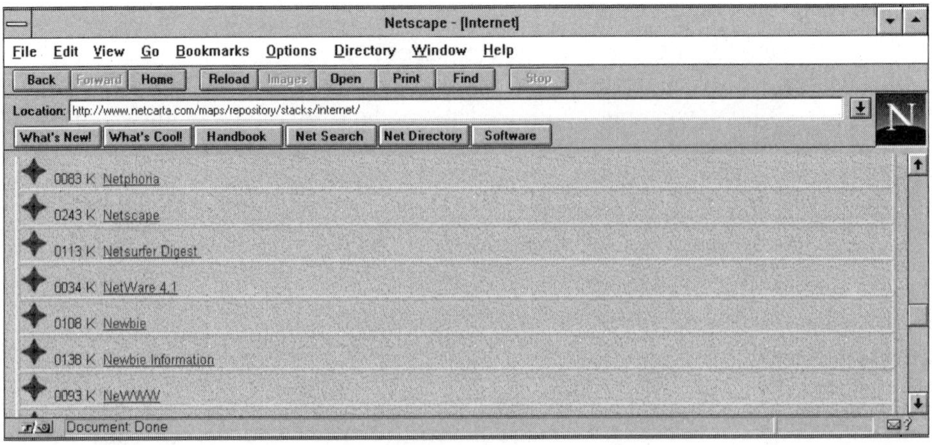

Figure 2.36 NetCarta library of CyberPilot maps created by WebMapper.

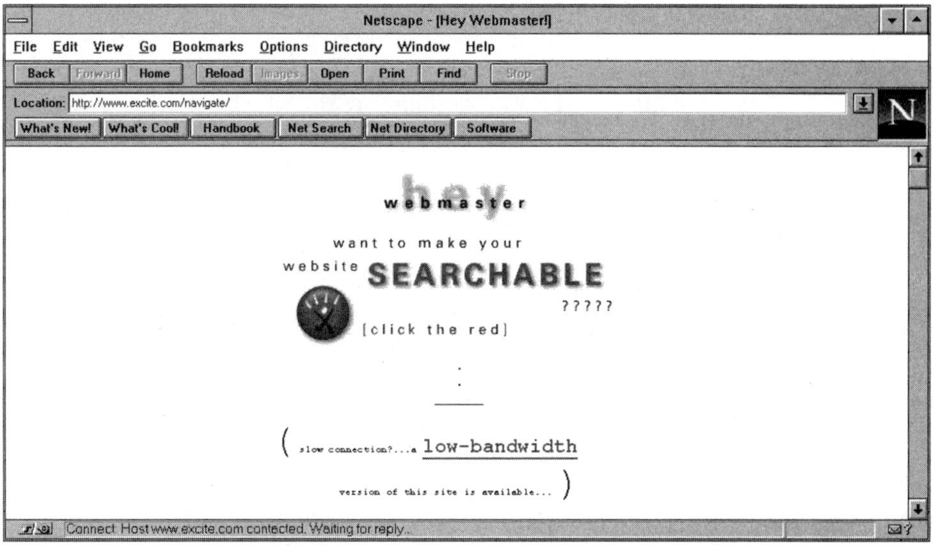

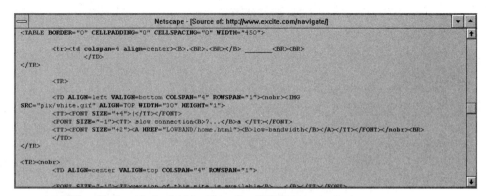

Figure 2.37 The Excite search engine is resolution and graphics independent.

The HTML code is listed in Figure 2.38. On the other hand, if you want to create an archetypal site with all the newest features, use a tool such as WebMate to design the site and load different modules as required to support the functionality of different browsers and versions of those browsers. WebMate commits your organization to multiplatform development problems, but at least, this tool organizes and simplifies many of the complications.

A technical document, called the NC Reference Profile 1, defines the hardware guidelines, Internet protocols, WWW standards, E-mail protocols, common multimedia formats, security features, boot protocols, and physical platform requirements for a device that accesses the Internet. The "NC" sets

```
<TABLE BORDER="0" CELLPADDING="0" CELLSPACING="0" WIDTH="450">

        <tr><td colspan=4 align=center><B>.<BR>.<BR></B> ________<BR><BR>
                </TD>
</TR>

        <TR>

        <TD ALIGN=left VALIGN=bottom COLSPAN="4" ROWSPAN="1"><nobr><IMG
SRC="pix/white.gif" ALIGN=TOP WIDTH="30" HEIGHT="1">
        <TT><FONT SIZE="+4">(</TT></FONT>
        <FONT SIZE="-1"><TT> slow connection<B>?...</B>a </TT></FONT>
        <TT><FONT SIZE="+2"><A HREF="LOWBAND/home.html"><B>low-bandwidth</B></A></TT></FONT></nobr><BR>
        </TD>
</TR>

<TR><nobr>
        <TD ALIGN=center VALIGN=top COLSPAN="4" ROWSPAN="1">
```

Figure 2.38 The simple code for fetching the other HTML page track.

standards for the "network computer" and it is a trademark. Chapter 3 defines this Apple Computer-sponsored profile in detail. Because most of the major vendors adhere to these guidelines, consider that part of your website development success will depend on your technical knowledge of how to create web pages that provide unlimited access to customers except where you specifically define browser and add-in requirements, or establish special security and authentication to access some or all parts of a site.

Untested, unchecked, unlinked pages.   A site with spelling errors; malformed or badly sized graphics; untested, unchecked, and unlinked pages; and services that simply do not work is the last, thirteenth, and most unprofessional of the web design sins. Spelling checkers work within most Word or Wordperfect HTML editing add-ins. High-end HTML editors include these tools.

This book discusses the process of building commercial sites with database transactional processing over the web and over private networks. You will need to test that integration. If you are building a site only with *freeHTML, freeDBMS, freeCGI, freeCredit,* and *freeHTTP* (that is, make-believe shareware or unsupported freeware editing and server software), you are playing games and do not understand the need to construct a viable, reliable, and functional cyberstore. In addition, various mapping tools, such as WebMapper, Web Doctor, and Web Analyzer, check the structure for broken, missing, changed, or nonworking links. There are even various shareware tools that do the same thing. I do not mean to suggest that shareware or freeware tools are insufficient to build a good site; rather, you need a full tool chest with functional tools (even if free) to check the site.

Finally, check your site personally. Check the links. Check the functionality. Do not let your users and customers be your guinea pigs. It is advisable to maintain a live "staging" site and have a secondary site for development and testing. This can be another URL on the same host or better yet another host. Check colors, links, speeds for downloads, browsers, and suitability. When you revise pages, move them to this intermediate site for testing. Only when all seems correct, use the File Transfer Protocol (FTP) to move the staging files to the live site. Check again. Check the file names and access rights. Make certain the links and paths are still correct, that permissions are set correctly, and that the site works as intended. There is nothing quite as bad as a message that says a surfer has insufficient security or rights to read your home page. There are also a number of design tools that map a website and look for broken links and other flaws. An interesting one is based at a website and shows some of the promise of actually doing business on the Internet. Doctor HTML (RxHTML) is free to noncommercial users, not for your cyberstore. Nevertheless, a secure HTML page might ask for credit card information, middleware might validate that field input, and after payment confirmation, this RxHTML function could actually be displayed, as shown in Figure 2.39. While many of the desktop tools and HTML editors would not even load the very simple first-generation pages at this site because of "fatal" HTML errors, Doctor HTML generated the very clean report, as shown in Figure 2.40.

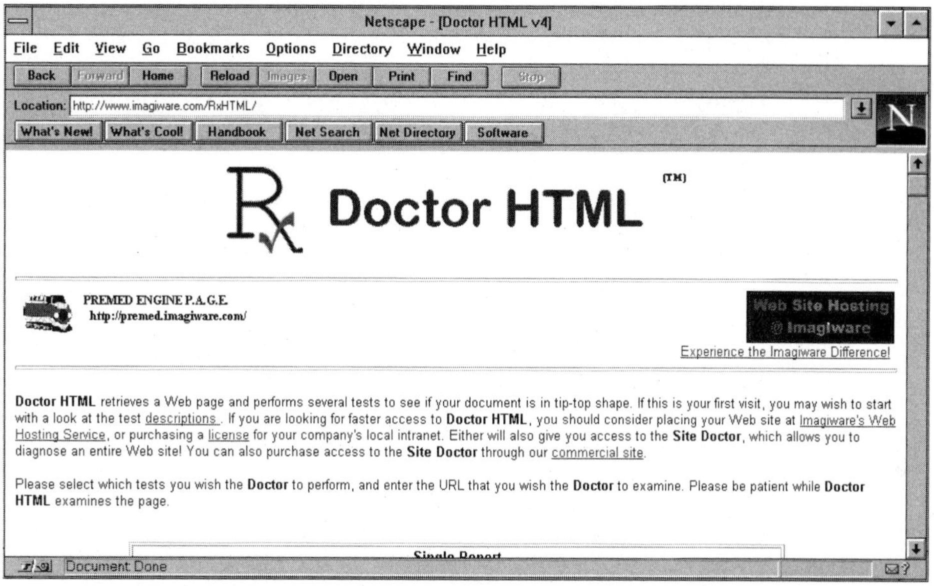

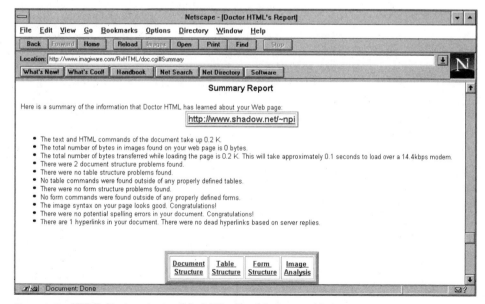

Figure 2.39 This website checks your website (specify the URL) for spelling, grammar, links, graphics, and other complex design or programming errors.

I suggest that you not rely solely on any one tool because WebAnalyzer points out broken links on this site but not other things, and WebMapper shows that one of the live pages is actually garbled and that the source file is corrupted. Use Quarterdeck Mosaic, NCSA Mosaic, Explorer, Navigator, the

Figure 2.40 HTML Doctor gives a (false) bill of health for my old site.

CompuServe Spry interface, WebSurfer, NetSurfer, versions old and new. Check access under OS/2, Windows, Macintosh, AIX, Solaris, and even AS/400 if you have access to an AS/400-Mosaic browser. Check various window and monitor sizes. Look at the graphics for legibility, resolution, and comprehension by a new web user, a non-native speaker, and certainly someone not intimately familiar with organization workflow, culture, and products or services. The site should convey the expected message without any predisposition, preferences, or prior knowledge. Since a cyberstore also includes some complex workflows required for creating customer accounts, taking orders, verifying credit, issuing credit for returns, and resolving customer complaints and technical difficulties, these processes should flow smoothly for the new on-line shopper.

Web design sources

The best source for design tips is other websites. Pick what you like. Pick the best concepts. Do not copy the pages and styles outright because you might run afoul of copyright laws. Also, do not copy them because your site becomes a "me-too," with a vaguely industrial character like everyone else's, or at least, certainly, the sites you copy. This same admonition is true for clipart because even though it is sold without limitations (other than its resale as a clipart collection) you do not want to create a cyberstore that looks like everyone else's. You will want to create a unique look. Just because another site works, does not mean you should do the same thing. Character and ambience is a style like hemlines, tie widths, and magazine cover styles. It changes based on the competition and what seems to work, as well as the industry and organizational character. You may have better ideas than those of designers at other sites. Design is plastic parameter. However, you should dissect other sites for ideas and, more importantly, the technical mechanisms that make the HTML work.

This is a technical design tip to use throughout your cyberstore design and development effort: most browsers (Mosaic and Navigator) include a web page source view option. Try the Navigator menu option *View / Document Source*. You can see how other cyberstores and websites implement most everything in the site. Explore how this window on design can be pertinent to your site. There are few sustainable secrets on the Internet. While most sites protect CGI applications to prevent viruses, security holes, and worms, the HTML in a web page defines everything. In addition, Netscape Navigator provides useful document file information from the *View / Document Info* menu selection, as shown in Figure 2.41.

Many HTML authoring tools add information to the page header that is not normally added when a designer creates a page by hand within an ASCII editor. The header information can include the file name (not just the URL), the name of the author, by what tool it was constructed, design dates, last edit dates, the version support for the HTML, and if the page supports secured http

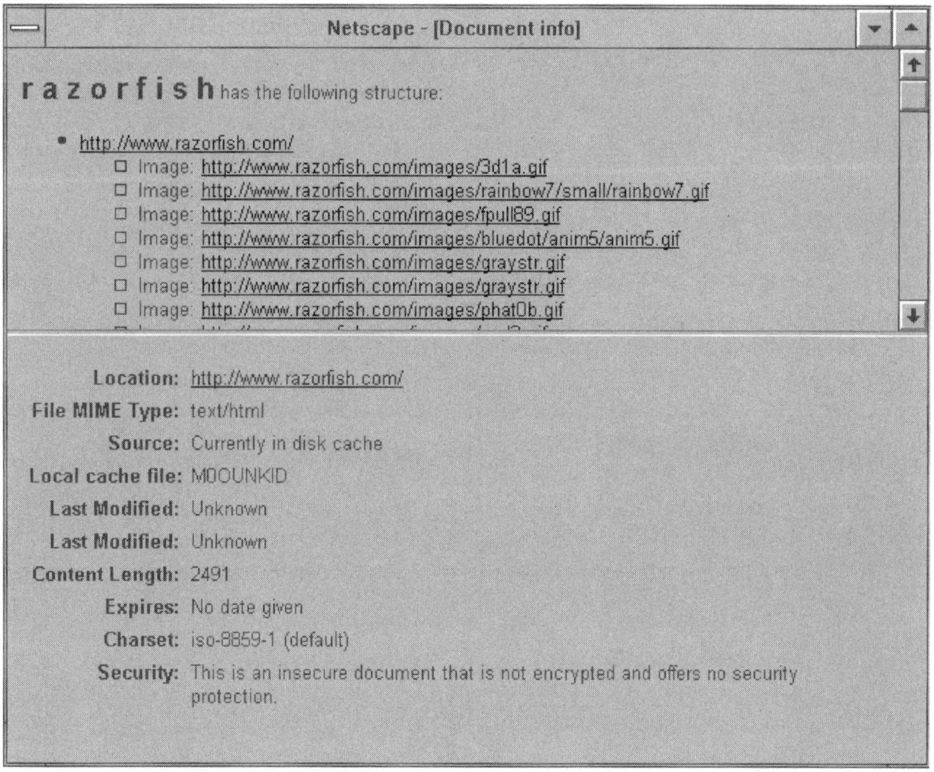

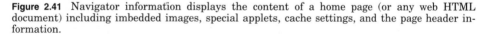

Figure 2.41 Navigator information displays the content of a home page (or any web HTML document) including imbedded images, special applets, cache settings, and the page header information.

transmission. It is even possible to include a page expiration date to prevent distribution of pages (and hence prevent sales of items no longer in stock or downloads of beta software that has since been released). If you desire some or none of this information, construct a template page with just a header, and imbed this template into all other pages or use it as the master design template with HotDog, BackPage, and Backstage Designer tools.

While some websites provide both good and bad examples in design for the cyberstore, and some tools include design templates and large art galleries, some of the most interesting sources for website design are actually websites hosting information about site design and including links to other useful sites. Keep my earlier admonition in mind because this web surfing can consume many hours and simple questions can lead to many more answers than you can possibly assimilate. Nevertheless, Figure 2.42 shows Weblings Graphics Home Page, some of the articles therein, and many links to comparable sites.

Some web design and information sites archive nice background material. However, you have to give the operators credit because the site is a promotion

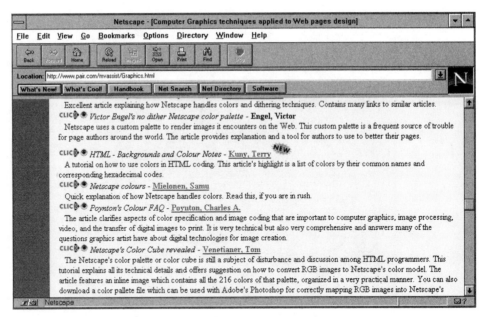

Figure 2.42 Web design pointers on the web.

for a product, service, other information, or newsletters. Activ Media pushes their research and expertise from their site, as shown in Figure 2.43. The better sites often contain commentary and interpretation on the meaning of various web tools, design techniques, and the basic transport and markup specifications. In general, specifications represent the concept of an idea, but the commentaries demonstrate how to actually implement that idea. Web Reference is such a site, as shown in Figure 2.44.

Even if you were to buy all the tools mentioned in this book, or pick the ones that I insinuated were the best, you would not necessarily achieve the best results. First, as stated previously many times, success with the cyberstore means success with integrating many tools, many parts, and many processes, particularly the point-of-sales and financial tracking systems. Second, web design is in a state of flux, mostly from its newness, and mostly from a lack of clear road signs to success. Third, many of the tools have yet to be even imagined. For these reasons, you want to remain plugged in to the home page for this book and the many sites it links to so you can track new tools. One such site is the Webmaster's Tool Chest, as shown in Figure 2.45.

Teaching sites exploring the potential of computer-based training (CBT) on the Internet represent not only a powerful website educational tool, but also an effective sales and marketing mechanism. In addition, CBT is useful for resolving technical support problems around the clock, offloading overburdened and expensive support personnel, and cutting the turnaround time for resolving customer complaints. The Professor Pete site shows some of the

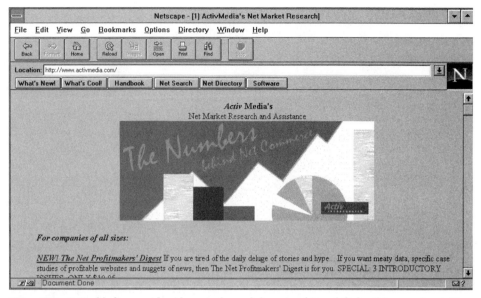

Figure 2.43 Activ Media provides ideas, tools, and demographics while hawking a subscription-based newsletter aimed at cyberstore developers.

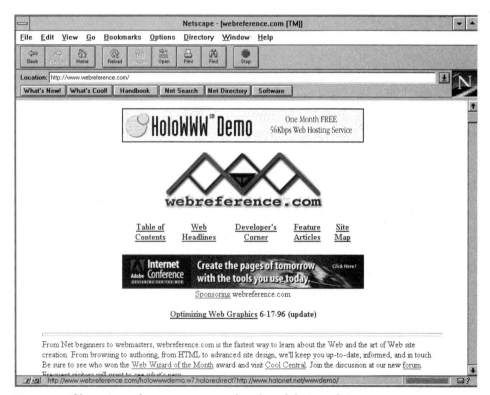

Figure 2.44 Glossaries and commentary on web tools and design policies.

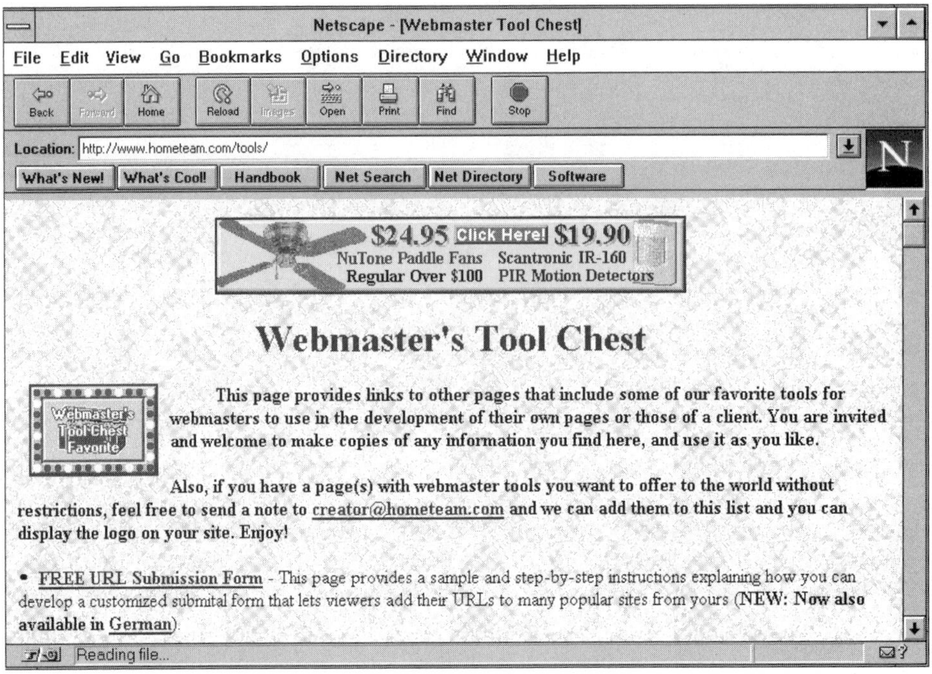

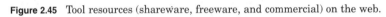

Figure 2.45 Tool resources (shareware, freeware, and commercial) on the web.

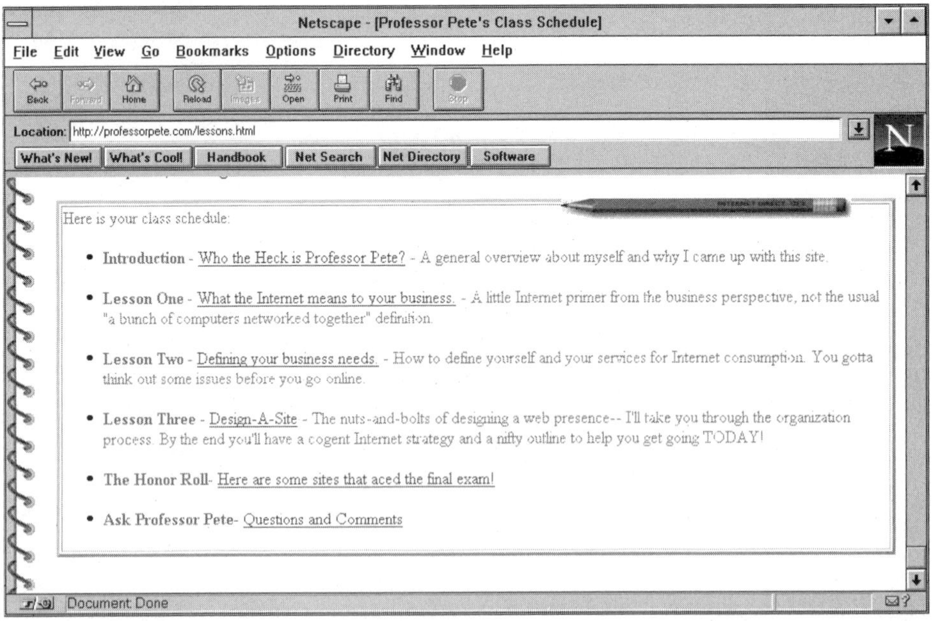

Figure 2.46 Website development training also demonstrates some of the CBT techniques that utilize the best of the Internet channel.

basic web design techniques and how to effectively implement CBT, as shown in Figure 2.46. Perhaps one of the most obvious reasons that the Professor Pete site is profiled here as a web design and development resource is the horse sense offered on such issues as website purpose, core business needs, integration with organizational workflow, and mesh with business functions, as shown in Figure 2.47. You need to understand website technology to design effective sites and create working implementations, but you need to precede that with business acumen.

The current state of the advanced web design site includes compilations of source information, commentary on that source information, libraries of tools, archives of CGI code, and links to other sites. Selena Sol's Online Library typifies the best of this aggregation, as shown in Figure 2.48.

By the way, Selena Sol's site includes at least four different libraries validating the CGI-coded cybershop concept. I think these CGI tools are sufficient for the cybershop with a limited product line, but not the complex cyberstore, and they are toys when it comes to the cybermall. You will find that expansion of the cybershop product line to full-service cyberstore will strain your ability (and any larger teams') to program all the options required. Even if you could support that task, I suspect that cloning the CGI code needed for each product selection will yield a high incidence of code errors and flaws. A DBMS integration with an accounting system ensures a higher likelihood of success.

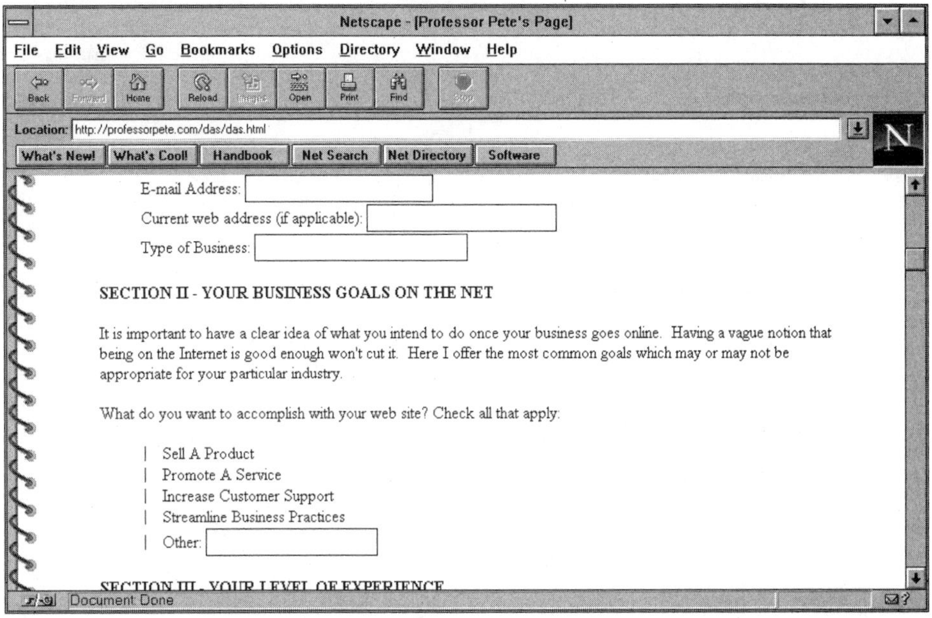

Figure 2.47 One of the more practical lectures by Professor Pete meshes with the purpose, financial tracking, strategy, and marketing themes of this book.

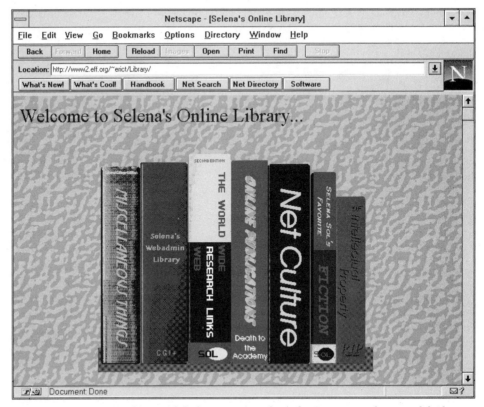

Figure 2.48 An aggregated site with links, sources, tools, and commentary, plus one of the largest sites for public domain CGI source and cyberstore programs.

Organization and structure

A website is like any communication medium. It has a start, an end, and various parts in the middle. When a website mimics the structure of an organization, it needs services comparable to phone directories, organizational charts, service phone books, and really smart secretarial help. After all, most sites do not have a person on call all the time to track user navigation paths, help lost users, or respond immediately to E-mail. You can do that if you want with pager services or connections to a call response center. However, it is expensive to integrate and activate. In general, for most websites and cyberstores, however, there are no artificially intelligent cyber clerks to help lost users or create better designs. Your site needs to compensate for that.

Complex sites that provide organizational information, calendars, glossaries, product information, technical support, and links to people in the organization need that basic table of contents. FirstFloor maintains a consistent image from page to page, as shown in Figure 2.49, to help with that basic table of contents. The table of contents represents a broad-brush view of a site. A good table of contents, both for a book and for a website, includes major chap-

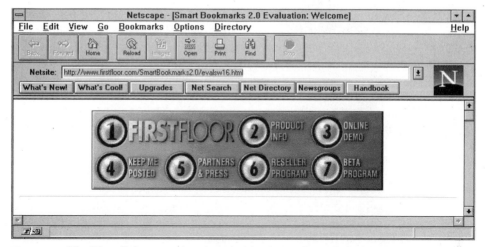

Figure 2.49 FirstFloor Software assigns its prioritization to the surfer's visit.

ters, sections, and subheadings. The image map shown in the prior site provides only the chapter information, not the details. WebMapper simplifies the process of developing a table of contents, as shown in Figure 2.50, once a site has been built. You can incorporate this hypertext map into the site with your own web page templates (using cut and paste, and it helps for that to have a

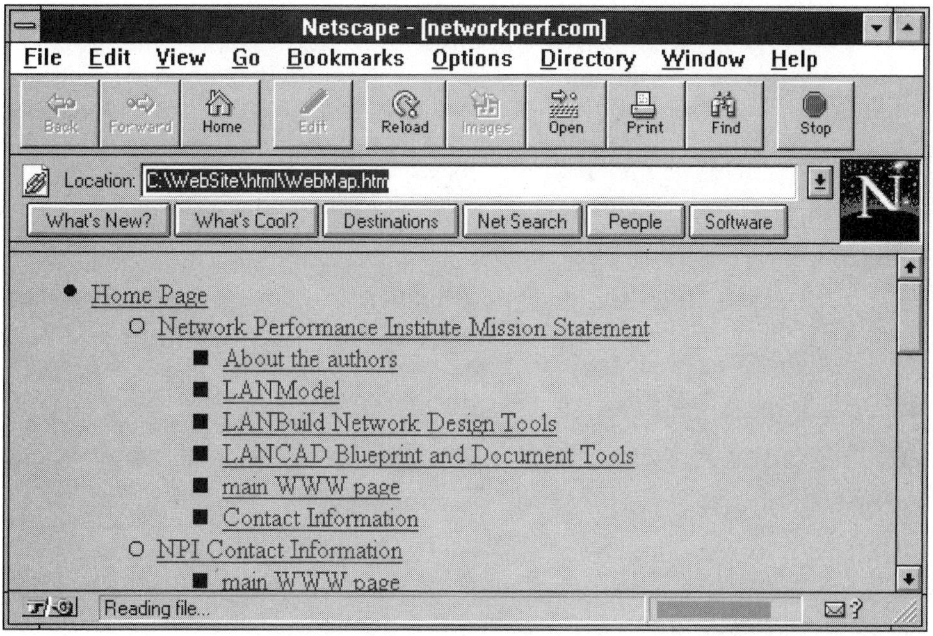

Figure 2.50 WebMapper and the client-side tool, CyberPilot Pro, create HTML pages in standard book index format outlining the site organization.

windowed HTML editor or two editors running at the same time). However, re-alistically, when you are building a cyberstore, you will want to design this structure in advance; first, to facilitate a clear and complete coverage and sec-ond, to provide an effective navigation path for customers.

Most men tend to be visually oriented and read highway maps, whereas women tend to prefer text-based maps and stepwise process instructions. This tendency has a biological basis driven by left/right brain connectivity and hor-mones. The ambience of the site ideally should reflect both sexes, or reflect the primary customer at the site and his or her needs. Do not allow your biases to define the predominant site mapping, organization, and navigation tech-niques. Recognize that other people may look at the site without graphics-enabled browsers or from the other view of website navigation. Create both types of maps, including the image map, which is discussed next.

Although MapInfo is a company that provides geographic and GIS mapping tools and datasets, it overuses map references and maps in its site. For exam-ple, the company details its international sales offices with a gratuitous world map that does not provide any new information. The map does not show re-gions or actual locations of offices on a geographic map; these are listed as mailing addresses and telephone numbers in text beneath the space wasted by the map. However, the site designers at MapInfo did have a good understand-ing of the complexity of the site and the many concepts and tracks. To help surfers navigate the site maze, they created this sparkling hierarchical tree shown in Figure 2.51. The text and images are mapped as hot spots linking to the appropriate pages.

The newest technique for website design is the multiple frame form. WebMaster, as shown by the screen capture in Figure 2.52, overdoes it with too many unfamiliar icons and a page-to-page flow that often makes a jump back between pages become a jump to the last *site*. This defect is a function of both Explorer and Navigator browsers. (You need to use the *right* mouse but-ton to go forward and backward in frames.) The back button saves the URL addresses for the entire HTML document and does not track documents within frames. This is a significant disadvantage overcome by imbedded tables in-stead of frames. I got lost in this site continually and got bounced back to other sites; and even though the hand pointer changed the URL indicator on the bot-tom of the window when placed over each icon, the HTML file names were not always concise enough to give a clue as to the purpose of each icon button.

MkzdK is the wildest site profiled in this book. It was not a commercial site and seems designed by someone with an overactive imagination and an excess of free time. Nevertheless, it is a marvel of design, organization, and the im-plementation of the latest HTML design tools and specifications. It uses design as ambience, and the philosophy of its science-fiction message is embodied by that ambience, as shown in Figure 2.53. The frames contain list boxes that tie together various philosophies and create a multidimensional structure to this website, not merely the typical format of a home page with chapters, or a branching tree structure with chapters and sections, but rather a cubic file cabinet with hypertext links between all those cabinets. However, the designer

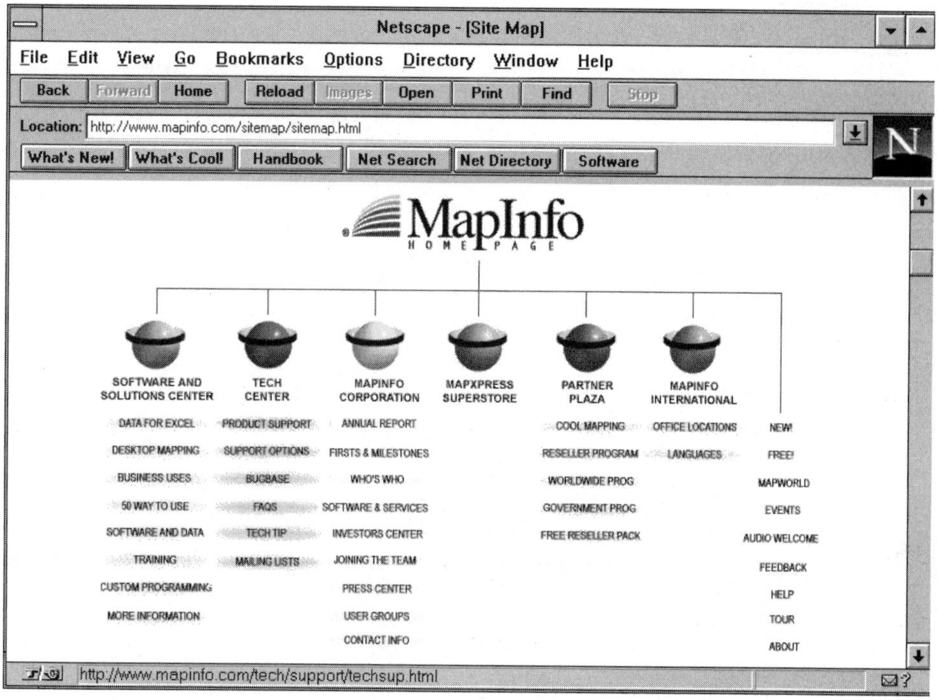

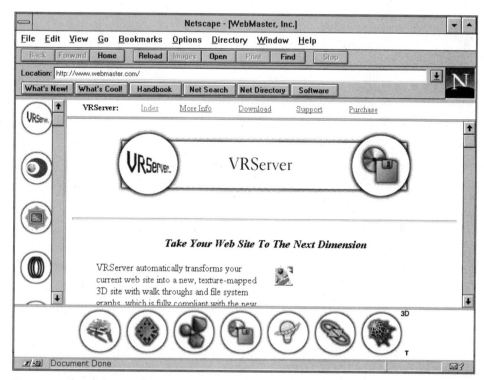

Figure 2.51 A graphical presentation of the organization of a complex website.

Figure 2.52 A website overdesigned with unfamiliar icon buttons.

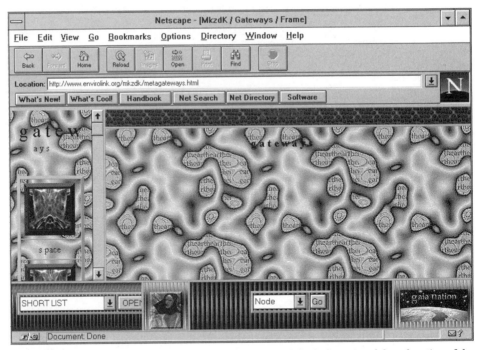

Figure 2.53 Hyperlinks can be anything and the density of the linkage is solely a function of design and the resources to create the linkages.

realized that the complexity and depth of the site required some visual and textual maps to help the new user navigate the site and understand the relationship between HTML pages. The cubic connectivity is reflected by the layered maps in Figure 2.54.

Site search and indexes

Promoting customer access to your cyberstore is not only a factor of listing your URL and key phrases and products with the commercial web search sites such as Lycos, OpenText, and Alta Vista. You also want to provide search and indexing capabilities once a customer is connected to your site. That means you want similar capabilities at the cyberstore as well. For example, suppose your organization carries 37,875 wire connectors and punch down blocks and a customer needs a four-wire connection, crimp-installation connector that is subminiature and conforms to the TIA/EIA 568 specification. The National Semiconductor and AMP sites use different database search techniques and are profiled in Chapters 4 and 5 as examples of database/web integration and an on-line cyberstore sales channel.

How will the customer locate that category of parts (you may stock thirty different types) or select from a range of possible matches? That's the power of

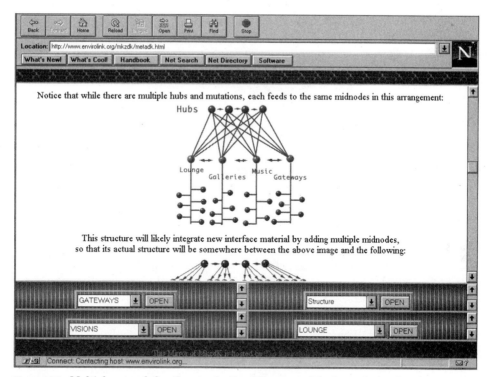

Figure 2.54 Multiple maps define the complexity of the site and the interrelationships between different paths through the site.

the search and index engine to locate connectors in a product-line haystack. Search capability is a very important marketing and customer support tool to get customers to your organization rather than to a competitor's indexed but printed catalog or to a telemarketing center with real people and only a two-minute wait.

There are several techniques for adding search capabilities to a website. The first technique is to add a search engine such as Alta Vista or Excite to the actual cyberstore site. These indexes only map the local site. You do not want to add a search engine that goes beyond local content, or add links and code into a home page that calls these global search engines. Those index traps filter from a larger Internet index, are slower, and may provide unwanted links to a competitor's site. These *local* search tools will read *local* document names, text within HTML files, and sometimes text within other types of files (such as .PDF, standard WinWord .DOC files, plain ASCII .TXT text files, and even visual content inside graphic files.) The minimum components needed for the OpenText LiveLink local search engines is shown in Figure 2.55. This is the most robust and user-friendly approach because it is a very powerful and complete index. The commercial search engines are expensive but easier to integrate because they generate matches on the fly and

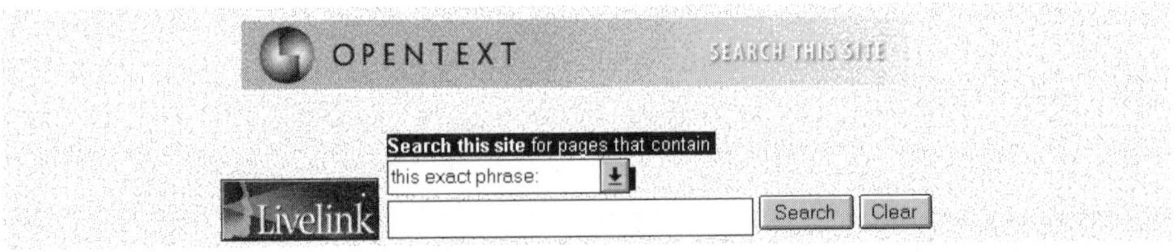

Figure 2.55 The fields for implementing the LiveLink engine.

provide more hits on large sites. Hewlett-Packard includes a full-search engine, as shown in Figure 2.56.

One of the benefits of the commercial interactive search engines is that the more advanced ones includes dictionaries of synonyms so that close matches and comparable ideas can be located, not just literal unions of Boolean terms. For example, a search with "Attention Deficit Disorder" and "children" should also yield hits based on the related terms of "ADHD," "ADD," and "learning disabilities." Many of the engines are not as intelligent as a good research librarian. That is where the second, noninteractive but nonetheless very automated approach proves its value for Intranet, commercial websites, and cyberstores.

There are many available freeshare CGI search tools that may search the text of the entire local website, search predefined indexes, or create HTML

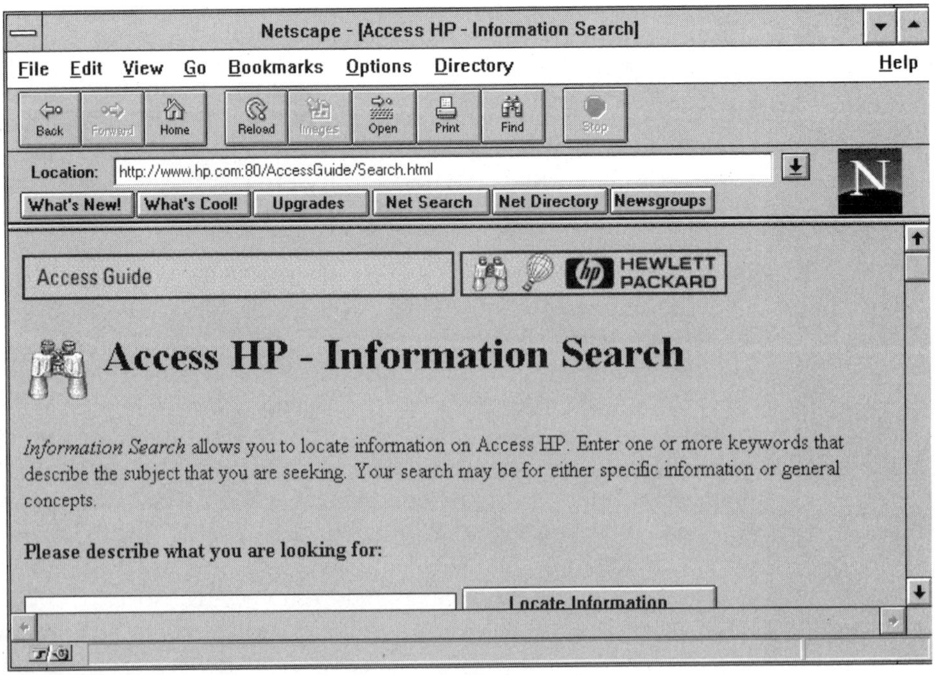

Figure 2.56 Commercial search engine for a commercial website.

search pages. The downside is that the CGI tools are difficult to configure, require careful manual construction of indexes, and need to be added to every page or imbedded in the page template. In addition, each running CGI script requires its own processing thread and therefore that overhead can be substantial. Since text searches are slow as computer processes go, the overhead should be avoided with other approaches.

The second approach is an indexing tool such as WebIndex that is delivered with WebSite Pro, assuming you are hosting the website locally on a WindowsNT Server, NT Workstation, or Windows95 platform. This is your basic indexing utility that should not be ignored on the smallest cybershop. The following sequence of screen shots shows the setup and indexing process, beginning with Figure 2.57. You will need to specify the types of files included in the website and attached cyberstore support, as shown in Figure 2.58. This index utility finds all unattached and unlinked files, so if you have included unreferenced files in the site home page, you may provide access to users to documents and resources not intended to be made available to them. This is

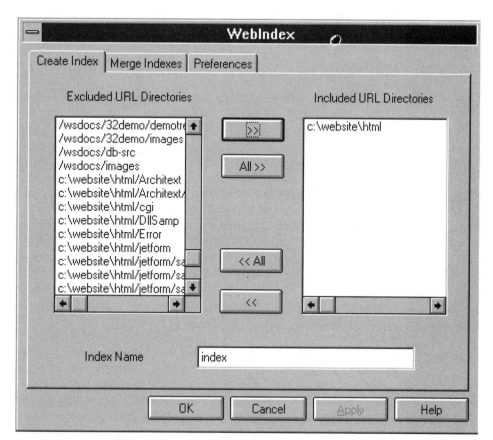

Figure 2.57 Indicate the root directory of the HTML files.

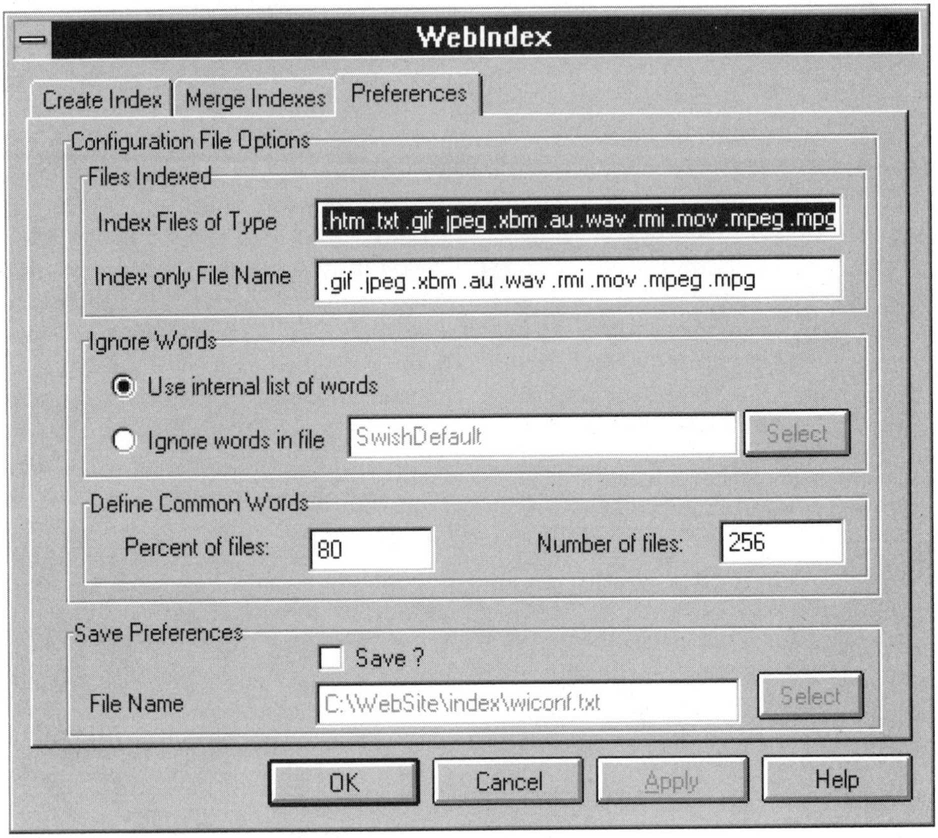

Figure 2.58   Specify the file extents and various index preferences.

one reason to check the structure, linkage, and correctness, and to test your website.

The process of creating the *table of contents,* although the tool is billed as an *index creation* tool, is painless, as shown by Figure 2.59. The output is similar to the website maps created by WebMapper, Web Analyzer, and other tools. The index file is called WebMap.htm by default and is saved to the root of the HTML document subdirectory. The map of my old website is shown in Figure 2.60. Notice that the page titles are the entries, hence the index is really a listing of the document titles.

Iconovex's PageAnchor tool creates HTML documents that are abstracts of the website. This is not simply a table of contents, but a true keyword index and an abstract of important topics. It is not an active search engine, but rather a content-driven extraction tool that creates reference pages (in HTML). Changes to website structure, organization, or content will require a regeneration of the documents previously referenced by AnchorPage. However, this is a simple, inexpensive, and very robust process. Content organization and indexing tools

Figure 2.59 WebIndex automatically builds a WebMap.htm file.

can locate information from within masses of information databases, dumps, and insurance; provide document tracking; and link related documents that are clearly not obvious. Consider the case of the very large insurance company that is converting all its accident report documents into text via OCR and perhaps storing fields within a searchable database. A secondary value is linking linguistically related documents by names, events, providers, services, and time frames to root out fraud, overcharges, and otherwise hidden actuarial problems.

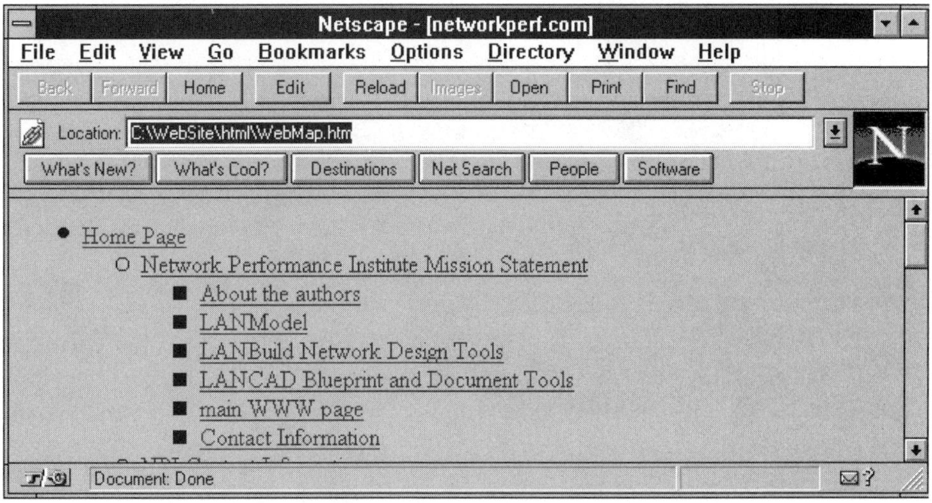

Figure 2.60 WebIndex page title "index."

I happen to like the AnchorPage indexing engine because it generates indexes based on multiple word phrases and has a better hit rate than the complex Boolean matches typical of the interactive search engines. In fact, the index for *Building Cyberstores* and all related web pages was indexed by Iconovex products. However, if you want indexes displayed in the site templates, you can integrate (again, that means cut and paste) the AnchorPage-created documents with a CGI-based interactive index utility for the best of all possibilities.

AnchorPage explores all the documents (or a subset) on a site and creates three new documents. Actually, it creates this header page, which I recommend integrating (by cut and paste) into one of your own home pages, three separate pages with a list of the alphabet pointing to 26 separate pages for each of these categories. This main page includes the table of contents, key concepts presented by the HTML pages, and keywords and phrases, as shown in Figure 2.61.

The subordinate phrase index for entries beginning with the letter "m" is illustrated in Figure 2.62. The subordinate concept index for entries beginning with "m" is illustrated in Figure 2.63. Note that "abstract" concepts are elaborated with a sentence or phrase defining the context for the concept. Since these are standard ASCII HTML pages you can modify the links and the descriptions as needed. The table of contents as generated by Iconovex AnchorPage is shown in Figure 2.64. This information is taken from the HTML page name, the page tags, or the headers. The process for creating these indexes is automatic. Basically, you fill out several forms and begin processing the website. Figure 2.65 shows some of the basic levels and details supported for index generation. You can target specific directories or individual

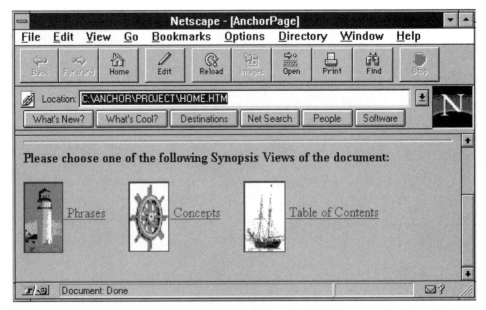

Figure 2.61   Iconovex-generated header page for indexes.

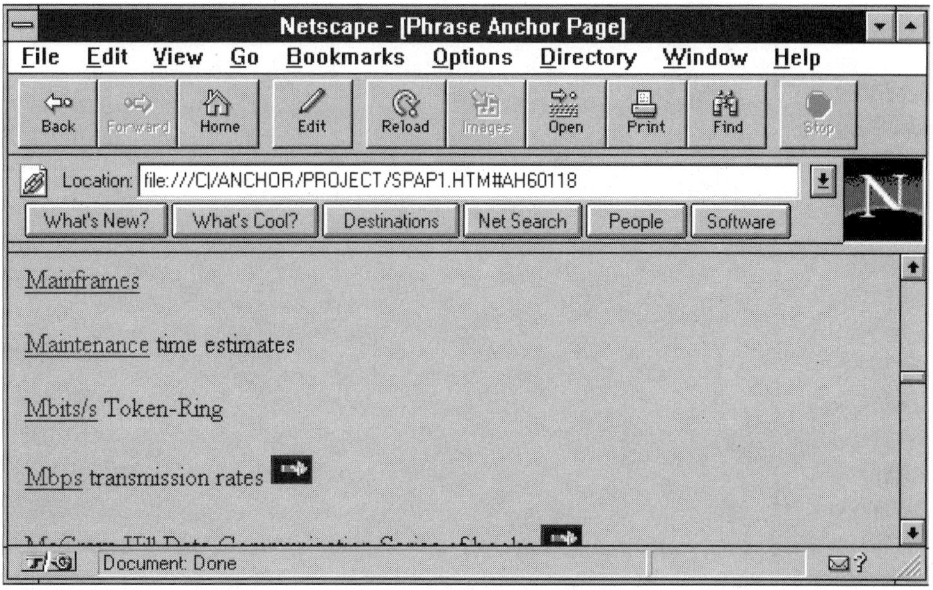

Figure 2.62 Phrase index items for alphabetic entries beginning with the letter "m."

HTML pages with the multiple selection listbox as shown by Figure 2.65. The process is automated, as shown in Figure 2.67.

As with most spelling checker applications and thesauri, you can create special dictionaries of phrases, words without importance, and words or phrases

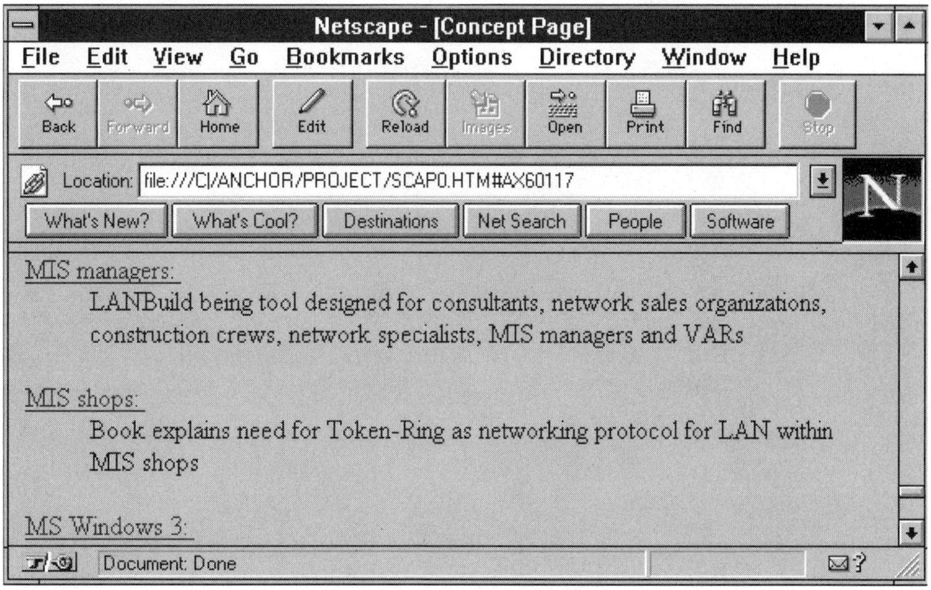

Figure 2.63 Concept index items for alphabetic entries beginning with "m" with context phrase.

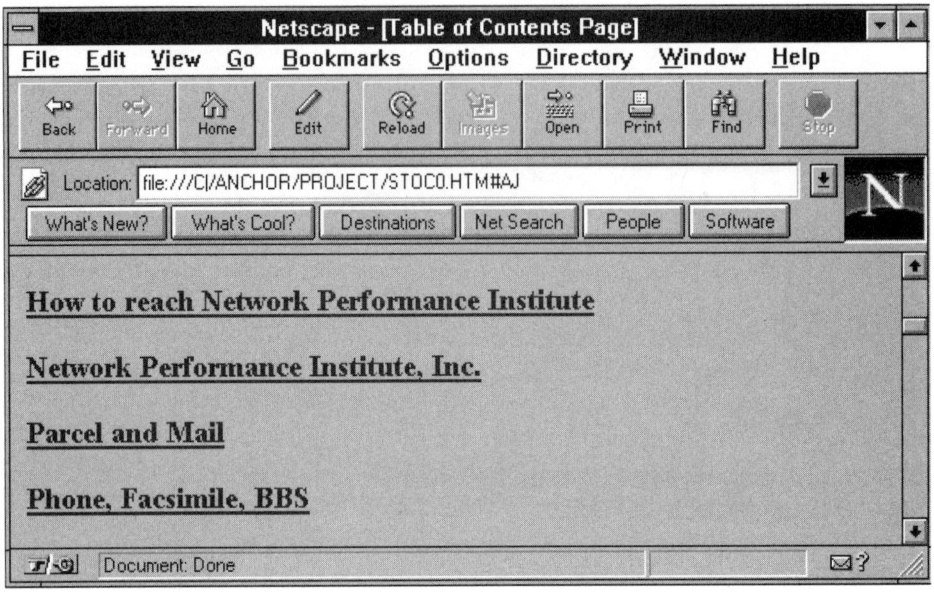

Figure 2.64 AnchorPage-generated website table of contents.

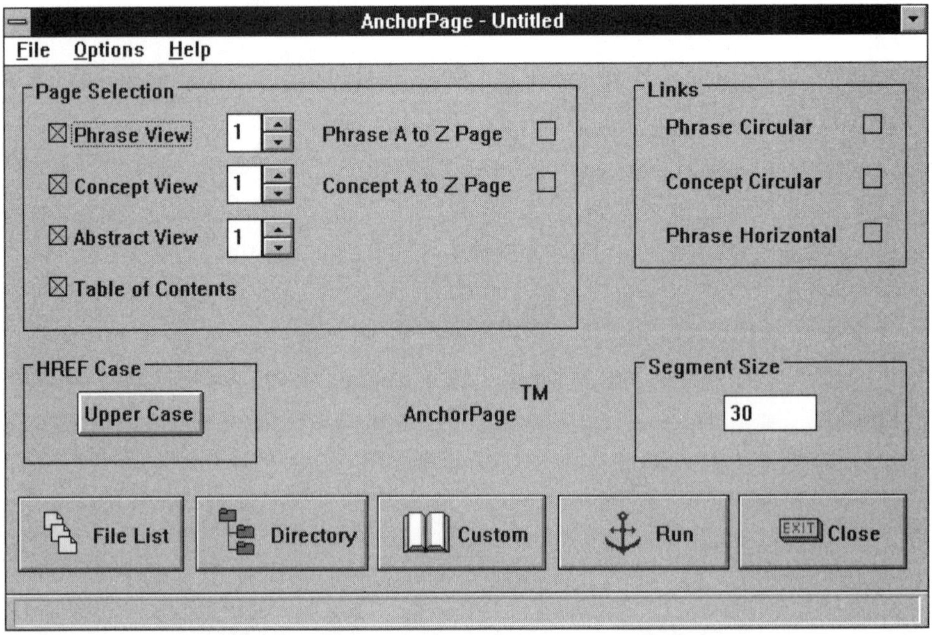

Figure 2.65 AnchorPage website indexing options.

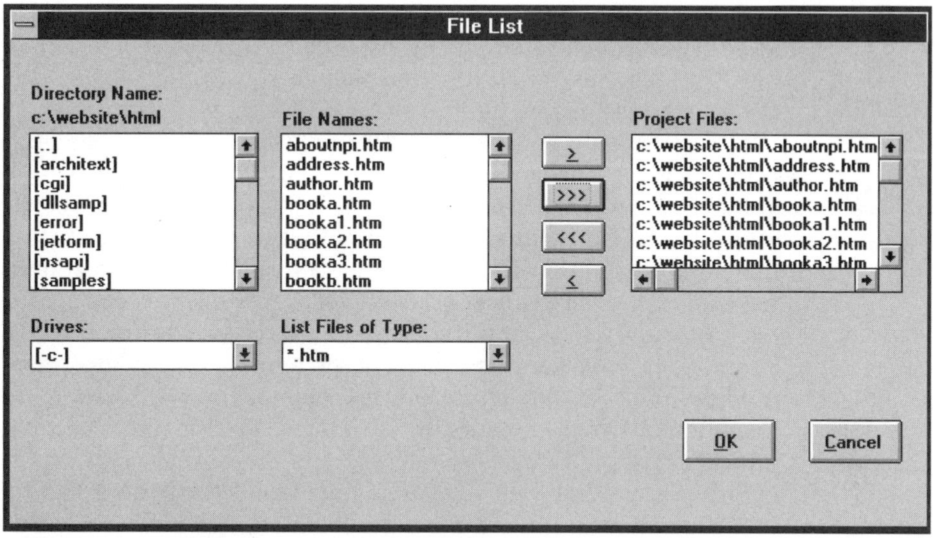

Figure 2.66 Site and specific page index inclusion.

specifically to be excluded. The development of industry-specific dictionaries is time-consuming but worthwhile for any designer or developer rebuilding sites on a frequent basis or for consultants and design firms frequently faced with complex cyberstore integration. Note that as with the interactive site index

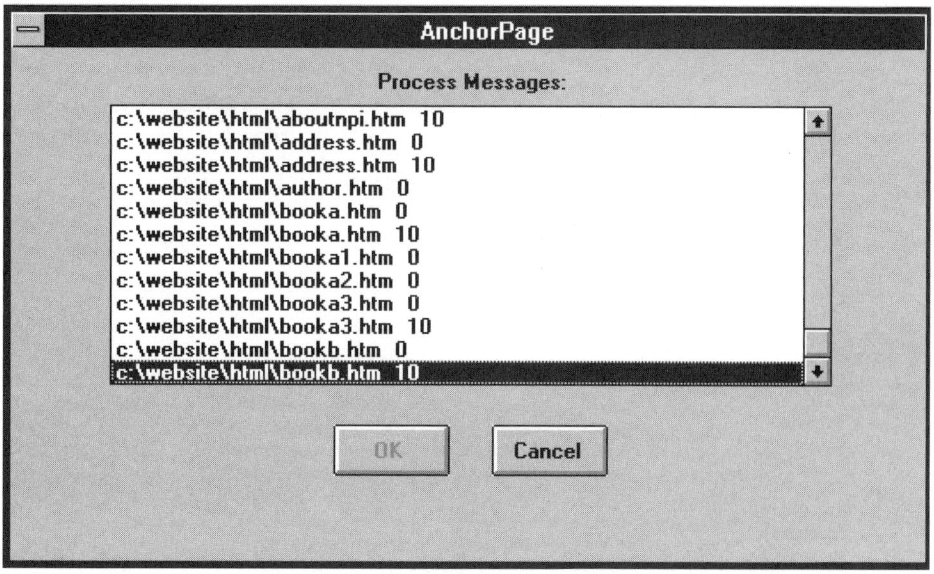

Figure 2.67 Automatic index generation message window.

tools, index generators do not find HTML pages created by database middleware tools or generated on the fly from databases because they do not exist until created. You might also consider integrating a database query tool into the search mechanism (on the same HTML page) for data navigation.

The third approach requires the Structured Query Language (SQL), the prime code for manipulating databases, or ODBC storage of HTML page texts and images with descriptive titles (metadata). An SQL or ODBC query engine searches the meta data or the contents of the tables within the database for matching terms. However, the significant caveat with this approach is that external users and even users authorized for access to some corporate data and not to others may locate information sources that they are not supposed to know about, have access to, or have the more privileged access of generating a report with the table details. Nevertheless, storage of data in DBMS formats, including HTML documents, links, images, multimedia, and sound is the powerful wave of the future.

There is another way to search that is not text-based and not directed at text-based content either. Specifically, Virage provides a search tool to select images by color, tone, overall balance, and composition. Since the web content includes more and more image or text, users and site developers will want to search for items (for example, in large on-line catalogs) by what they look like. Unfortunately, without a person cataloging the content of an image, this still cannot be accomplished. The tools that locate outlines and try to automatically identify the contents of an image are not yet ready for general consumption. However, Virage has a product profiled in the next five screen shots that matches images by color, composition, text, and structure. Figure 2.68 shows

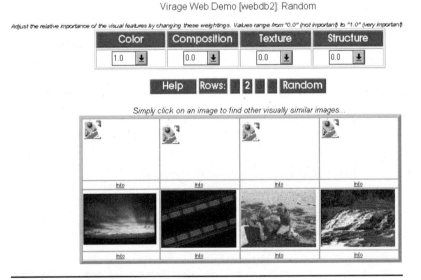

Figure 2.68 Random presentation of two images as a search starting point.

Virage Web Demo [webdb2]: Random

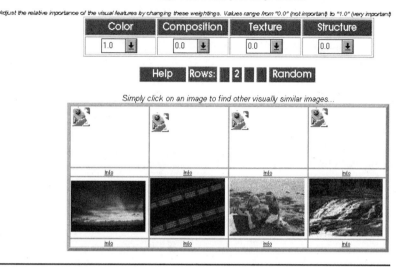

Figure 2.69 Expanded and focused match of original images.

the random opening starting point. When I select the people because I want to see people, I get the following sequence of four more images that somehow match this starting point. Indeed, one of the images has people, as shown in Figure 2.69. I see similar colors and textures in these images as seen in the original starting point. I still want to see people and now select the third image of the family. This generates the farming scenes in Figure 2.70.

Virage Web Demo [webdb2]: Query vs. Image #1222

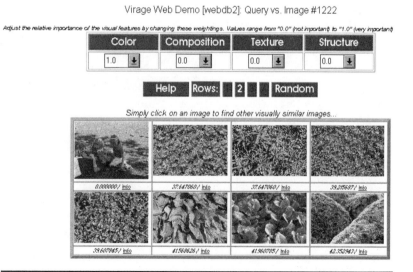

Figure 2.70 Color and texture in the background match the plants.

It is possible that the image database does not include more images of people. However, the search shows how overall tone of an image is used as the basis for locating other similar scenes. Rather than accepting any of the other seven images (top left is the base image), Virage returns eight new images as shown in Figure 2.71. This search netted two screens with people and several with animals. I still want people and select the cloaked child. This generates jungle-type images and the tiger lady on top. Again, you see that the matches have an overall tonality that is not content-related but you can see that the images are similar in the final screen shot (Figure 2.72) in this sequence.

Information for navigation

Tell your customers that if they are having trouble connecting to your page do not give up — "the cyberstore is available 7×24 unless something dramatic occurs." Here are some useful tips for you as a site developer and for your customers who may have trouble finding your cyberstore, particularly when you encounter messages like the one shown in Figure 2.73.

Hypertext Transport Protocol (HTTP) is the mechanism for accessing and distributing files over the Internet. HTTP requires a special site address called the Uniform Resource Locator (URL), which has the general form:

```
http://host.domain:port/path
```

The "http://" indicates the protocol; the protocol domain could also be WAIS, ftp, shttp, nntp, and a few other minor but nevertheless important network protocols. The host is often "www" and indicates the name of a server. The "do-

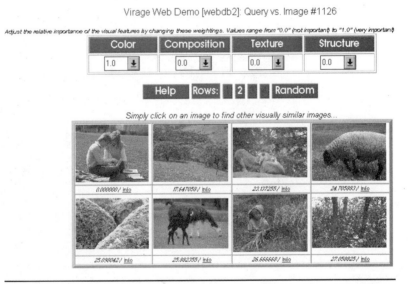

Figure 2.71   Images matching with the prior family and not background scenes.

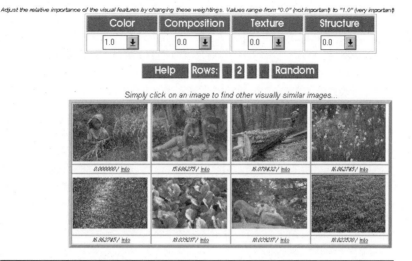

Figure 2.72 Continued searching yielded more backgrounds but a person, too.

main" is the fully qualified name of the host. The domain name could be an IP address, an Internet Service Provider (ISP), or your own webserver as registered with a domain name in the format of "company.com" as described in Chapter 4. The port address is used to distinguish between HTTP and FTP ports, which by default are different. In addition, web server farms consisting of multiple web servers in order to handle a heavy user load will often have different port assignments so that a domain name service

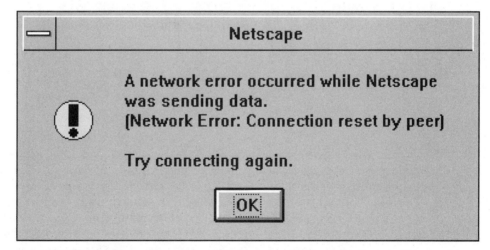

Figure 2.73 You (and your site users) need to know how to respond and cope with network connection or URL errors.

(DNS) or the load balancing front-end can actually assign requests to different servers as needed. However, note that the default HTTP port address is hexadecimal 80. If you are establishing an internal webserver, most software defaults to that address. If you plan to run multiple webservers, as you might if you choose to run WebSite Pro for its secure processing and E-mail facility and run WebMate for its integration into corporate databases, both servers can run concurrently on the same computer if you reset the HTTP port addresses to prevent the clash. In any event, I suggest you try to establish a simple domain name to map to the fully-qualified path if your site requires specific port addresses because users and customers are unlikely to correctly enter specific uniform resource location addresses like "http://network.ohios.edu:5060/~whirl/internet/notes.html." The final element in the URL is the path to the specific hierarchical reference for a file. If this is omitted, the default home page name is often "index.htm" or "index.html." Some servers expect different starting points and provide setup configuration for the home page. Even when the cyberstore website is driven by database-to-HTML middleware, you are likely to require a formidable home page to list basic information, provide a query form to start the database process, or catalog sales listings. If you are uploading files from Windows95, Windows 3.x or other platforms to WindowsNT or UNIX, realize that the default home page may require the different filename extent.

Chop off the last part of the URL of a default Web page or an index until you get a valid URL location. This is very important with cyberstore sites and other interactive sites that generate web pages from databases on the fly. Specific URL addresses are often randomly generated as needed, which results in bookmarks to pages that might never exist again. For example, if a customer marked some shirts at a cyberstore outlet site on closeout, the address may be temporary, generated by the database middleware, or even a random URL path to a temporary file. Consider that the bookmarked path may not work and that truncating the path as shown here may provide better starting points than the home page:

```
bookmark:http://www.landsend.com/closeout/mens/buttondown/saddle.htm
shorten: http://www.landsend.com/closeout/mens/buttondown
shorten: http://www.landsend.com/closeout/mens
shorten: http://www.landsend.com/closeout
revert to the home page URL: http://www.landsend.com.
```

You may also want to explore other protocol domains besides "http" because it may be a secure site or ftp site. Once connected, click to the page you want, even if it is generated from queries. Customers may spot your site from a name in an advertisement, on a jet ski, from product packaging, or products themselves in service. Try referencing the address with a tilde (~) and the name of the organization on the host site server. For example, Network Performance Institute (www.networkperf.com) becomes NPI, a user on the Shadow host ISP, or "www.shadow.net/~npi".

UNIX systems, as often found on ISP hosts (because the dominant operating system is Sun Solaris) reference documents as .html instead of .htm as found on Windows 3.x, Windows95, and WindowsNT. Home site files are often developed in Word for Windows or Macintosh development stations and copied by the FTP protocol to the host site. When changes are made to a site by copying the source files to the development station, the file name often changes and is propagated back to the host site. Try the variations on file extensions or look for an index.html or index.htm as a reasonable starting point for a site. The "index" file is the default name for a home page on most hosts.

Internationalization

Business on the Internet is international. The ability to support global business requires localization. *Localization* is the process of adapting to local markets, cultures, languages, and customs. Not only are internationalization and localization functions of the website, but also how you package and document products and services sold from the cyberstore. You do not want to sell English-only product with language problems when the website is internationalized; that suggests a misrepresentation of your organization. If the product is only designed for a local market, at least indicate this. Issues to consider include quality (such as ISO 9000), deadlines, language, government delivery customs and tariffs, local social customs, UNICODE support (for HTML, SGML, and software products), and product usages.

Face it. French is not the lingua franca of the web. Neither is English the universal language for web commerce. The technology is available to create multilingual websites and maintain them. The driving technology for this magic is database storage of data, database storage of cultural translations, good computer tools to automatically translate pages into pidgin versions of another language, and the Internet itself to link up website authors with bilingual translators. Note that there are 2,000 language and/or dialects in use throughout the world.

The screen shot in Figure 2.74 is clearly designed for English speakers. The Access Software product is really a client-side tool to translate sites in foreign languages (to you) into something that you can comprehend. However, this site itself shows the provincial mindset of the designers. The main logo contains text that does not change and cannot be translated because the text is part of the image format. The flags do convey a more worldly flavor, much like the international symbols now used in airports worldwide. However, even here, the text describing the nationality of the flag is part of the graphic element and will not translate either with the Access product or any language translation product.

The flag captions should be in the native language at all times and if there must be a graphic element (for reasons of fonts and the direction a language reads), it should be separate. Text on graphic buttons creates design havoc. If you want to take an English site and convert to Japanese, not

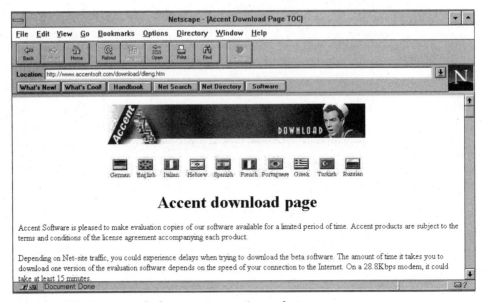

Figure 2.74 The home page for language transaction product.

only does the text need translation, but also the graphics need substantial reworking. The general rule is that all English labels require about 40 percent more text when translated into another language. English is denser than any other language, except on occasion, Japanese. Take the concept of the international symbols and abstract that to web design. Allocate the space in page template designs for that extra 40 percent needed for labels and text translated into other languages. If you are translating from French to Spanish, for example, you do not generally need to allocate more space for text. If you are supporting Arabic, Hebrew, Hindu, or Farsi sites, realize that the text direction is right to left instead of left to right as with European languages, and that the design will look funny if left aligned and translated to a right-aligned text. Language is even more complicated with Chinese dialects as the pictograms can be read in virtually any direction.

Figure 2.75 shows what happens when Access translates the Access Software website into Russian. I would guess that the choice of words and the translation have been optimized to best demonstrate this product. I couldn't tell due to font set substitution. However, one of the funny problems of internationalization appears. The several sets of Cyrillic (that is, Russian) fonts I have do not map to the translation. The translation used extended ASCII codes, and by default this mapped to the Windows Arial font and the TrueType symbol font. This translation is Greek to me. Notice also the English-centrality of the page. The banner is still in English and the flags (which activate selection of an HTML document in another language) are still very parochial.

Internationalization is not only about website design and appropriate cultural translation. You also want to provide clear explanation detailing how to send facsimiles and make phone calls, when it best to call and how the language differences can be handled, how to send mail or correspondence, and bulk shipping information. Phone numbers and postal codes vary from country to country and where they are supposed to be positioned relative to a country name. The global 800 phone number is very new, not widely implemented, and may be different from the local 800 telephone number. Include full access codes, country codes, area codes, city codes, and special access process information. For example, if you address a parcel with this format:

```
Abbadua Karreem
Electronique Industries LTD
3749 Route 67, Zula Building 1
West Lakeland Grace
Namibia 44121
```

the odds are better than 50 percent that this package will first get delivered to Minnesota before being returned as "undeliverable—no such address" because the postal code looks like a U.S. zipcode and it gets the priority sorting. You might also stipulate the best (fastest or cheapest) method for shipments before you or your customers get stung too many times by a worldwide delivery carrier (with a "base" cost of $27.50) that is delivered by pony cart in a very rural area of India or Denmark and generates a final delivery cost of $88.00. This

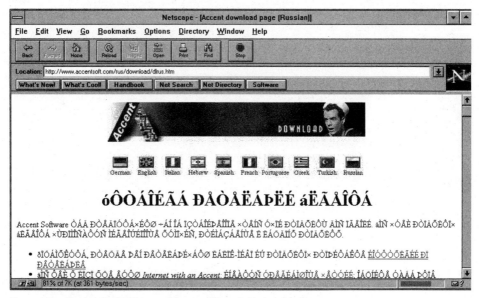

Figure 2.75 Font substitution problems with website translations.

has happened to me more than once. When you have billed by credit card and already collected for the sale and the delivery, you are likely to be burned by this undercharge mistake.

If your organization handles significant inbound telephone calls or letters, consider establishing a correspondence center to handle and translate these. A number of service bureaus in Belgium, Denmark, and Sweden specialize in these services and they are typically less expensive than local providers or establishing an in-house support group.

Competitive intelligence

Information on the web is made public, that is, "published." Corporations and organizations are eagerly publishing information about themselves, their people, their products and services, and even future prospects. This information is all over the Internet and is useful to those who know how to interpret it. Of course, you can legally use the information on competitors' sites. Just be careful how you reuse copyrighted or protected text, images, video, and sound (as explained in greater detail in Chapter 4). Perhaps, more to the point, understand what you are posting on your site and how a wily competitor can infer from that information and other public product reviews about your next product release.

A good electronic source is patent filings, Securities and Exchange Commission (SEC) 10-Ks and quarterly reports, proposed tariff rates, and public filings with other regulatory agencies. Although each electronic filing is never intended for any other purpose than meeting a mandated deadline or protective legal process, many electronic sources can be compiled together to create a powerful overview never conceived by the individuals publishing each filing or HTML page. While all this information seems like a garbage dump of minutiae, dumpster diving is a practical and *legal* method of effective *industrial espionage*. This process is now much cleaner on the Internet. When enough is at stake, the little electronic details, and there may be an awful lot of them, provide a cogent competitive picture.

Also, understand how references to people can initiate an E-mail dialog with individuals within the organization that can compromise security and trade secrets. The following banner (screen shot in Figure 2.76) displaying top management credentials at Extensis Corporation is more effective at furthering individual careers than the cohesiveness of the organization as an entity.

Who's kidding who? Don't the venture capital people see this? I understand that startups are notoriously unstable and the management teams, particularly creative people, tend to burn out and be hard people to fit within an emerging corporate culture, and are often replaced early on during the maturation process. This advertising appears most effective for the individual and not the team. Somehow this seems to be a perilous and divisive concept.

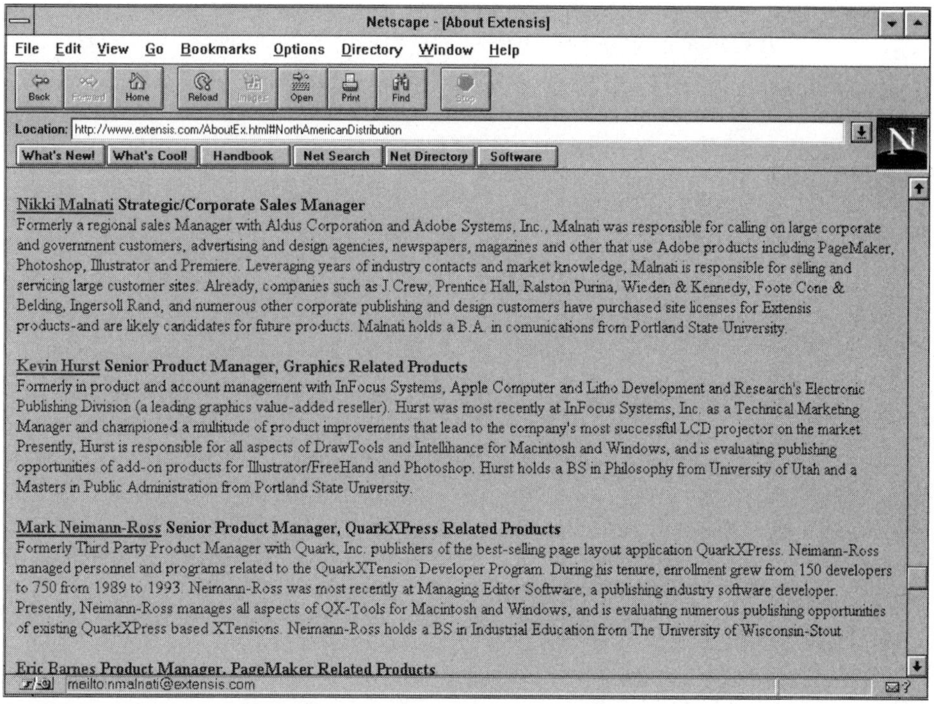

Figure 2.76 A treacherous supplemental web page.

Are these people hoping to get better jobs or attract the attention of corporate headhunters? Even when the details and track records are not so elaborate, this proliferation of insignificant detail can provide a fertile ground for elaborate intelligence accumulation. For example, a reference to a developer by the name of Dave Cooley can become the likely address for davec@company.com. If the mail is returned as undeliverable, consider dave@company.com or david@company.com. Sooner or later, you will figure out a functional combination. Perhaps the well-meaning mail or site administrator will read undeliverable messages. If you create a compelling message, or even simple requests that seem to have been lost, the administrator will forward the message to Dave. Dave might respond that he has no idea what the message is about, but that response will contain a valid return address. That is your pay dirt.

Create a new message to davec@company.com who may respond to questions from a supposed customer that fill in gaps about things you hadn't known and the company as an organization probably preferred you didn't know. Insignificant details become important puzzle pieces to a tenacious and crafty researcher. That researcher may be working for a competitor, a venture capital fund, Standard & Poor's, an industry research firm, or a brokerage firm that is watching your stock. Most organizations have a very smart senior person providing media relations, investor relations, and corporate communications. The Internet and a website can undermine a lot of the very formal structure.

This is not an isolated problem on the web, either. While many people and organizations complain about the losses of freedom and privacy through government, financial tracking and information accumulation bureaus, and many aggressive market research organizations, we also want the right to self-publish a tremendous amount of superfluous facts mostly self-serving. Furthermore, some privileged information does not fit the premise of the cyberstore. Although RadMedia actually has a nicely organized commercial site (with supplemental Spanish support) directed to promoting its web tools, my sense is that the details about major customers, principles, employees, current employee counts, as shown in Figure 2.77, do not favorably embellish or promote this organization. Key customers are encouraging, but the risk is that extensive customer information is useful for competitors.

Although some organizations have very formal rules for employee/community interactions, these have yet to be extended to the Internet. Some small organizations haven't even considered that the Internet and a website is an intrusion in business privacy and a potential liability. For this reason, I have compiled some Dos and Don'ts for website designers in Figure 2.78.

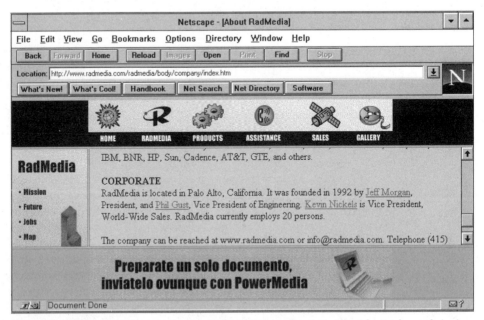

Figure 2.77 If less detail is enough, does each person need a page about his or her upbringing, schooling, and personal life?

Dos	Don'ts	Reason
Use a real name	Do not disguise yourself	You can be traced
Use a real name	Do not misrepresent yourself	You can be traced
Read competitor's sites	Do not steal trade secrets	Legally actionable
Post prices and features	Trade competitive price information	Violates antitrust laws
Ask for information	Make a bribe for privileged information	You can be traced
Post addresses for an official informational contact	Do not provide employee names, E-mail addresses, or phone numbers	Jeopardizes rights to privacy and opens doors for employee recruitment
Retain E-mail messages	Forward E-mail	Could be indirect and privileged information
Know confidentiality rules	E-mail competitors, contractors, customers without formal authorization	Could violate laws, confidentiality contracts, or legal restrictions
Post real information	Do not post misinformation	A website is very public and easily copied in full.

Figure 2.78 Dos and Don'ts for website content designers.

Java, VBScript, JavaScript, ActiveX, and Add-ins

Java, VBScript, JavaScript, and ActiveX are programming languages that facilitate the construction of complex websites. These languages are in addition to Perl, CGI, and any specific web server application programming interfaces (APIs). Java, Netscape add-ins, and applets are like viruses. If you have it, the user will get it. If the user has some, he or she will ultimately get all of them. The feasibility spreads in this way. Add-in tools add functionality to a browser, but each one takes up disk space and potentially can destabilize the browser, the linkage, the platform, or the ISP connection. A user's browser will not be enabled with the functionality until the user downloads the add-ins and adds them into his or her browser. Examples include Java applets, streaming sound, streaming video, and VRML. VRML is the acronym for Virtual

Reality Modeling Language, a method of providing real-time control of three-dimensional image environment. If you plan to develop a website with any of this add-in functionality, you need to provide users with the ability to download the tools either directly from your site (increases the FTP load to your site) or better yet, from a linkage to the home page for each add-in vendor.

The ActiveX approach creates some significant limitations on site design and universal access. Most notably, ActiveX is limited to a Windows client-side platform. Server-side applets will run just fine, but anything that is downloaded to the client is not functional. This is an issue of design, but it is also raised in Chapter 3. Although ActiveX lets developers integrate Internet functionality into applications; store data anywhere on the desktop, network, or Internet; run a web application without a user interface, facilitating remote execution and automation of web pages particularly with regard to commercial operations and workflow, it excludes all browsers who do not run under Windows95 or WindowsNT since Netscape Navigator and Microsoft Explorer (supporting ActiveX) versions 3.0 and greater are so far only available for those platforms.

However, I suggest this reality that you aim to keep functionality on the server side. Most add-ins are client/server development tools, with one part residing on the server development station to master the applet and any data files, whereas the other part becomes an HTML tag with a web page, and a third part becomes a client-side runtime library and/or a downloaded file. Most of the functionality for these add-ins is trivial, but that is not always the case. Some add-ins, such as a spreadsheet or stock ticker, really have a special value for your cyberstore. Make that assessment according to your needs. Nevertheless, customer-coded Java, CGI, Perl, and other scripts are time-consuming, expensive to build and maintain, and possible (maybe even probable) security breaches. Often this same functionality is available through server-side components that simplify client distribution and server design and implementation. Even so, simplify the server-side development process, too, if you can avoid website programming, especially in light of the potentially incendiary client-side support problems. There is a whole lot more to building the cyberstore than simply animation, clever sounds, and piecemeal integration.

Hit Counters

Site designers, marketing planners, advertisers, and product managers want to know how many people access a website. It also becomes a badge of honor or social acceptance to include hit count information at website home pages. The reality is that the fad itself will pass, but true usage statistics will become important management tools. Usage statistics reveal important information to assess the popularity of the site, effectiveness of any advertising, and actual load on the website server hardware. Statistics are important for planning, customization of sites, and the creation of analogous retail store "end caps" or "closeout" bins on cyberstore pages. Marketing information should include customer paths through the website, interests, and address confusions.

Any access to a website is called a *hit,* which means many different things from an unrestrained access to a file on a web or FTP site to an audited access by an indicated person. A hit count is not necessarily the full story for *access* and *readership* of a web page, or a Nielsen ratings measurement of enjoyment. A hit can refer to a site hit, a page hit, or a system counter accumulating the number of resources accessed at the website. For example, a server or operating system process counter could run up by one for each file accessed by the main HTML document. Each file load represents a different process. Cached pages can be hit indefinitely as long as that page is in the cache memory; the hit counter is not incremented. One of the newer measurement tracking methods is the "click through" from a banner advertisement on search engine sites to the site of the advertisement.

If a CGI, Perl, or Java hit counter is imbedded in a page, the HTML call to that process increments the system process counter by one, the process itself (running) generates a second increment, the access to a data file is a third, and the fourth is that the number from the data file is then used to generate an image of that number, which in turn is imbedded in the HTML presentation for a total of five system hits. By the way, if you want to optimize server overhead, minimize the number of files embedded into each page. For example, as Figure 2.79 illustrates with the various images — even

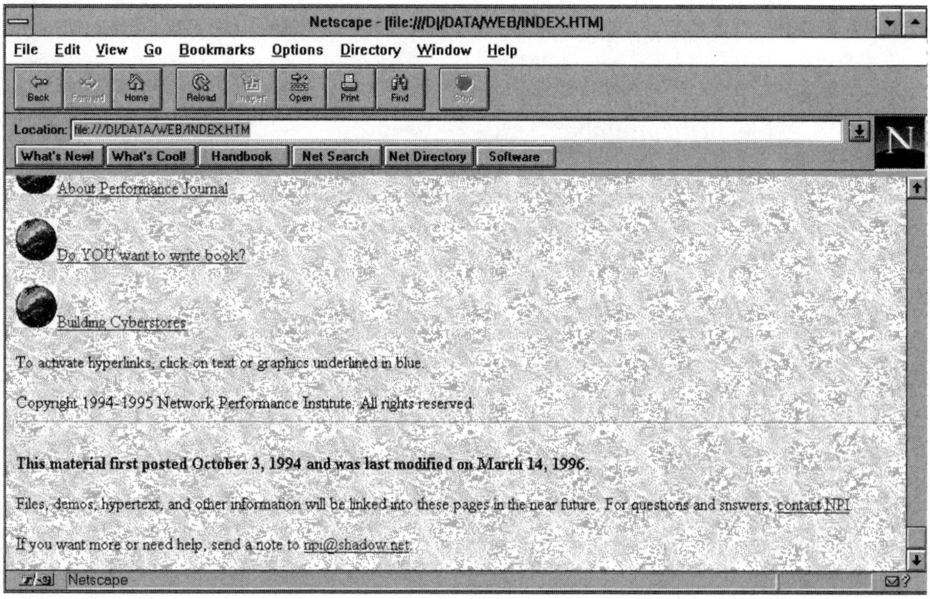

Figure 2.79 This screen shot (which is only part of a larger page) uses many imbedded graphic files and other HTML references that bump the counter up by 14 for just a single access.

the little items bullets—and references, a simple access to this page returns the false impression that 14 people accessed this page based on the web server or UNIX system process ID statistics.

If a surfer clicks on one of the references or the active bitmaps to go to another subordinate page before returning back to this same page, and the user's browser does not cache this page, the counter will accumulate 28 hits on just this single page. That is not right and it is not useful information. In fact, if a browser issues a Reload or Refresh, the effect is to increment the process and imbedded page counters all over again. This is mindless in the greater scheme of things. There was a big turmoil at the *Penthouse* magazine site because site management used process counters as an "official" site access audit. This perhaps provided more publicity for *Penthouse* than was warranted by the actual number of users surfing the site and created concern at many large companies that perhaps users were surfing for pornography rather than accomplishing work and fueled the perceived need for censorship. Statistics can be used and misused for various purposes. You must understand the technology behind them, how they might be audited, and the truthful ramifications of them.

Often, a Perl, Java, or CGI script is imbedded into a home page to increment a counter in a single separate or multiple data files every time the page is accessed. A few of these scripts, called "hit counters," are included on the CD-ROM for Windows NT or UNIX operating systems. They need to be placed in the \CGI-BIN or \CGI-WIN subdirectory, which are the directories where CGI scripts are stored. Because other files, such as password files, are often here, make certain you do not alter security to that directory or the other files stored within. These hit counter programs work as follows. Every time an HTML page is accessed, the counter program is run from the HTML document to increment a sequential number in a separate data file. This number is then used to construct an odometerlike image file, which is imbedded in the actual presentation, as shown by screen capture in Figure 2.80. HTML code to call a CGI hit counter is illustrated by Figure 2.81. This odometer process is shown in the following sequence of illustrations. Figure 2.82 shows generic annotated HTML code for calling a hit counter.

Figure 2.83 shows a screen shot of File Manager with the file structure for a hit counter (WWWCOUNT.ZIP on the CD-ROM should be in \CGI-WIN), the actual program counter script (COUNT.EXE), a subordinate utility script (MKSTRIP.EXE) to set the number of leading zeroes and convert the ASCII number string into an image file of the specified font and color type, a sample number image display style, and the actual ASCII data file with a large number of hits.

Figure 2.84 shows a screen shot of a fancy LED-style hit counter imbedded as an image inside a web page. You might also note the time display on this French-language page. This illustration is a reminder of the text and format (for times and especially dates) changes required when posting an interna-

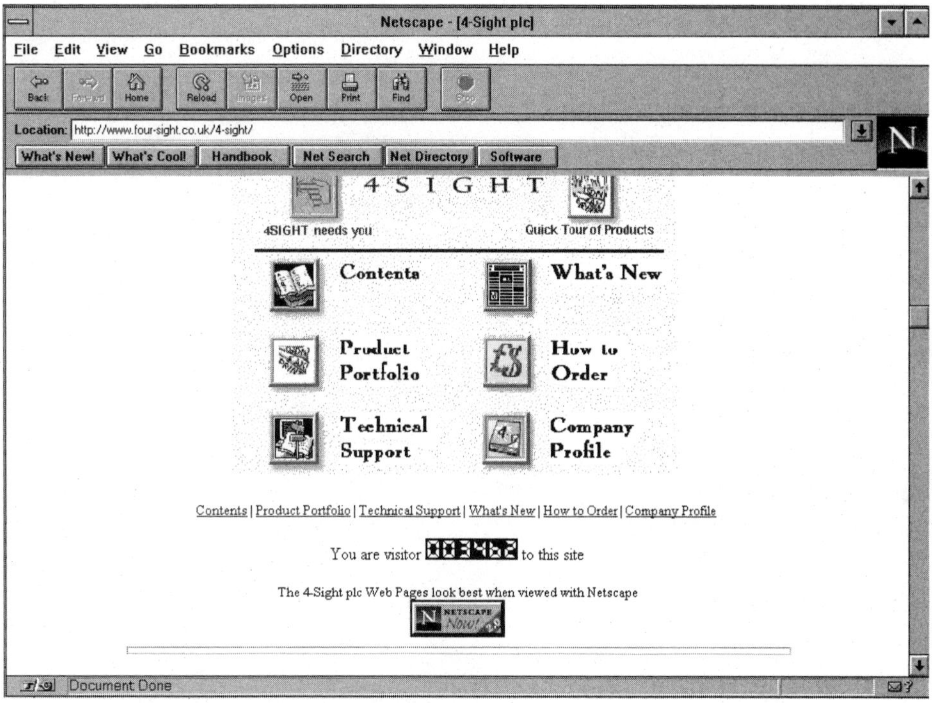

Figure 2.80 LED style hit counter generated by CGI code.

tionalized website. Most counters are available for UNIX, a few for Win NT or Win 3.x, and there is even Count WWWebula for the Macintosh.

There are a few important things you need to know about hit counters. First, the hit counter requires several I/O events that slow page loading. It is really hard to get around that except to recode the CGI counters to display the counter value first and *then* increment the data file value. Second, since

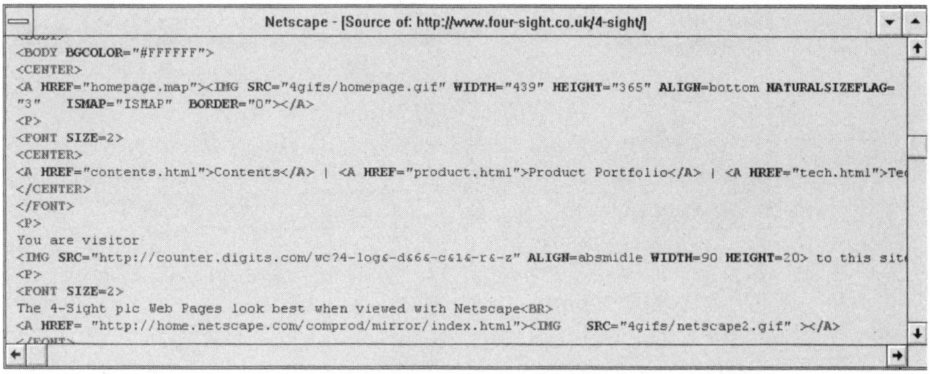

Figure 2.81 HTML code to invoke the CGI application to count hits to this page.

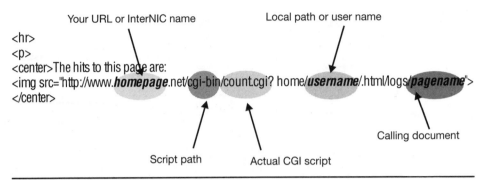

Figure 2.82 This annotated HTML code shows the very simple method for calling a hit counter script from a home page (master) or any subordinate page with supplemental parameters specifying secondary data files.

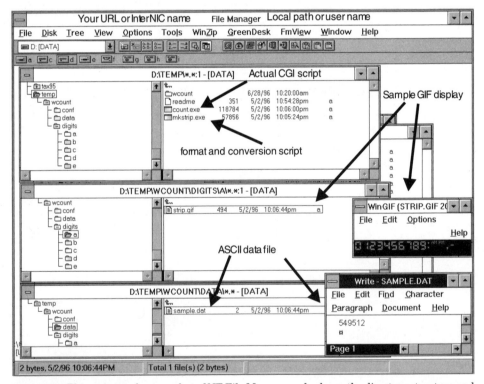

Figure 2.83 This annotated screen shot of NT File Manager code shows the directory structure and necessary files for the WWWCOUNT demo on the CD-ROM. This is similar to other C++, Perl, or Java hit counter scripts.

Figure 2.84 The hit counter script results on this French-language home page.

the counter is converted to an image, display that image with a height and width to improve page composition speed:

```
<img height=20 width=75 src="cgi-bin/wwwcount.exe ? ...">
```

The width is a function of pixels, which varies depending on the selected font for the image display. In this case, the width of 75 corresponds to 5 numbers each of which is 15 pixels. The pixel width measurements have no bearing or effect on web client screen resolution because pixel widths are device-independent. When you test your counter and the digits do not remove size information. If the counter does show the least significant digit changing with each hit, adjust the picture size information so it is wider. Third, the counter is not accurate; it will not count users hitting the page with nongraphical browsers, with pages and graphics cached, with graphics turned off, or if the user hits the "stop" button before the HTML code for the counter is loaded. WebTrends provides more detailed statistics.

The screen shot from the Taligent home site in Figure 2.85 shows accumulated hits in the last year as well as hits on a daily basis. (Those six site hits are all mine because printing crashed this connection a few times.) This does not provide any better or more accurate information than other counters as described here, but it is a useful tidbit for users browsing a site.

Figure 2.86 shows a page hit counter that says it all, as far as I am concerned. It is an animated image that displays random numbers. Since it is a looping script, the numbers recycle over time. Unless you activate more complex site tracking such as WebTrack profiled in the next section, hit counters

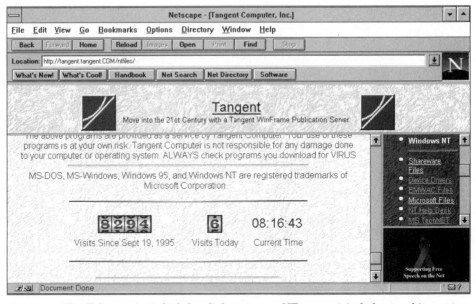

Figure 2.85 The Taligent site (which has links to many NT sources) includes two hit counters stored in two different files. It is interesting for the user, but adds to the file I/O and slowness with browser page display.

seem to be more a matter of developer pride and self-promotion than of value to customers surfing your site.

Audited statistics

Many advertisers are sold on web space based on unaudited site hit statistics, as typified by the Nielson PC-Meter Sweeps report shown in Figure 2.87. Although these statistics are based on a total audience figure, this is misleading because it is generated by standard survey methods. For example, "as an Internet user, do you use America Online?" tracks name recognition without the background, and so this type of survey information is uninformative.

Figure 2.86 The random animated hit counter script (AG_COUNT.GIF).

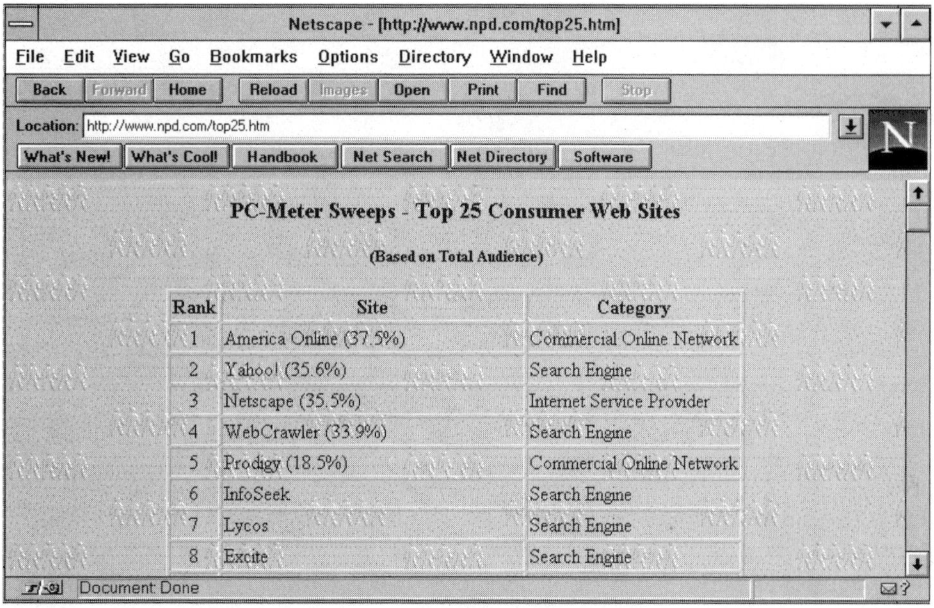

Figure 2.87   PC-Meter (by Nielsen Ratings) tracks site hits.

Net.Analysis will track distributed server sites with hundreds or hundreds of thousands of hits per day. One of the limitations of CGI-based hit counters and other primitive tools is that the data files can only sustain one hit during the instant that data file is open because it is hard to lock, read, increment, write, and unlock that file fast enough so that other server processes do not time out or ignore the file. One approach is with specialized server tracking tools. The screen in Figure 2.88 shows hit counts correlated by site type (as determined by the URL path designation) and hits from specific URLs.

These Net.Analysis statistics can be filtered and presented in pie and comparative bar charts for various types of site load and page hit analysis as illustrated in Figure 2.89. Nevertheless, even these detailed statistics do not differentiate separate user hits, hits with reloads, or backtracks to the same page. When you need accurate information about website usages, user statistics, and who is using your website and how, you build into the site a complex cookies or CGI tracking mechanism with an identification, password, and user authentication. However, the compressed development times make this unlikely, if not impossible, because the task requires enormous understanding of the type of information needed, a firm understanding of CGI, and coding and integration skills for building the scripts. Instead, you might try Surf Report, a tool that is profiled in this section, because it creates a different cut on site usage, audits, and other statistics. Figure 2.90 shows the configuration screen running with a Mac-based version of Netscape Navigator. If you read the next screen in Figure 2.91, you will see that visitors and customers to a site are tracked by frequency, source, referral source, and even the specific names of visitors.

Domain	Hits	Percentage	Cumm. Percentage
com	99955	41.84	41.8
none	55268	23.13	64.9
edu	42183	17.66	82.6
net	25579	10.71	93.3
org	4082	1.71	95.0
gov	2576	1.08	96.1
ca	2188	0.92	97.0
us	1691	0.71	97.7
mil	850	0.36	98.1
Other (46)	4189	1.75	99.8

Top Domains

Domain	Hostname	Hits	Percentage	Cumm. Percentage
org	gatekeeper.mitre.org	846	0.35	8.30
org	dopey.mtpc.org	205	0.09	22.00
org	pc199-189.nf.oclc.org	174	0.07	24.58
org	mac115.mactcp10.edc.org	108	0.05	35.83
org	app3.osf.org	102	0.04	37.16
org	oclaggott.gnat.org	100	0.04	37.02

Figure 2.88   Page hits quantified by site URL and site designation.

net.Analysis Beta v1.0

File   Edit   View   Utils

Report Palette

Time Stamp	Hits to HTML	Hits to HTML
11/17/95 01:00:00 AM	346	176
11/17/95 02:00:00 AM	278	122
11/17/95 03:00:00 AM	185	52
11/17/95 04:00:00 AM	100	39
11/17/95 05:00:00 AM	169	59
11/17/95 06:00:00 AM	270	150
11/17/95 07:00:00 AM	555	256
11/17/95 08:00:00 AM	1313	585
11/17/95 09:00:00 AM	1828	668
11/17/95 10:00:00 AM	1945	730
11/17/95 11:00:00 AM	2190	751
11/17/95 12:00:00 PM	2286	1001
11/17/95 01:00:00 PM	2486	934
11/17/95 02:00:00 PM	2527	970
11/17/95 03:00:00 PM	2480	976
11/17/95 04:00:00 PM	2469	983
11/17/95 05:00:00 PM	2141	970
11/17/95 06:00:00 PM	1486	641

Hits Over Time

■ Hits to HTML   ■ Hits to HTML From Com

Filter	First Time Stamp	Last Time Stamp	Maximum Hits	Minimum Hits	Total Hits	Average Hits/Hour
Hits to HTML	11/17/95 01:00:00 AM	11/30/95 05:00:00 PM	2527	2	32817	1058.61
Hits to HTML From Com	11/17/95 01:00:00 AM	11/30/95 05:00:00 PM	1001	2	13172	424.90

Figure 2.89   Net.Analysis comparison of hit rates for two pages.

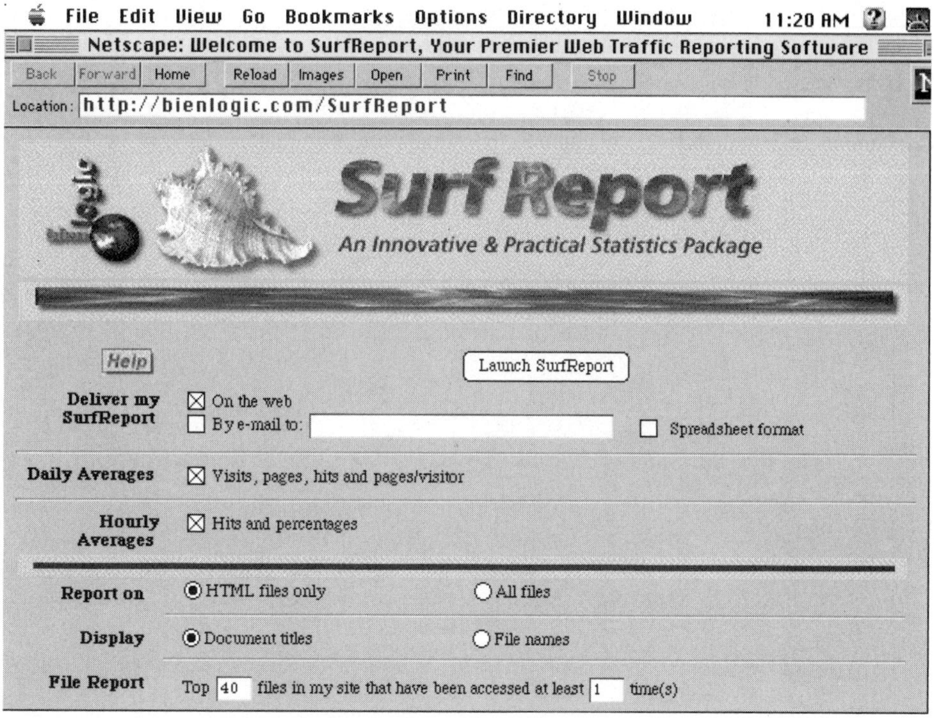

Figure 2.90 Remote configuration of Surf Report

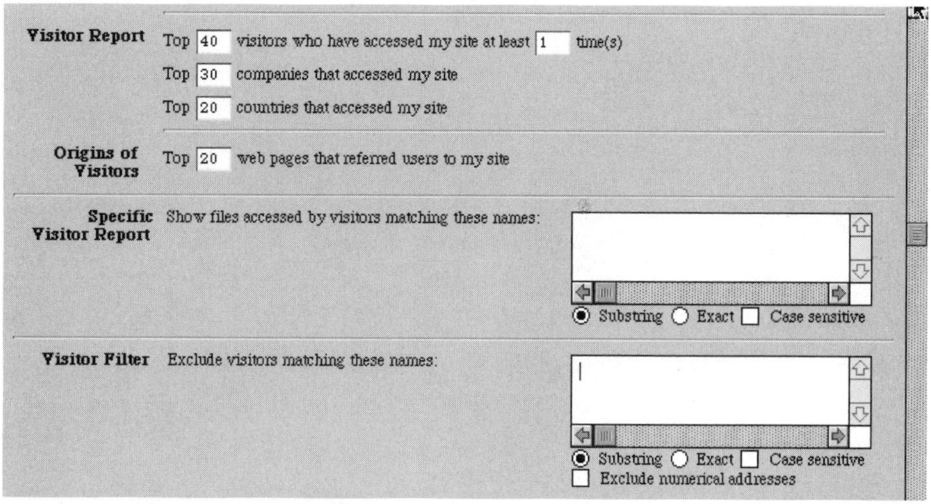

Figure 2.91 Tracking of customers to a site by sources, names, and even exclusion of users with specific names.

Since the web browsers are provided with information about what they are, Surf Report can log and create statistics on the frequency for browser usage. This is useful information since plans to upgrade a website with tables and frames are sidetracked by a lack of information about site visitors. Surf Report generates unequivocal statistics showing a breakdown by numbers and percentages, as shown in Figure 2.92. The resulting report will show who will be able to see your site upgrade as intended and even who can use the various add-ins and scripts that add dynamic functions to your site.

One of the statistical charts is shown in Figure 2.93. It separates out the pure functional hits from page accesses from those of actual visitors. That smaller bar shows the number of unique visitors (about 100 each day) during the specific week, and provides a better handle on the true value of a website, in this case, the Bien Logic site, developer of Surf Report. Figure 2.94 confirms my earlier assertions that hits and even page accesses provide spurious information at best. Rather, Surf Report defines true unique hits that correlate to unique visitors each day.

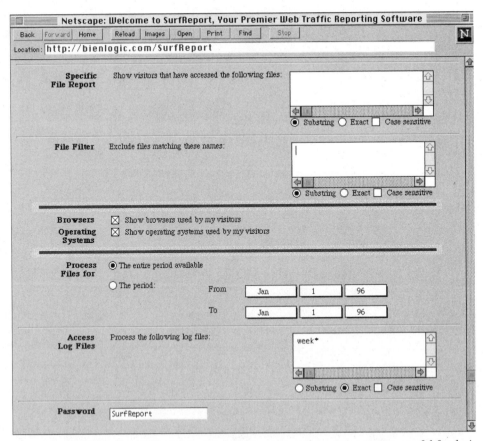

Figure 2.92 Surf Report will aggregate visitors by browser and operating system, useful for deciphering the effectiveness of complex site designs and add-in functionality.

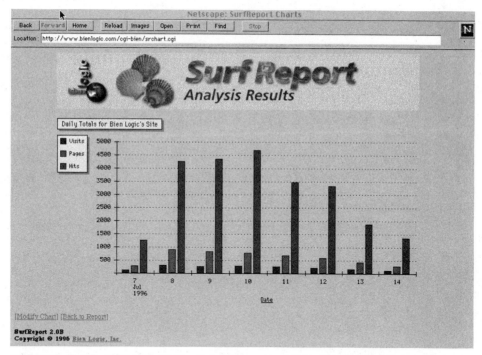

Figure 2.93 "Audited" hit, page, and actual unique user visits to the Bien Logic home page.

SurfReport 2.0B
Copyright © 1996 Bien Logic, Inc.

Location: http://www.bienlogic.com/SurfReport/surfreport/sr2/surfoutput.html

Surf Report
Analysis Results

Access Report from   Sun Jul 7 1996   to   Sun Jul 14 1996

[Totals] [Averages] [Visitors] [Files] [Other Info]

Daily Totals for Bien Logic's Site

Date	Visits	Pages	Hits
Sun Jul 7 1996	116	292	1258
Mon Jul 8 1996	307	896	4270
Tue Jul 9 1996	258	825	4362
Wed Jul 10 1996	275	797	4682
Thu Jul 11 1996	252	701	3471
Fri Jul 12 1996	219	591	3323
Sat Jul 13 1996	156	420	1881
Sun Jul 14 1996	110	286	1361

All Visits Pages Hits

Period Totals for Bien Logic's Site

Unique Visitors	Visits	Pages	Hits
1232	1693	4808	24608

Figure 2.94 The number of visits including repeat visits is separated from unique hits to this site by this unique site statistic report.

   WebTrends is a leading tool for website performance and generating exact statistics on advertising click throughs, page hits, reader hits, repeat reader access to a site, and the paths through a site to track effectiveness of special offers, discounts, and highlights. E.G. Software's WebTrends provides the type of immediate feedback and constructs the long sought-after goal of advertising because the tracking tools include that granular ability to track specific users. However, WebTrends is not necessarily a better tool than standard website statistics and ill-defined hit rates unless you take the time to learn the tool, imbed specific values to target in the web counting, and explore the available results in content to your needs and what *reasonable* conclusions you can make from the reports and graphs. Your website marketing people will want to accumulate and cross-reference various statistics, customer information, and externally purchased marketing information to generate likely resale customers, customers likely to buy ancillary products, or craft new product lines and services to fit the lifestyles of the customer base. The application window is shown in Figure 2.95. Some of the canned reports (which are inherently useful for a commercial website) are listed in Figure 2.96. You can customize and construct graphs and charts with

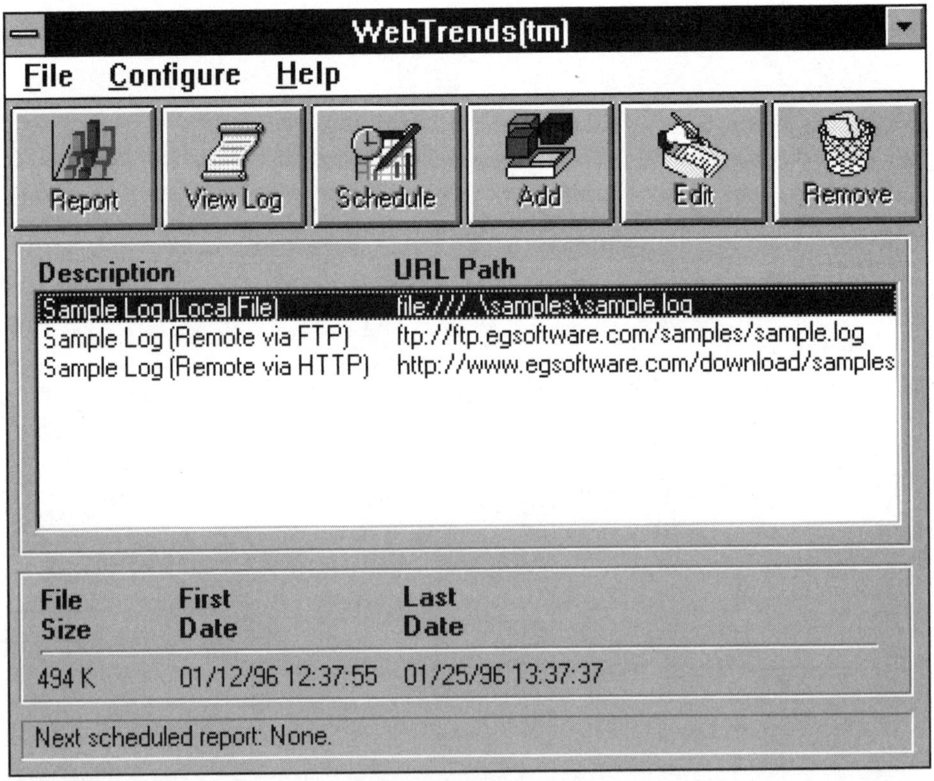

Figure 2.95 WebTrends runs as an application or Windows NT service to track more in-depth website usage statistics such as page hits, user hits, repeat access by user name or referring site, click-through access, and route through a complex web site.

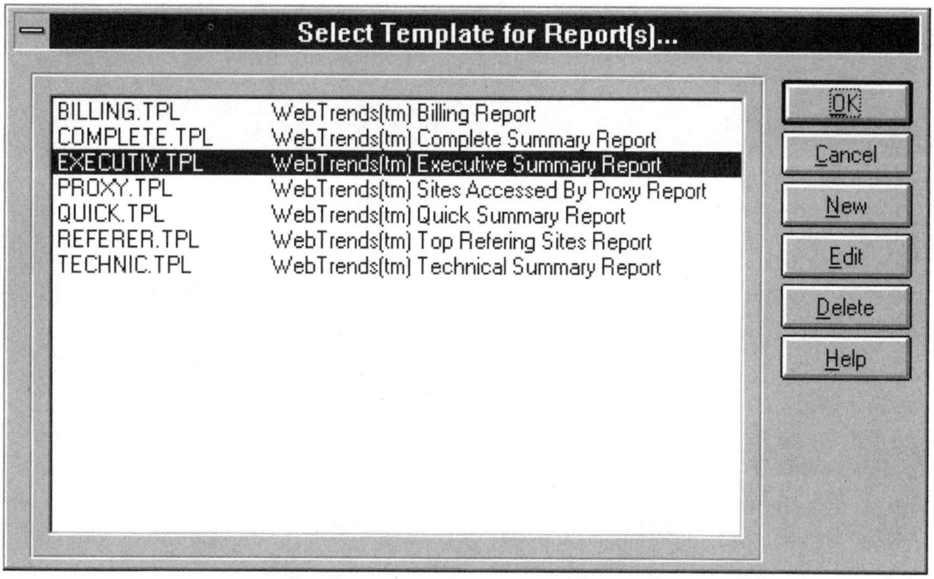

Figure 2.96 WebTrends canned reports delivered with the tracking tool.

the built-in Excel-like chart generation tools included with the generous and flexible report generator in WebTrends, as shown in Figure 2.97.

Scripts

Common Gateway Interface (CGI) scripts are not written in a programming language called CGI. That is just an umbrella terminology that is strictly a description of any programming code written in C, C++, Java, ActiveX, Visual Basic, Delphi, csh (UNIX C-shell), or Perl to pass information between HTML forms, the server environment, a database server, the operating system, and secondary server or client applications. These scripts are not typically raw sequences of interpreted commands (although they can be), but rather compiled programs. CGI scripts may be platform-dependent (Visual Basic and compiled in C for a specific CPU and operating system) or portable (Java and Perl) when they are not compiled. These scripts make anything possible . . . if your organization has the time and resources for it. Most don't and shouldn't!

Scripts are supposed to be secure, but there are a myriad of possible security holes as itemized in Chapter 4. For these reasons, I encourage you to visit other solutions that are more secure, easier to administer, and typically integrate better into the website as a whole. In addition, CGI scripts are terrific for small and simple processes on marginally loaded sites. However, when the site becomes busy and the number of processes and variations on a theme become large, software development, maintenance, and debugging render CGI solutions suboptimal. Even the enhanced versions of CGI that provide single threads for multiple processes, compilation to machine code native to the server environment,

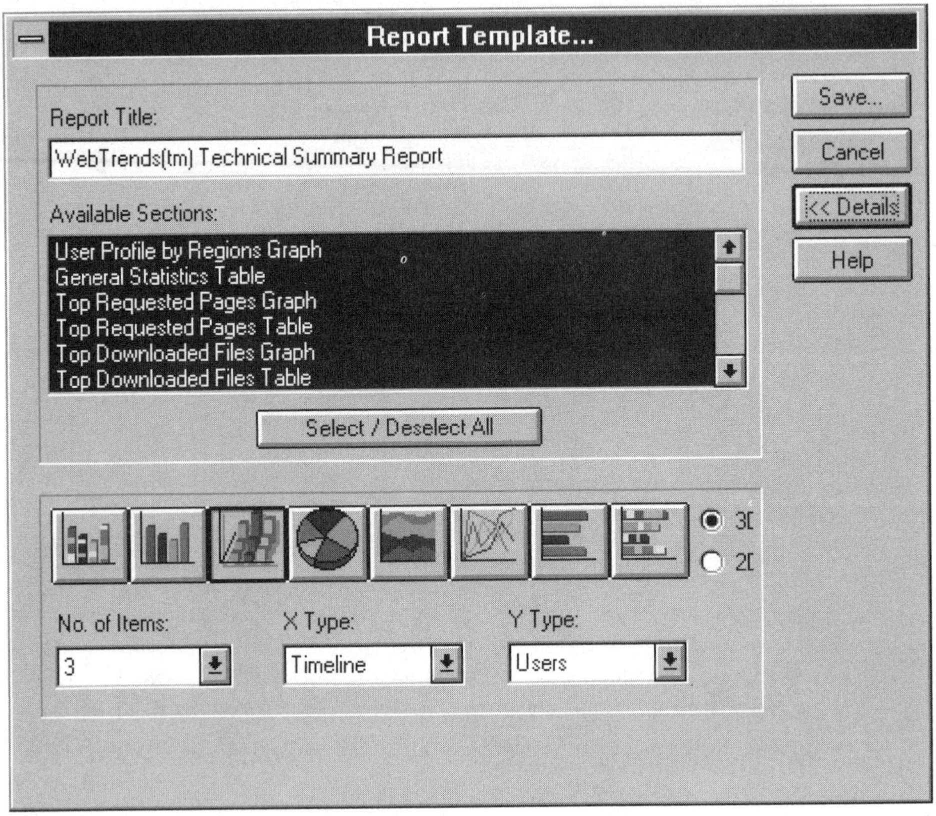

Figure 2.97 WebTrends canned reports delivered with the tracking tool.

and other performance and security additions represent more risk than are acceptable to commercial websites and booming cyberstores.

Nevertheless, you have seen some CGI scripts for displaying a hit counter and the CD-ROM has some scripts for the following: the cyberstore, a visitor's guest book, a changing fortune cookie (that is, the random useless message or a pertinent application tip of the day), user password authentication, keyword search, log file of hits, type of user browser, and various public domain CGI libraries. Most of these scripts are from the Selena Sol website on the Electronic Frontier Foundation (EFF). Notice that these scripts share common CGI libraries. You cannot mix scripts unless you rename libraries from different sources that have common names. For example, "CGI-LIB.PL" is a common name. Another good site for scripts for just about every conceivable platform and operating system is the NCSA CGI archives. Other sites are listed on this book's home page.

Note that many CGI scripts assume UNIX web server platforms, Sun Microsystems Solaris operating system in particular, but the Perl and Java ones are portable. Realize that the ISO 1660 (the definitive standard for CD-ROM file naming and directory structures) limitations of the CD-ROM means that many file names have been renamed to mesh with the DOS 8.3 filename format. This will likely create problems if you do not rename the imbedded file references. This problem is a prevalent development and server platform issue, which is addressed in Chapter 3; it is one you need to understand within mixed platform organizations. Your organization may support DOS, Macintosh, Windows, NetWare, IBM MVS or OS/400, while the organization hosting your site may be AIX, SGI, or Solaris. You will encounter surprises unless you recognize the trouble with cross-platform issues early during your planning and development.

Realize that the logger script (which collects user names of all people to hit your site) requires that the web server identd checking is enabled and accessed by surfers. In addition, the web server and development environment must be enabled for scripting and include supplement code libraries and run-times for P-code (or interpreted applications); all the scripts require either the compiler, interpreter, or run-time libraries. The CGI Perl 5 and classic libraries are included on the companion CD-ROM. In fact, if you want to implement most anything with 3-D and databases in CGI without software acquisition costs, download the NCSA version of W3Kit as shown in Figure 2.98 (and available at http://www.geom.umn.edu/software/download/W3Kit.html).

Selena Sol's CGI archives at EFF contain at least four cybershop scripts, one of which is shown in Figure 2.99. I emphasize that these working scripts are suitable for organizations that envision the website first as a presence, and second as a practical and convenient transaction processing channel for selling a handful of products. Cyberstores have more complex inventories and involved financial tracking requirements than to tackle site development with CGI code and a massive integration effort, risking the failure of building an office tower

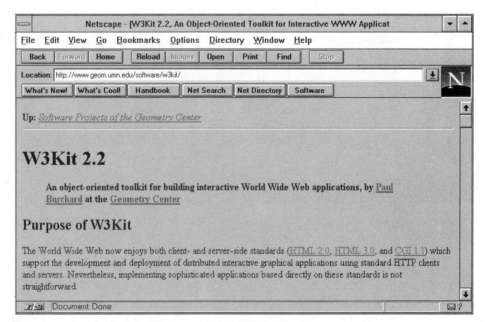

Figure 2.98   A multiplatform database and 3-D CGI toolkit.

Netscape - [Selena Sol's Public Domain CGI Script Archive and Resource Library
File Edit View Go Bookmarks Options Directory Window Help
Back Forward Home Reload Images Open Print Find Stop
Location: http://www2.eff.org/~erict/Scripts/
What's New! What's Cool! Handbook Net Search Net Directory Software
Selena's Electronic Outlet (HTML Version)
Selena's
Announcem
Scripts
Selena's FAQ
Netscape - [Number mart]
File Edit View Go Bookmarks Options Directory Window Help
Back Forward Home Reload Images Open Print Find Stop
Location: http://www2.eff.org/cgi-bin/Selena/Shopping_cart/Html_web_store/html_web_store.cgi?p
What's New! What's Cool! Handbook Net Search Net Directory
Available Options
Font: Times New Roman (No charge)
Color:
Red
Blue (+ $1.00)
I'd like to buy a number
View/Modify Cart
Return to Frontpage
Checkout Stand
Document: Done
Document: Done

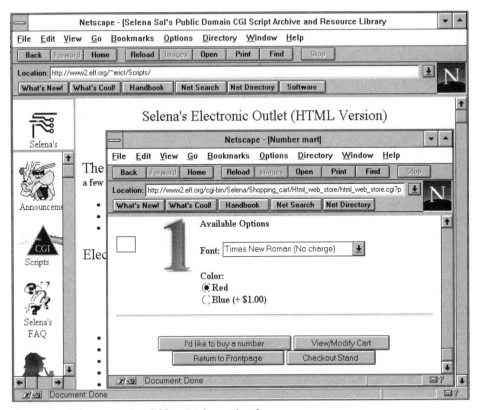

Figure 2.99 A demonstration CGI script for a cybershop.

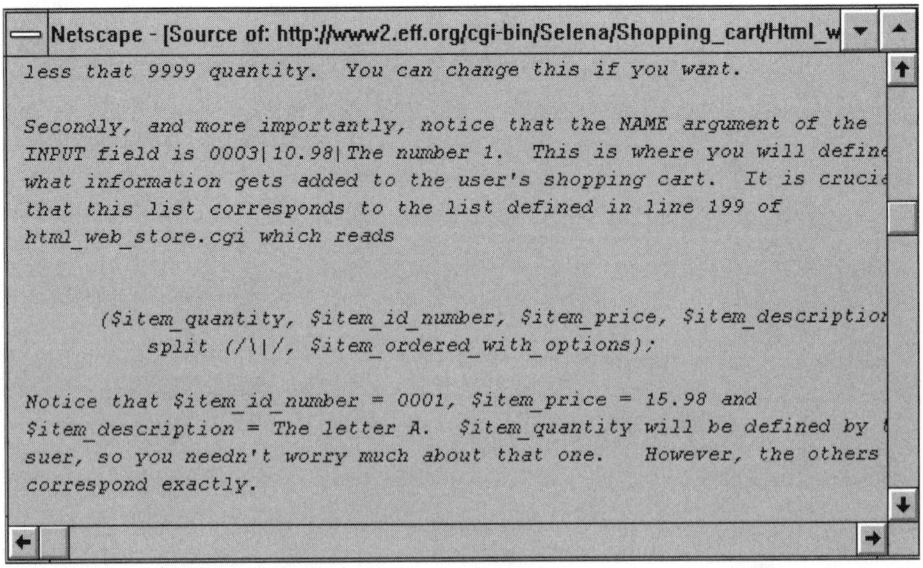

Netscape - [Source of: http://www2.eff.org/cgi-bin/Selena/Shopping_cart/Html_w
less that 9999 quantity. You can change this if you want.
Secondly, and more importantly, notice that the NAME argument of the
INPUT field is 0003|10.98|The number 1. This is where you will defin
what information gets added to the user's shopping cart. It is cruci
that this list corresponds to the list defined in line 199 of
html_web_store.cgi which reads
($item_quantity, $item_id_number, $item_price, $item_descriptio
split (/\|/, $item_ordered_with_options);
Notice that $item_id_number = 0001, $item_price = 15.98 and
$item_description = The letter A. $item_quantity will be defined by
suer, so you needn't worry much about that one. However, the others
correspond exactly.

Figure 2.100 A multiplatform database and 3-D CGI toolkit.

from cards or match sticks. The cyberstore truly requires more significant component building materials and integration with financial accounting systems.

The HTML code in Figure 2.100 shows the complexity and method for building the cybershop functionality with the form in the prior figure. In reality, the code is simple, easily readable, and very modifiable, but becomes just too much for significant product or service sales activity. The problem is not so much that the code will be hard to write, but rather that in quantity it becomes difficult to debug and upgrade.

Graphics

There are special versions of images that are viewable as part of a web page. They are specified by the graphical interchange format (GIF) and Joint Photographic Experts Group (JPEG) image format. GIF files are named xxxxxxxxxxxxx.gif and JPEG images are named xxxxxxxxxxxx.jpeg or xxxxxxxx.jpg to comply with the DOS 8.3 and ISO 9660 filename limitations. Kodak and Iterated Systems are proposing a new image format that supports multiple resolutions on demand. In fact, Iterated Systems provides a tool to create .FIF (for Fractal Image Format) and an add-in for the web browser to support denser compression and faster displays. Generally, most web sites will stick to the common and NC Reference Profile 1 image formats, either GIF or JPEG and ignore special formats like FIF.

Some general tips to get the most mileage and speed from imbedded images are described here. First, reuse common components because they get cached in memory on the client browsers and local corporate cache servers. Menu icon bars and logos are good bets. Gradient and textured backgrounds can consume excessive memory and bandwidth but can be optimized with the use of subtle tones and simple gradients. Simplify the palette (that is, the available number of pure colors) in textures, gradients, and even basic images to dramatically reduce file size and thus transmission times.

Palette reduction with various tools also results in significant image size reductions. You can even use specific color schemes for better JPEG compression. Color depth reduction (from millions of colors) to 24-bit, 16-bit, 8-bit, 4-bit, or 2-bit (monochrome) reduces image sizes dramatically for both JPEG and GIF images. However, do the color reductions before you dither and anti-alias the images or you will create grossly large palettes and odd moiré patterns or stair-steps if the color reduction occurs after the dithering or aliasing. GIF compression is minimal unless you convert from 24-bit or 16-bit color schemes to a 4-bit reduction.

Since none of the database tools profiled in Chapter 4 includes provisions for building pages with images extracted from a database and stored as part of the database, you will need special "middleware" for that process. When you store images inside a long-binary object (BLOB) field in a data table, typically you will need to extract the binary data (stored as JPEG or GIF formats) and create a temporary file with a temporary filename for reference and inclusion within an HTML page created on the fly. If you are doing that much work to integrate a database with HTML, consider using the fractal image formats from Iterated Systems to achieve compression ratios of 25:1 to 300:1. While it is possible to extract and convert image formats, process speed for large images becomes a critical factor, so the best advice is to store the images in a web format. Since the image display mechanism is implicit with HTML, long-binary extraction is very simple. You can use MS Access, Oracle, Sybase, SQL Server, or any major database with a dBase-like memo field. The trick is getting the images into the records in the first place.

The reason this technique and essential workflow issue is mentioned here is that large cyberstores are likely to include at least one image, perhaps multiple images, and even sound bites and video to show each and every product or service in its best light. A big cyberstore is very likely to have thousands of products. Management of an image portfolio is possible when images are bundled within the structure of a hierarchical database. By the way, read "possible" as "impossible" and "unlikely" to manage without good controls. Some of the many document management databases, such as Watermark and the New Wang/Microsoft Window95 API and toolkit, include support for scanned documents and images. When these databases use Oracle, Sybase, DB2, and other major DBMSs as a platform, cyberstore design, management, and integration are several steps easier.

The standard JPEG and GIF formats are interchangeable in HTML image tags and they are functionally interchangeable as far as website development is concerned. The file contents are not interchangeable but can be converted from one format to the other with WinGif, PaintShop, Photoshop, and other graphical editing or conversion tools. Basically, most people pick one format, generally GIF because it is simpler and smaller (for minimized color palettes but continuous tone photographs), as the predominant file type for images. If you expect to include many large and detailed color images, the JPEG format might be compressed to smaller file sizes. JPEG compression is lossy, which means that the file size is reduced with a loss of color depth, detail, and resolution. This probably doesn't matter for web images unless the images are compressed 100:1 or greater. However, both image types tile for backgrounds and can be positioned and sized with HTML commands. Both formats are likely to provide a better image than can be displayed in a web browser, given the color palette limitations and screen dot pitch resolutions (from 72 to 96 dots per inch [dpi]) for most browsers.

Color palette

Web browsers limit the graphic images to surprising sizes and typically a lower resolution than when created. Although the source image may be suitable for a *National Geographic* color impression of 133 lines per inch (lpi), that same image will display differentially in a web browser at 72 or 96 dpi. Note that 133 lpi is not 40 percent greater than 96 dpi. 133 screen lines (used by *National Geographic* for its typographic output) correspond to roughly

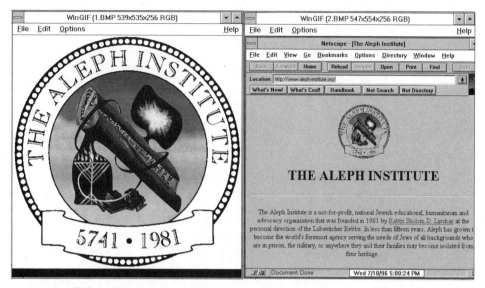

Figure 2.101 Web Analyzer captured the contents of the entire Aleph Institute site and showed the full size (539 × 531 pixels) and resolution (256 bits at 300 dpi) of the logo in contrast to the muddied display on the HTML page (47 × 47 × 256 bits but at 96 dpi). This site is profiled in Chapter 5 for a makeover.

2450 dpi. Figure 2.101 illustrates this point with a comparison of a very strong source image and the resulting browser output.

Notice that the browser version even with 216 colors is illegible. The banner name and dates break apart at these lower browser resolutions. The image in the crest is unclear. As a result, the logo is not only a waste of space for this page, but because the logo is also centered in the page rather than offset left or right, it also wastes the entire line of space to either side. The nice details and shading are lost on browsers limited to 16 colors, grayscale, or monochrome (1 bit in black or in white). Preview your images across a network, with different systems, different browsers, and different Internet connection speeds. Even when images look good on a development system, you need to validate how they look and work in a real downloaded web page.

Image densities.   When you create image buttons with source language as text and provide alternatives for other languages, be attuned to the legibility of any text when image color palette and density are reduced. Blue text on a red background is the same gray in black and white or grayscale. Images clear at 300 dpi might not resolve at resolutions of 96 dpi or less. So many sites have very pretty buttons with dysfunctional captions made even more ineffectual by URL tags that provide few clues to the meaning of these icons. For example, while I liked the frame design for this home page in Figure 2.102, nothing worked, not even the E-mail link.

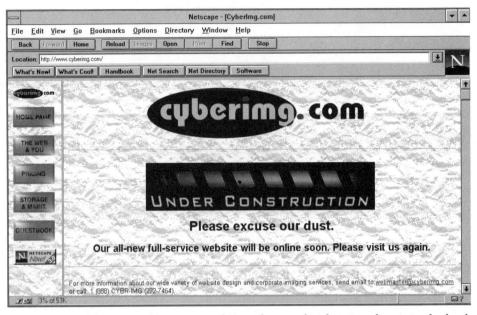

Figure 2.102 A page dominated by images and image buttons that do not resolve at standard web browser screen resolutions.

GIF formats

In the simplest format, and most flexible for website design, GIF is a format describing a bitmapped image. A more complex format allows for transparent display of GIF files so that parts of the bitmap allow a background to show through, a format called *transparency*. This technique is useful for the superimposition of images. The GIF89a specification (approved in 1989) includes the compilation of multiple image frames within a single GIF file for very simple and effective animations like a movie. The images can overlay each other to show filmlike motion or appear at different sizes and screen positions to create a presentation.

GIF89a also includes two file storage formats that show the image unrolling like a window shade (*noninterlaced* or *noninterleaved*), or a progressive display with greater depth and color (*interlaced* or *interleaved*). There are no storage differences, substantial file size differences (relative to other bitmap formats), or display time differences—just one anomaly that site designers sometimes like. The interlaced format shows a ghost image on a web page almost immediately so that users can get an idea of the content of the page. The noninterlaced format delays text display until the image is complete; this creates pages that appear ever so slowly with large holes that suddenly fill with floating image frames and a surge of text. Overall HTML page display time is identical. These formats are compared in Figure 2.103.

The only viable web/Internet image formats for your cyberstore are JPEG, FIF, and GIF. The Fractal image format (FIF) is a special lossless image compression format from Iterated Systems that requires a special compression ap-

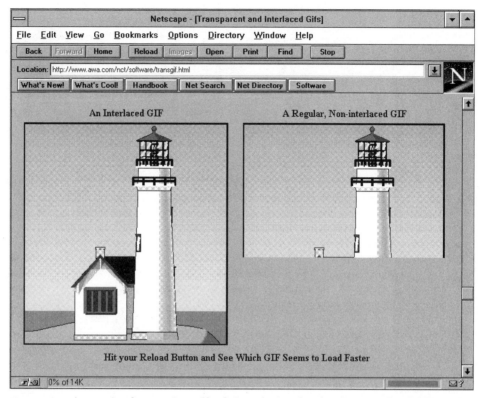

Figure 2.103   A very visual comparison of load times for interlaced and noninterlaced GIF images.

plication and add-ins for client browsers. This is not convenient for most cyberstores unless you want to exclude some users or maintain a secondary method to show uncompressed images with GIF or JPEG. This often requires coding and a CGI/server environmental variable for each client connection to indicate the browser type, operating system, and if special graphics are supported. The compound screen shot in Figure 2.104 shows a bitmap and its file size in different formats.

The most important information is that this original 71,988-byte, 256-color Windows bitmap file in a GIF format compresses it to 8377 bytes or 8772 bytes (in 216 colors) when the GIF image is interleaved. The JPEG version of the file requires 69,545 bytes, 8 times larger than the corresponding GIF file. The message is to use GIF files unless you need the full-color range or the JPEG compression yields a smaller file size than the GIF image, which is not usually the case unless you specify significant lossy compression. Interleaved images are approximately the same size (when you compare one to a JPEG or Windows .BMP or .RLE format) as noninterleaved GIF formats, although in actuality they are from 6 to 15 percent larger. This difference for GIF image formats on sites with images that range from 4000 to 14,000 bytes is immaterial.

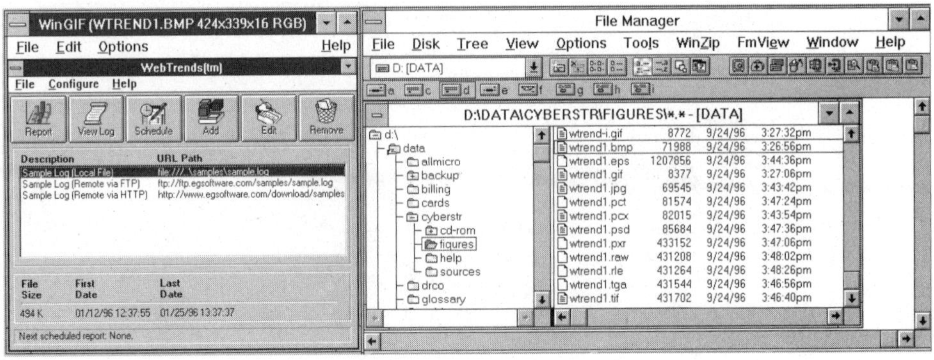

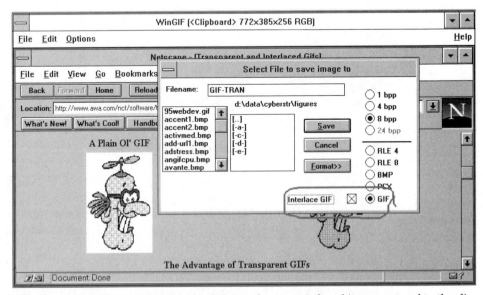

Figure 2.104 Image format size differences for supported Photoshop formats.

Overall loading times for a page with noninterlaced or interleaved GIF images are identical, but a user can see the interleaved image sooner. The difference between the interlaced and noninterlaced image is simply a matter of the file format and how the image is saved, as shown by the check box in Figure 2.105.

The transparency format is a more important attribute and one you should understand and know how to create and apply. The image in Figure 2.106 on the left includes a blank background. Blank means that the background has never been specified or the background color has been designated as the transparent equivalent of no color. This is similar to the blue screen concept used in film mak-

Figure 2.105 WinGIF is one shareware tool that makes any windows bitmap captured to the clipboard and pasted into the program an interlaced web-compatible format.

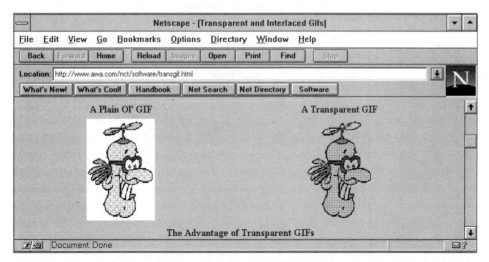

Figure 2.106 A very visual comparison of a standard GIF and a transparent GIF loaded over a background color or base image. The transparent image is visually more attractive and more flexible with color or image backgrounds.

ing for layering special effects behind actors filmed in front of a blank blue background. The background transparency color is noted within the GIF header. Any part of the image using this color will defer to an underlying or background image and let that color show through. The transparent color can be any chosen color. If the software (usually the graphics design tool and the client's browser) does not support GIF transparency, that part of the image may display as blank or white. Recent browsers now support the GIF89a transparency and frame extensions, so transparency support really isn't a major concern that should affect how you design web pages. The transparent GIF provides a means to overlay images and text into a more uniform and integrated presentation.

Not all image tools support GIF images and particularly the GIF transparency feature. PaintShop Pro is probably the best and simplest tool for GIF construction and it is bundled with a number of commercial HTML editors and web servers. If you want to create frames for standard or animated GIF images, Corel XARA provides a transparency feature not found in the mainstream draw tools that are useful. PaintShop Pro as shown in Figure 2.107 also provides the functionality to create single-frame GIF images and transparencies.

Microsoft and Adobe have also updated the Photoshop GIF add-in to support the alpha channel transparency capabilities for GIF89a. It works only in Photoshop versions 3.0.4 or later. This add-in file can be downloaded from Microsoft Developers Only pages or from Adobe's website. Figure 2.108 shows one of the Photoshop dialogs for setting the color for transparency. You might note that you cannot set multiple colors for transparency, so it is best to set a single likely background color for each image. This background color could be black, white, or the Microsoft 25 percent gray. Because Photoshop has the best

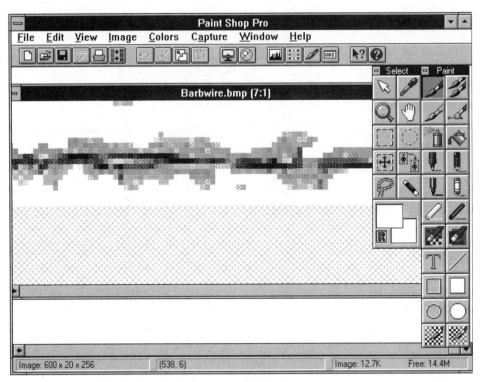

Figure 2.107 PaintShop Pro bundled with many HTML editors and web servers converts bitmaps to a transparent format, as this barbed wire separator shows.

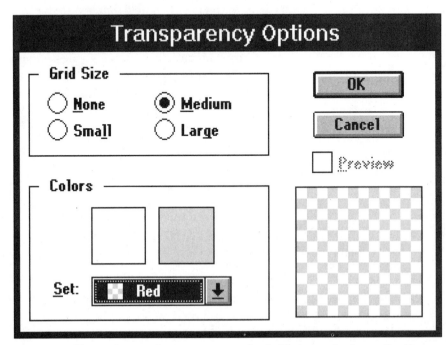

Figure 2.108 You need to set the transparency color in Photoshop (and save the file as a GIF format) in order to overlay text and images in HTML pages.

tools for bitmapped design and provides more control and functions than other image editors, this may be a better environment for designing transparent images and the base frames for animated sequences. Note that Photoshop requires a couple of weeks to learn and master.

Image animation

Although you can create Java (or ActiveX, Javascript, CGI, Perl, AVI, QuickTime, MPEG, or other coded) sequences to animate images, this requires the user's browser to be enabled for Java or the other add-ins and that the whole sequence including the Java code with the imbedded images downloaded to the user. It is faster and more respectful of web bandwidth limitations to create image animation sequences with GIF89a formats. A stream of separate frames or images can be imbedded within a single GIF file. The use of frames implies that images of identical shape are played in sequence to create the illusion of motion. The use of images played in sequence creates the illusion of a presentation with images of different sizes, screen placement, and fades. You can also create slide shows with waterfall images, display text and banners, and support various transitions from one image to the next frame. Specifically, you can have control over:

- x and y pixel of each frame
- Delays for user input
- Delays (specified in microseconds [1/100 seconds]) between frames
- Color transparency
- Interlacing display
- Text displays
- Fades and other special effects (transitions)
- Repeats and infinite loop
- Comments

One of the better sites for GIF information, tools, and many samples is the GIF Animation on the WWW site, as shown in Figure 2.109. Although you can see the animation effects with a browser or GIF viewer supporting the GIF89a extended format, you can view the images with most of the newer web browsers.

Figure 2.110 illustrates the process of GIF animation. Notice the sequence of descriptions for each frame in the center of the image and two frames displayed on either side. You can animate objects, texts, and words, and create special image fades with this extended format. Basically, the format includes a series of individual frames that are displayed as defined by each frame sequence and an overall program. Yes, an animate GIF file is larger and slower

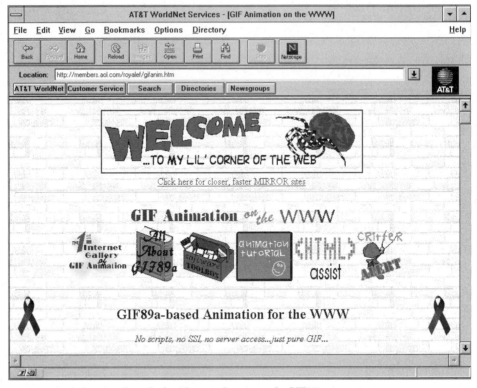

Figure 2.109 Animation described without code using only GIF89a.

to load. A file with ten frames is about ten times larger than a single GIF image. For example, a simple GIF file that is 4127 bytes and is modified to show a smile over ten frames in a GIF89a file will probably require 41,270 bytes (plus some sequence and other overhead) to store. If you must use

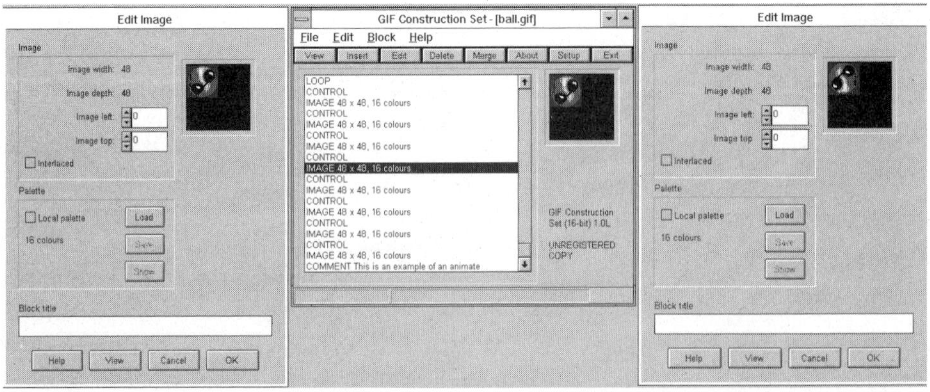

Figure 2.110 GIF Construction Set (included in the CD-ROM) running more than once showing frame animation.

interlaced images, figure on 49,000 bytes. Here the difference in standard and the interleaved format becomes substantial enough so that you might want to redesign a web page with a neutral background.

The CD-ROM includes information (GIFABOUT.HTM) describing the structure and techniques for applying animation in GIF files. I use WinGIF and CorelPaint to create a master image and then modify a little bit for each new frame. This is how cartoons are constructed, and this is how animated GIFs are built. The best animation is smooth because it has many intermediate steps, as shown by the image downloaded from an Internet site in Figure 2.111.

The next sequence of illustrations shows the construction process for an animated GIF. This particular sequence is obnoxious because it flashes an image and its inverse. Inverse and flashing are HTML attributes for text, but either attribute is unfriendly on a web page because it is like placing a flashing neon sign on a respectable street. The same artistic sensibility remains true for animated images. The next screen shot in Figure 2.112 shows the setup process for GIF Construction Set. Here is the Netscape color palette. It is really important to recognize that although your development workstations or users may support 24-bit color, support for images inside an HTML page is realistically limited to the 216 red, green, and blue (RGB) colors supported by the Netscape browser. Even if some users use Mosaic, a browser built into an application, or Explorer, some 75 percent of all surfers use Netscape (on Macintosh, OS/2, UNIX, and other platforms). The problem with using unsupported colors is lack of contrast, wild color substitutions, other shade conversion problems, or a moiré display. Figure 2.113 shows the available mix of RGB colors. Failure to

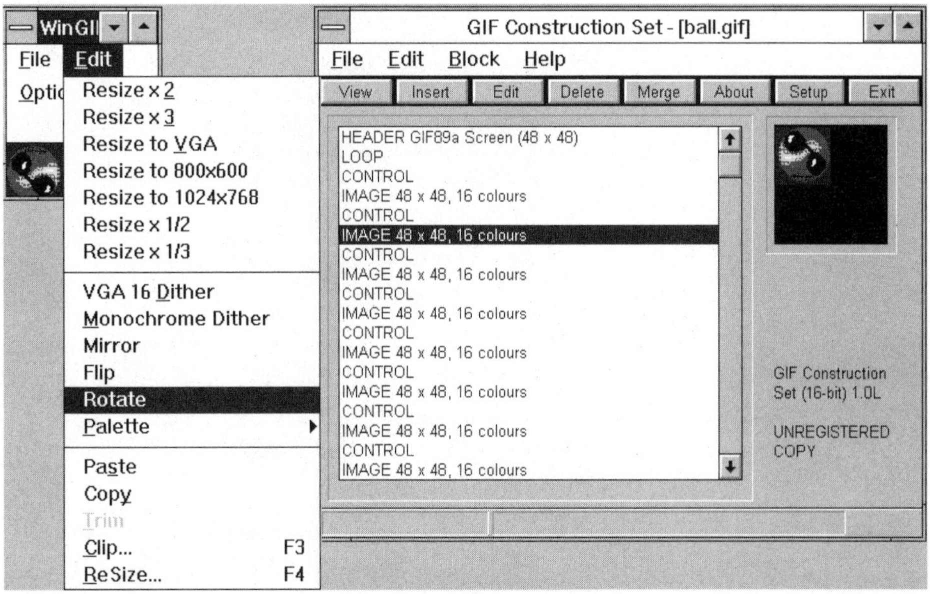

Figure 2.111 WinGIF used in conjunction with various other simple bitmap utilities and the GIF Construction Set can rotate or overlay parts of images to create the necessary animation effects.

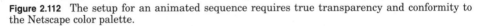

Figure 2.112 The setup for an animated sequence requires true transparency and conformity to the Netscape color palette.

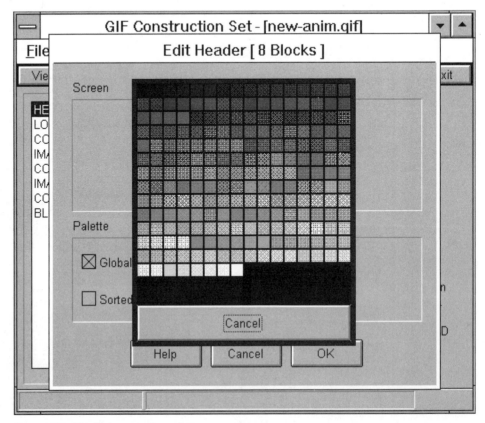

Figure 2.113 The Netscape color palette.

compensate for the Netscape palette conversion and dithering results in the following muddy presentation, as shown in Figure 2.114. Victor Engel demonstrates the color effects on both black and white page backgrounds in an organized color wheel. More information can be obtained about the Netscape color limitations from his white paper at www.onr.com/user/lights/netcol.html. The color wheel is shown in Figure 2.115.

The next illustration shows the insertion of basic images into the sequence that becomes an animated GIF. I made a CorelDRAW! image (full-screen size) of the star burst with the "NEW!" text inside, scaled it down to a useful display size, and created an inverse mask with the LView program. However, PaintShop Pro or Photoshop are better tools for manipulating single pixels for animated images because you can zoom to any size. You see both images on the left side. Netscape browser version 2.0 supports the LOOP command, which means that this animation will repeat endlessly. The CONTROL command sets transitions between the individual graphical elements, as shown in Figure 2.116. You can see two images listed above each other. One was loaded from the clipboard and the other was loaded as a file. I suggest you create a subdirectory for each animated image and store the individual frames as separate files numbered in sequence. This is just in case the GIF89a file ever becomes corrupt on your website host or on the development archives and you need the individual frames to reconstruct the sequence. In addition, you might save a print-screen to show the sequence.

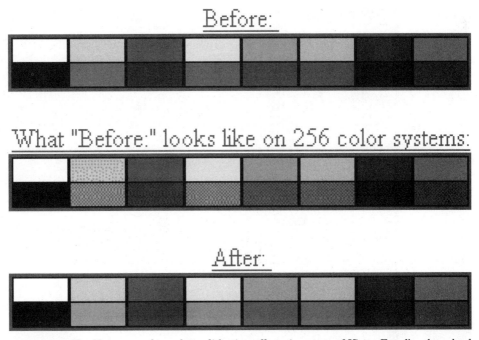

Figure 2.114 The Netscape color palette dithering effects (courtesy of Victor Engel's color wheel white paper).

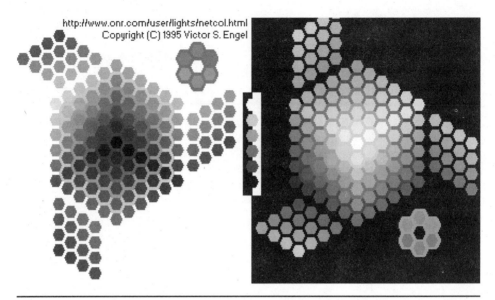

Figure 2.115 The transparent Netscape color wheel with contrasting backgrounds (courtesy of Victor Engel's color wheel white paper).

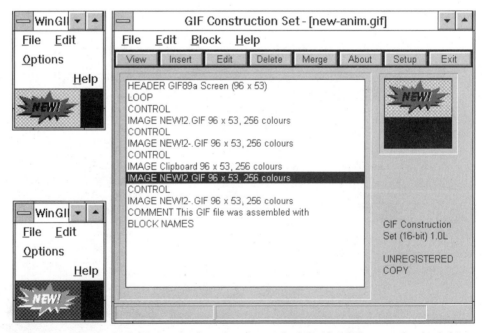

Figure 2.116 The two basic images for the animation on the left side can be pasted or loaded into the GIF89a file.

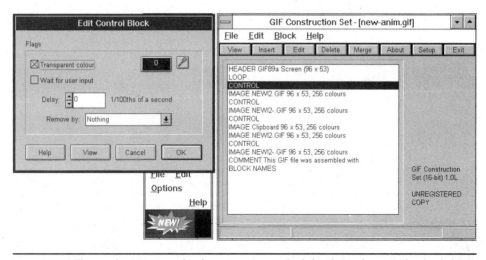

Figure 2.117   The two basic images for the animation on the left side can be pasted or loaded into the GIF89a file.

Figure 2.117 shows the check box for transparent color, which can be important when the animation is shown over tiled background, text, or another image.

Figure 2.118 shows the parameter for the LOOP command. Although the GIF Construction Set will display the animation sequence the specified number of times, most browsers will recognize the LOOP command and display the animation just once (when the command is not included) or endlessly rerun the sequence. Since the iteration counter is meaningless and the animation will run endlessly anyway, the duplication within the GIF wastes disk space, your development time, and Internet bandwidth. Figure 2.119 shows the simplest format for the animation. However, if you have special transitions for more images, you will need to construct a complete sequence.

Figure 2.120 shows the types of fancy transitions (or wipes) that you can use between frames. The following screen shot (Figure 2.121) shows the venetian blind effect as an image is added with a special transition. This sequence of four images also shows a presentation sequence that is not a framed animation and probably should not include the GIF89a LOOP command.

If you want animated graphics over complex or colored backgrounds, then be certain to save the master image as a transparent GIF. Use that image to construct the animated sequence. If you forgot this step, you will have to go back into each frame and replace each bitmap. Otherwise, the web page will end up with an unmasterful hole as the frames burn away the colored background. Large animated presentations and even small GIFs should be saved as interlaced images to improve the time required for parts of the

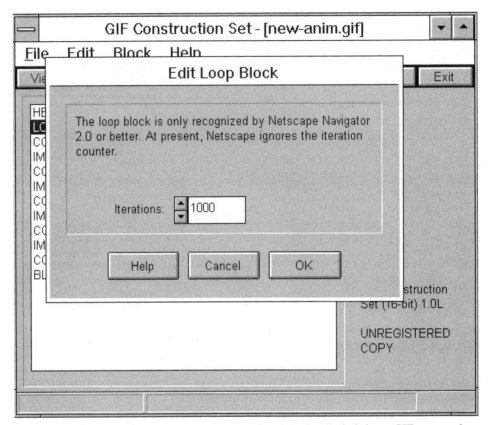

Figure 2.118 The loop parameters are not supported except when included as a GIF command.

page to show. Additionally, animated GIFs do require some minimal CPU time, each about 2 to 3 percent depending on the type of processor and available cache. Figure 2.122 shows a momentary load to 13 percent as the frames move through RAM. The real limitation is that most displays cannot repaint the screen as fast as the processor can fetch the next frame. Therefore, avoid haphazard and frequent use of animated GIFs on the same page, or the page will be blank until everything has loaded and paints very slowly.

Image maps

An image map is a graphical image usually of large size (not a thumbnail or icon) that contains multiple hyperlink areas that map to different URLs. For example, you can create an image of a spaceship console with buttons and knobs that actually request different HTML resources with the hypertext link. This is useful when the image has a universal quality to it, but very parochial when text is imbedded in the image. You can create rectangular or polygon shapes to define regions as complex as a class photo, in which every visible

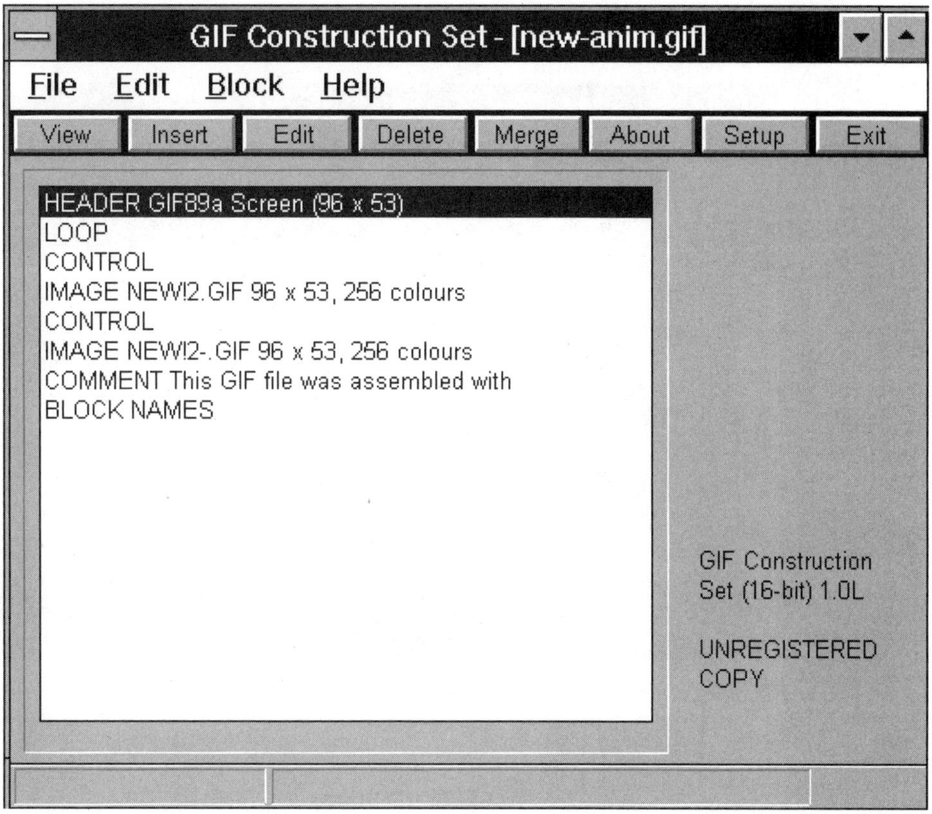

Figure 2.119 The duplication of the two files (NEW!2.GIF and NEW!2-.GIF) can be removed to simplify the animation, in this case with no change in the animation and savings in file size and complexity because the two images are identical.

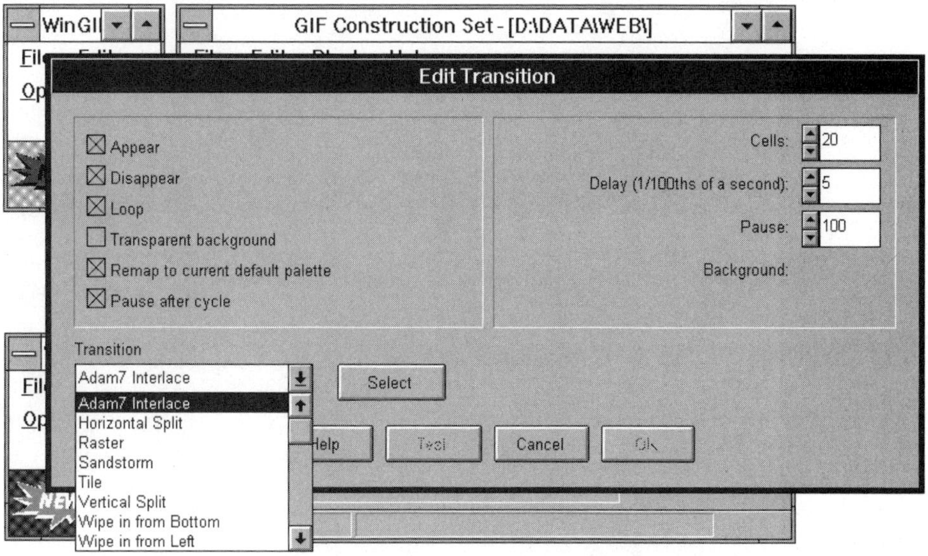

Figure 2.120 The loop parameters are not supported except when included as a GIF command.

Figure 2.121   Waterfall effect as images of varying sizes are positioned around the screen in overlay and transparent modes.

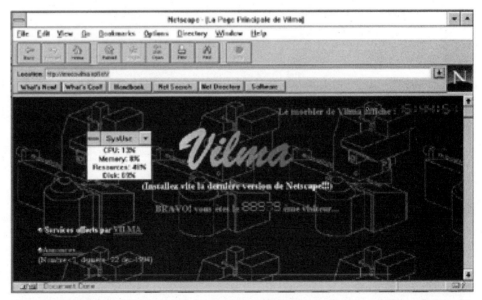

Figure 2.122   Minimal CPU overhead for looping GIF89a images (relative to Java, Javascript, VBScript, or ActiveX).

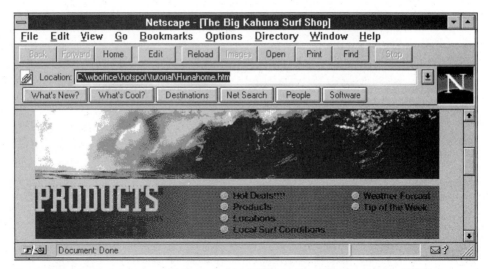

Figure 2.123 A complex image with balls and text intended to activate secondary HTML pages.

person is mapped to a different URL. Note that you do not use the Netscape-specific HTML commands defining images with regard to width and height when using hot spot maps. Instead, make the images the exact size that you want them to display at the web browser resolution. The image in Figure 2.123 shows a sample of the Kanahuna Surf Shop that comes with the Blue Sky HTML suite being mapped with HotSpot Studio. The hot spots are shapes literally drawn on top of the image. In Figure 2.124, you can see a rectangle mapped over a button and assigned to a particular URL. When a user clicks

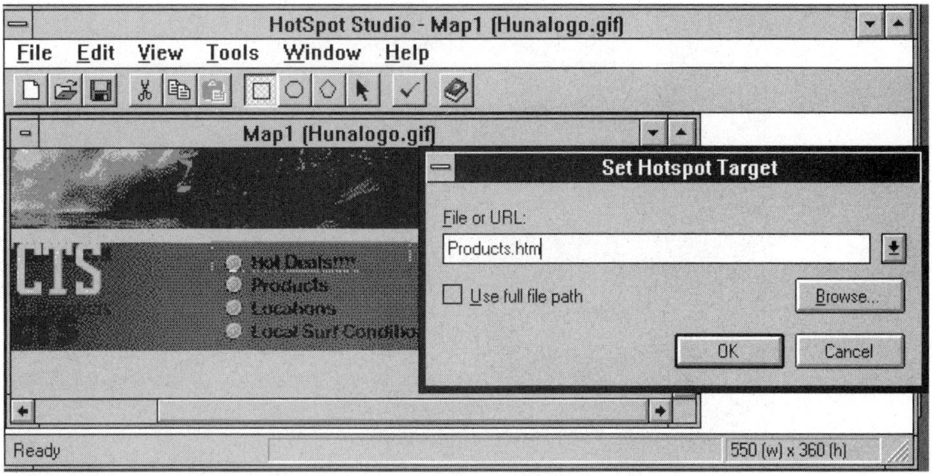

Figure 2.124 A "button," its text, and the area around it are mapped to a URL.

on that particular area of the image, the indicated HTML file (PROD-UCTS.HTM) will be displayed just as though the user clicked on underlined text mapped as text to the URL for PRODUCTS.HTM.

Create a larger border around images so that the user does not have to be so precise to activate the hyperlink. Buttons and hotspots in larger images do not have to be rectangular or circular. It is also possible to create polygons or multiple rectangles with overlapping circles to define more complex shapes as shown in Figure 2.125. Areas that are not represented by mappings often generate a visible (x,y) pair of coordinates on the web browser; the mapped sites generate and display the URL associated with the hotspot. It is best that all parts of the image have a default URL in case the user misses the hotspots.

Once you have defined all the logical hotspots and mapped these to the URL addresses, you need to save the file. What file? The image file is already saved; it exists unchanged and can be displayed as a standard image. The mapping information is stored within an overlay file, often referenced by the same file name as the image file with a .map extension. There are three standard map file formats, but the NCSA format is the most common, as shown by Figure 2.126.

You can create multiple map files for each image and reference a difference map file for different HTML pages. For example, if a user is viewing the home page, the hotspot for the home need not be defined and mapped to a URL. That way the button is not functional on the home page. If it were, the user would only be reloading the image from your website over and over with each redundant click. Give each map file a different name and reference the toolbar with the appropriate map file in the HTML statement. This requires a consistent naming convention so that you do not mix up files.

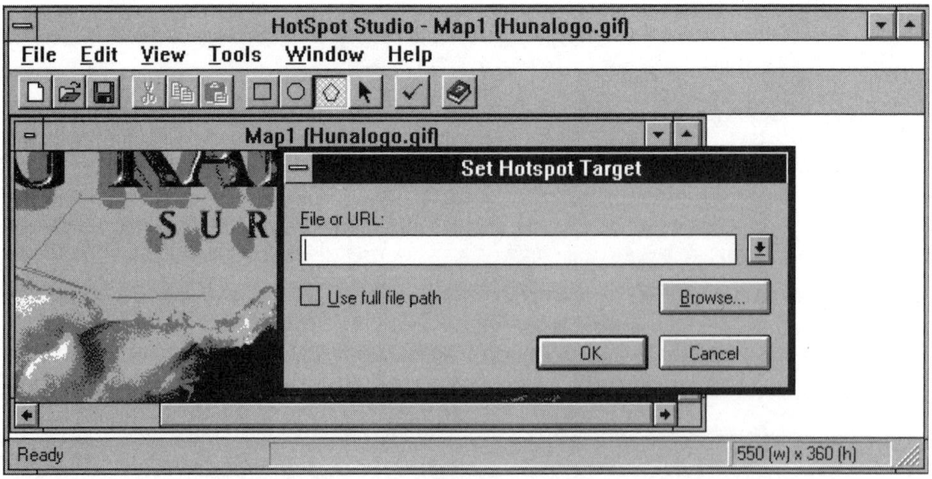

Figure 2.125 Mapping a hotspot with a polygon.

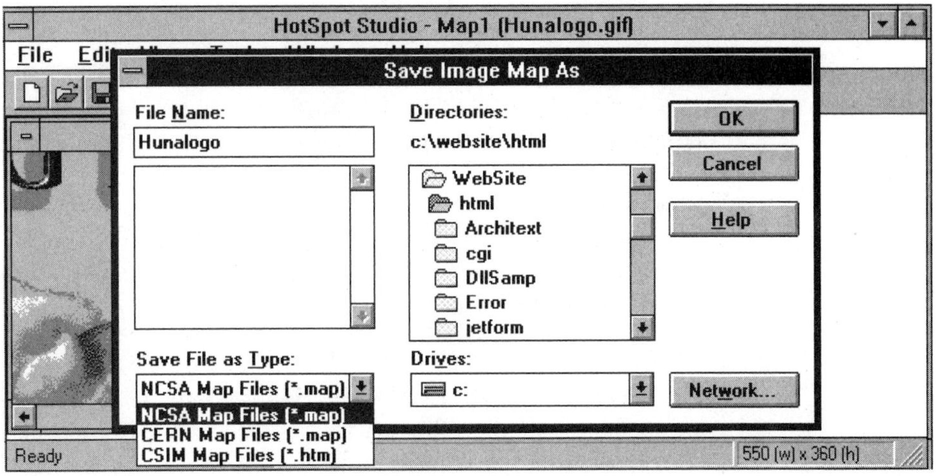

Figure 2.126 Various map file formats. Note that tools exist for format conversion.

The following screen shot in Figure 2.127 shows a bad image map from a demo for L5R. It is not that the image is bad, but the map file is overly restrictive. The hotspot area defined as Miami is just a small circle corresponding to the downtown area and is almost too small to activate with the

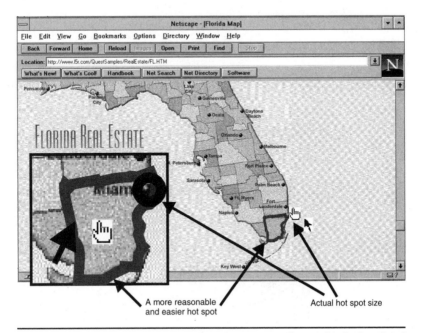

Figure 2.127 The active hotspot (small circle) is so small as to be dysfunctional when the spot could be more appropriately defined as a county area as annotated at the lower left.

hand. Instead, the hotspot should be the regional county as shown by my insert at the bottom left. Since this relates to the real estate cyberstore, the enhanced hot spot defines a more realistic and also meaningful search range.

You can capture screens from accounting packages and create order screens and hot spots very easily, as shown in Figure 2.128. HotSpot Studio is not the only tool that creates NCSA maps. WebImage with WebSite works too. You can use WebImage to create special effects to your screens. The conversion in Figure 2.129 just isn't readable, useful, or usable given the source image. However, it can be applied to mask QuickBook forms after you adjust the scheme for monochrome. The next figure (Figure 2.130) shows mapping the (stocking unit) SKU button to a CGI database function to query the inventory. The URL doesn't need to be a specific HTML filename or link, but could also be a function that invokes WebDBC or other middleware tools. This tool saves incidental information in the map file so that this programming can be maintained at a later time. WebImage also includes a feature that allows you to view and step through the hotspots and the associated mappings. It is very easy to overlook a button or to map two or more buttons into a single URL. Figure 2.131 shows how you can adjust and delete mappings.

The creepy site at Activision supporting the CD-ROM game called SpyCraft (partially authored by William Colby, former head of the CIA, and his Russian counterpart) includes HTML pages almost totally devoid of text and activated only by graphical hotspots as shown in Figure 2.132. The Activision site is profiled in Chapter 5.

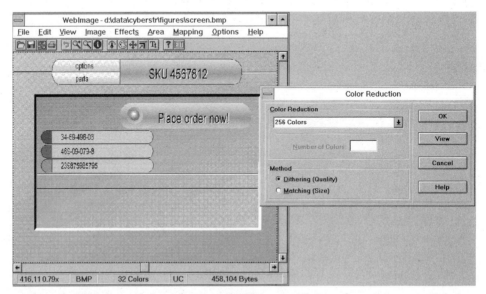

Figure 2.128 WebImage reduces a screen to the Netscape palette and creates an unsatisfactory moiré pattern. The source will require some color simplification.

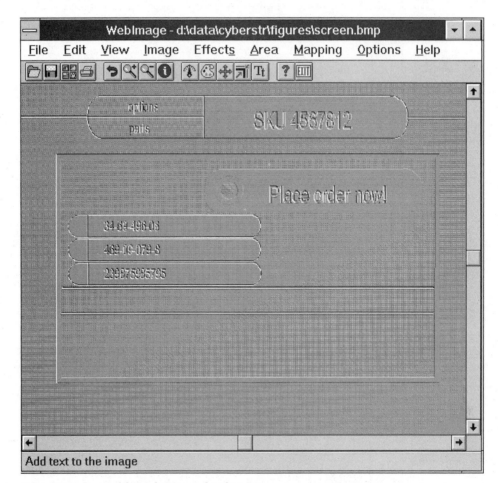

Figure 2.129 Image color reduction and embossing.

Mapped images are not just for fancy or contrived web sites. The screen shot in Figure 2.133 shows boxes constructed in CorelDRAW! and text overlaid to define the purpose of the hyperspots. The use of alternate fonts is inadvisable, but if the use of specialized fonts is part of the organizational logo or reflects a special image, the use of fonts inside images assures that the user will see what you designed regardless of the browser, operating system, or available replacement fonts. Note that any fonts you select in the design of web pages are typically substituted by the web browser and the platform as defined by preferences and the font-mapping table. The clean Helvetica font (sans serif) gives a nice look in imbedded graphics.

Most HTML editors and web servers include hotspot mappers. In case you do not have one, the companion CD-ROM includes a very good one called

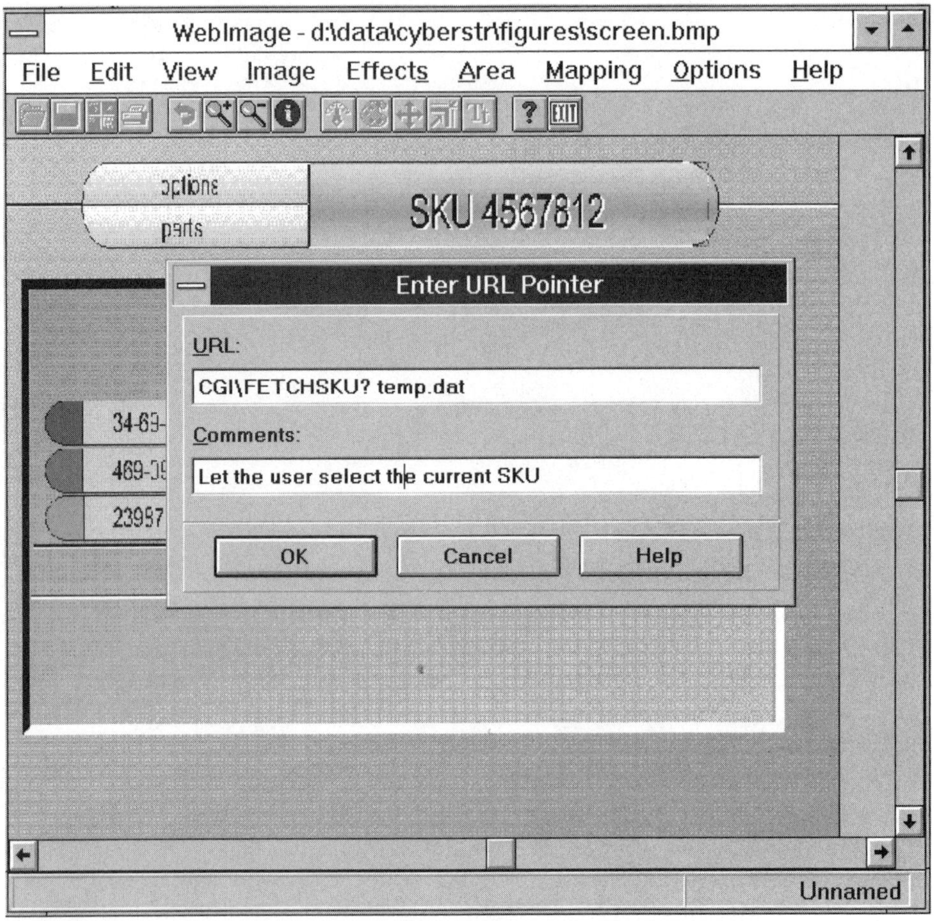

Figure 2.130 Mapping a button on an image to a (CGI) middleware function.

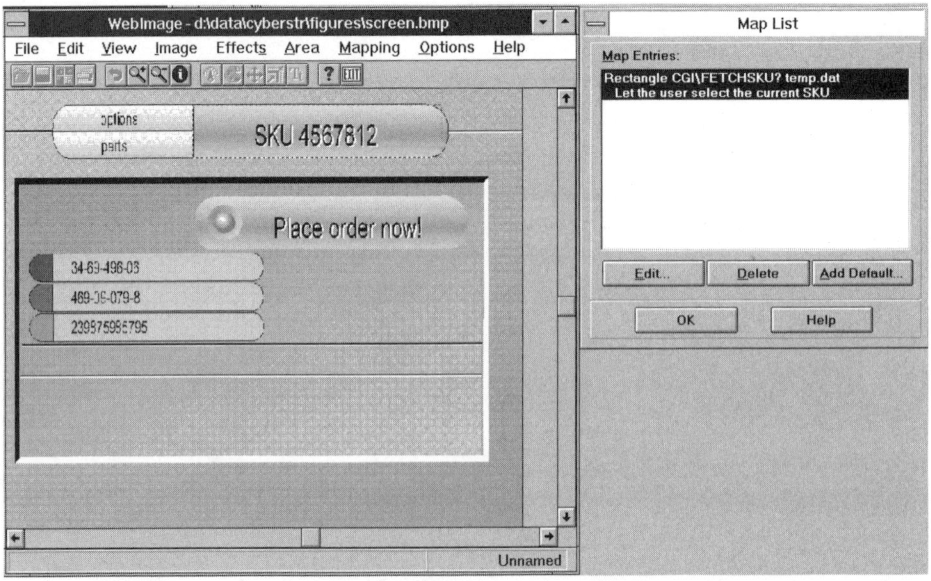

Figure 2.131 Reviewing and repairing hotspot maps with WebImage.

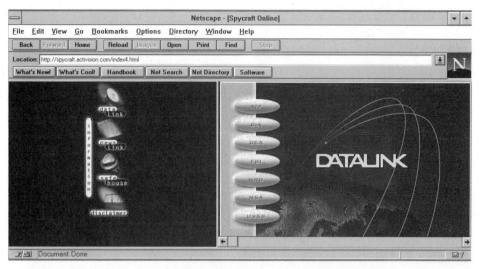

Figure 2.132 Framed images with polygon hotspots to enhance the SpyCraft CD-ROM game by providing an interactive and current events component.

Figure 2.133 Clean buttons in a single mapped bitmap assure alignment and the desired look and feel for your site.

Map This!, which links the map file to the GIF shown in action in Figure 2.134. Note that you can create multiple map files for the same GIF image so that different HTML pages activate different secondary pages. This is important when the icon bar includes a nonessential link to the current page or for special pages available to customers, users that have registered for your site with a cookie, or when a database middleware tool builds pages on the fly.

Image maps are actually implemented from either the client-side (browser) or a server-side implementation (SSI). SSI is most applicable and widely accessible because the implementation is browser-independent. However, the match-up between mouse movements, the image name, and the map coordinates requires a CGI script for interpretation. Instead, consider a simple client-side implementation and save CGI development time. The next two examples demonstrate the HTML code for map enablement:

```
<A HREF="http://www.companyname.com/image.map">
<IMG SRC="image.gif" ISMAP><A/>
```

Simple images can be mapped using only HTML code. The format for this is illustrated as follows:

```
<MAP NAME="testmap">
<AREA>
  SHAPE=POLY'
  COORDS="0,0,25,50"
  HREF="http://www.companyname.com/MAP1.HTM">
<AREA>
  SHAPE=POLY
  COORDS="25,0,50,50"
  HREF="http://www.companyname.com/MAP2.HTM">
<AREA>
  SHAPE=POLY
  COORDS="50,0,75,50"
  HREF="http://www.companyname.com/MAP2.HTM"></MAP>
<IMG SRC5"image.gif" USEMAP5"#testmap">
```

If you want client and server independence, presuming you have defined an HTML map definition in addition to the map file, try this code:

```
<A HREF5"http://www.companyname.com/image.map">
<IMG SRC="image.gif" ISMAP USEMAP="#testmap"><A/>
```

Virtual reality

Virtual reality and the pages constructed with the virtual reality markup language (VRML) represent photorealistic, surrealistic, or even hyperrealistic renderings of real places, people, products, and an onscreen representation of the shopping mall and shopping cart. VRML provides motion through a site in addition to 2-D hotspot mapping. Changes in image orientation alter the placement, perspective, and view of the actual website display. For the most part, the connection speed for users ranges from 14.4 to 28.8 Kbps with aver-

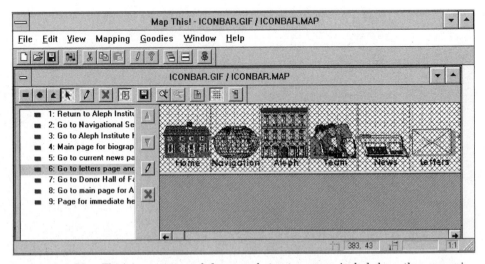

Figure 2.134 Map This! is a very good freeware hotspot mapper included on the companion CD-ROM here shown creating the map for the Aleph Institute makeover profiled in Chapter 5.

age throughputs of 0.2 to 1.3 Kbps. This narrow delivery, in spite of faster modems and even bonded ISDN digital connections, precludes effective use of websites that are graphics intensive. It is possible, pretty, and even practical to build websites with large, single-pane images (assuming you provide alternatives for nongraphical browsers), but showing motion and active 3-D graphics are impractical for most cyberstore customers. Of course, use the 3-D VRML effect if it is important for entertainment, virtual aisle shopping, or for some other competitive advantage that is not readily clear to me yet.

When depth of field and motion are important to your product or services, then 3-D and true VRML may represent a competitive advantage. Most cyberstores are complex enough that adding more complexity raises the development risks, tends to confuse and repel customers, and complicates the heady business of transaction processing and user navigation. Some designers suggest that photorealistic images, like the gallery shown in Figure 2.135 simplify user navigation by using intuitive navigation techniques. Click where you want to go, and you will be there.

Hyperrealistic images set the tone for a catalog of goods and services. For example, a restaurant wants to put on the best image of the food and convey the exultant feeling that a customer might have during dinner. The hyperrealism is just an artistic statement, perhaps not a promise of absolute product and service quality. In a sense, it is a style reminiscent of the Bauhaus period, but the reality is that it is a new style portraying no specific identification. That can be very powerful and useful for creating a unique identity for a cyberstore or advertising site, as Figure 2.136 illustrates. The message of the

Figure 2.135 An image suitable for 2-D hotspot mapping to facilitate physical site navigation.

Figure 2.136 A still life is a nonspecific message gaining meaning from the biases and predispositions of the viewer, a useful technique for advertising.

wine and fruit is timeless, and implies whatever the viewer wants to see, which is perhaps why still life painting has endured for four hundred years.

While the depth and size of a mall can be conveyed through virtual reality images and mapped with hotspots, website presentations can include displaying products, as the furniture and interior design services do for the next website. The vitality here for virtual reality is in defining in complete detail for a customer what is possible and leaving nothing to the imagination. Obviously there are customers who lack imagination or an ability to abstract; the result is that precision of view—assuming that view appeals to the customer—becomes a competitive advantage. Figure 2.137 highlights the power of facsimile for advertising physical products and services.

When three dimensionality is added to a cyberstore site, it must mesh with the purpose of the site. Simply showing an image, in this case a cow, in order to select the cut of beef desired, links the reality of the source of a product to its consumption. Although the cow has no expression and is clearly not anthropomorphized (that is, given human traits), it makes me uncomfortable scrolling very slowly around the figure to select sirloin or top round cuts, as shown in Figure 2.138. Scrolling in closer or on top is also confusing given the slow process speed over the TCP/IP connection. It is a gimmick that might work for complex part replacement selection, for example in a 3-D representation of the jet ski engine, but it cuts too close to home for food choice.

VRML is like a movie but it is not linear, as planned by the designer because it provides a framework so that the person viewing the presentation can determine the progression of the frames. Think of VRML as a movie with a fixed

Figure 2.137 Hyperreality with virtual reality addresses the needs for some customers to see exactly how products and services will fit their needs.

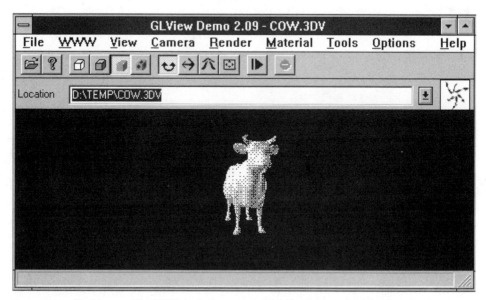

Figure 2.138 Problems with VRML include excessive bandwidth required for downloading, overloading of CPU, jerky painting, slow mouse control, and image resolution limitations as shown in this demo.

plot and cast of characters but a little freedom to adjust the viewpoint. Ray Dream Studio includes a wizard interface to speed the process of specifying backgrounds, lighting, and major objects. Planning viewing angles, object deformations, and creation of various Internet video formats are simple although time-consuming even with fast hardware. If you foresee a beneficial use for the VRML presentations, you can create your own site-specific plug-in or use one of the standard Studio APIs and viewers for integrating these "movies" into the website.

Downloading 3-D presentations improves performance, as shown by the .AVI-style flyover shown in Figure 2.139. However, the linkage is broken between the cyberstore sales process and the demo because the runtime is not provided with a browser, browser add-in, or movie player with any browser functionality. The connection to the sales process is tenuous at best so that any urge to include new technologies like this should be balanced against implementation and maintenance costs and should mesh with a clear marketing message.

Streaming video and motion

A number of products and techniques provide audiovideo presentations over the web. The simplest is an FTP site or WWW hyperlink to automatically

Figure 2.139 When the 3-D presentations are downloaded to improve performance, interactivity is limited (and slow) and the linkages to cyberstore commerce are lost and the message is weak at best.

download a .AU, .AVI, or .QIC movie. In addition, Freelance and ScreenCam presentations fall within this category. It is important to realize that these presentations are typically two- or three-step procedures. First, the file must be transferred to the local client. Second, the file then must be expanded. Third, the file is played. This is not dynamic like VRML. Several tools, including Shockwave from Macromedia, minimize the number of steps required to view presentations and video. This *streaming* presentation method automates the process so that the movie plays as it is downloaded and it is not saved to the local client. This is faster, but replays require that the stream be transmitted again. Streaming presentations are possible with audio, video, and audiovideo materials, and increasingly for multimedia training and technical support. This technology is very useful for computer-based training (CBT), but questionable when added to dress up a site. Streaming video is useful to profile a product or service that cannot be described with a static image, that is complex or new, or that elicits an emotional response. For example, the stunning sounds and wave-jumping action of a jet ski is a perfect product to portray because it is a complex and emotional product. Figure 2.140 illustrates a streaming presentation as part of a web page.

Video phone connectivity and multimedia

The latest new gadgetry on the Internet are virtual movies, streaming video, and video conferencing. The significant limitation is connection speed and bandwidth. Video usually includes synchronized sound, too. However, video

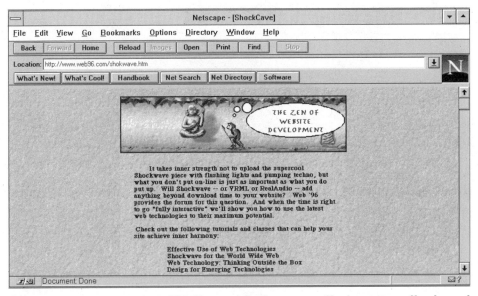

Figure 2.140 A page promoting a Web Show and Conference uses Shockwave to profile advanced technology. It is not clear to me how the panning video motion improves or clarifies the message for this site, although it is useful for CBT.

makes on-line help and CBT very possible and useful. For example, you could show a product in operation, people having fun with a jet ski, or the romantic mood possible with a new fragrance. This is new technology, as I mentioned, and is profiled in greater detail in my book, *Web Video Toolkit* (McGraw-Hill, 1997). The figure in 2.141 shows an exterior view of a window for a web-based streaming commercial.

Streaming video and multimedia is not the only possibility. It is also possible to "page" website technical support and get that cyber clerk on a video screen to explain where to go and what to do in real time. This technology is also profiled in Web Video. TEDDY.MOV is shown in Figure 2.142 and is included on the companion CD-ROM. Although this video is not relevant to most cyberstores unless you are selling toys (such as teddy bears) or providing a teddy bear repair service, you can extrapolate the value of it to other products or services.

Graphic libraries

Many web tools, particularly HTML editors positioned as complete website development kits, include galleries of images. Often, these kits contain a gallery thumbnail tool to help you search by name, topic, usage, or content, or to actually browse through the images to locate the one you want. Most of the libraries contain simple images of star bursts, 3-D balls and buttons, and con-

Figure 2.141 TV-style commercials and CBT are possible with video.

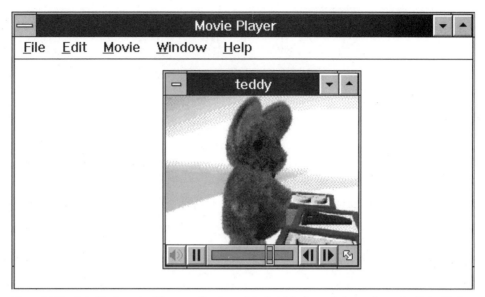

Figure 2.142 A teddy bear builds a word using alphabet blocks and shows the potential of inter-active training or video motion with sound.

versions of public domain bitmaps into the GIF or JPEG formats. Some sets, such as the WebOffice toolkit, include some more unique and interesting libraries, as shown in Figures 2.143. In fact, even the demo from Blue Sky Software included in its entirety on the companion CD-ROM includes a sizable collection of good advertising web art. The WebOffice contains some unusual

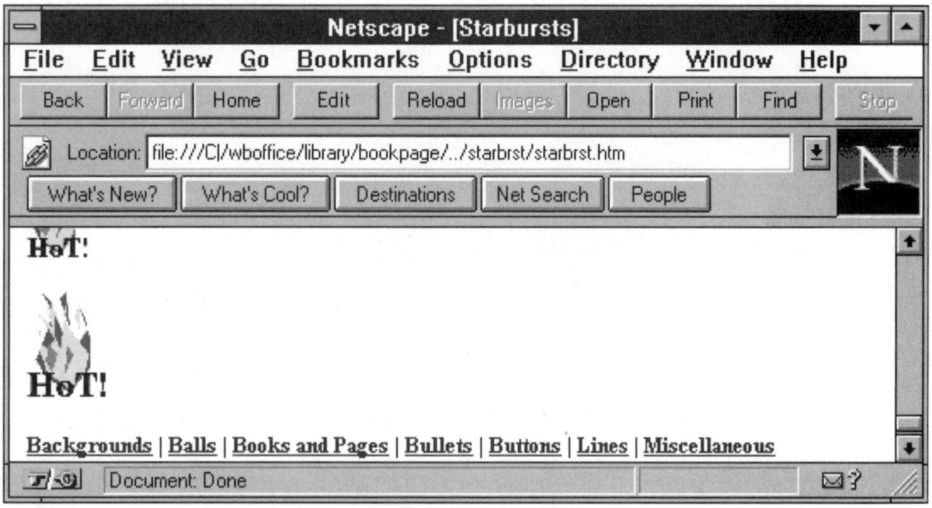

Figure 2.143 Starburst galleries "searchable" as HTML pages.

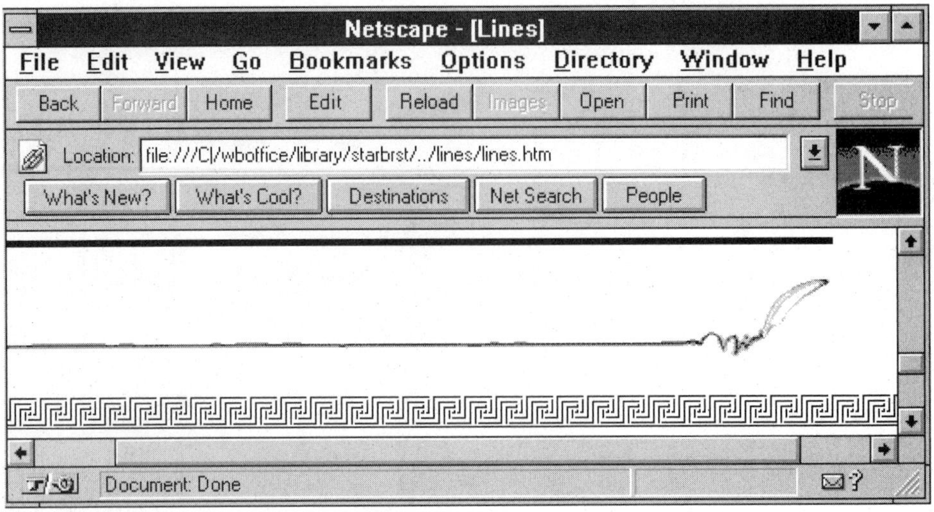

Figure 2.144 Line art galleries "searchable" as HTML pages.

separator lines, as shown in Figure 2.144, that can add impact or set the mood for a site. Figure 2.145 shows the "thumbnail" view of part of the CD-ROM library that Blue Sky provided for this book.

I mention that Visual Web (a Windows95 and WindowsNT tool) includes a complete collection of GIF images for credit cards. This library might be

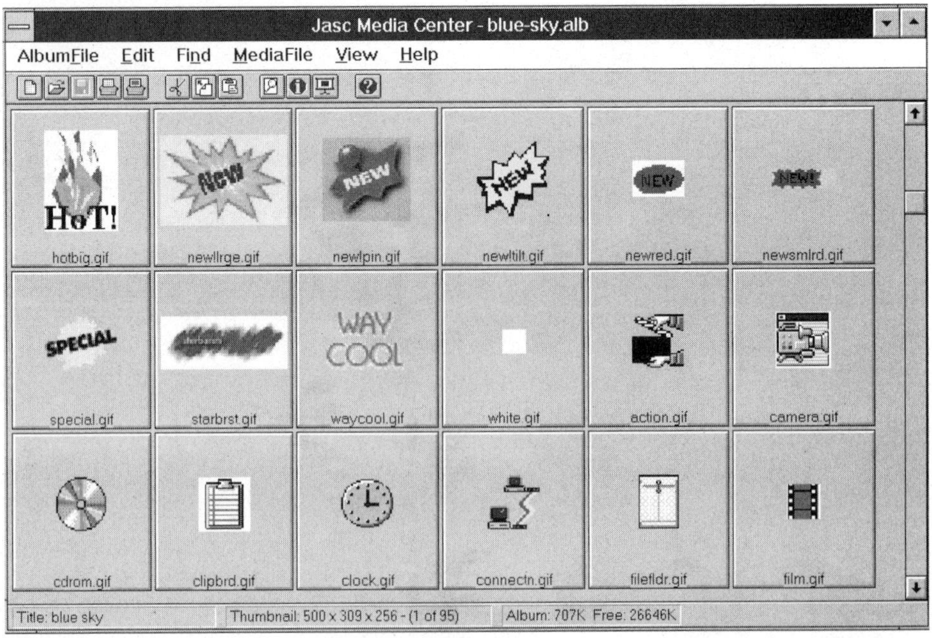

Figure 2.145 Clip art from Blue Sky on the CD-ROM.

more appropriate to cyberstore development than the Corel clip art collection in that it includes the major credit cards and some of the private label department store and gasoline cards. Realize that GIF clip art images are flat drawings made of color pixels that are very hard to modify and alter. If you want to use them, do so judiciously, but not to provide an unanticipated advertisement for the tool or clip art vendor. Promote your own site with its own unique ambience.

In general, most serious website developers will not use clip art images unless they use them as a basis for more complex and unique artwork. The problem with using clip art in a commercial website or cyberstore is that your site will look like every other basic website and hold no unique look and feel about it. On the other hand, some of the basic balls, check marks, lines, and simple symbols are useful for general-purpose design. In contrast, I often use CorelDRAW! clip art as a basis for designing sites because the images are not bitmaps. Instead, the CorelDRAW! clip art are vector images that can be separated from the backgrounds, altered in subtle or significant ways, and combined with other elements so that the clip art becomes very alien to its original source. The end result is unique art that will qualify for copyright status and can become the basis for logos, trademarks, or business-specific symbols. You can do almost anything new and imaginative when the basic vector clip art is combined with artistic text.

The Blue Sky Web Graphics locator provides a different metaphor in that it searches a hard drive or removable media for all suitable files, lists the file names, and shows a larger view than thumbnail of each highlighted image. If you create your own site logos and art, these thumbnail tools become important for locating your creations in your own site library. The Web Graphics Locator is shown in Figure 2.146.

You need tools like MediaCenter, Corel Mosaic, or the Web Graphics Locator to simplify sorting through thousands of images as thumbnails. Tools like Web.Gallery are proprietary and contain a core of images that cannot be expanded and are good only insofar as the images suit your requirements. The mechanism for looking for artwork within HTML pages is tedious because even with a local file and fast hard drive, HTML loads slowly. However, the Corel Web.Designer toolkit includes a handy thumbnail (that is, a small, often low-resolution representation of the entire image) gallery tool to organize and search your image libraries, as shown in Figure 2.147.

Capturing graphics

Any graphic on a website can be captured, even if it is protected by copyrights, trademarks, or the locked images and text with tools like Maximizer Image Guardian. There are ownership laws regarding all web material, text, images, sounds, and video as detailed in Chapter 4. Some are relinquished by a specific designation that the materials are available as public domain, but many are indicated as protected and misuse may be legally enforced. Tools such as WebWhacker, MilkTruck, or WebAnalyzer can grab an entire website, includ-

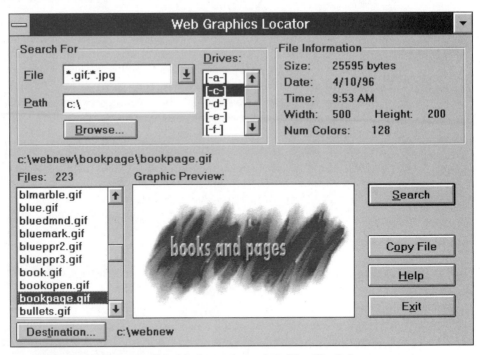

Figure 2.146 Volume (that is, disk drive) art selector from Blue Sky Software.

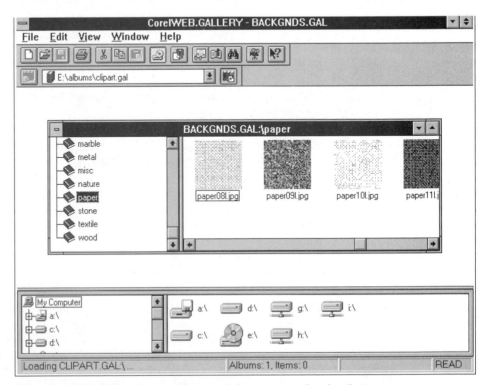

Figure 2.147 Web.Gallery shows galleries and the necessary thumbnail view.

ing HTM (HTML), GIF, and JPEG files. This requires disk space sufficient to host the structure and the text with graphics of the captured site. This is a useful procedure for me when I rework a client's site. Not only do I get a complete copy of the live site, but I save this "before" view to compare with the "after" enhancements, as you will see in Chapter 5 with the makeover for Aleph Institute. However, if I am hunting for useful images and background textures, I want to save the images in a very structured resource hierarchy so that I can find the files later when I need them. There are three approaches to grab individual graphics and background textures: the brute force method, the print screen or screen capture process, and the right mouse button in Navigator. The first two work no matter what browser you use.

Brute force. The first method is to view a page with the images you want. When the document is "done," use the menu option to view the source. In Netscape, you will get a secondary window, as shown in Figure 2.148. (Mosaic and HotDog will show a split screen.) Therefore, the URL for the logo image resource is www.iconovex.com/apglobe1.gif. Cut and paste this string or type it into the location. The other images include iconbar.gif, webanch.gif, echo.gif, and indxcn1.GIF. Although you are unlikely to want to use an organization's logo, you may want to use part of the globe to construct your own identifiable

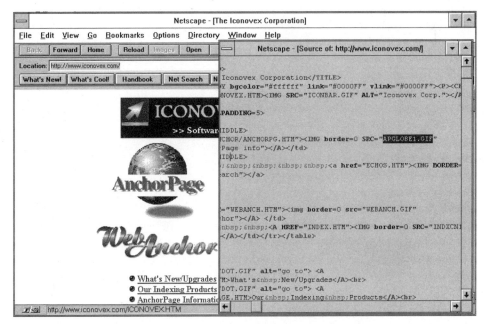

Figure 2.148 The subordinate window displays the HTML source. Note that the image file for the globe is referenced as "APGLOBE1.GIF" at www.iconovex.com.

and unique logo from parts of these others. The "http://" is optional with most browsers since they complete partially specified URLs with the formal address. The result is shown in Figure 2.149. The image is then saved (File/Save as . . .) under a filename in a directory of your choice. Tiled background images (whether GIF or JPEG) can be captured using only this technique. For example, Professor Pete's Webmaster 301 page has a nice tiled image. This spiral-bound notebook background is unusual in that it tiles only vertically. Notice the extended HTML code in the source code window to achieve this. The image is shown in Figure 2.150.

The image URL (all HTML source files, imbedded applets, and graphics have URLs) is entered into the location field, displayed in the browser window alone, and then File/Save As . . . to local file, as shown in Figure 2.151. Notice that this image fits together vertically and when it is tiled creates the illusion of the spiral-bound notebook. You could modify this image with light blue lines as found in a composition book, as shown in Figure 2.152. However, realize that the line leading (that is, the space between lines) is a function of user browser configuration, screen display resolution, and screen device drives so that any designer attempts to use a special font, such as a felt marker or an architectural handwriting font to fit on the lines and between the lines, is likely to fail for these reasons.

Print screen.   If you cannot get an image with method one, the second method is to create a screen shot of the completed document (ALT-PrintScrn in Windows) or the special Macintosh keyboard screen capture button (that is, ()). This captures the image in the active window, but does not work well for animated GIFs since the image is composed of multiple frames. Images protected by Maximixer Image Guardian can be captured to the desktop and cropped and corrected with various imaging tools in spite of the website URL protection scheme.

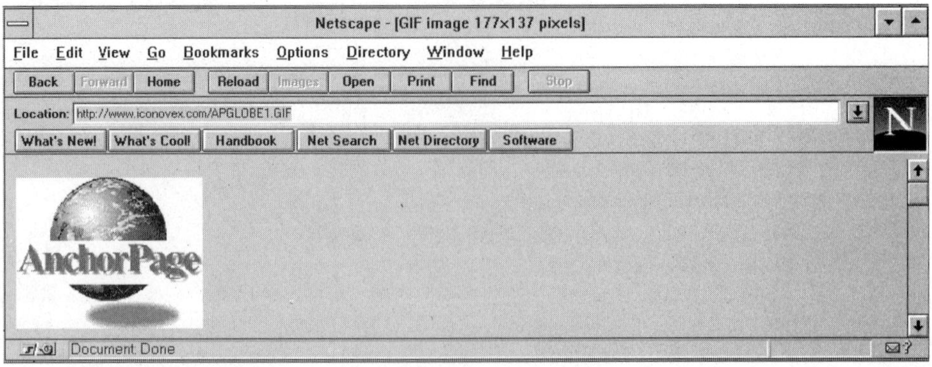

Figure 2.149   The path is constructed from the site URL and the file reference for the particular image. This can include GIF files and tiled JPEG backgrounds.

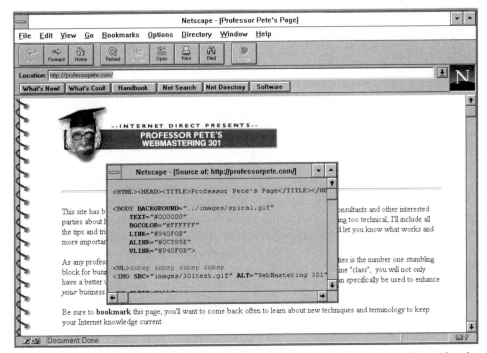

Figure 2.150 The code window shows how the GIF file is tiled only vertically and provides the name to capture this file.

Recall that there are ownership laws regarding all web material, and while you can capture and dissect just about any web building and design technique, you need to tread carefully so as not to infringe on others' legal rights. Chapter 4 details these protection mechanisms so that you know where not to trespass and understand how to protect your hard work. If you organize

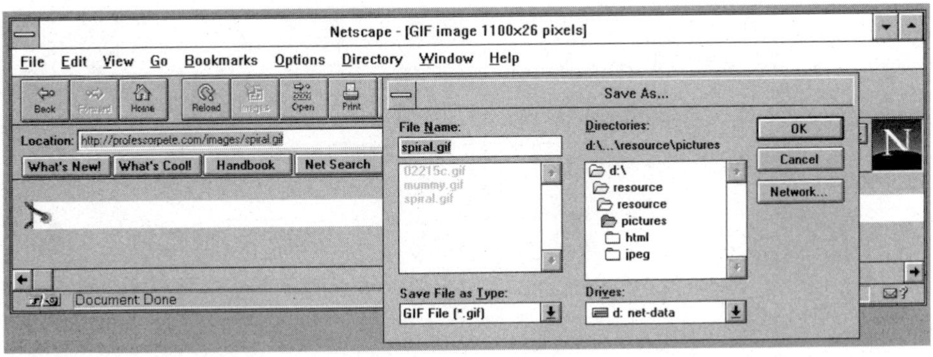

Figure 2.151 The URL shows how the image was captured and can be saved to a file in your image resource subdirectory.

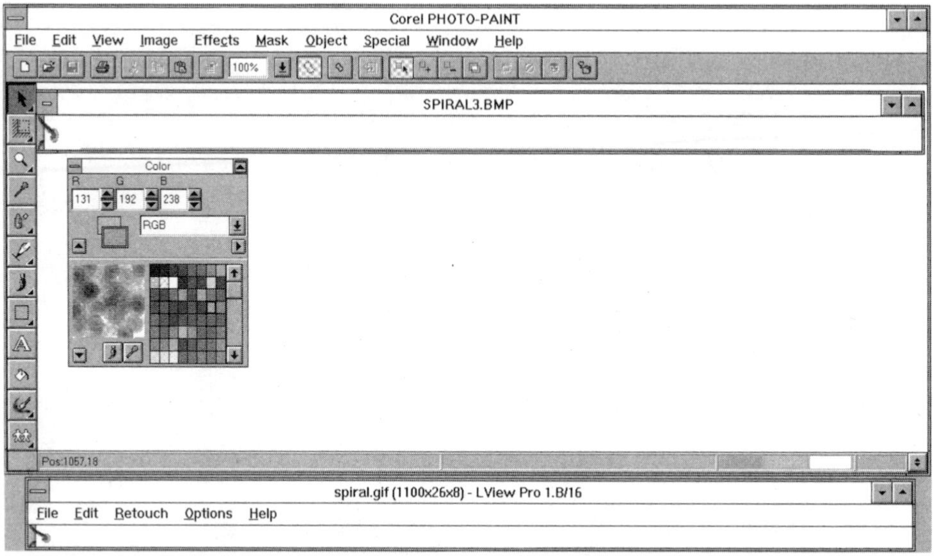

Figure 2.152 The GIF can be stretched vertically in LView, copied as a native Windows bitmap into Corel PHOTO-PAINT where a line is added to the image, and copied back through the clipboard to LView for filing in an interlaced GIF format.

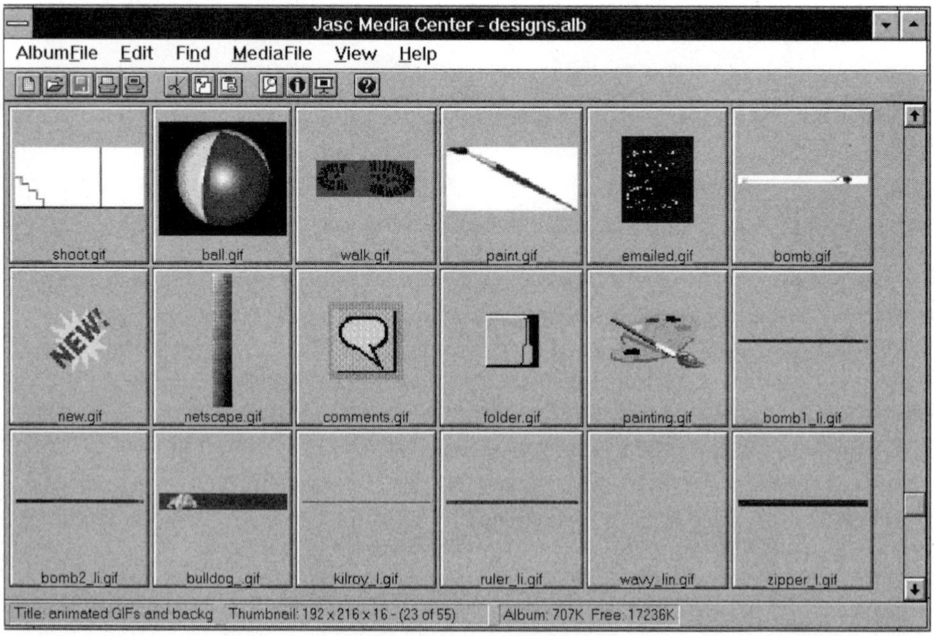

Figure 2.153 An image cataloging problems that displays pages of thumbnails is invaluable for selecting appropriate textures and figures.

captured images in subdirectories, Jasc Media Center or Corel Mosaic displays and prints thumbnail catalogs, as shown in Figure 2.153. Note that the obscured line backgrounds indicate GIF89a animated images, but some animated images with transparent backgrounds are shown only by the first frame.

Right mouse button. The third technique is the most efficient for capturing and categorizing individual images. It uses a special feature of Netscape Navigator. Click the right mouse button while positioned over an interesting image. The popup menu can show the individual image on its own frame or save it directly to file on your local disk, as demonstrated in Figure 2.154.

Some web pages are so full of animated GIFs that the page is slow to display and reload. View an individual image to see the animation in its own frame without the distorting influence of other animated images. This technique is useful for creating your own personal library of images and storing each image into an organized subdirectory structure. Note, however, this technique does not work for backgrounds as previously mentioned. You will still need to use the first technique to capture tiled JPEG or GIF images.

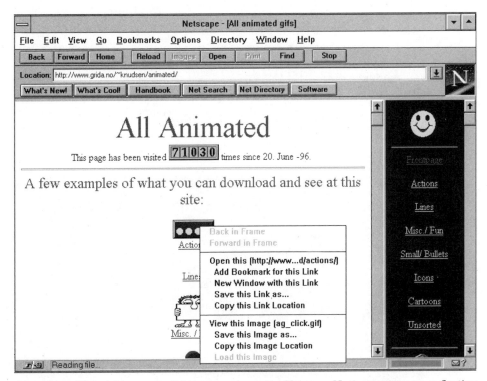

Figure 2.154 The right mouse click over an image in Netscape Navigator pops up a floating menu to view or save the image to specified path. This is useful to create a structured collection of images.

Getting pictures

The best source for royalty-free, industry-specific, and content-oriented images is a camera. There are two approaches that work for a website. You can take snapshots and scan them into computer file format with almost any black-and-white or color desktop scanner, you can take snapshots with a digital camera that captures the images in a computer file format, or you can hire a professional photographer or art studio to create glossy-large format images that you can then scan into your web pages.

In general, the better the source image, the better the web conversion. However, realize that the maximum browser resolution is about 72 to 96 dpi, so that a studio photograph has a resolution about 100 times better (from 2450 dpi to 8000 dpi for fine-grained Panavision film). You do not need that depth of color, resolution, and information for web images. In fact, Figure 2.155 illustrates a perfectly suitable image for a website of a low-end digital camera made with the very same camera. Cameras like this one from various manufacturers cost from $500 to $1,500. The quality is sufficient, not great, for Internet advertising and web pages. The snapshots in Figure 2.156 show a construction site useful for a corporate project report or a view for a condominium buyer and a consumer product.

If the images used in the cyberstore are also to be included in printed catalogs, the Polaroid digital camera takes pictures with a resolution at least 8 times better than the low-end digital cameras. As Figure 2.157 shows, these images are outstanding, and suitable for printed reproduction. I mention this camera because the $3,500 price is a good value in terms of image quality and relative cost. Studio photographers are happier with studio format cameras, such as Hasselblat, Nikon, and Canon cameras, which use standard film and offer the full complement of camera accessories, flashes, and filters. The Kodak

Figure 2.155 Kodak DC-50 Digital Camera as seen by the Kodak DC-50 Digital Camera, enlarged 4 times.

Figure 2.156   Uses for digital snapshots in cyberstore advertising.

Imaging group provides replacement backs for these cameras that capture images as digital files instead of film. Resolution is 16 times greater than the Polaroid digital camera, and the single lens reflex (SLR) camera frames support all the standard interchangeable lenses, long telephoto lenses, and other accessories. These conversion backs are shown in Figure 2.158. The key to

Figure 2.157   The Polaroid digital camera sets a new price-versus-quality point.

Figure 2.158 Conversion backs for digital photography with stock SLR cameras.

transferring images from the cameras to the computer is an interface, as shown in Figure 2.159 that connects to a standard serial port.

Background colors and textures

The home page for this book includes many links to websites with background images. One of the largest organized collections is at Netscape's website, illustrated in Figure 2.160. Some of the images are JPEG or GIF backgrounds, both of which can be tiled to create a special sensation for your site. Frankly, it just isn't worth your time searching for the right texture when there are easier and faster ways to generate your own unique and royalty-free background. Searching websites and downloading large image files is time-consuming and unnecessary when there are much easier ways to create an image. When you create your own background, there is limited possibility for copyright infringements. The best method is to create a solid color with an HTML command:

```
<body text=#FFFFFF bgcolor=#000000>
```

The body text color code and background color code is a six-position hexadecimal code corresponding to an RGB color. For instance, 0 is black and

Figure 2.159 The Kodak digital camera-to-computer serial port interface.

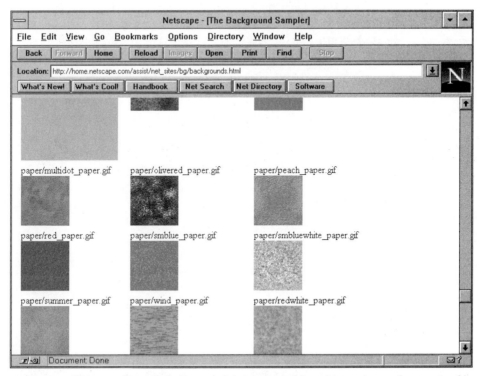

Figure 2.160 Netscape Communications maintains an archive of innocuous and unserviceable tiles for frame backgrounds.

FFFFFF is white. The ALLCOLOR.HTM file on the CD-ROM demonstrates all the possible solid text and background colors. The text color and background color should provide appropriate contrast (in color, grayscale, and black and white) if you want viewers to have complete site access. On the other hand, you can set text to black (default) and background to black (where 25 percent gray is default), or text to white and background to white when you want to hide text for the various web search robots to find and insert as index entries. This color selection is the most efficient method used to set a background. However, it lacks texture and pattern.

Even if a site states that the images are free, it is always possible that a site owner pirated an image from somewhere else. Create or scan your own images. Use CorelDRAW! (as explained) to create tiles. You can always place a piece of cloth on the scanner, scan the material, and use a graphics tool like Photoshop to create a mosaic, posterize, blur the image, or create other special effects. You can also use Photoshop filters to minimize the number of palette colors or complexity. Photoshop frost or glass filters tone down intense images, too.

Remember that resolution is probably unimportant. Recognize that a background should convey a pointed meaning yet not be intrusive to the site text. You do not want to detract from the message with an imposing background. Gratuitous backgrounds are a waste of resources. In addition, the background image file should fill the entire browser frame, but should be repeated in an interlocking tile pattern. The mechanism for tiling is automatic in HTML with this code:

```
<body text=#FFFFFF background=image.gif>
```

or

```
<body text=#FFFFFF background=image.jpg>
```

The body text color code for use over a tiled background is the same six-position hexadecimal code corresponding to an RGB color. As before, 0 is black and FFFFFF is white. The text color and background image should provide appropriate contrast (in full color, grayscale, and black and white) if you want viewers to see it.

Background tiling

Tiling minimizes the size of the image and the download time. Figure 2.161 illustrates this point as the outlined leather tile is automatically repeated. The rainbow wash is manually tiled to show problems with tiling unsuitable images. The leather tile on top fits together without seams, gaps, or pattern clash. This image would work for a cyberstore selling leather coats, handbags, briefcases, or for even an underground sprinkler company since the pattern looks like dried, baked earth. Be imaginative, and use humor when it works to

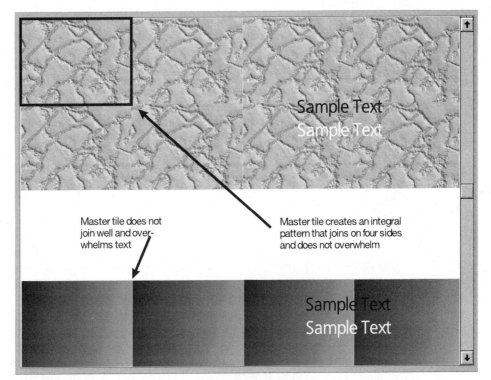

Master tile does not join well and overwhelms text

Master tile creates an integral pattern that joins on four sides and does not overwhelm

Sample Text

Sample Text

Sample Text

Sample Text

Figure 2.161   A background should be a repeating tile pattern that adds to the web page message.

present a message and when that humor is not offensive. Standard rules for studio art apply to web art and backgrounds. It might also work for conveying the lifestyle decision of buying the Honda Accord Sedan with an optional leather interior. Showing a leather interior is something that cannot be done with a printed catalog because some buyers might infer that the car was beyond their budget. This technology can coordinate personal tastes, budgets, needs, and sensibilities to create an advertisement targeted to a singular user on-the-fly. The dynamic web presentation is also cheaper than the $400 cost for a dealer at a car dealership showroom to demonstrate a car.

You could make this leather background lighter or adjust the colors to fit the product. The display resolution is very flexible, too. The message of the image needs to fit the theme. The red to blue color wash does not tile and will create a very distracting background. In addition, text is obscured by the brilliant color. The image is very sensitive to display resolution and is likely to show banding at lower resolution and pixel density. I suppose this image might work for a party store or day care center, but this clownish impression does not convey strength, integrity, or the reliability a consumer would want to find at a cyberstore. Check an image for its tiling symmetry and the overall implied message. Realize that other people may infer totally different and unexpected interpretations from your background selection. Test the impressions of a wider audience.

Do-it-yourself backgrounds

Although you can search the Internet, buy CD-ROM packages with backgrounds, and acquire HTML editors and other web tools that include galleries of possible images, the simplest and fastest source is CorelDRAW!. Create a rectangle, set the border line attributes to nothing so that the image does not have a black border, and add a texture fill. There are at least one hundred basic designs that can be endlessly modified by light source, light direction, density and transparency, and the colors used to form the patterns. Look for symmetry, simplicity, and congruence with the site message. The smaller the tile you create, the faster the pages will load. Export the object as a JPEG or GIF file. You can even run these images through Photoshop (as profiled in the next section) and its special effects filters (or third-party plug-ins) to create unique shadows, blurs, or mosaic patterns. Figure 2.162 illustrates five different basic tile patterns.

The best background is HTML-assigned color-code, preferably white. It is simple, professional, and easy on the eyes to view. White text on black backgrounds is bold, but hard to read. If you create a background tile for your

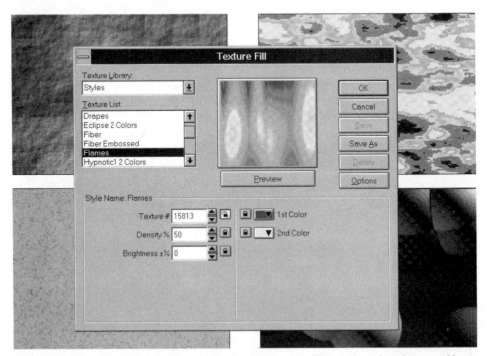

Figure 2.162 CorelDRAW!'s (versions 3 and up) object texture fill provides a broad range of basic textures and infinite ability to adjust color, brightness, and density.

home page, repeat the same pattern throughout the site. This is one way to instill an overall integrity to the site. If you want to use background colors to coordinate page or section types, create a handful of basic patterns. Use green hues, for example, for pricing information and the actual forms for ordering and transactions, blueprint colors for documentation and design, and screened reds for important messages. Repeat this scheme in page or section icons so that users get the symbolism for each color. Keep the number of color schemes to three or four so that users readily understand the concept. Too many color schemes overwhelm and detract from a unified message.

Image quality

Photoshop is the professional choice for bitmap image manipulation for Macintosh, Windows, and UNIX platforms, and is thus appropriate for any website graphics development. It is the tool of choice of art professionals and advertising agencies. It connects to ISIS or TWAIN scanners and provides many tools that rival the best physical darkroom techniques. For websites with the marginal 72 or 96 pixel (dpi) resolution, digitized images are very adequate. Scan snapshots. Scan publicity photos and professional artwork. However, you will have to adjust these images for the best presentation on the web. Extensis Intellihance is an add-in for Adobe Photoshop, Corel Photo-Paint, Director, and other multimedia production tools. If you are commited to cyberstore development internally or you are hoping to create a business as a consultant designing and implementing sites, learn Photoshop. It is not easy to get past the intensity and complexity of this tool, but it supports more plug-ins and special effects than even an expert darkroom developer.

When I am in a rush and do not have the hours (or do not allocate enough time) to manipulate images, I have trouble adjusting gamma, contrast, hue, saturation, the color balance, or any of the other 100 or so parameters in Photoshop. If I get started with this tool, I often go in the wrong direction with the sliding controls. I often end up with green-hued flesh tones, purple leaves, and image posterization or solarization. Intellihance speeds production for me so that that image adjustment occurs at the typical web-development speed. There are also some new plug-ins that provide batch processing of scanned images, a useful technique when building a product catalog, stuffing images into an object-oriented database, or creating image BLOBs in a standard DBMS.

You can use Paintbrush or Photo-Paint if you are really desperate and need to annotate an image with lines, text, or overlaid images. You do not get the full benefit of 256-color palette support or tools that convert true color, 24-bit color, or even 16-bit Windows images to the Navigator palette. These tools are not as flexible or useful as Photoshop for photographs as you begin creating multimedia video streams. If you need to get up to speed quickly, use the Intellihance add-in with Photoshop to compensate for overexposure and

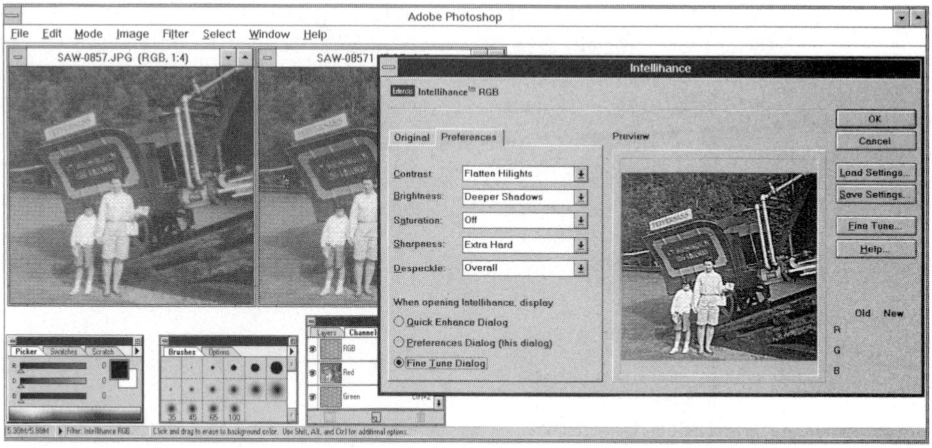

Figure 2.163 Intellihance makes it easier for casual users of Photoshop (and Photo-Paint) and other tools supporting Adobe plug-in filters to adjust marginal images for better browser display.

Figure 2.164 Even enhanced images represent a meaningless addition to a web page unless you compensate for resolution and size issues.

oversaturation. This interface and its results are illustrated in Figure 2.163. A dark, blurry, and shadowy image converts into a usable picture. This is like the NASA conversions of fuzzy satellite images from Jupiter Explorer or Mars Viking into clear images of another world. This same enhanced snapshot will appear normally in a browser at the size shown in Figure 2.164 on the left side. If you manually set image width and height (to improve the speed of browser page formatting and reload) and retain native image size, the user will see the image on the right. This is a function of the lower resolution. You should use Photoshop and Intellihance or other tools to reset the resolution so that an image remains meaningful.

If you find it necessary to include a snapshot, scan at the highest resolution, interpolate, enhance the digitized image, and reset the resolution to 72 or 96 pixels per inch. Enhance the image for best display at both 16 and the Netscape 216 color depths. If the image still provides no message to the page, simply do not use it or use it on a supplemental hyperlinked page. Site space is at a premium and should be allocated judiciously.

Color reduction can minimize image file size, browser page loading times, and server presentation speeds to increase the effectiveness of your on-line catalog. Colors (as in shades) are reduced to a smaller palette and the effect of complex washes and color changes are emulated with screens so that the eye perceives the same effect as with the original image, as shown in Figure 2.165.

A savings of almost 50% in file size with little or no loss of image quality. You can see other examples of the filter in action on the Photoshop f/x Online Companion. You can also download the demo version of the filter there.

According to Digital Frontiers, the plug-in works by simulating the way the human eye perceives color and by modifying the graphics file accordingly. No, I don't understand it either, but I don't care. HVS Color installs like any other Photoshop plug-in. After creating

Figure 2.165 Digital Frontiers provides a Photoshop plug-in (Win NT and Win 95 only) that intelligently reduces color and file size without altering the image.

Sounds

Most browsers support adds-in for playing sounds. There are the SoundReality, CoolTalk, and Crescendo tools for streaming sounds. Sounds can be useful for creating ambience, a powerful draw for a customer to return to a site, although the page designer needs to understand the impression that a particular sound, speech, or background loop will add to the page. Like backgrounds, some sounds, songs, or noises convey connotations completely different in different cultures. If you foresee an international customer base for your cyberstore, recognize the cultural pitfalls from background sounds. For example, the Japanese find pig noises hilarious, while Americans find them distasteful.

Sound formats vary and include .AU, .WAV, and .MID. Different add-ins are required to play each, and the user's browser needs to be configured to recognize the sound download as a tool that an available utility can play.

If the user does not support sound (that means, the system does not have a sound card or sound support), the user's system may abruptly crash. This does not bode well for providing universal user access. Avoid background sounds (even small looping files) unless the message or ambience of the sounds significantly adds to the cyberstore.

For example, a record, tape, or CD-ROM cyberstore and a music product studio should include music and even sample clips of products because it is consistent with the products or services offered at the cyberstore. Lifestyle products, such as a trip to Russia to copilot a MIG, should include jet sounds, while a trip to a roller coaster could include the sounds of screaming people. Nevertheless, if you are certain you want to add sound to your site by a client-pull/server side mechanism, and you want the music to play automatically when the HTML page is loaded, the necessary HTML tag is defined as follows:

```
<META HTTP-EQUIV=REFRESH CONTENT="99; URL=XXXXXXXX.XX">
  where the 99 indicates a delay time in seconds and the
  XXXXXXXX.XX is a sound filename.
```

Consider how long it typically takes for a page with all its imbedded images and database query to load. This may be as short as 5 seconds or as long as several minutes depending on user modem speed, ISP performance, host performance, and complexity of the page. Tables, frames, and other special formats increase loading time. Add another ten seconds so that the user can see the page and start understanding it before blasting the music. Note that the Meta tag is not the best way to play background sounds since it requires an open connection between the client and server. If you have a busy cyberstore and want to create a musical ambience, you will need more web server horsepower to support this method. The Crescendo LiveUpdate approach is enabled with this HTML code. Notice the EMBED command which is more efficient of server-side resources:

```
<CENTER><embed src="XXXXXXXX.mid"
  width=200
  height=55
  autostart=true>
```

```
<H6>Crescendo plugin &copy;
  1996 LiveUpdate. All rights reserved.</H6><BR>
</CENTER>
  where the XXXXXXXX.mid is a specific MIDI sound file.
```

E-mail enablement

Most browsers include built-in connections for sending E-mail. Proper functionality is a user issue and requires that each user configures a return address. Alternatively, most browser/mailers query the user for a from (return) address on first use. A standard E-mail form is illustrated in Figure 2.166. Although it is possible to construct a fancier HTML form with CGI code, the standard is probably advisable. If you want to collect detailed information about a hit and want to integrate this with a database, use Cold Fusion, WebDBC, or the JetForm. The simplest way to enable E-mail is to insert HTML commands:

```
Click here to
<A HREF="mailto:info@company.com">
request company info</A>.
```

This displays the very functional line:

Click here to request company info.

If you want to imbed more information into the hotspot modify the text between the paired A and /A tags. More advanced HTML editors hide

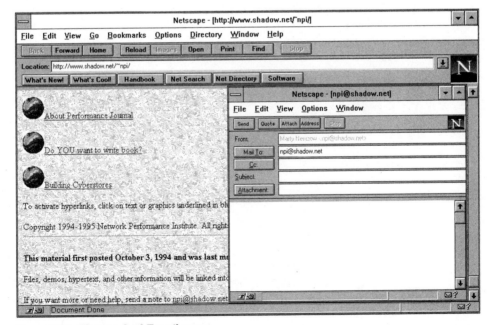

Figure 2.166 The standard E-mail popup.

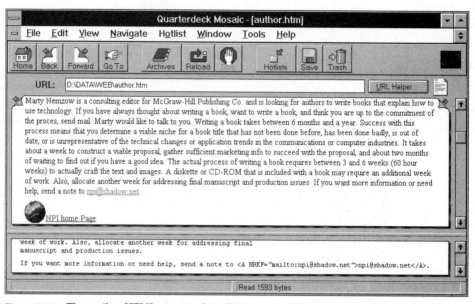

Figure 2.167 The mailto: HTML command is all that is necessary to invoke the standard E-mail form. Note that <A...<A/> tags repeat the address as a color-coded hotspot so that users understand the concept and can see the address.

these tags with special explanations. Figure 2.167 shows the text and HTML code in the split browser screen to enable the popup in the previous figure.

Some organizations want to customize the E-mail, as Riva Yamaha does in Figure 2.168. The standard E-mail form is too generic and does not con-

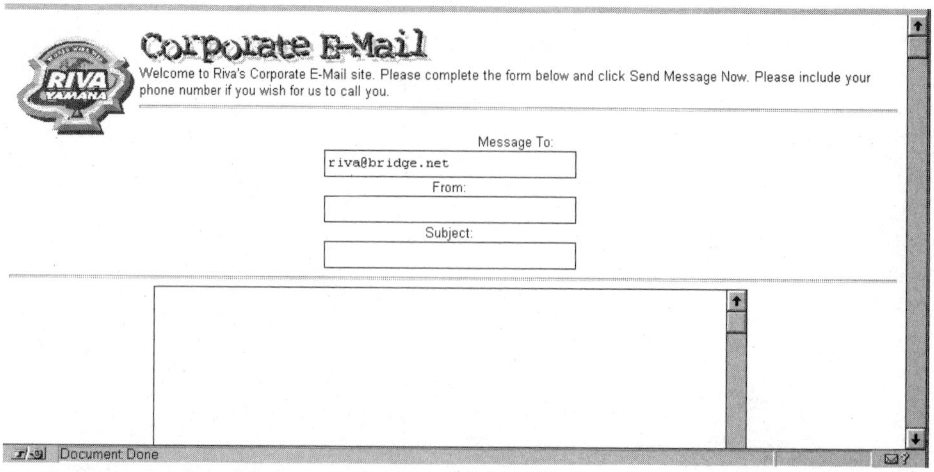

Figure 2.168 An HTML form sets an image for lowly E-mail and perhaps increases the incentive to send E-mail to an organization . . . but do you really want to add incentive for more E-mail?

vey the "importance" of the message when embellished with corporate logos. You can judge the effectiveness of a special HTML or CGI code to map the fields to the standard MIME E-mail message.

Database Integration

HTML is a text format for browser display. HTTP is the browser transmission protocol. A database is a structured file storage system. The integration of database technology with web page presentation runs the gamut from CGI code to extract delineated strings and put the parsed data into a flat data table, to the server process generically represented by WebDBC that creates forms and matches data with a relational record structure in a database management system. The decision is very complex. I suggest that your approach integrates with existing computer operations. For example, if your organization runs on Oracle Financials, use the Oracle WebServer and its multithreaded HTTP web server. Do not try to integrate Sybase web.sql, Computer Associates Jasmine web plug-ins, or Informix's Illustra Web DataBlade solution. Those solutions might work in environments with other financial systems, supporting ODBC drivers and developer toolkits.

Similarly, the lower-cost Microsoft IIF and SQL Server approach opens a can of worms. Although all the products (and many others) include ODBC drivers for "open" interconnectivity, any integration creates personnel and technical conflicts. Unless you want to test the migration to a new platform as part of your strategy, web-to-database integration probably also means web-to-database-to-organization workflow integration as well and how the organization does business on a daily basis, simplify the environment with as few dissimilarities as possible.

Notes Integration

Lotus Notes 4.x with the Internotes Web Navigator fetches content from the Internet and puts it into the Notes format database. The Internotes Web Publisher goes the other way and converts Notes databases into HTML documents accessible by browsers. The screenshot in Figure 2.169 shows how Notes and the conversion tools provide for web-enabled viewing of Notes documents.

The major difference between Notes and the various other tools available for web-integration and workflow enablement is that every piece of information in Notes becomes an organized detail accessible through various keys and linked by users to other related facts. While it is possible to enable an Intranet to provide the same types of services offered by Notes, the platform is not as mature and full of the development tools found with a standard Notes installation. In fact, the *USA Today* database, shown in Figure 2.170, shows some selected documents organized by user-defined criteria. I bet you cannot guess the search terms. This is one of the hallmarks of a good

Lotus Notes - INACOM LANDS MAJOR EDUCATION CONTRACTS IN PENNSYLVANIA AND NORTH
File Edit View Mail Compose Text Tools Design Window Help
AT&T
PR Newswire
September 6, 1994
INACOM LANDS MAJOR EDUCATION CONTRACTS IN PENNSYLVANIA AND NORTH CAROLINA
OMAHA, Neb., Sept. 6 /PRNewswire/ -- Inacom Corp. (Nasdaq: INAC) today announced it has been awarded two major education contracts. Under the terms of the State of North Carolina IBM K-12 Convenience Contract and the Pennsylvania Education Purchasing Program for Microcomputers (PEPPM) contract, Inacom will provide and install IBM/EduQuest computer hardware for schools throughout both states. Both contracts were previously held by the IBM PC Co.
"These contracts are very important for Inacom," said Lloyd Mahaffey, vice president of marketing for Inacom.

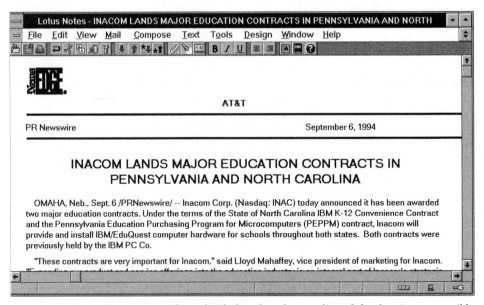

Figure 2.169 Notes documents (within a local, distributed, or replicated database) are accessible with the Internotes conversion tool.

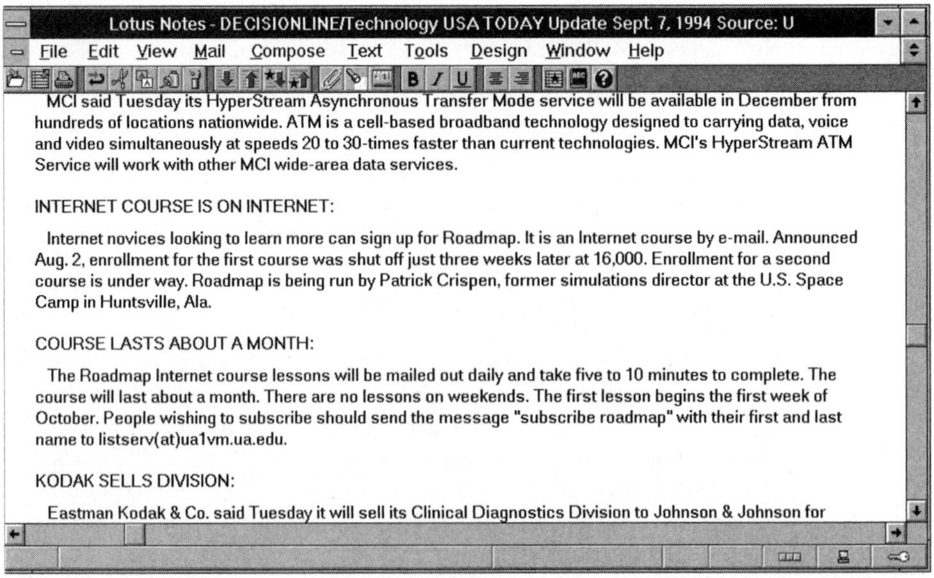

Lotus Notes - DECISIONLINE/Technology USA TODAY Update Sept. 7, 1994 Source: U
File Edit View Mail Compose Text Tools Design Window Help
MCI said Tuesday its HyperStream Asynchronous Transfer Mode service will be available in December from hundreds of locations nationwide. ATM is a cell-based broadband technology designed to carrying data, voice and video simultaneously at speeds 20 to 30-times faster than current technologies. MCI's HyperStream ATM Service will work with other MCI wide-area data services.
INTERNET COURSE IS ON INTERNET:
Internet novices looking to learn more can sign up for Roadmap. It is an Internet course by e-mail. Announced Aug. 2, enrollment for the first course was shut off just three weeks later at 16,000. Enrollment for a second course is under way. Roadmap is being run by Patrick Crispen, former simulations director at the U.S. Space Camp in Huntsville, Ala.
COURSE LASTS ABOUT A MONTH:
The Roadmap Internet course lessons will be mailed out daily and take five to 10 minutes to complete. The course will last about a month. There are no lessons on weekends. The first lesson begins the first week of October. People wishing to subscribe should send the message "subscribe roadmap" with their first and last name to listserv(at)ua1vm.ua.edu.
KODAK SELLS DIVISION:
Eastman Kodak & Co. said Tuesday it will sell its Clinical Diagnostics Division to Johnson & Johnson for

Figure 2.170 This screen from Notes shows how it provides press release organization based on important words, dates, and other keys.

Notes resource task. In contrast, as the indexing and search tools showed earlier in this chapter, the webmaster or website builder often must anticipate the uses for the database and possible indexes to get the broadest results possible.

This "freestyle" Notes keyword search is particularly effective when your cyberstore or commercial website will provide customer support or complex access to technical documents. Although some of the specialized Help Desk tools that integrate with HTML provide similar flexibility, Figure 2.171 shows that you have comparable results with Notes. This is useful if Notes is already in use within your organization.

Whereas the Help Desk and web integration provide "comparable" and effective tools for customer support, the flexibility of Notes is best shown when the same site provides internal support services and access to the organization flow, as shown in Figure 2.172. It is not clear that Notes is better or worse than other Internet, web, cyberstore, or Intranet solutions, but it represents a flexible and multi-faceted solution that may not require SQL, middleware, or CGI coding. If Notes is already in use, integrate that platform with the web rather than replicating similar functionality through the database middleware tools. The user interface in this Windows version of Notes (shown in Figure 2.173) is not that different from a hierarchical list from a website home page.

Figure 2.174 shows that a travel authorization application built with Notes can be run within the native Lotus platform or integrated with a web

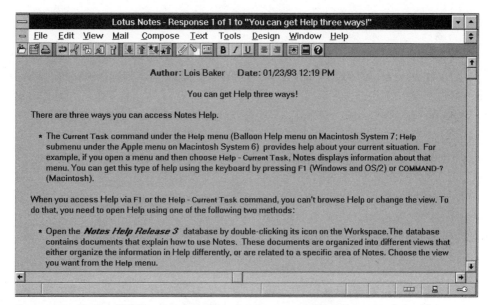

Figure 2.171 On-line HTML access to technical and support information using Lotus Notes.

Lotus Notes - Sales Force Automation Applications
File Edit View Mail Compose Text Tools Design Window Help
*Client Correspondence: Stores client names and addresses. Includes an easy-to-use way to draft customer letters, mail merge documents and faxes.
*Sales Management/Client Tracking: Tracks overall account activity for monitoring lead status, closure, issues and problems related to each account. Company becomes more responsive to the customer. This application is particularly useful for new sales reps picking up an existing account. Corporate headquarters can review and comment on any relevant customer activity.
*Monthly Status: Serves as a central repository for Field Status reports. Maintains a history of all account activity. Allows top management to drill down for information on accounts across their field organization.
*Telemarketing: Captures information about the caller during the initial call, and then helps manage the fulfillment of the customer's request with scripts to insure consistency and accuracy of information being given to the caller. Notes forms make it easy to include and change these scripts. The user can simply read the script from the Notes document and record the customer's input in fields in the document.

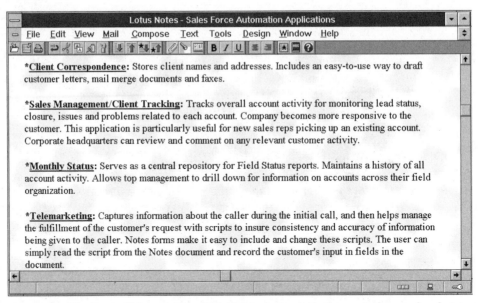

Figure 2.172 The key to Notes success with web integration is that many tasks are already integrated and do not require a new application development path.

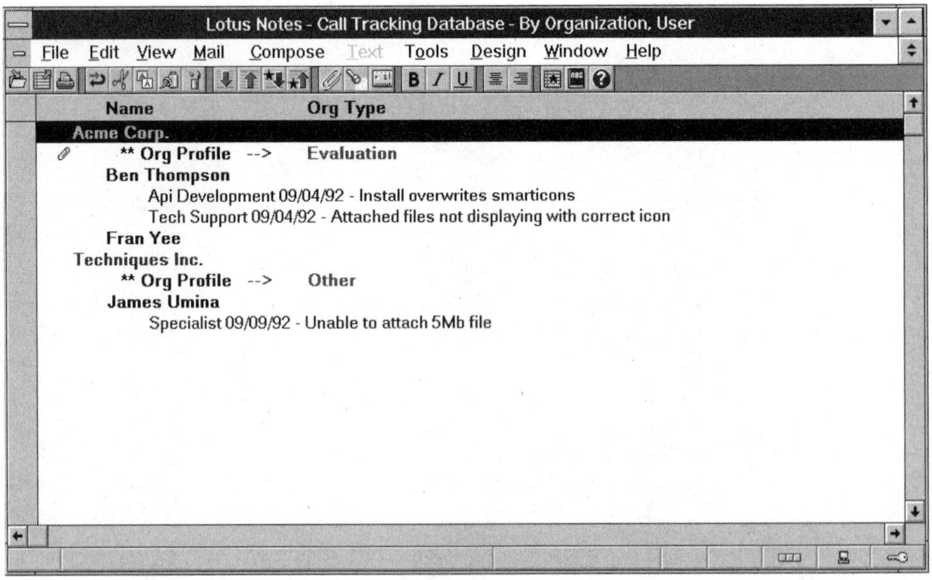

Lotus Notes - Call Tracking Database - By Organization, User
File Edit View Mail Compose Text Tools Design Window Help
Name
Org Type
Acme Corp.
** Org Profile --> Evaluation
Ben Thompson
Api Development 09/04/92 - Install overwrites smarticons
Tech Support 09/04/92 - Attached files not displaying with correct icon
Fran Yee
Techniques Inc.
** Org Profile --> Other
James Umina
Specialist 09/09/92 - Unable to attach 5Mb file

Figure 2.173 The Notes topic selection page is not unlike a Web home page.

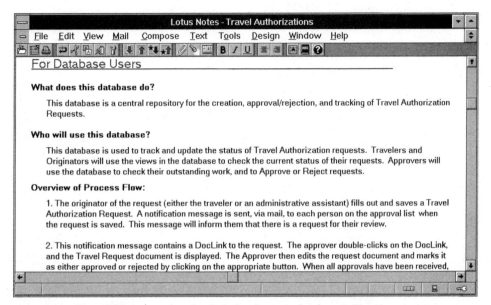

Figure 2.174 Notes/Web integration also includes dynamic database integration.

browser interface. You lose some of the Notes menu bar commands unless they are implemented as functions or hotspots on the web pages. Tile (described in Chapter 4) shows comparable conversion tools. The new Domino web toolkit and server provides more interactive access to Notes documents, including the dynamic integration with the Notes database and other ODBC databases.

Conclusion

The next chapter describes the comprehensive effects of choosing a web server platform. Not only is the cyberstore platform an operating system to support a web server, the cyberstore platform also will necessarily include SSL, SHTTP, and/or other encryption tools, dynamic database-to-HTML conversion, electronic payment methods, E-mail, threaded BBS-like conversation or chat services; it will also serve as the integration spearhead for point-of-sales financial accounting and tracking. Chapter 3 provides important technical selection and implementation details for the choices of building a local or hosted web server and connecting to homogeneous databases or mainframe platforms.

3

Platform Shoes

Introduction

The most profound and comprehensive cyberstore decision is the choice of the platform. This is not a monolithic decision at the present time. Not only is the cyberstore platform an operating system to support a web server, it also will necessarily include Secure Socket Layer (SSL), Secured Hypertext Transport Protocol (SHTTP), and/or other encryption tools, dynamic database-to-HTML conversion, electronic payment methods, E-mail, and threaded Bulletin Board System- (BBS-) like conversation or chat services, and in addition, it will also serve as the integration spearhead for point-of-sales financial accounting and tracking. There is no reason that these functions are represented by single hardware platforms or hypertext links to Intranet resources provided by local area network (LAN) servers, host mainframes, or a farm of PC- or minicomputer-based CPUs. By far the biggest decision is the linkage between databases, web services, and accounting. There is a lot of impassioned press information and misinformation about connectivity between databases and accounting systems. However, this is mostly noise or basic merchant credit card (such as MasterCard, VISA, and check verification) interfaces.

Only Oracle, Quest, WebBase, and Sybase bundle database servers and web front ends together and, notwithstanding, these are unlikely to represent complete solutions. Most other cyberstore implementations represent an integration of many complex components. Integration and administration are not usually easy. Every component typically creates trade-offs that affect security, performance, simplicity, cost, and the workflow.

It is also important to realize that the cyberstore itself may run on a platform different from the database, information sources (such as file servers and local networks), the administration and management environment, and the design and development platform. For example, many large sites will include IBM 3090 mainframes, AS/400 hosts, or RISC-based AIX clusters connected into an NT workstation or NT server platform protected by a router and firewall. Additionally, the actual web page design work is likely to have been accomplished on a Power Macintosh at an outside advertising or graphics agency. This results in some subtle complications and not so subtle operational and integration problems. The cyberstore components include:

- Web server (preferably secure or supporting encryption)
- CGI library support (for automating "what's new" lists)
- Database middleware
- HTML editing tools
- Graphics construction tools
- Language translation or conversion tools
- Site mapping (client- and server-side tools)
- HTML page validation
- Firewalls
- Settlement tools

The purpose, focus, and breadth of the cyberstore will define the need for other special services and hardware. For the most part, the cyberstore consists of a catalog display, a "shopping cart," and a transaction processing mechanism. The catalog display is built in HTML as either static web pages using traditional page editing and layout tools, as static reports using text or database to HTML conversion tools, or as dynamic web pages generated on the fly from database information. Any multimedia services, such as CoolTalk, HyperWire, and VDO require separate multimedia construction tools. The "shopping cart" is a metaphor for an order entry process that overcomes the limitations of stateless Hypertext Transport Protocol (HTTP) and server operations. Somehow, the ordering process must save user information, user selections, and other details necessary to complete an on-line transaction.

The shopping cart can be a Cookies transaction record (stored on the client machine), a special dynamic HTML page, or a series of related database records. The Cookies method lacks security and integrity, whereas the construction of dynamic HTML pages means that the process is likely to be frail, generate a lot of temporary files, and require considerable CGI code expertise and development time. The database method presupposes integration with existing systems, and the expertise will require focus on integration and financial systems skills. I favor the database method if only because cyberstore transaction processing requires fiscal controls anyway. Since these are likely to be integrated into existing business workflows anyway and since they test both organizational and computing integration skills, it seems worthwhile to integrate the order entry shopping cart process into this flow as well.

Success with a cyberstore depends on the platform. The platform is not just the choice of a server operating system or of web server software, but all the factors that are used to design, construct, protect, serve, host, and process the cyberstore activity. It is also a factor of outsourced services, such as designers and Internet Service Provider (ISP) sites. The selection is a complex business and a strategic, technical, and cost-driven process, often one not fully within the website designer's control. Preexisting equipment, networks, services, and the way an organization does business may drive the initial and hence, later platform decisions. Nevertheless, you are responsible for dealing with these preexisting conditions and integrating them into the cyberstore. Preexisting conditions typically drive secondary choices. As such, you need to be aware of the implications of every platform component choice you make. You are responsible for making the decisions and for the outcome.

In many cases, the issue is not functionality, but time frames. Sometimes you will not have a choice between what works better, but rather what works at all. Building the cyberstore is a function of workflow integration. You may start by creating a web site, adding in credit card transaction processing, and taking orders on the web and shipping by a worldwide delivery service. However as Chapter 2 explained, a cyberstore is about more than that. Ultimately, you will need to integrate the credit card payments into a financial tracking system. That is an integration project predicated by prior decisions and existing platforms. Although your platform shoes themselves may program the choices you can make, consider how you can simplify as much as possible, and purchase from vendors as much as is possible.

Internet Plumbing

The most obvious platform issue is the Internet plumbing. This refers to the interconnectivity between a cyberstore and the virtual Internet. It includes the physical connections, such as the web server, the firewall, hosts, and other local area networks or connections to IBM 3090 congregations or clusters of AS/400 processors. The plumbing also includes tie lines from local web servers to ISPs or the Internet backbone. However, the plumbing also includes the physical connections, which are "flows" between these components. These flows might consist of transmissions of data over various telecommunication channels. The selection and architecture has a profound effect on performance, integration, and compatibility. The logical software component for interconnection includes the Transaction Control Protocol/Internet Protocol (TCP/IP) stacks, firewall software, web services, E-mail services, and any of the middleware that converts data formats for display, processing, and accounting. This physical and logical plumbing flow is illus-trated in Figure 3.1.

It is useful to think about the cyberstore as both a physical entity with phys-ical plumbing that handles flows of information and also as a sequence of tasks or events themselves. You can look at the overall physical plumbing for band-width limitations, loops, bottlenecks, and clogs. The flows map a process, but the tasks and events map into middleware. Also, consider that an external hy-pertext link represents a powerful *logical* flow to other documents, services, platforms, or logical processes. Although the HTTP protocol and client-side browsers are stateless, you can link dispersed documents, services, platforms, and processes with browser "Cookies" (described in Chapter 4), process logs, or transactions stored in a standard database format. The solution to this state-lessness is some middleware application, best embodied by DBMS transac-tions. One way or another you are going to buy or build the middleware or a hodgepodge of components that perform necessary specific tasks. Some of the connections and the events that are pertinent to a cyberstore include those illustrated in Figure 3.2.

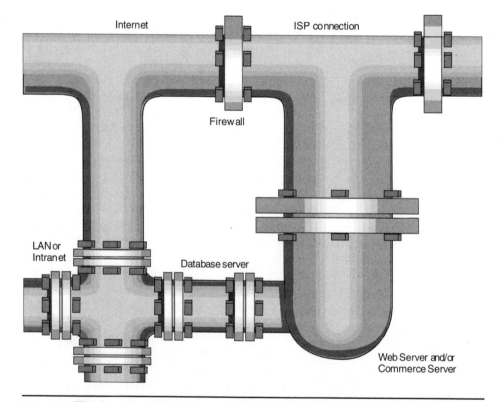

Figure 3.1 The physical and logical connectivity required for the cyberstore (or any web site) is called by the picturesque phrase "Internet plumbing."

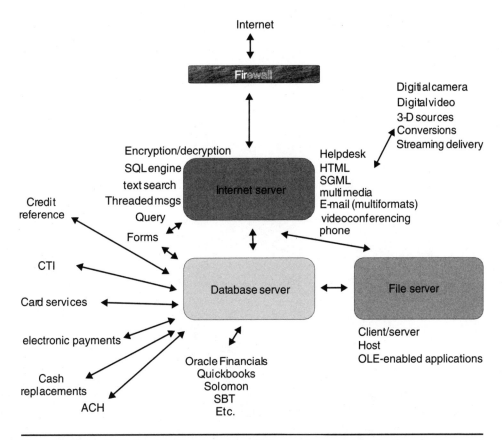

Figure 3.2 If you think the plumbing is linear, add the services necessary for the cyberstore, and then look at the integration that you need to plumb.

For most of this book, the cyberstore has represented a physical and virtual entity that exists at the web server, as though the server represented the entirety of the cyberstore. It is likely that for larger cyberstores one server will be insufficient for the site; rather, there will be a number of firewalls, a number of linked web servers, an application or middleware server, and other mainframes and smaller hosts providing database and financial processing. That clustered "server farm" is not the entire cyberstore. The World Wide Web (WWW) HTML file is just a page format transmitted by an HTTP server to an HTTP client. Without that client, nothing is really visible to see, no transactions can occur, and no cyberstore exists for the user. The cyberstore—really any web page presentation—exists as both client-side and server-side activities, as shown in Figure 3.3.

Most web operations are not stand-alone. In fact, the web component for both the client side and the server side are increasingly integrated into

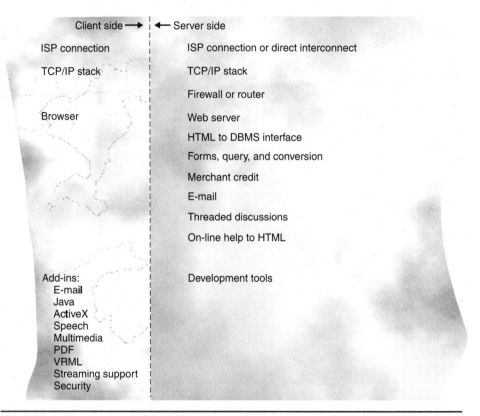

Figure 3.3   The complexity with cyberstore development is entirely on the server side, the organization side, with its need for web, HTML, security, workflow, and DBMS integration. The client side is only a presentation device, but one compatible with the server side.

existing networks, wiring infrastructures, and desktop hardware. Figure 3.4 shows a typical architecture for a client-side connection for a local area network to the Internet. This is a typical support configuration for an advertising agency or internal web development group. In fact, this architecture is also sufficient for a cyberstore if the connection from the enterprise hubs through to the ISP is sufficient to handle the traffic loads. One of the local nodes in this architecture may be a web server.

Figure 3.5 details the protocols required to LAN and cyberstore activity with Internet connectivity. When the cyberstore represents a significant activity, the network infrastructure must be more robust to support both internal network loads and external Internet services. This logical network design is illustrated in Figure 3.6. You might note the addition of a stand-alone firewall in addition to normal organizational backbone security and typical website security. These security issues are addressed at length in Chapter 4.

It is important to recognize that local area networks, particularly NetWare operations, will require a coresident TCP/IP stack and WinSock

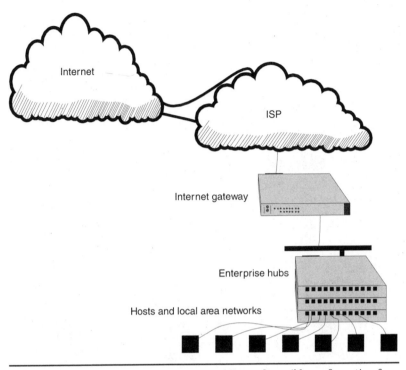

Figure 3.4 Basic client-side Internet connectivity and possible configuration for a small cyberstore operation.

application to support Internet access. Networks based on NetBIOS or other stacks will require the TCP/IP and WinSock services for each local user, a fixed IP address or a temporary IP address server. The IPX-to-IP gateway is needed unless Novell networks are converted to use IP as a native LAN protocol.

The domain name service (DNS), dynamic host configuration protocol (DHCP), Simple Mail Transport Protocol (SMTP), HTTP, File Transfer Protocol (FTP), database, and proxy services could run on the same station, although larger sites will typically split these services. The DNS service translates the English language domain names into IP addresses. The DHCP server allocates local and reusable IP addresses for LAN users for temporary Internet or even Intranet access. An SMTP server translates internal and proprietary mail systems (such as CC:mail and Exchange) to the MIME, POP3, and other common Internet E-mail formats.

The HTTP server on the backbone provides Intranet services, development, and test facilities for web pages. The proxy server is a local caching and access limit for LAN Internet and Intranet clients. The public web, database, and FTP servers are required for hosting the cyberstore; the FTP service is necessary only when your site is handling a tremendous delivery of packaged

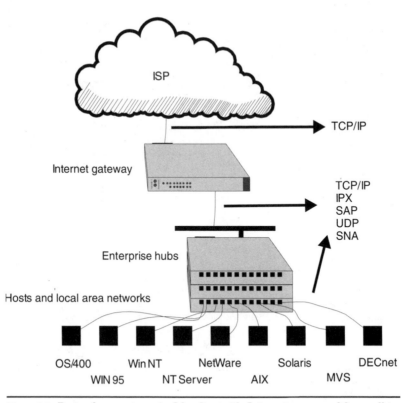

Figure 3.5 Protocol support required for client-side Internet access and for small integrated cyberstore operations.

information or software. In addition, sites with special services, such as newsgroup support, multimedia, and lots of mail may require supplemental services for newsgroups, a media server for the streaming or downloadable audio and video, and a public E-mail server.

Tie-lines

If your cyberstore is hosted by an ISP or a special facility such as OpenMarket, the cyberstore "exists" on that host. The files are stored on that host and orders are typically processed as E-mail messages and a credit card settlement report. The messages and reports are typically stored as E-mail files on that host and are downloaded with a client browser or E-mail application. Database integration is not possible unless the host provides that type of service, or your organization makes special provisions to run CGI or server applications that connect to a database. Since few ISPs are financially savvy and are basically providing modem banks and file storage, the most likely location for small sites or fully enabled cyberstores will be local to the organization. This

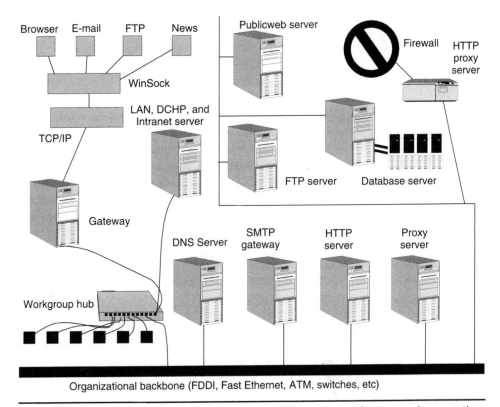

Figure 3.6 Larger organizations and cyberstores attached to existing data processing operations are likely to include extended Internet plumbing.

means that the local servers need to connect to the Internet with a dial-up phone line, a digital circuit, or a fiber tie-line.

These connections can attach directly to the Internet backbone or to an ISP. Typically, only circuits with capacities greater than T-1 (for example, T-1, T-3, or multiple circuits) connect directly to the Internet through a local telco provider, such as BellSouth or NYNEX, or a long-distance carrier, such as AT&T, MCI, or Sprint. A T-1 circuit provides 1.534 megabits per second (Mpbs) while T-3 supports bandwidth to 44.736 Mbps. In Europe and other locations, the E-1 circuit provides 2.048 Mbps, E-2 yields 8.488 Mbps, and, where it is available, E-3 serves 34.368 Mbps. It does not matter whether you configure these circuits for Integrated Services Digital Network (ISDN), Private Rate Interface (PRI), frame relay, Synchronous Optical Network (SONET), Switched Multimegabit Data Services (SMDS), or Asynchronous Mode Transfer (ATM) protocols because the underlying circuit defines the maximum bandwidth. In general, the protocol that runs on top of the circuit must be negotiated at both ends and must be supported with appropriate Channel Service Unit/Data Service Unit (CSU/DSU) devices. Similar capacities and less can be repurchased through an ISP for piggybacking to the Internet backbone or rerouting through the ISP host servers. These two options are illustrated in Figure 3.7.

You might note that these two options are really three subtle options. It matters which you choose because there are price, reliability, and performance factors for each. On the left, the direct Internet connection costs the installation for the circuit and monthly costs. These monthly costs might be a combination of line charges and actual usage charges, although more likely, T-1 circuits and greater entail no local usage charges. This is expensive because a typical T-1 line costs about $1,800 to install and an equal amount per month. If your organization does not need the full 1.534 Mbps, the cheaper alternative is to repurchase service through an ISP. However, you will still need a circuit installed to the ISP, so the savings will typically be the portion of the contracted bandwidth you do not use. Note that there may be minimum fixed charges and severe penalties if you exceed the allotted bandwidth. This yields equivalent response time as a direct backbone connection because you are basically wiring your tie-line into some or all of the ISP's tie-lines.

The third option is typically the first installation for a cyberstore test. Your organization establishes a local web server and links this to the ISP web server. The ISP host resolves domain name issues and rerouting. The performance hit is multifold. First, there is another server in front of your web pages

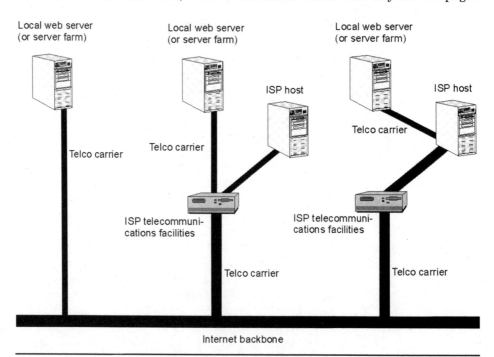

Figure 3.7 Direct or subcontracted Internet access shared with an ISP or routed through the ISP host.

and all that attendant overhead and latency. Second, your traffic must be routed, leading to another delay. Third, your rerouted traffic is competing for server CPU bandwidth with all the other host traffic. The compensation for this setup is that the connection between your local server and your business can be anything from an analog phone line or multiple lines added on demand to dial-up ISDN, a dedicated ISDN (which means you hope the circuit stays live all the time), bonded ISDN lines, or T-1 services. You can grow from small to larger in reasonable increments.

A dial-up phone connection to an ISP is unlikely to provide bandwidth for more than one or two users at time, while each ISDN channel provides about 20 TCP connections at a time. Of course, you have to balance all these generic statements against the type of Internet traffic generated *from* the local web server. An ISDN line will not provide more than a single streaming video or videoconferencing connection at a time but can support a handful of cyber-store shoppers rolling their shopping carts down your cyber aisles. Of course, until video codecs are better, analog phone lines are unsuitable for graphic-intensive sites and really not sustainable for serious cyberstores.

In any event, whatever the tie-line routing to the Internet backbone, consider the need for redundant connectivity. Backup ISDN lines can replace failed T-1 circuits in a crisis, while even a bank of 33.6 Kilobytes per second (Kbps) modems can substitute for failure and at least provide some presence to users. These options will not be fast, but at least they offer some backup. The best approach is to pair lines to the ISP or central office through multiple paths. For example, Access Loop Diversity is a service offered by a Regional Bell Operating Company consisting of multipath communication connections to a customer site in case a backhoe cuts an underground conduit or a central office switch fails. Access Loop Diversity is about double the cost of the base circuit, where it is available. Some places, like islands and rural areas, just do not support that comprehensive multilink connectivity. If backup and absolute integrity are required at all times, consider the Hughes VSAT services or DSS (like the satellite services) for continuity.

Authentication and Passwords

Although this section may seem like an unusual topic better included in the Security section of Chapter 4, authentication and passwords are an important aspect of web server platforms. Security is important to protect your website from both internal and external attacks to the web pages, FTP files, configuration or administration files, and most particularly to the cyberstore data sets. The data sets typically contain privileged customer information and credit card transactions. Debit transactions are sensitive, but the credit transactions (to customers) and the ability to create more of these is very vulnerable. In addition, security becomes even more important when the web server reaches through a firewall, exposing a LAN or enterprise network, mainframe databases, mainframe processes, or any LAN-based OLE or secondary processes and data sets. Security is often specified by a user authentication user name "ID" and a corresponding password. For example, the following list shows typical web applications and services requiring authentication IDs and passwords:

- Operating system administration
- User and password administration
- DNS administration
- Web server administration
- Web server home page write and execute access
- Web server SSL or SHTTP private key administration
- SQL Server (or other database engine) administration
- Database data set administration
- Middleware (Quest, R:Base R:Web, Cold Fusion, etc.) administration
- Web server/database connection administration
- ODBC administration
- SQL library administration
- Forms design and administration
- Merchant credit card administration
- EPS administration and private key management
- LAN management and administration
- Packet and network analyzer access
- Website management tools (WebMaster)
- Firewall administration

Thus, the important reason for including authentication and passwords in this chapter is simple—because the web server and other functions require an ID and an associated password. Some products may allow you to create a generic user called "administrator" or something as simple and obvious as that with a null (that is, a blank or unspecified) password. Many programs try to protect you from yourself and will not let you do that, and rightly so. If some-one can access your server in a Telnet session (even when the server is running on Windows-based platforms), that hacker can access all parts of the system. A hacker, perhaps, can even modify the passwords so that your administrator can no longer access the system. Hopefully, when events like this happen (and they shouldn't), you can restore administration files to provide an access override; however, realize that if lost system passwords prevent any file access to these files, you may have to rebuild the operating system and then restore only the web server, data, and middleware from backup.

Therefore, one of the serious web server platform and site management issues is to provide all user IDs and include passwords when requested. You are likely to require from 5 to 15 sets. It is tempting to create the same authentication user name and duplicate the password for every need, but resist that bad instinct. Instead, create a list of services, users, and corresponding passwords and store it in the safety deposit vault. If you need a list for active and ongoing operations, use some of the new password management tools or create the list as an on-line file and set very narrow access rights for only the operating system administrator. If you want to create fully verified security (that conforms to what is required by most Generally Accepted Accounting Principles [GAAP] public accounting rules) apply file encryption to the list that a person apart from the administrator knows, and that person must also not know the operation system administration passwords. Therefore, two separate people must collude or agree to view the complete password list.

Although large websites do require 10 or 15 people for design, data, control, and ongoing maintenance activities, it is still likely that a single person or several people will have access to these passwords and services. When the operating system, web server, or other application provides for a password list (more than just a single authentication and password pair), rather than creating a single administration user and password that everyone shares, create a real user (for example, I would be "MNemzow") and ascribe administration rights to that user so that you can track individual access. These security issues need to be defined in advance of building the Intranet or Internet. You cannot add security to a testbed web server and all the middleware tools after you have built it and want to make it public. It is just not practical to do after the fact, so plan security into the platform selection and installation process as you go.

Domain Name Services

Domain name services (DNS) is the software application that matches a domain name to the Internet Protocol (IP) number mappings on all computers. The name www.microsoft.com maps to 221.119.110.3, while 221.119.110.3 maps correspondingly to www.microsoft.com. Think of one as a human name and the other as a computer address. DNS is a hierarchy as you can see by the four-part number scheme (and more with Ipv6). The Internet is supported with a small number of domain servers who are responsible for tracking the top level domains (roots) and determining what domains and named sites are in them. The root servers know all the domain name servers, which ultimately provide for the domain roots. The root servers are the authority without ambiguity. Figure 3.8 illustrates this hierarchy of domain names.

When changes are made to domain servers, they are slowly propagated to all machines on the Internet. Specifically, if primary and secondary domain name servers are on-line when a root update occurs, a change will propagate

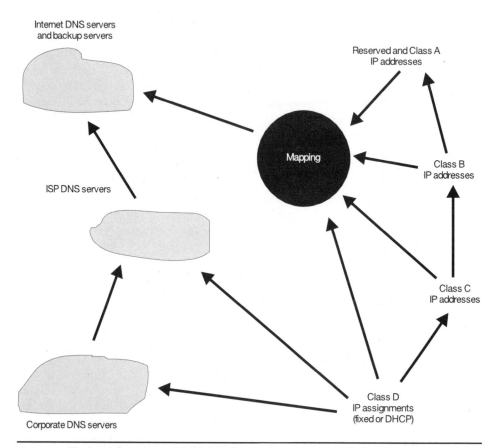

Figure 3.8 The logical structure of DNS with Intranet servers and TCP/IP addresses.

```
┌─────────────────────────────────────────────────────────────────────┐
│ ▬                            NSLookup                          ▾ ▲   │
├─────────────────────────────────────────────────────────────────────┤
│Default Server:  janus                                               │
│Address:  0.0.0.0                                                    │
│                                                                     │
│> dns                                                                │
│Server:  janus                                                       │
│Address:  0.0.0.0                                                    │
│                                                                     │
│res_mkquery(0, dns., 1, 1)                                           │
│                                                                     │
│───────────────                                                      │
│SendRequest(), len 21                                                │
│     HEADER:                                                         │
│         opcode = QUERY, id = 1, rcode = NOERROR                     │
│         header flags:  query, want recursion                       │
│         questions = 1,   answers = 0,   authority records = 0,  additional = 0 │
│                                                                     │
│     QUESTIONS:                                                      │
│         dns, type = A, class = IN                                   │
│                                                                     │
│───────────────                                                      │
│timeout (5 secs)                                                     │
│▬                                                                    │
└─────────────────────────────────────────────────────────────────────┘
```

Figure 3.9 Command-line application to establish local DNS services without an active Internet connection, a TCP/IP link, or even a local network.

within all zones after all zones refresh. The specifications for DNS and zone propagation and for official DNS machine and system names are listed in RFC 952. All of this information is very interesting for a network manager and Unix guru, but it actually has significant bearing on the cyberstore development process, internal support activities, and Intranet operations. In fact, if your Intranet is based on WindowsNT Server or WindowsNT Workstation and you have enabled Dynamic Host Configuration Protocol (DHCP) to use and assign temporary Class C subaddresses, you will also need to configure the DHCP server for the local network and match the web server domain name with a floating IP2 address. (Note that BootP and the Reverse Address Resolution Protocol [RARP] do not support IPv6 and the longer IP address format.) For example, Figure 3.9 shows a simple NT/DOS-based utility that creates a dummied local DNS service.

While this is one approach, the Windows and web-based DNS server installation and configuration method is shown with MetaInfo DNS 2.0 in Figure 3.10. Note that the configuration uses a wizard that gathers some of the DHCP or TCP/IP information directly from the Windows registry.

If your web site only provides web services in the form of HTTP pages, configure a web server only. Do not create security holes by adding addresses for phantom mail, FTP, or news servers. In fact, if you are using a threaded conversation BBS, such as WebBoard or Allaire forums, you do not require a mail server. The

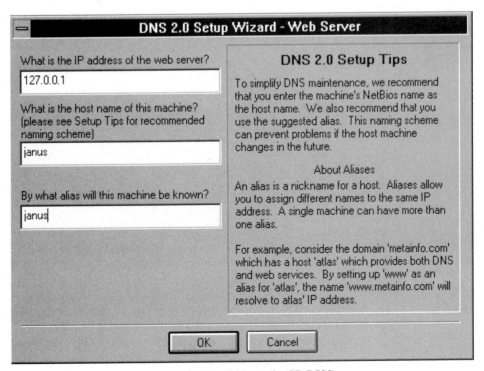

Figure 3.10 MetaInfo DNS server setup (available on the CD-ROM).

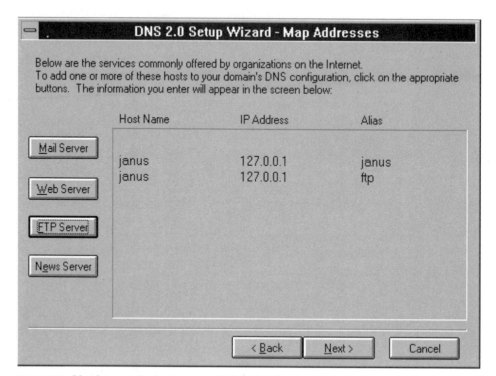

Figure 3.11 Matching up the host name with the IP address for Intranet or external web services (Note: do not use the IP loopback address as shown).

master HTTP page (linked from any other standard web page) handles all "mail" activity and automatically provides mail services through the HTTP protocol. Figure 3.11 shows the DNS configuration for FTP and web services.

Some of the newer DNS servers provide management utilities that run in a standard client-side web browser. This is convenient for mixed-platform environments, and in general, provides a simple interface as shown in Figure 3.12. Although DHCP, TCP/IP, and network configurations are modified from Control Manager applets, this changes with WindowsNT 4.0. Nevertheless, browser management means that the interface is constrained to be simple, as shown in the figure.

Specifically, most of the web server and server operating systems do not include a domain name server software application. However, UNIX and the thousand or so of its derivatives (such as AIX, Solaris, and Linux) do include host domain services as part of the delivery bundle and are administered through /ETC/HOSTS. Even Linux has a built-in DNS server. Operating systems with included or free DNS servers may not be good or may be sufficient. You can replace a DNS server with various freeware, shareware, or commercial DNS servers. The commercial variety often includes a simplified window for setup, configuration, and ongoing maintenance. Although DNS is easy to administer—I did it twelve years ago with the UNIX stream editor (SED) and

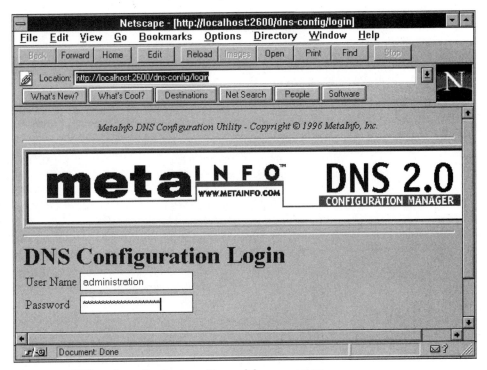

Figure 3.12   DNS configuration begins with a web browser access.

other flat files—the new commercial tools might save you two hours on initial setup and configuration and an hour (or even more in large internal sites) of weekly time updating the lists. However, realize the importance of the DNS services and include it in your website design budget and strategy.

Do not forget to put the IP numbers back to front for the reverse lookup file. While most web server operations are likely to fail when domain names do not map to corresponding IP addresses, reverse name lookups in IP format will not match to the corresponding domain names. For example, while a secondary server entry typically looks like this in a named boot or the DNS address file:

```
secondary   company.com   161.34.224.21   s/company.com
```

the secondary listing for the reverse resolution lookup will look like this:

```
secondary 34.161.in-addr.arpa 161.34.224.21 /s161.34
```

You are also likely to require a forward mapping file. This is in addition to the named boot file. Some of the newer WindowsNT domain name service applications and commercial files generate all the information required for forward and backward address look-ups from a single administration file generated within a tabbed dialog. If you are uncertain that the domain is configured properly, the nslook-up command (under UNIX) will return the other address format. By the way, address matching becomes even more important when your website maintains a SMTP server and E-mail forwarding facilities. For example, if you have addresses such as postmaster@company.com, webmaster@company.com, and info@company.com referenced in the HTML tags, the lack of address resolution will likely cause the ensuing misrouted mail to end up in some administrative subdirectory. Your site could generate a lot of mail and the webmaster might never know it until the mail directory got so large that someone got curious.

The Commerce Server from Netscape is billed also as an Intranet server and still does not include DNS. You need the LiveWire functionality. If your server platform is WindowsNT, try the Microsoft DNS Server on the companion CD-ROM. Microsoft has a free version of their NT-based DNS server, which is available on the CD-ROM (as DNS.ZIP).

NetManage sells Chameleon NFS for Windows, a product that will run on Windows 3.x, WindowsNT, and Windows95. Although this product is primarily designed for client TCP, IP, and NFS services, the bindery function (or "Bind" application) provides DNS services appropriate for Intranet or developmental testing. However, Chameleon NFS includes its own winsock.dll and you may need to adjust registry settings and system configuration to prevent dueling stacks and other network access conflicts.

In general, there are various dialog boxes to set the TCP/IP address. If you access the rest of the world via the Internet, these numbers are real and should be defined by InterNIC for your organization. The IP numbers need to be unique to prevent mapping clashes. See Chapter 4 for information on registering IP block assignments and Uniform Resource Locators (URL) domain names. In any event, you establish a local DHCP or a fixed IP address, usually from control panel (shown in Figure 3.13) in Windows, or with comparable UNIX or TCP stack utilities. The IP address assignment is usually defined in the /etc/hosts file on UNIX and derivatives.

If you cannot find the local address and cannot establish DNS service mappings between domain name URLs and an IP address, try this trick that seems to work on many different web servers. Type the specific URL "http://127.0.0.1/dateTime" to test that the local web service is working, verified in Figure 3.14. The local *loop-back* test uses the TCP/IP address of 127.0.0.1 by default for all network devices and web servers. Do not use this address for explicit TCP/IP device configurations except as a functional local test of TCP/IP services. You can use this same IP address for local site testing and Intranet access, but it is unfriendly for most users, so you will want to get DNS services running eventually. WebBase, which is both a web server and a database middleware tool in one package, shows this IP name and request resolution in Figure 3.15.

This issue becomes important when the site development team creates a local network to design, write, code, and test the server before it is live and after the site is operational on live web server or hosted on an ISP. The local site may

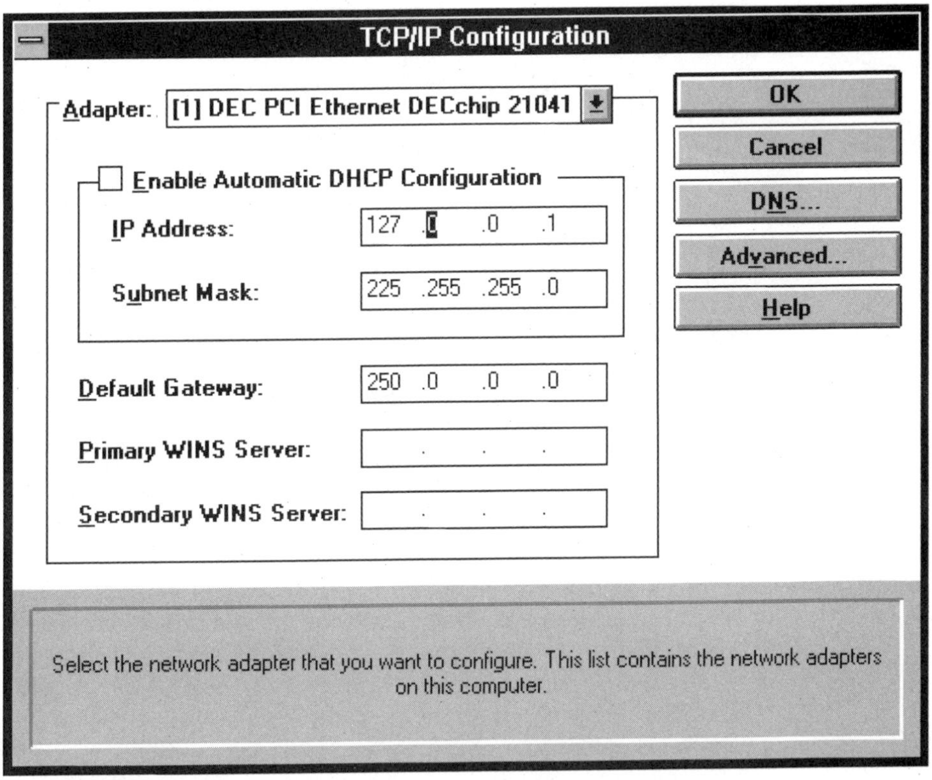

TCP/IP Configuration

Adapter: [1] DEC PCI Ethernet DECchip 21041

☐ **E**nable Automatic DHCP Configuration

IP Address: 127 . 0 . 0 . 1

Subnet Mask: 225 .255 .255 .0

Default Gateway: 250 .0 .0 .0

Primary WINS Server:

Secondary WINS Server:

OK
Cancel
D**N**S...
Ad**v**anced...
Help

Select the network adapter that you want to configure. This list contains the network adapters on this computer.

Figure 3.13   Windows control panel applet for setting DHCP or IP address.

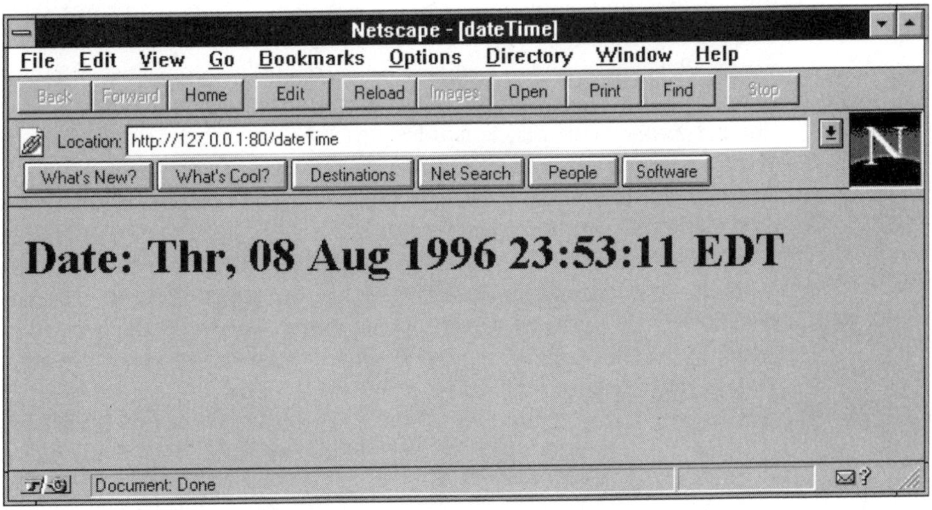

Netscape - [dateTime]

File   **E**dit   **V**iew   **G**o   **B**ookmarks   **O**ptions   **D**irectory   **W**indow   **H**elp

Back   Forward   Home   Edit   Reload   Images   Open   Print   Find   Stop

Location: http://127.0.0.1:80/dateTime

What's New?   What's Cool?   Destinations   Net Search   People   Software

Date: Thr, 08 Aug 1996 23:53:11 EDT

Document: Done

Figure 3.14   This default location should return the date and time (notice the case sensitivity) from a local and functioning web server.

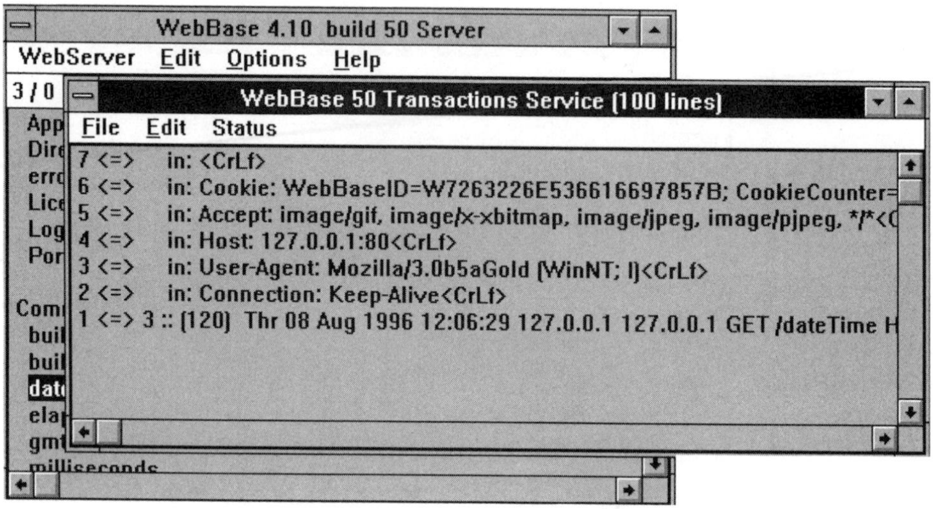

Figure 3.15 Confirmation that the date and time comes from the web server.

retain the domain name for obvious reasons and not be connected to the greater Internet. If it were, the domain name server conflict would create a problem, and in addition, you really would not want the test server accessible to customers, hackers, and others. Security is often not as tight on a development station or local network, and the firewall is usually not configured for it because it is not expected to be a live site. You do not want competing DNS servers pointing to different IP addresses as the "formal" location of the named site.

This means you will need DNS services strictly for the LAN environment and development stations. The alternative is to create local IP addresses and reference all calls to the various web servers, database integration tools (web-DBC, WebMate, and other tools) by the IP address. Since this actual IP address will be imbedded in all the functions and calls instead of the relative domain name, you will run into some serious replacement problems when the code, data tables, and HTML forms are migrated to the live server or host. Consider implementing DNS on development stations and the local network to forestall this problem in advance.

DNS services become painful when websites are served by many interlinked web servers (same software or even different software) with 7×24 backup, RAID, fail-safe cutover, and load leveling. When individual machines handle millions (in the case of a Netscape) of hits per day, the DNS address becomes a generic link to a particular site and a DNS Round-Robin or DNS load balancing algorithms, and the master IP address is matched with multiple IP addresses that, in turn, specify individual servers. DNS Round-Robin is used at many websites and Intranets because it is simple. For example, this scheme assumes that all website servers are identical in performance, have identical loads at the instant of request, and are up and running. DNS load-balancing has a fatal flaw in that crashed servers show no activity and hence no capacity for new requests. You might note that there are bugs in the DNS server implementations, particularly with caching, that can create some load and process allocation problems, but these scaling problems will have solutions in the near future because many large websites and busy cyberstores are experiencing hit overloads and several vendors are testing new solutions. For example, HydraWeb is selling a more sophisticated load-balancing product that runs on WindowsNT (on Pentiums, Pentium Pros, and Intel786 series) and UNIX (for Sun and SGI). I cannot vouch that this product is any better than other DNS servers or cluster controller schemes because I did not test the product. This information is included to corroborate the importance of web server load balancing for large corporate sites and database-driven cyberstores and the forthcoming hint of new technical solutions. In any event, you might note also that Netscape had 20 SGI platforms answering 6,000,000 hits per day using a proprietary DNS load balancing solution that has shown to scale well and is in fact *linearly* scaleable. Netscape is creating dispersed sites (POPs) with DNS servers provided to cut telecommunication costs and increase reliability one more notch.

Client Browser Platform

Chapter 2 referred to the NC Reference Profile for a client access device to the Internet. The current reference is labeled "Profile 1" and includes design input from Oracle, Sun, Microsoft, IBM, Netscape, and Apple. Just as multimedia standards for Windows have evolved through several definitions, be certain that the reference profile will as well. *NC* refers to the trademarked entity called a *Network Computer*. The complete profile (included on the CD-ROM as NC-REF1.HTM) defines the *minimum* functionality required for a client Internet access device. It is important to recognize that websites do not represent the ultimate in Internet services, and cyberstore functionality is not specifically but at least implicitly mentioned. In fact, NCs are expected to be highly scaleable and to span a product range from the palmtop to the desktop. They attach to the network and interoperate with other network nodes and network content in an IP-based network. They are enduser devices. NCs adhering to the NC Reference Profile support a common Java-based programming environment enabling network-resident applications, as well as stand-alone applications, to execute on them. They are typically dependent on the network but may offer stand-alone functionality.

A variety of NCs will likely emerge in a number of different arenas. It is desirable that they support a base level of standards, and that classes of devices, which may provide unique features and functions specific to their particular market, do so consistently and based on open system standards. As unique requirements or technologies emerge, the companies plan to recommend new profiles so the standards supported by these various NCs are selected thoughtfully and support a broad range of open network-based applications and content in a consistent and comprehensive fashion.

NCs are not intended to replace personal computers. Today's personal computers are fully capable of supporting the draft NC Reference Profile. However, unlike personal computers, NCs are designed from the outset with the network, Internet, and Intranets in mind. Additionally, NCs that comply with the NC profile have the following attributes:

- Architectural neutrality
- Lower total cost of ownership than personal computers
- Lower entry price than a typical personal computer
- Significantly easier to use and administer
- Enable security

The NC Reference Profile consists of a set of open standards and guidelines that form the basis of an NC. The initial NC Reference Profile was finalized by participants in August 1996. The initial NC profile includes:

- Minimum screen resolution of 640 $\times$ 480 (VGA) or equivalent
- Pointing device
- Text input capability
- Audio output
- Persistent local storage not required

NC devices participate in an IP-based network and will support IP as an underlying protocol. Specific hardware attachment to the network is not specified. The following are IP-based protocols:

- TCP
- SSL (secure connections, if supported)
- FTP
- Telnet
- NFS
- UDP
- SNMP

Web and Internet protocols include:

- DHCP
- Bootp
- HTML (including CGI).

- HTTP
- Java Application Environment with the Java Virtual Machine and runtime environment and Java class libraries.

In addition, the NC Reference Profile includes the following mail protocols:

- SMTP—Simple Mail Transfer Protocol
- IMAP4—Internet Message Access Protocol Version 4
- POP3—Post Office Protocol Version 3

The Reference Profile includes the following common multimedia formats:

- JPEG
- GIF
- WAV
- AU

The Reference Profile Security features are optional at the present time and only supported through emerging APIs:

- ISO 7816 (SmartCards)
- Europay/MasterCard/VISA specifications

The point of this information is that the NC specification represents the lowest common denominator for web access. Your site design and future plans need to reflect who you want to visit your site and how universal you want access to be, as Chapter 2 outlined in the deadly design sins section. If your customer base is consumers, the lowest common denominator is advisable. If you are selling to businesses, they are likely to have powerful systems that exceed the NC minimums. However, if the value of a business-to-business link is preeminent and the value of sales or margins is high, you can subsidize the latest and greatest for your customers. Rent systems, lease them, or subsidize customers. Perhaps the best technique to subsidize customers is to provide hefty initial discounts (less, but still substantial discounts after six months or a year) for on-line cyberstore purchases and that way encourage the customers to acquire, set up, and maintain their own client web stations.

Client-Side Browser Platforms

The first stop on this tour should be the comprehensive site at Browser Watch. This web site is listed at my book's home page and information archives. It is also included on a file copy of this home page, which is included on the CD-ROM. You want to be aware of this site because it contains current information about the capabilities and compatibility for each type of browser.

This is a user decision that you have to understand. For example, at the time of this writing, Netscape browser 1.1 was selling for $24.99 at a computer store chain, while version 2.0 was selling for $39.95 with a mail-in rebate of $10.00 interlaced on the same retail endcap with identical packaging. You had to realize that the pricing was not a stocking error and that the package had the 1.1 printed on the box under the shrink-wrap and that the new boxes included a sticker under the shrink-wrap. Very subtle difference in the store. However, Netscape browser version 2.0 supports SHTTP and secure transactions and the new HTML table and frame formats, whereas the prior version does not.

For the cyberstore vendor, this means you have to create a workaround for receiving credit card information or shipping privileged information and software. For Microsoft Explorer 1.0 users, customers with a Mosaic, older Netscape, Sun, or Chameleon browsers the information contained inside tables and frames loses its format. This physically looks like badly OCRed annual reports; it is a jumble of mixed up columns and tabbed information. As I said before, you can force the browser choice. In this case, a user may choose not to explore your site at all if you do not provide text-based viewing or provide an alternate composition for more primitive browsers. Nervous shoppers who get through the mess may choose to make purchases by telephone or fax; make it obvious that there are alternatives to the secured browser transaction process.

Development Platforms

Development platforms are personal choices adjusted to reflect the cyberstore and DBMS environments. Since HTML is ASCII with markup, any platform is functionally suitable. When possible, simplify, simplify, simplify. If you can save text files or at least convert them from EBCDIC to ASCII without surprises, any Burroughs or IBM mainframe or AS/400 system is fine, presupposing that you have useful web layout software for those platforms.

Realize that most UNIX-based systems (SGI, Solaris, HP-UX, AIX, Xenix) create text files that include line endings and an extra line feed for each line. You will want to check how these files appear when viewed inside a browser before committing to a particular editor and HTML creation process. There is nothing quite so bad as a UNIX text file that formats nicely on a terminal but looks very ragged with blank lines when viewed in a browser. UNIX-based HTML editors automatically resolve this difference, but if you add code to a pre-existing HTML file using EMACS, or other file editors, watch out for extra line feeds. Most creative agencies prefer Macintosh equipment because they have invested money and experience in using it for printed page layout and image processing. Windows is a leading choice for corporations if only because of the preponderance of suitable web, HTML, and image applications available.

Even if you choose to host your web site on an ISP or other server specifically provided and promoted as commercial web sites, cyberstore hosts, or cybermalls, you *will* want to maintain a local staging version of the web site—if only to create local backup and make backup tapes of CD-ROMs. Do not fully trust an ISP or host for the integrity of your site. The same holds true for independent advertising agencies and consultants because things can go wrong and source materials do become corrupt or get lost. You need a development or redevelopment and deployment platform. If you are developing a site in-house (either for ISP hosting, Intranet deployment, or public display with a local web server), you need a development platform for HTML, database, and web services. This can be the same machine or separate units. When the cyberstore goes live, and the development platforms are converted to support the live site, you still need secondary platforms for ongoing maintenance, management, backup, statistics tracking, testing, and redevelopment. It is probably best if these secondary platforms are not connected to and are distinct from the live server.

In addition, if the web server is a local machine, not just a series of directories on an ISP server host (or distributed over several machines), consider backup in the form of spare systems, lots of parts, and even clustered or live backup systems. Consider also main and backup telecommunication channels. You will also want to match development and deployment environments. For example, if you create dynamic HTML using Javascript or VBScript and export to port the pages to a UNIX-based ISP host, you will run into compatibility problems. If you have a wonderful local site using Cold Fusion, SQL Server, and Oracle Financials and think that the ISP will support NT applications and tolerate an SQL database application running on the ISP hardware, you had best be prepared for the multiple platform integration effort and clear negotiations with the ISP. In addition, you may need assurances verified by audits that corporate financial data does not leak around the ISP administration staff or leak through the host firewalls.

I cannot tell you what type of platform (or platforms) you should pick for website development. That is a function of convenience, integration, and performance. WindowsNT seems to be the leading choice by vendors for HTML, middleware, and graphics tools. WindowsNT is also a leading choice for low- to mid-range web servers. Since you are likely to maintain an Intranet web server not connected to the Internet (so as to resolve possible DNS conflicts), NT might be a good choice. WindowsNT Workstation and particularly NT Server run anything that Windows 3.x will and even Windows95. As noted later in Chapter 4, some long filename problems and some applications are specific to Windows95 and will create port problems and other functional ramifications. However, if your ultimate server is based on Windows95, it might make a good choice for development, too.

However, that is not the end of the story. You have to look at the other integration platforms. If you are running Sybase on UNIX or SGI, or Informix on HP-UX, or DB2 on AS/400 and expect to integrate the web server into these databases, plan where the web server will reside, where the middleware will execute, and then decide on the development platforms. Page layout is best on the Macintosh with PageMill, SiteMill, or on any comfortable and compatible Windows platform running any of the Windows tools profiled in Chapter 4. However, you need to integrate the scripts, the middleware, and the transaction processing on whatever platform is compatible with the DBMS.

In addition, you have to assess loads. WindowsNT will not sustain the millions of daily hits at a site like Netscape, even though WindowsNT can run on multiprocessor systems and can cluster to multiple servers. If you realistically expect millions of hits every day, SGI provides a better platform that scales. However, since SGI runs a unique version of UNIX, plan for development and deployment of design, middleware, and database tools that work reliably in that environment. Just because a vendor promises a port to UNIX from NT and provides a Solaris adaptation does not mean functionality or satisfaction on SGI.

When 7×24 uptime is required, you need redundancy and some software to move processes from a failed machine to a functional mirror. Although some of the DNS load-leveling tools will provide this, the redundancy is not only a function of the web server itself. You do not want your cyberstore to be muted because database queries cannot be fulfilled because the data server has failed and is waiting for someone to notice this fact and reboot it. The cyberstore needs a standby database server (in case of primary failure), mostly a service or data replication and standby cutover. NetWare, Vines, SGI UNIX, AS/400, and IBM 3090 with MVS will support this; however Sun does not, and Windows does not with reliability. Although some third-party software does enable Windows servers for standby cutover, you need to realize that the transfer may require several minutes, not the seconds or milliseconds with an IBM mainframe assemblage or VAX cluster.

Table 3.1 explores my preference for client-side access to the Internet and development under Windows 3.x. It is clear that Windows 3.x does not support

TABLE 3.1 Comparison of Windows95 Versions of Windows.

Product functions	Windows 3.x	Windows95	NT Workstation
System resources	64 KB stacks	expanded	unlimited
MS-DOS support	Yes	Yes	Most
Multimedia APIs	Yes	Yes	NT 4.0
Win 95 Interface	No	Yes	With add-in
Network client support	Yes	Yes	With RAS
Protection from Win16	No	No	Yes
Protection from Win32	No	No	Yes
NTFS	No	No	Yes
Automatic system recovery	No	No	Yes
Security	No	Some	Yes
Typical system requirements	18 MB	40 MB	90 MB
Typical RAM requirements	8 MB	20 MB	16 MN
Multiplatform CPU	No	No	Yes
Wide web tool support	Yes	Some	Yes
Wide web server support	Some	Some	More

VRML, streaming services, or provide the level of security and reliability of Windows95 or WindowsNT, but the lower resource requirements, the availability (mostly through sunk costs) of workable tools and solutions makes Windows 3.x effective as a client-side development tool. Obviously, while many corporations have resisted the upgrade to Windows95 or even WindowsNT for the desktop, development is shifting to the 32-bit platforms. At some point, probably during 1997, Windows 3.x will only provide a low-end functional, but superseded by the WindowsNT workstation platform. This will become true as database middleware, streaming video, and VRML become mainstream development tools under NT and UNIX. At that point, I will reassess my choice of primary development platform.

Personally, my preference is Windows 3.11 for most design and development work because I like the older user interface best and the tools are comfortable—like an old shoe. (I finally gave up my 1978 copy of CP/M WordStar in 1994 because it couldn't create rich text format [RTF] files necessary for Windows help development.) Tools that run only under Windows95, UNIX, or WindowsNT get used within the networked environment as needed when they provide functionality that is superior to or impossible with older or current Windows 3.x tools. Windows 3.x performance is typically better than WindowsNT and Windows95 as well since I am unwilling to upgrade to the 32-bit versions of the software. Frankly, Windows 3.11 is good enough. I am not unaware of the pressure to upgrade and have a local network of many machines running different operating systems and different versions. The network supports Windows 3.0, Windows 3.x, WindowsNT in various releases and versions, OS/2, Windows95, some beta versions, Linux, Solaris for Intel, and a few other oddities. This provides distribution and test platforms for software development, although most work is performed under Windows 3.11.

In fact, some of the management software for multiple-participant videoconference calls runs only under UNIX (such as the CU-SeeMe reflector) and you may need similar diffusion. Nevertheless, the native Microsoft networking software provides file server access, local file sharing, and INT12 access to SCSI and other external devices such as scanners, CD writers, ISDN terminal adapters, and cameras across all these platforms. NetWare does this to a degree, Vines supports a heterogeneous environment, but both require a dedicated file server, which the Windows peer-to-peer environment does not. You can substitute NT Server and achieve the same service centralization with a dedicated file server, or connect in existing corporate or departmental LANs.

WindowsNT provides a better server platform than Windows95 because the user interface is standard Windows 3.x, it includes very good security, and it is faster and more reliable than Windows95. However, realize that WindowsNT is really two separate products that have important limitations as far as website server development and hosting are concerned. Specifically, WindowsNT is available as a workstation version for the client and a server version. The differences are minor and typically do not matter for NT version 3.51 but do matter with releases since NT 4.0. Specifically, the NT Workstation costs about $149 per copy for the upgrade (or $325 as a new package) and NT Server costs $1,495. In the scheme of the cyberstore and the costs associated with each minute of downtime, costs for the software are not material. However, you do need to realize the differences between the server and client products. Specifically, IIS, SQL Server, and the Microsoft commerce tools geared to cyberstore activities will run only under NT Server. Most other NT products, including DNS 2.0, WebSite Pro, Cold Fusion, Quest, Sybase SQL, and Sybase WebServer do run under both versions of WindowsNT.

Some tools only run under Windows95, such as the HVS color reduction plug-in for Photoshop and Visual Web. To resolve these needs, my organization has various Pentiums, Pentium Pros, and cloned 486 and 586 systems running on a network. Some CPUs are not based on Intel chips or motherboard designs. I would like some dual processors or certainly more robust and resilient servers, but all are based on single CPUs. Most machines include a removable EIDE boot disk that is stored in a locked caddy so that different configurations, different versions of an operating system or GUI (for example WindowsNT 4.0), or demonstrations can be tested without compromising existing and working configurations. In addition, a second caddy provides disk-to-disk backup and OS mastering as needed.

Because the cost for large disks is dropping and 2GB of hard disk space costs about $200 right now, you can also think of the hard disk as a removable device, comparable in cost to magneto-optical (MO) removable media but about 10 to 40 times faster. Just label the hard drives and caddies so you know what each drive has on it. I frequently exchange the C: drive with a D: drive and spend ten minutes wondering why a system will not boot, or worse, mismatch different D: drives and wonder why Program Manager or registry information doesn't point to working applications or data sets. Because it is invasive to open cases to swap drives and align the 25-pin or 50-pin cables, and because doing so is not very good for the cable connectors and the little pins on the drive, consider installing a drive bay device designed for frequent swapping of drives, as shown in Figure 3.16. These caddies are available for about $16 per unit in VAR quantity for common disk drive formats, such as IDE, EIDE, and SCSI (with an ID selection switch).

Two units in a single machine provide a direct disk-to-disk copy facility. While this seems far afield from website development, a great deal of development effort and time are lost to process controls, project overhead, details, bad or insufficient management, lack of development planning and controls, and platform confusions. With the release of new browsers and new development on Windows 3.0, Windows 3.x, Windows for Workgroups, OS/2, WindowsNT, Windows95, UNIX, Solaris, Linux, NFS, and other operating systems, the forthcoming Daytonia and Cairo, 16-bit .VBX, 16-bit .OCX, 32-bit .OCX and remote Procedure Calls (RPCs), and OLE distributions, Java, Javascript, ActiveX, various other add-ins, the website support and development tracks are exceedingly complicated. In fact, how would you test DOS FAT partitions versus NTFS, or the new NTFS 2.0 version with NT 4.0? How

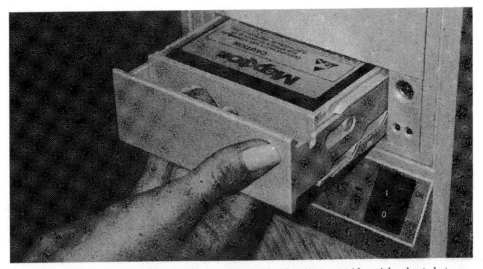

Figure 3.16 QUIKDRAW and other products with similar functions provide quick reboots between versions of DOS, Windows, UNIX, and other platform configurations.

would you try different DNS servers or fixed versus DHCP IP address assignments?

The one disadvantage of swapping hardware and portable drives is that operating systems and drivers, particularly the registries, have become very device-dependent. If you want to create a flexible environment, build systems from standard hardware, include standard devices (such as mice), and install the same size hard drives, same make and model CD-ROMs, and isolate the SCSI devices to a single machine that is different or standardize your use of SCSI across all the platforms.

The benefit of these removable hard drives over magneto-optical cartridges is an access speed that is 10 to 40 times faster. I would not advise benchmarking website performance with a magneto-optical system, but performance is exactly the same with this QUIKDRAW hard drive configuration as it is with a standard hard drive installed inside a PC case. By the way, the removable frame for drives protects them from some of the normal abuses otherwise visited on exposed drives.

However, even with all these tools, desktops, and network resources, I can frequently overload 2 or 3 fast Pentium Pro and faster 133 MHz Intel 486 systems simultaneously running website downloads, moving sites with FTP to the host, keeping software development on track, while juggling billing, payroll, and collections at the same time. Graphics, and Photoshop in particular, eat resources, and the need to use different operating systems and applications at the same time creates a lot of network traffic; swiveling from system to system and switching keyboard and monitors with gang switch boxes creates website development confusion. Premiere, and other streaming video presentations, represent management of multiple large images at the same time and require even more power and memory. In larger teams, focus developers to specific systems to cut hardware costs and training time, but realize that you will probably need as many platforms as possible to test performance, compatibility, integration, and displays of web pages on different colors, monitor depths, and browsers.

Host WWW Site

The previous section addressed some of the compatibility issues with local website development and integration with rollout to a different host platform. Obviously, there are even more issues involved when choosing to host a dynamic website within a shared Internet Service Provider (ISP) environment. If your organization has a policy of *outsourcing* MIS, DP, and other services, website hosting is a natural outsourcing venue. Some people liken hosting web sites locally to the process of buying printing presses, bindery equipment, and mailing tools to create a company newsletter. The ISP host is easily accessed from the development site, is equally accessible by advertising agencies or outside design consultants, and technical support and backup are generally part of the service. Outsourcing web services is only as good as the quality of the ISP and your relationship with them. The important ISP selection issues include:

- Cost
- Flexibility
- Technical support
- Reliability
- Security
- Technical support
- Willing to write CGI scripts or specialized programming
- Ability and willingness to provide load and bandwidth usage reports
- Expansion or upsizing possibilities
- Performance
- Service

In general, ISPs are a business like any other, with their share of exceptional and poor providers. In addition, the market pressures are stressing both small and large providers in terms of performance, technical support, and pricing. It is important to differentiate client-side Internet access from server hosting. While AT&T has created free access for clients, you do not get free access for host sites. A few providers are offering hosting with pay-as-you-go schemes where you get charged for hits or on-line sales, but the reality is these services may be more expensive and less flexible than a standard ISP.

Web hosting services can mean anything from a UNIX shell account to a service that builds and designs everything for you—you just provide pictures and text for the site. Then, of course, there is everything in between. Here is a measuring stick that you might find useful for evaluating an ISP:

- Check references
- Visit the site
- Verify number of hops between ISP and Internet backbone
- Check ISP financial background
- Check ISP technical background
- Ask about expansion capabilities

The ISP will tell you everything that is glowing and positive, but not detail how difficult it can be to get through to a technical support person or solve billing problems. You want to ask other customers how they feel about the services. Visit the site to see how well run the organization is. Messes and chaos indicate growth, lack of true management skills, or even possible problems. Look at the equipment, the people, and the organization structure. You probably want an organization committed to the state of the art in technical, routers, firewalls, and scripting. You also want to see backup facilities and a system to move services to other sites and backups to secure facilities in case of significant site disasters. When it comes down to the final ISP selection process, consider the points in the following list. You want to communicate the website objectives very clearly and involve senior management in the process. The bottom line for a cyberstore that is wholly dependent on 7 × 24 operations is that the outsource provider provides what they are supposed to provide. It is especially important to include financial people and contract negotiators, if your company has them. The important contract issues include:

- Know the objectives in procuring a web service contract
- Establish quantitative yardsticks and service benchmarks
- Involve senior managers who understand overall objectives
- Communicate these objectives throughout the organization
- Structure flexibility into contracts to allow change as technology evolves
- Have an escape clause in case the vendor does not perform
- Have the same staff work on a new service agreement from negotiation through implementation to sidestep important oversights
- Contract with a reputable ISP vendor
- Use good consultants or external support experts if the organization lacks the internal expertise to negotiate the website hosting contract

My service provider got hit by Hurricane Andrew in 1993 and had some minor problems, but not as severe as some major corporations because the service provider was better prepared. When the ISP is not connected directly into the Internet backbone, the router and service delays increase with each hop in the daisy chain. In addition, each hop adds significant questions about the validity and reliability of the service. When the ISP is connected directly, the only question becomes how does the telco provide tie line backup and response time to catastrophe? You should also check the finances and technical background of the ISP. After all, you do not want an ISP that goes broke and leaves you hanging without the sources (HTML and scripts) to your commercial cyberstore. You do want an ISP that can build complex scripts (for SHTTP and SSL transactions) and make modifications quickly in the event of security problems and technological changes to HTML or HTTP.

The reality is that you will be charged at least your fair weight, maybe more, if your site does not generate the level of traffic you hope for or expect. If your site becomes a mecca for traffic and on-line business, the ISP will want to renegotiate. This is a double-edged sword because your site may represent a cybermall anchor or a very big and very powerful slice business that is attractive to other ISPs or cybermall operators. Nevertheless, that presupposes a sales track record and hit load to make your site attractive to customers and hence advertisers, operators, and ISPs looking to ride successful coat tails.

One of the first questions to ask is whether you want a national or local ISP. Since everything is done by telephone, from making agreements and signing up for domain names to shipping HTML pages to the host, proximity is not a valid issue. I suppose you can make a case for reducing telecommunication charges for tie lines, but the reality is that almost every Internet access provider supports a local point-of-presence (POP), so it really is a moot point. Three years ago, line charges mattered when I located a local commercial provider. Now it is not relevant.

The decision process is one of checking references, making long- or short-term commitments, recognizing the contract and integration nightmares that can occur, and avoiding confusion over ownership and portability issues over domain names. Ultimately, realize just how interchangeable a website and a web host really are. I would recommend that you investigate domain-name aliasing (to save money) and add flexibility for site hosting. I also recommend this list for validating high-performance cyberstore hosting from an ISP.

- 24 × 7 monitoring
- 24 × 7 problem resolution (not a 9-to-5 operation)
- 10 Mbps access to an Internet backbone or router
- Redundant Internet connections
- Proven high-performance servers

- Shared or dedicated servers
- Proven response time and performance
- Secure Internet access (SSL, SET, SHTTP, etc.)
- Third-party auditing services

Table 3.2 shows average statistics for my site and for my client sites. These are average figures and take into account dialing problems and Internet access problems at a specific server, service, or protocol.

You own the InterNIC registration unless you do not read the fine print on the contract from the Internet service provider. It is a mistake not to fill out the InterNIC domain name registration forms yourself or at least check that they are issued to your organization's name. You do not want the registration in the name of the ISP on your behalf. Flexibility is a key issue. In many cases when you are not happy with a provider, there may be contract cancellation fees and you can negotiate moving the domain name.

Moving a website from one ISP to another—if you make a bad choice—is not traumatic if you plan appropriately. Since DNS services are transportable, you can take your domain name and all your files and merely change access phone numbers. Domain name is simply a matter of propagating the IP address matches to all the secondary and primary Internet domain name servers. That takes about a day, or maybe three or four, to funnel down to tertiary and Intranet domain name databases. However, if your site has specialized CGI code, relies on specific CGI libraries, or has functions of the operating system and configuration of the ISP, moving to a new ISP can become involved. If you contract for SHTTP code, CGI code, special Perl scripts to update the "what's new" page automatically, and link into merchant credit card services, make sure that the contracts state your ownership of the CGI and Perl code, merchant account numbers, and other scripts. If the scripts are not based on standard public domain libraries, make certain ahead of time that you have rights to these libraries. These scripts may run just fine on any ISP or after the appropriate script libraries are included, or may require some minor reprogramming.

Causes for poor web service performance

The reasons for delays on an Internet server, whether it is a stand-alone local server, a server cluster connected directly to the Internet backbone with a

TABLE 3.2 Actual Experienced ISP Response and Uptimes

ISP	UUNET	PSInet	Netcom	Hooked	Ultranet	Shadow
Response time	8.8 s	12.8	165 s	47 s	18.2	4.6
Uptime	99.999%	99.999%	96.3%	95.8%	96.7%	98.2%

telecommunications connection, a local web server attached with a dial-up or commitment connection to an ISP, or even a website based on an ISP host, are:

- Many hops (routes) in the connection
- An overloaded server
- A server running too many CGI scripts
- Poor web server device drivers
- Overloaded disk access
- Slow or inefficient disk controllers
- Slow or inefficient disks
- CPU stalled 50 percent or more while waiting for data or instructions
- Fragmented disks or small disk blocks and segments
- An inefficient operating system
- Overloaded CPU
- Overloaded or inefficient cache
- Improperly configured server
- Slow or inefficient disks
- Poor database designs (table structures and relationships) and processes
- Too many layers (OLE, DDE, CGI, and macros)
- An inadequate WAN connection from the server to the Internet
- A poorly written HTTP daemon

Web server performance benchmarks are available through a number of sources and there are tools that will measure site performance. Neal Nelson & Associates has been providing a web server benchmark called Webstones for UNIX systems and now has made it available for WindowsNT. The idea is to analyze the speed of common functions, profile performance under light and extreme load conditions, profile clustered or load-leveled servers, and identify the causes for dramatic slowdowns. Ideally, you will want to test performance on the local development site, the local web server, and contrast this with ISP services. Be certain you connect into the website from the server, from a network workstation, from a remote connection, and with a dial-up or dedicated connection. Check permutations, different times of day, and different background loads. When performance is a problem, you want to isolate the delay to bandwidth, network interaction, server loads, web page complexities, and configuration issues.

It is really an enjoyable puzzle to solve performance problems. It is my specialty as evidenced by the consulting work and the McGraw-Hill performance books series (*LAN Performance Optimization, Computer Performance Opti-*

mization, and *Enterprise Network Performance Optimization*). However, it is unfortunate that when website performance problems occur, the tension is very high, stakes are high, and tempers are equally high. The real problems occur when political infighting and finger pointing outweigh relatively solvable technical problems. As outlined in my books, performance optimization is an administrative task of creating a consensus of what constitutes a clear and concise outcome, the resources available for that outcome, and the degrees of freedom for effecting that optimization.

Local WWW Site

Your choice of a web platform will have significant effects on the success of your cyberstore. A web server at the simplest level is a file server accepting requests for specific documents and responding with the delivery of those documents over a TCP/IP connection to a web browser. The documents can be text (in any language), images, sounds, or any data that can be represented by a binary file format. The web server is just a responsive machine delivering a stream of bits. There are web servers for most platforms, from Macintosh to OS/2, Windows, and UNIX, as mentioned in the last section. The only proviso for a functional server is that it have a connection into the Internet. Since this connection can be as simple as an analog modem line, any computer with at least one communication port can be a server. Freeware and shareware HTTP products have their own Yahoo search category and there are many more packages available in various archives. However, you do not want to base business on unsupported software.

Platform issues

By the way, your cyberstore is likely to require multiple servers. Large operations may need to partition or cluster the web server into multiple units for a cyberstore web server farm. A cyberstore operation requires the following features in the main web server:

- HTML file service
- E-mail enablement
- Secure transaction processing
- Relational database management system

Although the generic web browser represents the most uniform user interface in the world to date, there are many technical, implementational, and managerial ramifications for each choice. The bottom line is that you cannot assume that "plain vanilla" is the simplest or the best, or that the newest and most advanced is the best either. There are substantial trade-offs in your choices, some of which have effects beyond your control over your web site. Platform issues include four major choices: site development platforms; site web servers; site hosts; and the choices for end user browsers. You do not normally have the choice over the end user browser, which may have a major effect on your cyberstore, but you can force a choice in some cases. In general, you need to be aware of the ramifications of the end user browser choice and many of the other platform issues because bad choices, poor technical decisions, and disagreement over strategies can cost extra time and money.

Platform choices

Almost any computing platform can provide web service. It is best if that operating system platform supports multitasking, so that several users can interact with the site at the same time. UNIX, specifically SGI hardware and operating system, provides the most robust cyberstore platform at the current time. AIX or Solaris is a close second, while WindowsNT is viable for small sites. Current development of DNS load distribution software and the continuing integration of web server, database, and operating systems will provide more "web server farm" possibilities. This track represents the more robust cyberstore platform.

If your cyberstore is a small operation and begins to outstrip the horsepower of a single CPU, multiple CPU servers are available from IBM, SGI, Sun, Hewlett-Packard, and DEC. Each additional CPU increases the horsepower by about 80 percent of the prior one. Because cyberstore transactions are more likely to create loads because of database query overheads rather than an absolute crush of web server requests, consider moving the database operations to a separate CPU or server farm before addressing web server request server overloads. Most transactional sites I have engineered or explored run out of bandwidth to the Internet first, then create excessive database latencies, and then, finally, overload the web server. Obviously, this generalization is not true when a cyberstore provides no FTP file service, is designed to minimize database-to-HTML traffic and loading, and has simplified the complexity of web pages and the data entry process. Channel bandwidth will still saturate before the web server does, but the web server will likely overload before the database structure creates the critical path.

A number of dual-Pentium or quad-Pentium motherboards and processors are available. These are suitable for enhancing the performance of small commercial websites and cyberstores. Although it is possible to run UNIX and NFS on a Pentium, WindowsNT workstation represents a simpler, less costly, and more flexible platform for installation, integration, and management. There is a wide range of web servers, databases, and support tools that will run on WindowsNT. In fact, you can connect through to Sybase, Oracle, DB2, CICS, and other database platforms from an NT-based web server. Figure 3.17 shows the motherboard of an Advanced Logic Research (ALR) dual-Pentium server. I do not put much stock into dual or quad CPU servers because performance and load-leveling are still primitive; I do appreciate the redundancy

Figure 3.17 Dual-processor Pentium motherboard. The most relevant issue for a web platform is not really that the computer has two CPUs, but rather that it has redundant power supplies, handles hot replacement of boards and disks, and is built more robustly than a traditional desktop computer.

and hot-swapping of components with dual or quad server-rate hardware that become an essential issue for 7×24 website operations.

Since the connection through the Internet provides the multiple communication channel support for multiple sessions (or thousands of sessions) simultaneously, the external hydras of modems required with remote dial-in and BBS systems are not required. The ISPs provide those for FTP uploading, E-mail, and site management, or a direct connection to Internet backbone bypasses any need for that. However, when you build a local web server, you have a lot of choices. There are many products available—some are free, some are free if you have the right hardware platform, and some are commercial products. Table 3.3 lists commercial web servers.

Web servers are available from commercial sources and also from Internet sites as freeware or shareware (which you do have to pay for). These tools are worth what you pay for them and the cost of the service, technical support, and administration. However, most commercial and free products do not include secured transmission or encryption services. This is anathema to the cyberstore, not for real and confirmed on-line security problems, but rather for perceived and legal responsibilities, as outlined in the Security section in

TABLE 3.3 Commercial Server Platforms and Web Servers.

Platform	Commercial Web Servers
AIX	Commerce Server
Amiga	
CMS	
DOS	-none-
Macintosh	InterServer, MACHTTP, Web Server 4D, WebStar
NetWare	Purveyor Encrypt, SecurServ, SiteBuilder
OS/2	Internet Connection
OSF	Cheetah, Esplanade
SGI	Cheetah, Commerce Server, Enterprise Server, Esplanade, Fast Track Server, Secure WebServer, WebForce
Solaris	Cheetah, Commerce Server, Enterprise Server, Fast Track Server, Esplanade, Netra, Secure WebServer, WebForce
SunOS	Esplanade, Enterprise Server, Fast Track Server, Netra, Secure WebServer, WebForce
UNIX BSD	Cheetah, Commerce Server, Esplanade, Enterprise Server, Fast Track Server, Netra, Secure WebServer, WebForce
UNIX var.	AlphaServer, Cheetah, Commerce Server, Enterprise Server, Esplanade, Fast Track Server, GNNServer, MMB Teammate, Netra, Secure WebServer, WebForce
Vines	WebServer
VMS	Cheetah, Purveyor Encrypt
Windows 3.1	Quarterdeck WebServer
Windows95	Cheetah, Commerce Builder, Secure WebServer, WebSite 1.1, WebStar
WindowsNT Workstation	Cheetah, Commerce Builder, Commerce Server, Enterprise Server, Fast Track Server, GNNServer, Purveyor Encrypt, ISYS Web, MindWires, Safety Web, Secure WebServer, SuperWeb, WebSite 1.1, WebSite Pro, WebStar
WindowsNT Server	Cheetah, Commerce Server, Enterprise Server, Esplanade, Fast Track Server, ISYS Web, MultiNet, Purveyor Encrypt, Safety Web, Secure WebServer, WebSite 1.1, WebSite Pro, WebStar
source code	

Chapter 4. WebSite Pro, Commerce Server, Secure WebServer, and some of the commercial products include various levels of security. These may include private/public key schemes, DES, digital signatures, or authentication, or all of these features. Realize that you may also need to negotiate with a service provider (for a fee) for assignment of private certificate, for digital signature, or for cyberstore vendor verification. This might include legal and private investigation into the operation and personnel of the organization.

The free products do not generally include security and encryption built into the web servers. The exceptions are the Apache SSL (for U.S. use only), and the IBM Internet Connection Secure Server. By the time you read this,

Microsoft Internet Information Server (IIS) will probably still be free, but the Merchant Connection (with security) will be a commercial add-in. The most famous of the freeware servers is the IIS from Microsoft, which runs only under NT Server. However, it does provide most of the desirable cyberstore features, integrates with SQL Server, has tools for database connectivity, and is as easy to administer as a Microsoft OS gets. Table 3.4 details the availability for various platforms.

It is important to differentiate WindowsNT Workstation from WindowsNT Server. Although WindowsNT generally refers to the workstation GUI, the NT Server designation refers to the WindowsNT Server software. These are different products. A file server typically runs the NT Server software; it is similar to Vines, NetWare, and other network operating systems in that it provides network log-in, file services, and print services. However, it is not a desktop operating system and generally is not as robust for that type of limited

TABLE 3.4 Server Platforms and "Free" Web Servers.

Platform	"Free" Web Services
AIX	IBM Internet Connection, W3C httpd
Amiga	Amiga Web Server, IBM Internet Connection
CMS	Webshare
DOS	-none-
Macintosh	FreeMAC
NetWare	-none-
OS/2	Apache, IBM Internet Connection
OSF	CL-HTTP, Spinner, W3C httpd
SGI	CL-HTTP, Spinner
Solaris	CL-HTTP, Spinner, W3C httpd
SunOS	CL-HTTP, Spinner, W3C httpd
UNIX BSD	Apache, Apache SSL-US, CL-HTTP, IBM Internet Connection, NCSA httpd, Spinner, thtppd, W3C httpd, WN
UNIX var.	CL-HTTP, IBM Internet Connection, NCSA httpd, Spinner, W3C httpd, WN
Vines	-none-
VMS	OSU DECThreads Server, Webshare
Windows 3.1	-none-
Windows95	Fnord Server, Windows htppd
WindowsNT Workstation	EMWAC Server, Fnord Server, IBM Internet Connection
WindowsNT Server	EMWAC Server, Fnord Server, IBM Internet Connection, IIS
source code	Apache, Apache SSL-US, CL-HTTP, Fnord Server, NCSA httpd, Spinner, httpd, WN

service. It is important to make this distinction because most web servers run best on the NT workstation software; only the Microsoft Internet Information Server (IIS) specifically requires NT Server. This is a clear positioning statement and marketing strategy.

All the testing for this book was performed with NT versions 3.51. Microsoft has made a decision that NT 4.0 Workstation will only allow 10 TCP/IP connections within a ten-minute period, thus forcing users to deploy the more expensive NT Server rather than the NT workstation client as a web server platform. (There are ways around this with third-party communication servers though.) Mike O'Reilly of O'Reilly & Associates has stated that this is an artificially-created restraint of trade, and it is not clear whether legal action will be necessary to adjust the Microsoft position or if it will help. This artificial limitation may not withstand the pressure from the marketplace as it will stifle development of small cybershops and deployment of small sites. Nevertheless, this represents one of the serious technical decisions affecting web platform choices.

If you want to imbed ActiveX components into web pages, realize that Internet Component Download is not universally supported with browsers. However, Internet Explorer (3.0 and greater) issues a web server-independent request for the referenced executable file. In the same vein as the warnings about restrictions and hosting server limitations, you need to be aware of the various application programming (API) languages built into web servers. There are basically two generally accepted APIs at the current time. It is unfortunate that there is more than one. The APIs are ISAPI (Microsoft specification) and the NSAPI (Netscape Communications definition). Other APIs include the original but anemic National Computer Security Association (NCSA) design, as well as IIS and Netscape Commerce Server, and the Open-Market Commerce Server. Note that not all database-to-HTML middleware tools for building your dynamic and interactive cyberstore will work on all web servers.

For example, while WebBase works on NT Workstation, it does not work with WebSite Pro, even though WebSite Pro works on NT Workstation. The discrepancy is due to the APIs themselves and to the fact that WebBase includes its own web server. Since WebBase lacks the SSL encryption technology, you may have to choose between a dynamic database and WebBase. On the other hand, you can bypass these problems by running both WebSite Pro and WebBase web servers and assigning different ports to the server. The default is typically 80hex, but this parameter is configurable. As such, you can allocate different HTTP pages to each server by including the port address in the URL. You could also run the web server software on different platforms and link them together with external HTML hyperlinks in the same way.

Solutions like these are clunky and, ultimately, limiting. Of course, most problems can be solved by technical excellence and perseverance. I suggest otherwise, since you are trying to build a commodity, that is, a simple and functional web-based transaction processing environment. As such, realize that you can select solutions that simplify. For example, Cold Fusion (a "lite" version that comes with WebSite Pro) and WebSite Pro with WindowsNT Workstation 3.51 are all made for each other. WebSite Pro includes encryption, a CGI library, and some goodies for enhancing the site. In addition, WebBoard fits right into WebSite for threaded conversations and technical support. So far, so good.

Realize that these products do not run under UNIX yet, and thus do not scale as well as AIX, UNIX, or AS/400 solutions. Furthermore, you would have to craft ODBC solutions through Cold Fusion to add sales data to accounting system, and perhaps even force transaction commitments from Cold Fusion to make certain that they are fully added to the financial system. You would need a programmer familiar with SAP, PeopleSoft, or Oracle Financials to correctly make those changes. This process is not for the faint of heart or the ill-trained. Consultants with those skills are hard to find and are expensive. This aspect is something to consider in the platform selection process.

On the other hand, Mustang Software makes WildCat!, which now also includes WWW services since the release of version 5.0. Wildcat! is one of the best bulletin board systems (BBSs) available and has done most of the things that the best web servers and supplemental tools do for the Internet. Specifically, the BBS supports mailboxes (you need an E-mail server application with many web servers), threaded messages (you need a conference system like WebBoard), security that puts most of UNIX and Windows to shame, and a file archive that is functional and includes multiple lines describing each file. This format is very dated when you can see a browser list the files on an FTP site or enhance a file listing with unlimited text, pictures, and sound in the calling HTML documents. In effect, WildCat! (and other BBS servers) provides the types of services every website should have but it does not require the banks of modems (or ISDN terminal adapters) that are required for most BBSs. If only it were so easy to build the Internet BBS and have all those services.

Two significant limitations for this hybrid platform are its lack of internal connectivity for Intranet services and its lack of DNS functions; also, it does not yet support SHTTP for secure transactions. While there are other ways to activate secure transmission of information or delivery encrypted packets, the pace of web server development makes this an interesting platform only if you need to support dial-in services or are migrating from existing BBS activities to Intranet and Internet support.

Local to Host Process

The structure of a tested website should be preserved when you port that site to the ISP host. You also want to check filename compatibility, directory structures, and access rights. Although this is generally a manual and specialized task requiring a webmaster, new tools like WebMaster check links, structures, and URLs and can automatically adjust the paths and names to maintain that integrity. Try WebMaster from the CD-ROM (limited to 30 days). Alternatively, you should know how to set up a site remotely. You may build a site and need to post it on an ISP or at the client's local and live web server. This section outlines the steps necessary to move the files, set security, and assure integrity of the site. Do not forget to test the site with HTML Doctor, RxHTML, WebMapper, or Web Analyzer as a final step (before *and* after the move).

Use FTP to select and move files from a local system to the remote host. Long path names, Macintosh file formats, and full path with drive root pathnames will break on the host site. In addition, DOS, Windows 3.x, Windows95 and WindowsNT all use the "/" as a directory/subdirectory delimiter. UNIX uses the back slash, that is "\", which creates havoc with maintaining path names. You may notice that WindowsNT and Netscape Navigator are slash blind and use the forward (regular) slash interchangeably with the back slash. While you can get away with some of these sins on a local web site or as a user with a browser, the path names, the fully-specified, and file names should be normalized for ISO-9660 consistency. This means that filenames are best formed with the DOS 8.3 file name.file extent format, but in addition, only alphanumerical characters are valid. This simplifies mixed-platform development and hosting.

The trick to moving files from a local development station to a host is with the FTP protocol, and probably with a windowed FTP application such as WINFTP, as shown in Figure 3.18. You connect into the FTP server at the host site. This may be the same physical hardware as the web server, but larger host sites, such as UUNET, have hundreds of servers and some specially dedicated to FTP services. The host name is typically of the format ftp.hostname.net.

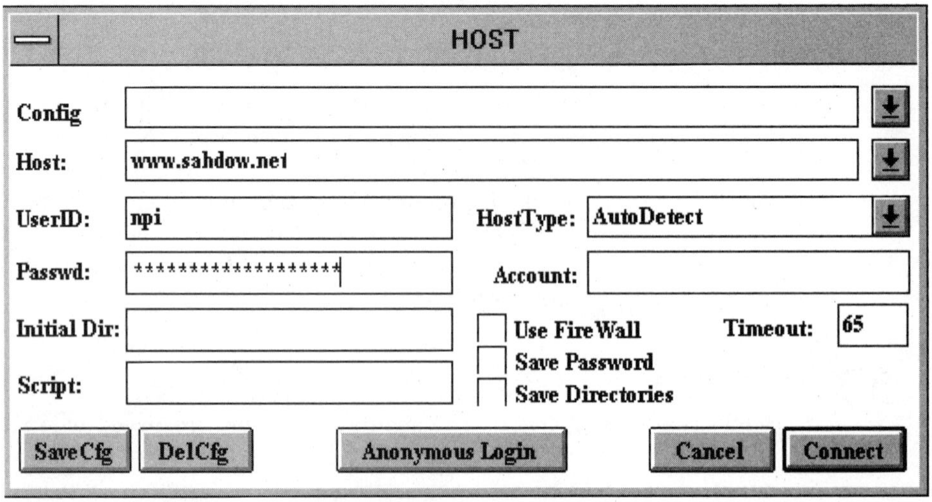

Figure 3.18 Specify the host name to move the site to the host.

Once you are connected with a password, logged into the FTP server as your user name, you will move files from the local site to the host site. If you log in anonymously, you are unlikely to have the correct security and privileges to copy files to the host site. The function is a matter of selecting files, dragging them, and dropping them into the host directory, as shown in Figure 3.19. This immediate operation may require ten seconds, but the open FTP connection for the file transfers may require minutes or hours, depending on the speed of the connection and the number of bytes to transfer. The transferred files will have file privileges of the home page administrator and at this point should not be accessible to the world or anyone with web browser at your site. If a customer goes to the site, the URL will generate an error that states that the user does not have security access to this site or alternately that the site does not exist. You need to log into the site in character mode and change the rights to the files and subdirectories. This is

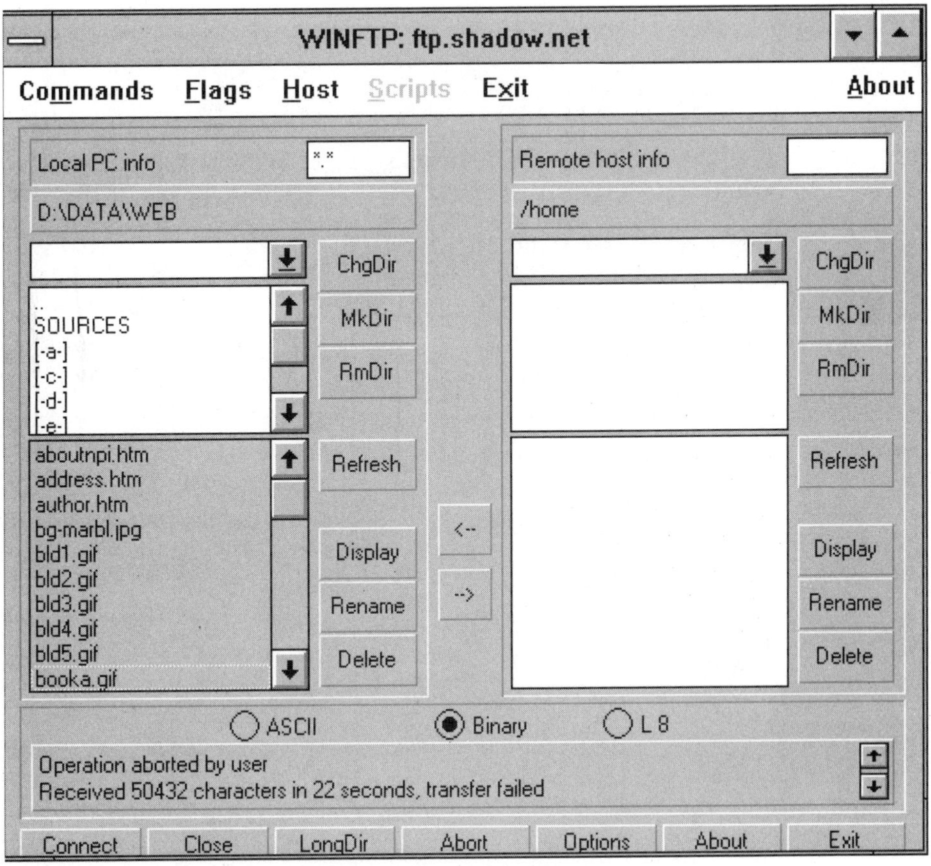

Figure 3.19 The Windows GUI makes drag-and-drop work between development stations or local testbed web servers and live ISP web sites.

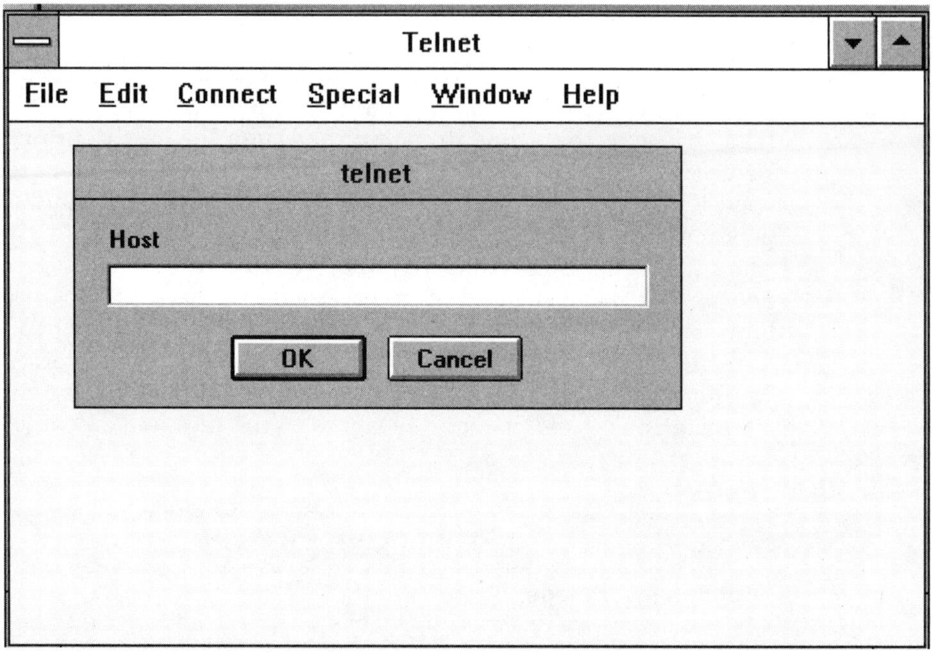

Telnet

File   Edit   Connect   Special   Window   Help

telnet

Host

OK   Cancel

Figure 3.20 You need to Telnet to the website to check and change directory and file rights for the website files.

shown with the Windows-based TELNET application in Figure 3.20. Once you are connected into the host in character mode and have a csh, bourne, or other UNIX character-based operating system shell, you have full access to the website or the file location where the website will exist. The UNIX file structure is usually designed with these salient structures as shown in Figure 3.21.

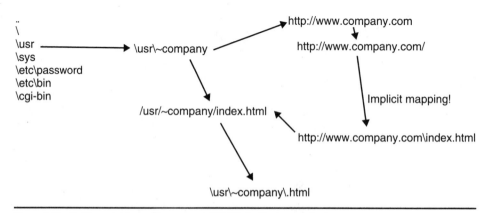

Figure 3.21 Setting rights to files using a UNIX shell command.

The ISP will have created a user directory referenced directly when you as a user log in as ~ name. The downloaded files will be in the root directory. UNIX files have three security attributes: files can be read, written, and/or executed. The attributes are exclusive, so that files could be executed but not read, or read but not executed. In addition, the security ring structure includes three levels of security, which include group, owner, and world. The system supervisor usually has complete access to all files unless the operating system includes another security layer. Make this user directory executable to the web world with this command:

```
chmod o+x~
```

Create a subdirectory under your home directory with this command:

```
mkdir .html for a directory called ".html"
```

or

```
mkdir .htm for a directory called ".htm"
```

Make this directory readable and executable to the web world with this command:

```
chmod o+rx .html
```

or

```
chmod o+rx .htm
```

You want to move all the *.html, *.htm, *.gif, and *.jpg files to the ~company\.html or ~company\.htm subdirectory. Alternatively, you could FTP the files to that subdirectory directly, assuming you created it first. The command to move files in UNIX is *mv,* as shown below:

```
mv *.htm .htm\.
```

This command allows you to move all the *.htm files into the subdirectory of the same name. You would repeat this for all other linked files so that the relative URL paths established on a local development system are correct on the UNIX host. Some sites will require a complex tree structure of subdirectories for databases, engines, and many separate layers of documents. Obviously, that structure is beyond the scope of this book because every site will have a different infrastructure to support the commerce, help support, documents, E-mail, and other activities geared to the middleware running on the host and the need for middleware file structures.

Web servers versus commerce servers

Do not make much of the differences between web servers and commerce servers because this is mostly a vendor marketing position. A web server is a file server that fulfills the HTML URL request by providing an HTML document. A commerce server is a web server that includes integrated services to simplify the construction of the cyberstore. These services *might* but not necessarily include:

- Secure transmission
- E-mail encryption
- CGI gateway support
- EPS toolkit
- Database to HTML integration toolkit
- On-line catalog builder
- Common scripts and applets

Most of the packaged deals for commerce servers represent overpriced and anemic bundles. In general, the commerce servers are ten times more expensive than comparable web servers. The most important addition is the secure HTML page function, which is available in several free and many commercial web server bundles. WebSite Pro (from O'Reilly) is twice as expensive as the basic WebSite product. It also includes a subset of Cold Fusion database middleware. Included tools such as Mosaic and HotDog are nice additions, but are not really important in the greater integration efforts. However, if you do plan to take credit cards via Internet, you will need the secure page function.

If you plan to distribute intellectual property by Internet (pay-per-view documents or software), you will need a distribution application such as 20/20 or Cryptolopes, which encrypts a password inside a mail message and distributes an encrypted file that can be opened by the password. This procedure is discussed in greater detail in the Electronic Software Distribution section of Chapter 4. Whatever your cyberstore needs, define them clearly and pick the packages most applicable or integrate what you need.

Site Development Platform Effects

Little things become very important in site development. For example, if you create links under a UNIX or Windows environment supporting long file names, web page files are likely to be named "NPI MASTER HTML HOME PAGE.HTML" and include links to other pages like this:

```
<IMG SRC="button.gif" ALIGN="BOTTOM"><A HREF="npi master home page.html">NPI
home Page</A>
```

Although this is perfectly correct, you can create problems for everyone when the file names are converted to 8.3 file names. The file name is likely to become "NPI~.HTM," which is no longer referenced by the tag within the "NPI MASTER HTML HOME PAGE.HTML" file also renamed to something like "NPI~1.HTM." Although this appears to users as broken links, it really indicates platform and operating system differences. What can really be worse is when long path names such as "HTML PAGE 1 in progress.HTML" and "HTML PAGE 1 live.HTML" both become "PAGE1.HTML" either as file names or tagged references. This can create infinite loops in the home pages that drive users crazy and give webmasters fits trying to figure out the intended hierarchy and sequences of pages. If a user has a Windows 3.1 16-bit tool such as WebWhacker, Grab-a-site, and other site upload utilities and is using the DOS file system, files uploaded from a Macintosh, Windows95, UNIX, WindowsNT, and AIX webserver are likely to be broken on the user's machine because of file-naming convention differences. Be thoughtful and sustain simple file-naming conventions even for users who grab your entire site . . . after all, they will be browsing it offline and that is the idea of the site after all.

Conclusion

This chapter described the practical problems of web server platform selection and subtle integration issues. The choice of the website platform is a profound decision with significant ramifications for the successful design, implementation, integration, customer usage, and maintenance of the cyberstore. As shown, the website platform is not a monolithic decision; not only is the cyberstore platform an operating system to support a web server, it also will necessarily include SSL, SHTTP, and/or other encryption tools; dynamic database-to-HTML conversion electronic payment methods; E-mail; and threaded BBS-like conversation or chat services. In addition, it will serve as the integration spearhead for point-of-sales financial accounting and tracking. Chapter 4 illustrates these assertions and shows the practical implementation issues and the techniques for building the cyberstore.

Service Implementation

Introduction

This chapter outlines the implementation issues for coding, implementing, and maintaining a commercial website and fully integrated cyberstore. The key topics raised in this chapter include budgetary issues for site development, domain registration, Internet connectivity, local and hosted site selections, legal implications and ramifications for the developers and for the site as an entity, HyperText Markup Language (HTML) creation, forms creation, database integration, and security concerns. This chapter is complete with technical details that you need to know to succeed in building a successful cyberstore, as well as the practical steps to "go live" with your cyberstore.

Budgeting Site Development

This section is an afterthought, but its introductory position in this chapter accentuates my view of its true importance. Site development and service implementation are an application development project similar in all respects to any in-house software development or shrink-wrapped product development. If there are differences, they are manifest in that the end product is delivery of information and dynamic transaction processing and in the complexity of the integration process. Website development is a function of hardware, software, telecommunications connections, site hosting services, web development, process integration, and web page design.

Since it is possible to host a local web server and build a minimal site without the need for any hardware (other than a development platform and even that can be the Internet Service Provider [ISP] host) the major investments are labor. If you recall from Chapter 2, I can build a small commercial website that costs a client about $40,000 running on an ISP host. This compares with an installation of a local site and server with T-1 connection for about $80,000. Commercial database integration with workflow planning begins at $150,000. It is not the cost of the tools or the complexity of building a dynamic database-to-HTML connection, but rather the need to craft a workflow and all the applets to perform the full range of point-of-sales (POS) operations.

If you believe the Forester and IDC estimates and surveys, some of the ad agencies and other major players are building sites that begin at $1,300,000 with annual support costs roughly equivalent to that. I estimate that in-house development and development costs for most customers break down into the percentages shown in Figure 4.1.

For example, a low-end web server (including hardware, software, and security) costs about $4,500 installed. The Integrated Services Digital Network (ISDN) connection with the ISP dedicated port will cost about $400 per month, whereas a faster T-1 connection will cost about $1,500 per month. A low-end financial accounting package with the appropriate developer's toolkit to simplify transaction process integration runs from $600 to $6,800. Mid-range software and developer's extensions cost from $18,000 to $38,000, whereas something like an SAP, PeopleWare, or Oracle Financial setup begins at $120,000, plus another $12,000 for the development toolkits. In addition, if you foresee the need for such high-end accounting packages or your organization is already running such an operation, web operations will require separate facilities to support high-end DBMS applications. A mid-range server costs about $12,000 with all the backup and support paraphernalia, while a Redundant Array of Inexpensive Disks (RAID) or clustered configuration adds from $8,000 to $40,000. If you foresee the need for 7×24 reliability, AIX, VAX, SGI, Novell SFT, and some of the Solaris hardware and software add-ins start at $3,000 and can add up to $100,000. The

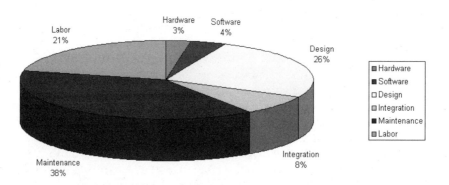

Figure 4.1 Percentage costs for website implementation.

total cost is a function of scale and the acceptable time allowed for a fail-safe cutover.

Planning

Websites should appear as free-form sculptures, but they should be planned in detail in advance, with a full accounting of construction costs, risk assessments, and, of course, some estimation of the financial return on investment (ROI) to the organization. This requires planning tools, including spreadsheets, database designers, a story board for the site concept and particularly to define the paths a customer can take through a site, as well as source code control for middleware, web pages, CGI code, and all security templates and keys.

Planning tools are outstanding and will improve the odds that your cyber-store will succeed. These tools require a commitment in terms of effort to learn them and then to integrate them into your development environment. Although there is an initial negative payback, if you can jump that hurdle, the resulting payback is hundreds of percent. The biggest hurdle I saw was really in the design phase: scoping out projects; understanding the integration of tools, services, and functions for the overall website; and matching a design with the right business strategy. I think the problems that kill projects really occur before implementation begins. My website development joke I give at presentations is a derivative of my application development failure joke. Basically, development failure is designed into the process within the initial day of the project, but unfortunately the managers and developers do not recognize the cause of the failure until months have elapsed. While it is possible to ameliorate many development problems with more money, more people, and performance optimization, these last-minute fixes represent Band-Aids for massive structural damages. Such damages are really only fixable during the initial design process when strategies, goals, and workflows are discussed. In as much as website development is a technical challenge, many of the fundamental design choices are business or organizational decisions.

If you want a metaphor, web designers who take the long, high road and lack the tools, experience, sponsorship, strategic input, and fighting spirit will fail to complete the task. The designers should have taken the low road and used project management tools, database designers, and Rapid Application Design (RAD) tools. Most likely, it will take from 6 to 18 months to create a website, but "web development time" allows mere weeks or a couple of months at most to go from concept to live public viewing. This time frame is possible (and has been demonstrated by many organizations) if you set clear goals, refrain from surfing the net for better ideas, and stick within a narrow scope. Create a plan. Stick to the plan. The plan is your success factor.

On the other hand, most of the other commercial developers I know and have talked with about HTML and web-oriented database tools (especially Java, JavaScript, and VBScript) all complained about the team development problems that occurred as they staffed up to handle the increasing requirements for a commercial website and to deal with integrated transaction processing workflow. Code gets lost or overwritten with various Common Gateway Interface (CGI) libraries, it becomes absurdly difficult to test, and management overhead grows faster than the size of the team. New team members create the most havoc, because every team has a culture and every application has a style particular to its primary designer and developer. Plus, code design and development must integrate into another structure predicated by HTML layers, the cyberstore flow, and reasonable scripts defining a sales process. Many organizations rapidly integrate process utility tools such as version control, source code control, bug tracking, and automated testing scripts after the first serious failure.

Source code control (SCC) is available specifically for web development, but almost any SCC will work just fine. That type of failure is the wake-up call to do something. Managers at some organizations wait until that wake-up call is the Klaxon voice of an angry boss insisting that they had better do something to get the website up and running . . . or consider looking for another job.

When they assessed the benefits to the bottom line, managers of all organizations that used tools said that they paid for themselves within a month or six months when they tallied the fully burdened human and organizational costs of the new tools. More complex tools, like entity-relationship diagrammers, database designers, and database controls, met with mixed reviews. However, consider the importance of database design tools since most cyberstores will require connectivity to Database Management Systems (DBMSs), which are very useful for mapping structures of preexisting databases that are part of POS and other financial accounting systems. These specialized tools have a learning curve significantly higher than that of the process utilities. In some cases, these "metatools" require "metaknowledge" about programming and application design that just do not fit the culture of the organization or the concept of website implementation. When they do work it is usually because there is an individual behind the process driving it—someone perhaps more interested in the quality of the process than in the end results. Furthermore, the cost is high for the first project, but less for subsequent ones, which usually works out better for well-staffed organizations than Spartan ones, or for consultants and agencies building sites for clients.

An idea is not sufficient to champion a web project. If you want buy-in, you need to present a proposal that includes risks, finances, people for the team, resources, and time frames. The most effective tools for this process include design specification tools, a project management tool, and a financial spreadsheet. It is possible to use a word processor and a spreadsheet for all aspects of this process; however, larger projects typically incur greater costs, involve more people, and have critical paths that are not easily tracked by simple tools. Furthermore, success is more likely with complex projects when you can track incremental and midpoint events with a time line.

Planning is critical with shortened business cycles. Products changed over decades in the early part of this century. Note that change is in cycles of 6 to 18 months—or the hectic 2 to 6 weeks typical for the website project. Product development goals should correspond to this short cycle and be carefully tracked since an overrun of 2 weeks to refine database integration or convert a template CGI applet into a working one represents an overrun of 33 to 100 percent. Although two weeks may seem insignificant, the overrun can be serious for small clients, damaging to large clients who want to establish a presence to match other advertising programs, and very costly for reputations.

Planning begins with an assessment of user requirements and project goals. Often this information is listed in a document created in a word processor. Answer the questions, What do users want? and What do users need? Temper this with management and strategic information about the goals for the project. The goals should be very specific and measurable. You do not want to simply make something "better" or "faster." You want to "increase transactional processing time by 30 percent" or "lower labor content with workflow integration and increase data accuracy by 40 percent." Those goals are specific and measurable. Clearly, the goals must fit the technology and the technology must be available to successfully complete the task. For this reason, this book is about showing how trivial some types of workflow integration are to implement, and how to create modules that can stand apart from the core application.

Examples include credit card on-line transaction processing, and report generation. Electronic Data Interchange (EDI), which is used by large retailers and manufacturers is also included, because EDI may be the preferred method for financial remuneration for Internet-based transactions. Figure 4.2 details

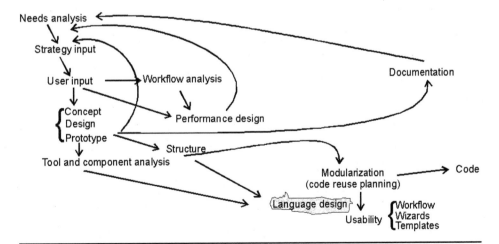

Figure 4.2 Determining application requirements and performance strategic assessments, and doing the necessary development planning is an involved and iterative process.

the steps required to map requirements to technology with quantifiable strategic goals.

You might prioritize requirements and goals, numbering each from 1 to 10 in terms of importance, complexity, strategic value, and resource requirements. You might note that documentation weighs in heavily at this stage because good documentation becomes a design tool for subsequent steps, and can be recycled later to prepare demonstrations and actual end-user documentation. There are very few planning tools that will help you create systems specifications. Each cyberstore integration project and complex workflow automation endeavor is different from every other one. You might find that an outliner can be helpful to prioritize needs and work forward from partial concepts to implementable functions (see Figure 4.3).

When you have a simple prototype for demonstration, you can create a requirement specification, functional specification, design specification, and testing procedure, and both demonstration collateral and end-user documentation. Most organizations save documentation for the middle or end of a project.

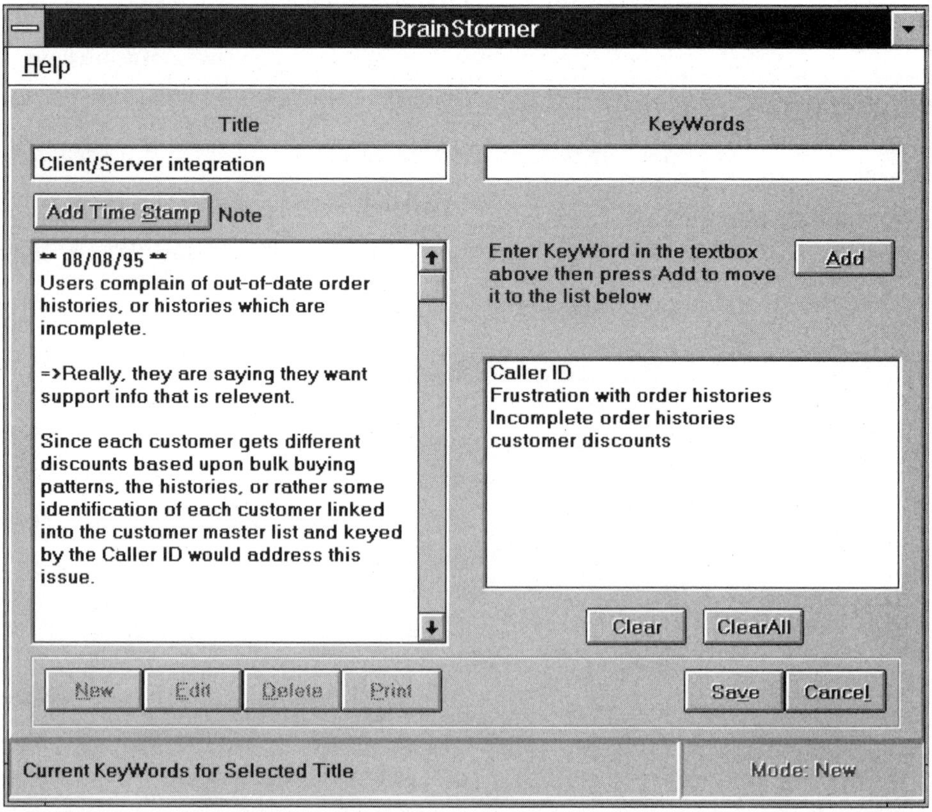

Figure 4.3 An outline tool with keywords (and relational or item linkage) provides a means to organize and prioritize functional specifications and strategic goals.

First, the confidence in project success usually just isn't there until some application code is actually running and working. Second, resources are not available for this part until later. Third, there often is nothing a writer can use to document until that running, working version exists. However, the documentation process is usually the step where workflow disasters are discovered, because purpose and process are actually defined step-by-step. This really needs to occur earlier in the development cycle.

The most important step in the planning process is to convert the designs into a project plan. Elsewhere I have said that a word processor or a spreadsheet (or even a plain paper notepad) is a sufficient tool for small projects. If you have integrated Word, Excel, Access, and the other parts of the Microsoft Office Suite, you really have all the tools you need. When projects have significant resource requirements, multiple developers, dependencies, necessary milestones, and critical paths, you need a more sophisticated project management tool. The downside is that a manager can spend all his or her time just updating information for this tool. Instead of the manager controlling the project, the project management tool controls the manager and adds a level of fear and panic to all team members. Constant status information is important, but too much of it is used against people. However, this combination spreadsheet, schedule, resource leveling, and Gantt chart are very effective as tools to detail the flow of the development process, estimate resource requirements, track budget and progress, and uncover delays or other fundamental problems (see Figure 4.4).

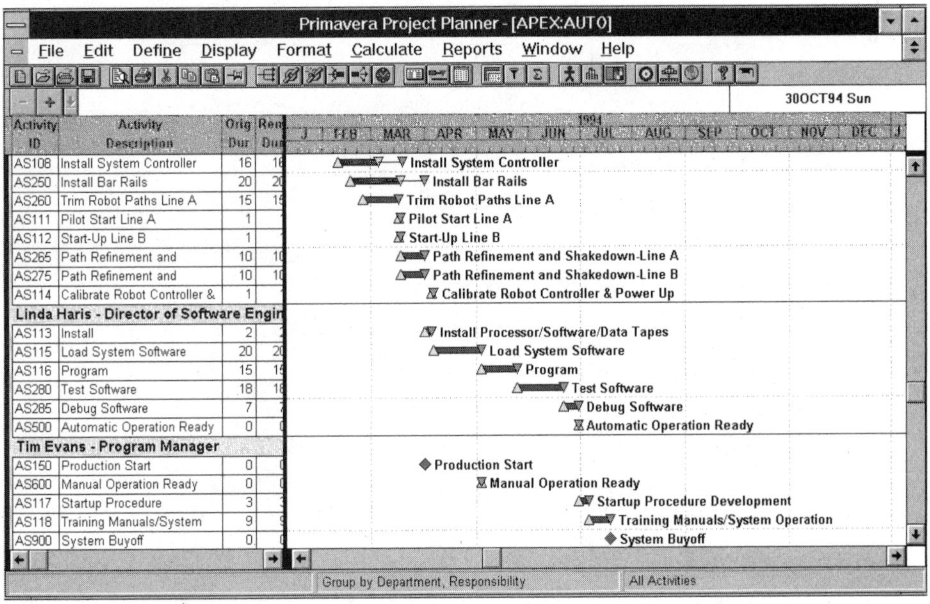

Figure 4.4 Project management processing software code development critical path.

Project planning is a game of estimation. It is not a science, and typically there isn't enough prior development information to create accurate forecasts. Many corporate development teams have lots of experience with COBOL, Job Control Language (JCL), ReportSmith, and other host-based tools, while product marketing or press groups have experience with outside agencies, story boarding techniques, and demographics database, but little hands-on experience with website development requirements. A project management tool partitions the project into discrete activities that can be further subdivided into unique steps. Each step follows other steps and has a resource requirement in terms of people, equipment, software, time, and support facilities. All projects have fixed resources. Every person on the team has a different skill set, but only up to 20 hours available per day for working. A tool like Project, Time Line, Milestones, CheckPoint, or Project Manage levels resource requirements and checks so that you do not overcommit to the project (see Figure 4.5).

A project management tool lets you adjust your estimates as you go. For example, if one team member is ahead on progress by 20 percent, but another is hopelessly behind by at least 50 percent, you can adjust your estimates of resources and completion time based on the accelerated pace of one person and the slippage by the other. Figure 4.6 is a screen shot from Primavera Project Planner (P3), showing how we all would like to see our projections match the actual results.

If you are uncomfortable or unwilling to implement a full project management tool, try something like Project KickStart, which is a cross between a

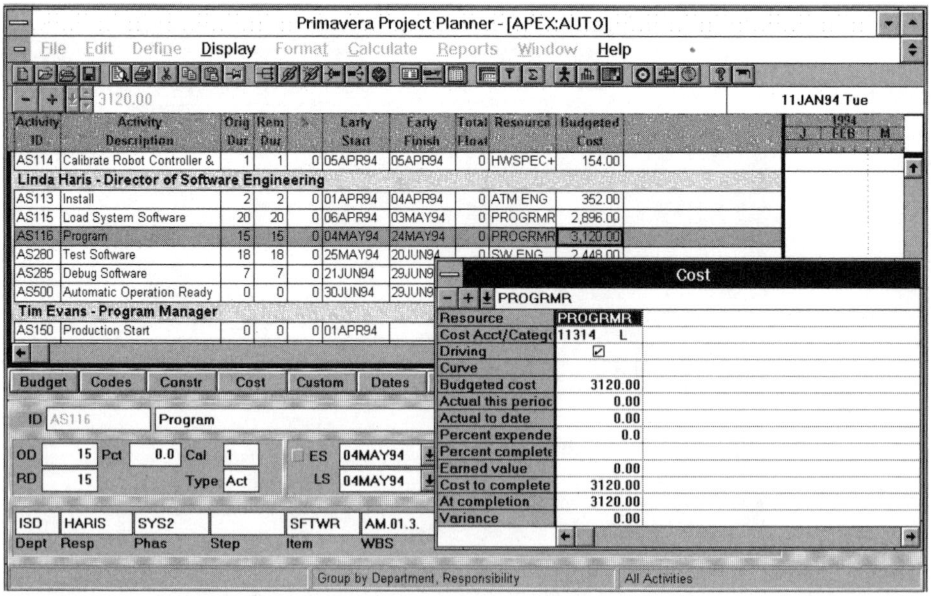

Figure 4.5 Project management showing site dates and the costs associated with that programmer.

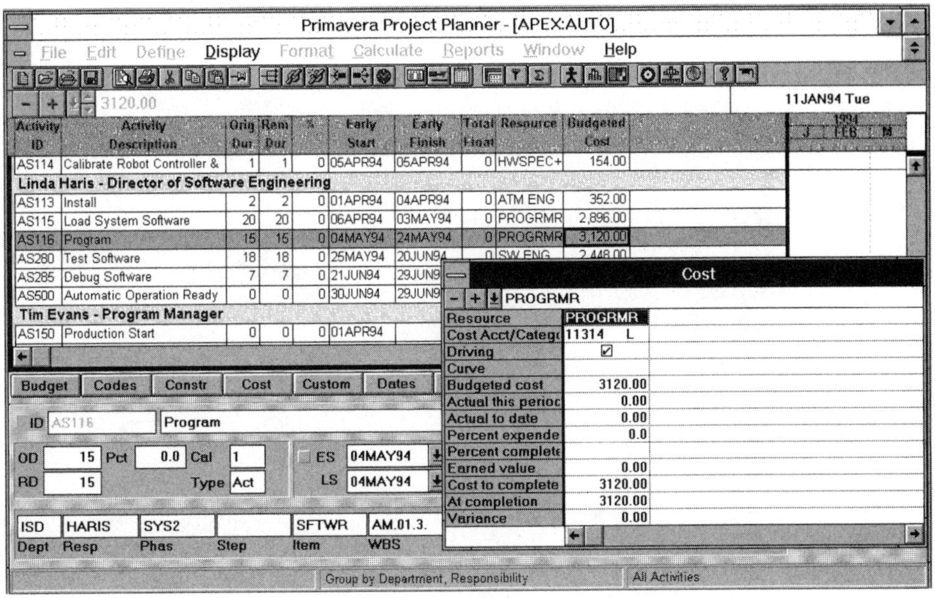

Figure 4.6 A programming task budget summary, on time and on budget. If only it could be true, and later maintenance and upgrades (after deployment) did not add to the budget and resource requirements.

brainstormer or outliner and a project management tool. It pushes you to prioritize your project goals, strategies, and technical issues in terms of tangible steps (see Figure 4.7).

If you notice, the goals, strategy, phases, and obstacle libraries represent stock phases and starting points for times when you cannot verbalize the planning process. They are very much aimed at action-oriented phases and steps. Since software projects often fail due to obstacles never considered, Project KickStart also encourages you to define the possible problems. There is no writer's block here, as the developers have included lists of many possible problems you are likely to face. Figure 4.8 shows some hurdles you will likely encounter in upgrading to Windows 95 to use tools like Visual Web.

The problem with many metatools is that they stop short of completing the task. While an outliner gives you an outline that might go nowhere, or a brainstorming tool creates linked lists of ideas that still might go nowhere, at a minimum, Project KickStart gives you a hierarchical list of phases and steps within each phase with basic resource linkages that you can import into MS Project, or P3 and Timeline (because these support data exchange through DDE, OLE, or comparable file formats; see Figure 4.9).

When all is said and done, the website project plan is crucial to the planning process. Obviously, you can use it for budgeting, but most importantly it is the roadmap for determining where the project is between the start and the end. You need this information if you are to adjust the functional specification and

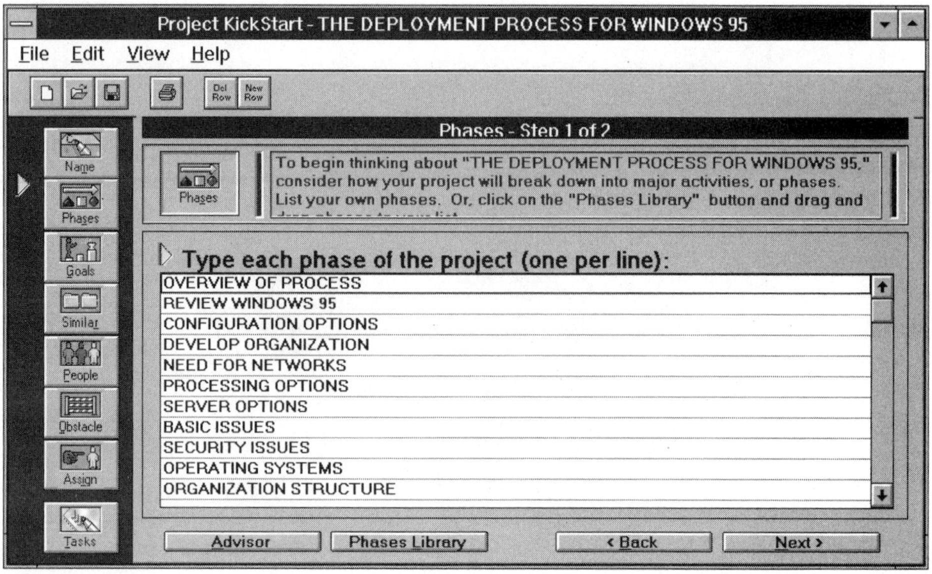

Figure 4.7 Project KickStart is a pre-project manager or outlining tool for organizing thoughts about a complex development project.

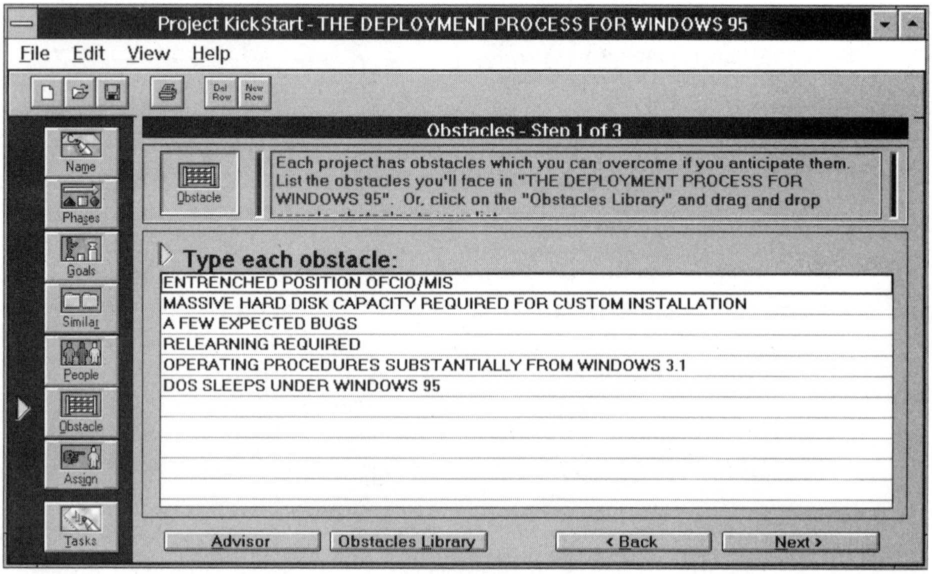

Figure 4.8 KickStart helps you define possible obstacles and prioritize them.

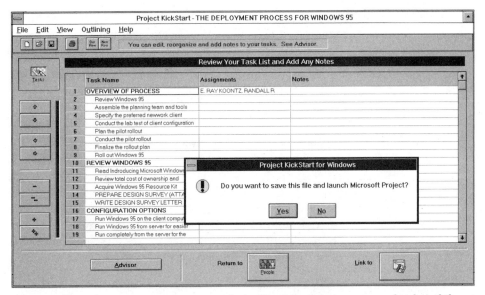

Figure 4.9 Not only can you organize your project without the learning curve and technical threat of a full project management tool, you can also export the hierarchical outline into MS Project.

remove features to hit a window of opportunity (likely) or add features because you have uncommitted resources available (unlikely). More likely, planning helps you assess your need to add new people, what the likely learning curve will be for those team members, and also how new development tools will alter your completion time.

Domain Registration

Every website needs a unique name. Duplicate addresses are not allowed. The name can be as obscure as http://members.oal.com.royalef/gifanim.htm or as simple as GTE.COM. Most names are not case sensitive, but are character-position-, and port-dependent. Since imprinting is as old as the Babylonians, there must be a good reason for it. Imprinting is now called *brand marketing, product name recognition, trademarks, service marks, copyrights,* and *patents.* Although it is important for physical products, it is equally important (if not more so) for intangible Internet sites. If you host a site yourself with local hardware or post a site on an Internet Service Provider (ISP), you are likely to have an obscure address such as www.shadow.net/~npi. This says Network Performance Institute (NPI) is a user on Shadow Information's ISP site as the user named "npi." However, WWW.NETWORKPERF.COM also maps into this local path name. Names are the jurisdiction of the Internet Network Information Center (InterNIC). Each name must be unique, and the assignment is called a *domain name.* A domain name can be acquired for a fee from InterNIC, but with a considerable amount of paperwork, hassling, and configuration. Figure on two or three passes before the name is correctly established with a top-level domain (TLD) server with the correct IP address and E-mail and contact information. A TLD server is one of the main Internet sources for matching domain names with actual IP addresses.

By the way, a domain name can map to a range of IP addresses with CIDR block request. This can be useful for larger organizations supporting WWW, FTP, WAIS, Gopher, and cyberstore activities and may also have a busy outbound load from the organization to the Internet. This is called a class B or class C license, and is useful if your organization is a big Internet site.

The application for a domain name is not complicated. Forms and information are included on the CD-ROM as text files (for example, DOMAIN.TXT) or go to the InterNIC site. The CD-ROM includes forms and instructions for domain names, class licenses, and CIDR block registrations. Fill out the forms and submit them by E-mail. An ISP may charge from $75 to $150 to perform this simple task for you. When InterNIC accepts the name and assigns it to you, you need to pay $100 for the first two years ($50 per year after year two) to retain this name.

Note that the InterNIC assigns domain names on a first-come/first-served basis, so that it might be possible (and was very easy in the past) to register www.bugsbunny.com or www.bugsbunny.net with the InterNIC for use on a TLD. Warner Brothers probably holds the trademark and rights to Bugs Bunny. However, Network Solutions, Inc. (NSI) now provides the commercial registration of .com domain names and its policy since November 1995 has been to respect preexisting registered trademarks and refuse, reclaim, and return misappropriated uses to the trademark holder. Since capitalization is often a part of trademarks (such as NBC or IBM), and because www.ibm.com, www.IBM.COM, and even www.IbM.cOm map through the TLD to the same IP numerical address because domain names are case insensitive, some issues remain inconclusive. Legal briefs are available at *http://www.mids.org/legal*.

Network Solutions, Inc. is the billing service organization for InterNIC, and they have been overwhelmed by and unable to adequately handle the growth in registrations. You will still need an ISP to broker a connection from your local site and a telecommunication connection or hosted site at the ISP, or an LEC to provide T-1, T-3, SMDS, or ATM connections to the Internet backbone. Figure 4.10 shows the main page of the InterNIC site.

Go to *http://rs.internic.net/cgi-bin/whois* and type in the name you would like to register. If the name is available, you can sign up then and there. While there is a limit of 30 characters (standard keyboard values allowed with some exceptions) for the domain name, shorter names are probably better. This is a function of the two-tier domain name service limitation and also the name length limitation for most host names. There are prefaces that include *rs, www, home,* and many others. Additionally, there is an extent in the domain name. Examples include *.edu, .gov, .mil, .net, .com,* and *.bus.* Foreign sites often include a country code after the extent. The .edu prefix is reserved

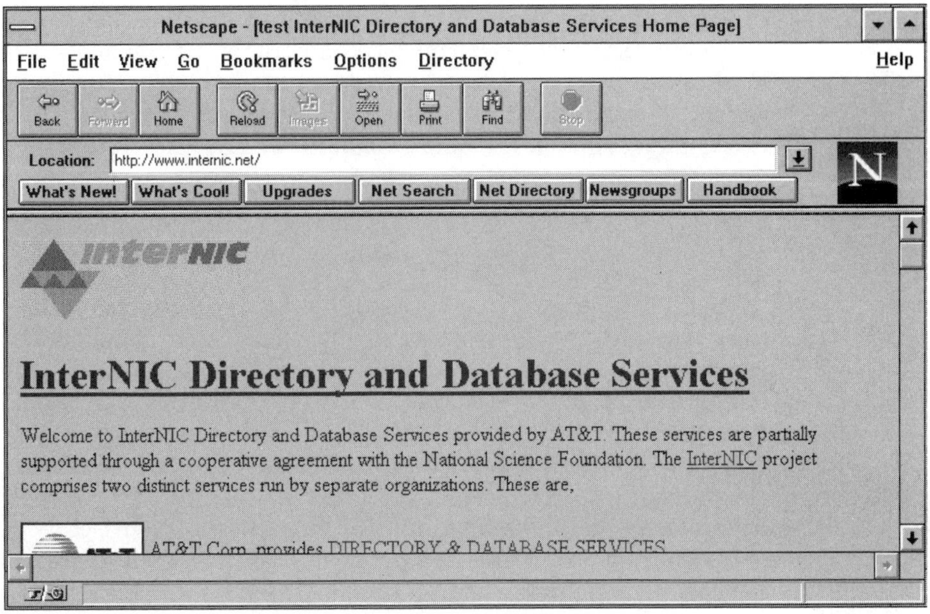

Figure 4.10 The main site for InterNIC information and registration.

for educational institutions, .gov for governmental groups as initially designated by the IETF when the Internet was first established, *.net* for ISPs, and *.com* for commercial sites. Since the commercial domain space is nearly full, *.bus* has been designated for more expansion sites. However, before you jump for this new suffix realize it has some serious limitations. Not all firewalls, routers, and other devices or ISPs will allow information to map and pass through this unusual address (yet). A site in Australia may be designated as www.anu.*edu.au* to distinguish it as an educational university.

If you are a penny-pincher, you can register a name in the *us* domain for free. The format will look like "www.companyname.state.us", and the registration is free. You can obtain the details from *www.isi.edu/in-notes/usdnr*. Note that some firewalls and routers will filter out commercial sites and cyberstores if they are not set to accept Uniform Resource Locators (URLs) in this format. That is the downside for saving $50 per year for owning a more dependable and ordinary domain name.

There are a couple of rules for domain names. First, the name must be unique. It cannot previously have been registered and still be in use. Second, it cannot be a trademark or other registered device or name. While there has been a thriving blackmail business in registering important names or competitors' names, InterNIC will not defend your misuse and you may forfeit the filing and initial fees. For the record, you can register a copyrighted name or trademark, or service mark whether you or your organization has rights to it or not, but the burden falls on you or your organization to defend the use of that name with NSI. Part of the name becomes the domain name, and that part is protected by a copyright, trademark, or service mark. However, the domain name itself (which is a construct of web addressing and other names) cannot be copyrighted, trademarked, or protected by a service mark; that entire name itself is in the public domain. The InterNIC states:

"Registering a domain name does not confer any legal rights to that name and any disputes between parties over rights to use that name are to be settled between contending parties using normal legal methods."

This is further described by the IETF RFC 1591, which is included in its entirety on the CD-ROM. In fact, misuse of registered and trademarked names can be prosecuted under various local and federal statutes. Some misuse falls under international laws promulgated by the Berne Convention.

Legal Limitations

The Internet is a minefield of legal hurdles and surprises. A cyberstore that provides transaction processing with a public clientele represents a minefield of city, county, province, interstate, U.S. federal, and international laws. You will likely cross paths with local departments of revenue, tax bureaus, and the Internal Revenue Service (IRS). Because the Internet is a new metaphor, perhaps similar to catalog sales, those laws are most similar and pertinent. Even if you are already taking payment by credit card and shipping merchandise, you still need to check with your attorney because there are always surprises with new technologies, businesses lacking "local" presence, and local business laws.

A cyberstore's tax liability may be local, state, and federal. Taxes include sales taxes, excise taxes, property taxes, taxes on cash balances and inventories, payroll taxes, unemployment taxes, and insurance. There are other local, state, or federal fees (not really taxes), but they have the same effect as taxes. Fees include local services, business registration certificates, licenses, and site inspections (for fire safety and other building code issues). Local, state, and federal agencies use the following factors when determining the imposition of such fees and taxes:

- Jurisdiction
- Tax base
- Source
- Rate

The jurisdiction is the identification of the state or county that has the legal right to levy taxes and fees. The tax base is the definition of what products, services, or property are taxable and which might be exempt from taxation. The source defines the process and source of taxable revenue and property. The rate or taxation structure defines the fees and percentage or fixed rates applied to the tax base and source revenue for taxation purposes. I mention these legalistic details because many definitions, primarily of the cyberstore location and whether it really transacts business, do not fall within the taxable juridiction. It can be a profitable or an expensive legal fight. Large cyberstore operations could benefit substantially from fighting for jurisdictional exemptions. There are no clear-cut standards or legal rulings, or an obvious direction for the cyberstore taxation question.

For example, one up-and-coming cyberstore, called Auto-By-Tel, listed automobiles for sale with classified advertising. Web surfers who identified a car they wanted more information about and a location to see it would leave an E-mail message. This provided the mechanism for brokering the deal. The advertisements were both text-based and included snapshots of vehicles. The advertising itself was free, but the referral to the owner or commercial used car dealers was charged on a per referral basis. No other fees were paid.

Advertisements were pulled when a vehicle was sold to maintain currency for the site. However, lawyers for the Motor Vehicle Division of the Texas Department of Transportation issued an edict to desist for violating an obscure state law because a selling referral "holds the organization out to be a broker" and the Chicago company lacked a brokership site and license in that state.

The issue is not so much that the Auto-By-Tel lacked these facilities and a license, but rather that entrenched businesses will try to prevent competition from outside organizations that can cut transaction costs from $307 per vehicle to $25. While Auto-By-Tel can acquire a small, already licensed organization to meet Texas laws, and has in fact done this, this $368 million per *month* organization can afford that small expense. However, many on-line sites cannot afford it. Furthermore, this complaint is only the first round as attorneys are paid in advance to defend merchandisers selling high markup and high transaction cost products from out-of-town cyberstores and international companies. A lot is at stake as businesses with high fixed costs, large physical inventories, expensive sales personnel, and costly transaction fees are undercut by more efficient paper-pushing cyberstore operations. Although this seems most relevant for consumer retail sales, I see the largest opportunity undercutting business-to-business VARs, resellers, brokers, and gray marketers.

In addition, there is a confusing array of sales (value-added) tax laws for interstate, international, and credit card sales. The U.S. Supreme Court ruled several years ago that credit card sales are subject to a state sales tax if the organization has a physical presence in the state of the sale; the legal terminology is a "substantial nexus." It is not clear what that means for a cyberstore that lacks anything but a logical presence and a single physical disk presence that can be anywhere on earth or soon even in orbit and perhaps beyond the jurisdictions of any authority. Some states, in lieu of protracted legal battles with the Supreme Court and with mail-order businesses, have negotiated consent decrees with the businesses directly so that they collect taxes for the state. Since many states assess an ad valorem tax or business assets tax, sales taxes are effectively assessed on business property. This has a bearing on corporations buying inventory and products through cyberstores because the burden is placed on the buyer to pay local state taxes on the yearly value of cyberstore purchases. Since this is true for all productive assets uniformly, the cyberstore impact is a red herring.

European value-added taxes are applied to every sale at every step in the value chain, and taxes are to be paid to the appropriate countries. This gets very complex, especially when defining locations, since a cyberstore may not have one; when it is difficult to classify whether an organization has a physical presence in a particular location; sales, shipping, website design may be accomplished in several different places; and ISP access is typically local. Countries such as Guyana and the Cayman Islands, and other tax havens, are trying to encourage cyberstores to set up shop in their countries to elude these local tax and legal hurdles. This may be as simple as establishing a legal business incorporation and a tie-line to the Internet backbone from these countries. These tax and license issues will become the weapon of choice by entrenched organizations to fight the introduction and success of cyberstores.

Local taxes can buffet the cyberstore. Tacoma, Washington has levied a 6 percent tax on gross revenues of any firm providing Internet connections in that city. Fort Collins, Colorado assessed Internet service providers with a 3 percent value added tax. The state of Florida will impose similar measures beginning in February 1997, pending legal review of taxation on enhanced interstate services. The real division with these local levies is that they place burdens on locally-based businesses that do not need a local presence because of the telecommunications infrastructure. This results in a shift to tax-free locations, even international ones, as local municipalities assess taxes on services and pass along tax increases to customers. Large customers are likely to move to other locations and create alternatives to bypass these fees. I suggest the NASA space station as soon as possible. That may be funny, but there is significant truth and there will be a forthcoming flood of opportunity and legal wrangling when orbital platforms for cyberstores (not just laser weapons and cruise missiles) become viable. It might just be worth the $500,000,000 to buy a launch site on an Ariane rocket or space shuttle payload.

Ownership of site and materials

Ownership encompasses patents, trademarks, services marks, and copyrights. All these source ownership stipulations may be in effect and enforced (by the respective owners) on the Internet. When employees in an organization create a website, a copyright is automatically created. The creator then owns the copyright, and since employees are bound to the employer, the Berne Convention copyright rules provide an automatic transfer of the material to the employer. However, when an organization pays an outside consultant, freelance artist, graphics agency, or advertising affiliate to create the site or any part of it, the outsourced party owns the copyrights to the content it created and the rights to your site. If an outside agency (by this I mean any external individual, organization, or entity) registered your domain name on your behalf, they may own it. That is the law! A written work-for-hire agreement should stipulate that the contracting organization gets the copyrights and the sources for a website. Sources that reference libraries (such as Perl or CGI libraries) should be transferable to you as part of the contract and with an additional fee if necessary to purchase a usable copy of these libraries. If you are building a cyberstore and you subcontract the work and want to reuse it, rework it, or include it in other materials, you want to hold all rights to that work and all rights to materials that make it work. The ownership to that work and the content should be negotiated up front. Rights to content are partitioned by media. You typically want "press rights, book rights, and electronic rights in all known formats of media and hereafter deployed."

There is a significant tension, particularly on the Internet, between the exploitation and consumption of intellectual property with its commercial and private ownership rights of its creator. This is most evident with the cyberstore concept and the increasing interest in pay-per-view information using micromoney and electronic software distribution methods. This tension is bound to increase despite the current copyright laws and the forthcoming modifications to the field of intellectual property rights. I suggest you create a folder labeled "Intellectual Property" or "Copyright Filings" and track all the new creations you make with the U.S. Copyright Office Form TX submissions and all the clippings and articles that pass your desk on the subject. This combination will not only remind you of the value of your work, but also of how to stay out of jail for free. For example, here is the copyright notice (Figure 4.11) for the L. L. Bean website; it is clear where they stand, what belongs to the organization, and how they are likely to respond if their ownership is infringed.

Perhaps the most significant issue for the commercial website operation and cyberstore are the liabilities of *vicarious* copyright infringement and *contributory* infringement. This means that your site is liable for using, showing, or distributing copyrighted material submitted by others or acquired under the as-

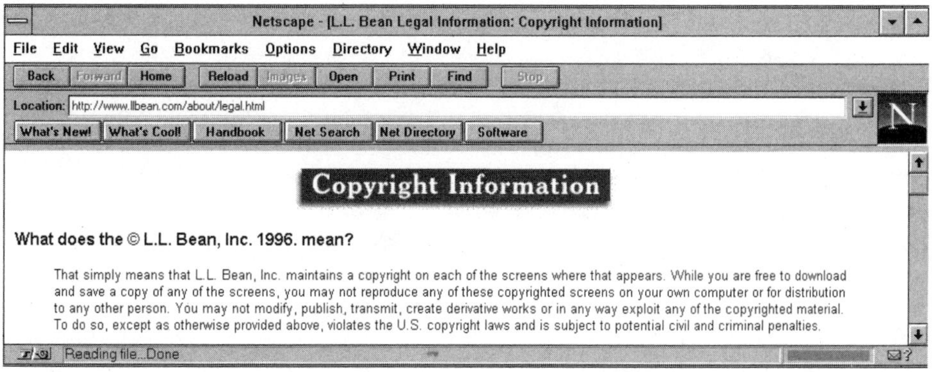

Figure 4.11   A very clear and strong statement of copyright ownership.

sumption that it belonged to the public domain when it remained a true copyright by the owner. In this case, ignorance is not bliss, and the operative bottom line might be to use only what your organization creates or commissions.

The Copyright Protection Act of 1995 (still pending ratification by Congress as of this printing) strengthens some of the rules concerning Internet distribution and ownership for your benefit and protection from infringement. Nevertheless, under the current Berne Convention rules (which are international in scope) the *absence* of a copyright notice does not mean the material is *not* protected by copyright. Under U.S. law and the Berne Convention, any original work in a tangible medium is *automatically* protected whether a filing is submitted to the U.S. Copyright Office or other national or international registration bureaus. Specifically, the copyright owner has exclusive right to transmit copyrighted material on-line. Libraries can use transmitted materials. It thus becomes (more) illegal to alter or remove copyright identification from an electronic document.

Reuse of preexisting content

You should always assume that material is copyrighted and someone or some organization retains that copyright. Material on the Internet and specifically on a website is copyrighted by default unless the site specifies that the material is in the public domain. Do not assume that a lack of a copyright notice gives you permission to use the material. The law does not require a copyright notice, although the power to litigate misuse of copyright materials is enhanced by a formal notice. Anything published before 1922 is in the public domain, with some exceptions; these include works for hire and many books for which ownership is held in trust by estates of the author.

You can reuse public domain materials, but you need indications that they are public domain property. Some images I captured from websites marked as being in the public domain were indicated as copyrights of specific people at other sites. Usage was granted by specific permission, by written permission, for noncommercial uses, and with other limitations. Be careful what you recycle. You can also reuse copyrighted materials with the copyright holder's permission. Written permission with a handwritten signature is best. E-mail response, even with a certification of source authenticity, may not be sufficient. Reuse of copyright can entail a fee or might be free. For example, many songs sung around the campfire at children's summer camps are not in the public domain, and the organizations using them are supposed to pay royalties. These include such common songs as "God Bless America," "Puff the Magic Dragon," and even "Happy Birthday." In fact, the songwriters organizations are trying to collect for royalties owed and for past infringements.

Also, understand what is copyrighted. A website operator downloaded the contents of the PhoneUSA CD-ROM, converted it to another format, and posted it on the site. Because the names, addresses, and phone numbers were not protected by copyright (in fact are excluded explicitly from copyright), only the CD-ROM software and search engine on the CD-ROM were protected, thus letting this operator off the legal hook. You can cite copyrighted material, quote it, and reference it as part of the "fair use" doctrine. This does not mean you can cite material in its entirety, imbed it within something else, and thus be free of copyright restrictions. It doesn't work that way. If you notice, with this book's website and the material *not* included on the CD-ROM, some material was merely cited so as not to infringe on copyrights. The website URLs were referenced so that material is "included" but not taken, copied, or in any way misused.

Even if you created an entire site with your own content or have acquired the copyrights to all sounds, speeches, images, multimedia, texts, and backgrounds, you still could run afoul of the rights to publicity and privacy. The rights to publicity give everyone the ability to profit or control the commercial usage of his or her own identity. This means that photographs, recordings, likenesses, caricatures, impersonations, and anything that is similar to someone else belong to that person (unless the person is an employee). The owner can sign over the rights without a fee or for payment for specific and defined uses. The permission to use a likeness is called a *model release*. For example, permission to use an image on a brochure does not provide for permission on a billboard or website. The best example of infringement was "Wheel of Fortune"'s Vanna White's fight against an advertiser who created an advertisement with a wig-clad robot in a futuristic game show who looked like her and violated her rights to privacy. A person who is famous but does not choose to use his or her likeness has a right to privacy and can prevent any use of that likeness, in terms of image, voice, or singing.

By the way, anything "protected" by "trade secret" on a website or part of an HTML page is probably in the public domain. A trade secret is only possible when a limited number of people are privy to the creation's special techniques, and only in so far as these secrets are somehow kept from the vast majority of people. Competitors who can infer how the creation process works or break the trade secret through reverse engineering (when not protected by copyrights and patents) can make use of what were *once* secrets. They are not secrets anymore. The function of copyrights and patents is literally to make something public and open, thereby creating a monopoly on its usage through a legal injunction. If an organization opts to keep (that is, try to keep) a trade secret instead of publishing or patenting it, maintenance of that secret is difficult and tenuous.

Malice, libel, defamation, and opinions

The Internet is a publication medium protected and supported by First Amendment rights in the United States and limited by other laws, and by laws of other countries. Since the Internet crosses country boundaries, some of these rights, freedoms, and even limitations must be carefully observed. In general, news groups, websites, and particularly your cyberstore are not the places to cast competitors in a *false light*. This can mean stating anything that is "highly offensive," misrepresentative, or distorted about another person, organization, service or product, or even another website. Stating something that is false or untrue is *libel,* even within the seemingly public and free forum of the Internet, and to say something libelous with the intent to do harm becomes *malice.* The statements must be made to a third party for them to be actionable. In other words, if you say anything with malice or that is libelous or defamatory to the insulted party and no one overhears it, it is not a legal problem, although it can become a moral or even business problem.

People or organizations *believed* damaged by libel or malice can seek legal damages; the cost, time, and heartache defending against these charges can exceed any legal judgment assessed you. Be fair, be honest, and weigh the perceived benefits of making statements that may be *perceived* in a false light.

If you are offering an opinion, emphasize that the assessment is indeed a statement of your personal belief rather than a categorical analysis or scientific fact. In addition, since web text and images can be recycled from other sources assuming copyright permission, you can also misuse that material by reusing it in a false light. For example, you should not show a screen shot from a competitor's product with another one from a general protection fault message transparently overlaid. That creates a false impression with potentially serious legal problems.

It is possible to create an electronic bulletin board or threaded conversational message system (such as supported by Wildcat! or WebBoard) that will allow customers to post comments, questions, responses, technical help, and suggestions. This requires minimal effort, keeps the site content fresh even when site developers (at a cyberstore) do little to upgrade the site, and could make a site very attractive. Several court cases, namely *Stratton Oakmont vs. Prodigy,* created a differentiation between site control, site editing and screening, and a laissez faire attitude. The ruling cited in so many web-related articles is that legal responsibility for site content is upheld only when the site tries to screen and edit content. However, the Communications Decency Act (CDA) of 1996 *may* overrule prior cases with the provision called "Protection for Good Samaritan Blocking and Screening of Offensive Material." A Philadelphia judge (in contrast to the Philadelphia lawyer) has overruled parts of the CDA in that federal circuit court. The strength of the CDA provisions for the Good Samaritan seem to imply some protection for content providers and site managers; however, it remains unclear if Congress intended the act to cover on-line access providers specifically and an "interactive computer service" provided at a commercial website or cyberstore. The law will need to be tested, and you do not want to be the test case. If you have doubts, involve an attorney in your website design and basic site management decisions.

HTML Design (Layout) Issues

HTML is simply the name given to codes imbedded in standard American Standard Code for Information Interchange (ASCII) text files. Even when you connect an IBM 3090 or other EBCDIC-based computer systems and DB2 databases to a website, the resulting HTML pages are still plain ASCII with HTML tag markups. HTML can be written on punch cards, DOS, Windows, OS/2, Amiga, UNIX, Macintosh, as extracts from .DOC Word files (as with WebAuthor or the Internet Assistant), and as calculated reports (from Crystal Reports, JetForm, L5 Quest, or Cold Fusion)—as long as they are ASCII files. As I asserted in the preface and in Chapter 1, HTML tools are primitive for the most part. They are either macro add-ins for a word processor, stand-alone word processors, tag insertion tools, or browser overlays. Most support HTML 2.0, some include that support along with support for the popular Netscape or Microsoft proprietary extensions, and none as of yet include full support for HTML 3.2. (HTML 3.0 and HTML 3.1 were proposals that have no current reality). I typically use more than one tool for site development on more than one development platform because each tool has a different focus, supports different tags, and does different functions. It is also handy to cut and paste between different tools.

This book will not detail the use of the different HTML tags. The CD-ROM companion does contain the HTML specifications for those who want them and the book's home site includes links to the latest revisions and commentary on applying the HTML codes. Quite frankly, you can get bogged down very rapidly by adding codes for sounds, enabling CGI applets, imbedding JavaScripts, and handling tables and scripts. It is unquestionably not worth your time. Use one of the tools profiled in this book or another one that is newer to automate the results you want to achieve. Also, most of the tools have a number of serious bugs that stop development cold and the vendors have yet to provide a workaround. For example, WebMania makes great tables and frames (unlike most other tools), but Web.Designer or Visual Web provide pretty templates to define the basic page layout. I prefer Internet Assistant because I can click through an entire site and not need to load individual pages one at a time. WebAuthor is also a good Word macro that preserves the power of a fully enabled word processor supporting spelling and grammar checking, as well as a number of other useful add-ins such as Iconovex, Doc-to-Help, and RoboHelp.

Realize that you can also modify tags with any ASCII editor, such as WRITE.EXE, NOTEPAD.EXE, or CLIPBOOK.EXE. Even if HotDog or Spider will not load your HTML file because it does not recognize the tags as valid HTML, you have other viable options. For example, Spider, which is shown in Figure 4.12, tags these HTML "errors" when my company's old home page is loaded.

The rest of this section demonstrates how to use many of the HTML development tools and enable web pages for interactive and dynamic generation of information for database integration. Web.Designer, shown in Figure 4.13, is a good entry-level program and provides effective templates. Note that the alternate text defines how images will display if a user has disabled graphics or if Fast Forward cuts off the image download.

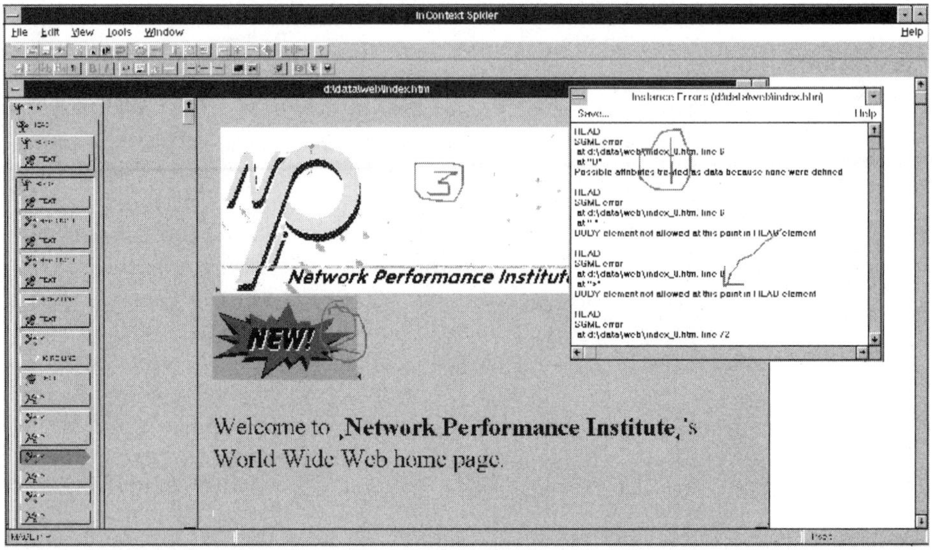

Figure 4.12 Spider locates HTML errors on this old file created by hand.

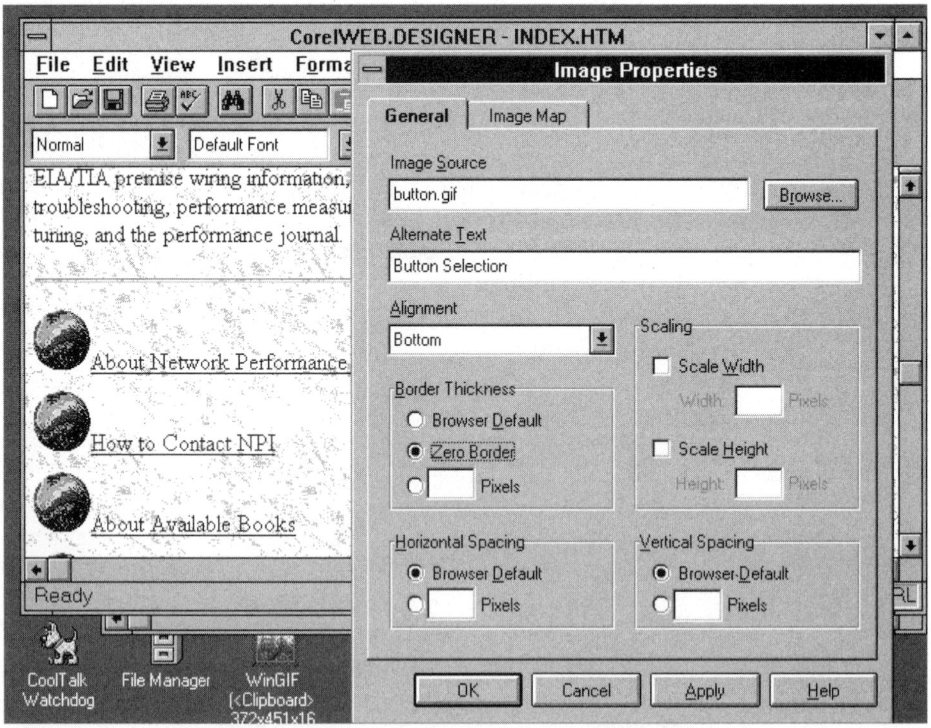

Figure 4.13 Universal page access requires definition of a replacement for an image that may not appear for a customer. Unfortunately, it gets very difficult and contrived to support these features with multiple languages.

For example, see Figure 4.14 to see how my company's home page would look without a graphical browser or graphics enabled. The lost images do not even appear as images, just lost "(Image)" text placeholders. As it turns out, these images are not important and are better left out of a commercial cyberstore because they convey nothing new or different.

Although many sites include a background image that covers the entire page or is tiled, the code shown in Chapter 2 is more easily inserted in a pop-up window within Corel Web Designer as shown in Figure 4.15.

Although Internet Assistant and WebAuthor utilize the spelling and grammar functions of Word, stand-alone HTML editors need to include this feature as shown by Web.Designer in Figure 4.16. If your favorite tool does not include spelling checks as an option, open the HTML files in one of these tools. The benefit of running spelling checks within an HTML editor or the Word macros rather than opening an HTML file inside Word is that these high-level tools are smart enough to ignore HTML tags and file names with paths. Otherwise you will need to add the HTML tags to a personal dictionary or step through each false-positive spelling "error" and manually ignore it.

Visual Web is functionally a Windows 95-only tool; I experienced significant problems converting it to run under Windows NT because of long file names and the websites I created using its templates and graphics included the long file names. When these files were moved by File Transfer Protocol (FTP) to an

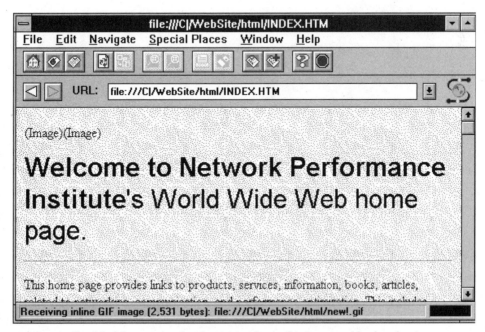

Figure 4.14 Graphical home page showing text only . . . this is a very bland and not a very promotional view.

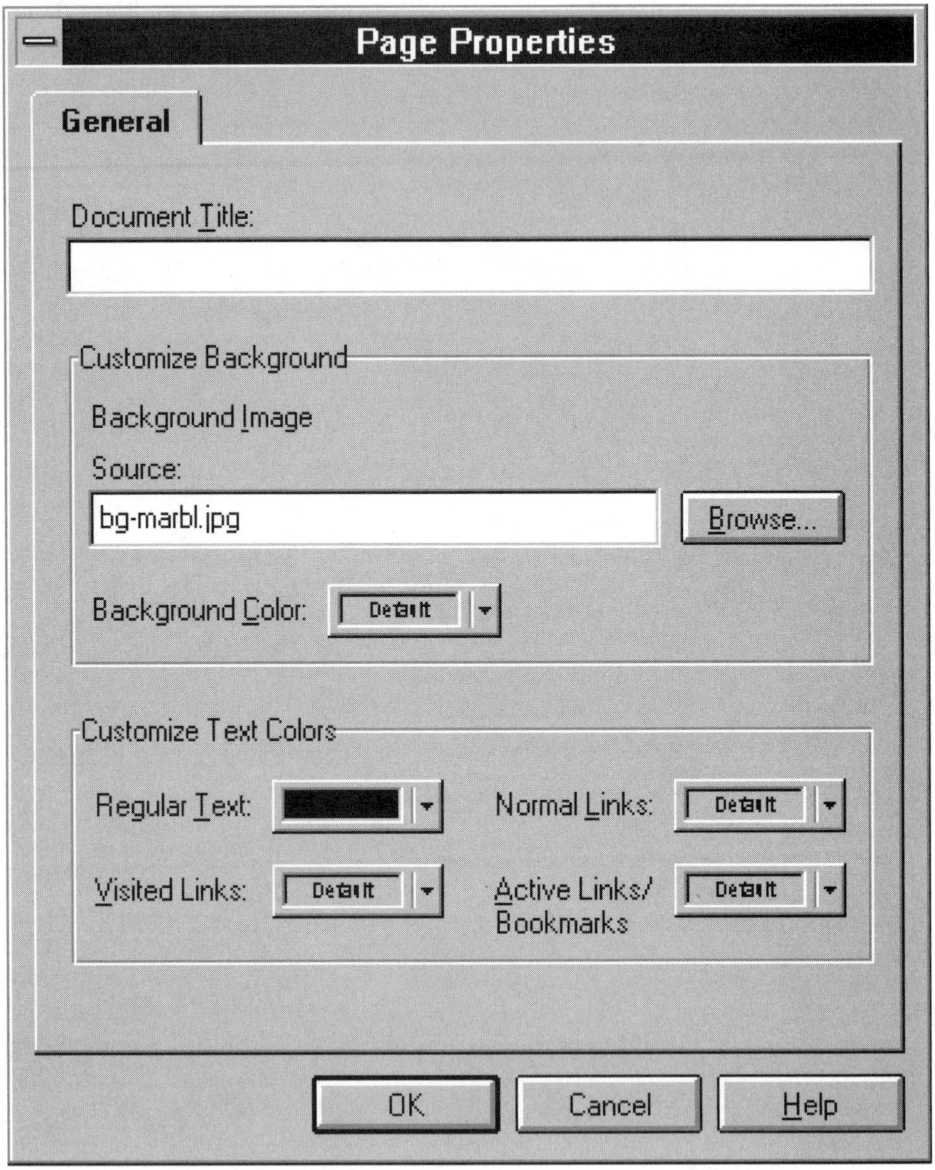

Figure 4.15 Adding a tiled background is as simple as specifying it in the pop-up dialog box in Web.Designer.

NT host and even the ISP UNIX host, these names needed reconciliation. However, Visual Web is a good initial design tool because it focuses the design efforts on the big picture. Specifically, it forces you to recognize the need to acquire a domain name and define it for the website you are building, as shown in Figure 4.17.

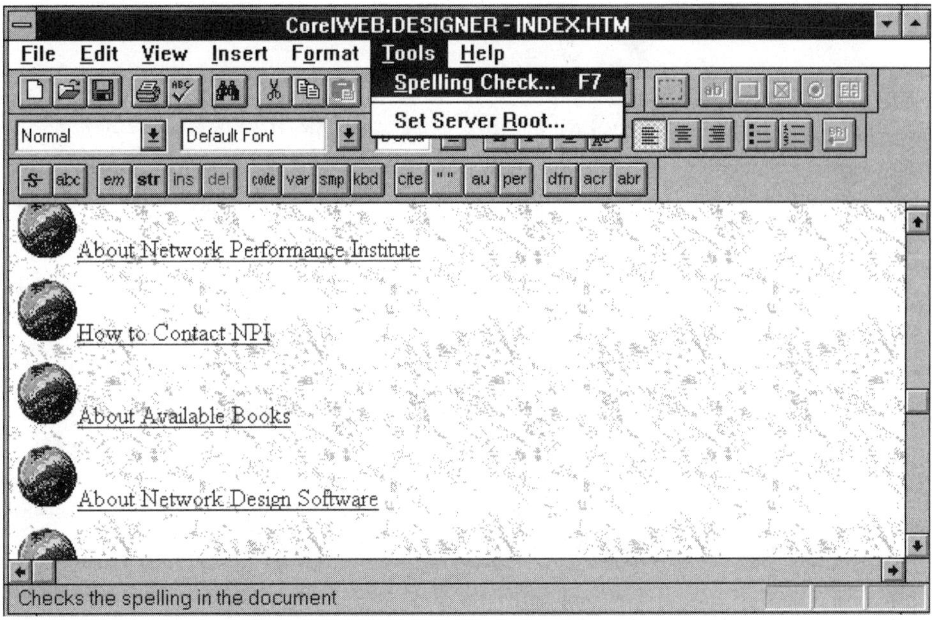

Figure 4.16 The lack of spelling verification is a website sin.

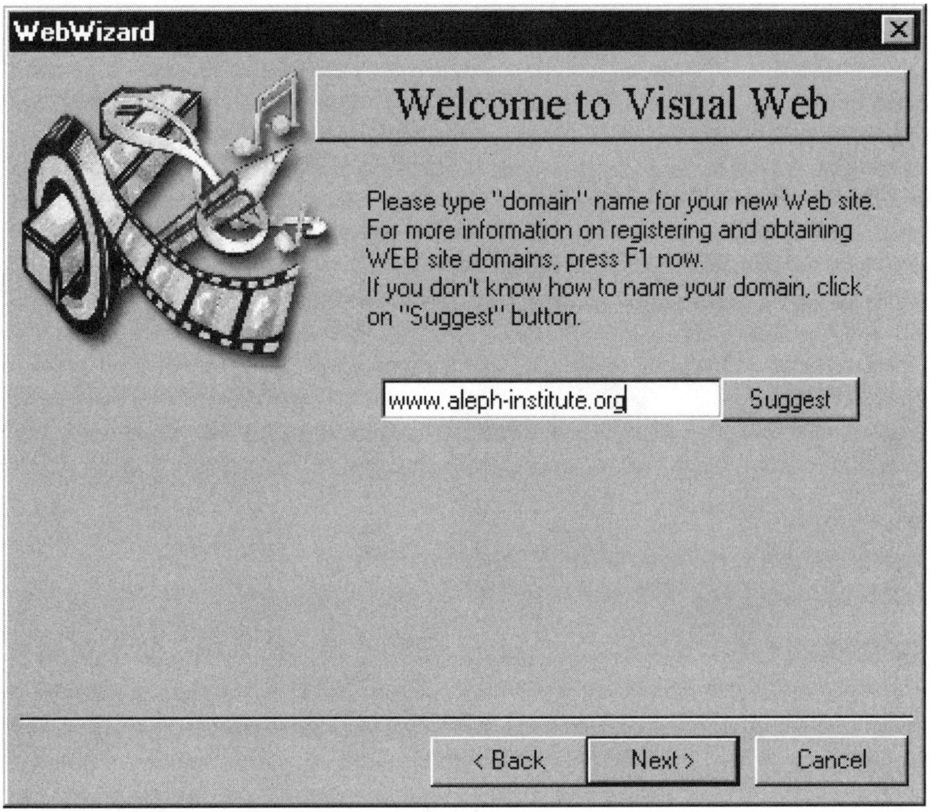

Figure 4.17 Visual Web starts from the big picture.

In addition, the focus is on the purpose of the website. The selection process for the included templates suggests a look and feel based on the type of site and the image you want to project. Figure 4.18 shows the template selection and the objectives behind each choice.

The Visual Web WebWizard walks through the process of background coloration and tiled image selection. The look and feel is addressed with emotive information and is coordinated with prior site type and purpose selection, as the screenshot displays in Figure 4.19. Corporate sites are black on white or white on black, marketing sites are very colorful, and public sites are dull and businesslike.

The site even includes the default inclusion of a "home page" graphic. The image revealed in Figure 4.20 is a waste of space for cyberstores because it does not add anything to the site message. However, it is easy to substitute a logo, an icon bar, an advertisement, or a banner from this dialog box. Although it is easy to work with the defaults, this often leads to any of the thirteen design sins described in Chapter 2.

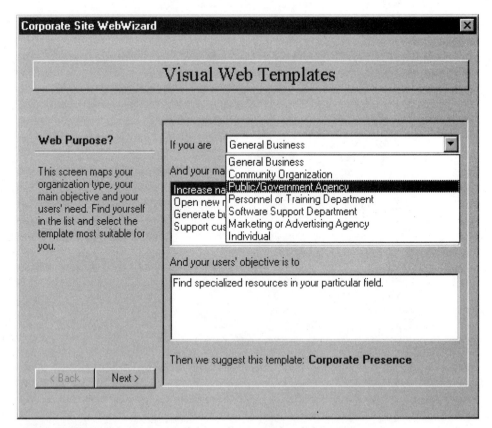

Figure 4.18 The template selection is driven by site type and objective.

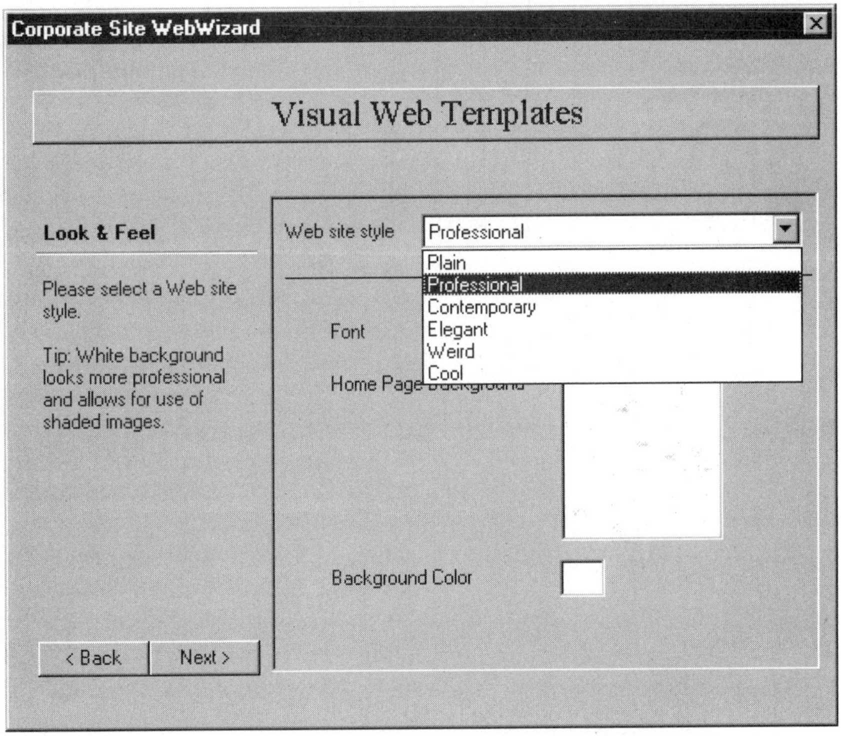

Figure 4.19 You are guided through colorization based on prior selections.

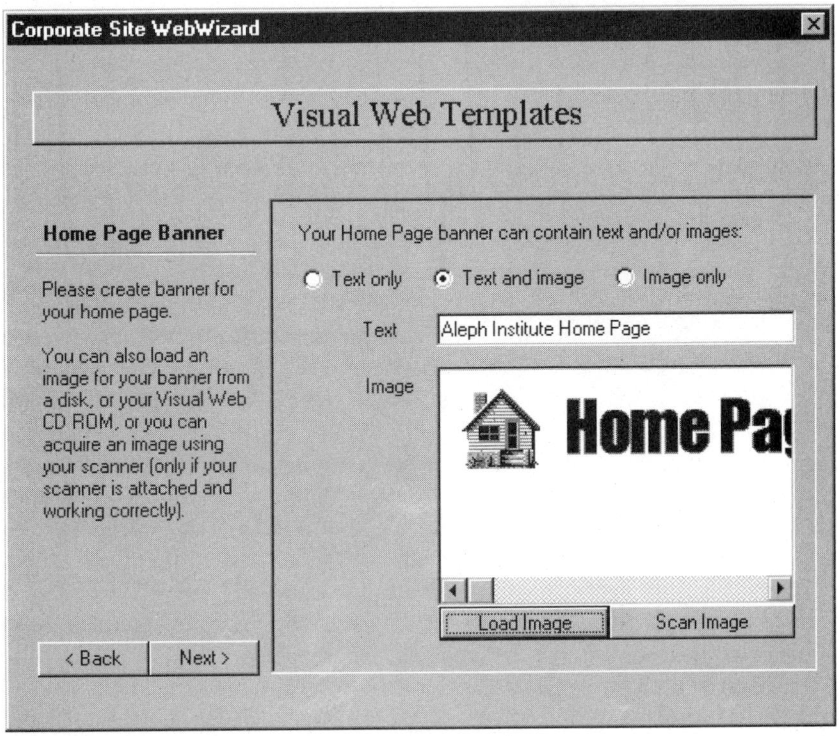

Figure 4.20 Home page with a default banner.

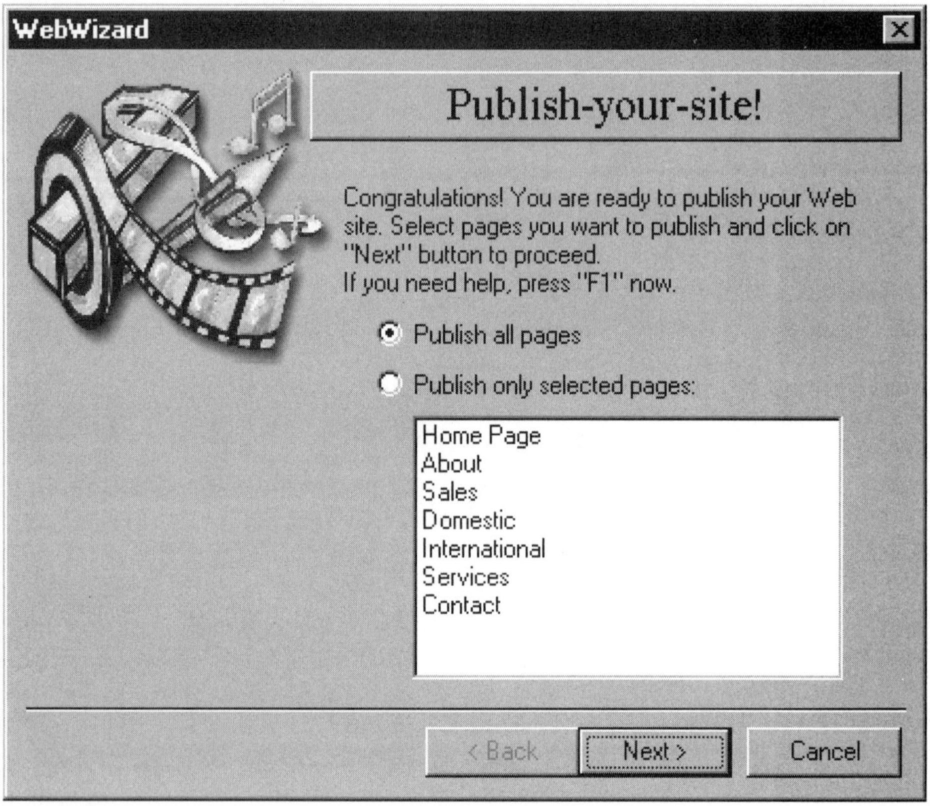

Figure 4.21 Automated FTP distribution to the host web server.

The WebWizard even creates basic constructs for the typical commercial website. This screen in Figure 4.21 leads you through the automated generation of a home page (title page), a what's new page, about the organization, copyright information, and a text-based navigation bar to these other pages.

You can define the elements to include on each site page. The check boxes in Figure 4.22 allow you to include at the site a table of contents, guest book or registration form, copyright notice, and navigation toolbar. Note that the navigation bar is built with text hyperlinks to the other supplemental pages.

A pulldown menu activates a dialogue box for defining the background, text colors, and sizes for the home page and supplement pages at the site. As Chapter 2 suggested, it is probably better to retain the "standard" Web settings and not override the color schemes and font selection configured in each user's browser. These settings are shown in Figure 4.23.

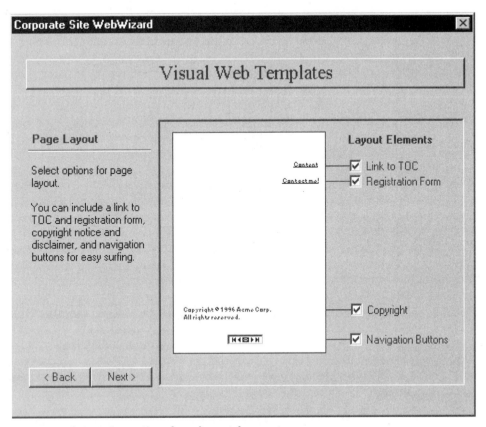

Figure 4.22 Automatic creation of supplemental support pages.

The background dialogue tab shows how to set a background color, a tiled picture, a background image, and even a looping sound file for ambience. The tool inserts the necessary code for all types of files to display correctly, even the sound file listed in Figure 4.24.

Unlike most other web development tools, the WebWizard Visual Web includes an FTP daemon to move the pages from the development directories to a live HTML subdirectory, to another host on the same network, or to an ISP linked through an active WinSock. This is easier than using the manual process described in Chapter 3. This automated process is demonstrated by Figure 4.25.

Although Navigator Gold builds tables, HotMetal and WebMania build tables and frames. Although you can copy code from other framed websites and cut and paste that code into your master home page, you can use the frame wizard that comes with WebMania to automate the process as shown in Figure 4.26.

In addition, WebMania automates the process of creating specialized HTML forms for credit card transactions, guest lists, ListServ registra-

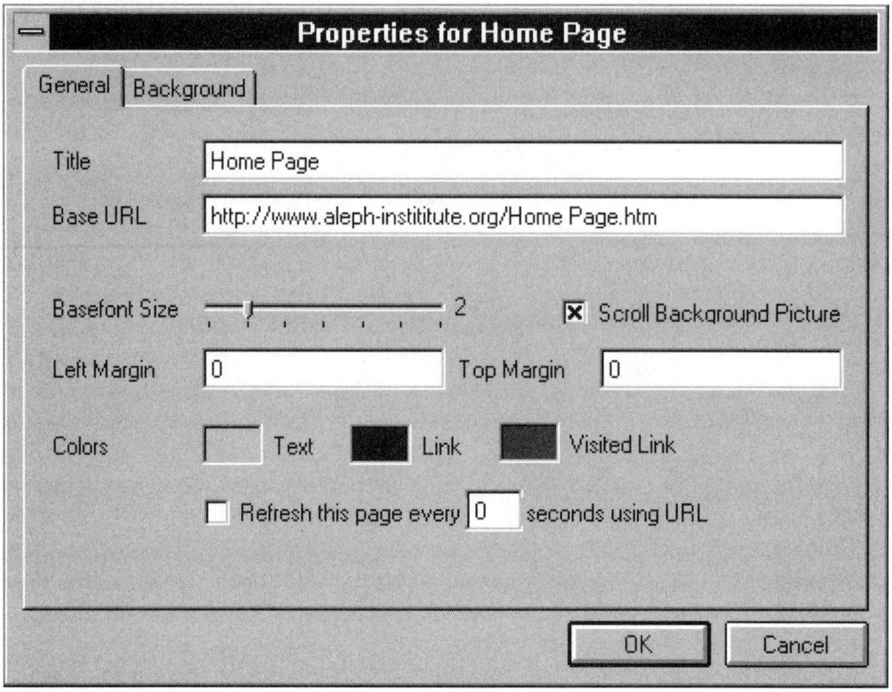

Figure 4.23 Color settings for the page; do not alter link settings.

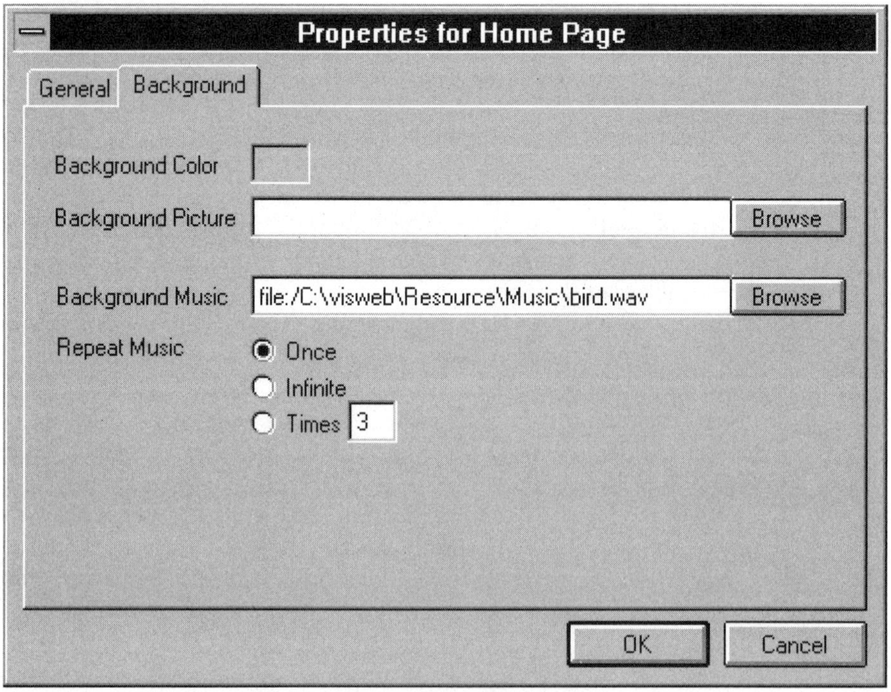

Figure 4.24 Automatic selection of a background sound.

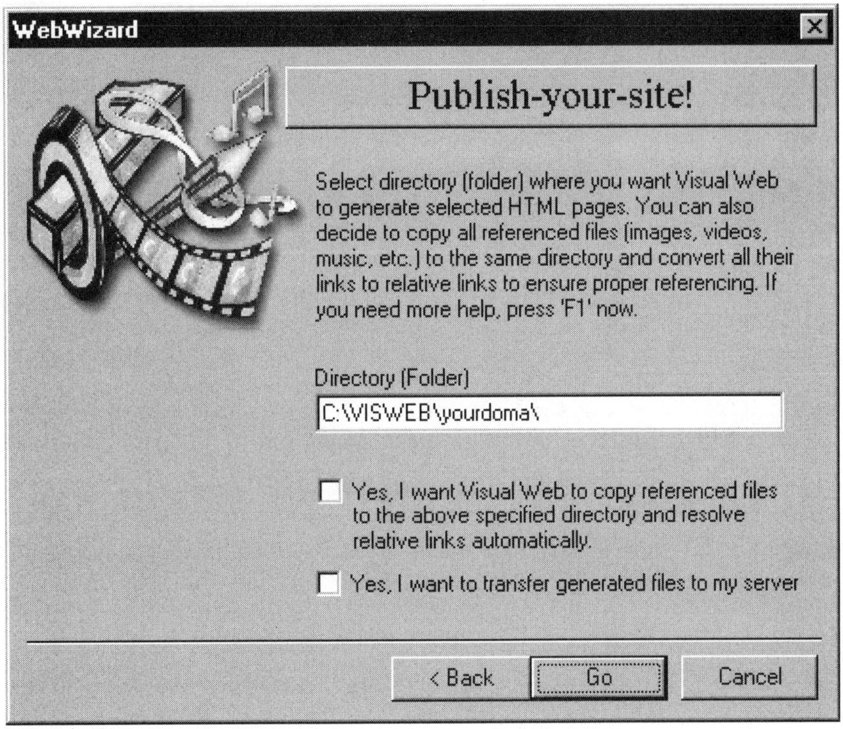

Figure 4.25 Automated publishing of a local website to the host.

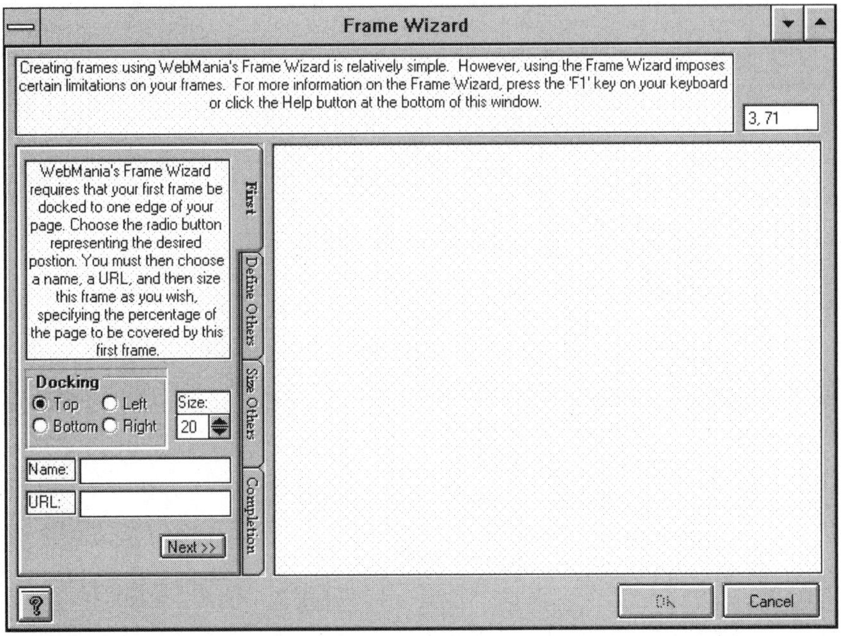

Figure 4.26 WebMania does tables and frames . . . and even includes a wizard.

tions, and personalized E-mail forms, as shown in Figure 4.27. Why code an E-mail form by hand when a wizard will create the basic template with a few mouse clicks? You can load that form into Web.Designer or WebAuthor and dress it up with a background, colors, banners, or other images and sounds.

Although a later section talks about validating the HTML code, URL links, and some of the tools represented in that section include spell checking, some of the HTML editors include spell checking, as HotMetal does shown in Figure 4.28.

The free version of HotMetal is included on the companion CD-ROM. Realize that free tools are worth what you pay for them. Many are good, but the incentive is not available for the designer and developer to increase or improve them. Some of the free tools are given away as promotions and hints to upgrade to the current commercial version. HotMetal version 3.0, shown in the next series of screen shots, includes conversion and construction from scratch support for tables and frames defined in HTML version 3.2, shown in Figure 4.29.

Note that not only do you get a useful template, but the CGI code and tips on how to use this code from the server side are also included with HotMetal.

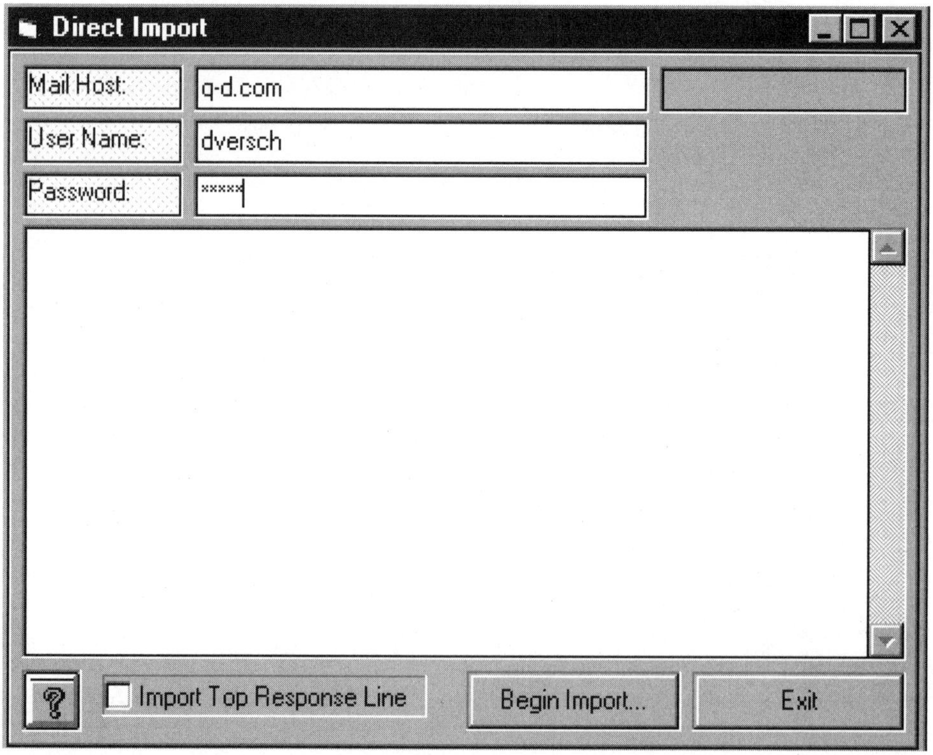

Figure 4.27 The WebMania wizard can create an HTML E-mail form.

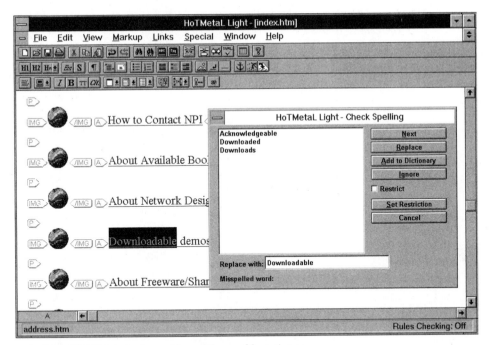

Figure 4.28 HotMetal checks spelling with possible options.

Since CGI scripts are complex for beginners or designers pressed for time, the CGI script tips outline how to modify the corresponding code to match any changes you make in the forms. That is more thoughtful than the norm. Although the Quarterdeck WebAuthor includes the ability to create forms, delivery and processing are only by the built-in E-mail Simple Mail Transport

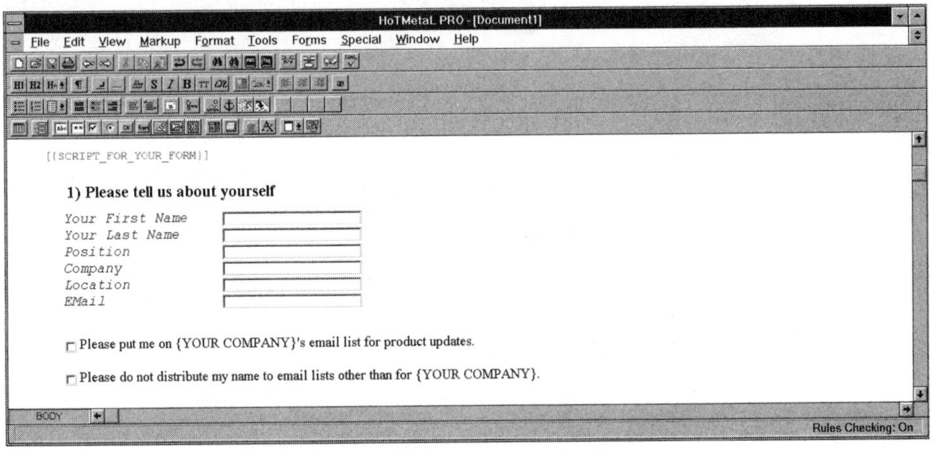

Figure 4.29 The commercial version of HotMetal includes copious templates that are complex, useful, and above the norm in designer utility.

Protocol (SMTP). The scripts here include field validation and more complex processing.

Frames are hot on the web. Although both the Navigator 2.x and 3.x browsers and the Internet Explorer browsers do not implement the Back and Forward buttons with frames as might be expected, designers like the flexibility and presentation style with frames. In fact, Navigator uses the right mouse button to scroll forward and backward through frame contents. You might want to communicate this fact in your website if you implement frames so that users do not bounce completely out of your site to other sites with the Back, Forward, and pulldown menu Go option. Figure 4.30 shows the basic starting point in HotMetal for designing a frame.

Since web development time is so compressed—what might be allocated 18 months to complete in a software development project is given 4 weeks—you need to start with templates. Although many of the web editors include images, page templates, or even a Visual Web that walks you through the steps of creating a superlative consistency in the look and feel of a website, they do not contain the depth and character of the HotMetal templates, as shown in Figure 4.31.

Document-to-HTML conversion

One of the quickest approaches to create a live web presence is to convert existing documentation into HTML. Although the web display format is different from trade magazine advertisements, multiple page brochures and mailings, or video tape, sometimes the primary business strategy for the cyberstore is just to be there first. Beautification, embellishment, and complete hypertext linkage and workflow enablement become a secondary need. Two approaches are available for expeditious conversion. First, you can scan documents and

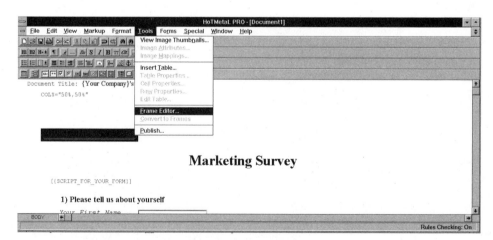

Figure 4.30   HotMetal construction of HTML 3.2 frames.

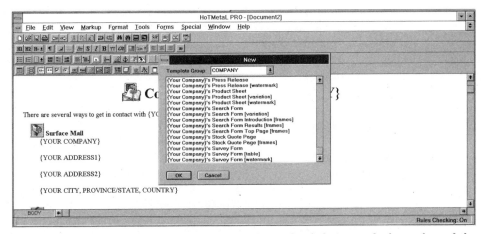

Figure 4.31 HotMetal templates include a range of typical web design needs that go beyond the basic home page, about the organization, what's new, and index.

convert them with optical character recognition (OCR) into the HTML file formats. Second, you can convert computer formats into HTML file formats.

Figure 4.32 illustrates the TextBridge Pro conversion into a flat ASCII file. Notice the complete translation. Had I lassoed the image and marked it as a graphic, TextBridge would have created a separate imbedded GIF file, too. Recognition accuracy is quite good, but not as good as the OmniPage Pro engine for small and skewed text by about 15 to 25 mismatched characters and a couple of words per standard letter-sized page. Nevertheless, the TextBridge direct scanner input and direct output to HTML with a Visioneer PaperPort desktop or keyboard scanning hardware is very attractive. Realize that this technology is so easy and fast that you might be tempted to take years of old

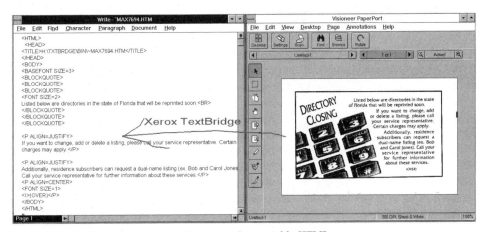

Figure 4.32 TextBridge conversion of a postcard to a viable HTML page.

and obsolete marketing literature and brochures and convert them for web use. As the design sins of Chapter 2 cautioned, quantity in lieu of quality makes a big, impressive site but not always a useful or effective one. The web is a different medium that does not tolerate such direct and massive conversion. Use the converted text and some of the HTML markup from TextBridge, but see to it that the material suits the format, character, message, and purpose of the website.

Complex documents generated from a database or a word processing file include intrinsic markup. While this may not conform to the SGML superset of HTML, it is still very useful. For example, the word document in Figure 4.33 shows part of a chapter from my *The McGraw-Hill Essential ISDN Sourcebook*.

Notice the heading markups, lead paragraph formats, hidden figure references, and the imbedded image. This structured file is easily converted into a formatted, camera-ready set of page proofs or on-line hypertext help. Similarly, the structure of this file makes it easy to convert it immediately into a structured HTML document. Figure 4.34 shows InfoAccess's HTML Transit program converting the document source into an HTML structured file. By the way, Corel also bundles a subset of this tool inside the Web.Designer package.

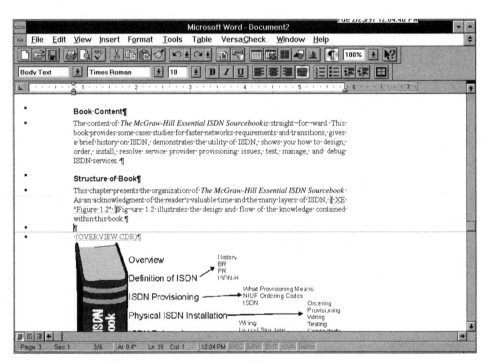

Figure 4.33 The page layout of a typical structured document.

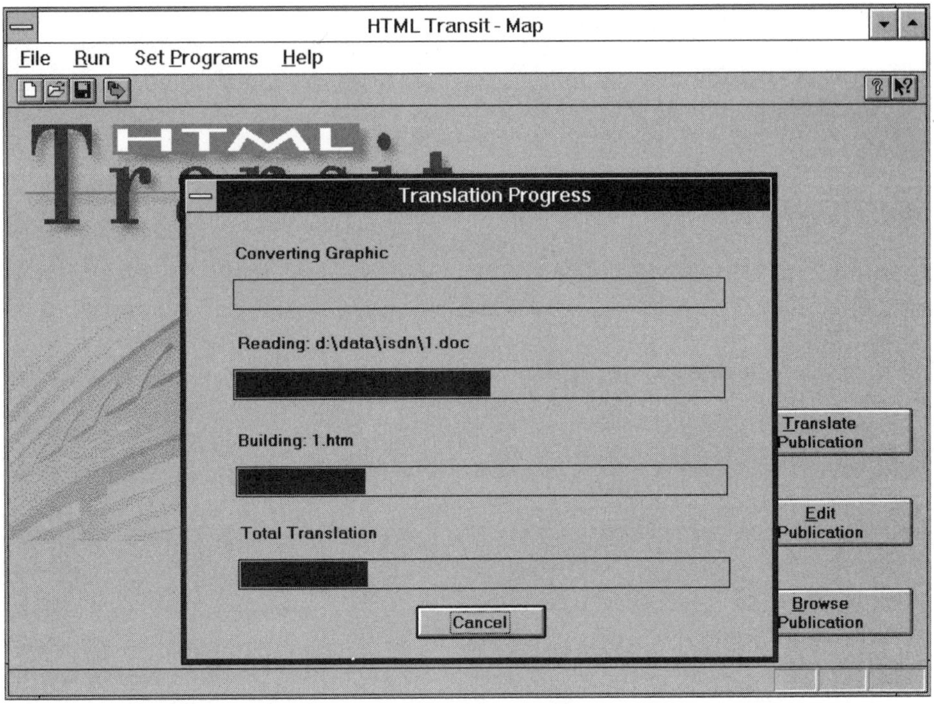

Figure 4.34 HTML Transit converts a document into HTML.

The structure of the original document is important because it simplifies creation of a structured and immediately useful web page. Figure 4.35 shows the hyperlink hierarchy of headings and subheadings that are fully functional.

Although this document requires some clean up to convert a page- and chapter-oriented document into a screen- and section-oriented HTML view, the conversion of this document is surprisingly clean and functional. You will likely need to remove headers and footers, adjust image resolutions, and add additional links between chapters. However, if you spend time up front tuning the conversion templates, all index, table of contents, and associative links in a Word document will be correctly converted. In fact, a click on the hypertext "Structure of book" subheading will jump to the section shown by Figure 4.36.

Data-to-HTML conversion

Data-to-HTML conversion is a simple process of building reports with codes compatible with HTML rather than for printing on various hard-copy printers. Data-to-HTML conversion is a one-way process that is useful for cyberstores, primarily management reports, job tracking, and sales information, but it is

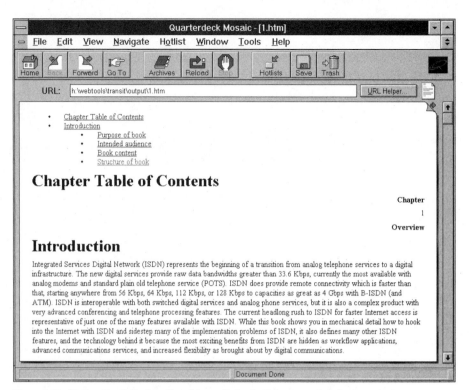

Figure 4.35 Notice the fully functional hyperlinks in this converted document.

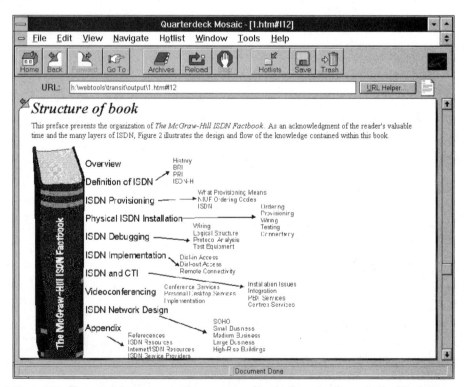

Figure 4.36 Hypertext jump to a section corresponding to the prior figure in the Word document. Notice that the image and the structure are preserved intact.

not enough to enable on-line transaction processing. The conversion is both static and dynamic. The static conversion is the simplest because the website developer selects a database and creates an HTML representation (often a list or table) of the data. The dynamic representation requires a CGI query process driven by the user or another CGI process to define the data subset to display. Dynamic conversion is usually part of a database middleware useful for other cyberstore transaction processing.

As such, Concentric, Crystal, and many other vendors selling report writers have added a module for HTML report writing. You can even use a DBMS tool. This process is not complex. In fact, if you have an older report writer, you can imbed HTML codes (that look like tags, text, or field codes) as part of the output file and then output the report as ASCII (text-format) so that a server daemon can fetch and display the file as a standard web HTML file. It works. However, it is complicated because you need script OLE or CGI processes that create the report and spool it to the server. In fact, the conversion process is detailed in Figure 4.37.

Even Microsoft FoxPro includes an Internet wizard so that web browser can query a database with a stand-alone executable application (you do not need FoxPro) that uses the CGI pipeline. Download the utility from Microsoft from the *developers only* forum. More complex tools include

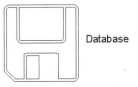

Database

Select tables

Select fields

Select records

Create a report format

Generate a report

Output to file

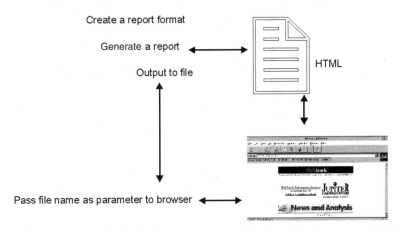

HTML

Pass file name as parameter to browser

Figure 4.37 The steps required for data-to-HTML conversion and display.

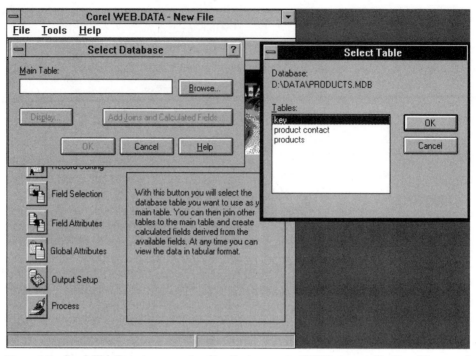

Figure 4.38 Corel Web.Data is a report writer that converts ODBC, Access, FoxPro, dBase, and other common databases into HTML pages.

Web.Data. The Corel version of this product is demonstrated starting with Figure 4.38.

As with any report writer, you define the table, the fields in the table, and even individual records. This Web.Data process is static and is driven by the web designer. Figure 4.39 demonstrates the selection of field records and the text and tags inserted with each field. The pad on the bottom of the dialog box automates insertion of HTML codes. Note that this product does not check the pairing or integrity of your HTML code, so you are fully responsible for understanding it. Web.Data directs output to a file (as shown in Figure 4.40) instead of a standard output device or printer.

The report conversion process creates standard ASCII output with HTML markup. This is established by the Microsoft WRITE applet display of the report file in Figure 4.41. This file is displayed as a table in Figure 4.42 in the Netscape browser. Note that the output scrolls left and down because it is a very large table. The next screen shot (Figure 4.43) shows this same data displayed as text with the table display function disabled. Realize that the data display format is constrained by the table size and width and by the abilities of each browser to present it well.

The report format can be rearranged to present database record entries as separated items, as shown in Figure 4.44. The Edit/Find feature will allow a

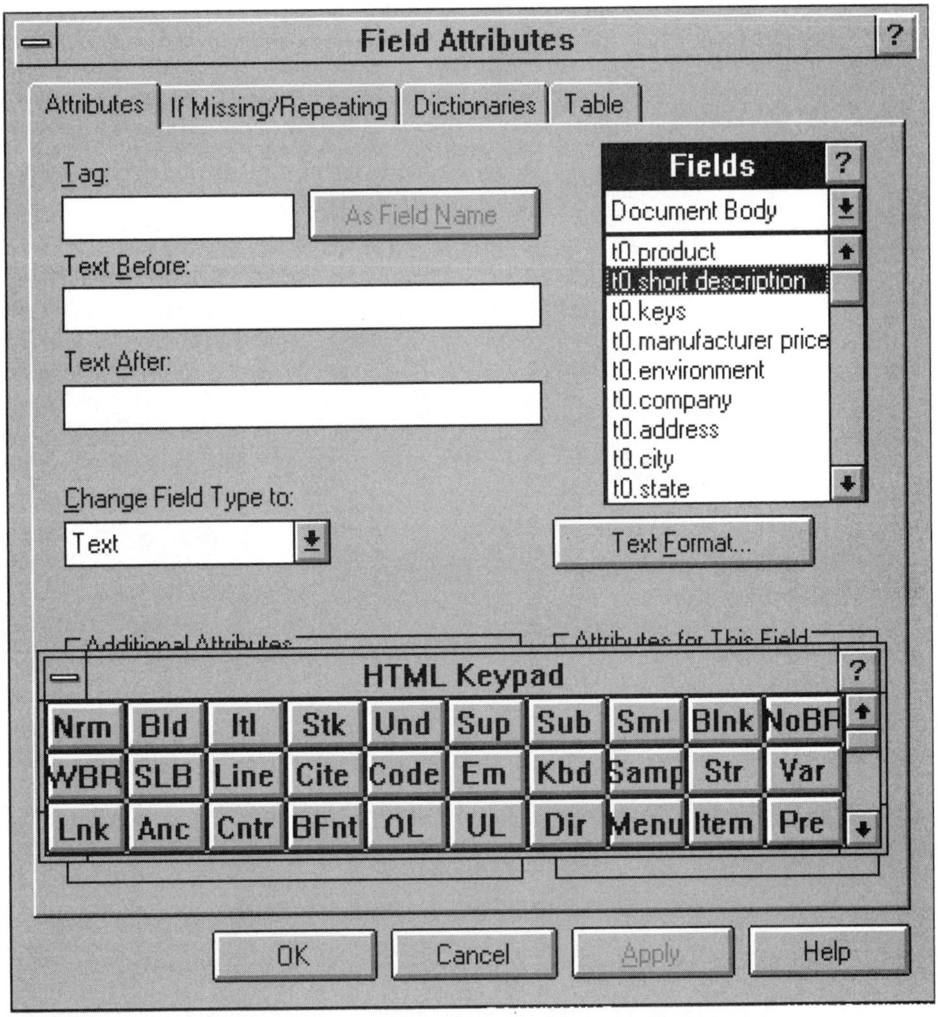

Field Attributes

Attributes | If Missing/Repeating | Dictionaries | Table

Tag:

[   ] As Field Name

Text Before:

[   ]

Text After:

[   ]

Change Field Type to:

[Text   ▼]

Fields ?

Document Body ▼

t0.product
t0.short description
t0.keys
t0.manufacturer price
t0.environment
t0.company
t0.address
t0.city
t0.state

Text Format...

☐ Additional Attributes   ☐ Attributes for This Field

HTML Keypad ?

Nrm	Bld	Itl	Stk	Und	Sup	Sub	Sml	Blnk	NoBr	▲
WBR	SLB	Line	Cite	Code	Em	Kbd	Samp	Str	Var	
Lnk	Anc	Cntr	BFnt	OL	UL	Dir	Menu	Item	Pre	▼

[OK] [Cancel] [Apply] [Help]

Figure 4.39 Each selected data field can include text tags and HTML markup.

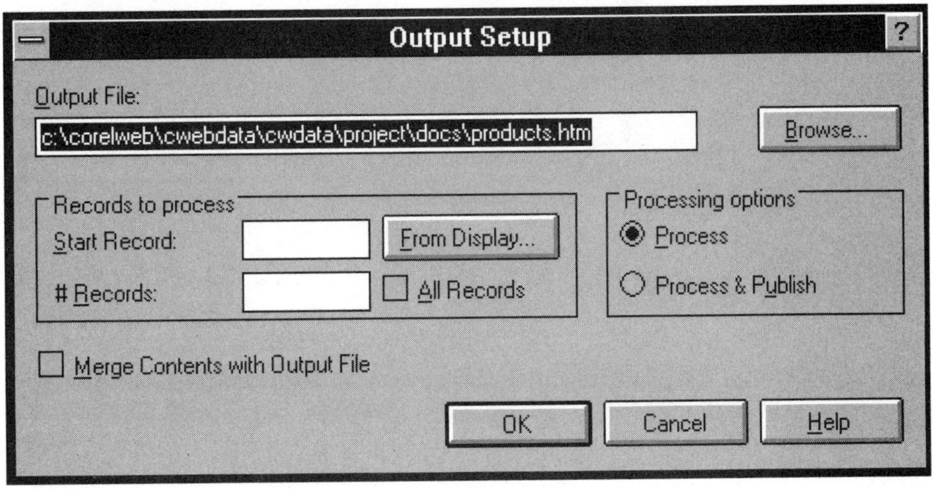

Output Setup ?

Output File:

[c:\corelweb\cwebdata\cwdata\project\docs\products.htm] Browse...

☐ Records to process
Start Record: [   ] From Display...
Records: [   ] ☐ All Records

☐ Processing options
◉ Process
○ Process & Publish

☐ Merge Contents with Output File

[OK] [Cancel] [Help]

Figure 4.40 Redirection and generation of the report as an HTML file.

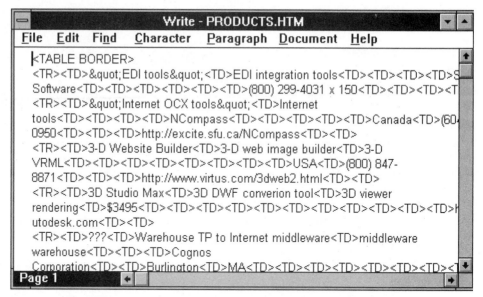

Figure 4.41 The HTML report file is standard ASCII with HTML tags.

user to search for particular information. Note that the Web.Data only handles text conversions and will not include large binary objects (BLOBS) in its output. However, since this is standard HTML, any HTML editor with an insert image feature and full support for HTML image alignment will simplify the

Application Security Toolkit	CyberSafe		http://www
Astound Web Player		(408) 982-0200	http://www
Authorware	Macromedia	(415)-252-2000	http://www
Autobahn	Speedware	(800) 447-0745, x250	http://www
BackStage	Macromedia	(415)-252-2000	http://www

Figure 4.42 Standard browser display of converted data.

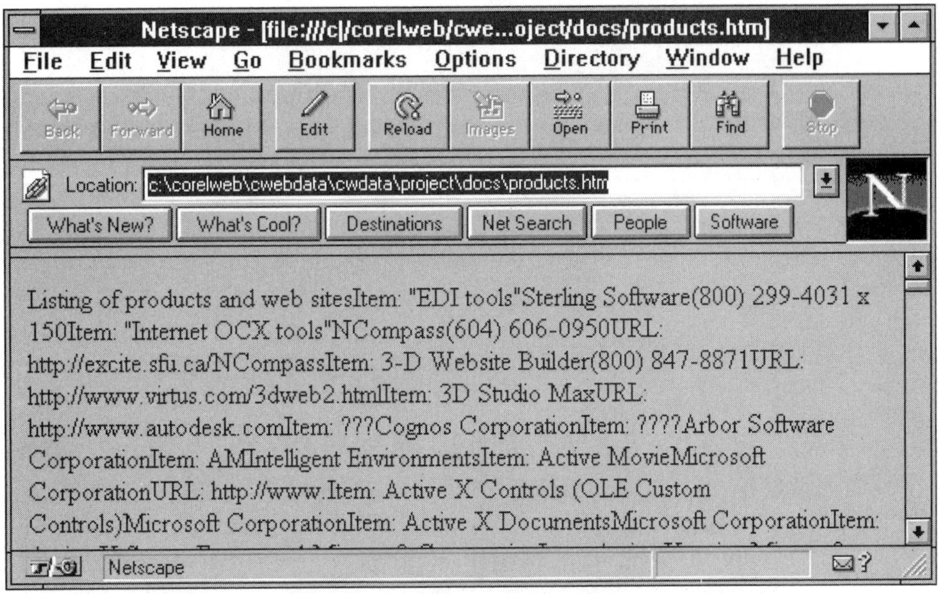

Netscape - [file:///c|/corelweb/cwe...oject/docs/products.htm]

File   Edit   View   Go   Bookmarks   Options   Directory   Window   Help

Back   Forward   Home   Edit   Reload   Images   Open   Print   Find   Stop

Location: c:\corelweb\cwebdata\cwdata\project\docs\products.htm

What's New?   What's Cool?   Destinations   Net Search   People   Software

Listing of products and web sitesItem: "EDI tools"Sterling Software(800) 299-4031 x
150Item: "Internet OCX tools"NCompass(604) 606-0950URL:
http://excite.sfu.ca/NCompassItem: 3-D Website Builder(800) 847-8871URL:
http://www.virtus.com/3dweb2.htmlItem: 3D Studio MaxURL:
http://www.autodesk.comItem: ???Cognos CorporationItem: ????Arbor Software
CorporationItem: AMIntelligent EnvironmentsItem: Active MovieMicrosoft
CorporationURL: http://www.Item: Active X Controls (OLE Custom
Controls)Microsoft CorporationItem: Active X DocumentsMicrosoft CorporationItem:

Netscape

Figure 4.43 Yuck! Table data displayed without table functionality.

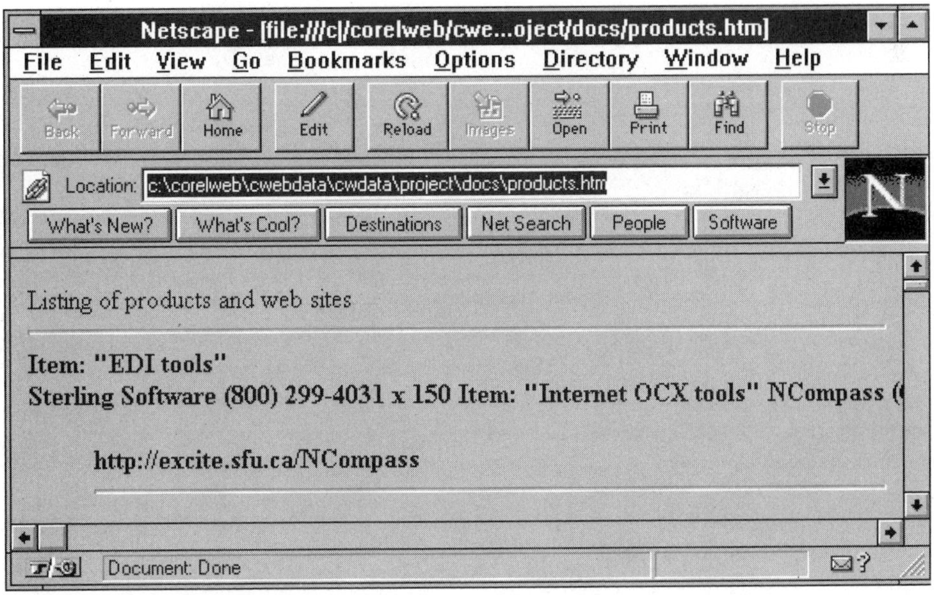

Netscape - [file:///c|/corelweb/cwe...oject/docs/products.htm]

File   Edit   View   Go   Bookmarks   Options   Directory   Window   Help

Back   Forward   Home   Edit   Reload   Images   Open   Print   Find   Stop

Location: c:\corelweb\cwebdata\cwdata\project\docs\products.htm

What's New?   What's Cool?   Destinations   Net Search   People   Software

Listing of products and web sites

Item: "EDI tools"
Sterling Software (800) 299-4031 x 150 Item: "Internet OCX tools" NCompass (

http://excite.sfu.ca/NCompass

Document: Done

Figure 4.44 Basic on-line catalog. It can be supplemented with images using almost any HTML
editor to insert product snapshots.

process of inserting the corresponding graphic for each entry. This format is useful and appropriate for on-line catalogs with images; in fact, the samples from National Semiconductor and AMP show how on-line databases can be constructed.

The final Web.Data figure (Figure 4.45) illustrates the use of tables and a restricted presentation of the fields included for each data record. This provides a more useful look at the data because forcing a user to scroll over to get the entire listing is bad design. If you want to include additional information, create a simple, narrow table like this one and a full listing as shown in the prior screen shot. Combine the two reports into a single file. Edit the table and add hyperlinks within the document from each table entry to the corresponding full entry. This technique, although somewhat laborious if you have many data records, provides search capability and master/detail presentation as only possible in a browser with full database middleware.

This conversion is strictly static. If you want the user to be able to search the database for hits, the reporting function must be dynamic. A number of tools from the free toolkits available with Structure Query Language (SQL) Server and IIS to NuTech's WEB2SQL provide this one-way query and reporting function. However, when you want to update information or add transactional information back into the database, the process is no longer as simple

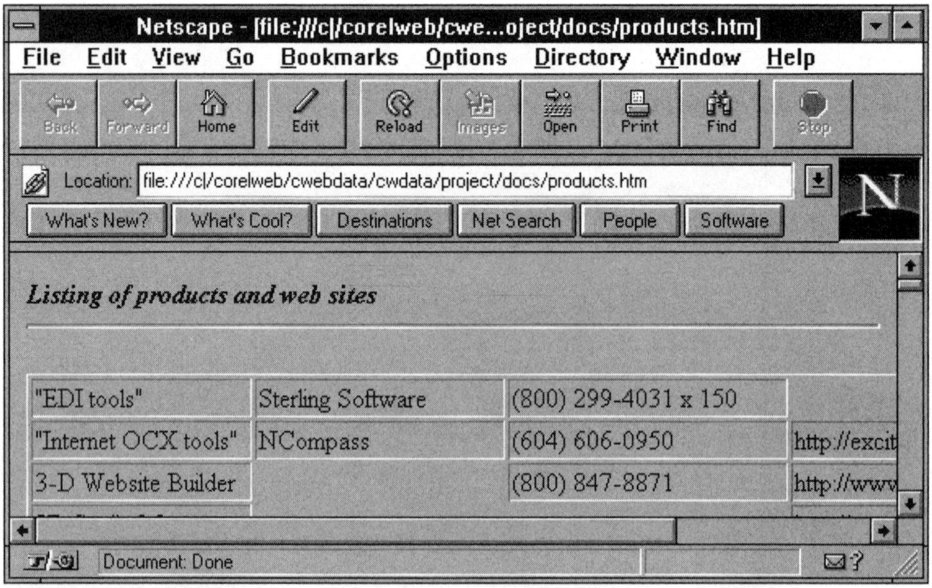

Figure 4.45 Notice that the table data scrolls in two axes, and thus is awkward.

as conversion; it requires a more complex middleware interface as detailed later in this chapter.

Help-to-HTML conversion

On-line Windows help (HLP) is a structured database. Indeed, the Rich Text Files (RTF) used to construct the on-line help file also represent a structured database. Either format can be converted into HTML very easily with a number of conversion tools. The HLP format is converted to HTML format and images are linked and converted to GIF-formatted files. Because RTF is highly structured as a document, or series of documents in the table of contents with sections and subsections, the RTF source can be converted into a series of HTML pages linking to the GIF files. Any graphics with the RTF files are converted to GIF-formatted (noninterlaced) files. Figure 4.46 shows the starting point for Help-to-HTML from Blue Sky's Web Office Suite.

Help-to-HTML is really that simple. The next step is watching the Win95 progress bar, as shown in Figure 4.47.

It is important to recognize that the bundled structure of a single help file gives way to the chaotic structure of layers of HTML files. Any macros imbedded in the help file are not converted, so if the source help file called sounds

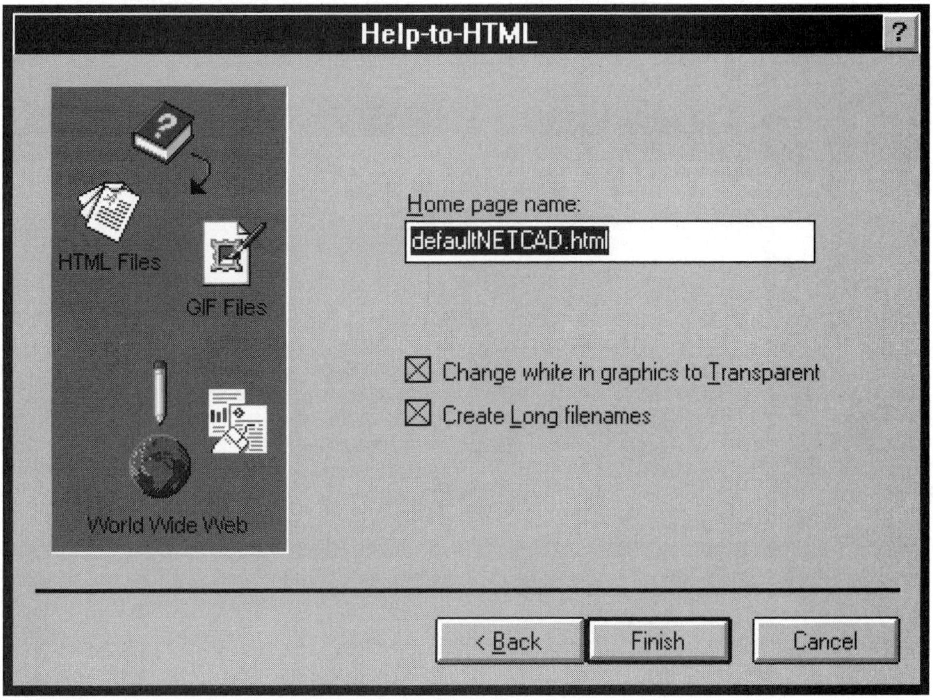

Figure 4.46 The Help-to-HTML conversion process.

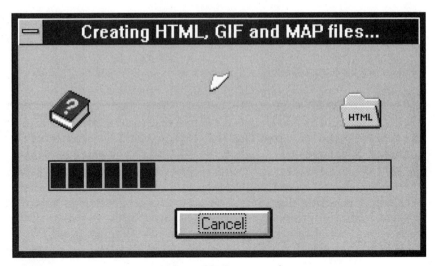

Figure 4.47 Windows 95 shows Help-to-HTML progress bar.

and multimedia, and activated other applications, they are not supported with this tool. However, the same functionality might be manually transferred with Java, JavaScripts, VBScript, HTML calls, or CGI applets. The file list for this conversion is shown in Figure 4.48. Note the loss of file name uniqueness and

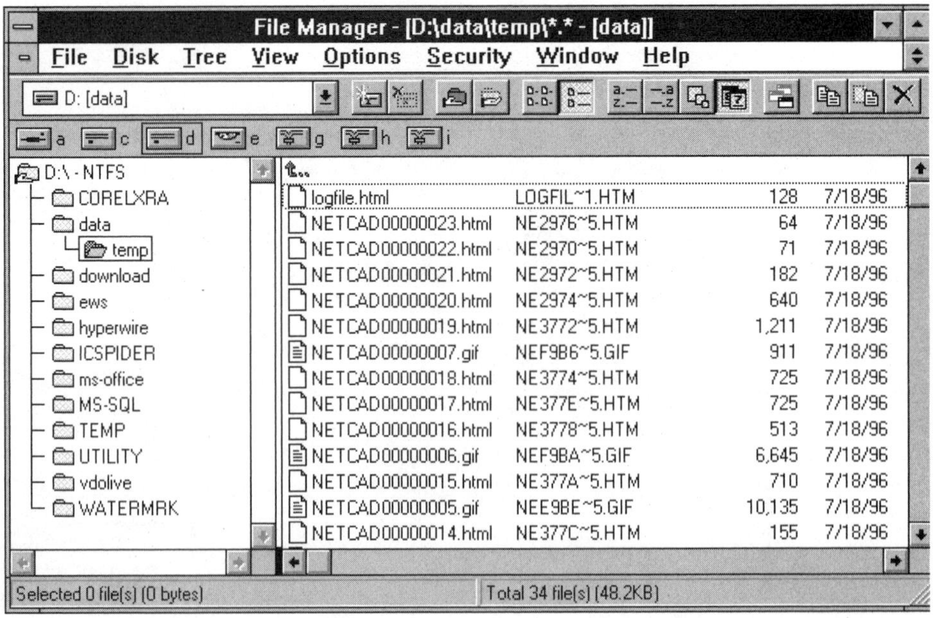

Figure 4.48 The WinNT display of the converted help file to the associated and linked HTML and GIF files.

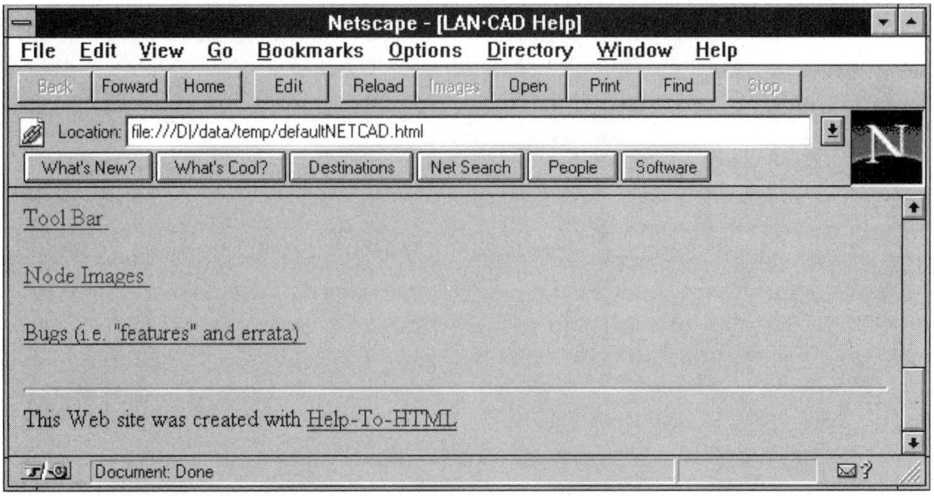

Figure 4.49   The HLP contents becomes an HTML home page contents.

the long file names for the HTML files (with converted ones shown by this Windows NT file manager). Microsoft has stated that it will abandon the .HLP format in favor of an all disk-based and Internet support in the HTML format. Since tools such as VBNET, Internet Tool Pack, and other C, C++, VB, Power-Builder, and Delphi toolkits include browser components, it is as easy to call a local or even remote site for an HTML help file. This is an important migration that you will want to watch and be ready to support. The keyword search, abstracts, and contexts engines provided with the new Win95 help compiler and viewer are not immediately supported in HTML unless the site manager adds this functionality with AnchorPage, CGI search applets, or full-scale commercial search tools like Alta Vista.

The standard contents menu becomes a standard HTML home page, as shown in Figure 4.49. Images and page layout are retained pretty much intact. The graphics are not bundled within the same file so that loading time is slower. Note that any Help files bundled with 256-color graphics and a macro to support bitmap display and dithering will convert with great looking graphics (assuming you map them to the 216-color Navigator palette). Most help files only include 16 color images, whereas browser display supports at least 216 colors. The conversion results of a help topic with a graphic is shown in Figure 4.50.

Link Etiquette

As the last section explained, you link HTML documents and other functions together with HTML tags or file references. The links "thread" the documents together. These hotspots (which default to the color red and turn

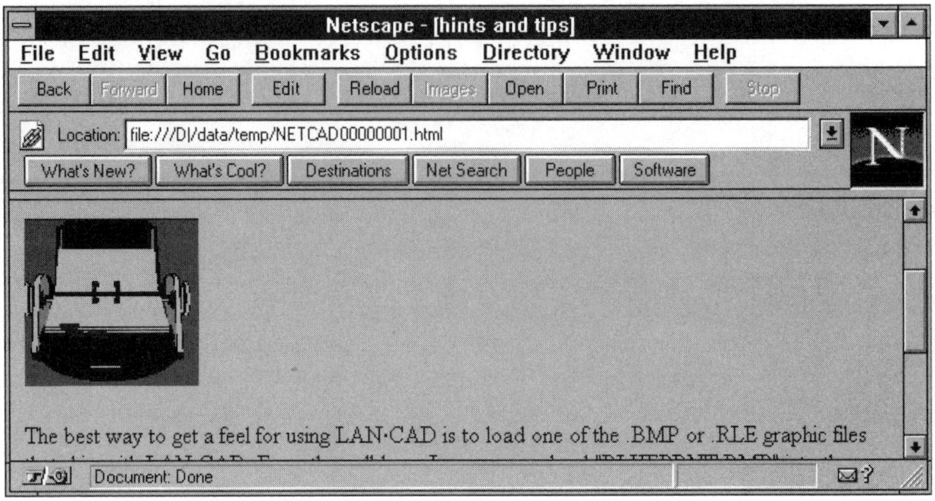

Figure 4.50 The help topic converted as an HTML page.

purple after a user has selected them by default) are *hyperlinks*. The last section implied that hyperlinks interconnected documents at your own website. In addition, hyperlinks can also link your documents to documents at any other site on the World Wide Web. A URL is supposed to be a global address. Instead of specifying "index.htm" for example, you can specify "http://www.fbi.gov". In fact, the *Building Cyberstores* Informational Site Links page included on the companion CD-ROM or the actual book site demonstrates this process.

There are two approaches. First, you can list the URL with a description tag:

```
<IMG SRC = "button.gif" ALIGN = "BOTTOM"><A HREF = "npipage.htm">NPI
home Page</A>
```

This hides the actual URL address. Second, you can include the URL address as a visible part of the page:

```
<IMG SRC = "text.xbm" ALT = ["TXT"]<A
HREF = "http://www.fbi.gov/security.txt">http://www.fbi.gov/security.txt</A>
```

I suggest that you hide local URLs but display the full path for remote URLs. My reasons are threefold. One, remote URLs tend to change over time and may not be viable. The user will need to search for a new path or may try to correct the path. Two, a path description adds to the information about a particular site. Three, most browsers retain URL hits and will color code prior hits. (By the way, these URLs are retained indefinitely or for 30 days depending on how a user sets the optional browser configurations).

A more pernicious issue for link etiquette is the legal liability. Links represent a thoughtful way to share information without repeating it or violating copyrights and also a means of improving web research and making it more useful. The legal argument can be phrased like this: "Your link might send a user to someplace and that user might suffer injury as a result—economic injury, physical injury, emotional injury, or a security breach that is actionable within the tort justice system." You could be responsible for the liability of sending the user to that someplace.

Legal precedent does exist, and it is called "negligent misrepresentation." For example, a general practitioner might suggest you seek a second opinion or see a medical specialist. Since medical problems of this type are novel to you, you ask the name of a suitable medical specialist. That representation, if it includes a description of the physician's qualifications— for example, "Oh, he's the best at that surgery"—can be exercised as a professional referral for responsibility if the medical specialist performs malpractice.

Get this hint and be careful of how you portray your links. They should be a convenience, not an endorsement. The rules for responsibility require that you quantify, qualify, endorse, approve, or lend one's name to another product, site, or service. If you are a publisher of information, there is minimal claim for responsibility. If you review the links for content, this puts you in the position of an editor, site censor, or republisher, which renews the potential legal risk. Consider including a prominent disclaimer, such as:

> "These links are provided as a matter of convenience only and do not endorse the sites or what you may find there."

You will see this at the *Building Cyberstores* Informational Site Links home page. Similarly, you could also create legal jeopardy by creating links to the "5 percent worst pages on the Internet" or setting judgments on websites. There are several sites just like that. Insults directed at sites, site designers, or the contents therein can become a basis for a slander, misrepresentation, or libel law suit. If you are certain you want to pursue this route, make sure you are correct or at least have sufficient professional evidence to validate your claim. The libel issue is not really pertinent for most commercial cyberstores. However, many people have assumed a certain anonymity and autonomy in using the Internet to achieve personal objectives. However, as more organizations pursue websites to conduct business and negotiate financial transactions, the consequence of websites will be the equivalent of TV, radio, or magazine advertising. You can compare and contrast services and products on a website. The rules for an autonomous journalistic review are very different from a jaundiced competitor's review. Understand the difference and play fair, honestly, and with integrity. People will take it seriously, as will the competitors. Do not denigrate competitors' products, services, sites, presentations, or technique. In contrast, just make yours better.

Lastly, you may want to check who is linking to your site. Partners and related organizations should be, but are they? Competitors and disgruntled former employees maybe shouldn't, but are they? You might discover favorable awards, recommendations, and pointers to your site. On the other hand, you might also discover things you did not want to know, but must do something to fix. Similarly, you may discover wrong URLs that generate server load like wrong phone numbers that tie up the hapless receptionist. You may also discover wrong or out-of-date URLs that point in your general direction but do not complete the connection. You can correct those with E-mail to the webmaster at those sites.

Several approaches work to identify links to your site. The first method is listed in Figure 4.51 from the tips section of the Alta Vista search engine.

In addition, you can provide this same information to WAIS, ARCHIE, FTP, and full-text retrieval engines or to multi-robot search engines. Some of these tools run on the server of an ISP or particular Internet sites and return results in the form of an E-mail or an HTML document. Full-text searches are useful for locating references to your organization, your products or services, trademarks, or key people who might not be part of an HTML URL, but could be listed as a passive reference or listing. Since these extensive searches may require several days to complete, pick a server that will tolerate your activity and does not often fail or get restarted at midnight every night.

Another approach is best demonstrated by NetCarta WebMapper software. This tool identifies incoming links because the "back URL" is passed as a browser parameter. While you can write CGI code to trap this and other use-

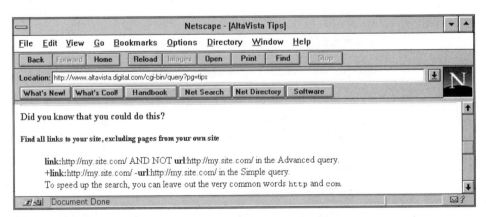

Figure 4.51 Use Alta Vista for URL keyword references to your site.

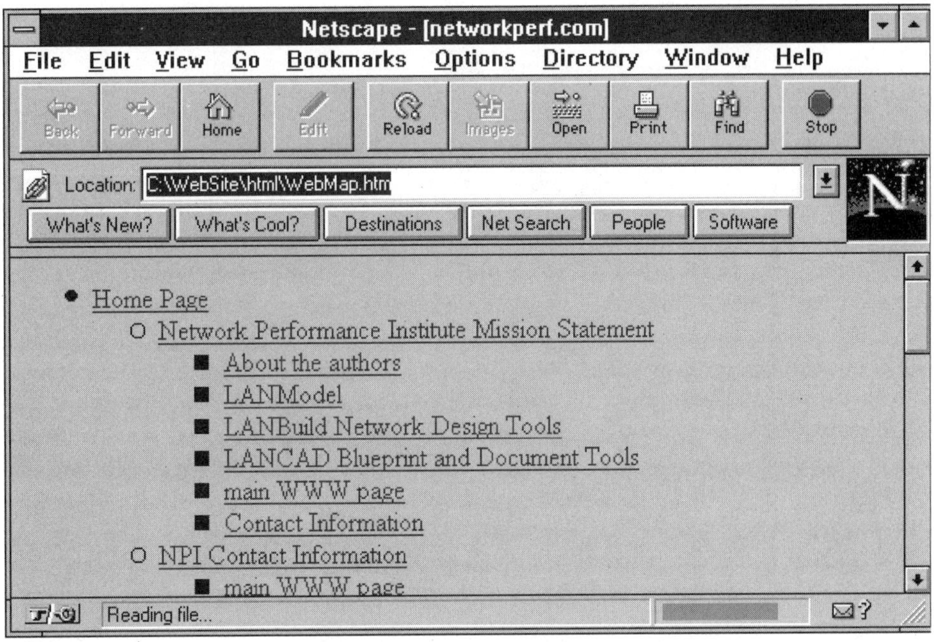

Figure 4.52 WebMapper traps incoming links.

ful information (such as user E-mail address, browser type, and IP address), WebMapper does it directly, as shown in Figure 4.52.

Another useful technique is to review the web server logs and error logs. Malformed URLs indicate search engine problems, old links, bad directory (Yellow Pages, Search Engine, List Servers, and other sources) entries, and other Internet plumbing problems. By matching this information with the URL source, you can track backwards and get the owner of the site to correct the entries. A high number of hits (and here, "hits" means a visit to a home or subordinate page) of short duration could indicate bad, meaningless, or useless directory information. I suppose if you want hits to bolster your advertising success image, this listing may be useful. However, most advertising agencies want more meaningful web statistics—bad linkages and bad directory information are unnecessary server overload.

Site and link validation

The sins of web design stated in Chapter 2 are explored further here. There is nothing worse than to jump to a link that does not exist. The result is any number of messages, one of which is shown in Figure 4.53.

Given the number of tools and interactive websites that will validate HTML code, hypertext links, spelling, and layout, there is no excuse for this. In fact,

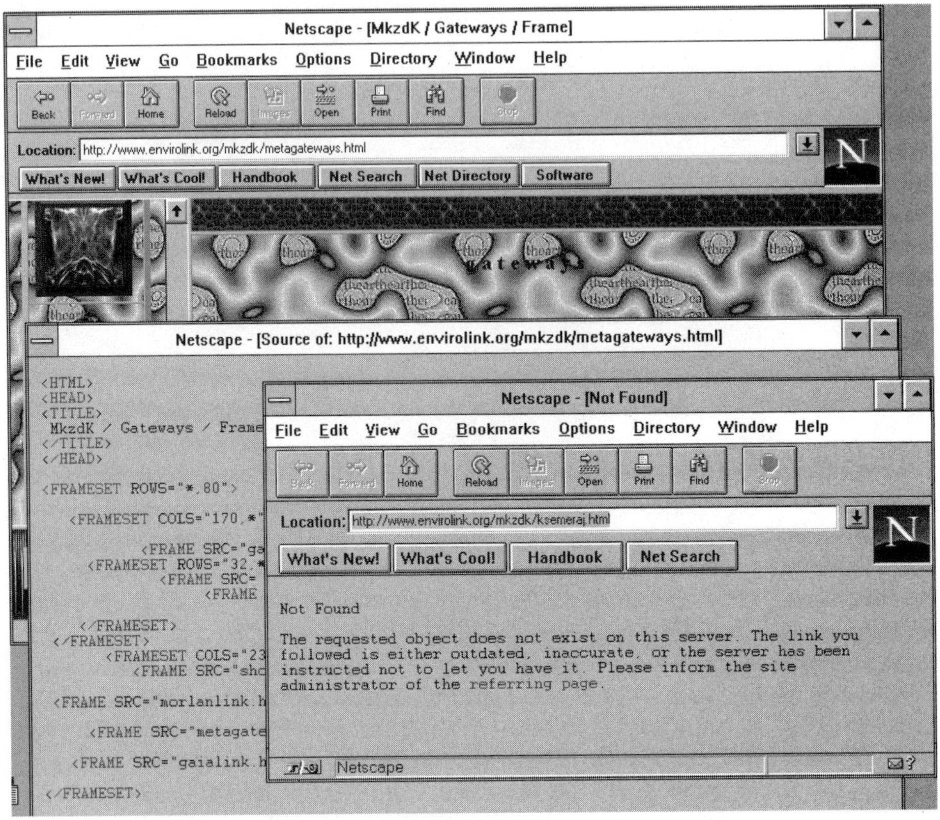

Figure 4.53 A broken link, a resource missing, and a dead end for a customer.

if your cyberstore includes links to other organizational subsidiaries that host their own cyberstores, these tools will also check these external links. Web Doctor is a tool from the Blue Sky Web Office suite and is shown in action on the sample website shipped with the product in Figure 4.54. This is a good tool for occasional use.

Web Doctor is driven by dialogue boxes. You can limit the scope of the validation process as shown in Figure 4.55. Web Doctor can also generate an interesting report detailing the download times for particular web pages. If you suspect that a framed and tabled page with significant graphics, and animated GIF images at that, is abusive to customers, Web Office will calculate approximate download times, as shown in Figure 4.56. However, the times are approximate and do not include ISP, telecommunication overheads, server delays, and cache effects common with most Internet connections. The 14.4 Kbps speed highlight in Figure 4.57 shows download time that is exactly twice the 28.8 Kbps time shown in Figure 4.58. Since I often

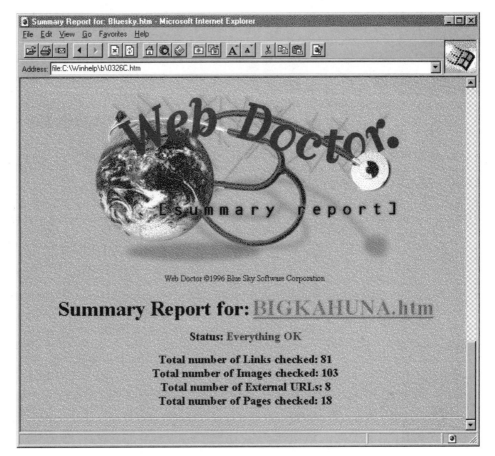

Figure 4.54   Web Doctor traps broken links.

see 1.3 Kbps transfer rates at 14.4 Kbps and 0.47 Kbps at ISDN speeds, these numbers are roughly estimated and trivialized. However, it is a good start to test your basic site design.

Figure 4.59 shows Web Analyzer, This tool is industrial strength, as is WebMapper. These tools check all internal and external links, map the structure of the site, and show broken links. In fact, this map shows a total of six documents, four of which are corrupted HTML documents and not readable on the ISP, and two ZIP files that do not exist anymore. By the way, Web Analyzer is like Milk Truck and Web Whacker in that it will grab an entire site, images and all, for storage on a local site. This feature is useful for agencies and consultants repairing or upgrading existing sites.

WebMaster is similar but includes a functional interface that activates a browser and an editor, and maintains an overall integrity to a website. For ex-

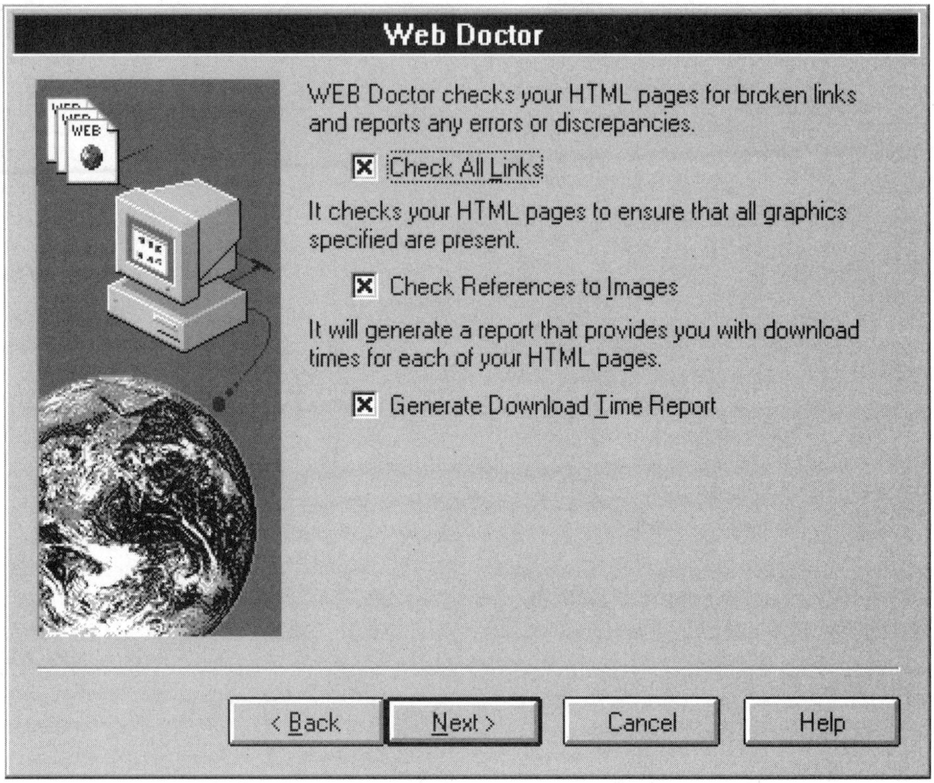

Figure 4.55 Web Doctor validation range dialogue.

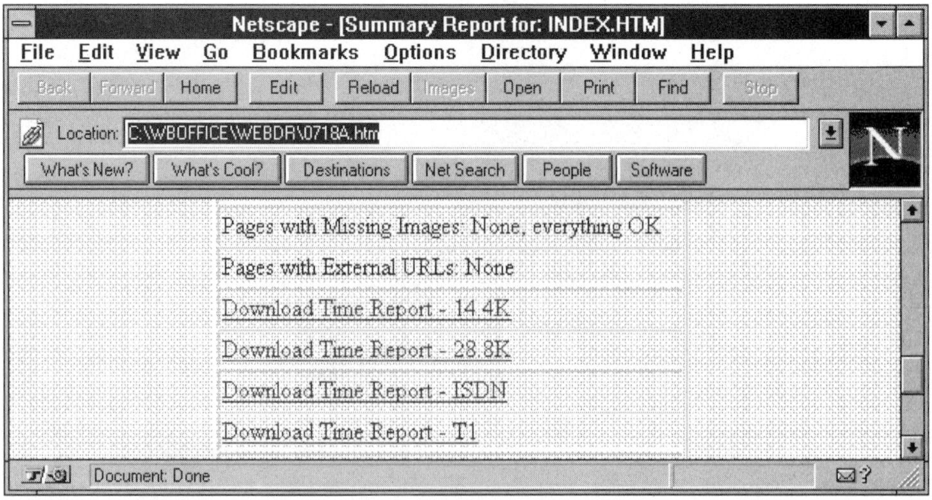

Figure 4.56 Approximate download times for a specified web page.

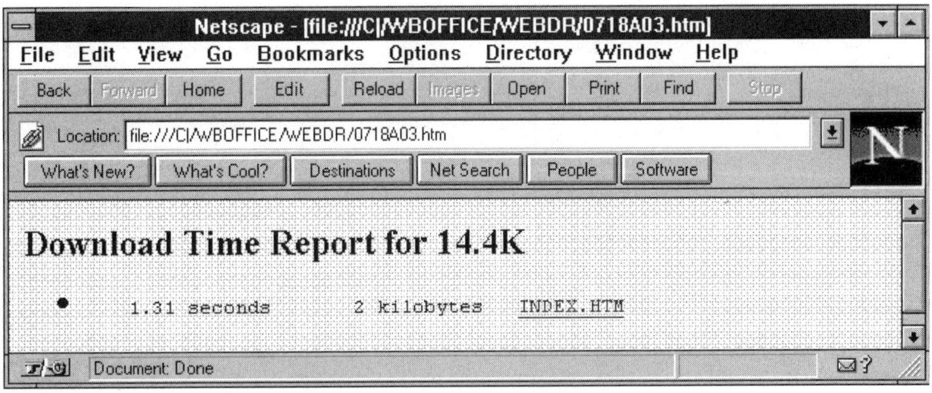

Figure 4.57 Page download time at 14.4 K modem speeds.

ample, WebMaster is searching for broken links and trying to automatically match up the URLs to the missing HTML page names from within its URL/page name database, as shown in Figure 4.60.

WebMapper, Web Analyzer, and most other HTML validation tools also miss an interesting problem. Specifically, how many times have you created a document called TEMP.HTM or EXTA.HTM with material cut from other pages and forgotten about it? How many times have you created a contact form, E-mail form, about the organization HTML page and simply forgotten to link those pages into the website? This is not a case of links being broken, but rather of orphaned pages that are not linked. Figure 4.61 shows that WebMaster searches for lost resources.

The various tools create a graphical representation of the website. The table of contents is often a list of page titles. Instead, customers may want a road map that shows how to traverse the site. The WebMaster screen shot

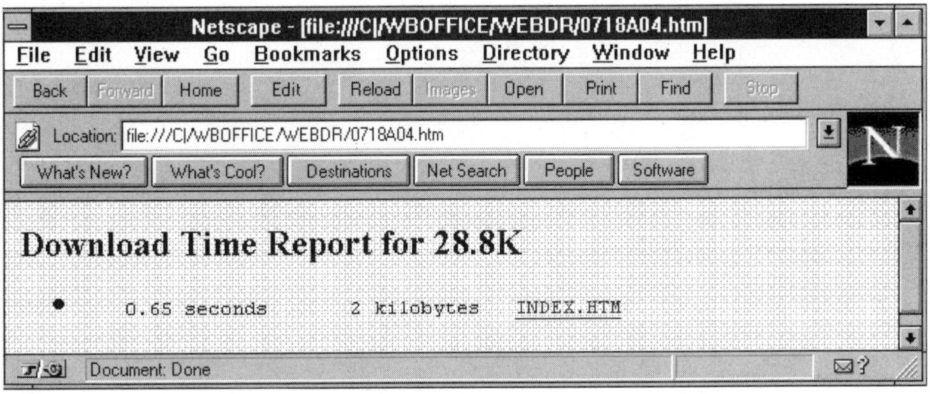

Figure 4.58 Page download time at 28.8 K modem speeds.

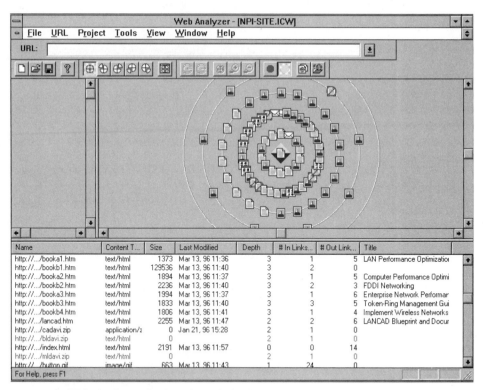

Figure 4.59 Web Analyzer displays hyperlinks between documents and references to missing links.

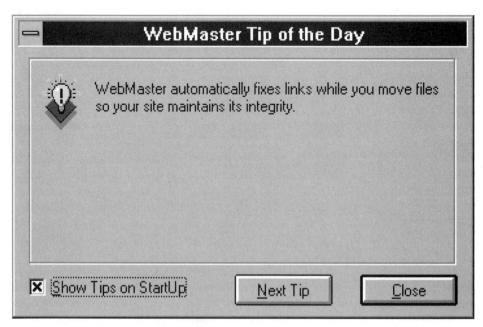

Figure 4.60 WebMaster repairs missing links automatically as you move files, rename files, or alter the basic directory structure.

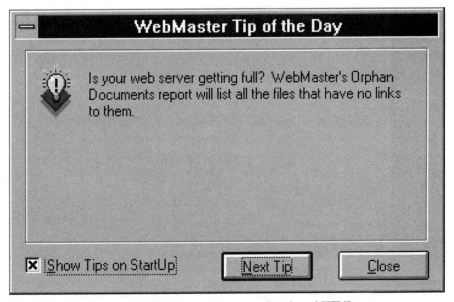

Figure 4.61   WebMaster searches for lost resources and orphaned HTML pages.

in Figure 4.62 shows one approach to this type of map. Both WebMapper and Web Analyzer create similar maps. The map from WebMapper can be exported as an HTML file and a GIF file with a hotspot map. You can also make a screen shot of the map you like best and create the image map in MAP-THIS.EXE (on the CD-ROM).

While most maps show the hierarchy of a site from the home page, Web-Master also displays the site from the view of a specific resource. In this example shown by Figure 4.63, a missing document is referenced by three different documents. If that document is missing, this map shows the broken links ($\times$) or what documents need repair if that document is no longer necessary in the website.

As I mentioned previously, WebMaster is a taskbar for browsers, editors, image editors, and map makers. When you click on a particular resource, an associated tool is activated so that you can directly view or manipulate the contents of that web resource. Figure 4.64 shows this. O'Reilly includes Web-View with the Web Site server and it does the same thing. This is not a unique service; however, WebView does validate the links, too. Detailed information about the components in a website, not just maps, is shown in Figure 4.65. Web Analyzer provides this same information with its split, three-window design.

Security

Cybershop, cyberstore, and commercial website security are many things ranging from physical site security, backup, site text and image source control to limited access to data records and financial transactions. Ideally,

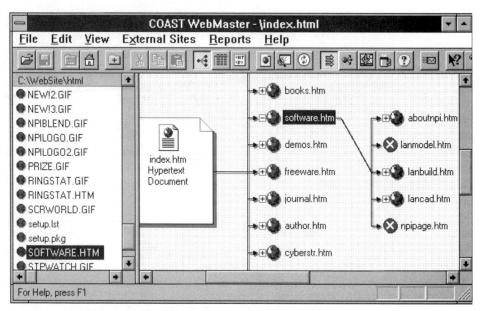

Figure 4.62 WebMaster displays an image map of the site, useful for tracing broken links but is also source for creating a graphical representation of a site.

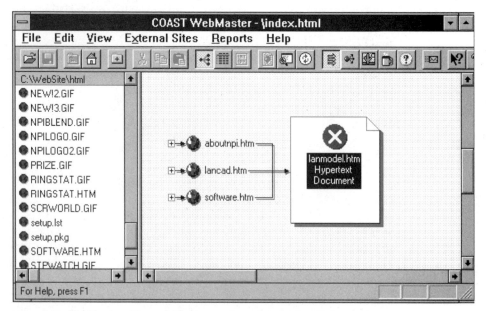

Figure 4.63 WebMaster shows which documents contain broken links.

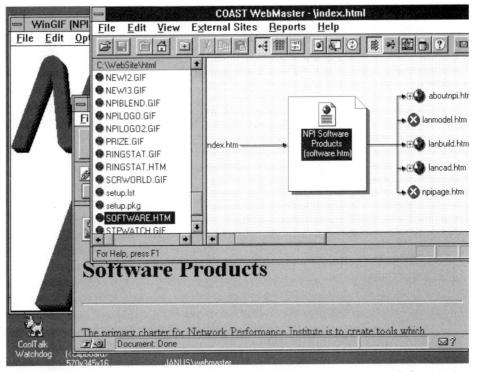

Figure 4.64 WebMaster serves as a task bar to activate secondary functions, including viewing and editing images.

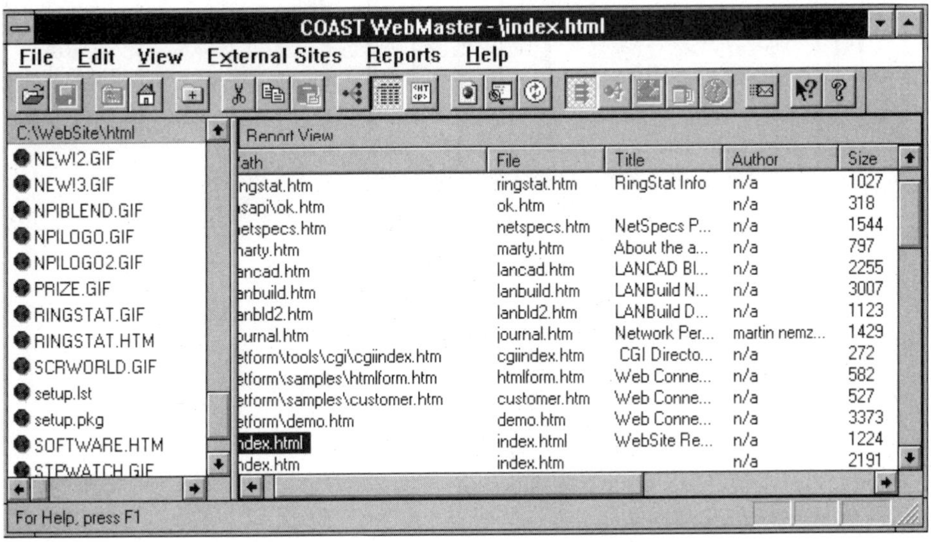

Path	File	Title	Author	Size
ingstat.htm	ringstat.htm	RingStat Info	n/a	1027
sapi\ok.htm	ok.htm		n/a	318
etspecs.htm	netspecs.htm	NetSpecs P...	n/a	1544
narty.htm	marty.htm	About the a...	n/a	797
ancad.htm	lancad.htm	LANCAD BI...	n/a	2255
anbuild.htm	lanbuild.htm	LANBuild N...	n/a	3007
anbld2.htm	lanbld2.htm	LANBuild D...	n/a	1123
ournal.htm	journal.htm	Network Per...	martin nemz...	1429
etform\tools\cgi\cgiindex.htm	cgiindex.htm	CGI Directo...	n/a	272
etform\samples\htmlform.htm	htmlform.htm	Web Conne...	n/a	582
etform\samples\customer.htm	customer.htm	Web Conne...	n/a	527
etform\demo.htm	demo.htm	Web Conne...	n/a	3373
ndex.html	index.html	WebSite Re...	n/a	1224
ndex.htm	index.htm		n/a	2191

Figure 4.65 Website resource details.

website security is part of IS and physical employee security, not different or separate from standard defensive measures. If your commercial site is hosted by an ISP, do not completely trust their backup, security, firewall, and service measures. In fact, my ISP of the last three years has been breached four times, lost my website three times, provided partial but nevertheless incomplete restoration of corrupted partitions at least twice, and I have reloaded the website from a local drive at least six times with an FTP transfer and once from QIC80 backup tape. In fact, links seem to be always broken, HTML files invariably corrupted, and the site takes constant maintenance even when nothing changes. The message is that things do go wrong and security is a daily, escalating endeavor.

The most frequent security breach of cyberstore information is by employees or former employees from the inside using inside information. Inside thefts are the most profound and expensive, and create the most chaos. The number of hackers who profit by illegal activity is estimated to be a few hundred in the United States, about the same in Germany, and several thousand in Russia. However, these numbers are dwarfed by bored teenagers with nothing better to do on AOL and who are looking for the most challenging puzzle they can find. This is war—serious to you as the designer and responsible party for a cyberstore operation—but for the most part, a safe war for the reprobate hackers. In fact, *www.gte.com,* the website for GTE, was attacked within five minutes of going live with a telecommunications line to the Internet backbone.

Security is also not a technology as much as it is a faith and a confidence. It is important that customers believe that your site supports security, will protect their privileged information, and will provide a level of integrity consistent with their expectations. The use of firewalls, security IDs and passwords, and other techniques is only as effective as the weakest link in the chain. Site management has to walk that chain looking for breaks, bypasses, and corrosion. Security becomes a policy, not a tangible result or product. The U.S. General Accounting Office (GSA) published an internal document after a two-year security and consulting study. The 10-point program as distributed includes these steps:

1. Establish clean and consistent security policies and procedures.
2. Define a hierarchy of responsibility.
3. Run vulnerability assessments to identify security weaknesses at all sites and hosts.
4. Make mandatory corrections of identified host, network, system, and security weaknesses.
5. Perform mandatory reporting of attacks to better identify and communicate vulnerabilities and necessary corrective actions.
6. Record damage assessments to reestablish the integrity of the information jeopardized by attack.

7. Teach an awareness training so that users understand security risks, information value, organizational security methods, personal responsibility, and good computing practices.

8. Provide assurance that all employees have sufficient time and training to provide security.

9. Use firewalls, security access cards, and other technical solutions.

10. Develop a tracking system and proactive capability to aggressively detect and react to attacks and to prosecute attackers.

Additional security measures include ID badges, access control, pass cards, and inventory checks. A policy of *zero tolerance* for theft goes a long way in communicating organizational policy, business practice, and legal intent should a problem occur. This policy should be added to the employee handbook and referenced occasionally. I mention inventory checks, specifically physical inventories, because most fraud and security problems begin from the inside. Without viable financial systems (and inventory controls) valuable products can disappear, with all the blame placed on the cyberstore. Who is to know?

Create a team atmosphere so that organizational employees and outsourced contractors feel some obligation and partnership. Threat assessment and security might become a weekly walk-through and challenge. You might even consider awards for employees who discover problems. However, the emphasis should remain on creating a team that works together to prevent problems rather than snitches on each other after they occur.

Also, as employees work from remote sites, these and roving laptaps represent security holes. Frequently, passwords and IDs are imbedded inside log-on scripts. A stolen laptop or appropriated desktop unit becomes an open door into the ordering, shipping, payment, and even bank statement reconciliations on the cyberstore. In fact, the security risk does not end with the cyberstore because if you integrate cyberstore operations with existing workflow, a thief with a stolen laptop or a disgruntled employee can create a paper trail so that a trailer can pull up to the loading dock with appropriate bills of lading and empty a warehouse. Enforce laptop encryption if you can, or at least perform security audits for remote users to check their access and potential vulnerability to your cyberstore.

Beyond the standard network and IS security countermeasures, security is partly a red herring for the functional cyberstore. Security for on-line transmission of credit card information is an overblown issue. Consider the total lack of security of cellular phone NAMs and the content of conversations over this wireless link. Contrast the almost nonexistent reports about the theft of credit card information from an Internet transmission to the frequent news reports of sales clerks passing on account numbers or hospital workers getting account information from unconscious patients or hospital billing systems. I rarely hesitate to send my credit card information over the Internet as part of a form, data transaction, or E-mail if I know the company and regard it as legitimate. That is my practical view of the issue. However, press reports of fraud and problems may scare away some potential customers. Reality and legality, or rather "what a prudent person should do," become a different website commerce issue. If you require security to protect payment information, lock in the delivery of information on software, or provide external access to corporate data, security measures are required on a practical basis.

Since it is common knowledge that security problems exist with authorization of credit card purchases over the Internet, the legal standing *realistically* means that you as a cyberstore merchant have to exercise some security measures to prevent credit card fraud. There are simple solutions available that require no advanced technology, only some simple logic and modifications to the sales transaction workflow.

Although the Internet traffic is open in the same way that a party telephone system is and everyone could possibly "listen in," the reality is that there is so much information that it is virtually impossible to filter except by a direct tap of an organization known to be submitting credit or debit cards. While it is also possible to filter for strings in the format of 9999-9999-9999-9999 99/99, which is the U.S. format for credit card information, or 999 999 99999 99/99, which is the format for most other places in the world, the hit ratio for useful credit card information is going to be very small. If names and addresses to match with credit card numbers are made available, as most vendors and the credit card clearing houses are now requesting, the transaction is likely to be rejected and the card holder does not have to substantiate the fraud.

In addition, U.S. federal law, specifically the Fair Credit Billing Act, limits credit card liability to a maximum of $50 for fraud per occurrence. If you use a single credit card solely for Internet purchases, loss exposure is limited to $50. In addition, consumers (anyone who uses a credit card, even within a corporation) can dispute charges while they are being researched. Unless you have lost the physical card or been very immature with its use, most credit card companies do not assess the $50 fee. In addition, AT&T Universal Credit Card in conjunction with AT&T WorldNet Internet service (free to AT&T customers) provides full financial liability protection in addition to lost wallet protection. This means a card holder has no liability. This can be confirmed by calling AT&T at (800) 400–1447. I have included this information as a useful tool to dispel any doubt for customers at your Internet site. In addition, Columbus Bank and Trust Company is offering the WebCard VISA with guaranteed security against unauthorized purchases. You can post this information as a marketing tool so that customers are less concerned about payment risks.

Customers can call an interactive voice recognition system or a touch-tone computer system to corroborate, order, and provide credit card information. The more advanced systems store voices and convert spoken numbers into computer data. Older systems and more reliable ones convert the sounds from the touch-tone pad into numbers. This represents the most automated order-taking system.

If providing credit information over the Internet or by touch-tone phone seems to be a substantial risk, a customer might prefer to provide credit card information by facsimile or to phone personally. Since any form fill-in process (even CGI) can activate a fax-back service, order information can be faxed to the customer for confirmation. The customer can then sign the order form and add credit card information to fax back to you. If a customer is still queasy about this process, your organization can phone the customer for credit card details. Most people buy products from catalogs over the phone and provide credit card information. As such, they should not be averse to providing this same information that most people already do. The cybermall at eShop realizes these concerns and posts this security guarantee in listed Figure 4.66.

Practical responses do not often satisfy the lawyers or answer the more complex technical issues, some of which are addressed in the next section. Security for web and Internet transactions is a function of both logical and physical security. The reality is that everything on the Internet is in plain view. Logical security refers to the aspect of the Internet as one large network that has no real physical presence. The closest a user comes to physical Internet presence is the access phone line. Everything on the Internet is open, even "secured" or password-protected data and transmissions are broadcast in *plain view*. *Encryption* is the processing of data under a secret key in such a way that the original data can only be determined by a recipient in possession of a secret key. It is the application of a specific algorithm to data so as to alter the appearance of the data to make it incomprehensible to those who might attempt to steal the information. The process of decryption applies the algorithm in reverse to restore the data to its original appearance. At the physical level, security usually means passwords, access cards, and servers that are physically locked up and also placed inside a secure room.

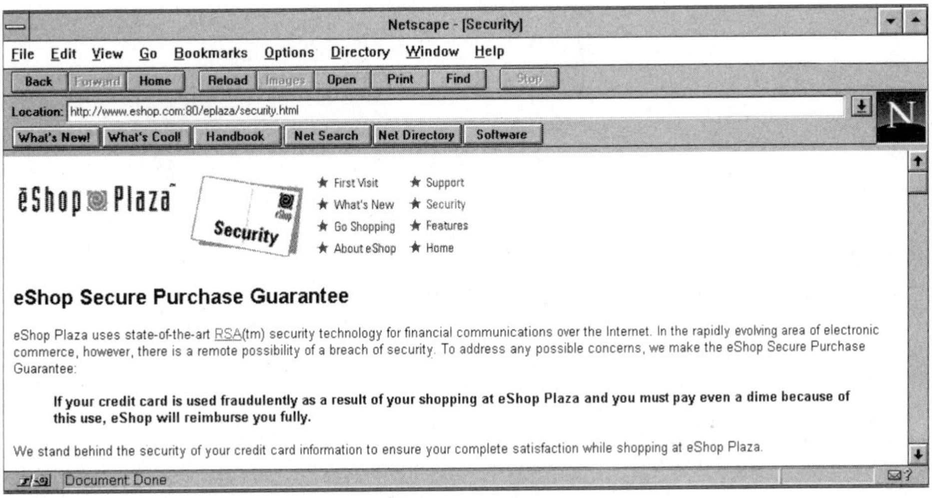

Figure 4.66 The on-line security guarantee for eShop.

At the simplest level, cyberstore security means protecting the site from external attack. HTML pages, CGI code, and scripts need protection from a motivated hacker who typically adds graffiti to a site. This external protection entails setting passwords, limiting file access to read only, and hiding the scripts from all eyes. Since it is also possible that someone internally could accidentally or unwittingly alter the HTML page flow and modify or create a new script with adverse affects, you also want to create some internal controls too (Figure 4.67). This is likely to include source code control and periodic site backup; a master site staging image is best because it is complete. Encryption techniques typically protect information provided by customers; it rarely protects the merchant (except for the legal risk of "not doing enough" to protect the financial interests of a customer). The two exceptions are when products are delivered to a customer in an encrypted format and when the merchant uses a digital certificate to authenticate that the user is who he says he is. Most of the security risk is inside the operational side of the firewall, where most webmasters think the Intranet is safe, the site is safe, and their jobs are safe.

Security is only as strong as the weakest link. If you construct the cyberstore infrastructure with many tools and components, realize that security is not a factor, summation, or additive combination of the chosen tools, but rather of the strength of the least secure component. For example, consider an environment composed of a firewall, Netscape Commerce Server, WebDBC, JetForms, and

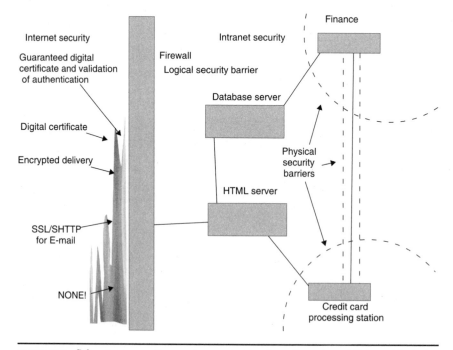

Figure 4.67 Cyberstore security requires protection from the external Internet but also attacks from within.

MS SQL Server. The firewall will prevent certain types of intrusions as you define them. The Netscape Commerce Server with SSL protects transmission of credit card information. Both WebDBC and JetForm will maintain appropriate path flows through transactions. However, the transaction database could be unsecured to FTP transfers from remote sites, lack security passwords and encryption for access to credit card numbers and expiration dates, and may be completely open to insiders over a local network. That represents the weakest link. Even if you are already familiar with firewalls, physical security, passwords and authentication, public key cryptography, web server and development software is easy to misuse; if you don't use it properly, much of the security you could gain by using it might be deeded to the weakest link.

Several client and server tools are available. The "best" client-side tool is probably Pretty Good Privacy (PGP). This tool runs in most environments, from Amiga, OS/2, UNIX, and DOS, to Windows, and GUI front ends are available to simplify the parameter setup for this tool. E-mail messages and enclosures can be encrypted with a private key for distribution and unpackaged by users and customers with a posted public key. The benefit of the PGP approach is that some E-mail applications include PGP linkages or OLE support. The next screen shot shows the PGP website at MIT in Figure 4.68.

All versions of PGP generate a private key that should not be released to anyone and also a public key, which is distributed for E-mail decryption and extraction of software or other computer-formatted files. The key is typically

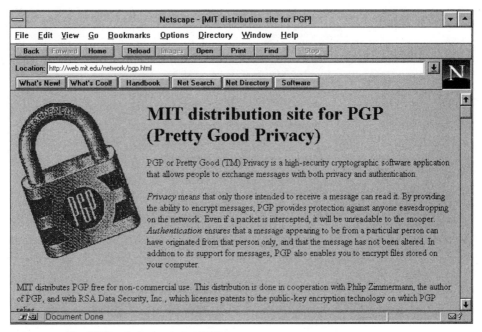

Figure 4.68 The PGP website hosted at MIT.

stored as a file. This file is often delivered to trading partners, but otherwise, despite the notation that it is "public," you do not want to post it for everybody to see. The PGP encryption keeps out most prying eyes, and lack of access to the public key keeps out all others including those with PGP software. The key is displayed in Figure 4.69.

As with all security and encryption tools, do not forget your password. There is likely to be no one else who can break the password and restore your files. A user interface to the strictly character-based PGP lets both website administrators and clients automatically process E-mail and files. One such tool is shown in Figure 4.70.

PGP is strictly an add-in tool to other processes. When you want to enable file security and encryption as part of the process, the encryption and decryption must be integrated directly with the other applications. Microsoft has only recently released a security and encryption API library, while other vendors have been selling specialized developers' toolkits for quite a while. One such example, the Carrick .DLL library from Azalea Software, is shown with a primitive Visual Basic front-end in Figure 4.71. It is important to realize that Carrick is not based on DES, triple DES, PGP algorithms, or other common public/private key systems. The single key is used both to encode and decode.

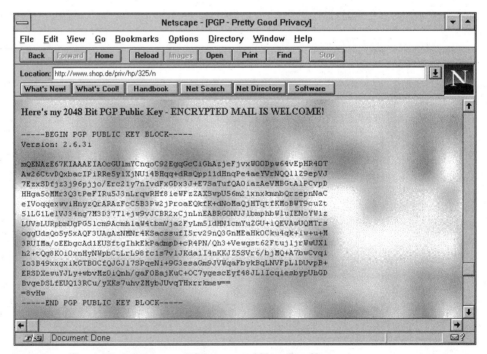

Figure 4.69 The public key for *some* PGP encrypted E-mail or files.

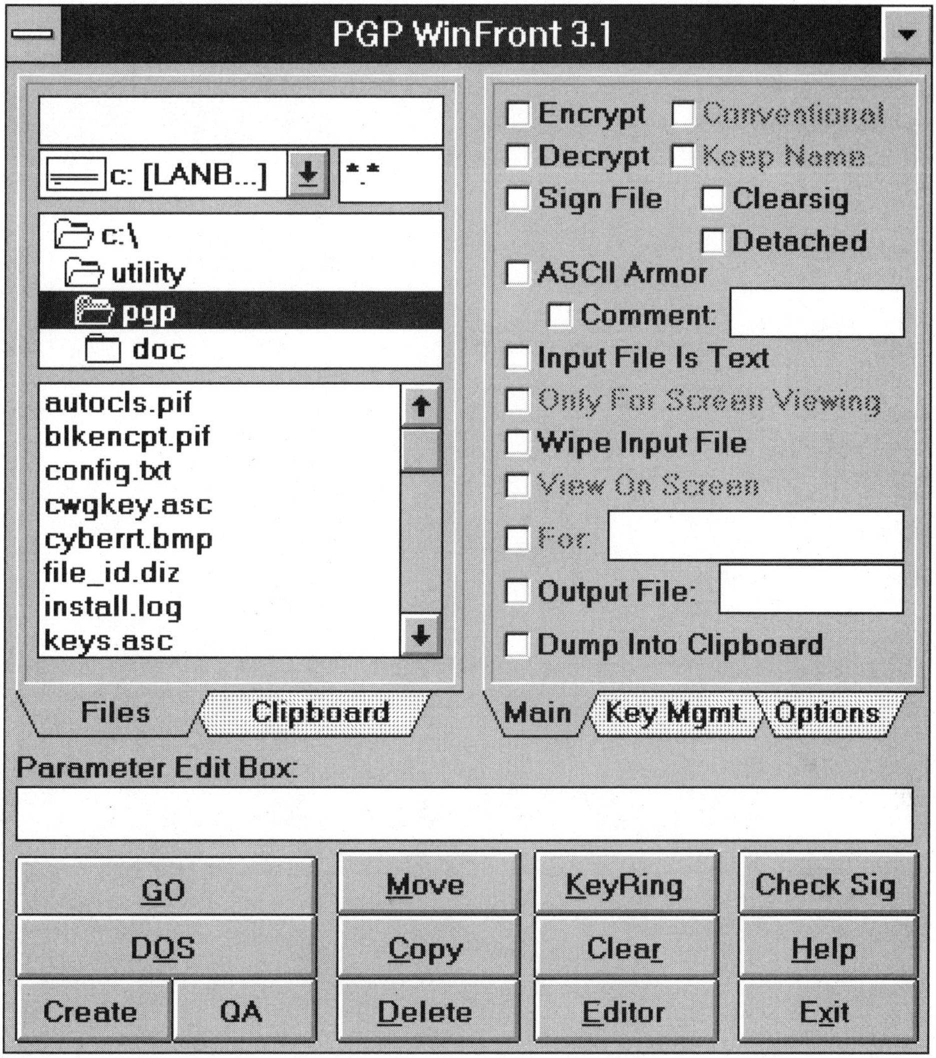

Figure 4.70 A GUI front end to PGP.

Security costs. The first part of this chapter included a budget and a break-down by percentage for the "typical" cyberstore. However, security is likely to become a serious and rabid expense should any fraud, security breaches, or suspected hacking occur. While the ISP will provide a considerable amount of security and perhaps chargeback for construction, coding, and activation of SSL or SHTTP forms, all these problems become website implementation and management problems when the web server is part of a larger local network

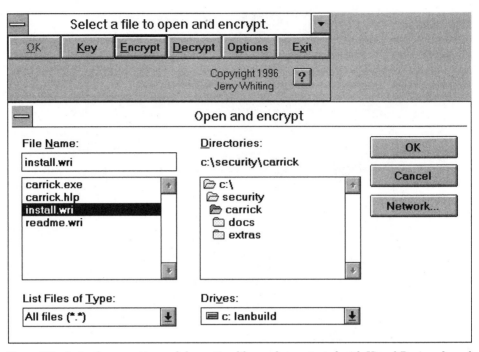

Figure 4.71 A simple encryption and decryption library demonstrated with Visual Basic code and a common dialogue box.

or resides locally with either a connection to an ISP or to the Internet back-bone. Table 4.1 addresses security hardware, software, firewall, and audit costs for an operation with 100 network users and a thriving cyberstore.

Plugging server leaks.   Web server leaks may or may not exist. You do not know about them until someone defeats your security implementation. That is the realistic and hard approach. If you want to proactively address potential leaks and breaches, the best technique is to search the web for security information about your platform, web server, and any middleware or utilities used to process cyberstore transactions. Realize that server security can be under-mined at the firewall, the web server, the security settings on the applications or source HTML files on your web server (or even ISP host site), the CGI scripts, database middleware, and potentially any VBScripts, Java applets, or JavaScript code. About 42 percent of all web server security breaches have oc-curred at sites with firewalls. Most of these leaks were not detected by the fire-wall and did not circumvent it, but did break through with IP spoofing, au-thentication failures, and other tricks. The list below details some specific se-curity information sources:

```
JavaScript can obtain an E-mail address:
  (see http://www.popco.com/grabtest.html)
```

```
JavaScript can surreptitiously track web usage
  (see http://www.osf.org/~loverso/javascript/index.html)
JavaScript can map local disks:
  (see http://www.osf.org/~loverso/javascript/dir.html)
Java can attack servers behind firewalls:
  (see (http://www.cs.princeton.edu/~ddean/java)
Security leak from IIS to NT Server:
described at http://www.omna.com/iis-bug.htm)
but the fix available at:
http://www.microsoft.com/infoserv
```

These are not the only sources. Check vendor sites and newsgroups about
your platform or server software, follow hyperlinks to other sites, and view the
security entries for this book's home page. The latest and best source of security information is dynamic.

NCSA security testing. The National Computer Security Association (NCSA)
has created a lab to test and certify firewalls that protect organizations
from intrusion but still allow business functions to be accomplished. NCSA
has created the Firewall Product Developer's Consortium, a subgroup that

**TABLE 4.1   Security Costs for a Network Enterprise
with an Attached Website**

	Cost
LAN security	
Encryption (local)	$ 15,000
LAN auditing utilities	$ 2,500
Desktop security utilities	$ 10,000
Security add-ins	$ 5,000
LAN single sign-on control	$ 5,000
Virus protection	$ 2,500
WAN security	
Router encryption	$ 14,000
Passcard control	$ 8,000
Remote access control	
Access control	$ 2,000
Central management tools	$ 18,000
Internet security	
Firewall	$ 26,000
SSL	$ 500
Encryption (E-mail, etc.)	$ 2,000
Security-related services	
Audit	$ 8,000
Implementation	$ 24,000
Policy documentation	$ 3,000
Training	$ 8,500
TOTAL	**$154,000**

has defined a suite of attacks that the firewall must withstand while allowing a set of business functions to pass through, such as E-mail, FTP, and web access. This product testing and certification is no guarantee that use of a particular firewall will protect you from security break-ins, but it represents a minimum seal of approval. Certification of a firewall is not an endorsement. Physical access to a web server or other host hardware, internal access to an Intranet, and weak control (as in passwords and IDs) can undermine firewall protection. The following is a list of certified firewalls:

- AltaVista Firewall
- Black Hole
- Borderware
- Checkpoint Firewall-1
- Eagle
- Gauntlet Internet Firewall
- OnGuard
- PrivateNet
- Secured Network Gateway
- SunScreen SPF-100
- TurnStyle Firewall System

It is important to note that the certification is based on testing a particular software or hardware release on particular platforms and operating systems. Firewalls are not necessarily certified for use on other platforms or with a mixed platform environment. In other words, a firewall that is certified for NT 3.51 may not pass certification for Windows 95 or Windows NT 4.x. The Internet home page for this book lists the current NCSA firewall testing results in greater detail.

Proactive security. Haystack WebStalker is a software-based automated web protection tool. While most other security measures, including passwords, firewalls, and router filters are gatekeepers, proactive tools such as WebStalker are like Doberman pinschers and cable TV cameras. This new wave of network management tools looks for problems as they happen and creates various events logs so that problems can be unraveled later or the method of security compromise can be understood. While immediate or passive prevention is the mainstay for firewalls, this new breed of tools can prevent or terminate user access even when the password, IDs, and other authentication suggest that the user is valid. However, the audit trail of events becomes a very valuable ally to curtail future attacks. The configuration screen for WebStalker is shown in Figure 4.72.

Attacks can generate various alarms through monitoring stations, beepers, pagers, E-mail, or phone calls. The screen shot in Figure 4.73 shows an alarm on the system server. This information could be propagated through other communication channels or sent in addition to the basic server monitor if an alert is deemed severe enough. In addition to the configurations tracked, WebStalker traces and audits the procedures listed in the screen shot in Figure 4.74.

Indexing flaws.   The website should include only those files material to the site and should not contain unlinked and unreferenced files. These files could represent temporary files, old information, out-of-date information, privileged sources, and mistakes. The file rights (security settings) are not frequently monitored, with the result that an unscrupulous hacker could replace these files with ones specially designed to pierce security. Even some of the firewall products, such as TrueSite and other tools, will not notice these files because they are not linked into the chain from the site home page.

While it is generally unlikely that a random hacker can pierce the veil of home security, almost all of the site indexing tools can, by creating special

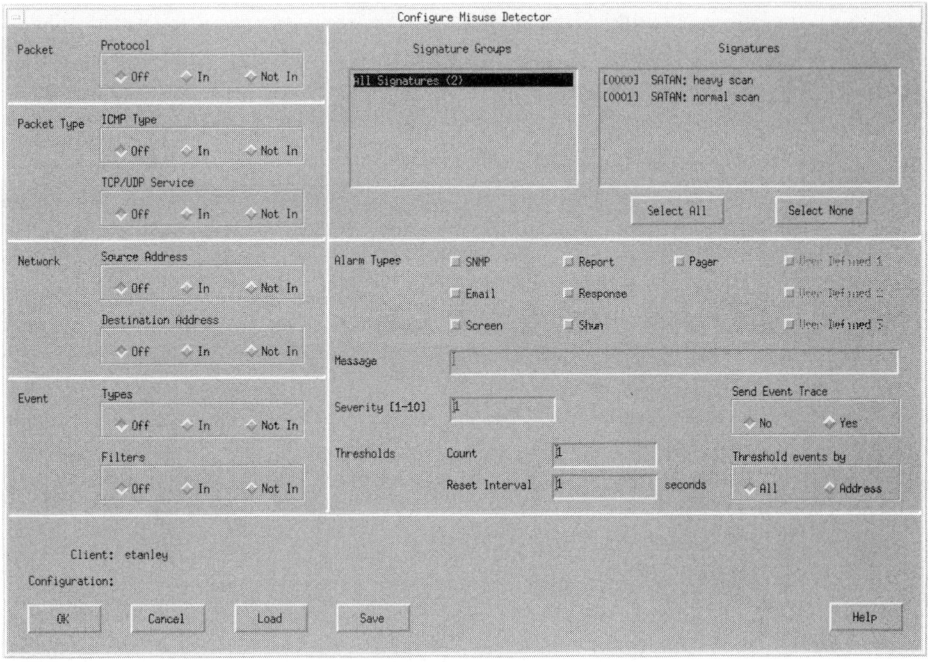

Figure 4.72   Profile and configuration screen of WebStalker.

Figure 4.73 WebStalker shows attacks interactively and categorizes these by severity and frequency. The filters can be set higher so that normal or nonessential messages are ignored.

HTML pages with tables of contents, indexes, keywords, phrases, and references to these files even though site developers never intended these pages to be available and visible. The bottom line for security is to check your indexes and get debris out of the live site; save it for development on the development sites.

Page caching. You might note that this document information report shows that the page is currently available in cache on the browser's system. This

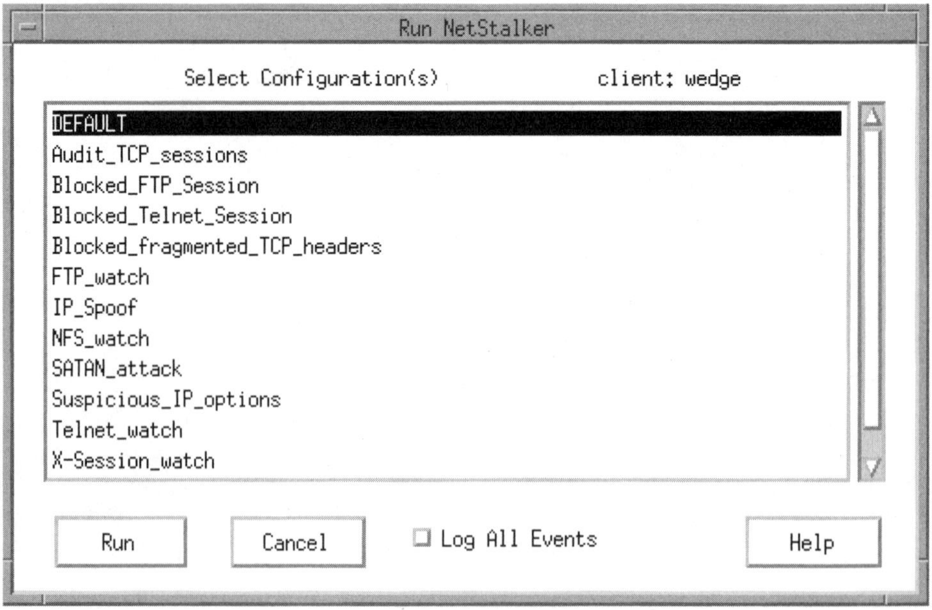

Figure 4.74 WebStalker activation screen for performance audits.

improves performance, but can create a security problem with encrypted pages. For everyone's satisfaction, make sure that your secure web server disables caching at the user's browser before transmitting a secure page, flushes the cache after receiving back the contents of the secured transmission, and then reactivates the cache for the user. The issue is not that private information is transmitted over the Internet but that cache pages with private information remain after a transaction is complete and can be found in the browser (by moving page forward or backward) or stored as a temporary text file on the hard disk of the computer running the browser. The local cache file name is identified as M0OUNKID, which is shown in Figure 4.75.

WindowsNT security breaches. WindowsNT includes a better file system than DOS or Windows95. Unix and the many derivatives provide good security once you are aware of the holes and install the appropriate patches. However, WindowsNT 3.51 and WindowsNT 4.0 provide a platform more familiar to most organizations and with a wider range of commercially supported toolkits. Unfortunately, Numega Technologies created a public domain utility (NTFSDOS.EXE on the CD-ROM) for DOS and Windows users to open on a read-only basis all files stored in the NTFS (NT File System) file format. You can download this utility and later releases from the O'Reilly and Associates website at *ftp://ftp.ora.com/pub/examples/windows/win95.update/schulman.html*. It really isn't a long stretch for someone to decompile, modify, and recompile a version with read and write access. The utility ignores security settings and bypasses all file security. Microsoft has stated that this isn't a serious concern because it only demonstrates the need to restrict physical access to the web server and NT Server or NT Workstation disk units. Anyone

Location:	http://www.razorfish.com/
File MIME Type:	test/html
Source:	Currently in disk cache
Local cache file:	M0OUNDKID
Last Modified:	Unknown
Last Modified:	Unknown
Content Length:	2491
Expires:	No date given
Charset:	iso-8859-1 (default)
Security:	This is an insecure document that is not encrpyted and offers no security protection

Figure 4.75 Document information shows how cache status can compromise secured information.

who really wants to break the security can take the disks to make a disk copy by tape, CD-ROM, or direct disk-to-disk transfer.

Java security breaches.   Java and JavaScript are secure to all but the most concerted attacks, but can become carriers for viruses and for other executable files with viruses. The problems as outlined in various papers (some referenced by the book website) include the bytecode loader, which checks for forged pointers, access from a known hostile computer, access or object restriction violations, but does provide some holes to get around these checks. Although the loader can prevent many types of attacks, it is not secure from repetitive and malicious attempts to defeat the system. WebScan from McAfee and other viral scan tools often require too much memory and CPU time. Although the users cannot get into the system, an ongoing denial of service brute force attack eats up system CPU cycles or cripples part of the platform and its services. However, failure to scan for security traps and viruses can potentially move these viruses and other problems from the web server, the web page cache, out to the users' desktops.

The application of security and virus protection is an implementation and managerial issue that most often needs to be addressed by web users and sites of web users, rather than by designers of websites and cyberstores. At best, the cyberstore is a file store with minimum connectivity to other hosts and is basically an information distribution site rather than a collector. However, realize the potential for damage to product and inventory databases, transaction and payment logs, and EPS systems. In addition, recognize that some users may not be enabled for Java or JavaScript, or may be prevented by their own firewalls from using scripts with these embedded tools; you do not want to build a site that excludes access for potentially lucrative customers.

Illicit knowledge about the host system, the operating system, hostile applets, HTTP and FTP proxy servers, and interapplet sabotage can compromise security. In addition, multiple party attacks can leave components on a server that in and of themselves are not hostile and may actually be useful, but when combined like some two-part nerve gases, create a hostile virus or security breach.

- Open architecture
- Broadcast communication
- Easily tapped
- Limited hardware security measures
- Easily jammed transmissions (point-to-point)

It is also possible to capture the E-mail address from any browser supporting an E-mail applet, such as Navigator, with a little bit of code. You, too, can see this demonstrated at *http://www.popco.com/grabtest.html.*

The key part of this web page is the JavaScript applet that includes this line:

```
<BODY onLOAD = "document.mailme.submit()">
```

This is useful for the cyberstore operator, but invasive for web surfers. Netscape has plugged the security in later releases of their browser, but I suspect it is only a matter of time until someone figures out a new approach to gathering browser information, if only from the Cookie file.

Cookies security breaches

Version 2 of both Netscape Navigator and Microsoft Explorer include the *Cookie* functionality, which is defined in the specifications as *persistent client-state HTTP Cookies*. Realistically, this is the file called COOKIES.TXT in the browser subdirectory, which looks like a Windows 3.x .INI file (a file storing configuration and registration information). Each entry itself in the file is called a Cookie, and the file contains multiple Cookies. It is important to realize that the http protocol used for web browser is designed to be stateless. The Cookie is designed to store information between requests and overcome some of the difficulties that arise in more complex web transaction processing, when commercial transactions are best when not truly stateless. For example, you would not want a customer to order a monogrammed dress shirt twice (because an accidental system error did not recognize an aborted transaction), pay for it twice, receive two of them, and then complain that the nonreturnable duplicated order was a vendor mistake.

The COOKIE_S.HTM on the CD-ROM or that is available from the Netscape website details the standard parameters and their uses. In general, the parameters define the user name, mail address, dates, registrations, and other information stored from one browser session to the next. However, shrewd marketing organizations (examples include DoubleClick, Focalink, Maximizer, Sapphire, and Interse) have exploited this need feature in browsers and have begun target marketing. The concept is to limit the number of times users see a banner advertisement (for example, at Yahoo) or cycle through a list of advertisements, and then use this information to track the user who is hitting various sites and when. Figure 4.76 shows the COOKIES.TXT text file, sanitized somewhat with the removal of sensitive encrypted and personal information.

Although user information is not stored per se in the COOKIES.TXT file (note that much of the literature incorrectly refers to a phantom file called COOKIE.TXT, without the "S"), a Cookies program could ask a user to fill out a form, receive that information, and store it within the file. Some Cookies sites are innocuous. This site in Figure 4.77 includes the code (which is also on the companion CD-ROM) and demonstrates site access counting.

```
─                           Notepad - COOKIES.TXT                      ▾ ▲

 File  Edit  Search  Help

# Netscape HTTP Cookie File                                                    ▲
# http://www.netscape.com/newsref/std/cookie_spec.html
# This is a generated file! Do not edit.

.netscape.com    TRUE   /custom FALSE   946638779       version  01.50E00
.netscape.com    TRUE   /custom FALSE   946638779     . custom   n00FFFFFF000000CC0000006699n09yny10::Wel
.netscape.com    TRUE   /custom FALSE   946638779       p1       blank
.netscape.com    TRUE   /custom FALSE   946638779       note     Reminder: Add this page to your bookmark
.netscape.com    TRUE   /       FALSE   946713599       NETSCAPE_ID    c65ffb1e,c71c06bf
.focalink.com    TRUE   /       FALSE   946670400       SB_ID    ads03.036848305210475779 43
cgi.netscape.com     FALSE  /       FALSE   946713599       NETSCAPE_VERIFY c65ff94b,c75f3504
www.sapphiregroup.com    FALSE  /       FALSE   884610153       PBCookieSupport Yes
206.7.214.133:80     FALSE  /       FALSE   884610167       PBCookieSupport Yes
www.PageBlazer.com       FALSE  /       FALSE   884610212       PBCookieSupport Yes
206.7.214.170:80     FALSE  /       FALSE   884616644       PBCookieSupport Yes
www.SapphireGroup.com    FALSE  /       FALSE   884610776       PBCookieSupport Yes
www.15r.com      FALSE  /       FALSE   945046800       QuestKeys      2016,52722,53892,57330,66960,128
.infoseek.com    TRUE   /       FALSE   866950383       InfoseekUserId  84EF2751BD0D9D4D6746D3BF7CC2FDE5
maximized.com    FALSE  /       FALSE   946688399       INTERSE ppp-mia-295885836575204837          ▼
◄                                                                             ►
```

Figure 4.76 The COOKIES.TXT file used to store browser information.

Once the "Cookie" has been initialized with an integer counter, the number is incremented at every access to the site, as demonstrated by Figure 4.78. This technique could also be applied to track access time and other duration or paths through a site. Every HTML page could add a different tag to the Cookie entry. The *New York Times* news site uses the Cookie for user identification and password authorization.

So far, Cookies can be used in combination with user authentication, site-specific user name and password, site path tracking and usage, site access, and even commercial transactions. For example, the Cookie could check a user's access to a site (pay-per-view) or a balance available for purchases. Cookies storage of a prepaid service is similar to prepaid phone cards; however the security risk is greater for both user and vendor.

Figure 4.77 The COOKIES.TXT file is not initialized for this site.

Figure 4.78 The COOKIES.TXT after it is initialized. Note that it will display actual site accesses as an integer.

In such cases, the Cookies file contains proprietary information that becomes a security risk for both users and cyberstores. Although a cyberstore is not legally responsible for a lost or damaged Cookies file on a customer's hard drive, good business practice means that the cyberstore will have to indemnify a user for unused service credits even if it is lost, stolen, or hacked. It is also important to realize that there is limited documentation on how applications at various websites modify the COOKIES.TXT file, so that reconstructing damaged files is impossible. There are no norms for Cookies formats and no central repository or design registry. Which user, as of yet, thinks to back up this file?

This means that credits stored in a Cookies file represent a financial liability for the cyberstore; and even more risky is the fact that an altered Cookies file represents an interesting pathway for commercial fraud by increasing credit availability or altering account names, numbers, and passwords. Central site storage of prepaid credits or billed services is probably better secured than dispersed Cookies files.

Although I am opposed to the invasion of privacy possible and maybe inherent with Cookies, one good use of this technology is to gather effective marketing information. An early morning call (7:20 am) on a Sunday from AT&T Long Distance offering special rates to Canada to a customer who almost never calls Canada is a disservice to both AT&T and a sleepy customer. AT&T should have the information to target receptive customers because it should have my billing information available. In this same way, a Cookie can be used to trace Internet usage and target appropriate users. For example, the sample Cookies file shows my interest and access to Sapphire Group, PageBlazer, Maximizer, and L5R. The next time I surf to a site hosted by a database middleware vendor, an applet could infer from my Cookies that I am serious about connecting HTML to ODBC for commercial transactions. The conclusion should be that I am a likely prospect for a follow-up phone call, access to more in-depth information at the site, and other direct marketing attempts through E-mail, official registration, or a very forward push to download a demo or multimedia presentation to my local hard disk.

Website Security

Attitudes about website security are changing, not because theft and abuse are so common, but because the stakes have become so high. Computer processing and networking technology are no longer simply tools isolated from organizational operations; cyberstore transaction processing is the lifeblood of many organizations. For these reasons, a concerted effort is required to divert attacks on web servers, database storage, interconnected hosts, and the firewalls ostensibly protecting them all. Most importantly, ongoing vigilance is required to counter threats, address attacks, and maintain the integrity of the website.

There are four types of security issues pertinent to website and cyberstore protection. First, you want to protect integrity of your website from damage or site content replacement. Second, you want to protect the integrity of data generated during the process of cyberstore sales. Third, you want to protect the content of data distributed over the Internet. Fourth, you want to protect and retain ownership of web materials, including website text, images, logos, and the arrangement that defines the uniqueness of your organization's site. The first three security requirements are immediately obvious, while the importance of the last item is not clear until you see your site copied or duplicated, or materials from it pirated and recycled. This section and subsequent ones address these implementation details.

Literature and movies have long had a special fascination with computer crime and abuse. Reports of yet another clever intrusion, massive white collar theft, or another computer virus scare are the grist for good reading. Like everyday burglaries, breaks in security are something that happens to someone else. In general, only minimum protection measures are applied, although such steps provide a false sense of security.

Security, while hard to define, is even more difficult to implement. What one software or hardware designer invents, another can crack, given enough incentive. Website, system, and network users invent new problems because they hit upon novel methods to attack the protection mechanisms, just as viruses and their designers adapt to new protection measures. Hardware security has been the traditional route of control because it has been possible to limit physical access to equipment. Yet, with the increasing distribution of equipment onto the factory floor, or into individual offices, and with remote links via the Internet and via Intranets to corporate networks, the cost and difficulty of applying security have increased significantly. Traditional security is a secluded room; however, that is no longer realistic with websites and particularly with dynamic cyberstores. Physical restrictions prevent physical attacks to the computer. Levels of access rights once restricted the logical access to the computer. However, the computer is no longer the homogeneous object it once was as the mainframe, and large cyberstores may reveal a farm of separate servers.

The mainframe has given way to tens, hundreds, or maybe even thousands of computers. Many units are important. However, even more important than those few units is the structural integrity of the network, the value of the ongoing operations, and the value of the data as a whole. Attacks upon one unit can propagate problems throughout the whole network. The acceptance of networks raises the organizational cost and significance of a careless, dishonest, or disgruntled employee damaging the machinery and information, or stealing information. Common reasons for security breaches include:

- Inadequate control over physical access
- Inadequate designation of sensitive materials
- Lack of locks on computer equipment
- Lack of organizational security policy
- Inadequate authentication and password implementations
- No access logs or journals
- Lack of records of attempts to break security
- Inadequate end-user security training

Security windows and techniques

Security, particularly with open and evolving websites, is an ongoing task. The best security is not to include anything on your website that you cannot afford to lose and hence reconstruct. Since most of the HTML and FTP files are for public access and download anyway, you need not be concerned about anyone "stealing" these files because they are free and available anyway. However, you do not want anyone except those who are authorized to alter or replace the website information. When access to some HTML or FTP resources is controlled by authentication and passwords, or enabled only after a customer has paid to receive information, security of these private resources becomes important. Consider granting no authorization to these files and encrypting them on the web server. Only when the server needs to deliver these files do the attributes get reset for E-mail delivery inclusion and a separate E-mail message with the password is then delivered. The Electronic Software Distribution section later in this chapter details this process and mentions A/Pay and Cryptolopes.

Although you should initiate the highest levels of security when you build your web server or hosted website as detailed in Chapter 3, security management does not end with the installation process. It continues—or at least it should—on a daily basis. Cyberstore sites become particularly vulnerable because there are so many pathways from the HTML interface through to the corporate databases, Cookies, and processes that automate the Internet POS process. At a minimum, you want to search the Internet sites of vendors for products that you are running and locate any new items relating to key words listed below:

- Security
- Virus
- Hacking
- SSL
- SHTTP
- Encryption
- Firewall or firewall breaches

You might also note the Princeton security website listed on the book's home page. There are other security-related sites listed on there, and links from those pages should provide more information than you can possibly read, let alone absorb. The following list suggests the simple tasks you should implement at your websites or client sites to maintain, test, validate, and audit website security:

- Examine server log tiles, such as process accounting, syslog, and lastlog, for unusual activity. This step is not foolproof because intruders often cover their tracks by editing these logs. Check the file time stamps, and/or create a daemon to generate a series of hourly log file copies.
- Look for unusual or hidden files—files that begin with a period and are not normally displayed. These files are often password-cracking systems.
- Examine all *setuid* files. Intruders leave these behind for later system access.
- Check systems binaries to ensure that no changes have been made. Compare the installation with the original tapes because a backup program may also have a Trojan Horse.
- Examine all tiles that are run by *cron* and *at* commands. These can provide intruders with backdoor entry to an operating system. In some cases, intruders get back onto the system through these access points even after an administrator has kicked them out.
- Inspect the *etc/inetd.* configuration files for unauthorized changes or additions, especially for shell programs. Be on the lookout for entries that execute a shell program, and verify that all programs in the *etc/inedn/osh* area haven't been replaced by Trojan Horses.
- Technicians should examine system and network configurations. The plus sign and inappropriate nonlocal hosts often point to an intrusion.

- Examine all computer configurations. In particular, check hosts that share NIS- or NFS-mounted partitions or are referenced in /etc/hosts and equivalent files. In addition, examine all remote hosts for possible entry.

- Check the *letc/host file* for any new domains that can break into the development, operational, or extended Intranet.

- Check the *letc/passwd* file for any new accounts, accounts with no passwords or User ID changes to existing accounts. You can create a duplicate and compare versions daily and verbally verify any changes.

In fact, because a cyberstore represents a massive integration effort, examining logs, validating sales activity, and matching payments with orders become important to catch fraud, hacking, and other normal errors or disruptions before they go too far. For example, if your site is used for the wrong merchant credit card number, a monthly settlement and reconciliation should limit the window of error to about 40 days. Some problems can be reversed. If you are rightly owed money, you can correct that problem within one or two billing cycles. Beyond that limit, however, the problem becomes your organization's responsibility.

Notice that security is both a technical issue and also a business and organizational one, too. If you are a webmaster in charge of security, you need assurances from the finance department that electronic payments are correct, if you do not audit them yourself. In contrast to the billing cycle protection in which you as a merchant are protected from errors and fraud, your organization could owe money to a bank or clearinghouse for up to a year after settlement. After problems happen you can only close the door to prevent the specific discovered problems from continuing.

Internet lacks security

The Internet FTP, HTTP, IP, and SMTP mail protocols provide no security, neither network security nor data security. The Internet is designed as a simple and open physical medium for data transmission. Furthermore, the Internet is not immune to snooping and spying, nor diversion of information because it is a broadcast technology. These basic vulnerabilities may surprise some readers. How could a network exist and succeed where security is either virtually impossible or comes at very high cost? However, the various Internet transmission protocols are straightforward, and thus allow for transparent transmission of encrypted data. Additionally, virtual switched and node switched technology increase security by limiting the range of the broadcasts. Firewalls and partitioning minimize some risks as well, but global and remote network access increase the security exposure.

The Internet, like UNIX from which it was primarily built, has begun its rise to be the enterprise connectivity solution because of its speed options, area coverage, and wide range of uses. While some specialized networks succeed solely because they meet strict government security criteria, or enforced contract bidding specifications, other networks have succeeded because they are simple enough to promote equipment interconnection and a generic platform. The Internet and the WWW fill this description admirably. Both are simple and robust. The Internet does, however, face security threats.

Threats to the website

There are four categories of website security threats: external threats, internal threats, physical risks, and data-related risks. Externally, an organization is at risk from events that might compromise the physical integrity of the website. These external threats are posed by Internet tie-lines, modems, or PBX telephone tapping performed by computer hackers, disgruntled or former employees, the occasional career crook, and motivated competitors.

Internally, the organization is vulnerable to profiteering employees and contractors, disgruntled employees, and the random disaster. Inventory shrinkage and accounting system manipulation are particularly lucrative when websites support cyberstore trading of hard goods or any monopolized or unique service. If the website is perceived as a toy and that data never have value, and all users agree that work accomplished on the website is totally exposed and expendable, then and only then is security an unnecessary constituent of website design and administration. Figure 4.79 uses a simplex matrix to illustrate those website components that are at risk.

Component	Internal	External
Power lines	√	√
Telephone lines	√	√
Remote connections	√	√
Premise wiring	√	Maybe
Wiring closets	√	
Website facilities	√	Remote components
Wireless RF/IR signals	√	√
Microwave long-links		√
Website nodes	√	
File server/host data	√	√
Inventory	√	Somewhat harder
Record embezzling	√	Somewhat harder
Output devices	√	
Intermediate nodes	√	
Wastepaper	√	√

Figure 4.79 Website risks and vulnerabilities.

External threats. A website is exposed to external threats from physical attacks and, to a significantly greater degree, from data tapping. Most websites are contained within a single building, and as a result are usually secure from physical affronts. The Internet presents a broader risk because the remote network channels and tie-lines are apt to run between buildings and through city blocks, and thus are apt to be fairly exposed. A saboteur cannot cut website wire or cable if it is locked away, nor disrupt power if power lines are underground and are similar in appearance to many other lines. While this issue is often overlooked by many organizations, computers, particularly mainframes, have been attacked by terrorists and competitors. An organization like QVC, Home Shopping Club, or the Internet Shopping Club is completely dependent on computer and Internet resources. As with all Internet and other websites, you can only do so much to lock away a website.

A destroyed mainframe, web server, or severed website is not only an expensive item to repair or replace, but also the data or time lost can bankrupt a cyberstore, especially when the transactional data are the lifeblood of the business. Think of the effects to a cyberstore should a student group protesting a political decision (e.g., investment in the Botswana sale of animal skins, or products tested on animals) decides to cut the Internet website in multiple locations, or worse, to bomb the wiring centers. Last, do not discount the possibility of catastrophe: computer damage from chance events such as fire, flood, hurricane, tornado, explosion, lightning and power surges or power deficits, or a collapsed building could set the organization back more than need be under such extreme circumstances. For example, the Oklahoma City bombing collapsed the entire building.

Fire damage is not merely the direct damage from the fire and heat itself, but also from fire axes, foam, debris, and water. The Internet tie-line links are also at risk from construction, excavation, and poor documentation. While extrinsic damage to a website might occur (it is best not overlooked), dial-up modem and remote connections are the more frequent avenues of assault on a website. Most websites, and everything on the Internet, see the external world through telephone connections, T-1 or T-3 links, and wireless signals. There is no reason to prohibit such contact, although there are many reasons to control it or limit it with routers and firewalls. Most organizations have local offices and satellite facilities, and communicate professionally and academically with others that are off-site. The problem is to prevent unauthorized entry onto the website to delete files, modify files, power down the website, spread viruses accidentally or maliciously, access privileged information, copy information for profit, or disseminate information to the public to discredit or supplant the organization. The potential dangers that must be guarded against are:

- Catastrophe

- Power disruption

- Terrorism

- Website jamming

- Website HTML and file replacement
- Website tapping
- Theft of information
- Destruction of information
- Data diddling (tampering)

Computer viruses. Of relevance to many website managers is the Internet virus propagated by a computer science graduate student. This Morris virus replicated itself without causing overt damage other than filling disk space and memory with its copies. It propagated by reading the Internet address tables and then reaching out across websites to infest all the other machines on the LANs and WANs. Some website managers may rightfully argue that the Internet virus did substantial damage. Not only did it halt networks and flood FTP and E-mail sites, but it also caused the attached machines to attend to the high-priority processing of the virus itself. Note that it did cause loss of use of the computers, lost time, and data loss, which amounted to tens of millions of dollars. While PC websites are prone to destructive viruses like *PC is stoned,* the *Jerusalem virus, Michaelangelo, Ping Pong,* the *disk killer,* and the disk boot sector virus primarily from Pakistan called *Joshi,* other websites with other types of platforms could easily be damaged by viruses specific to their hardware or software, or could be carriers for PC-based viruses.

In fact, many websites based on Windows95 or WindowsNT support DOS FAT partitions and even NTFS disks are sensitive to DOS viruses. A handful of Macintosh, OS/2, and UNIX viruses exist, but are relatively rare. Java and website script problems are possible but have yet to be documented. While personal computer viruses are disruptive, a website expands the damage by providing an easy path for website infection, or as is described later in this chapter, there may be no local effects but retransmission of the virus to customers. A new virus infects Postscript-PDL printers and damages the CMOS setup configuration. Other new viruses, called *stealth viruses,* attempt to hide themselves to outwit virus-detection software.

The availability of object-oriented programming and menu-driven virus design toolkits have simplified the process of creating new viruses. Even shrink-wrapped software from reputable vendors is not immune to these attacks. Sometimes attacks create no effects on the primary attack site. For instance, DOS viruses can propagate fairly innocuously on OS/2 and UNIX websites. While these diseases will change files and corrupt data when executed, the results tend not to be as immediate. However, when these viruses reach DOS stations through the website or through disk masters of software, the damage is typically immediate. To date, no one has died as a result of a virus; that may change, though, as computers control more activities, as more networks are controlled by HTTP and SNMP interfaces, and as the next generation of air traffic control computers are based upon nonproprietary computing platforms. It is easy to imagine situations in which a computer is monitoring a patient or controlling aircraft, a nuclear power plant, or chemical additions on an assembly line. A virus could unwittingly and unintentionally halt a host-based website or local server with devastating effects.

It is also possible to piggyback any manner of exploration tools, destructive viruses, or site analysis Trojan Horses through E-mail attachments, web scripts, Cookies, and other channels when web usage is not strictly partitioned from web construction. You probably do not want designers mixing surfing activities with designing activities, so as to protect your own site and customers from inadvertently spreading problems that do not affect web servers but that may affect the software or platforms used by browsers. In other words, like Typhoid Mary, your website could be immune from the effects of a virus or stray piggyback script, but could be a carrier of it to users, who are your trusting customers.

Virus damage protection and access prevention are available through software and hardware. Realize that the hardware is mostly called "firewalls," and that most of the website attacks have occurred in spite of these firewalls. Virus prevention and protection are not free, perfect, or faultless. New viruses can defeat current prevention methods, which require overhead in terms of CPU cycles and website bandwidth. In addition to the obvious cost of the virus software or hardware, there are costs for storing it, times to execute it, and the overhead related to running Terminate-and-Stay-Resident (TSR) and background operations. In fact, firewalls that protect internal networks from the external Internet and the web servers meant to provide cyberstore operations and technical support add latency and degrade overall performance.

Some software creates extensive checks and encoding tables so that in the event damage does occur, the damaged files can be repaired. As such, the overhead and process required to track viruses may be in effect worse than the actual virus itself. Additionally, some software that "cures" virus infestation is not innocuous itself and may corrupt files and damage the contents. In fact, files not damaged may still be targeted and "fixed" by virus correction software. Assess the requirements and access to the website accordingly.

Novell NetWare users should be aware that there are programs that unravel the security system and provide an entry point for unauthorized users. One such program, called HACK.EXE developed by students at Leiden University in the Netherlands, makes NetWare think the user has supervisor privileges. Another program, called KNOCK.EXE, was distributed over the Internet and provided unauthorized users access to a NetWare website. Novell now has patches to prevent KNOCK.EXE from working and a SECURFX.NLM to defeat HACK.EXE, both of which were developed in response to security breaches. However, these may not prevent future programs for NetWare, or for other ID and password systems, from being developed to defeat website security. I have included NTFSDOS.EXE so you can explore the extent of the Windows NT security breach.

As of yet, there have been no reports that anyone has decoded the password tables for many mainstream website operating systems. It is certainly possible, though, and, when so much is at stake, it is a certainty that it will happen. However, realize that physical access to most any NetWare, UNIX, Windows, or MVS server would allow a person to reboot the server with a boot disk or operating system tapes and replace or edit the password file. There are also several companies selling utilities supposedly for the purpose of recovering lost supervisor (or superuser) passwords. In the wrong hands, these can compromise website security.

Internal threats. A website is under scrutiny internally as well as externally. Once the basic physical security of the website is breached, or as often is the case not even considered, the website equipment is at risk. Unauthorized access to information is simplified, and prevention and detection are progressively more difficult to achieve when there is an amorphous intrusion. The simplest security flaw is caused by users not logging off their machines. This is akin to leaving a door ajar, so that anyone can enter. While remote website links can be tapped between buildings regardless of the media, internally the website can be physically tapped like a common telephone eavesdrop. If someone can walk into the server room without any sort of challenge, your credit card data, inventory levels, and proprietary customer lists are unprotected. The Internet, as previously explained, expands the horizon for eavesdropping since it repeats the IP transmission packet globally to all website nodes. Although the technology for tapping the Internet is more difficult and costly than Ethernet or Token-Ring, it is not impossible. An intruder with a means to promiscuously read packets can also intercept information without anyone being much the wiser. A protocol analyzer can tap the website remotely.

A highly sophisticated user can override any software protection by directing falsified IP packets to a target station or node; this scheme progressively modifies those software protection schemes for an eventual intrusion. These IP packets can spoof most firewalls and even sidestep the web server and reach the networks and databases supporting cyberstore activities. The source and destination addresses could both indicate the target node, and few protection schemes are designed to protect a user from harm. This level of power is possible because IP is open, and most operating systems key upon frame address information. As a consequence, protection stops far short of top security. Some of the more advanced tools, such as Haystack WebStalker, function with the Russian Communist mentality that anything not explicitly defined and configured is probably best deferred.

While eavesdropping has its many risks, such as breach of organizational secrets and theft of information, modification of data can be more devastating because it can remain hidden indefinitely, or be propagated and disseminated before errors are detected. Money can be siphoned from accounts payable and redirected to other pockets, trade secrets can be tampered with, private files can be read, development efforts can be hindered, and "ironclad" results can be scrambled, discrediting the innocent. Security can be breached internally both by physical damage and data access such as:

- Power disruption
- Telephone line disruption
- Remote service disruption
- Website sabotage
- Equipment damage
- Website jamming
- Website tapping
- Theft or loss of information
- Data diddling (tampering)

Physical access to the website equipment raises the possibility of sabotage from a disgruntled employee or an authorized visitor. The physical website cabling and devices, the servers, and the data residing thereon are at risk from someone throwing a shoe (that is, *sabot* in France and hence "sabotage") into the works. Most organizations assume no need to protect the equipment from employees. Unfortunately, this is often an expensive assumption.

Protection countermeasures. There are some straightforward measures that will protect the website. These include physical website isolation and microsegmentation, various firewalls, standard password protection, limits applied to outside access, occasional changeovers in website operating policies, data encryption, and the monitoring of access channels, both physical and logical. Loss-limiting measures include fallback provisions and a good website backup policy. Progressive countermeasures for enhancing security include:

- Physical website equipment and infrastructure isolation
- Identification and password authentication
- File security
- Firewalls
- Internal microsegmentation
- Occasional policy changeovers
- Encryption
- Access control for website monitoring devices
- Vandal detection and incorrect password logs
- Application access and usage limitation
- Hierarchy of access (user, group, and limited file access)

- Fallback countermeasures
- Website backup (hardware, services, and media backup)

Physical website isolation.   The most effective website protection is simply to lock up the website and make it unavailable. Obviously, this severely cripples its usefulness to an outside world where most of the potential cyberstore customers exist. However, when more emphasis is placed on physical security and when access to the website is controlled, the website is more secure. This holds true for both physical and logical devices. However, most websites provide necessary communication channels for cyberstore business, usually as transactions, electronic mail, change notices, meeting announcements, and other normal messages, and thus such draconian measures are inappropriate.

Furthermore, many E-mail and groupware packages are not encrypted; the data is publicly accessible in spite of any physical security. While Lotus Notes and Novell NetWare provide security and encryption tools, the use of them is not assured and users tend to ignore them. SSL and SET do address these issues, and you should apply them up front as Chapter 3 most sternly suggested.

You cannot not lock up access to the website without curtailing business. There is no "physical" access for web users because it is all logical connectivity through the Internet. However, you can create user IDs and passwords matched with customers validated by prior credit card transactions. This can be one way to provide services to customers who have actually bought products (and paid for them) and hence are likely to need or want support services, more information, and access to special data.

However, the concept of physical security can be extended as far as necessary to meet requirements and protect website equipment from internal events. The rule is to lock up as much as possible. Mainframe and website file servers should have limited and controlled access. If printed or drafted output (fighter plane plans, for example) is confidential, then certainly lock up the printers and delegate one person to burst, collate, and distribute all website output. For additional confidence, bond that person and shred paper and magnetic media trash. Move credit card information and customer information once processed to machines without physical or even logical access from the website.

Since data storage mechanisms often use removable medialike tapes, disks, punched output, or removable magnetic or optical platters, a cautious approach is to restrict access to these classes of devices and their active media. Log all mountings, and catalog all purchases, uses, disposals, and distributions of storage media.

If more security is required, lock up the local and remote tie-line transmission channels. Place cables beyond reach, in a plenum, in locked corridors, or in restricted areas. Position multiplexing hubs beyond occasional reach and protect the Internet connections. If this is unfeasible or impractical, then at the minimum, restrict access to as much of the physical website as possible. Run external optical cable in armored bundles. Establish alarms, with beeper activation if necessary, to provide notice of *any* loss of connection on these vulnerable links. Even a brief inexplicable website service loss could indicate that someone may have installed a tap or signal splitter (such as a new patch cord from a server) on the website. As such, maintain physical cabling documentation.

The server equipment is always vulnerable, although on a broadcast transmission medium like the Internet, each server provides a window of vulnerability to all other website equipment, including caching servers, E-mail servers, DNS devices, database servers, hosts, and data storage farms. Multiport hubs, which are not fully populated because some ports are unutilized, offer a ripe invitation. The lobe is already in place and invisible to the website monitoring tools. Therefore, it is wise to disable the extra unused ports where security is an issue, and periodically inspect all lobes for unauthorized tinkering. A lobe cable could be diverted from a single station node via a concentrator without anyone being the wiser unless a periodic physical inspection is actually performed. Figure 4.80 illustrates a common node with an added hub. You might want to document unused ports and remove unused hubs to a secure locker.

Password protection.   At the website software level, password authentication protection is the most effective mechanism for website protection. Passwords prevent unauthorized access to files and website devices, and protect information from diddling, theft, and tampering. All operating systems can be breached when physical access is granted to the equipment by partially creating a new operating system. However, for most novice users, passwords keep out prying eyes and are also effective in protecting websites from competent

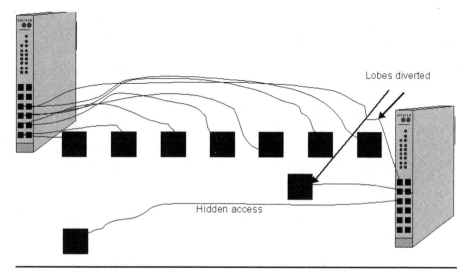

Figure 4.80 Wiring hubs and switches provide an opportunity to spy.

external hackers. Most serious data thefts have been perpetrated by novices who exploited a hole in the system. Password protection limits software access to a node, thus limiting access to the website. Additionally, contingent upon the website software and the underlying operating system and support services, password protection may lock individual files. In situations where security is of utmost concern, tools that analyze files at the bit and byte levels can be entirely removed from the system or locked away from the casual user. Such tools can invalidate bit-level protection mechanisms. You should also lock up OS and NOS distribution media so that they are not readily accessible.

Password protection is only as strong as the weakest link. User log-in names and passwords that are freely disseminated ease access to the system. Public keys that are freely available on the website rather than distributed as needed by E-mail defeat SSL and SET web protocols. Common passwords that everybody knows or can easily break breach the security. Hired consultants with external dial-in privileges (who have built or upgraded web content) can be a serious security problem. Prudent management of security requires that passwords be changed regularly, and that when an intrusion is indicated, passwords be deleted from the log until ownership of a log-in is requested again by a user. Good policy also requires that when people leave a company, their passwords be removed from the log, especially when a person has left under questionable circumstances. You may not want to immediately remove the user ID until the files from that user have been examined and transferred to a new owner. New user log-ins not matched with people, multiple log-ins for the same people, and guest log-ins possibly point to a breach of supervisory access and security.

There are also a number of tools that test password files for common names, frequently used words, or typical values for both IDs and passwords. Transliterated, mixed cased, and compound or hyphenated words foreign to the local language are good choices.

As Chapter 3 detailed, password protection is the most readily available website protection. Most websites provide password protection as a minimum security measure, and at different levels. You have operating system security, file level security, web server access, DNS access, and database passwords, plus all the inherent skills and complications of the website that in and of themselves add to basic security. Password protection is, however, the most easily applied countermeasure, although it requires vigilance.

Encryption.   Encryption is the transformation of data into a format that is not readable by anyone who does not have the key for decoding it. There are various formats for encryption, which include substituting bytes with a code from a code table, replacing byte values with calculated mathematical value, or transforming entire blocks of data through a key encryption algorithm. This latter method is finding the most use today with commercial Internet transactions since it is virtually impossible to defeat. The data encryption system (DES) method is one such system, while the Internet has defined a new standard called the privacy enhanced mail (PEM), which relies upon a two-part key: a published public key and the user's private key. SSL and SET are similar, and will be more widely implemented in the future. The problem remains how to assure the authenticity of the public key, a need fulfilled by organizations registering, validating, and storing keys. Verisign is the leader in this area. In the future, we will see more and more of this, with the increase in electronic commerce and electronic payments.

Although anyone who desires complete privacy should encrypt data, files, and mail messages, there are problems that generally preclude this. For example, it takes time to convert the information into and from the coded format. Additionally, it may require more space in terms of storage or transmission time. The loss of a key also precludes recovery of the information contained by an encoded message or file. Consider what would happen if a person lost her code key or if an employee encoded all his data, and when fired refused to reveal the key or code. The administration of messages and files containing gibberish is made that much more complicated. On the other hand, when secrets must be kept, encryption provides the most reliable method to do so.

For example, the following screen shot (Figure 4.81) shows a standard HTML page encoded for SSL security in order to access credit card informa-

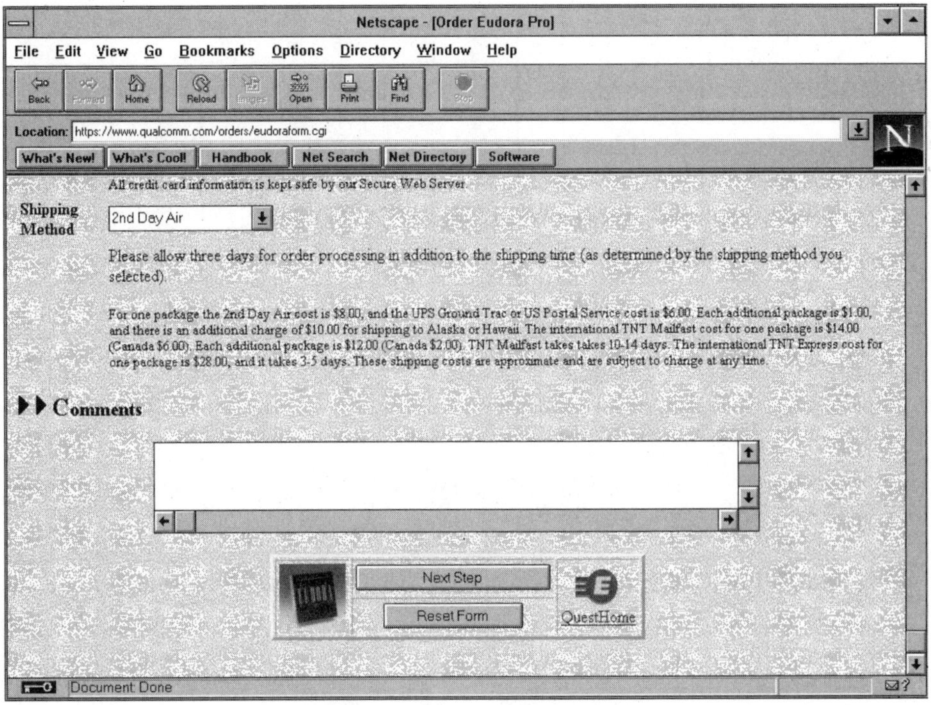

Figure 4.81 Secure ordering of Eudora software. Notice the key icon in the lower corner indicating that the form is secure. The path also refers to "https."

tion in payment for software delivery. Although software (and even documentation) could be delivered via electronic delivery, Qualcomm chooses to ship boxes to users who order new or upgrades to its Eudora Pro software. This is a business decision that you might have to consider if your cyberstore sells software, information, images, or other computer-formatted products.

When the form is submitted, most browsers indicate that the information is submitted either as a secure or unsecured transaction. The following dialogue box confirms that the Eudora request is secured, as shown in Figure 4.82. Secured HTML forms are indicated in Navigator (and other browsers subscribing to SSL) with the key shown in Figure 4.83. This implies that the data provided to you may be encrypted and response is also likely to be encrypted, too. In contrast, unsecured transactions may often generate another dialogue box explaining that the data sent back to the web server are not secured. You will note that the key is broken, thus indicating a lack of security, as shown in Figure 4.84.

When security is combined with downloads, users at your site will also see a dialog box reminding them that you are a possible security hazard. This is true regardless of the type of file (whether a script, executable, multimedia, or video), as shown in Figure 4.85.

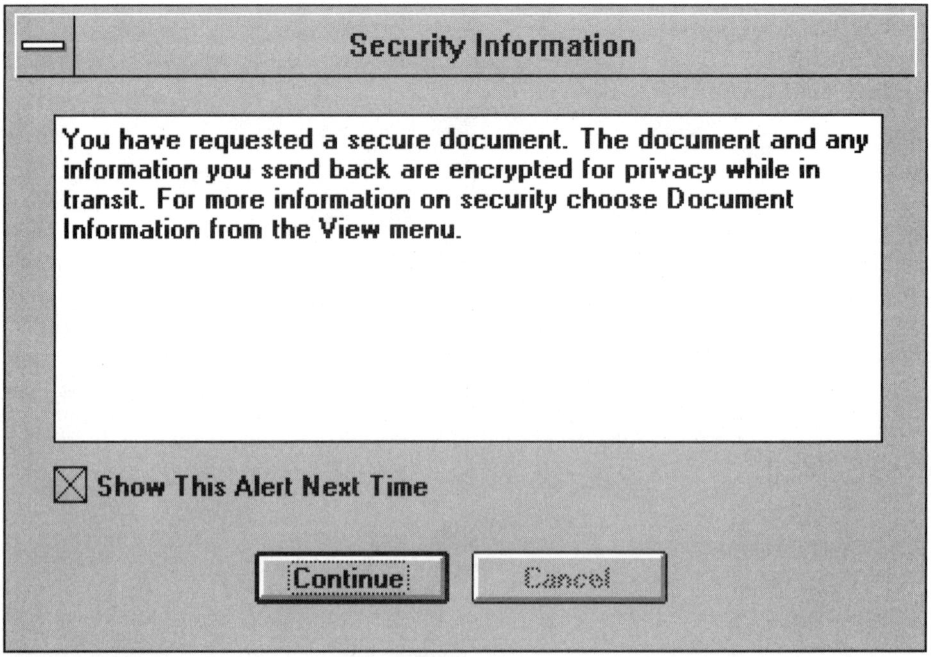

Figure 4.82 Confirmation of secured delivery.

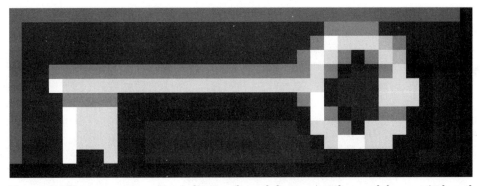

Figure 4.83 The secure transaction indication (lower left corner) under a web browser (enlarged 100×).

External access

Most published security breaches have occurred through phone access modems. The most frequently perpetrated breaches are a result of trusted employees or careless procedure and password controls. A phone line is a doorway into the website, the modem is a lock, and the password is the final key. Therefore, the best protection is not to have any protection at all, but also not to have any external phone access to the website. When external phone lines are necessary, several precautions are relevant. Do not publish access phone numbers. Change the phone numbers frequently, or at least recycle them internally. If you have premise wiring, you can easily assign switch numbers.

Use modems that wait for a tone from the caller. This has the advantage of not accidentally informing a dialer that a computer exists at the number dialed. Install callback modems that do not accept calls without verifying the identity of the caller, the phone number, and the password. ISDN improves security as long as its devices use Caller ID and callback, and do not default

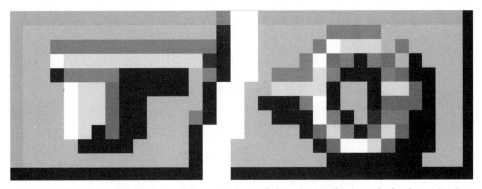

Figure 4.84 A broken key in the web browser (lower left corner) indicates a lack of security (enlarged 100×).

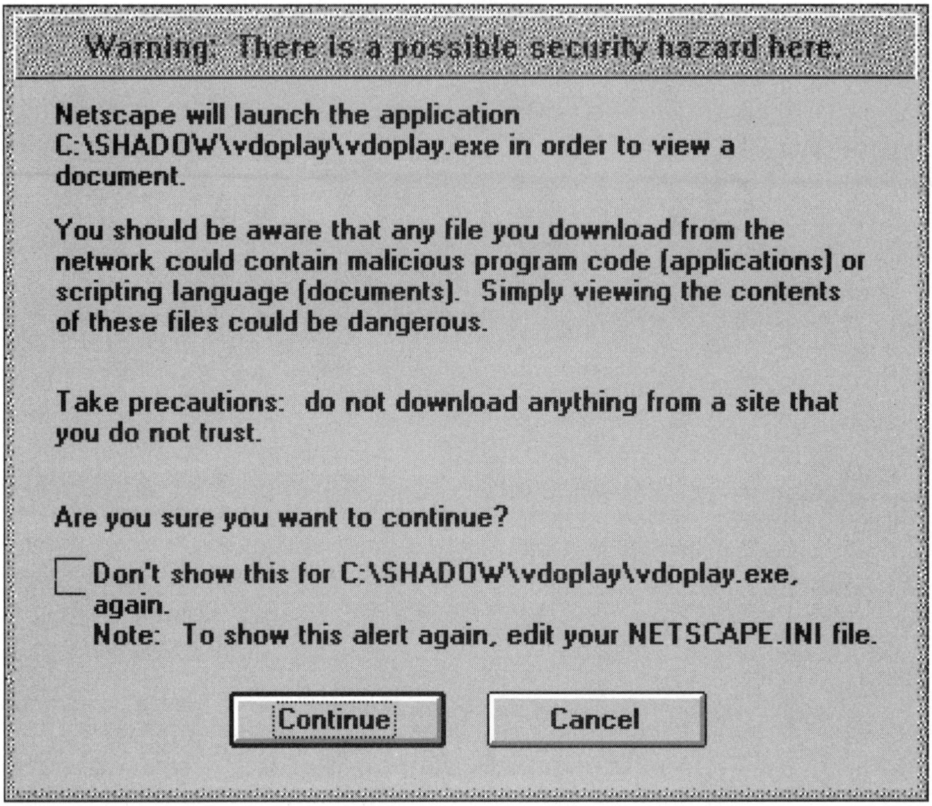

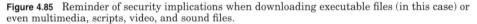

Warning: There is a possible security hazard here.

Netscape will launch the application
C:\SHADOW\vdoplay\vdoplay.exe in order to view a
document.

You should be aware that any file you download from the
network could contain malicious program code (applications) or
scripting language (documents). Simply viewing the contents
of these files could be dangerous.

Take precautions: do not download anything from a site that
you do not trust.

Are you sure you want to continue?

☐ Don't show this for C:\SHADOW\vdoplay\vdoplay.exe,
again.
Note: To show this alert again, edit your NETSCAPE.INI file.

[Continue]   [Cancel]

Figure 4.85 Reminder of security implications when downloading executable files (in this case) or even multimedia, scripts, video, and sound files.

to analog service instead of the still rare digital service. Install specialized modems that are difficult to use (many modems talk only to others identical to themselves) or that scramble transmission. While data encryption usually adds a dramatic overhead, it may provide assurance for external links. Additionally, where feasible and available, install Caller ID and related technology to verify the actual number of the calling party at the time of the call by the second ring. If so, make certain that modems do not establish connections before the Caller-ID information is received. By April 1995, the FCC had ordered Caller-ID services between Regional Bell Operating Companies (RBOCs), so even long-distance numbers will be included.

Note that there is some concern that Caller ID can be defeated so that no identifying telephone number is provided, or that a phony number is supplied. Install Caller ID to log the originating numbers of all callers. While Caller ID can be disabled with a few widely known tricks or given a fake phone number, the phone call without a number or with an unknown number is likely to represent a problem unless rejected. Until these concerns are resolved, Caller ID should be installed in conjunction with other security measures. Crucial procedures for remote security include:

- Avoid dial-up connections
- Don't publish the dial-up phone numbers
- Change the phone numbers frequently
- Use modems that don't supply a carrier tone
- Install callback equipment and/or Caller ID
- Control distribution of log-ins and passwords
- Change passwords frequently
- Install specialty modems

Where a website runs between buildings, lock up the cable or install optical fiber, which at least for the present, is expensive to tap. If these possibilities are unfeasible, inspect the connections daily for signs of possible intrusion. If microwave or a radio frequency is used, scramble those transmissions. There are few legal remedies once an eavesdropper is detected spying on public RF signals, even though the Communication Act of 1985 makes it illegal to tap the airwaves. Select sideband or multiband transmitters rather than single frequencies. Be aware of the possible security leakages at the time of installation, understand the need for organizational security, and weigh the benefits of applying the necessary countermeasures. On-site, physical security includes:

- Lock-up access to wiring closets and hubs
- Check for intrusions
- Install optical fiber (more difficult to tap)
- Alter transmission frequencies
- Apply SST and sideband transmission methods
- Scramble or encode transmissions
- Root out anomalies
- Remain vigilant
- Maintain website blueprints

Websites isolated by bridges, routers, switches, and gateways provide additional security. Every step taken to microsegment a website from public access increases the inherent security. While interwebsite access is frequently required, subnets add a buffer when they filter the frames that are forwarded. All transmissions destined for nodes on the originating website are not globally broadcast beyond that website. A router or gateway filters only the traffic that must be transferred to the other websites; source or destination address explicit forwarding effectively retains sensitive material. As noted previously, this does not preclude the conveyance of doctored packets unless transmission is a one-way process. In this way, a website could be constructed with a centralized and rigorously secured website facility. This secured website would lock out all remote links and dial-up access. On the other hand, the central secured website could reach out and remotely access the other websites and their resources, including dial-out telephone communication lines. Many such secured subnets could be constructed with access to a general-purpose website backbone. Once one-way transmission is established from the core area, a vulnerability is nevertheless established.

Occasional policy changeovers.   The best security relies upon sudden change. The most complete physical security systems—the best password and encryption systems—depend upon new people, new passwords, and *new* keys. You cannot bribe someone who is new and cannot break what you do not know; any security system is improved by constant and unpredictable variety.

Website security can implement such changeovers. Access codes, passwords, sign-in procedures, and front desk guards can be rotated with frequency. Although changing the domain name is akin to altering access phone numbers for local sites, you really cannot do it with public websites. That defeats your efforts at advertising the website. Website page changes and upgrades do disrupt efforts to hack sites. Just realize that changes and upgrades may leave all sorts of security vulnerabilities previously closed. In general, though, change upsets the best-laid plans, and improves the odds that a trail of evidence will remain if an intruder actually breaches the website. Security measures that should be changed frequently are:

- Sign-in procedures
- Access process
- Guard personnel
- Location of computer
- Door keys
- IDs and passwords
- Security and encryption codes
- Media delivery and recycling policy
- Website links
- Remote access
- Locations and names of files

Data encryption.   The Internet transmits anything placed in the data fields, and easily supports data encryption. The Internet, like the party-line telephone system, is blind to the nature of the conversations. Anyone who wants to listen to a party-line conversation is welcome, but unless the listener understands the key, the conversation is privileged. Just as a telephone will handle foreign languages, the Internet will transmit encrypted data or information in foreign languages as easily as English. Even promiscuous capture of packets will prove valueless if the data are properly encrypted. Data encryption is the most easily implemented security measure. It is, however, expensive in terms of the computer time needed to encrypt and decrypt data, and should be applied judiciously. Furthermore, a motivated intruder could break almost any encryption scheme. The Data Encryption Standard (DES) is a good tool for use within the continental United States, but DES is not yet approved for export due to government restrictions. I expect the U.S. government to alter its current policy with respect to SSL, SET, and other encryption methods because it is stifling American business; anyone can go offshore or build an offshore website to bypass these "export" restrictions.

Access control for website monitoring devices.   Certain monitoring devices, like the protocol analyzer, allow promiscuous access to all Internet traffic, particularly on a backbone. The push from vendors supplying analyzers is for full Open Systems Interconnect (OSI) 7-layer decodes for virtually all transport layer protocols. When such a tool is easily available, the data payload is easily read unless encrypted. Realize that the volume of traffic on the Internet backbone from 45 Mbps to 6.2 Gbps makes it unlikely that your cyberstore transaction will be targeted. Nevertheless, with such a device, mail, file transfers, and all website traffic can be passively, selectively, and silently captured. In fact, all mail, all data, and all files can be cracked, read, and understood (unless encrypted). While the traffic may provide only a glimpse into the full information desired by an intruder, such a device can clearly unlock private secrets. Hidden connections that are not authorized are more difficult to spot, but once noticed are obvious for what they are. Not only is such a monitoring device highly effective at uncovering secrets, its presence is easy to hide. It is a suitable piece of website equipment and it belongs.

An analyzer, or website software like SNMP or RMON with certain packet capture features, will allow anyone with enough skill to capture and analyze the Internet frames transparently and unobtrusively. Note that SNMP and RMON capabilities in terms of PUT and GET are as sophisticated as any hardware analyzer when enabled through NMS software, but usually very difficult to use when the front end does not include promiscuous features. This promiscuous data capture technique raises a first line security issue. Additionally, many protocol analyzers will allow a sophisticated intruder to build falsified Internet frames or any other protocol packets that could crack security locks by forging valid keys. However, if a website administration removes, limits, or monitors usage of all such tools, a minimal measure of security can be achieved. Other measures are required for more certain protection.

A protocol analyzer's inherent danger is so obvious that it can be overlooked. While there is a clear need for it, unauthorized usage constitutes an invasion of privacy and breach of website security. Therefore, lock up such devices when possible, and monitor their usage when they are in use.

Intrusion detection.   While the protocol analyzer can actually intrude on private communications, it can also uncover unauthorized website access. Users who shouldn't be on the website will appear as unknown Internet addresses, or will transmit at unusual or unauthorized times. Furthermore, access to unauthorized devices, supposedly prevented but actually achieved, can indicate vandalism and so can be disclosed. Active intrusion detection devices, of which WebStalker is the first of this new breed, look for events and processes not specifically authorized.

If transmission facilities on the analyzer were disabled to prevent such inadvertent data diddling, the snooper would still seek website access. This access is most often provided through an unauthorized connection or a secondary hub. When security is an issue, precise website blueprinting becomes critical. Furthermore, a detailed impedance chart should indicate any present or past unauthorized tapping. Twisted-pair and wiring hubs can be more difficult to tamper with when the wiring closets are locked. Other clues to intrusion include:

- Lost or damaged password files
- Telltale log-in times
- Unusual log-in names
- Duplicate or overlapping log-ins
- Signal irregularities
- Website transmission interference
- Unusual errors or log entries
- Missing printed output
- Missing or altered data files

Although data encryption will foil some vandals, time works against it. The key can be lost, passed around the office as passwords often are, broken with enough time and poor key recycling procedures, or broken by a clever person. However, there are additional techniques to thwart data theft. While the website monitor allows a sophisticated user to capture and read packets, it also can indicate who is utilizing website resources and thus indicate the possible presence of a spy. While the promiscuous mode of data capture is invisible to the website because the Internet signal is a global broadcast, certain clues can correlate excessive CPU load with limited website access. Sooner or later, an unauthorized node is bound to request a retransmission. This, however, requires good detective skills to uncover.

A crook does not play by the rules, which is the prime danger, of course. In order to counter such danger, it is important to understand the value of the data on the website and the damage that can be perpetrated; this knowledge will point to the possible danger and to the people who will benefit from such intrusion or damage. The information resident on a website has no value except to certain parties and there are usually warning signs in security breaches. Train the website operators to spot anomalies since they often monitor all website traffic and could uncover problems as they happen.

Most of the administrative emphasis should be applied to prevent vandalism. The original website design should factor in security as a basic configuration constraint. Daily operations should be altered occasionally to disrupt the norm. Such strategies protect the website in anticipation of vandalism and snooping, but in no way completely preclude them. After most intrusions, there are traces that can be analyzed to prevent further access. These traces include log files, packet traces, time stamps, improper website impedances, unusual website interference, computer server problems, and missing or changed data files. The website analyzer can indicate other software and traffic disparities as previously explained.

Hierarchy of access

There are several categories of security access created to clarify and evaluate the growing number of protection methods and escalating secure operating systems. As users acknowledge the need for security as an integral part of the operating system and network landscape, vendors are listening. However, confusion reigns with this proliferation of user requests (primarily the Department of Defense, or "DoD") and vendor offerings. To address this problem, the National Security Decisions Directive created a framework for security evaluation. This so-called *Orange Book* framework, which is used by most vendors and the Internet Engineering Task Force (IETF), is outlined below:

A—Verified protection
    A_1—Verified design
B—Mandatory protection
    B_1—Labeled protection
    B_2—Structured protection
    B_3—Security domain
C—Discretionary protection
    C_1—Discretionary security protection
    C_2—Controlled access
D—Minimal protection

Note that this security outline has become outdated because it was really designed for host-based mainframe environments. LANs and intranets create new hazards, and C_2 security is not great even in the corporate environment. The highest level is the verified subcategory under the verified protection level. To date, these exotic systems are merely in the design stages. Previous attempts at complete security failed either through excessively slow response time or under the concerted efforts of expert system crackers. UNIX, UNIXWare, and MS Windows NT, for example, are both C_2, although with a little effort they can meet the higher C standard. Multics, CMS, VMS, and other like systems also fail at C_2.

Fallback countermeasures

Website access audit trails, transaction logs, physical inventories, and website security audits are standard procedures when security is an important website concern. Often, the logs will indicate an anomaly suggesting an intrusion. If an intrusion has been detected, it is necessary to act. If the intruder is known and the access point revealed, the problem is solved, although damage may already have been done. On the other hand, if the intruder is unknown, there are two courses of action. The first is to watch and wait, and then trap the intruder. The second is to lock up the website without hope of catching the intruder. Which course of action appears to be the best depends upon the costs of continued damage, the repair of that damage, and the vindictiveness of the affected organization.

There are clear detective methods for trapping an intruder. Sherlock Holmes' style of observation is likely to reveal even cautious intruders. However, when the danger is clear and acute, and the identity of the intruder is less important than protecting the website, a staged shutdown of the compromised website doors is the best course of action. Elements of both hardware and software that can be shut down are:

- Disconnect modems (used for site maintenance or upgrades)
- Change site maintenance dial-in telephone numbers
- Encrypt
- Inspect cables and links for tapping, tampering, or intrusion
- Inspect website software and files for tampering
- Change ID and password file and purge outdated entries
- Alter executive code file ownerships
- Relocate and/or rename critical data files
- Disconnect firewalls, bridges, routers, switches, and gateways
- Lock up printed output and storage media
- Restore physical or data damage
- Limit access to remote devices
- Change door keys
- Alter card key codes

From the hardware viewpoint, change as much as possible and disconnect as much as possible while retaining the required minimum cyberstore functionality. The procedure is as follows: disconnect all dial-in lines and change the access numbers to prevent future intrusions. Power down all remote transmitters and alter the transmitter frequencies. Inspect all twisted-pair, coaxial cables, optical fiber cables, and connections for signs of tampering, splicing, and all other indications of line tapping. If you suspect that the intruder may have discovered information derived from wastepaper or from stolen printed material, make rapid plans to alter paper disposal methods and output distribution. Lock up the printers and hand deliver printed output. Shred wastepaper. Certainly, data storage media hold the entirety of the organization's secrets. Lock up those media, both on-line and on backup tapes. Furthermore, log the disposition of the data storage media. Change keys, codes, and access procedures.

Many steps can be taken in software to locate signs of tampering. They may appear as missing or altered data files, or as unusual log entries. Look at database server logs, web server logs, E-mail logs, password files and log-in histories, and any fundamental changes to the operating systems. Restore whatever damage is discovered. Additionally, change the password access. Purge outdated password entries. Limit remote access to other website nodes and website devices. Change the access to website software that might allow data tampering and data snooping. This includes programs that read protected disks or files at the bit and byte levels, and programs that override disk- or file-level protection schemes. Restricted access is possible for security-sensitive materials by moving them or changing their names.

Access to any machine in the website where sensitive data reside might require a magnetic access card like an automatic teller machine card or a credit card. Additionally, keyboards might have software locks to deter casual use. In any event, physical cases of website machines should be locked securely to prevent replacement, removal, or temporary installation of hardware components, including floppy disk drives, tape archival units, hard disks, security components, serial or parallel ports (used to link to a laptop computer for downloading data), or a nonsecured output printer.

These are generic techniques that work equally well when initially installing a website or at any time the organization suspects a problem. If the website is insecure, it is prudent not to tarry and wait until a problem is revealed before applying such countermeasures. Security entails a cost in time, materials, labor, and aggravation.

It is important to have adequate protection mechanisms; tight security could mean that it will be forever unnecessary to repair damage or prevent damage from recurring. Security is a series of applied techniques that are disruptive, inconvenient, and rarely transparent. The hope is that such techniques will never be required, but they are instituted purely on a prophylactic basis.

Website backup

The website is hardware, software, and data. This is true whether the website is hosted at an ISP or locally. The data consists of your HTML pages, FTP files, E-mail, threaded discussion groups, the structure of the site including the relationship of URLs and hyperlinks inside web pages, as well as the CGI or scripts used to link databases to HTML pages. If your website is hosted by an ISP, any secure CGI code they write to animate your cyberstore activity should be invisible to even the skilled hacker, but should be backed up for your ongoing continuity and business protection.

Realize that a website also includes the people, their skill sets, and how they interact. If you are creating a disaster recovery procedure, do not overlook this aspect. If the hardware were damaged, it could be replaced more easily than the information it contained or the workflow encapsulated by the cyberstore. Despite this relative ease of restoring hardware, do not overlook the need to have spare parts on hand. File servers and intermediate node components are good candidates for the spare inventory. Assess the damage if a key component failed and were irreplaceable for a given period. Keep spares of those units that could create a crisis if broken. Do not limit backup procedures solely to the data and software.

Many organizations are critically dependent upon data. Either they are the organization's product, or they provide records of funds payable and receivable. Data also can explain critical production or operational techniques. Website backup procedures provide a means to repair software and data damage. If a catastrophe occurs, backup media may change a catastrophe to merely a major inconvenience. As trite as that sounds, backups are a standard policy for most organizations with mainframe computer facilities. "Mainframe computer facilities" are referenced here mainly as an example of the attitudes and policies that have developed from the experiences now affecting the new website technologies. Many websites, however, developed from small components and therefore the organization and its managers lack the realization of the website's crucial importance. Enterprise websites tend to include many subwebsites where management jurisdiction is local. Backup, as such, may be locally administered and incomplete. As a result, backups are nonexistent, infrequent, or applied to that minimum of personally owned files deemed important. A critical portion of any website is resident in unique files that define the relationship of nodes on the website, the website operations itself, and scripts automating arcane processes that have become complicated over time.

In the final statement, braggarts will often reveal their activities and indicate problems and a security breach. Listen well, be vigilant, and evaluate the level of security required. Cleverness will undermine all security systems, and ruthlessness will sway the most secure system. Note well that the strongest security program will fail if the website operators and users who are assigned to protect the resources are compromised.

Encryption certificates

A secured server, such as O'Reilly's WebSite Professional, needs a registered certificate to provide secure web page and E-mail transmissions. The certificate is effectively a two-part key. One key, called the private key, resides on the server and is used to encrypt data flows to and from the server. The second key, called the public key, is sent to the browser upon request of the E-mail application or a CGI or HTML code inside a web page to establish a secure, encrypted link. This key is used to protect the information passed between the server and that browser. Typically, in the case of the cyberstore, the secured transmissions will be limited to financial and credit information. Examples include credit card numbers and expiration dates, EDI data, Automated Clearing Houses (ACH), Electronic Payment Systems (EPS) information for the various cash substitutes. There is increasing diversity in the encryption standards and transfer formats despite agreements between credit vendors for a common protocol. Realistically, this implies more complex integration of payment systems into the cyberstore implementation.

The installation process for any secured web server—and it does not matter whether the mechanism is SET, SSL, PGP, EDIFACT, CALS, WWW, or various other encryption techniques or certification keys—must be sent to the certification authority. In the case of WebSite Pro, the Certificate Manager Wizard walks you through the steps of creating a database and the needed information to submit to the public for certification to VeriSign, as shown in Figure 4.86.

Figure 4.86 The public key file begins with construction of a key database.

Figure 4.87   The WebSite Pro Certificate Request Wizard.

Figure 4.87 shows the certificate Request Wizard in operation. You need to move the mouse around for about five minutes to generate enough random points to create a random public and private key. I think this is very artificial because the Windows random generator generating 2048 integers based on 2048 seeds based on a time stamp will indeed be statistically random. However, Figure 4.88 shows this process.

The public key certification is generated by the Wizard and is stored as text file on the web server. This process is shown in Figure 4.89. This is not the end of the process. The text file with the public key must be submitted to a central key authority for certification, in this case VeriSign. This process is best performed by sending E-mail to the authority with the file attached to the message, as shown in Figure 4.90. By the way, the address in the prior screen shot is incorrect even for WebSite, but it is used in this next illustration only for consistency.

A sample public key certificate looks like the message in Figure 4.91. VeriSign charges a range of fees for digital certificates (IDs) based on classification for an individual. Currently, they provide four classes of IDs. Class 1 ensures uniqueness of name or E-mail for casual web browsing and E-mail. Class 2 ensures uniqueness of name or E-mail for casual web browsing and E-mail with a third-party proof of the name, address, and personal information attached to the ID. Class 3 is a Class 2 certificate with a personal ap-

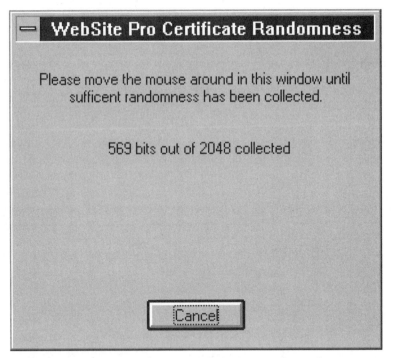

Figure 4.88 You create a random set of keys by "mousing" around.

Figure 4.89 The Wizard generates a public key file.

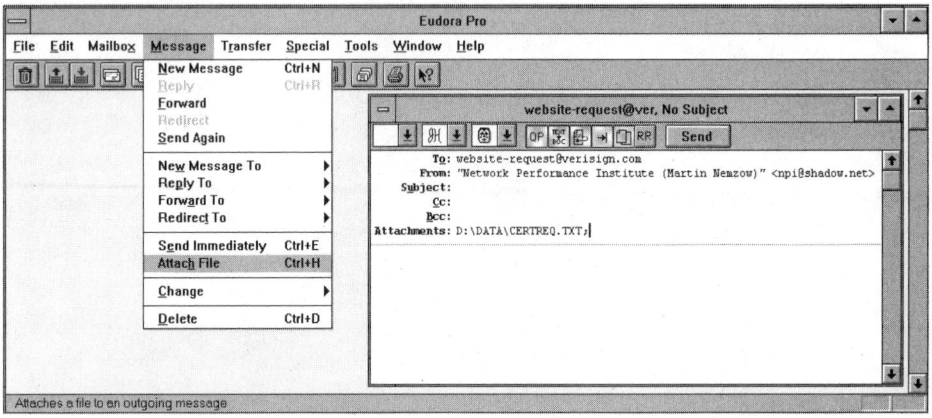

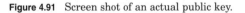

Figure 4.90 Submission of the certificate by E-mail. The attachment ensures that the sensitive text of the certificate does not get garbled when you paste it into the message part of the E-mail, and instead is sent as a complete file.

pearance and presence of registration credentials; it is typically used for electronic banking and payment for services through cyberstores. Class 4 includes the personal presence for certification and "thorough" investigation of the individual and/or organization that they represent. The certifications solve problems for a range of trust issues.

A digital certificate currently costs $290 for the cyberstore. Additional digital certificates are $95 per year. The "signed" response to this request must be loaded into the WebSite Pro certificate database. This enables the server to use SHTTP. For example, with WebServer Pro, save the certificate file under

```
-----BEGIN PRIVACY-ENHANCED MESSAGE-----
Proc-Type:4,MIC-ONLY
Content-Domain:RFC822
Originator-Certificate:
 MIICDDCCAbYCAQAwDQYJKoZIhvcNAQECBQAwgZAxCzAJBgNVBAYTA1UTMRAwDgYD
 Lm51dHdvcmtwZXJmLmNvbTBcMA0GCSqGSIb3DQEBAQUAA0sAMEgCQQDnSHCXKctL
 uIbpc2zX1tHUn9/csf3hsiyioJZSk+uUZ+yuuSQamIO23yxNx5clyzFRAjL1Rdia
 RtI/Fr6igApxAgMBAAEwDQYJKoZIhvcNAQECBQADQQBD1Z1GrJzSSJUVvGnouBRay
 VQQIEwdGbG9yaWRhMRQwEgYDVQQHEwtNaWFtaSBCZWFjaDEmMCQGA1UEChMdTmU0
 d29yayBQZXJmJmb3JtYW5jZSBJbnN0aXR1dGUxEzARBgNVBAsTCmN5YmVUyc3RvcmUx
 C9kYTsJz5NmbUn1/JjIgWRJq1IX7pLhTd9y2KA6sD4q4qm6Aa4Spu95mN3Brh7KQ
MIC-Info: RSA-MD5,RSA,
 d29yayBQZXJmJmb3JtYW5jZSBJbnN0aXR1dGUxEzARBgNVBAsTCmN5YmVUyc3RvcmUx
 5b+Hu2x6CECRXzksE0E7Yg==

U2ViU210ZSBQcm8NCg==
-----END PRIVACY-ENHANCED MESSAGE-----
```

Figure 4.91 Screen shot of an actual public key.

a special extension; O'Reilly suggests the server name, with ".cer" appended to it. Hence, mine might be "websitenetworkperf.cer". Note that this is a long file name, which works under UNIX, Windows NT with the NTFS, Windows 95, OS/2, or the Macintosh file system, but not for DOS 8.3 file name limitations. Back up this file and the private key file permanent media and store them in a bank vault. You do not want to or need to regenerate the private and public keys again, and you certainly do not need (or want) to pay the certification fee again except as a necessary annual renewal. Note that this procedure is still insufficient to provide secured page and E-mail transmission. Reference to a secured document is typically in the form of:

```
<A HREF "https://www.company.com/secure.html">Secured Page<A/>
```

or

```
<A HREF "shttp://www.company.com/secure.html">Secured Page<A/>
```

where the https or the more common shttps replace the standard http URL path name. If there is CGI code or other other scripts attached to this page, these will need to be created and added to the appropriate binary directory and security set so that hackers cannot alter, reverse engineer, or otherwise defeat what you intend. If HTML forms deliver user information (such as orders, shipping information, and credit information) by secured E-mail to a tool such as Eudora, do not allow this data to remain on-line once decrypted. That would defeat your entire security.

Site content protection

The previous sections have all dealt with protection of the physical and logical content of a website. This last section deals with the intangible values of a website, including text, images, layout, and process. While a number of tools exist that supposedly protect your web site, the text, and the graphics included within, the reality is that pursuing a copyright, trademark, or service mark infringement is costly and time consuming. Protecting the contents from reuse on a website is virtually impossible. The text and images are publically displayed, and meant to be so for the most part.

Any hidden information, such as copyright, specific wording, or other ownership assertions, is not always included when material is captured from a browser as text or as a screen-resolution image. Obviously, you might and probably should pursue egregious theft of your work, but the best protection is clear prevention. For example, do not post anything you do not want stolen. That is a bit severe, but is the wisest action. If you must include text on-line, then include some notice of copyright. If you create a logo or image, add a copyright, official trademark, or service mark symbol. Realize that U.S. federal trademark registrations often circumvent state registrations, unless the state registration was earlier.

The rules for marks are complex and will require an intellectual property lawyer. In any event, all images that you create can be copyrighted. In fact,

© 1996, Martin Nemzow

Figure 4.92 Official copyright symbol and text for protecting text or an image. Note that this image was constructed as a small, transparent GIF that can be overlaid to any other image file.

text and images are copyrighted by default under the Berne Convention. The symbol and date with the name of the owner are sufficient for most international usage, although an official Form TX improves your ability to litigate in the United States and elsewhere. The format is shown in Figure 4.92.

Although this symbol is text based, you can turn it into a GIF format by pasting the image of the text into a GIF editor, setting the background white to transparency, and saving that image. The GIF image can be layered on top of any other image in Photoshop, PhotoPaint, and the various GIF-centric tools referenced in this book. Figure 4.93 shows how to get the copyright (or registered trademark symbol ® five characters to the right of the © symbol) into your text in a graphic problem that includes a function for adding text to images with the Character Map applet, copy that standard bitmap into a GIF format, and save it as an image. By the way, most word processors, including Word, have an insert symbol menu option or keyboard sequence to insert a special character. In fact, most applications running under Windows will accept the ALT-0169 to insert © and ALT-0174 to insert ® into any string process when using an international character set such as New Times Roman or Avante Garde. Unicode sets are best. The symbol set used ALT-0211 to insert © and ALT-0210 to insert ® under Microsoft Windows.

It is surprising when large organizations manage the construction of Oracle databases for on-line commerce, use HTML with CGI, Java, or C++ tools to

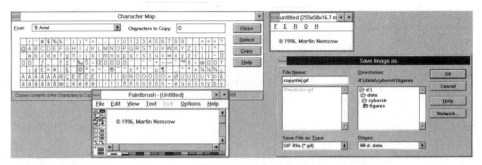

Figure 4.93 The process used to create a GIF overlay for a copyright symbol. It starts at the upper left to Paintbrush, to Lview, and then the image is saved at the lower right.

connect that database into a web page, and get all the actions integrated in beautiful web pages created by an outside graphics agency—only to be stymied by legal and organizational stumbling blocks like the trademark and copyright issue. It is often the case that when the corporate counsel sees what Information Systems (IS) has accomplished in on-line transaction processing for product sales, it throws the wet blanket on the project. Lawyers notice the missing symbols and security issues, and appropriate legal mumbo-jumbo to project real or feigned legal threats. Although the delay is not a big deal (at least it should not be), take these issues seriously. Demonstrate that there are appropriate solutions to solve all the potential problems in short order. This solution requires five minutes at most, and I am surprised that programmers and IS people frequently do not recognize how simple it is to implement.

You can include notification as part of any GIF89a animation sequence simply by adding in the copyright or trademark frame in the sequence, as shown in Figure 4.94. However, since it is as easy as deleting that frame with a tool such as the GIF Construction Set, consider also overlaying the notice on one or more frames. If you overlay the image in the same location on multiple frames (or even all frames), the copyright notification will be persistent. The next screen shot (Figure 4.95) shows a vendor's inclusion of a trademark with an image and the company name. It is unlikely anybody will knowingly copy all or parts of an image with such an obvious protection.

Two other tools are currently available that protect websites and their contents. Image Guardian, shown in Figure 4.96 from Maximizer Software, includes information such as a URL to prevent reposting (and thus reuse) of im-

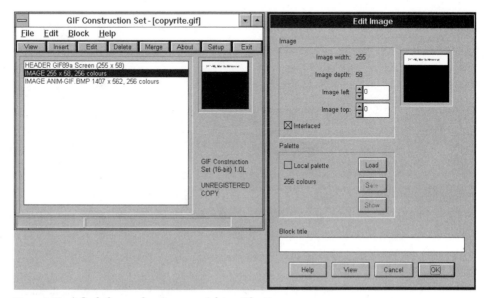

Figure 4.94 A flash frame showing copyright notification.

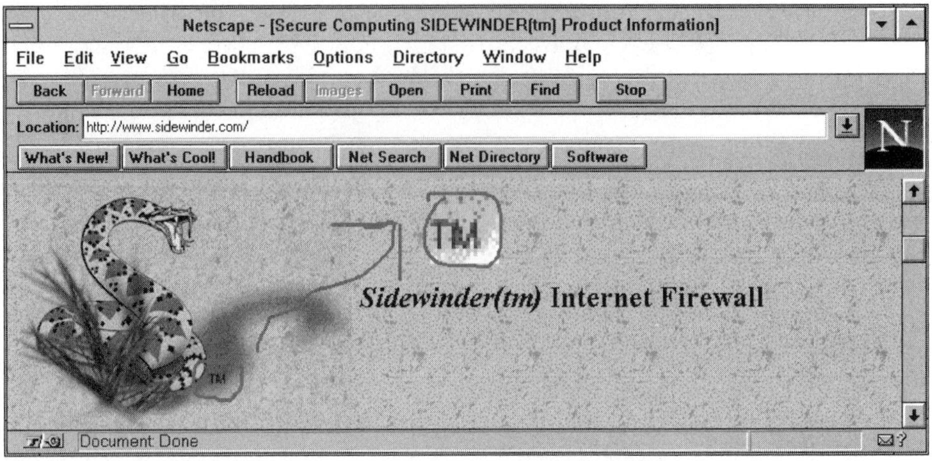

Figure 4.95 The trademark notices might discourage most misuses of the image and the product name.

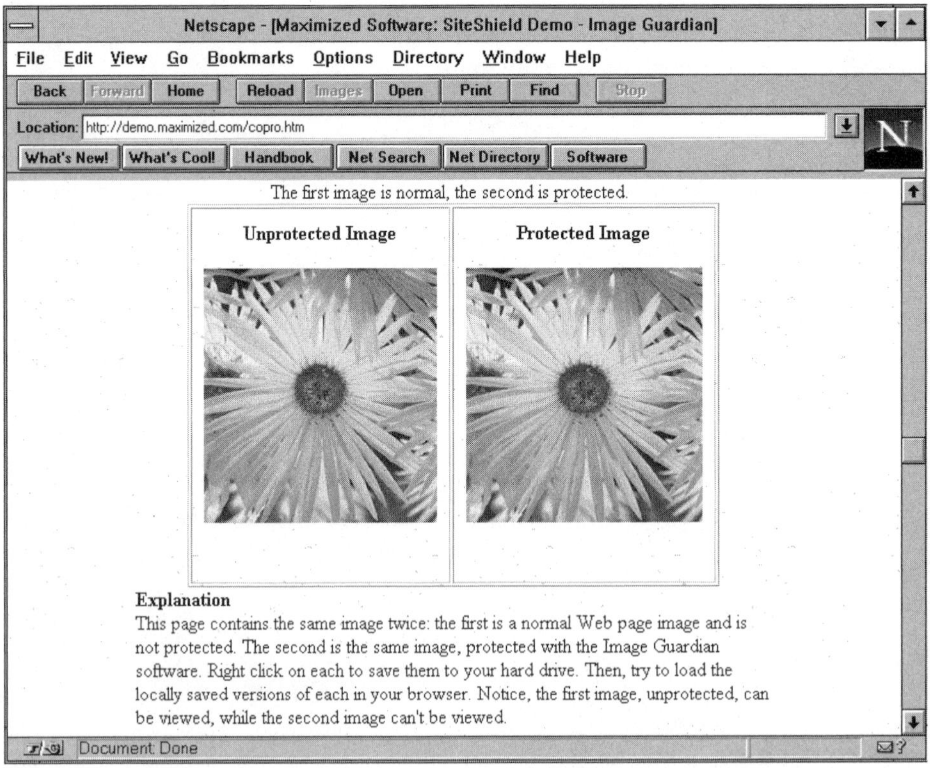

Figure 4.96 Image Guardian imbeds special information, including the official website URL into images and text documents to prevent unauthorized parties from copying and reusing that information. However, an inferior counterfeit is possible with Print-Screen and many OCR tools.

ages at other websites. When your HTML code tries to display an image (captured with a right mouse button) thus protected, the image will not display. However, this very screen shot shows that a simple screen shot is effective in getting the image and recycling it. I do not put much stock in the value of Image Guardian and think that an overt trademark or copyright notice represents an effective discouragement.

Website TrueSite software stamps website pages with a code and a URL, as shown in Figure 4.97. Notice the "TrueStamp Certified" logo. When a website or its contents are altered or moved elsewhere, a similar process as that of Image Guardian indicates that the site is defective, fraudulent, or hacked. TrueSite is operationally an independent audit guaranteeing the veracity of the website. Some commercial sites are using this service (about $10,000 per year per site and $1,000 per page per year). I think that it is an unnecessary service that increases website latency and overhead.

Although this is an ingenious service, I suspect that other approaches will be as effective as independent audits. The sole value of of the TrueSite Certification is that it indicates a financial commitment to a website not affordable by small sites. However, I would not trust that this type of audit implies any financial security, guarantee of cyberstore service or product, or integrity

Figure 4.97 TrueSite imbeds special information and URL functionality to check with the TrueSite administration to verify the integrity of a commercial website.

of the business because even criminals will invest enough money when the payoff is presumed to be great enough.

If you want to provide the same level of certification without an outside vendor and additional costs, enable website security, check the integrity of your website pages, and maintain a consistent image for your organization over time and despite site content changes. Although it is possible to get certifications of identity, key escrow, and sport logos from big names at your site, this name-dropping is not as important as building a viable identity for your own organization by your own internal efforts. Customers will come to see the level of integrity at your site as something not bought and paid for through an external organization. Hackers are always likely to subvert cyberstores and commercial sites, so your vigilance is thus always important.

Notes Conversion and Web-Enablement

Notes is a special flat-file database that is simpler than most relational DBMS designs. However, because it is different, and proprietary for the most part, the tools needed to access it are specialized and tuned for Lotus Notes web integration. InterNotes was the first primitive product. Now Lotus sells Domino, which is not only a secure web server, but also the dynamic Notes-to-HTML conversion tool. Many organizations have created significant workflow and process tools with Notes and now can create distributed applications over the Web with limited redevelopment effort. You might note that Notes already includes DES encryption because it is built as an enterprisewide networking tool. Because of this, security is built into the Domino web product at a fundamental level.

Third-party products abound for web integration. Some are conversion tools like HTML Transit, others look like Cold Fusion in that they provide a CGI command set that looks like SQL for querying and manipulating the Notes data. Tile is static, and is illustrated in Figure 4.98. As with HTML Transit, you need to understand what it is you are trying to present so as to best show an interactive environment as a series of HTML pages. Figure 4.99 shows the Tile conversion process.

The major difference between database conversion tools and Notes database conversion tools is that Tile understands that data can reside on multiple servers and that multiple Notes applications and databases can exist on each server, as shown in Figure 4.100. The output is a standard HTML page. Tile tries to preserve formatting and tabular formats.

Database Integration

All database middleware, conversion tools, and CGI scripts create results that are about the same as far as the customer is concerned. When you look at visual results, the tools process query forms and master pages conform to standard HTML forms. However, when you start to analyze CPU overheads, levels of support, platforms that the database middleware will run on, the upsizing potential and support for multiple server environments, ease of design and

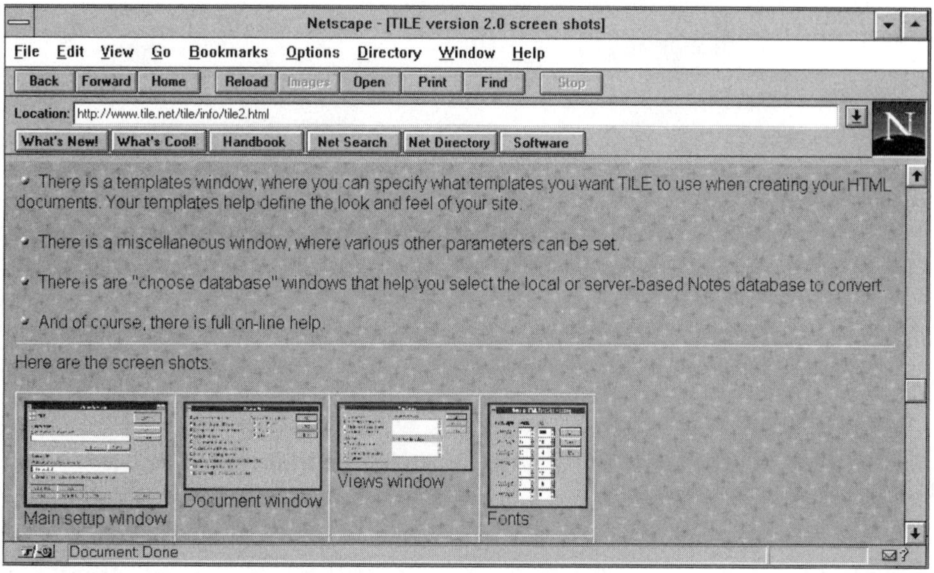

Figure 4.98   A web view of the Tile Notes database about converting Notes documents into HTML displays.

integration with the HTML pages and databases, integration with accounting systems, and the little implementation and operational details, the differences in the database tools become quickly apparent. My constant advice is to select the middleware and DBMS tools most consistent with an existing and

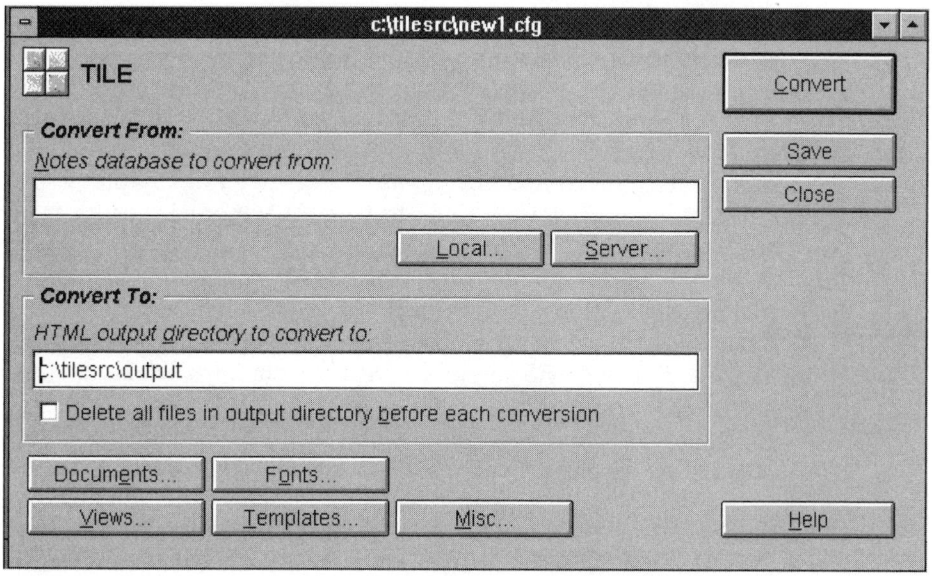

Figure 4.99   Tile converts existing Notes documents into HTML formats.

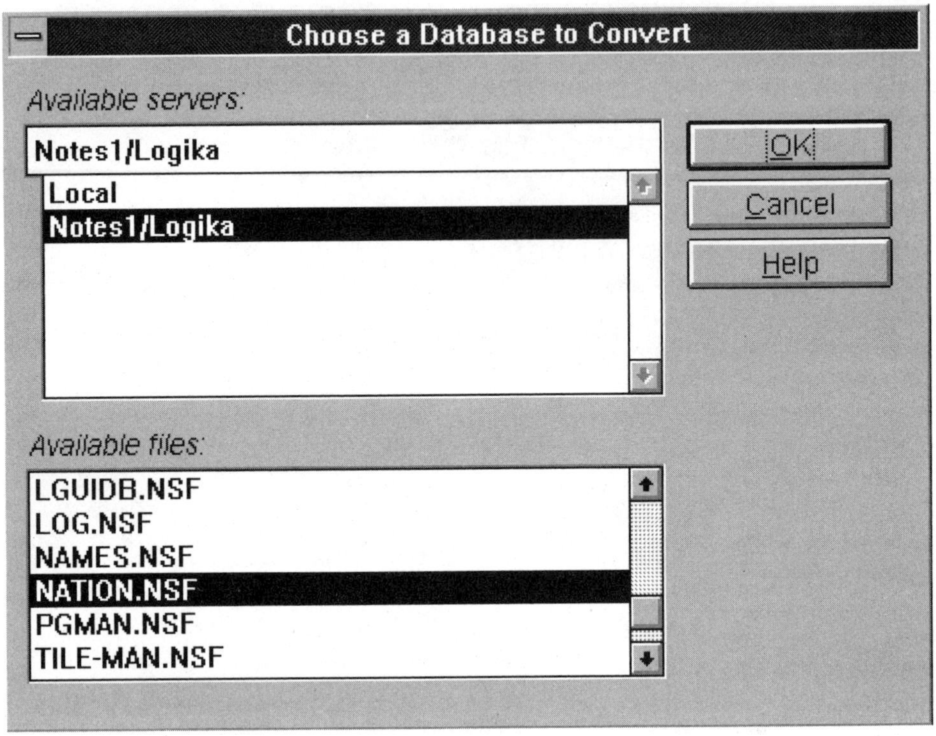

Figure 4.100   Tile conversion of a database from a Notes enterprise.

effective IS and accounting environment. You may be directed to select specific tools that can interface with SAP, PeopleSoft, QuickBooks, Great Plans Software, Peachtree, Platinum, other mainstream accounting packages, or accounting packages sent as code for such environments as Access, Foxpro, or SQL. The quickest route to failure is an inability to track sales, fulfillments, and inventory, and the lack of a tight fist on monetary flows and profit ratios. You need financial accounting, as was stressed in Chapter 2.

Database connectivity and electronic payment interface is the weak point with database/HTML interaction, and the one requiring the most attention. While any of the dynamic database/HTML conversion software programs profiled in this section work and will probably match your platform, database, and basic web integration requirements, the biggest choice will be what to purchase and how it will integrate with the business books. I want to stress that selection of the database middleware is not so much a technical solution as a trying integration task. Think of on-line database catalog sales as the POS extension needing the same tools as any POS operation.

In fact, you may discover that your database connectivity requirements may demand more than one tool. Although I stress the fundamental need to simplify as much as possible during the development of your cyberstore, I also see some instances where multiple tools are a godsend. For example, while Cold Fusion is probably the cleanest ODBC middleware solution with the fewest surprises, it is code intensive for many websites. For example, if a user wants to locate a "4-bedroom house in the Midwest with a sun room and all on one floor," the query process with Cold Fusion will be very awkward. How do you explain SQL syntax to a mere mortal user? Instead, you will end up encoding list boxes for this on-line MLS real estate service to replicate the functionality of complex queries and always build a full SQL query statement potentially with search strings set to null, default values, or the "*" value. For example, the typical list boxes included in real estate application on the web (built with Quest, Krakatoa, and Java) include:

- Location
- Neighborhood type (that is, urban or rural, high-rise or single family)
- Asking price
- Taxes
- Number of bedrooms
- Number of bathrooms
- Building style (that is, Colonial, ranch, modern, split-level, etc.)
- Distance from services or other special locations
- Other special physical house features (such as, garage, family room, finished basement, pool, deck, island in kitchen, etc.)

This results in an SQL statement of the form:

```
SELECT ALL FROM table
   WHERE location LIKE table.location AND
   WHERE neighborhood LIKE table.neighborhood AND
   WHERE cost LE table.cost AND
   WHERE bedrooms GE table.bedrooms AND
   WHERE bathrooms GE table.bathrooms AND
   WHERE style LIKE table.style AND
   WHERE distance LE table.location
```

Special features are not even considered or added to the query simply because the range of possibilities, spelling variances, and nuances is too great to effectively handle. In addition, notice that this search provides only exact or "greater than and equal" and "less than and equal" for specific fields. Typically, a person will ask for a house that is approximate to their needs. When you are starting a search, unless you know the neighborhood and a representative price range, the answers coming back are likely to be disappointing or meaningless. For example, look at the Krakatoa sample with the query that returned zero records. As a result, some of the fuzzy search tools or middleware incorporating more flexible searching parameters can be very valuable. Although Quest, for example, is based on CGI and creates a process thread for every query and can overload a server, it is a suitable choice for bundling with Cold Fusion for simplifying the query user interface because it will parse a request such as "4-bedroom house in the Midwest with a sun room and all on one floor" and handle it well.

Although the cyberstore might be seen merely as a test bed for on-line sales, and thoughts of working with the approved and formal IS department may be anathema, realize that you can quickly create a workflow and cyberstore process that will defy any future integration efforts without another implementation from nothing. You may not even be able to recycle menus, HTML forms, or any of the SSL or SHTTP CGI code for secure processing. Integration is very important, especially when planning database, middleware, and connectivity with standard business workflows and preexisting accounting systems. If the accounting system uses a two-phase commit process—common with high-end products like Oracle Financials—you will need to track completed web transactions that somehow remain in limbo in the database transaction log but not committed to the database. Web transactions in limbo represent both unsatisfied customers and lost revenue and are a common problem with database-to-HTML integration when account processing is included (as it should).

Match these middleware tools with the expected loads, or if you are creating a cyberstore trial, avoid CGI solutions (such as Java, JavaScript, ActiveX, and VBScript) that are cheap (or even free) and readily available unless you can confirm that these tools will upscale and handle the loads of a successful enterprise. Most programming solutions, except the 4GL database tools with hooks, such as Jasmine or Net Dynamics, have a weak point in terms of CPU loads and also demand management, programming, and debugging expertise. Jasmine is the integration of object-oriented database technology with HTML process. Net Dynamics converts SQL or user-compiled SQL statements (in preexisting libraries) into Java and a mix of SQL code.

The integration aspect of the database middleware includes a really nasty installation problem in many environments. It is important to recognize that many processes under Windows95 and particularly under WindowsNT run as applications invoked by a *load=* statement, an entry in the startup program manager dialogs, or as hidden services under the Control Panel. These services are like device drivers. You can envision them as part of the platform. Services may automatically start up at boot or require special circumstances to initiate them. A stub application may initiate a service and possibly terminate it when it is no longer needed. Problems occur when you are installing various products into the web server; you are likely to discover that active or even services merely installed on the disk with Windows Registry entries will halt the setup.

If you get burned by these problems, you can either call the vendor and ask if he has a solution or you can uninstall a conflicting application, which is probably the cleanest solution. If you cannot get an answer, install the new software, and then reinstall when you have uninstalled. I saw this frequently with SQL Server and ODBC device drivers. Nearly every database middleware product includes proprietary drivers or versions of Sybase, Microsoft, or Centura. Often these bundled drivers were older than what I had previously installed on a web or database server and the installation routines (even the Wyse or other InstallShield) would not recognize comparable or later versions of these device drivers. Windows95 and WindowsNT are supposed to be beyond those primitive problems, but the complexity of the registry, tracking active services, and finding distributed directories are still complex.

When you get a working platform, jot down the process you used to get everything working. Catastrophes do occur and you might have to rebuild a server at some future date. The installation sequence that works may save countless hours. Good things do happen, too, and you may find yourself building a secondary or supplemental web or database server and wishing you had only remembered the exact component installation sequence. In general, you will discover that you have to install the operating system and all bug fixes or service patches, create directories and users, and get the DNS services running properly so that URLs using the domain name for the server will correctly reference HTML files. Then, install the web server software. Add in any helper applications, including database engines, database middleware, CGI libraries, and finally the HTML sources. As previously stated, you may have to jockey SQL Server and other middleware libraries to get the tool sets installed.

All the database middleware that I reviewed work as advertised, but most are rough around the edges, which is to be expected with first-generation tools. Installation is clearly a sore point, as previously mentioned, because these tools integrate as services and drivers within the web server operating system (about what the web server really is) running atop the platform operating system. However, the complexity extends beyond simply technical issues. All the middleware tools create workflow, performance, presentation, and implementational time frames that are critical to consider. Tools have their best points. They also have their worst points. For example, Sapphire Web and Spider generator C++ or Java are great because you implement anything you can possibly envision. On the other hand, you need the skills and time to make that vision a reality. Cold Fusion or Quest make a reality almost instantaneously, but some visions are not possible because the tools are simply not that flexible. The remaining part of this section shows how these tools integrate with a database. Figure 4.101 shows Quest, listing investment-grade bonds in its own panel. As mentioned previously, you can see the "fuzzy" search capabilities in the menu bar above the line item listings. You can specify precise values or reorder and filter the data by predetermined ranges, in this example, the minimum or maximum call dates.

Quest can also imbed icons or symbols in the dynamic tables. This listing of cities and their defining properties shows happy faces of various colors and expressions to reinforce the text-based descriptions, as illustrated in Figure 4.102. Newark, for example, was listed as a "War Zone" with a skull and crossbones replacing the frowning face.

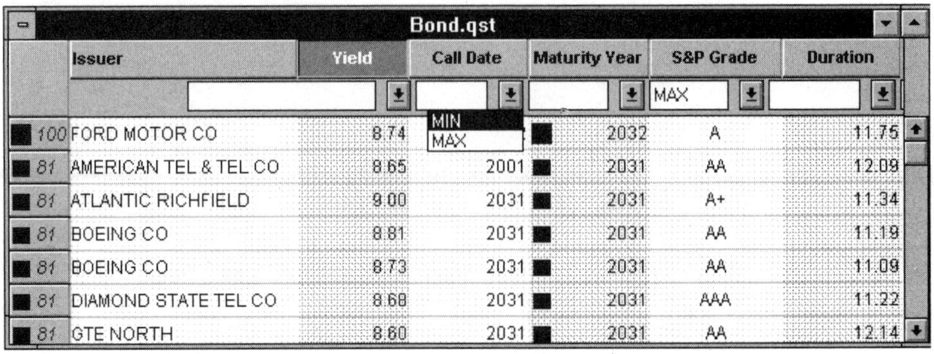

Figure 4.101   A brokerage house web listing in Quest showing current bond offers.

The next figure Figure 4.103) shows symbols in an employee review application. In addition, the HTML 3.2 frame, cell color control, and width variability are profiled.

The problem with tables, as shown earlier in this chapter in the discussion of static database conversion to HTML, raises its ugly head here, too. With the bandwidths available, it is awkward and slow for most users to scroll both vertically and horizontally through a web-based table. With some tools, the information not visible in the other horizontal columns is not cached and must be fetched again from the database for redisplay. This causes an unnecessary effort and really is not good use of the Quest middleware, as shown in Figure 4.104. Instead, create a simple table with a minimum number of columns that return only a few rows at a time. Although you might want to enable full row searching of a database, consider other presentation methods to minimize time-consuming conversions and presentation overheads.

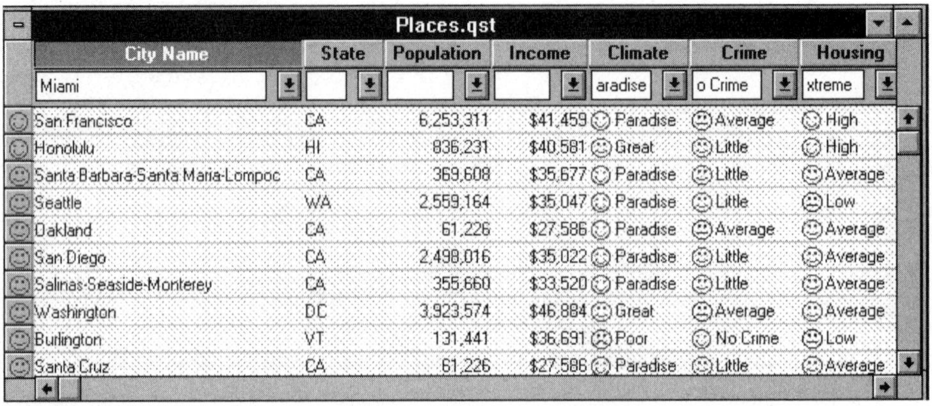

Figure 4.102   Quest can include symbols as part of a dynamic database table listing.

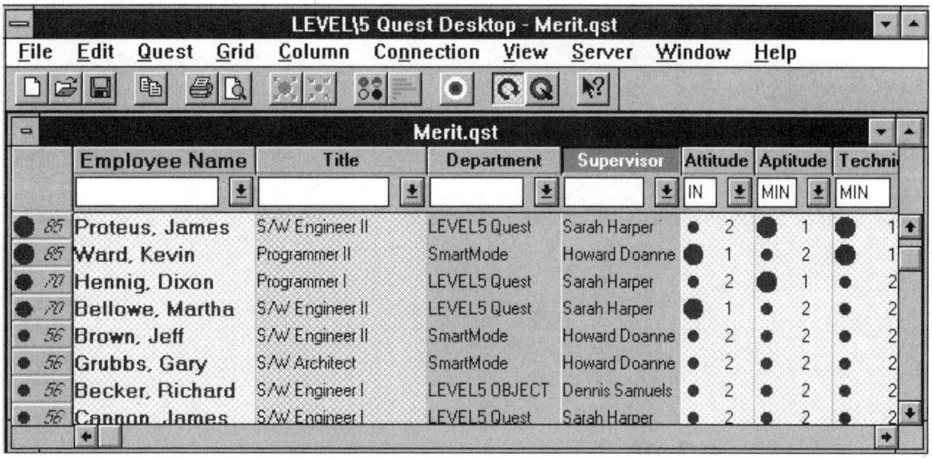

Figure 4.103   Quest implements the HTML 3.2 codes for complex table attributes.

Cold Fusion is activated like most of the ODBC-compliant middleware tools. You *add* tables to the administrator tool and specify preferences for access to databases, as shown in Figure 4.105. Preferences include named user access as well as read and write permissions. It is important to understand the relationships between master databases, replicated extracts, and what developers can present to users. There are security issues that are typically decided by a database administrator, not necessarily by the website designers. If sensitive information must be available to the Cold Fusion templates, you may need to create supplemental or extracted data tables specifically for web access.

Cold Fusion will work with MS Access, SQL Server, Oracle, Sybase, Paradox, FoxPro, and even dBASE data sources. The screen shot in Figure 4.106 shows the setup for access to a sample *Quest* database. This

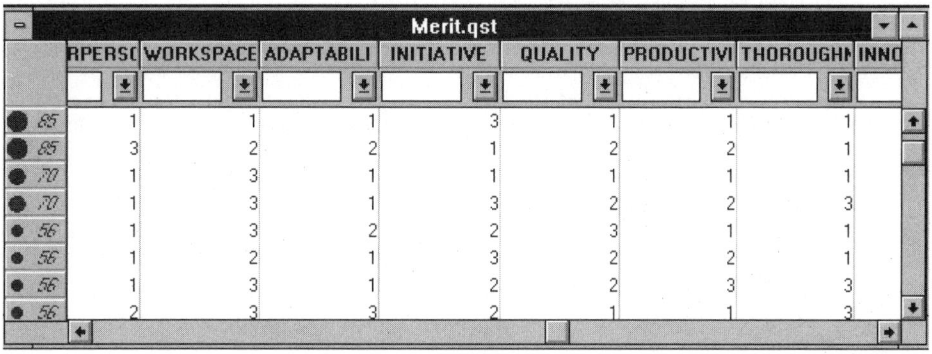

Figure 4.104   A Quest table that scrolls horizontally. Notice that you lose the row legends and thus the context for each row of information.

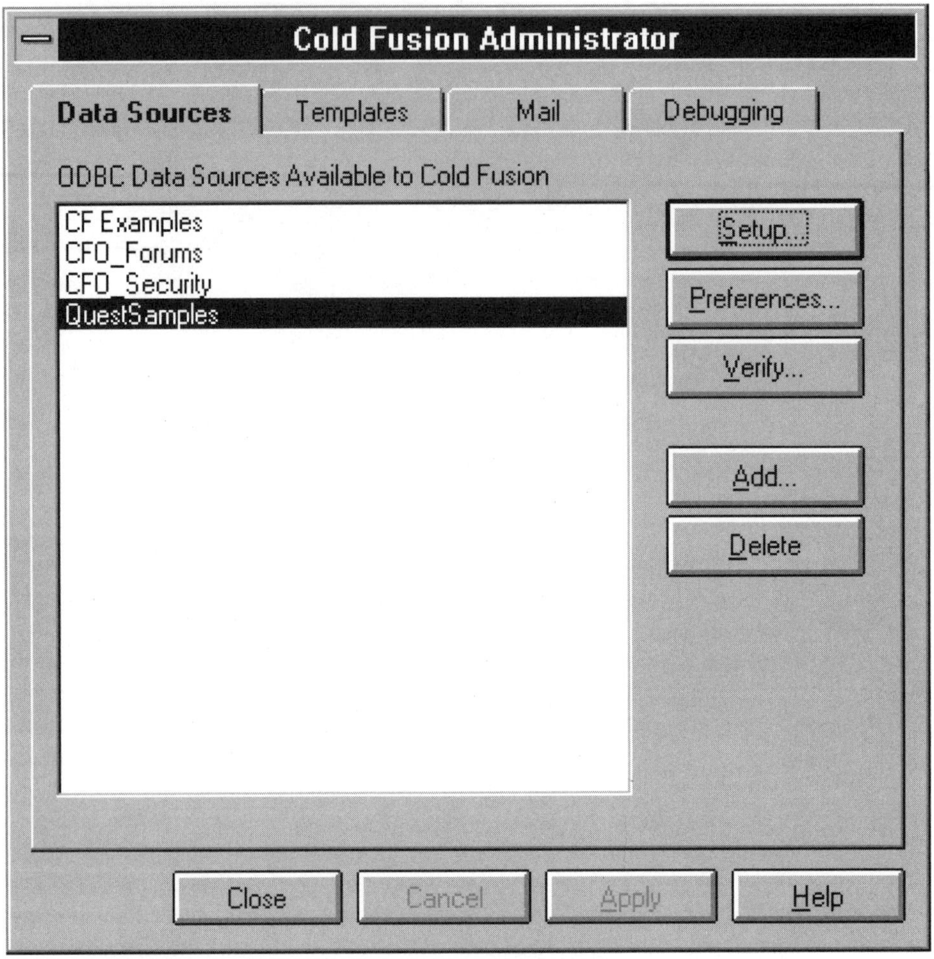

Figure 4.105 Database ODBC administration with Cold Fusion.

reinforces the interoperability and possible need to use more than middleware tools. It also speaks to the need to understand that ODBC driver setup with multiple middleware tools may overwrite and alter prior ODBC data-source configurations. You always want to validate the configuration before creating Cold Fusion templates and confirm that the web server connection and configuration matches what Cold Fusion expects, as shown in Figure 4.107.

The code for Cold Fusion is simply a combination of standard SQL statements and HTML codes. Accessing templates — each HTML file could reference one Cold Fusion template — is with an imbedded code:

```
<FORM ACTION =/cgi-shl/dbml.exe?/Template = insdata.dbm"
METHOD = POST>
```

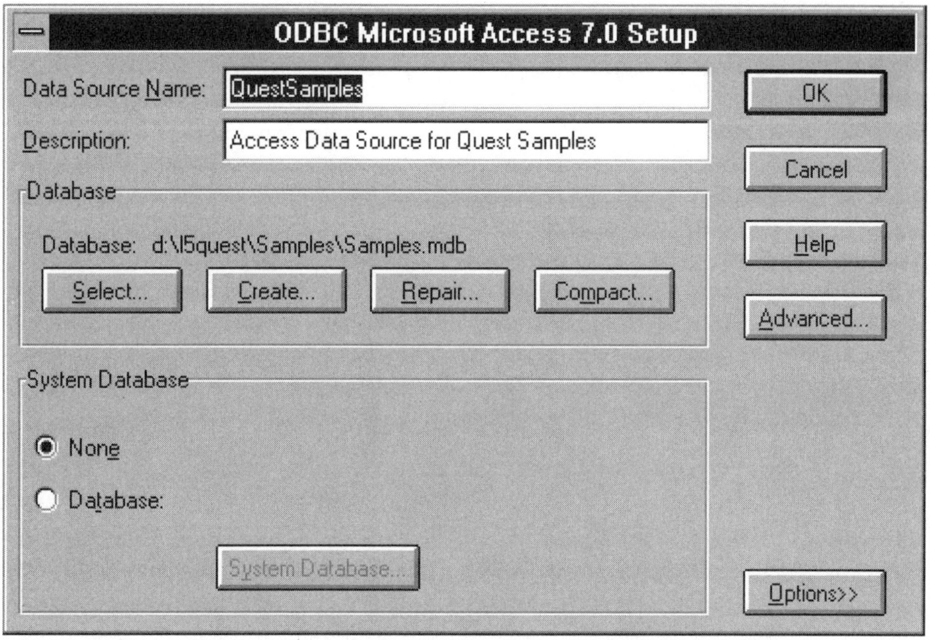

Figure 4.106 Accessing a Quest sample database with Cold Fusion.

Figure 4.107 Verify that a data source is active and valid before creating or using Cold Fusion templates.

When you want to create a database query with Cold Fusion, you create a mix of HTML and SQL that might look like this:

```
<HTML>
<HEAD><TITLE>Example Query</TITLE></HEAD>
<BODY>
<FORM ACTION =/cgi-shl/dbml.exe?/Template = insdata.dbm"
METHOD = POST>
<PRE>
State: <INPUT TYPE = "text" NAME"Customer">
Type: <SELECT NAME = "Type">
  <OPTION>Corporation
  <OPTION>Government
  <OPTION>Nonprofit
  </SELECT>
Size: <INPUT = "submit"VALUE = "Do Search">
</PRE>
</FORM>
</BODY>
</HTML>
```

If you notice the format carefully, you will see the CGI trademarks of the path to the CGI library directory and the "?" indicating a command process. When you want a more diverse platform support and greater scalability than possible with WindowsNT, organizations implement the database interaction with other tools that show a fourth-generation heritage (such as Forte and PowerBuilder) or generate C++ and Java code.

The query and display interface

There is technically a lot more to database integration than simply patching Domino, WebDC, or Cold Fusion to production database and building forms. The presentation, the workflow, and the process must make sense. This section profiles various sites and shows what works and why it was done. For example, the National Semiconductor site shown in Figure 4.108 illustrates the frame and HTML INPUT fields that are linked to the Krakatoa search engine.

As mentioned earlier, you want to focus and simplify database queries as much as possible. The hypertext in the left frame minimizes the search range and the amount of information returned from a user-initiated query. This shortens the database search, table building time, and transmission time to the client browser, as shown in Figure 4.109.

Additional hierarchical selections focus the ultimate query by providing another layer for the search criteria. Most users will not construct valid SQL or tolerate complex list boxes that parallel the SQL selection. Users do not think yet in terms of "this AND this OR that BUT NOT that," so that simpler specification processes are required. This specification hierarchy has the previously mentioned performance effects, and also makes it easier for users to find what they are looking for, as shown in the reduction presented in Figure 4.110. While most users will not know the part numbers or specific part titles, they will know that they are looking for an ISDN or ASDL encoder chip.

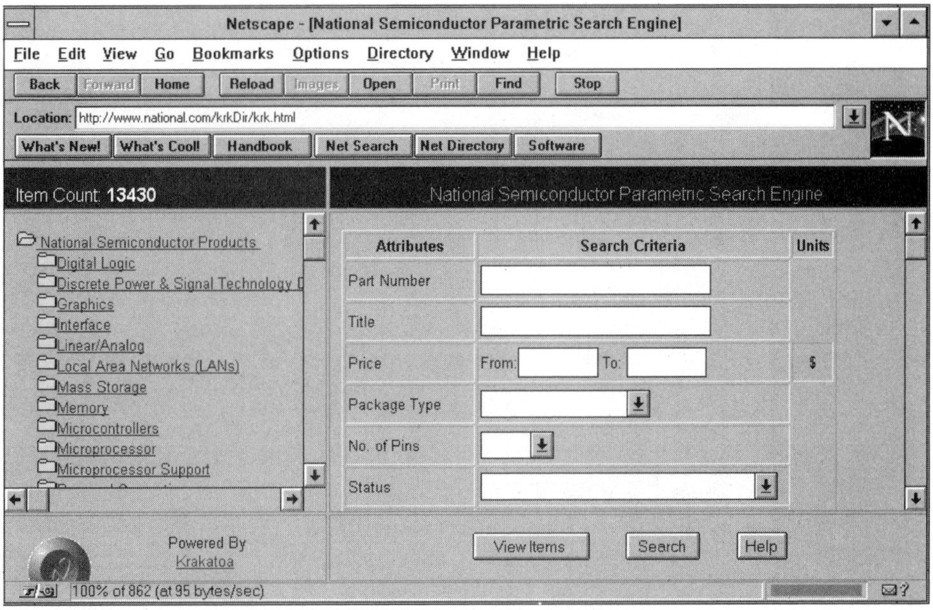

Figure 4.108 The home page for the National Semiconductor on-line parts and specification catalog.

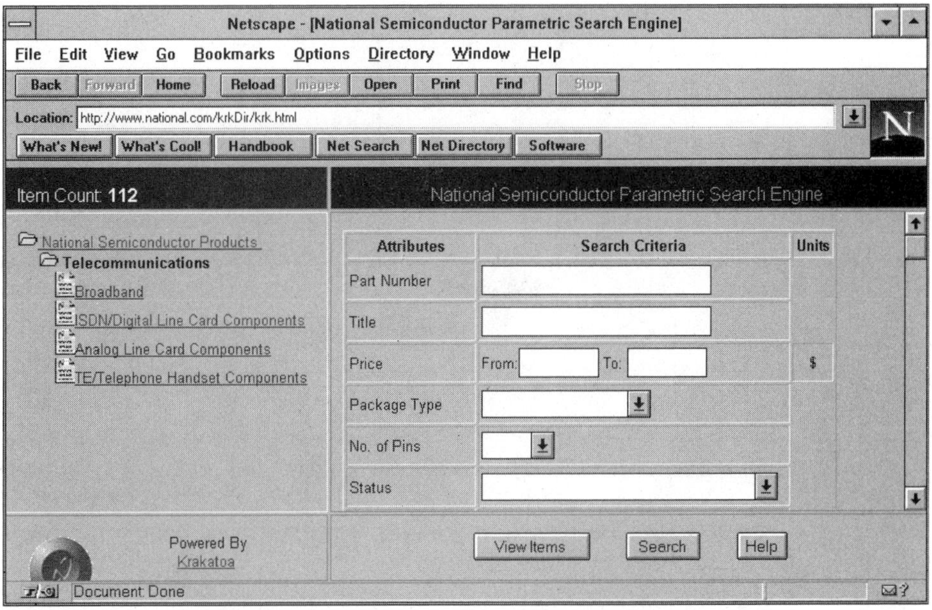

Figure 4.109 Selection of Telecommunication and ISDN components focuses the search and data return.

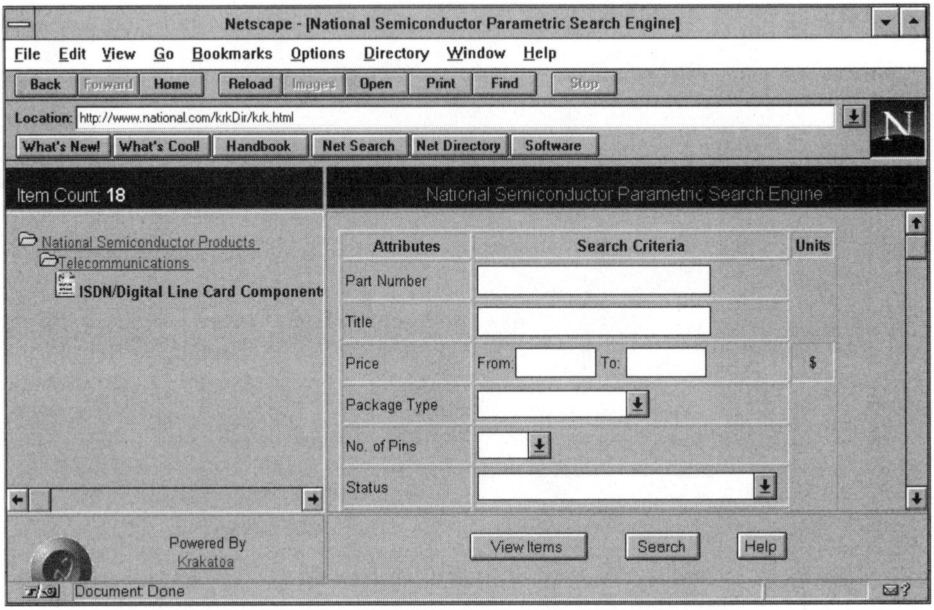

Figure 4.110 Another layer in the hierarchy is specified by the framed text.

At some point, the user will need to specify some or all of the part title. In this case, both "ISDN" and "*DSL" were entered to generate the tabular report dynamically from the database, as shown in Figure 4.111. Notice that the report is created as a new floating browser window.

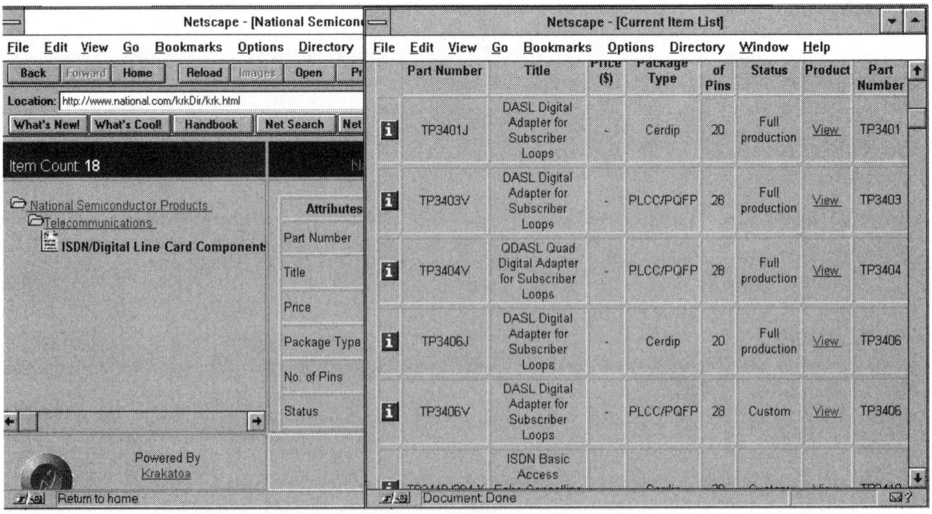

Figure 4.111 The dynamic data table as a secondary browser window.

A real estate application demonstrates another use for Krakatoa. However, I do not mean to imply that Krakatoa is the best tool for real estate cyberstores. In fact, you can use straight HTML, Cold Fusion, webDBC, or Quest, and most vendors will provide demos of real estate websites or give you URLs to customers who have built real estate sites with their products. This CADIS MLS site in Figure 4.112 shows that the queries need to handle unspecified fields and deal with combinations of specifications that can return no valid matches. As stated previously, you want to provide users with sufficient feedback so that they can easily and quickly expand the search specifications. Too many null searches waste time and do not sell the customer anything.

The real estate query also returns a floating window with results, as shown in Figure 4.113.

The floating results are not the end of the search. When a user clicks a specific row listing, the hypertext icon or "view" text requests the display of the line item listing. This integration of both text, memo field, and image components to a standard HTML web page is shown in Figure 4.114.

It is unlikely that unique and large-ticket items are sold over the Internet. New cars are sold on the Internet because they are identical and contain uniform warranties, which used cars do not.

There are also complex legal contract negotiations with homes. Thus, the catalog presentation of real estate represents only a first step in the sales process, but serves to accumulate large numbers of properties, provide a focus for a potential buyer, and also link that buyer with the listing agent. On-line database

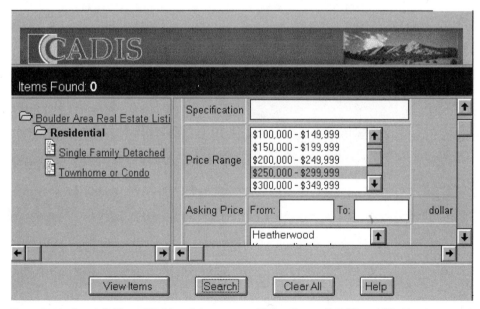

Figure 4.112 Input field- and list box-driven query. Notice the explicit "Search" button to prevent accidental processing of an incomplete request.

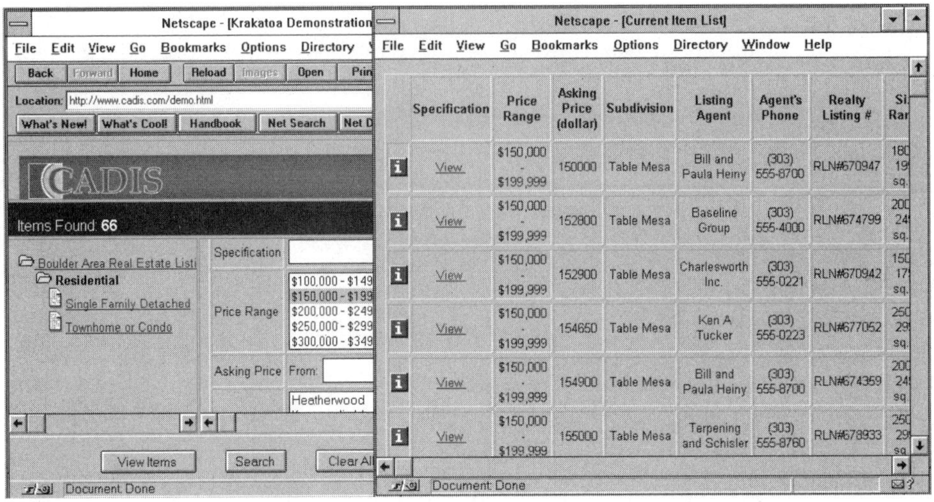

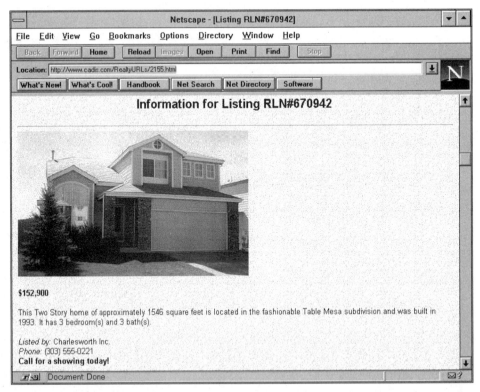

Figure 4.113   Notice the tabular results from the query.

Figure 4.114   The terminal real estate list. Note that the contact is presented as a phone number but could include a form for E-mail, automated paging, delivery of a prospectus, or enablement of a realtor's calendar to schedule a site visit.

listings of real estate seem likely to appeal to buyers from other cities or to professional buyers as a very focused announcement of product and its availability. Thus, the attractiveness of data-driven websites is that the products are complex, often change, and are diverse or the products and components are similar yet have differences that are important to a buyer. This aspect is pertinent for the sale of electronic components, automobiles, and homes.

However, database integration is not everything for these highly data-driven products. You cannot simply slap a web interface on the database and expect it to be enough. Sites need instructions, definitions, and preamble. Some consumer sites may make single high-ticket sales. You need to explain how to use the site, provide on-line help, and create a clear and simple interface for the user—who is always expected to be a first-time user. This is true even if users have seen competitors' sites. Other sites rotate stock, have new closeouts, and hype new products. You want to help the first-time user through the site, pick multiple items for his or her shopping cart, and effect electronic payment. Yet other sites, such that of National Semiconductor, sell industrial component lines with subtle differences and applications. These industrial sites are data driven and should be designed to optimize the time spent by an industrial buyer placing orders and setting up EDI transactions. Even so, you want to provide some preamble for the buyer and help apprentice and new buyers use the site.

For example, the National Association of Realtors (NAR) has spent more than $18 million building websites in California, New York, New Jersey, Texas, and Florida. Some of these separate sites were very expensive and include data-driven components, but lack a good preamble and interface to the search engine and database. In fact, the California site cost $13 million and is not as functional as the either the Texas or Florida sites. The home page for the Texas site is shown in Figure 4.115.

The Texas site is not limited to Texas properties. The search engine links into other sites because even real estate is becoming a global market and commodity, as shown in Figure 4.116. Foreign investors are buying housing, apartment buildings, vacation condominiums, and commercial properties to hedge against currency fluctuations, local economies, inflation, and political risks. The results of the national search show websites for local associations in almost every state. Notice the Florida sites in Figure 4.117.

The Realtor Association of Miami also includes a preamble. Although the listings are stored as database entries, the image and emotion shown on the home page can be very important not only for local buyers seeking to change neighborhoods or upgrade, but also for potential buyers from other cities. Notice the yellowed parchment map that emphasizes the history and antiquity (which is not really true) of Miami, as shown in Figure 4.118. Although most neighborhoods are new within the last five years, the image and emotion symbolize an important message for this local realty association. New cities and housing developments often lack a sense of community and instead impart an association of sterility, newness, and small trees. Notice also that the hotspots

Figure 4.115   The home page for the Texas NAR site.

Figure 4.116   National search for properties from the Texas website.

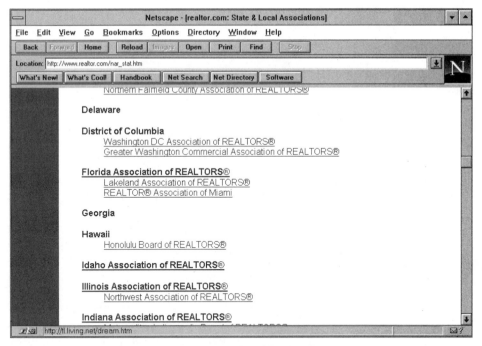

Figure 4.117 Local website listings for the NAR-listed local realtors.

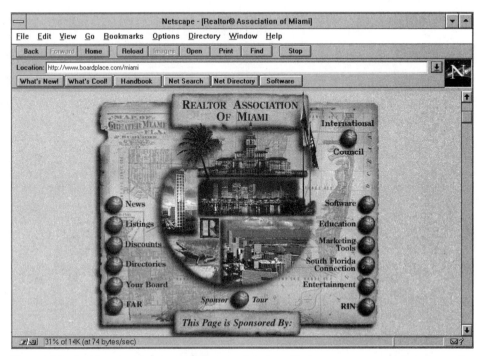

Figure 4.118 Ambience and message take precedence on the home page over technical superlatives, database interfaces, and technophobia.

include many local service options and directories, not just a limited jump into a data-intensive listing service.

Even when you want to search for a particular property, you have to negotiate the next neighborhood section. Although fast and efficient interfaces are important, realize that the message for this website seeks to overcome some serious negative impressions about Miami—its crime history, attacks on tourists, car hijackings, and the type of city that it has been portrayed as on various movies and TV shows such as "Miami Vice." The presentation of Miami as a series of neighborhoods softens the hard edge. Notice in Figure 4.119 that even the page is soft and fuzzy. However important it is to provide a useful database interface, the message to the infrequent buyer is even more important.

Even when you think you are getting to the MLS listings, you get another layer of publicity and puffery. Figure 4.120 shows another soft and fuzzy screen that tries to ease the hard edges of a major metropolitan area. Although one can suggest that the designers display an inferiority complex when compared with the faster growing adjacent city/county area of Fort Lauderdale/ Broward, this message is important when the product you are selling must face another competitor.

When you think you might actually get to the database, you get another view of the city, as illustrated in Figure 4.121, in the famous Art Deco style common in the area. Image is everything when marketing high-priced ticket, once-in-a-lifetime purchases tinted so much by emotional issues such

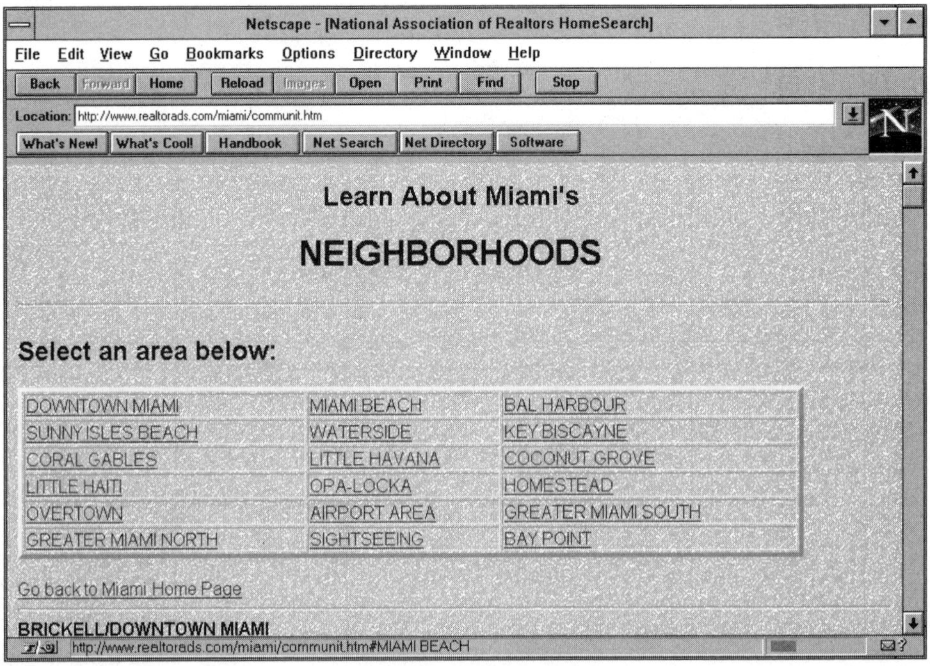

Figure 4.119 The multilayered front end to the database creates a semiotic message of history, antiquity, and a creation of neighborhood.

Netscape - [National Association of Realtors HomeSearch]

File   Edit   View   Go   Bookmarks   Options   Directory   Window   Help

Back | Forward | Home | Reload | Images | Open | Print | Find | Stop

Location: http://www.realtorads.com/miami/communit.htm#MIAMI BEACH

What's New! | What's Cool! | Handbook | Net Search | Net Directory | Software

MIAMI BEACH

Fashion models, writers, movie producers and assorted glitterati are the new players in Miami Beach's renaissance. South Miami Beach is a neighborhood on the move. Renovated hotels along Ocean Drive and throughout the Art Deco Historic District have captured national praise for an architectural treasure of Art Deco, Streamline Modern and Spanish Mediterranean Revival styles dominating a one-square mile area from 6th to 23rd Streets and from Ocean Drive to Lenox Avenue. Pastel colors, zigurrat rooftops and whimsical friezes have become Art Deco signatures, as well as a vivid backdrop for cafe dining, nightclub hopping and people-watching. Thanks to the tireless efforts of local supporters, the district earned a spot on the National Register of Historic Places, the youngest community to be so honored.

In the past few years, images of "SoBe" (the SoHo of the South, as South Beach is referred to) have permeated fashion catalogues, films and television shows from around the world. International crews can be found filming throughout Greater Miami and the Beaches from dawn to dusk. With the film crews, transplanted celebrities have converged to the area to work and play, transforming it into a year-round playground of the stars.

Just north of the Art Deco Historic District, multi-million dollar restorations have transformed many of the legendary hotels along Collins Avenue into inviting waterfront resorts. The spectacular new architecture and sheer beauty of the recently expanded Miami Beach Convention Center make it an instantaneous landmark.

Document: Done

Figure 4.120   Another soft and fuzzy pitch for the Miami Beach real estate market.

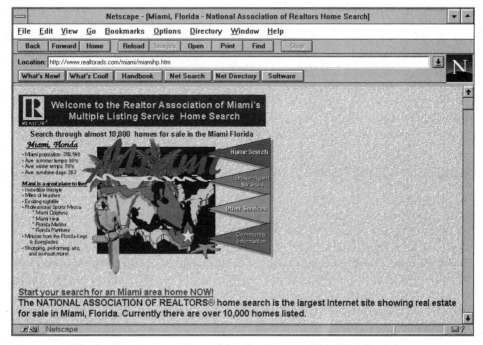

Figure 4.121   The database presentation is delayed yet again with a lifestyle pitch.

as a sense of home, safety, security, quality of school systems, and lifestyle. Miami makes a clear pitch for the tropical paradise lifestyle issue. Figure 4.122 shows a query screen for the MLS database. Notice the complexity in this screen. Although main buyer parameters are included here, the layout and complexity of the items are somewhat overwhelming. A report of the query is shown in Figure 4.123 simply as a continuously hyperlinked listing of properties, pricing, the MLS number, a description, and a photograph where available.

You might notice that these pages are generated on the fly because the hyperlinks are based on the particular query filters. Some searches will only return 10 or 20 matches, others just 1 or 2. While you could design an HTML file for every listed property (or product or service) and create a database with an HTML filename, the query would have to return a table of listings, which in turn hyperlink to each HTML file. The Krakatoa sample actually does this. Instead, these hyperlinked real estate listings link to each, the chief giveaway of a more dynamic data-driven website. In fact, Figure 4.124 shows a Quest-based demonstration of a Florida real estate catalog.

Figure 4.125 shows that this query is just a standard HTML form. You could build it with the Quest tools, with Web Author, or with HotMetal. The most difficult part, at least for me, is aligning the list boxes with the sets of radio

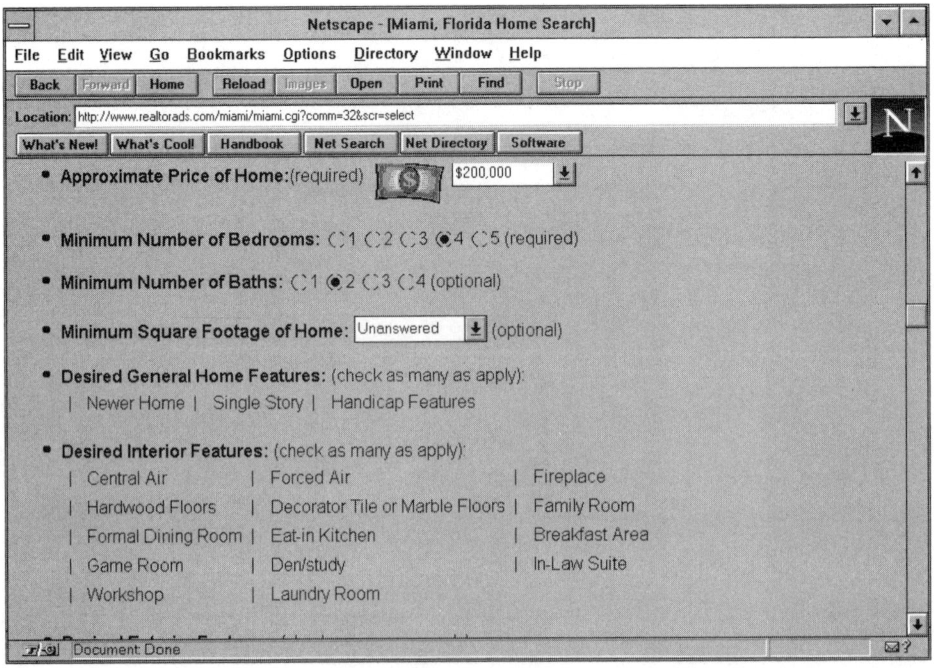

Figure 4.122 The actual query screen for a real estate search.

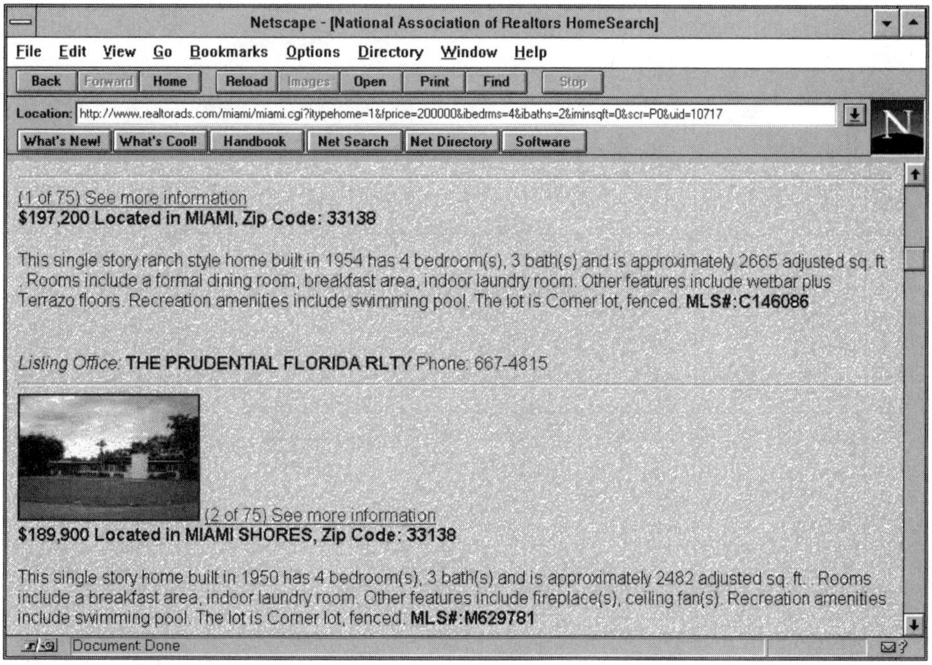

Figure 4.123 The database query result.

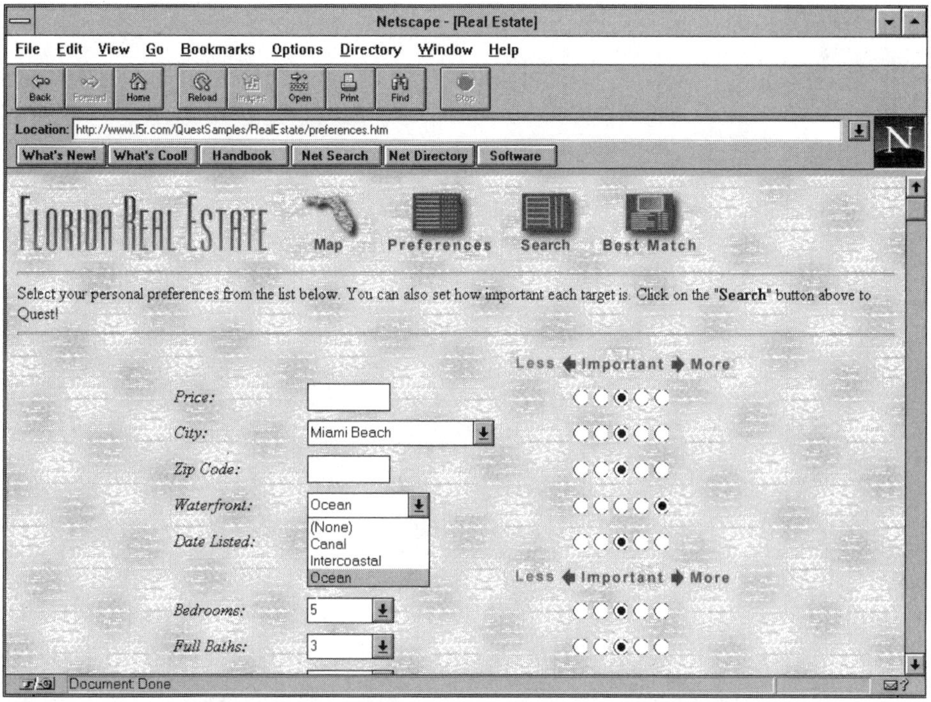

Figure 4.124 Quest-based query screen—note the weights given to various fields.

```
   Netscape - [Source of: http://www.l5r.com/cgi-bin/htmlplug.exe?RealEstate/pref
<tr>
<td><i>City:</i></td><td>Miami
</td>
<td><center><input type=radio name="RI_City" value="Least"><input type=radio name="RI_City" value="Littl
</tr>

<tr>
<td><i>Waterfront:</i></td><td><select name="WaterFront" size=1>
<option>(None)</option>
<option>Canal</option>
<option>Intercoastal</option>
<option selected>Ocean</option>
</select></td><td><center><input type=radio name="RI_WaterFront" value="Least"><input type=radio name="R
</tr>

<tr>
<td></td><td></td><td><center><img src="/QuestSamples/RealEstate/importance.jpg" align=bottom width=230
</tr>
<tr><td><i>Bedrooms:</i></td><td><select name="BedRM" size=1>
<option>(None)</option>
```

Figure 4.125 The query form is just a standard HTML document.

buttons on the same line. Database implementation and integration are not hard, as you can see, but the design and composition can be.

Quest is a standard CGI process, with all its benefits and limitations. The form above is parsed, processed, and passed to the Quest engine. The result is a table of entries, each of which is hyperlinked to a page providing house details, as shown in Figure 4.126.

ComSpace lists commercial real estate, a different market that is based on need, rates of return, and cashflow. Notice the home page for ComSpace in

88	12888	161000	South Miami	3	Ocean	No	French	199	
88	51120	458000	Medley	3	Ocean	No	Traditional	199	
88	67680	392000	Miami	4	Ocean	No	Mobile	199	
87	3060	95000	Pompano Beach	5	Intercoastal	No	Traditional	199	
87	4608	102000	Pompano Beach	5	Intercoastal	No	English	199	
87	32652	184000	Pompano Beach	5	Intercoastal	No	Contemporary	199	
87	35694	260000	Pompano Beach	5	Intercoastal	No	Traditional	199	
87	37242	170000	Pompano Beach	5	Intercoastal	No	Contemporary	199	
87	49500	260000	Pompano Beach	5	Intercoastal	No	Mobile	199	
86	51012	283000	Medley	2	Ocean	No	Ranch	199	
86	51642	269000	Tamarac	3	Ocean	No	Log	199	
86	61308	412000	Tamarac	6	Ocean	No	Traditional	199	
85	54324	461000	Sunrise	6	Ocean	No	Manufactured	199	
85	59436	632000	Sunrise	4	Ocean	No	Log	199	
85	59940	377000	Sunrise	4	Ocean	No	Mobile	199	

...brought to you by *LEVEL5 Quest Server*

Figure 4.126 The Quest real estate demonstration report.

Figure 4.127. Even this Miami site does not dump the user directly into a query page but also provides a preamble.

The secondary page specific to Miami makes no mention of the soft and fuzzy issues transparent in the MLS preamble. Instead, this website is all business. The data query is first partitioned by types of commercial real estate needs, not just ownership. In addition, notice that there are different types of commercial real estate, from retail to industrial. The page shown in Figure 4.128 has a table to create the main hierarchies. A standard query page helps a user focus the search on the properties that best match his or her needs and then returns a tabular listing.

I believe the greatest utility for the cyberstore is inherent in business-to-business sales of raw materials, industrial products, parts, and tools. This is presented best by the John Deere website. John Deere products are synonymous with industrial productivity. Although a new data-driven catalog is not yet available to the public (only internally to allied organizations), Figures 4.129 to 4.131 show where the static web pages will be enabled with the entry query screens.

Much like the AMP site profiled in Chapter 5, when you click on a particular parts line, you jump to the page profiling that parts line, as shown in Figure 4.130. The overwhelming image in this site is that of completion, support for both John Deere products and those of competitors, and the impression that you will find the exact part you need no matter how obtuse,

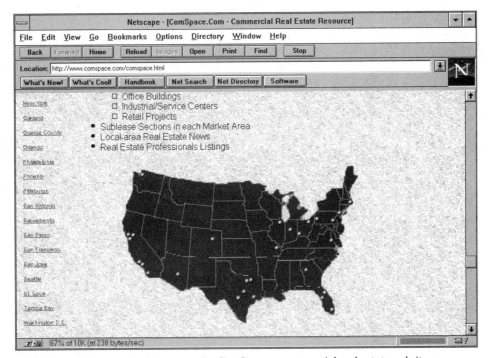

Figure 4.127   The preamble home page for ComSpace, a commercial real estate website.

Figure 4.128 The hierarchies into the database are listed on this secondary page.

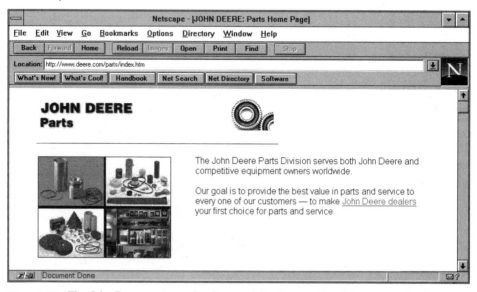

Figure 4.129 The John Deere parts catalog front end for the new data-driven parts database.

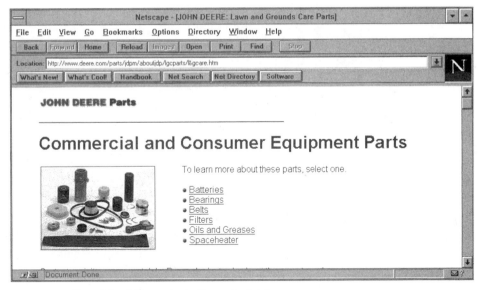

Figure 4.130   Second-level hierarchy to the parts database.

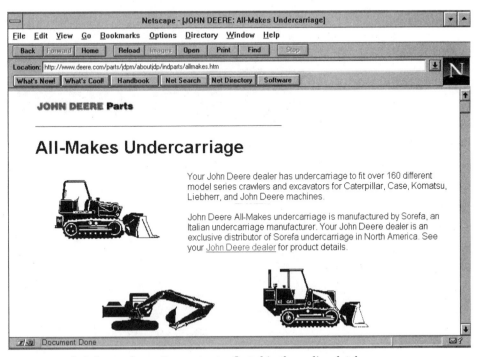

Figure 4.131   A stub page for an item not yet reflected in the on-line database.

old, or unusual. Since the database was not yet live at the time of this writing and previews of the interface were not yet allowed, John Deere does include the following stub screens (Figure 4.131) when you select a part not yet on-line. Notice that each stub screen does include some general information about the missing details and a contact for additional information. E-mail would provide an even better method of continuing the sales dialogue in most cases, except that when you need a part for construction equipment, you need it in a hurry, and even E-mail does not provide real-time response.

The web page for the Dodge Virtual Showroom shows another facet of the cyberstore integration process and database integration. You can select cars by model name, price range, and options, as shown in Figure 4.132. When you select the cars, the response is to sort through the database of model lines, option lines (if available for each model), and price ranges.

Although real estate is difficult to sell on-line, cars represent a known and warrantied quantity. Dodge does not in fact make transactions on-line—to its own detriment — while other dealer/brokers are creating brand names for Internet transactions, underpricing local dealers, and creating increased price

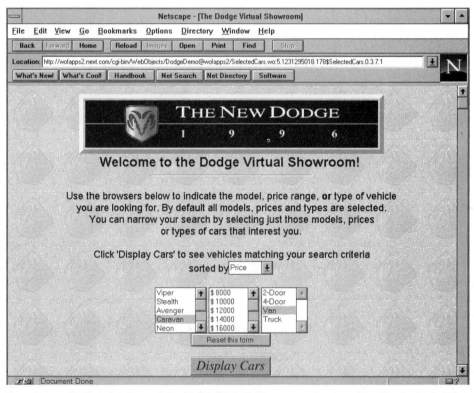

Figure 4.132 On-line database of the Dodge Virtual Showroom showing shopping for high-ticket items, such as cars.

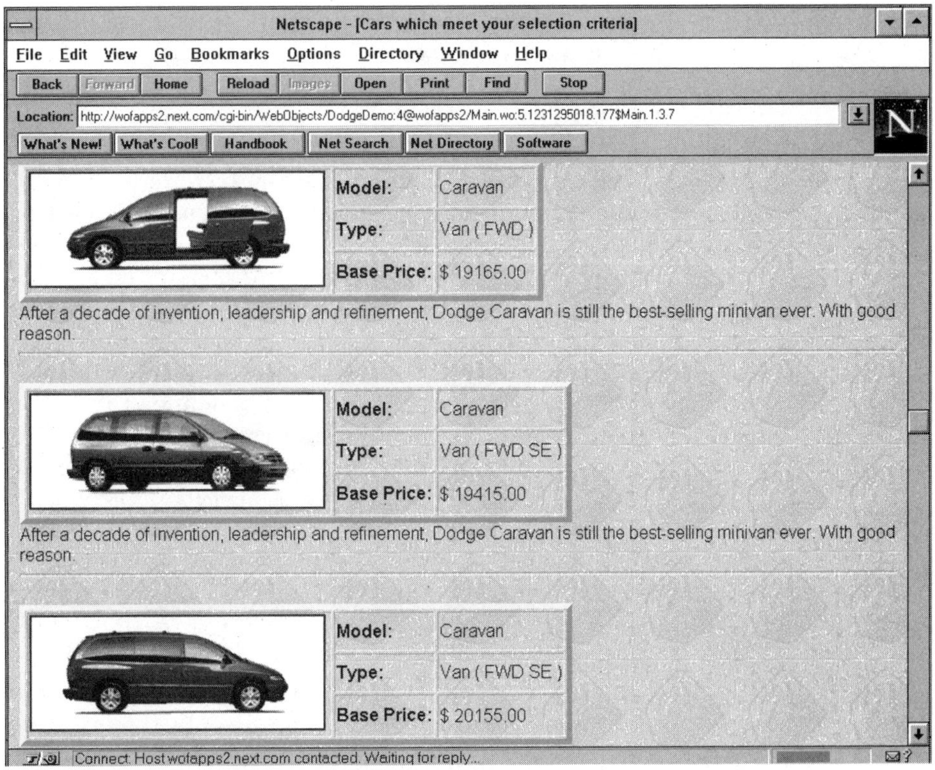

Figure 4.133 Dodge report on product returned from the prior database query.

pressures for Dodge and all the other car manufacturers. Figure 4.133 shows the simple HTML tables generated from the product database.

Web Application Enablement

A hot button for many developers and vendors is to add web support to their applications. There are four ways to do this:

- Add web-enabled help
- Add browser components
- Add integration components
- Enable an application to run as a web process

The Blue Sky Software WebOffice contains all you need to swap the Windows API help calls to URL requests. It is fairly easy to add a simple browser with functionality limited to the help URLs. This presupposes that your users will have a TCP/IP stack available. Basically the help-file file name becomes a

URL path, any help topics with a help file become a URL, and any jumps within a file become URL offsets.

If you want to add a browser component to your software, I suggest you question your motives. Netscape Navigator has about 75 percent of the market, unifies a fair number of Internet functions, and has more resources to enhance that single-purpose browser than you have to build a web-enabled application. I suppose you can look at the Internet as a big network, and just as you have enabled applications to be network sensitive and aware, it makes sense to make applications compatible with this new and bigger network. That is going to happen but you need to understand the ramifications and the resources required.

Although browser enablement seems like an attractive path to access remote help files, data sets, and even databases, define your focus. I do not think you can compete unless you are building a cross-platform application intended to access a cross-platform database and want to simplify the user interface. If your goal is to construct a viable and profitable cyberstore, special applications that are browser enabled create a barrier to entry and a large hurdle to getting users to your store. In a sense, you are creating a proprietary user interface for a website, when the very success of the Internet and of websites has been the openness of the browser. It is one of the reasons I suggest you avoid add-ins and client-side applets.

However, many tools, including the Crescent Internet ToolPak and VBNet, provide VBXs and OCXs to convert Windows applications to web applications. These tools work well, but you need to realize the effort needed to construct or convert existing applications to contain web functions. You need to add code and test, and then test that basic application functions still work as intended and in conjunction with the new browser features.

Internet enablement is essentially browser enablement as described above, but you might also add FTP or SMTP functionality. Of all the features that seem attractive and are in fact useful, the SMTP E-mail enablement means that an application can read and create messages to send to technical support, to other people who are part of an organization-wide process flow, or even to other processes. This can include list servers for product registration; mailing lists for announcements of new services, upgrades, or products; and reports and other results forwarded down the workflow chain to other applications or people.

Enabling an application to run as a web process is interesting and useful if you want to limit the scope of user access to Windows, Java, or JavaScript. Several conversion tools and design tools allow a software developer to take existing pieces of code, entire client/server applications, and even antiquated host-based applications and port them out to the web. There are two benefits to this conversion process.

First, you upgrade the user interface with old applications. This is pertinent to 1.5 million COBOL programmers maintaining and adding features to big applications. It also provides a means of distributing applications to remote users and even customers without creating wholly new applications from scratch. This is an important point when you are integrating a cyberstore operation into existing POS operations and need to interface mainframe accounting systems with credit card processing and web-driven transactions.

Second, you reuse existing code for new uses. This is primarily of value with PowerBuilder, Visual Basic, and any OLE client or in-server procedures. Recycling code can save development time. However, you need to balance these efforts against the costs of learning a new development and *integration* environment. Also, you need to understand that ActiveX and VBScript conversions will run only under Windows servers and clients. Similar limitations exist when you convert COBOL, C, C++, PowerBuilder, or Forte applications into web-enabled servers or applets for client-side processing.

Understand the limitations clearly enough. You need time, resources, and knowledge, and you also must understand what you will achieve with this migration and platform integration. For example, Figure 4.134 shows a mainframe-based librarian system enabled for web access.

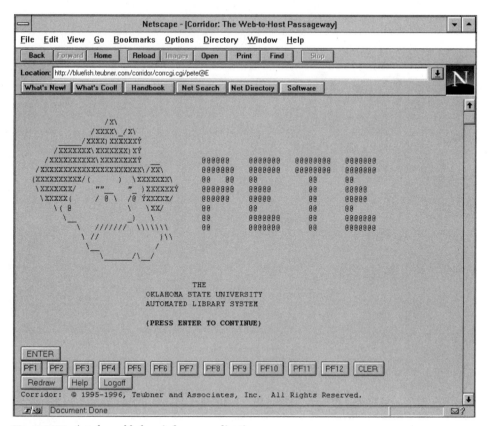

Figure 4.134 A web-enabled mainframe application.

Notice that the web version doesn't look much different from the original terminal display. This is both good and bad—you decide, and factor in your customer base. On the other hand, you can see that the IBM functional keys are now mapped easily into any PC or other desktop client station. Many organizations hoping to move the hardware from IBM terminals to desktops have had to create a gateway and deal with mapping the hardware keys. This application takes care of that process very simply by creating buttons on the web page.

Another major benefit of this web enablement is that people who previously had no access to a library catalog now can view that catalog remotely, in fact, from anywhere in the world. The power of interlibrary book lending is boosted by this refinement. Even when a library system is designed for a university, as it is in Figure 4.135, remote campus sites can attach to the library system without a specialized gateway, special access lines, or even a special wiring system for the library network—any web browser will do. Search capabilities are available with secondary web pages, as shown in Figure 4.136.

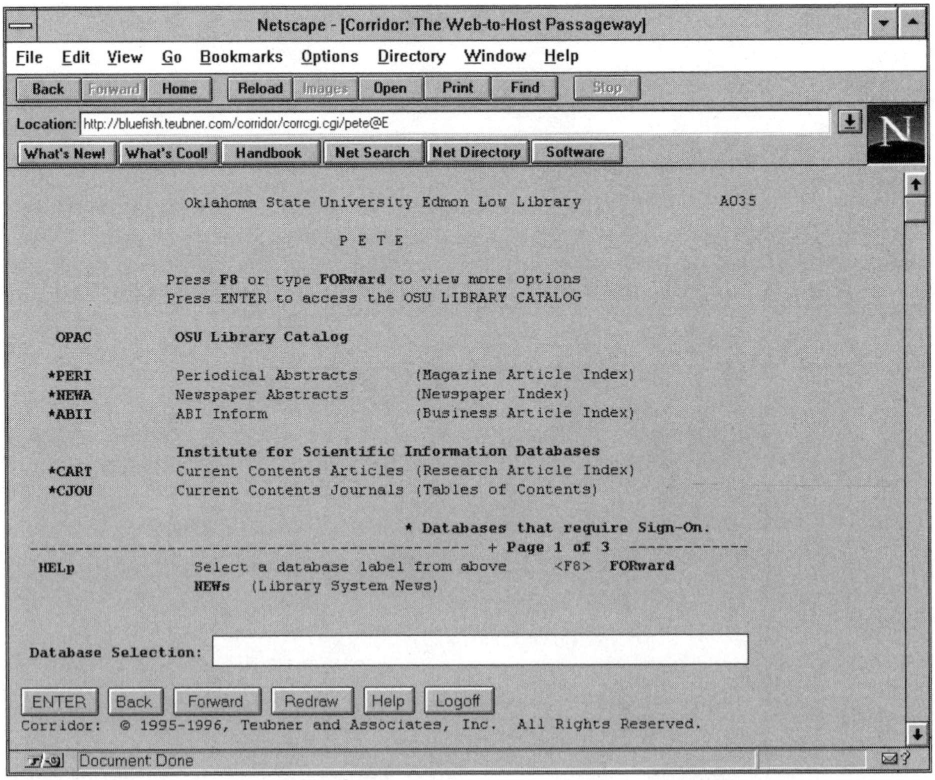

Figure 4.135 Stack search from anywhere with any web browser.

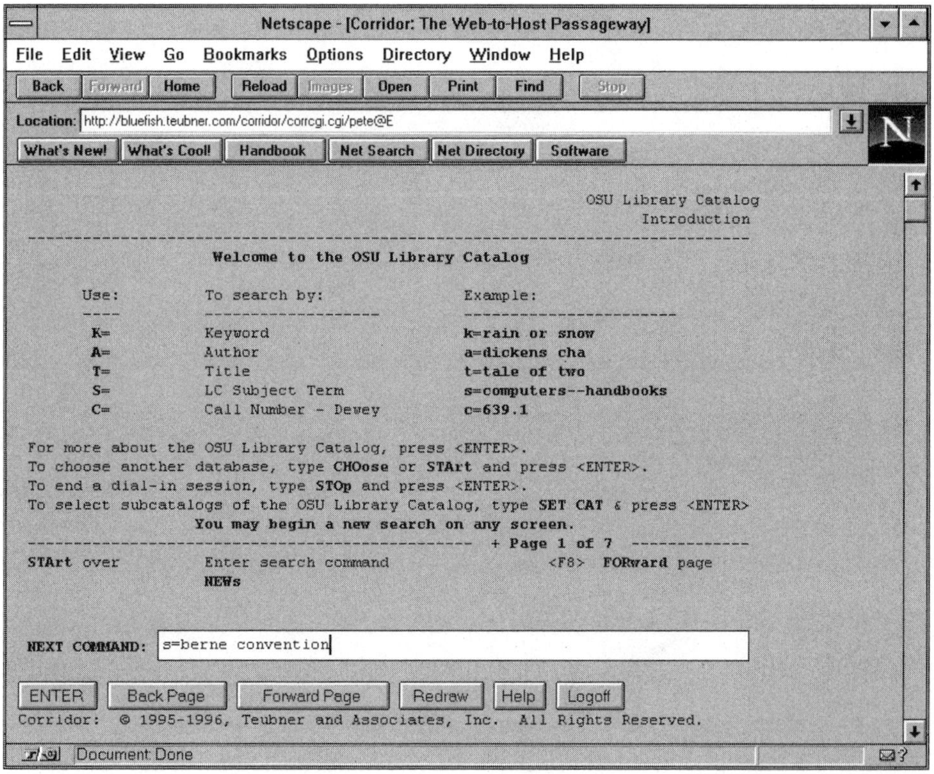

Figure 4.136 The full power of the original application is available through secondary web pages.

The web-database query returns the standard results in a format consistent with the original application. If each entry included a hypertext link, it is possible to see additional information about the resource that is not even included on the mainframe database. The report is shown in Figure 4.137. This information could include more details about the book, its location, sign-out information, and even a text-based copy of the material or perhaps images of each page of the book as more books are added to library image databases. New materials that are electronically based, such as computer disks, applications, CD-ROMs, and DVDs, might even be activated for the user.

Library applications do not have immediate value when building a cyberstore. However, IBM demonstrates the integration of a Communications Information Control System (CICS) financial application with a web interface in Figure 4.138. You do not need a company like Teubner and Associates for its toolkits; if you are a Big Blue shop and want to retain IBM tools, services, and account representatives without creating new relationships, you certainly can.

This looks the same as any standard host-based application, but it was accessible a thousand miles away without any unique hardware, communication

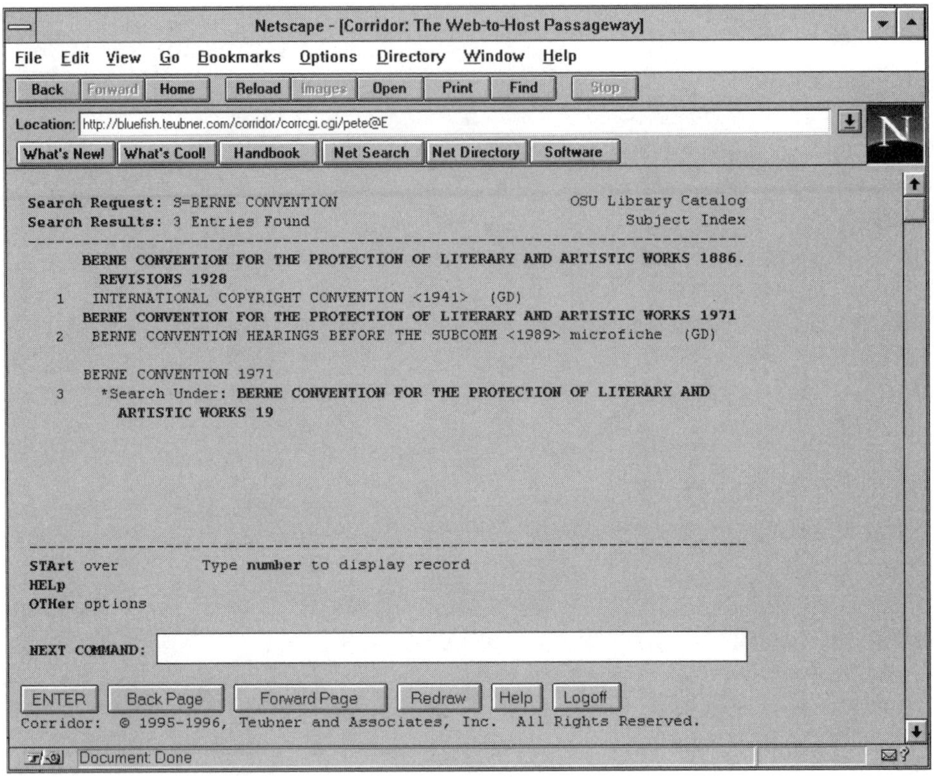

Figure 4.137 Response from the stack query.

hardware, or system administration. All that is necessary is an authentication ID and password. In fact, multiple CICS applications can be coordinated through a single home page URL, as shown in Figure 4.139.

With an HTML INPUT field in a web-based command shell, even system administration commands and operating system commands can be invoked, as illustrated in Figure 4.140. Obviously, this introduces a security risk, but one perhaps no more severe than a normal dial-up access method. CICS supports the standard authentication. While a dial-up line presupposes that a user knows the access number and has comparable equipment, reality is that the user is insecure with Caller ID and callback features.

Database integration, as previously defined in Chapter 2, includes static database publishing, interactive CGI, and binary gateway interface (BGI), which runs on the web server. Static database integration includes results generated by Web.Data, while more dynamic implementations include WebDBC, Perl, ActiveX, and the IS2WCGI interface delivered with the IIS server. Realize that each CGI application (that is, every query, report, and partial response) runs as a separate process thread under UNIX, Windows NT, and AIX. Although the overhead for each individual thread on clustered

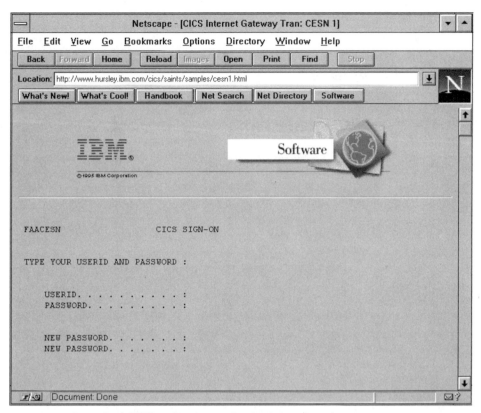

Figure 4.138 A standard CICS application can be piped over the web, too.

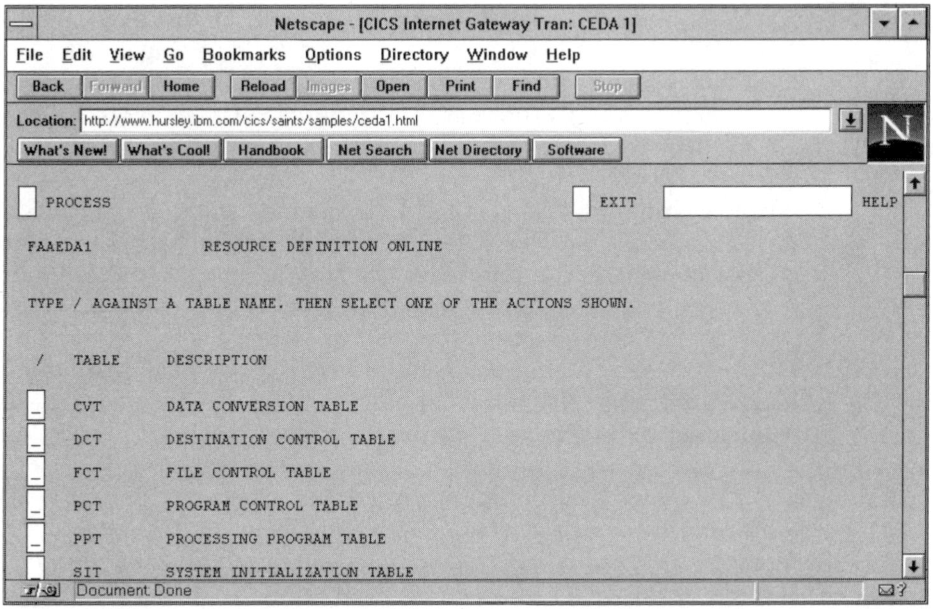

Figure 4.139 The standard function key-driven IBM menu is replaced with a standard, albeit bland, web page.

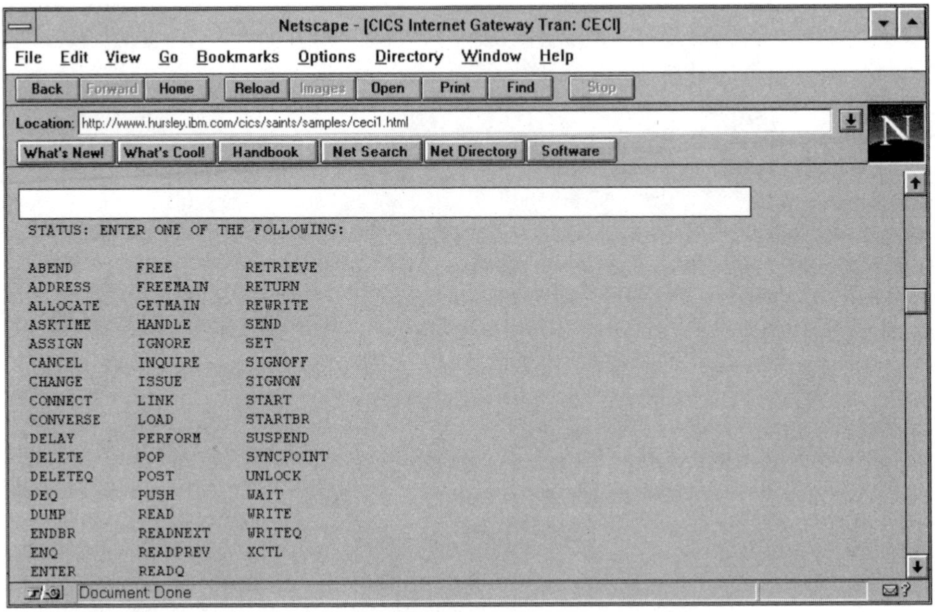

Figure 4.140 A web-based command shell for MVS.

and true multiprocessing web operating systems is minimal, the impact of many of these can easily overload the site. The problem is the overhead for managing and time sharing the threads. Instead, the active middleware tools, such as WebDBC, the BGI implementation of the ISAPI with SQL Server, HTTPODBC.DLL, and OLEISAPI.DLL provide a single instance of the service process, which is more efficient.

If you want to go the route of NT Server, IIS, and SQL Server, the integration of the database into dynamic HTML is actually very simple with the Internet Database Connector (IDC). Use the SQL Server Web Assistant, which is a wizard application, to create forms for the two-way connectivity between HTML forms and the database records and fields. Make certain that the IIS services are running under the system account, not the administrator or other log-ins. This guarantees a good level of integrity and security. Do not set the trusted connection option, as the security is not automatic. In addition, this also lets VB-based OLE services (with the OLEISAPI.DLL) provide unique functionality not possible with SQL or other middleware. VBScript is supposed to be thread scaleable to address the performance issues at busy sites and the interpreted speed limitations of VB code.

To solve some of the concern (read that as "scared," as opposed to valid proof of security holes), Microsoft has established a formal ActiveX registration process for application controls. Private developers pay fees of $20 annually, while larger organizations pay $400 annually to use the VeriSign signature inside a distributed component. For more information on this digital ID technology, refer to *http://www.digitalid.verisign.com*. This link is also included in the book web site. The VeriSign digital certificate does not qualify or guarantee the usability, security, or effectiveness of a control; it only guarantees that the control is from who it says it is, and that the organization or individual has a signature. In a sense, this process says the signature on the check is real, but it cannot tell you if the bank account is real or if there are funds in the account. This subtle difference and lack of full qualification does, however, go a long way toward improving trust in the dynamic website and tool market.

Database performance

For small cyberstores, MS SQL is a good choice for the database because it supports multiple clients better than MS Access, is ODBC-compliant, and provides a string development environment with hooks for BackOffice, Visual Basic, WebDBC, or Cold Fusion. However, one performance problem you should check for is the long running transaction, which is demonstrated with MS SQL. It is going to be a very common problem with web-based transactions at the cyberstore. For example, a user will decide to place an order and start the process, and then will get interrupted, and decide to do it later. On the other hand, a user may just decide to abort an order. The user's system might have crashed or the transport line or an ISP may fail. Also, the autocommit or BeginTrans and EndTrans pairs may not terminate this failed transaction.

Although HTTP and the web server are stateless and will drop the connection and throw away the HTML pages and its field data, the database server will not. It received notification of a pending transaction, started it, and will still be there waiting for it. The log file will still be open and will be getting bigger. By the way, if these log files are not periodically cleaned up, the server will crash for lack of disk space. Also, you will have an active thread that is being managed by the server, which is an unnecessary load. The solution is to search in the process log file (syslogs table in SQL) for an unmatched Begin Transaction that is missing the End Transaction, Commit, or Rollback. If you find a "zombie" process, try to commit it. Although it is an aborted transaction, it may contain a useful sales lead for a phone call. If the transaction is lost, use the Kill command to halt the process and free the tangled resources.

Several design flaws can wreck database performance for DBMS-to-HTML transactions. Although these problems are by no means new to Internet processes or cyberstores, website designers are very likely to ignore a very fundamental technical issue and not use modeling tools to design flows and the actual database structure. (You might review my book *Visual Basic Developers Toolkit* [McGraw-Hill] for database design techniques or *Computer Performance Optimization* [McGraw-Hill] for tuning database server performance.) A cyberstore is not much different from any other application development process, but it integrates with a lot more components than most. Specifically, three flaws will create performance bottlenecks. First, complex look-ups due to extreme database normalization will slow the query, reporting, and data entry processes. Second, very sparse tables create index and look-up nightmares that slow all data operations and are best solved by improved table design and relationships between tables. Third, Java, JavaScript, ActiveX, and CGI (particularly Perl) run slower than COBOL, C, and other typical development languages. Although the difference is really very minor, the reality is that these scripts must call the operating system or daemon functions to fetch records and results from the cyberstore databases. This secondary interface between the scripts and the database engine creates significant performance delays and high CPU loads. As a result, a fast web server, database server, or clustered web environment can spend 50 percent of the CPU time stalled while waiting for instructions and data.

Web help

Another important type of web commerce is product-problem resolution, better known as the help desk. Since people are inclined to communicate on-line when resolving complex high-tech problems and incompatibilities, there seems to be a shift towards similar capabilities for ordinary consumer and wholesale products. In addition, banks and credit card bureaus are providing more on-line and automated telephone-based billing-inquiry arrangements, which is a small step (and perhaps similar process) to integrate with websites. Tracking and delivery tracking are already available on-line through UPS and Federal Express on the Internet, as shown in Figure 4.141.

More businesses are seeing web opportunities for service-oriented businesses. While UPS and FedEx are using the web as a uniform and less costly transmission channel, other vendors are using the web to provide information and services that are current. TuneUp (at $3.95 per month) provides many of the services that Norton Utilities does for Windows95 without the user burden of storing the application on a local hard drive. However, you have to have a working system and an Internet connection. In addition, the tweaks and virus searches are supposedly always current. The implementation includes a client-side Windows95 application that runs in conjunction with the server-side knowledge bases and reporting tools, as shown by Figure 4.142.

Although I question how many users would be willing to allow an outside firm full access into their desktop systems and configurations, the potential for other types of interactive and dynamic help services is staggering. Consider that support costs for many high-tech products exceed manufacturing costs, and that support becomes either a very costly overhead or a cost center. In fact, a number of traditional help desk services and software vendors are seeking to define a common information base format to expand the market for these products. The most typical help desk product for the Internet is a translation of the data-

Figure 4.141   Internet package tracking with multiplatform software.

Figure 4.142   TuneUp is an interesting help service that includes server and client-side components to optimize disks and Windows95 setups, and check for viruses.

base-driven help desk to an Internet front end. Services such as ESP Li@ison, shown in Figure 4.143, are available only to registered corporate users.

The primary benefit of these services is similar to the concept that drove Microsoft to create on-line help desks, fee-based services, and the Developer's CD. The wait times and costs for solving trivial questions were too high. In

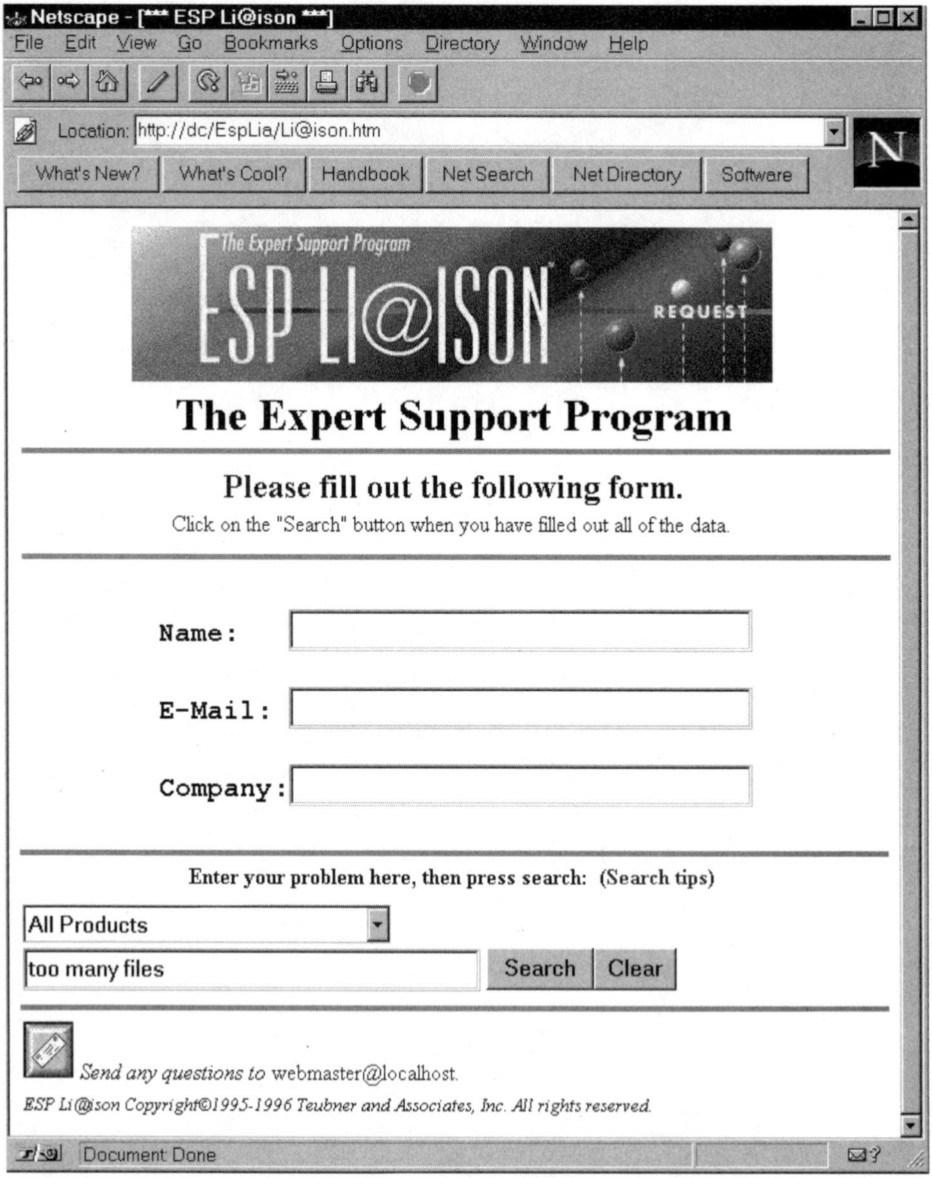

Figure 4.143 The ESP Li@ison help desk service is available through the Internet.

fact, many questions could be answered faster and better with on-line help, or at least, the on-line help could represent a first pass for the typical user to by-pass wait times and perhaps resolve the problem without personal technical support. The following screen shot (Figure 4.144) shows ESP responding to a typical software problem.

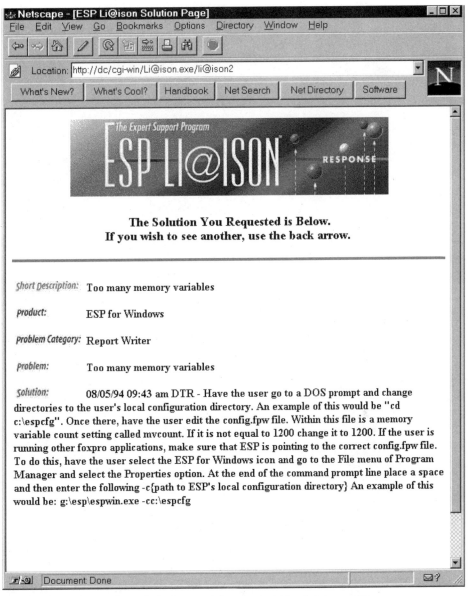

Figure 4.144 ESP provides technical support for a typical (simple) user problem.

Help desk databases, currency, and the rapid access that the Internet provides are a superior combination for on-line technical support. You see this exhibited in Figure 4.145, where ESP presents a weighting for proximity solutions. Not even a knowledgeable support person can find all the likely solutions without the help of similar tools. Since many computer problems result from configuration, platform, or integration, or from making connections be-

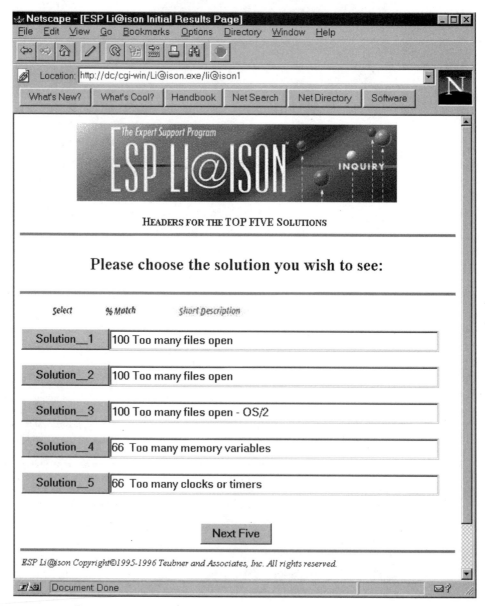

Figure 4.145 Proximity solutions narrow the range of possibilities.

tween unlikely facts, the integrated help desk database represents a powerful support tool for your organization.

The question is, "How do you add these tools to your site?" A number of products are available that link into standard HTML pages. You can differentiate the products into three categories. First are the external search engines and databases. Second are the corporate search engines and the organization that builds its own database. Third, are the companies providing the databases of industry or product-specific help. Unless you need the industry databases, you might consider integrating an Internet-enabled help desk tool into your site or building your own database and query engine. In this case, ESP is annual or per incident service, and if its database is pertinent to your needs, you can add HTML code to link to the ESP site. More likely, though, you will create databases with problems and solutions particular to your products and services, and then add the HTML code to activate the ESP search engine, which then searches the local archives.

If you do not need the specific functionality of the help desk tools or the pre-built support databases, consider building your own help desk facility. Although I suggest that you buy most solutions that can integrate easily into your website rather than build them, construction of a help desk is a basic task if you really only need to create a support database and populate it with data. You would still need to populate the blank help desk database with data; this query/report function is the easiest of the dynamic database/web integration projects in this book.

Since this book is about building transaction processing with DBMSs, database query through an HMTL form interface and on-the-fly generation of reports is quite relevant. It is also simple to implement with the tools profiled here. Whereas cyberstore transaction processing requires the creation of complex master/detail records (or a simplified flat-file E-mail representation of an order), help desk support is simply a process of defining a query, searching the database, and building a report. Some CGI code, WebAccess, IIS and SQL Server, or any of the more complex database middleware tools, are suitable. Cold Fusion, DBWeb, and Q5L are good examples. JetForm is the simplest tool for building a help desk because it builds forms; links into Access, SQL Server, or ODBC-compliant databases; and generates reports.

Graphical integration

Although it is early yet in the cycle of web-based graphical information system (GIS) products and servers, a number of websites and GIS vendors are developing them. For example, you can look up an address or phone number for a person, cross-reference either of them, and then construct a location map for a residence, organization, or business through the University of Buffalo AdServ and linkage to the MapQuest service. The state of Maine is using GIF images based on database information and also standard bitmapped formats to provide tourism, voting, services, and weather information, as shown in Figure 4.146.

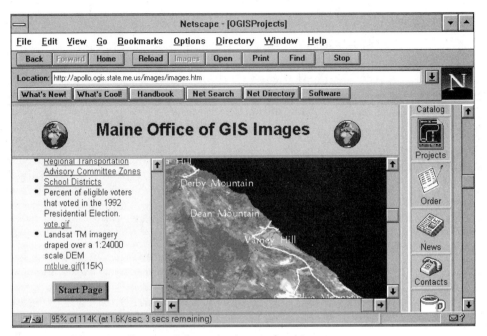

Figure 4.146 Maine provides state information in map formats.

It is important to differentiate a simple included GIF or JPG image from one generated from information sources on the fly. The MapQuest site is a good example of an interactive display of person, telephone, or address linked into a street map database.

Electronic Commerce

Electronic commerce means the ability to present information on the web and to effect transactions electronically. Any website is by virtue of its ability to present information part of an electronic commerce site. At a very minimal level, any website with an E-mail hook could qualify as an "electronic commerce" site. However, I think that is pushing the definition. Throughout this book, electronic commerce has included the ability to fill an electronic shopping cart with desired products and services, submit that order electronically, merge that order into a relational database, and then accept electronic payment for that order. SBT defines the process with a flowchart in Figure 4.147.

My business has provided electronic commerce for more than five years through CompuServe, a BBS system, and the Internet. It hasn't been truly interactive on the Internet until about two years ago with our first construction of a website. Orders were placed even then by CompuServe SWREG registration, credit cards, E-mail, fax orders, and faxed purchased orders. Internet and web enablement is proceeding as order volume dictates and the availability of

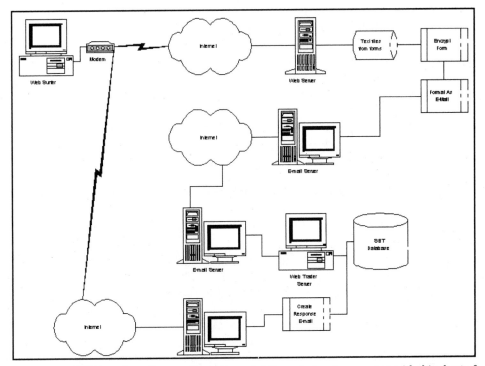

Figure 4.147 SBT (a maker of accounting software) defines electronic commerce with this chart of flows and processes. (Courtesy of SBT)

cost-effective and time-effective tools dictate. The Internet has attracted electronic commerce for several reasons:

1. It is based on standards derived from negotiation with various participants.
2. The infrastructure is reliable, interoperable, and robust.
3. Distributed directory services (search engines) locate addresses for people and organizations almost anywhere in the world.
4. There is an explosion of access points to the Internet.
5. The standards and references level the playing field so that competitors and participants will work together.
6. There is a large vendor base for EDI and Internet-enabled electronic commerce.

The types of electronic commerce available to the cyberstore designer include the following:

- Credit and checks
- Electronic data interchange (EDI)

- Electronic cash
- Automated clearinghouse
- Credit cards
- Debit cards
- Wire transfers
- Organization credit
- Cash account balances
- Arranging debits to creating accounts

These electronic commerce options are detailed in each of the subsequent subsections.

Credit and checks

While employees at many businesses may make small purchases with personal or corporate credit cards, the bulk of business-to-business commerce is done on trust and credit. Even if you build the cyberstore for industrial products, as AMP site shown in Chapter 5 has done, you will need EDI interfaces or credit verification services. Dun & Bradstreet, Equifax, TRW, and other service bureaus track the credit worthiness of publicly and privately held organizations. As the technology has advanced, these companies have installed AVR and computerized systems for clients to verify new or existing customers. These services are expensive, but less costly than collection efforts. It is an integration task to pass information to the credit validation request and interpret the response so that a transaction can proceed. You will need middleware, most likely designed and implemented specifically for your financial systems. Credit checks run from $30 to $150 per automated check, and more complex reports (which are hard to use for computerized decision making at point-of-sales) run up to several thousand dollars. However, these reports can be useful when establishing relationships for wholesale and bulk sales activities.

A less expensive option is a CD-ROM library of credit information, updated monthly. Integration is no less extreme; however several subscriptions are available at less than $2000 per year. American Business Information has the Credit Reference Directory, which will run under WindowsNT and can be automated with in-process OLE to interface with most any Visual Basic application. This directory can be used with any NT application server or database, and particularly with the IIS and SQL Server web database tools. CompuServe and American Business Information provide BBS reports for $3 per basic report. The problem is to get the information and parse it automatically for a go/no go cyberstore process.

Electronic Data Interchange (EDI)

My take on Electronic Data Interchange, or EDI, is that it is a computer process designed by accountants, implemented by accountants, and for the most part used by accountants. It is simple, messy, but reliable. EDI is basically a financial E-mail message transmission process where the message is a relational hierarchy typified by an order transaction sent as a structured form in a flat-file format. The delivery system is built from private networks or private value-added networks (VANs), which are similar to ISP businesses but serve the EDI community.

However, the downside to EDI is that every originator has unique rules for its syntax, and, therefore, your implementations need to handle origination errors. The Internet is pressing the VANs setup for secure EDI transmissions; they are more expensive than Internet E-mail, even with its necessary added security. Therefore, EDI will migrate to the Internet, and Internet payment schemes will include EDI for business-to-business payments, presale ordering, and other transactional transmissions. Vendors are beginning to create any-to-any mapping solutions, which are like the proposed universal in and out boxes for electronic communications, to interconnect EDI with EPS systems.

The push for electronic commerce is driven by the realization that the Internet is a great marketing opportunity lacking a secure transaction mechanism. Electronic Data Interchange is the technology for paperless trading. It is a communications function that spans industries, including the automotive, financial, government, mass market retail, sporting goods, health care, and hotel industries. The workflow advantages for EDI include its innate ability to span time zones, language differences, and staff levels. This is very relevant for multinational companies or those involved in international trade. The benefits of EDI include immediate acknowledgment of transactions so that fewer events are lost in the mail, a reduction in manual effort for transactions and shipping activities, reduced order entry costs, and fewer errors and changes in orders. You can sum up the benefits of EDI as timely workflow, speed, accuracy, and security. Thus, EDI benefits include:

- Reduced mail and paper costs

- Increased data timeliness

- Streamlined communications

- Improved productivity

- Improved information access and availability

- Increased productivity

- Reduced lead times for inventory management

- Reduced clerical workload

EDI is commonly defined as the application-to-application transfer of business documents between computers. Many businesses choose EDI as a fast, inexpensive, and safe method of sending purchase orders, invoices, shipping notices, and other frequently used business documents. Since the transfer of information from computer to computer is automatic, there is no need to rekey information, and the error rate drops to near zero. RJR Nabisco estimates that processing a paper purchase order costs its company $70. As I mentioned in several places in this book, most surveys peg purchase order costs at $150 per single order. Processing an EDI purchase order reduces the cost to a mere 93 cents at K-Mart.

EDI is also a method of improving customer service by filling orders faster. K-Mart and other retailers have implemented a program called Vendor Stock Replenishment (VSR). VSR requires that vendors to the retailers maintain appropriate inventory levels in all stores. With VSR, K-Mart pushes some of the inventory management responsibility onto these vendors, who replenish stock as the inventory system tells them it is necessary. Billing is also done automatically, via EDI. This process pares times from the order fulfillment cycle, and ensures that the product is always on the shelf. Because EDI documents are stored in a database (referred to as a "mailbox"), you have a serialized history of documents. Copies of invoices or purchase orders are shared between partners, so that photocopying and faxing are minimized.

I look at the strategic business reasons for using EDI from two angles. First, there is the efficiency angle. Second, business partners using EDI are like

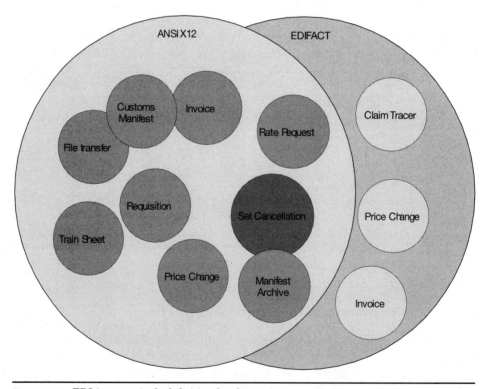

Figure 4.148 EDI is not a single definition for electronic transactions; every market segment has defined its own standards for communicating information between trading partners.

10-ton elephants; they sit anywhere they want. Many large manufacturers and retailers suggest that suppliers institute an EDI program or else!

The format of paperless trading varies by industry, and each industry adheres to a different hierarchy of protocols. Documents exchanged through EDI include invoices, purchase orders, payment orders, acknowledgments, shipping notices, shipping schedules, shipping information, planning schedules, reservations, requests for proposal, and shipment billing. EDI is not one single standard. In fact, there are many industry-specific EDI standards (no single uniform standard exists yet), and common protocols include ANSI X12 and EDIFACT. In some cases, trading partners have created their formats as a means to thwart security threats, or as simple resistance to other interest groups. In general, for an industry, document types are formalized by a standard code. For example, a lockbox is 823, whereas invoices are 810 for retail trading transactions. Sets are numbered from 104 to 998, and there are about 200 different definitions. The EDI standards can be envisioned as shown in Figure 4.148.

There are similarities between EDI standard codes. Invoices look like shipping manifests, and orders look like invoices. What is pertinent to this book is that the EDI transaction standard is a flat database definition. EDI is not a complex process; it just seems that way because it was first implemented in businesses with little experience in office automation. Before designing a VB application, it is worthwhile to review the list of EDI transaction types, find which might pertain to your organization, and get the exact file definitions. Not only does EDI provide industry-specific knowledge about the field types needed for transactions, it also shows very concise file formats. For example, here is part of an 810 retail trading transaction:

```
Pos Seg    Name                  · Req  Max  Loop
010 ST     Transaction Set Header   M    1
·020 BIG   Beginning Segment for Invoice    M    1
030 NTE    Note/Special Instruction    F   100
290 PER    Administrative Communications Contact    O   3   21
  LOOP ID-LM       Loop Repeat-10    21
300 LM     Code Source Information    O    1   21
310 LQ     Industry Code    M   100   21
010 TDS    Total Monetary Value Summary    M    1
020 TXI    Tax Information    O    10
030 CAD    Carrier Detail    O    1
  LOOP ID-SAC      Loop Repeat-25    1
300 LM     Code Source Information    O    1   21
310 LQ     Industry Code    M   100   21
010 TDS    Total Monetary Value Summary    M    1
020 TXI    Tax Information    O    10
030 CAD    Carrier Detail    O    1
  LOOP ID-SAC      Loop Repeat-25    1
040 SAC    Service, Promotion, Allowance, or Charge Info.    O   1   1
050 TXI    Tax Information    O   10   1
060 ISS    Invoice Shipment Summary    O    5
070 CTT    Transaction Totals    M    1
080 SE     Transaction Set Trailer    M    1
```

If you notice the loop code, it is the accountants' method of handling multiple line items within each order. This is a flat-file representation of a relational database. Despite this verbosity, EDI works because so many players have forced it to work. This partial definition (the full definition is much longer) shows the master record, non-null (that is, required) items, and the detail definitions. It isn't easy to read because the master/detail relationship is broken out into a flat list with detail line items that repeat. However, this layout is sufficient to extract field names and definitions. While MS Access and most SQL databases support an unlimited number of detail records for each master (that is, one-to-many), EDI sets a limit on the number of detail line items that can be submitted in a single transaction. The solution is to send subsequent transactions to complete the actual event.

Most organizations have not built their own transaction software or even translation software, because they have assumed it is complicated and difficult to implement. You can see that this process is merely tedious, because you have to map your database fields to EDI transaction fields, and deal with information that may be immaterial to existing operations. For example, the industry code may be irrelevant to an order, and unless a tax district assesses retailers a VAT tax, tax information may be unnecessary, too.

Because EDI data exists as a hierarchical (that is, strictly formatted) message in a mailbox, that message can be translated into various formats. The EDI message can be converted into a standard master/detail record, or it can be formatted for fax transmission. If you need other formats, you can decide the value of parsing the text directly into other needed formats, or of going through an intermediate master/detail database.

EDI has lacked the critical mass to be a mainstream application outside of industries that are hard-pressed to lower costs, automate, reduce headcount, and increase efficiencies. The lack of mass appeal is due to the fact that an EDI implementation is the grist for a 3- to 6-month outside consulting project. This means that only the largest business and governmental agencies have implemented EDI. However, that is about to change with the World Wide Web, simply because there are many new opportunities for trading that are now possible with the Internet, and because there is currently no widely available secure and cost-effective method to support these transactions. At the present time, credit cards are too expensive, costing $0.25 plus 2.5 to 7.5 percent per transaction. Bank wire transfers are also, too expensive, at $10 to $25 per transaction. Such high costs preclude software utility and data sales. However, EDI represents a serious contender as the medium for Internet transactions because it can cost a mere $0.93 per transaction. The other possibility is a global electronic currency like CyberCash, or some other form of electronic money.

You no doubt know that a breach in security is the major threat to Internet trading, just as it is for EDI. These threats include:

- Loss of data by the processing network or system

- Loss of data integrity

- Access (unprivileged) to data by a third party
- Modification of data by a third party
- Repudiation of receipt of data by recipient
- Masquerade of a third party as the sender or recipient of data
- Masquerade of a third party as the sender of data to send inaccurate information

Presently, the Internet Engineering Task Force (IETF) has proposed an extension for encapsulation of EDI documents inside a Multipurpose Internet Mail Extension (MIME) electronic message, the standard mail message on the Internet. Two options for this extension include the MIME Object Security Service (MOSS), also known as privacy-enhanced mail, while the other is based on an encryption tool called Pretty Good Privacy. Both proposals offer encryption, authentication, and privacy features. By the time you read this, both will be available as toolkits and complete EDI packages.

Tremendous resources related to EDI services for PC platforms, and EDI electronic data formats, rules, regulations, and tool providers are available over the Internet. A good first step is the American Bar Association archives, which are shown by Figure 4.149.

E-cash

Electronic cash (E-cash) is one form of electronic payment system based on a script exchange of money, a promissory note (like a check but often paid in ad-

Figure 4.149 This electronic data interchange website is a bigger commodity than actual EDI services. Nevertheless, the American Bar Association site provides reference materials and links to other EDI sites.

vance), cash cards (like phone cards), or smart cards. Realize that E-cash is not necessarily a better transaction medium than cash, checks, or credit cards. For example, not all the E-cash products provide transactions, secure payment, and shopping cart support for the cyberstore. In addition, these products may require special vendor and user software, complex brokerage or transaction procedures, and a lack of audit, confirmation, settlement, and proof against loss guarantees. Some of the primary vendors include:

- CheckFree
- CyberCash
- DigiCash
- FirstVirtual
- GlobalD
- Mondex
- Outreach
- NetCash
- Netchex
- Millicent Micropayments
- OpenMarket

Some people will want to use E-cash because it is anonymous. In fact, some Internet users will not make purchases if the purchase, their name, and other information is traced. It is enough that marketers send brochures, call at 7 a.m. to see if you are interested in lower phone rates to Canada, and cross-tabulate data with other sources to target you as the likely sucker for a new product, scheme, or sales pitch. E-cash represents the ultimate common and widely accepted transaction mechanism to date because there is a limited means of tracing its transfer.

On the other hand, the process for the return of product or services paid by E-cash has yet to be resolved. This makes E-cash a useful medium for intellectual property sales; since the transaction cost for E-cash transfer is a penny or less per trade, this medium is useful for selling news, reports, shareware, and commercial software. Technical support issues may require some sort of registration in spite of the sales anonymity. Vendors will want to know that they are supporting valid users or that competitors are not buying and reverse-engineering applications. The reality is that the Internet and commercial laws are migrating to support the open society where trade secrets are not legally or economically viable for many products. Besides, copyright and patent infringement and protections for intellectual property become easier to enforce, trace, and import.

However, that concern may be addressed by E-cash payments per event for technical support, too. You might note that technical support is an intellectual property as well and can be dispensed from pay-per-view databases or from live people supported by E-cash payment systems.

Credit cards

Credit card submission for payment is actually a very simple process and is easily made a part of data processing. I suggest that you purchase toolkits that have been authorized by banks and clearinghouses rather than building your own and getting the process certified. Your organization will also require authorization with a credit card clearinghouse to use their services. Fees generally start at $0.25 per transaction, with a discount rate from 1.5 to 7.5 percent per sale plus minimum fees on a monthly basis for merchants doing few transactions. The negotiating party is usually a commercial bank, often one used for checking, loan, and other financial services. The bank establishes an account for your organization through the clearinghouse, a middle-layer transaction processing provider. Large organizations, such as Wal-Mart, Federated Stores, and Hyper Marche, negotiate directly with VISA, MasterCard, and American Express and bypass the clearinghouse altogether.

The rule most commercial banks enforce for issuing a merchant credit card account is that the business include a retail site or retain substantial assets on reserve with the bank. This is the guarantee to protect against fraud and excessive charge backs. Some banks will issue accounts to businesses without a true retail presence or business site. These include mail-order businesses, catalog sales, and the cyberstore. The discount rate per transaction is likely to be higher than the low end of 1.5 percent because of the perceived higher risk. However, if the volume becomes substantial, renegotiate or take your business to another bank and clearinghouse.

The more complex issue is integrating the credit card processing into the financial systems and trapping the authorization to allow for continued website processing. PC-Charge, as shown in Figure 4.150 is Visual Basic application and also a VBX/OCX toolkit (hence ActiveX) that can be used to integrate the complete credit card flows into your cyberstore. These include charge cancellations, charge backs, and voids.

The next screen shot shows how the credit card processing information would get matched for inclusion into the financial tracking systems. The card number and ticket number become the index into your order numbers, as shown by Figure 4.151. Since PC-Charge is also a development toolkit, you can integrate Web operations into the PC-Charge for immediate authorizations and confirmations with ActiveX technology on WindowsNT Workstation and Windows NT Server. The VB development environment is shown in Figure 4.152.

CommerceRoom from WebMaster provides a more advanced toolkit in that it includes the switches and flags to integrate the credit card process directly as CGI or BGI threads. If your platform is AIX, HP-UP, or Solaris, or the website is running on a host so that credit card information is passed through

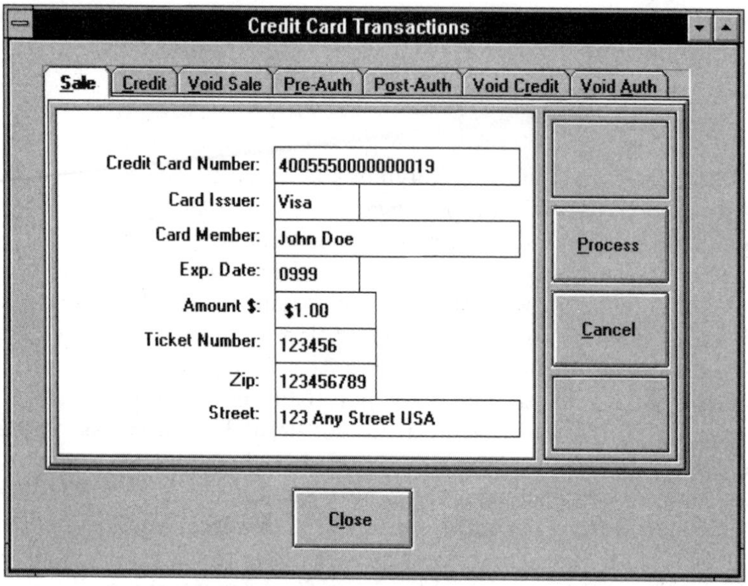

Figure 4.150   The PC-Charge Visual Basic application.

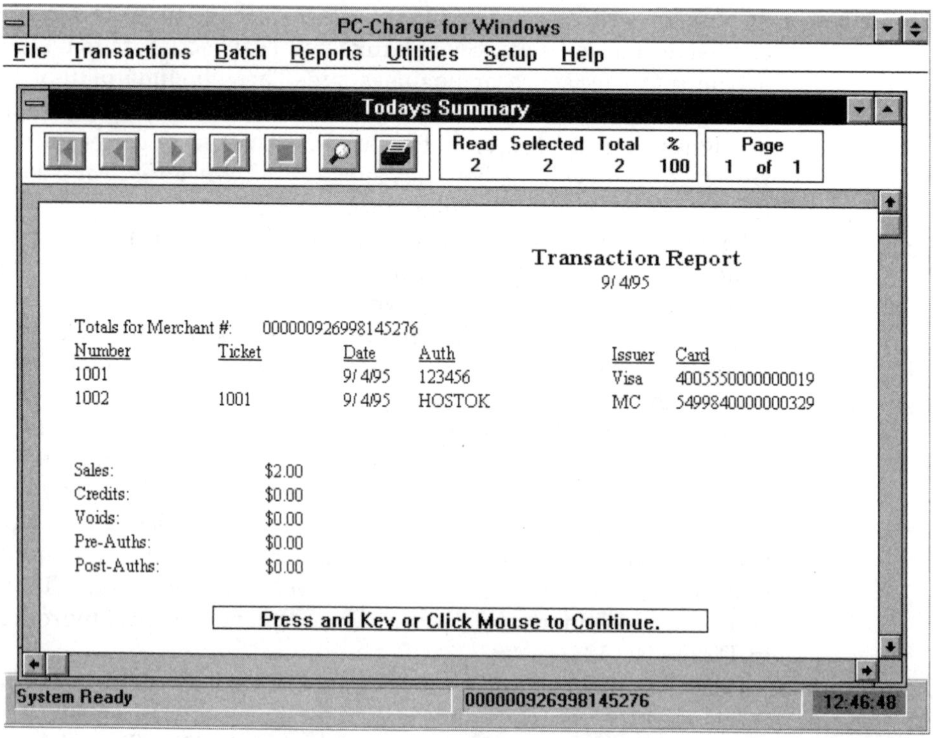

Figure 4.151   The credit card process creates unique card numbers, transaction numbers, and dates of service for indexing into transaction orders.

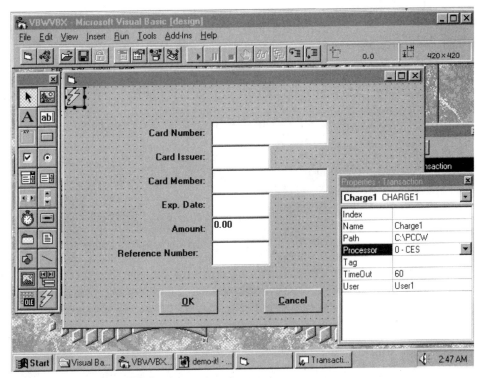

Figure 4.152   PC-Charge/VB development environment.

secured E-mail, then you will need to construct a daemon to grab the E-mail as it arrives, parse the information, create a credit transaction so that it can be submitted by modem, and then pass the authorization pack to the host server in about 14 seconds as a file that the host web process and CGI code can check as a process flag. Another option is to integrate the ICVerify API toolkits, which are available for most platforms, into the web process. This entails a significant amount of labor; however, organizations building cyberstores with links to mainframe hosts and clustered, RAID-based database servers are likely to have the programmers to implement the steps otherwise provided by CommerceRoom.

Merchant credit/debit services

Payment by "plastic" is a generic workflow integration process that includes payment by credit card (MasterCard, Diners Club, Discover Card, VISA, American Express, and private brand cards), debit cards, check authorization, check vouching, payment by wire, and bank-to-bank payments. This process is called a "Merchant Credit Card Service" and is offered by most commercial banks. Payment is typically arranged as bank-to-bank credits to a bank account. Costs for implementing credit card authorization include several thousand dollars for equipment and software, monthly fixed service fees, and a fixed cost plus percentage fee per transaction. As previously stated, transaction fees are usually $0.25, plus 2.5 to 8 percent of the transaction amount depending on the credit card clearinghouse and credit card used. Small businesses might not qualify for merchant credit card service through a bank, but often can arrange slightly more expensive services through clearinghouses, service agencies, and phone order center services. The structure of credit card authorization is shown in Figure 4.153.

Other services, such as check verification or check vouching, incur fees of $0.50 per transaction, but no percentage fees. They are an inexpensive means of minimizing bad checks. Banks typically provide phone services with a person or automated attendants (using digital touch-tone multifrequency DTMF codes), while the service bureaus want to sell the equipment. Because any PC with a modem (faster than 120 bps) is sufficient for on-line credit, debit, or check processing, you can integrate the process into VB at some level. The

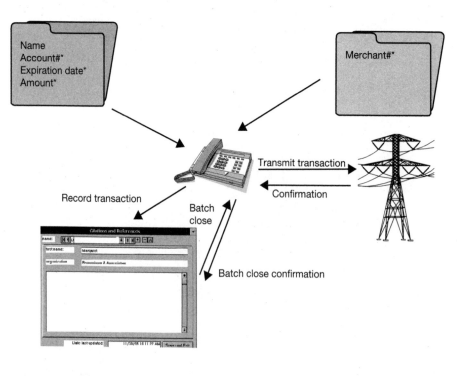

*required information

Figure 4.153 The full cycle of credit card processing.

caveat is that most software tools available are based on DOS, not Windows, or are built internally by or for each large organization that wants to automate these services. It can cost upwards of $25,000 just to test an application (stand-alone or client/server) for each card type for each service bureau. Because credit card and other electronic payments are regulated by individual states and by various federal agencies regulating interstate trade, commerce, and banking, legislation and rules change frequently. Designing a proprietary connection is a programmer's heaven—the job will exist forever. As such, if you can buy the drop-in components from vendors such as ICVerify Inc. or Credit Card Charge, and credit a single (or even multiple parallel) OLE server for authorizing credit, debit, or check transactions, the process and setup costs will be reasonable.

I happen to like this process because it simplifies the workflow for many transactions. For example, my company takes an order by phone for software, equipment, books, and shipping. I create an order (invoice) during the phone conversation. When the sale is to be paid by credit card, I get the name, credit card number, and card expiration date, and verify the credit before processing the order. With approval, I enter payment information and approval codes to a payment receipt that matches that invoice. I then attach a copy of the credit card authorization to both the buyer's order (no longer an invoice, but rather a shipping pick list, bill of lading, and receipt) and an internal copy. Even though each transaction costs 2.5 percent, this saves delivery of an invoice, follow up on past due or overdue invoices, the subsequent matchup of checks with outstanding invoices, and the creation of a deposit slip for the day's take of checks.

Benefits of a computerized merchant credit card service include reduced complexity of workflow, decreased need to revisit many invoices, and reduction in full-time accounting personnel, uncollectible invoices, and bounced checks. The actual process for submitting a credit card payment are as follows:

- Dial a modem to a credit card clearinghouse
- Submit a transaction
  Merchant account number
  Transaction type
  Card type
  Customer credit number
  Name
  Date and time
  Amount
  Tax
  Notes/memo
- Receive notification
  Rejection or
  Authorization number
- Print credit slip

This creates an in-process transaction, which has been submitted but remains open. At the close of each business day, all such open (or pending) transactions must be closed and submitted for execution. This process in no way jeopardizes your ability to collect, but is part of the workflow for the credit card clearinghouse. When you close all submitted transactions, funds (receipts less fees) are transferred to a designated bank account. The process for closing the batch is similar to that for executing a credit card transaction:

- Dial a modem to a credit card clearinghouse
- Submit a close batch transaction
  Merchant account number
  Date and time
  Amount
- Receive notification
  Rejection or
  Authorization number
- Print batch list
  Customers and amounts
  Daily batch
  All batches
  All rejections

ICVerify is very simple because it supports a text-based client/server polling process. A client creates the transaction, which is just a simple ASCII text file with a .REQ file extension (even in WindowsNT and Windows95) in the ICVerify batch directory. This file includes the credit card number, credit card expiration date, amount, terminal ID, processor ID, and merchant ID. The fields are delimited by commas and double quotations. Under DOS, the ICVerify application must be running. The ICVerify batch server (the serving agent) polls for changes to the directory contents every 3 seconds (average wait time is thus 1.5 seconds), and submits these transactions. Authorization or rejection requires 4 seconds if the modem is active and the software connection is open, or 8 seconds if the ICVerify must initiate a phone call. Some retail stores connect into the service with a digital line, and approval takes under 2 seconds. The transaction answer is provided as a simple ACSII text file with an .ANS extension. The client polls the batch directory for the file corresponding to the matching request file. For example, 00005703.REQ would beget 00005703.ANS.

The eight-second processing delay is a significant workflow issue. This delay can be compounded to become an intolerable delay if the credit card submission sequence is not slipped intelligently into the workflow. For example, the order entry process can be fine-tuned so that credit card approval is asynchronous. Second, billing and shipping information can be entered in the interim for a service bureau response.

Credit card transactions can be converted to EDI for increased workflow integration. Although ICVerify does provide its own database and database reporting tools, you can reverse the process and, at the close of the day, read all .REQ and .ANS files in about the same way as demonstrated above, then use the data to create and populate database records. The complexity is not in the process or code, but in how you integrate the functionality into organizational workflow.

A single ICVerify service agent can process at least 10,000 transactions per hour. Consider how many transactions each point-of-sales station, electronic cash register, or kiosk in a building can process. Factor that number by the number of point-of sales stations, electronic cash registers, or kiosks in the entire organization. Despite the large number of transactions, a bottleneck is not likely. The request and answer ASCII files are 200 bytes or less. Communication speed, even with 300-bps or 2400-bps lines, is not an issue either. The most substantial delay is the dial-up time, which can be solved with leased lines or by maintaining an active connection to the credit service bureau. Credit card service bureaus rarely have service bottlenecks because all lines into the host are limited to 2400 bps, and even with thousands of phone lines, the aggregate load is not very large.

In general, the cost of each paper-based transaction is about $5, and uncollectible losses are pegged at 5 to 15 percent, depending on the business type and the collection efforts. A credit card transaction costs about the same, but

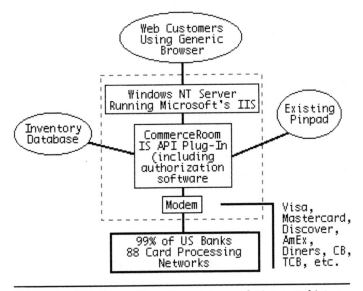

Figure 4.154 Existing credit card processing can be integrated into a web server with new software, modem, and web forms.

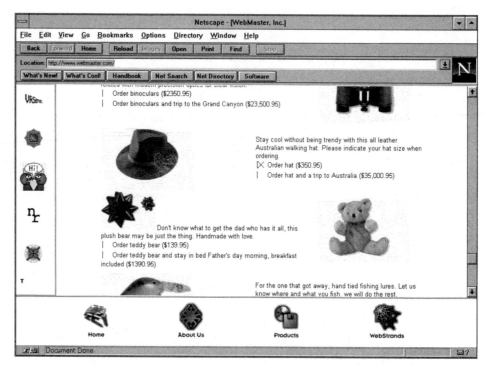

Figure 4.155 HTML forms and product graphics for cybersales integrated with shopping cost.

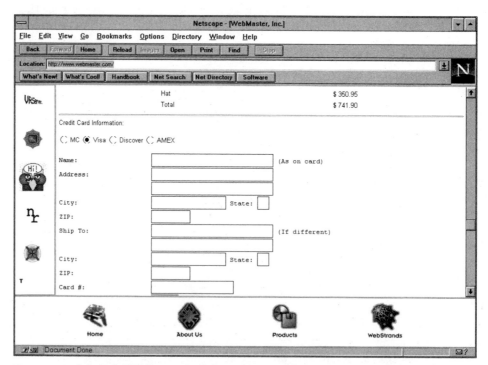

Figure 4.156 Cybersale HTML must include credit card information for automation of authorization. (Notice the broken key on lower left of frame that indicates a non-secure transaction.)

when the process is integrated into the workflow, you reduce the cost of registering that transaction to about $0.50. When credit card transactions are included into electronic data interchange, the cost of the entire transaction process can be as low as $1.20 plus the percentage credit card fees, as verified by large retailers. Data interchange and credit card transactions can be integrated into WWW page ordering, too. Security issues with WWW and credit card information transmitted by E-mail are discussed later.

It is important to build robust workflow so that the system will automatically handle or flag transactions lost in process, terminate connections broken in process, and transactions declined for payment by a credit card clearinghouse, as shown in Figure 4.157.

Secure internet transactions

The leader in electronic security is Ron Rivest of RSA who devised the RSA 40, RSA 80, and the current RSA 129 standards. The numbers refer to the number of digits in the public key encryption system. The larger the number of digits, the more difficult it is to crack the code. However, simultaneous attack over networked machines (the Internet is a suitable network) can break almost any

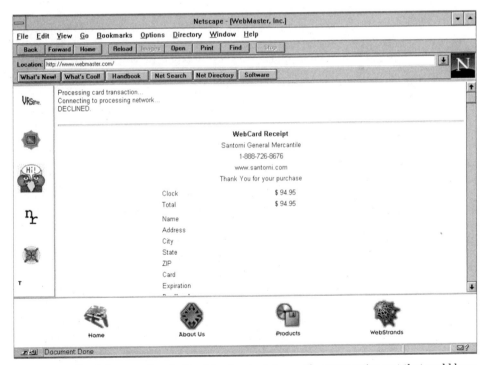

Figure 4.157 Partial transaction declined by clearinghouse with a transaction cost that could have been avoided by testing for blank or incomplete form entry.

code in time. However, the word "time" might mean months or years. SET is based on digital signature technology defined by X.509 certificates and RSA Data Security Inc. encryption technology. When security is important, you need to enforce it or at least assume responsibility for it at both ends of the Internet connection, as well as at the transport through the various linkages.

Although users are typically responsible for their password's secrecy and maintaining it as a secure key, a couple of things can compromise this. First, the Netscape commerce server caches data to improve performance, which can and should be disabled in the http header to read:

```
pragma:no-cache
```

Since this information is also likely to be cached on the user's hard drive as part of the user's cache, the user should use the pulldown "Clear Disk Cache Now" command to flush user IDs, passwords, and other information before it was encrypted by the secure browser process. Realize that the user types this information into the browser and the tool then secures it. However, the cache can become a temporary file on the hard drive that does not go away ever. It might even need to be specifically deleted and overwritten.

Electronic commerce foundations

Ari Services and Dun & Bradstreet have announced a standard ID number for electronic commerce that may carry some weight because of their reputation in the financial and credit services tracking community. The ID includes an organization designation built from the D&B DUNS designation and suffix designating who placed the order and where exactly within the organization it was placed. The classification is called an EC-ID, or electronic commerce identification.

Financial Accounting Integration

There is not much I can show about integrating web transactions with existing databases. Web-enabled POS systems do not exist yet, and no vendor (as of the time of writing) has a complete cyberstore solution. Great Plains Software promises transactional and reporting integration with its Marco Polo software, when released. A screen shot in Figure 4.158 shows table construction using the Microsoft FrontPage Editor.

However, the hard reality is that you will need developers to code web transactions into the preexisting accounting system. Most small business accounting systems, including Peachtree, Solomon, SBT, and Quickbooks include toolkits. Midsize products, such as Platinum, have a large after market of products from the vendor and from third parties, and even an interface for the Magic code generator.

The SQL or proprietary accounting packages are typically more complex. SQL and database tools are probably sufficient to hack into these systems and

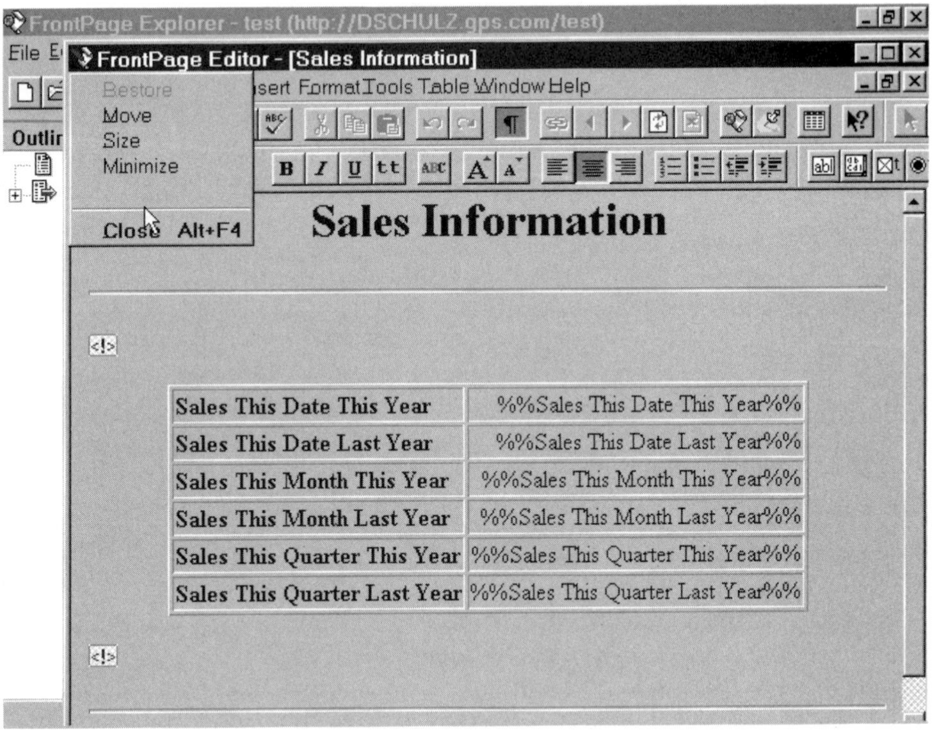

Figure 4.158   Construction of GPS report using FrontPage Editor.

extend them as needed, but the limitation really is one of understanding the interrelationship between database and tables, how the scripts process transactions, and how to preserve the database integrity. You do not want to break an existing mission-critical operation when you add a web point-of-sale system to it. Third party tools are available that simplify module creation, that reverse-engineer these systems and map their structures, and that have tools that document the data structures. InfoModeler and S-Designor are good examples.

However, integration is easiest when you have a developer's toolkit, as described in Chapter 2, and when you have dedicated or contract help to link HTML fields into database fields with ODBC middleware, CGI code, and any number of Java scripting tools. A number of SQL, Access, Sybase, or Oracle products are available as runtimes with source code that can simplify this migration and enablement.

Electronic Software Distribution

Electronic software distribution (ESD) has primarily focused on LAN management and on distributing new applications and updates of client software over local networks and organizational enterprise networks. In effect, ESD is the network opposite to uninstaller software. However, the Internet has created a unified channel for electronic delivery of information, demos, reports, software, and other products or services deliverable as bytes. ESD automates the distribution process with lists, encryption, and imbedded payment schemes. Solutions for the LAN include WinInstall, FUDN, LANDesk, NetWizard, and Norton Administrator. To date, there are no standards for ESD, although the Desktop Management Task Force (DMTF) is intent on creating a standard for a desktop management interface (DMI). The DMI includes a management information file (MIF) that is best represented by the Windows95 registration database. However, these specifications and implementations do not yet address secured information delivery over the public Internet beyond the LAN.

Specifically, delivery of information over the Internet requires that the "information" is paid for, is delivered intact and guaranteed, and is not susceptible to carrier hijacking or copying (so that it can be used by another party). This includes data, reports, updates, new software applications, and updates to existing and previously installed software applications. Since it costs at least $1 to master a 3.5-inch diskette and about $2 to master and packet a CD-ROM, plus an additional $5 to ensure delivery of each unit, Internet software delivery becomes feasible whenever ESD costs less than $6 or $7 per unit. In fact, EPS typically costs $0.40 per unit, including overhead.

Techniques for the actual ESD include CompServe Shareware Registration (SWREG), ZIP, Web Transporter, A/Pay, ZipLock and Cryptolope. Note that SWREG doesn't have to be just shareware, it can be documents, data, tools and techniques, or services. However, the cost at 15 percent per transaction is higher than credit cards unless the per unit cost is low. The most common delivery process creates a packed file (saves download time) with a password. The simplest approach is illustrated in Figure 4.159.

The following illustration in Figure 4.160 shows PKZIP with the WinZip shell setting the password option for a compressed collection of files. Note that if you use any version of Windows, you programmatically apply OLE, a recorder macro, and/or DDE to create a random password, pack the files using WinZip, set the password, and send the file as an E-mail attachment or as an FTP download. The automated process can create (another) E-mail message, a voice message, or fax with that random password. This secondary message can then be spooled for later (thus, marginally safer) delivery from a queue. If you are concerned about security, the password should be delivered by a different method than the file.

Realize that the encryption method used with PKZIP is easily defeated by various cracking programs that are readily available from Internet shareware sites. I did not realize this to be the case and have in fact bought keys to "zipped" software over CompuServe and the Internet. (I will still continue to "buy" the key because it is the right thing to do.) Even when you assign a unique key for each zipped file set, it is simple to break the encryption.

More secure ESD systems negotiate a secure connection and establish a private key and public key exchange. The information is packed and encrypted,

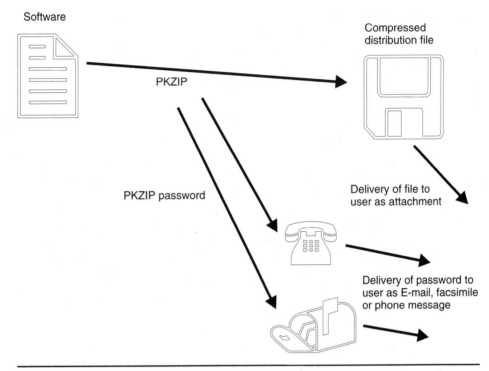

Figure 4.159 Electronic delivery using PKZIP and password.

then delivered to the user, usually by FTP controlled by a hypertext link in an HTML document. For example, the document often includes an HTML code such as *FTP://www.company.com/ESD/123786.EXE*, which the customer will move the hand over and click with the mouse to begin the transfer process. When the delivery of the file is completed, the code key or password

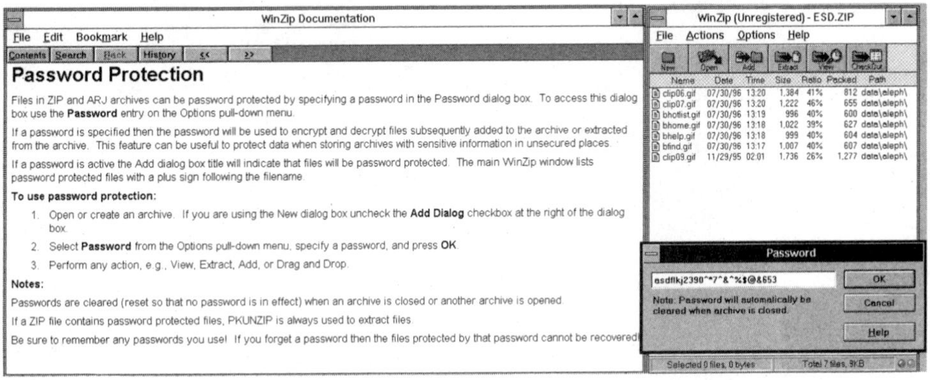

Figure 4.160 Electronic delivery using PKZIP, WinZip, the password help screen, and the pop-up window for specifying a password.

is then delivered as a secured E-mail message or a secured HTML document, as illustrated in Figure 4.161.

Many shareware or even commercial products are available as fully functional applications. In order to encourage registration and payment for these applications, the executable or its installation process may create special time data, an entry in a registration database, or even the older .INI format Windows file. These problems are difficult but not impossible to override. Vendors have created products such as A/Pay (demonstrated on the CD-ROM) or Time-Lock, shown in Figure 4.162, that use a secure encryption method to store date expiration information. Basically, the application stops working when the expiration date is reached, it has been run for a preset number of hours, or it has been tested a preset number of instances.

The most secure and integrated process is the Cryptolope or ZipLock process that imbeds transaction and credit card processing into the delivery packet as illustrated in Figure 4.163. The antelope is the cargo encryptically sealed inside the delivery packet and is not accessible until the packet holder pays for the right to open it with various electronic payment methods. The packet includes a header describing what it is, what it contains, and how to activate the payment mechanism.

Unlike other electronic delivery systems (EDS), ZipLock, A/Pay and Cryptolope can have lives of their own. Packet holders can copy, rename, and redistribute the packet while the contents remain encryptically sealed within. In fact, many vendors and resellers using these systems would like the packet to float around because more people might like what they see and buy. The ZipLock packet has a separate time-limited demo compartment so that software can be trial tested for some predefined time period. Typically, a demo or

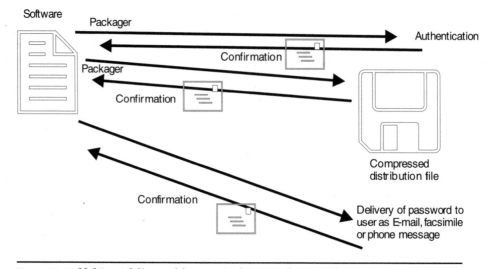

Figure 4.161 Multipart delivery of documents, data, or software with secure transmissions.

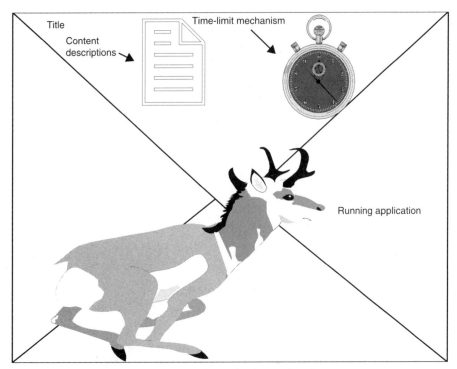

Figure 4.162 A time, usage, or frequency limited software distribution.

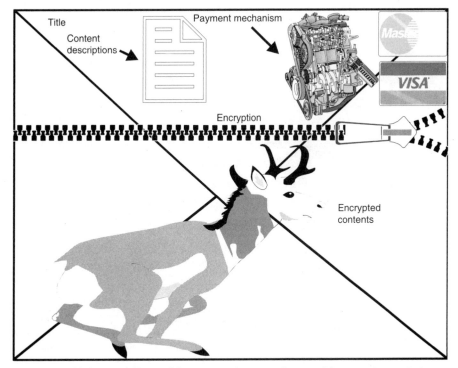

Figure 4.163 Multipart delivery of documents, data, or software with secure transmissions.

delivery file is listed on an FTP archive site or referenced on an HTML document. For example, the SSI code to imbed a demo is:

```
<IMG SRC = "button.gif" ALIGN = "BOTTOM">LANBuild .AVI movie(<A
HREF = "http://www.shadow.net/~npi/bldavi.zip">bldavi.zip</A>)
```

This is the standard method to highlight a demo for download. However, it is not the standard download. This particular sample is a packed file using PKZIP. Alternatively, the file might be a ZIPped file in a DOS.EXE format with an imbedded PKUNZIP or a UNIX TAR file. You want to provide a package that is convenient for the end user. Furthermore, the demo is not fully enabled. If the demo is a description of a Cryptolope document, that document is not fully accessible until the user enters a credit card and pays for the full delivery. The Cryptolope document is really a teaser with a description. The ZipLock and flexCrypt deliveries are similar, but they work differently. ZipLock provides a minimum functionality and delivery as specified by the vendor. Full access is only provided when the user enters credit card informa-

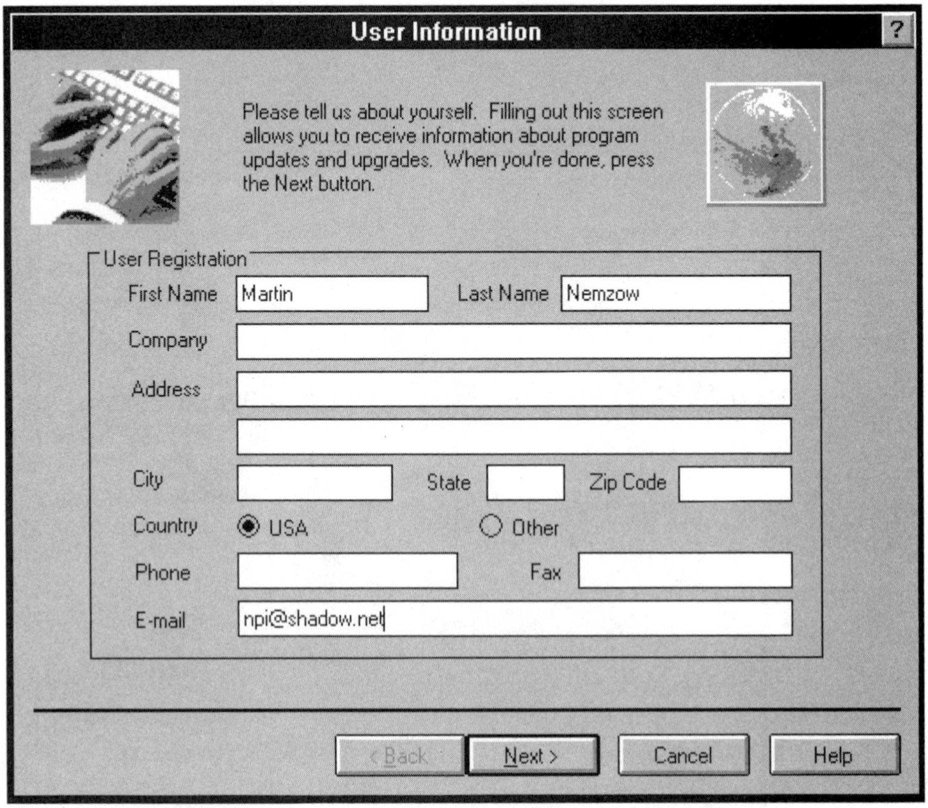

Figure 4.164 On-line payment for various information and software products.

tion and registers the delivery at a per delivery cost of $2.50. The flexCrypt product, on the other hand, provides full functionality, but it blows up after a preset number of days and cannot be reactivate until the user becomes a paying customer. The flexCrypt and A/Pay delivery systems also include an Internet-enabled credit card payment facility. For example, the next series of screen shots detail what happens after a time-limited application has expired and the user decides to activate a real copy or order a full copy (and some other merchandise). Figure 4.164 shows the user registration screen.

A/Pay can sell additional hard goods along with the software. In fact, Figure 4.165 shows my selection of a company T-shirt to go with the software. This process flow is useful for selling manuals, books, other related products, and the typical catalog soft goods like T-shirts. If your organization is like most, fighting over a limited supply of internal pens, pencils, company caps with logos, and other spirited promotional merchandise, you can add these inside sales features for employees. If you want to take it a step further, company products, office supplies, and lunches (on a daily basis) can be ordered and delivered with this secure ordering and delivery system. The payment process is as simple as selecting a payment method, as detailed in Figure 4.166. Purchase confirmation is shown in Figure 4.167.

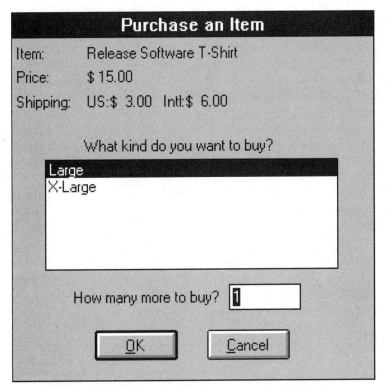

Figure 4.165 Software registration includes the sale of a T-shirt.

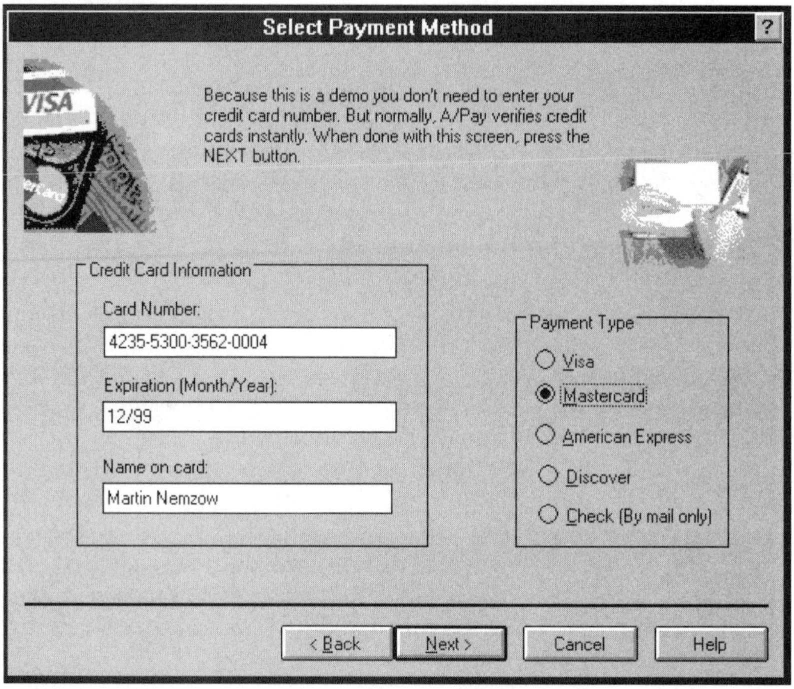

Select Payment Method   ?

Because this is a demo you don't need to enter your credit card number. But normally, A/Pay verifies credit cards instantly. When done with this screen, press the NEXT button.

Credit Card Information

Card Number:

    4235-5300-3562-0004

Expiration (Month/Year):

    12/99

Name on card:

    Martin Nemzow

Payment Type

- ○ Visa
- ◉ Mastercard
- ○ American Express
- ○ Discover
- ○ Check (By mail only)

[< Back] [Next >] [Cancel] [Help]

Figure 4.166 Payment method is a simple widget-driven GUI form.

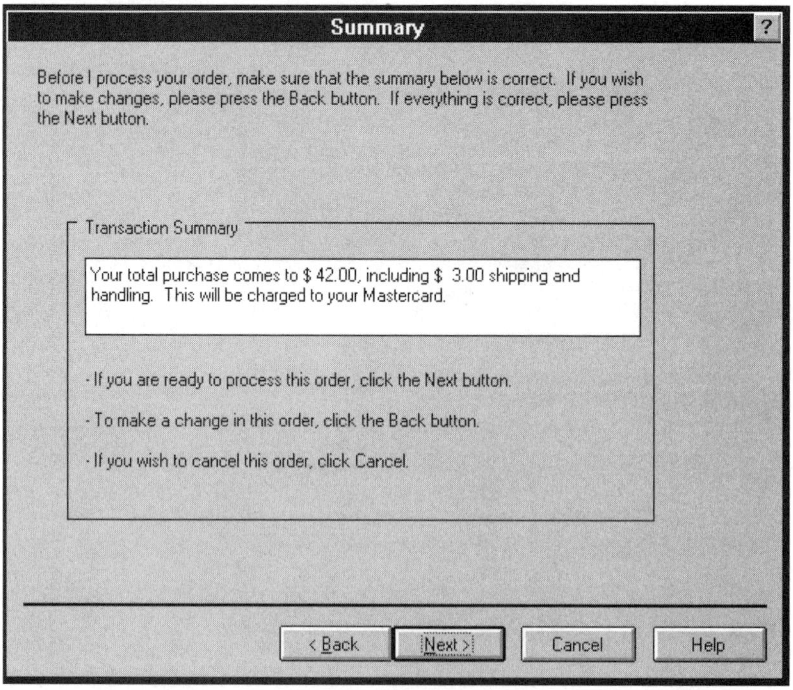

Summary   ?

Before I process your order, make sure that the summary below is correct. If you wish to make changes, please press the Back button. If everything is correct, please press the Next button.

Transaction Summary

Your total purchase comes to $ 42.00, including $ 3.00 shipping and handling. This will be charged to your Mastercard.

- If you are ready to process this order, click the Next button.

- To make a change in this order, click the Back button.

- If you wish to cancel this order, click Cancel.

[< Back] [Next >] [Cancel] [Help]

Figure 4.167 On-line payment and purchase confirmation.

A/Pay can process the payment in several automated or immediate methods, as listed in Figure 4.168. The process is designed to include this default information (which you have to program into the A/Pay delivery package) in order to complete the Internet-based credit card delivery process. A similar series of "programming" is required to set the standard modem-driven credit card verification and payment process in proper motion, as shown by Figure 4.169.

By the way, these electronic payment schemes absolutely require careful auditing. For example, consider what could happen if a site developer programs a merchant number or website that is not the official organizational number of the site. That developer (employee, consultant, or outside service firm) could siphon your sales without your knowledge. Several versions of the public distribution could contain a wide range of EPS payment addresses, which typically have a lifespan of several years, as my shareware distributions from 1988 reveal as very old copies turn up on BBSs, CompuServe forums, Internet shareware libraries, and even CD-ROMs mastered in places such as Taiwan, the Republic of South Africa, and France. This suggests a commitment to the process and a loyalty that can span many years whether the base cyberstore or source website is successful or not. These electronic distributions acquire an independent life of their own that can provide sales, royalties, and paid technical support calls.

Note that all these electronic software delivery systems handle some aspect of Internet delivery and payment for the product or service. However, they do not integrate financial tracking directly relevant for most cyberstore control systems. While the merchant clearinghouses will provide payment reports for each billing period, not all these products provide more than anonymous information about the customer or reports, which can be massaged and imported into the financial control system. If you want customer details, you will need to select the product most attuned to your information-gathering requirements.

Fulfillment

Cyberstores selling physical product must deal with the actual picking, packing, and shipment. As Chapter 2 clearly stated, any leaks in the cyberstore order flow, credit card payment, and verified shipment are likely to create expensive charge-back problems and even eventual charges of credit card fraud. Assuming you are building a long-term relationship with customers, you generally want to provide postsale product delivery and customer support.

This process is generically called *fulfillment* or *order fulfillment*. Many organizations have internal fulfillment resources, although some very small and other larger organizations are outsourcing the operations. Inbound telemarketing, inventory, returns, damaged good assistance, and collections are often provided with nationally based or even international providers that map phone numbers to their call centers. Examples include Precision Response

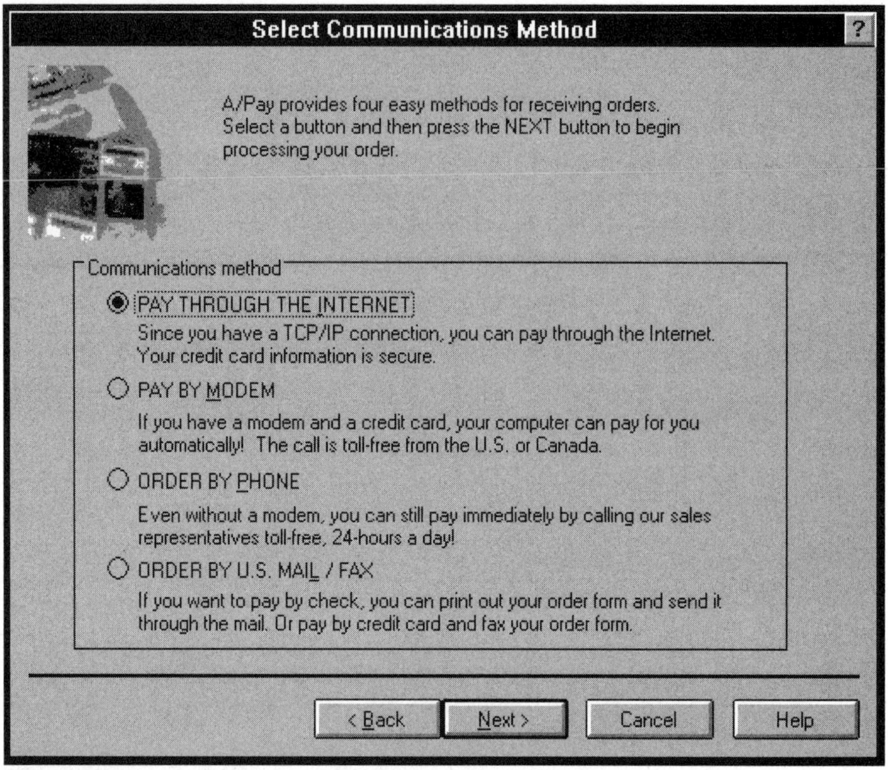

Select Communications Method

A/Pay provides four easy methods for receiving orders. Select a button and then press the NEXT button to begin processing your order.

Communications method

⦿ PAY THROUGH THE INTERNET
Since you have a TCP/IP connection, you can pay through the Internet. Your credit card information is secure.

○ PAY BY MODEM
If you have a modem and a credit card, your computer can pay for you automatically! The call is toll-free from the U.S. or Canada.

○ ORDER BY PHONE
Even without a modem, you can still pay immediately by calling our sales representatives toll-free, 24-hours a day!

○ ORDER BY U.S. MAIL / FAX
If you want to pay by check, you can print out your order form and send it through the mail. Or pay by credit card and fax your order form.

[< Back]   [Next >]   [Cancel]   [Help]

Figure 4.168 On-line payment by Internet, "old-fashioned" modem, or standby phone and mail processes.

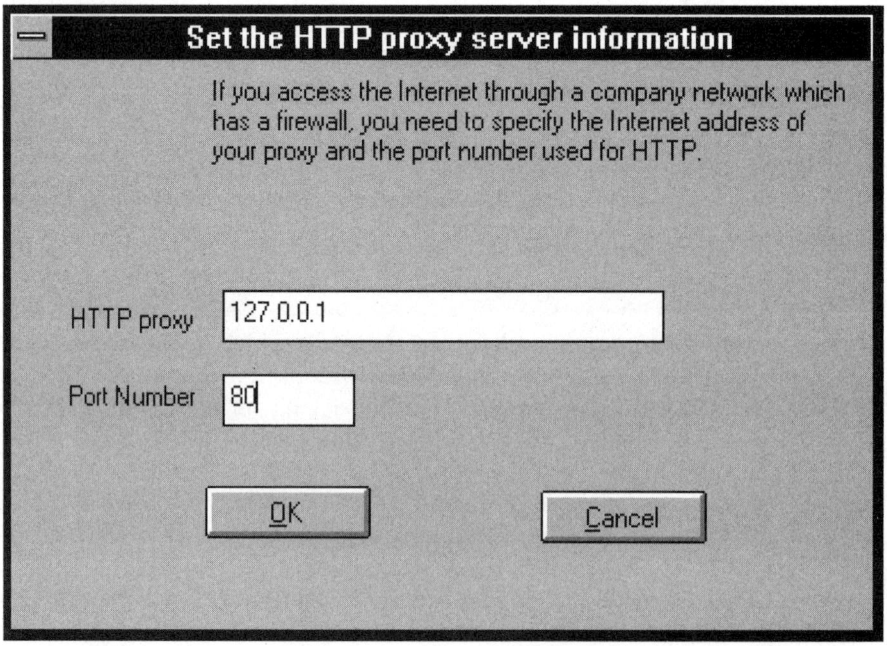

Set the HTTP proxy server information

If you access the Internet through a company network which has a firewall, you need to specify the Internet address of your proxy and the port number used for HTTP.

HTTP proxy   `127.0.0.1`

Port Number   `80`

[OK]   [Cancel]

Figure 4.169 Site developer programming to set the site name (could be a URL or IP address, phone number, or addresses) to enable the public distribution in order to pay the right organization.

Corporation, a company that takes orders by telephone, access payment by credit card, and actually picks and packs the product for registered shipping. One of the "boiler rooms" showing the telephone operators taking orders is shown in Figure 4.170.

Although the term *boiler room* is most often associated with fly-by-night scams, it also refers to the *telephone response center* or *call response center* necessary for telephone-based credit card orders. It is also possible, as shown in this book, to provide fully automated cyberstores (for information and software products), packaged software, and hard goods, but troublesome orders will get bounced to a person to complete. Because Computer Telephone Integration (CTI) in the call response center provides the same services as shown in Figure 4.170 to answer calls for Pond's, Ryder Trucking, Microsoft, and other companies, the utilization and efficiency levels for these composite operations often means lower costs for a cyberstore vendor.

Also, realize that fulfillment centers can route overflows as needed or add staff quickly, something most corporations, government organizations, and small start-up operations cannot do. Figure 4.171 shows a training problem for new operators. If you notice the color-coded screens, the operators are handling multiple customers as the software handles and tracks the calls automatically with automated number identification (ANI) and inward called number tracking.

The fulfillment organizations are integrating with electronic bulletin board services (BBSs), CATV advertising services, and the vendors to automate op-

Figure 4.170 Precision Response Corporation provides telemarketing services for customer support and fulfillment. (Courtesy of PRC)

Figure 4.171 As with most aspects of cyberstore integration, the technology is only as secure and effective as the workflow and as the training of the people supporting it (*Courtesy of PRC*).

erations and increase the effectiveness of business information. Home Shopping Club and QVC, along with a number of other marketers including the growing realms of cyberstore sales, need sales information to plug into inventory and shipping schedules. Notice the bank of modems on this site (in Figure 4.172) providing feedback to customers so that they can plan production, inventory shipments (to PRC fulfillment operations), and gauge the effectiveness of advertisement placements.

As a cyberstore operator, you will want to integrate website statistics with sales, fulfillment, and return information. For example, I discovered that puffery and over-excited advertising with my product line created excessive technical support problems and a higher rate of returns. Technical support and returns are costly. This is true for print media advertising; on-line BBS information; postings to USENET, news groups, and CompuServe forums; and our own Internet site.

It is *useful* to oversell some software to people who might need it or use it because it increases their sales volume and gross profits. Some organizations find it too difficult and costly from their end to return a product, while some buyers do not want to admit they made a mistake to a boss, so products become shelfware (do not get used) and too much time elapses to return a product for credit. You have to balance these inferior sales with the potential for future sales, the company's reputation, and a high return rate. Too many over sales create too many technical support calls or calls for merchandise return authorization (RMA). It is always possible to automate return authorizations

Figure 4.172 Precision Response Corporation supports sophisticated fulfillment services, including technical support, surveying, accepting credit card payments for order taking, and follow-ups on shipment receipts. (Courtesy of PRC)

with a cyberstore site, but realize that reversing credit card transactions incur clearinghouse fees and other internal paperwork. There is also the sensitive issue of authorizing on-line credit payments to customers directly from a website while still maintaining the integrity of that process. I suggest keeping the rate of inferior sales under 3 percent and returns under 1 percent. Higher rates will tie up the phone lines, the cyberstore site, and management attention, and detract from the more productive sales side.

The problem with too many technical support calls is that they cost money and some do not get handled well, which leads to returns. The problem with returns is that they are expensive to handle, at least on the order of $100 per return. Some customers seek basic product information and usage instructions that suggest the need for clearer product documentation and installation instructions, or better pre-sale information. You do want to track the sales channel (that is, the source of a customer sale, which could be from retail channels, resellers, direct by advertising, BBS, USENET and news groups, or Internet sites) on a per customer basis. Someone will want to cross-tabulate call information, technical support overheads, and returns to adjust product positioning, packaging, advertising, installation or usage instructions, or to address other problems.

The one clear benefit from cyberstore sales (particularly when the fulfillment organization differentiates sales channels), is that you can get rapid feedback when there is a problem. For example, if you are selling information or software on-line and delivering it the same way, you will want to create a simple installation process and initial running demonstration to minimize the number of initial technical support calls. In addition, if technical support is answering questions about why a software accounting product doesn't automatically read all prior transaction records into its format (as with TurboTax and Quicken) but requires a separate definitive menu step, consider incorporating a new intermediate release feature (for all on-line sales and deliveries) to minimize the support calls. The "fix" could be an automatic first-time installation feature, better documentation and demonstration, or clearer help sources that are integrated on-line at the cyberstore.

If customers are buying something from your cyberstore that does not provide the services they expected from the on-line sales literature, you will need to correct that error quickly. Adjust the cyberstore presentation. Alternatively, realize that mistake and reengineer a product or service or obtain additional product lines to address that unfulfilled need; this can be a wonderful market opportunity if your tracking systems and fulfillment systems are tied together. Since cyberstore advertising can be changed with literally a moment's notice, a cyberstore such as Lands' End can add product and make a new market if they can find a supplier in a moment's notice. Technical cyberstore sales and fulfillment issues like these transcend the technical issues of building a cyberstore and doing on-line database transactions, but nevertheless have significant effects on the operation and success of the cyberstore.

Website Performance Optimization

Websites consist of at least one web server. When the sites begin to handle more traffic and hits than can be supported by the failing infrastructure, more web servers and support servers are added to the site. When web servers are integrated with standard business and POS workflows, this implies integration with hosts, other servers, and internal networks. This often includes LANs, backbones, clusters of activity work groups, hosts, gateways to those hosts, multiple transmission channels (some that are even parallel, redundant, or idled for emergency backup), and all the infrastructure necessary to maintain a functional support network.

It is often unclear when a website is a single entity or just a collection of servers with a network of networks behind it. You have to realize that a website (unless it is wholly for Intranet, that is, for internal usage) includes a network of networks behind it. Every website is supported by the grand network or networks called the Internet. All such Internet performance bottlenecks typically inflict some penalties on your cyberstore. Problems can back up from around the world and affect your website. Websites hosted by ISPs or hosted locally with Internet tie-lines or leased lines through an ISP have additional, performance baggage. You have limited ability to optimize performance problems caused by backups around the world, saturation on an Internet backbone, or routing problems. Obviously, a direct link to the Internet backbone bypasses bottlenecks caused by local providers, but there are other performance issues. You can select which ISP hosts your website, and what size lines and what type of backup or alternate sites are included for the cyberstore; you can tune local networks, hardware, and the website architecture. The following section presents some of the technical issues and applicable solutions for bandwidth problems and optimizing website performance.

Network performance

You cannot avoid Internet bandwidth problems—they are beyond your control. However, you can select where your tie-lines connect and which ISP will host the website. You want to avoid connections that are overwhelmed and an ISP that cannot maintain a predictable service level. Even when you connect a web server directly into the Internet backbone, the implication is that your customers who access your website from the Internet will utilize from T-1 or E-1 to T-3 or OC-30 bandwidths. This utilization presupposes a website that can indeed process at least 1000 hits per minute and more. This load level is greater than most single platforms can support, and presupposes that a local website comprises multiple web servers and other devices networked together.

Currently, the prices are such that Fast Ethernet provides the lowest latency and greatest bandwidth, assuming that all website components can be wired within 100 m of the wiring closet. If you stuff all the website equipment in a single room, a Fast Ethernet work group hub might be a sufficient network medium. When you have more devices than can be supported on work group hubs (typically 8 to 24 devices), you can use enterprise hubs which will support 128 devices. Fast Ethernet with switching is advisable for websites with many devices because heavy loads will swamp it since the environment is primarily server to server and the traffic will be very high-support database transactions and the typical HTML requests. Although HTML files are typically small—about 3K to 15 K—the image files referenced are often large. Chapter 2 discussed the need for minimizing image file sizes in general, and for palette reductions in particular. You certainly do not want 1 MB background images clogging up a local website network.

When a website includes linkages to inventory systems, hosts, and networks that extend beyond a server room and include a typical office environment, Fast Ethernet or Switched Fast Ethernet provides suitably low latencies and bandwidths. When the local site extends beyond 100 m, the local network is better served by FDDI because this fiber-based protocol supports linkages between network devices at ranges up to 2 km.

If a network infrastructure uses FDDI or Fast Ethernet and still performs badly, the odds are that the performance problems are not in the network, but rather in the server structures, in the design of the cyberstore workflows, in database designs, in the loads imposed by inefficient CGI scripts, and in other web server-based problems. Refer to my enterprise optimization books for additional details about LAN and enterprise tuning. You might also explore delays in fulfilling user requests from hosts and main-frame databases.

Host performance

There are two performance issues with hosts. The first and most likely host bottleneck occurs with an ISP hosting your website. Performance bottlenecks on an ISP include tie-line overloads, lack of server horsepower, heavy loads, and, as is the case with UUNet, the overhead of coordinating requests arriving to some several hundred servers, matching them to the appropriate data files or databases, and routing these requests through a complex internal network. When you experience service delays of this type, explore a different ISP.

The second type of host bottleneck occurs when a mainframe responds to web queries slowly, updates records and transactions slowly, or seems to provide slow service for preexisting operations. You should not experience any new delays or performance latencies that are unusual with host-web integration when you are connecting into a preexisting POS or accounting system. Check standard performance lags against the extra step of converting the results into the format necessary for HTML presentation. If these lags are substantial, trace them to their sources. It is likely that poor gateway performance or network performance problems are the cause. The overhead to convert EBCDIC to ASCII and format the results into an HTML document is very low. If the database on the host has been designed specifically for web activity, you may want to explore database and relational designs for problems.

Transmission connection speeds

Transmission connection speeds are a factor of raw bandwidth, transmission overhead, intermediate device latencies, and delays at either end of the transmission channel. The ISP or local telephone company can provide channel utilization levels if you cannot. When utilization exceeds 60 percent and there is a lack of available slots, you may want to explore a larger transmission channel. If you are currently using a dedicated ISDN port, consider adding more channels or moving to ISDN PRI. If the T-1 channel is overloaded, consider migration to T-3. Realize that a wider pipe often requires greater infrastructure at the ISP or local server end to support the greater bandwidth.

Typically, channel utilization is less of a problem than server overloads. This can occur when the CPU or disks reach saturation. Under those conditions, bandwidth utilization is low, but server and CPU loads are high. You want to reassess the network infrastructure, but mostly the web server and database server load distributions in this scenario.

Transmission connection speeds are also a function of latency. Although a local site can have a very large pipe to the Internet backbone, delays at communication servers, ports, routers, local networks, and gateways will squander that available bandwidth. For example, routers and gateways, particularly firewalls, impose processing delays on both inbound and outbound traffic, which can create suboptimal channel utilization levels. The indications for this problem are low bandwidth and server utilization levels.

Database query performance

In general, web database performance is a function of database server performance, the CPU horsepower of the database server, the hit rate on that server, the overhead requirements to create the HTML conversion, and line connection speed (as the client sees it). Database queries are slow in general, so you need to realize this as a developer and compensate for it in your web page and process design. When the queries become too detailed, too many layers, and simply interminable, customers will go away. However, a database search can be much faster than searching for items in many layers and the tie-in to a database can provide details about a product or service that would not ordinarily be included in a static web page. There are three approaches for database optimization:

- Do nothing and warn the user that the process is slow

- Improve the server horsepower or distribute the loads

- Improve the query filters and process

Actually, doing nothing is a viable and reasonable alternative even though it sounds lazy. Sometimes there is not a lot that can be done to improve the infrastructure or enhance performance with the cyberstore budget. If the accounting database design came from SAP, Great Plains, or Oracle, you are unlikely to make design changes. However, compensate for that weakness; let the user know that the process is slow by providing a graphical or HTML display of progress and the expected completion time.

If you have the budget, you can move a database server off the platform with the web server, split the database server to a distributed architecture, or add more horsepower with more competent database platforms. It is also possible that the Internet network connecting the web server to the database server and to other resources is overloaded. If that is the case, you will want to upgrade it. See my performance optimization series of books for information on LAN, enterprise, and system (including platform hardware) analysis and tuning tips.

The biggest performance improvement is threefold. First, you want to protect the user from running queries accidentally. If the HTML form query is activated by the <Enter> or <Tab> keys, the user can activate a long-winded query unintentionally and wait for minutes cursing their uncoordinated fingers or the stupid form. Instead, add a specific button that states "Submit" or "Run Query" to activate the query and confirm that no other HTML links can activate the query. You may need to test the code or read the resulting CGI,

HTML, or scripts created by a database code generator to check for key-driven instances that activate the query.

The second way to improve database performance is through database structure design. Complex and hierarchical relationships and particular tables driven by external keys (in other tables) are locally slow with SQL. Use a database design tool, such as InfoModeler, to optimize or denormalize complex databases. Of course, when databases are linked into POS or accounting software, you probably have no recourse but to optimize that third party software. These requests are marginally slower when the results are shown in a web display. Some tools cache the entire subset and then display, whereas others display the results line by line in table-encoded HTML. This line-by-line approach is more desirable because it provides user feedback on the process. It is like displaying interlaced GIF files, as described in Chapter 2. The time to complete the entire table is identical, but a user can begin to read a query table as it is displayed by individual lines.

The third approach is to replicate and divide the databases. You can do this in one of two ways. First, you can create a read-only database specifically for web usage that is not part of the production database. This offloads the process to another platform and also protects the corporate data from external hacking. The product database might regenerate or replicate the web database when changes occur, either daily or more frequently. Second, the web database can be flattened (that is, denormalized or split into multiple tables), which will improve query performance. Again, the web database need only be a partial extract of the production database. If the cyberstore is writing transactions and updating a POS system and inventory levels, this process can be separate from the catalog query operations. This validates one reason to use different database middleware products in the same cyberstore. As such, the transactions can write through directly to the production database or to a temporary log.

One last note, which is more of a user convenience than a performance optimization hint. Use HTML forms for complex queries to retain prior searching parameters. Some CGI and even database middleware reset the query fields after every search. Do not turn off the cache facility in the user's browser. Some security operations will purge and turn off the user's cache. However, if the query is complex and not quite right, the user can go back to the query form (and sometimes multiple pages) with all field entries intact. This is a nice subtlety if your CGI or database middleware merely puts a front end on SQL code and does not create more user-friendly search routines.

Robot exclusion

Robots are indexing and content "spiders" that explore the web to build site maps (like NetMapper), build lists of topics and documents (from each HTML page header), or search documents for keywords, application index items, and content and substance. These robots can eat up web server resources because they can extract the fundamental information from a site. Although such spiders are best run at nonpeak hours, the web is such that what is nighttime and slow in one place, is peak time somewhere else in the world. It is not always obvious where a site is and what its load is. If you want to exclude robots from a web server, you create a root file on it called "ROBOT.TXT." This file will restrict access to individual users trying to access the site with this line:

```
User-agent: NetCarta Cyberpilot/USERID
Disallow: /
```

where the user ID is an entry from the webserver log. If you see a lot of traffic from site spiders, you can always post a local map because it cuts down on the number of users profiling your site and mapping it every time they hit it. Again, using WebMapper as an example, you would map your own site and create a sitemap.wmp file, accessible to browsers with this HTML code:

```
<A HREF="sitemap.wmp"> < IMG SRC="mapicon.gif" ALIGH=MIDDLE
   BORDER=0>Webmap of this site<A/>
```

This includes the hypertext jump to the Webmap so that CyberPilot will automatically display the available map and an icon and, in turn, users familiar with Webmaps and the CyberPilot icon will recognize the opportunity. Alternately, you can create a webmap.htm file with WebMaster, WebMapper, Web Analyzer, and other tools. This file is a text-based (with icons and images if you choose) hierarchical map of the site. Post it as a standard hypertext link. This site map appears as a text file.

Conclusion

This chapter defined some of the important implementation and operation issues for building and maintaining a cyberstore. The most important information in this chapter was the explanation of detailed methods for attaching databases to HTML forms in two-way, dynamic, and interactive flows for order taking, transaction processing, and site and historical data mining and abstraction. Chapter 5 details some successful, not-so-successful, and very pretty websites that show the range of not-for-profit information fulfillment, corporation information and dissemination, technical support, promotional advertising, and transaction processing. Also, the final section of Chapter 5 details a makeover of a flat website into a hierarchically ordered series of HTML pages with secure mail enablement for delivery of confidential legal documents and acceptance of credit card payments for donations.

5

Case Studies

Introduction

This chapter profiles various organizations' use of websites for information distribution, sales and marketing, and transaction processing. The profiles run the gamut from small cybershops to single-organization cyberstores and malls with many vendors. I have also profiled some government agencies, non-profit organizations, and graphics agencies to show the new, the good, and sometimes the questionable. Sometimes you can learn as much from seeing what doesn't work as you can from seeing what the leaders and cutting-edge shops are doing. In addition, this chapter profiles the makeover of a dull website first hosted by Aleph Institute to one that is livelier, more organized, and includes secure HyperText Transport Protocol (HTTP) delivery for credit card information.

Small Business Informational Site

The Annuity Research Center (ARC) is a one-man insurance-selling operation. However, it has a website. The complexity and lengthy sales process for most insurance sales precludes on-line transactions, but the message of this site is focused, businesslike, and presents old information in a very different light. A screen shot from the ARC site is shown in Figure 5.1.

I like this site because of the inclusion of graphical clippings from the *Wall Street Journal*, which are dressed, cleaned up, and presented to augment the message at the site. In contrast, many sites include gratuitous images—the world, spiders, logos, and rocklike tiled backgrounds. However, this site uses the graphics to reinforce the sales message, spread new information, lend the name of a higher and respected authority to the site, and, nevertheless, add cachet because of the shadows that graphics add to this otherwise plain and simple site. The site wouldn't work with just the text and the bullet items.

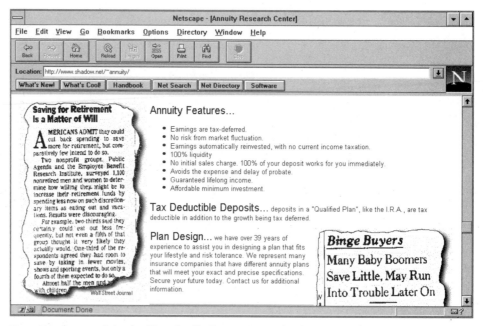

Figure 5.1 A very minimal, although effective, content-only site.

Manufacturer-Direct Commerce

Mainstream industrial and consumer manufacturers are singing the praises of company stores because of the control they have over planning, budgeting, marketing, and pricing. Additionally, manufacturers selling directly to the consumer and thus bypassing the middle reseller and the retailer are accumulating prime marketing information about consumer likes and dislikes. Note that this assertion presupposes that the manufacturer selling directly has initiated point-of-sales systems to the operation. This change of channel is very prevalent among manufacturers who were dominated for a long time by the power of retail giants and the confederated pressures of seasonal retailing cycles. However, this channel is nowhere more prevalent than among small software and intellectual property vendors who have never had access to standard retailing and reseller channels.

Many software companies develop from an idea and a technology, and are not marketing machines. The thought of resellers, channels, direct sales, and outlets does not come into play until the venture capital people or professional management teams come into the picture. As such, many ventures advertise on-line and provide product trials, credit card payments, and delivery by the Internet. Sausage Software does this in spades. By looking at the home page in Figure 5.2, you would not realize that this company is based in a small town in Australia. It shows that location is immaterial to product and position in today's global market.

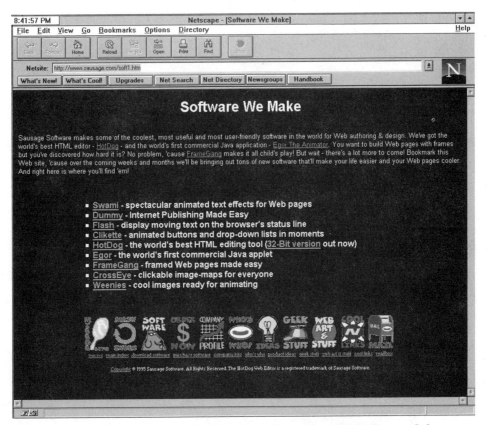

Figure 5.2 Worldwide distribution and on-line transaction processing from Sausage Software.

Institutional Wholesale

The AMP catalog site represents the direction I think the website and the commercial cyberstore will head. Although a number of manufacturers for retail will try to boost overall sales, create a name brand cyberstore presence, and force lower reliance on retail chains, new retail channel sales likely represent 1 percent of the market. Retail consumer sales represent less than 10 percent of all worldwide gross national product (GNP) activity, and while home computer use and Internet access are growing, they will not represent a substantial mainstream sales opportunity for some time yet. However, 90 percent of all transactions are between businesses, 40 percent of businesses worldwide have computers, and 23 percent of those have Internet access. Therefore, the market opportunity is between business trading partners. This includes AMP and all electronic product manufacturers or wire product users, or National Semiconductor and worldwide designers of electronic and electrical products. While the semiconductor chip is a basic material, buyers of retail product, raw materials, office supplies, and other production product or consumer goods can benefit from the business-to-business cyberstore.

AMP was an earlier player with an on-line catalog. While I consider this site difficult to use, slow, and not intuitive, the AMP website does represent some interesting technology, as shown in the sequence of website parts searches. The main page is shown in Figure 5.3.

The screen image in Figure 5.4 shows the typical pulldown list box of components in a cyberstore. Note that large lists can be slow to load and that multiple or hierarchically dependent lists are very bandwidth intensive. For example, if a user selects the N connectors as shown in the figure, a second list box would be dependently populated by specific types of N-type connectors. When this process is dynamically driven with a parts database, the hit is twofold. First, the database must be queried for record details; that process can be slow, as Chapter 4 outlined because of database overhead, network overhead, and the CPU processing by Common Gateway Interface (CGI) or database/HTML data conversion. Second, the filtered information, even when pared to a simple, single-column list of part details, must be transmitted to the client browser and stuffed into the list box. Although there are list-box widgets in Solaris, Windows, and Macintosh, the process of populating (and sorting) the entries is CPU inten-

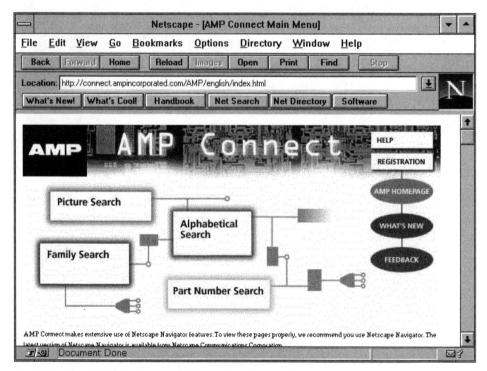

Figure 5.3 The AMP cyberstore and database catalog home page.

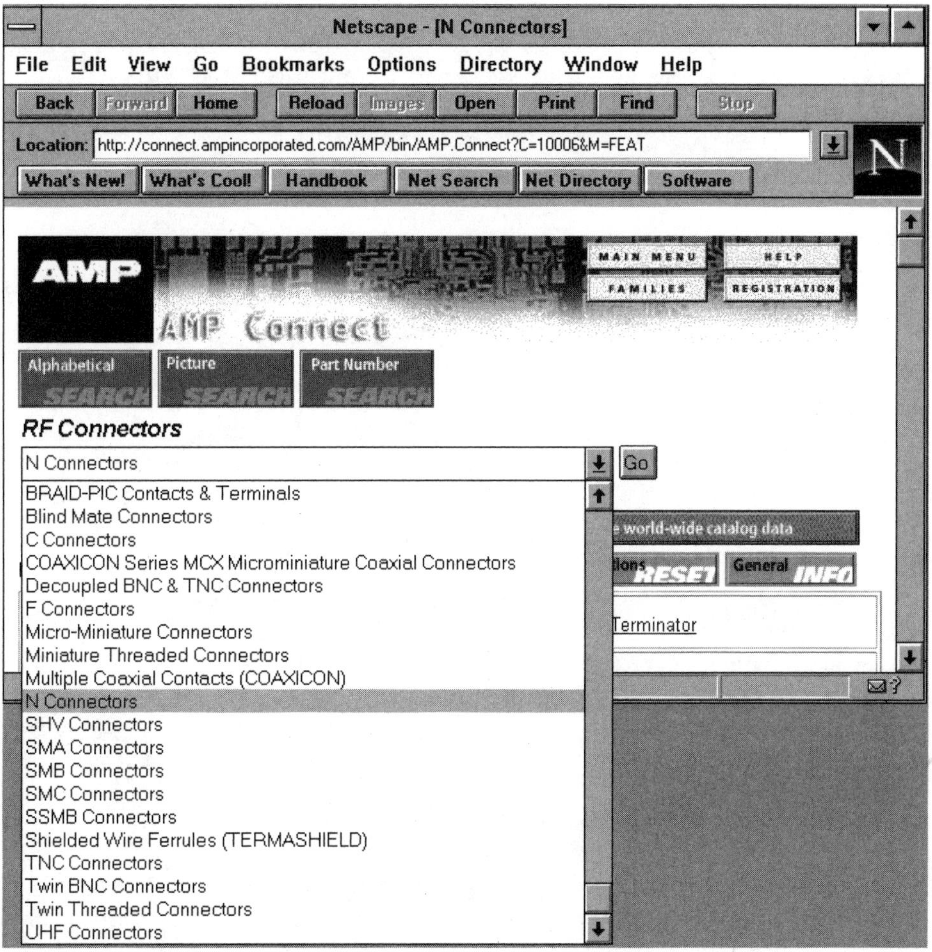

Figure 5.4 Component selection is possible by component purpose as is typical with most cyberstores, by picture, or by part number.

sive. Use discretion when specifying and designing pages with one or more list boxes.

Although the site is not intuitive, it is designed for part searches by what the components look like. The menu structure includes product categories, the ordinary categorization by product lines or organization for consumer constituency (for example, breakdown by sex or product costs), but the AMP site also includes categorization by what products look like. Although the screen shot in Figure 5.5 seems to group products by category, this basic search is expanded with subcategorizations by images.

Figure 5.6 shows the search hierarchy progressing through increased image detail. While most cyberstores force the user to surf through a hierarchy of product lines, products, options, and features, the AMP site lets a user match

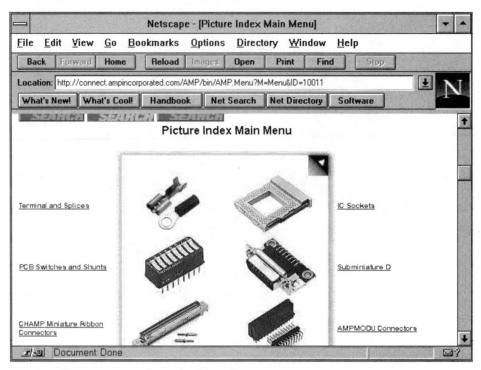

Figure 5.5 Categorization and searches by product images.

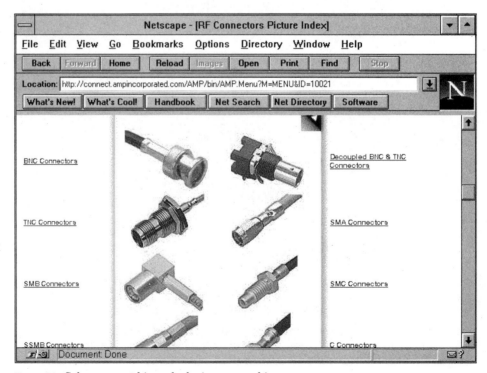

Figure 5.6 Subcomponent hierarchy by image searching.

his or her needs by the actual generic image. Notice that the text is subordinate to the images. The text is small and shown off to the side, thereby reinforcing the importance and centrality of the image search. It would be interesting to tie a product like Virage (profiled in Chapter 2) into product and component image searching. Ultimately, the image search ends with a family of components such as N-type network connectors. The type, sex, style, and connection type must be specified with more exacting textual details, as shown in Figure 5.7.

The final details are given as a data report dump as shown in Figure 5.8. These are the details needed by an industrial buyer. Realize that all raw materials have characteristics that can make or break a final product. Impedance, working voltages, and radio-frequency leakage are clearly important with a high-speed network connector. On the other hand, comparable characteristics such as pattern, color, thread density, fiber content (such as wool, cotton, silk, polyester, or rayon), sheen, sizing, stabilizing chemicals, cleaning options, and expected shrinkage with drying become very important for clothing manufacturers. This type of detail is shown simply in the field tag and tag value format, but could also be formatted into ruled tables or secondary pages, as shown later with the National Semiconductor website.

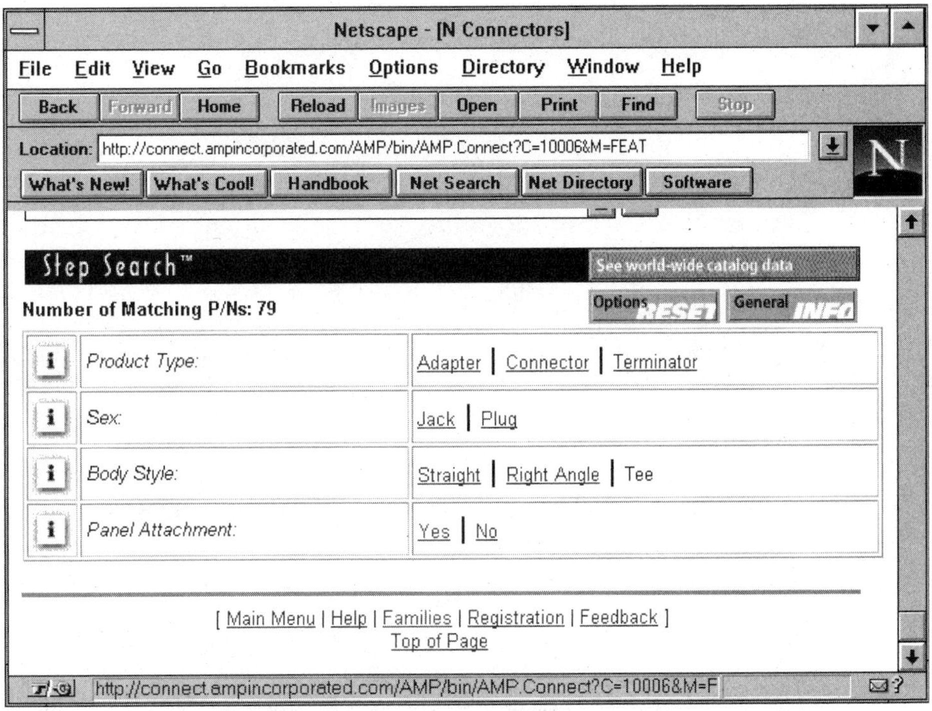

Figure 5.7 Specifying the details for a selected component.

```
┌─────────────────────────────────────────────────────────────────────────┐
│ ─ │        Netscape - [N Connectors General Information]        │ ▼ │ ▲ │
├─────────────────────────────────────────────────────────────────────────┤
│ File   Edit   View   Go   Bookmarks   Options   Directory   Window   Help │
├─────────────────────────────────────────────────────────────────────────┤
│ │ Back │ │Forward│ │ Home │  │ Reload │ │Images│ │ Open │ │ Print │ │ Find │ │ Stop │ │
├─────────────────────────────────────────────────────────────────────────┤
│ Location: │http://connect.ampincorporated.com/AMP/bin/AMP.Connect?C=10006&F=0&M=CINF&N=0&RQS=C~100│ ↓ │   │
│ │What's New!│ │What's Cool!│ │ Handbook │ │ Net Search │ │Net Directory│ │ Software │   N │
├─────────────────────────────────────────────────────────────────────────┤
│ Electrical Characteristics                                              ↑ │
│ Nominal Impedance-50 ohms                                                 │
│ Working Voltage-1000 volts, rms at sea level                              │
│ Frequency Range-0 to 11 GHz                                               │
│ Voltage Standing Wave Ratio (VSWR)-Straight Plug or Jack-1.3:1 max.       │
│ Right-Angle Plug-                                                         │
│    1.35 max. at 0 to 9.0 GHz                                              │
│    1.50 max. at 9.0 to 11.0 GHz                                           │
│ Contact Resistance-                                                       │
│ Outer Contact-0.2 milliohms                                              │
│ Center Contact-1.0 milliohms                                            │
│ Right-Angle-2.5 milliohms                                                │
│ Insulation Resistance-5000 megohms min.                                  │
│ Dielectric Withstanding Voltage-2500 Volts, rms at sea level             │
│ RF Leakage-Mil Type, -90 dB min. at 2 to 3 GHz                           │
│ RF Insertion Loss-Mil Type, 0.15 dB max. at 10 GHz                       │
│ Right-Angle Plug, 0.3 dB max. at 10 GHz                                  │
│ Corona Level-Mil Type, 500 volts min. at 70,000 ft. [21 336 m]           │
│ Terminator-                                                              │
│ Resistance-50 ohms ±1%                                                  ↓ │
├─────────────────────────────────────────────────────────────────────────┤
│ │‡ᴢ│ Document: Done                                          │     │ ✉? │
└─────────────────────────────────────────────────────────────────────────┘
```

Figure 5.8 The AMP cyberstore and database catalog home page.

Web Mall

Because the costs of advertising and implementing a cyberstore are quite steep and because the ability to shop from one place and compare quality, price, and character are so ingrained in shoppers, the mall concept is flourishing on the Internet. Cooperative advertising, pooling of developmental and implementational resources, and a uniform interface hallmark the cybermall. Although there is no definitive monopolistic or oligopolistic cybermall yet, this section shows the highlights and defects in the current consolidated cyberstores. One such example is Avante Garde, which is shown in Figure 5.9.

Real retail malls have a focus. They generally provide dense, high-margin goods with a high rate of turnover. Stores with lower margins, bulk goods, and items that require a more complex or lengthy sales process cannot afford the expensive space at malls and instead opt for convenient locations, low-rent districts, or strip malls. They often build large space stores or congregate along a highway strip, often popularly called the "Auto Mile" or "Furniture Row." There is a defined concept of what malls sell. This includes soft goods, clothing, and household goods, and impulse items, but less often appliances, furniture, automobiles, consumer electronics (except specialized and

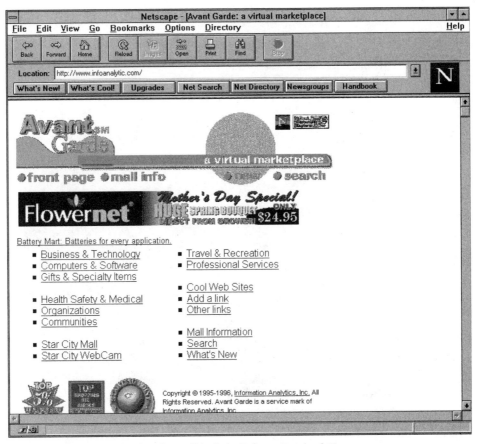

Figure 5.9 The Avante Garde cybermall built by Information Analytics.

very high-margin goods), and expensive toys such as motorcycles, motor homes, and jet skis. In contrast, many commercial websites lack focus, as shown in Figure 5.10.

Chapter 2 makes a big point about keeping the path to your cyberstore clear and the advertisements in traditional media copious. The following figures demonstrate a case of common names and sites vying for business with the same names. One is a regional cooperative information website for Hong Kong merchants (as shown in Figure 5.11), and the other is the commercial cybermall enabled with leading edge technology and on-line transaction processing.

The screen shot in Figure 5.12 profiles the eShop, a venture started in 1994 and acquired in 1996 by Microsoft, to advance that company's Internet presence and provide a tasting ground for cyberstore commerce and fully automated transactional processing.

The progenitor of all Internet cyberstores and cybermalls is the Internet Shopping Network (ISN), patterned after the marketing TV shows like the

Figure 5.10 The everything-to-everybody chameleon cybermall.

Figure 5.11 E-SHOP muddying the cybermall message.

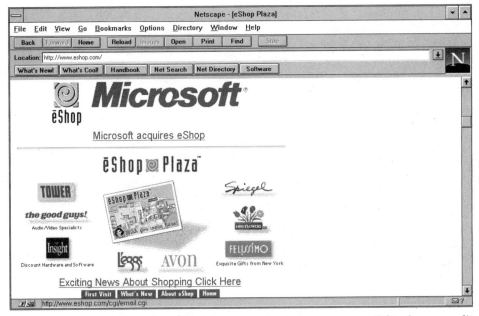

Figure 5.12 A leading-edge cybermall with a guarantee to assume responsibility for any credit card fraud related to on-line sales at its customers' cyberstores.

Home Shopping Network and QVC. In fact, QVC owns the Home Shopping Network and recently acquired the Internet Shopping Network to test new marketing techniques, old marketing tactics, and the new on-line channel. A presentation from ISN is shown in Figure 5.13. ISN is glitzy and expen-

Figure 5.13 TV marketing takes to the Internet with ISN.

sive, and it remains to be seen if it will thrive in a very competitive market. There is a considerable amount of funding behind ISN (as there is with eShop), but this cybermall is driven with database and financial integration, marketing expertise, and a wealth of existing product channels, all of which may be more potent than new technology and glitzy presentation. Content and substance are potent combinations in consumer mass marketing and especially for business-to-business sales.

Figure 5.14 shows a new twist on the cybermall concept by putting trade show information and people on-line. This means live web video (see my *Web Video Toolkit* book) and desktop teleconferencing tools such as Video-Phone and CU-SeeMe, or streaming video presentations with LiveVideo will now be available as significant communications media. I actually like this technique because it saves physically traveling to far-off places, walking through huge exhibition halls, and missing the technical people who seem to be always at lunch or on break at the shows. In a sense, the actual booths can be established with hypertext links to vendor home pages and a secondary entry point specifically with show deals and special pricing information that typify the high-pressure sales tactics at shows.

Activision Games On-Line

Interactive games and on-line gaming have been suggested as the next big wave in entertainment. However, the functional bandwidth of the Internet is

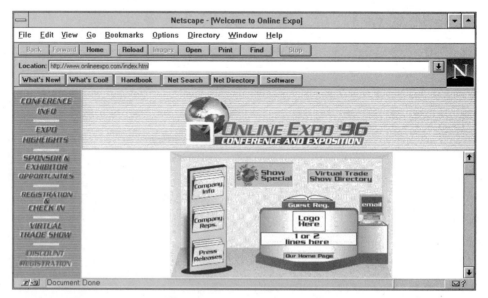

Figure 5.14 High-tech conference and trade show marketing takes to the Internet with Online Expo.

no better than that of commercial on-line services (such as CompuServe, AOL, and Prodigy), and in fact given the bottlenecks seen at most ISPs, the service is probably even less. Nevertheless, the combination of CD-ROM games and on-line components reached a new stature with the Spycraft strategy and adventure game. This game is crafted to take advantage of new information, news, and other databases to enhance its play and currency. The Internet connection (through Activision, market maker for the game) includes a special ambience attuned to the secrecy and espionage promulgated by the game. Even the download process as shown in Figure 5.15 reinforces this mood. The standard Navigator pop-up window dispels the myth of the game for a moment until the player defines a download path and file name, as shown in Figure 5.16. This is still a game, for sure.

The currency of the game and its relationship to real news and events are emphasized with the latest bulletins on the death of William Colby, retired CIA director, spymaster, and one of the two design consultants of the game. The news is shown in Figure 5.17. The connection between the game (on CD-ROM), the Internet, and the datasets and news is crafted with a very well-defined user interface that both matches the environment of the game and is functional, stable, and reliable. These details make this commercial use of the Internet work well and illustrate the value of the cyberstore channel.

Travelocity

The outstanding distinction for Internet-based outlets is the speed of communication, the currency of the information, the absolute consistency of the user

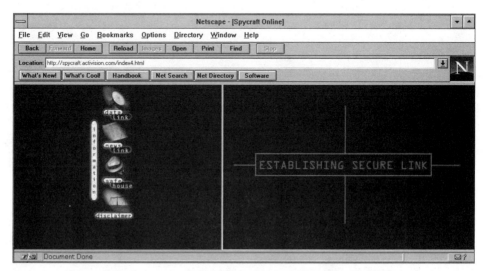

Figure 5.15 Secure links for a game download? Is this a game or the real thing?

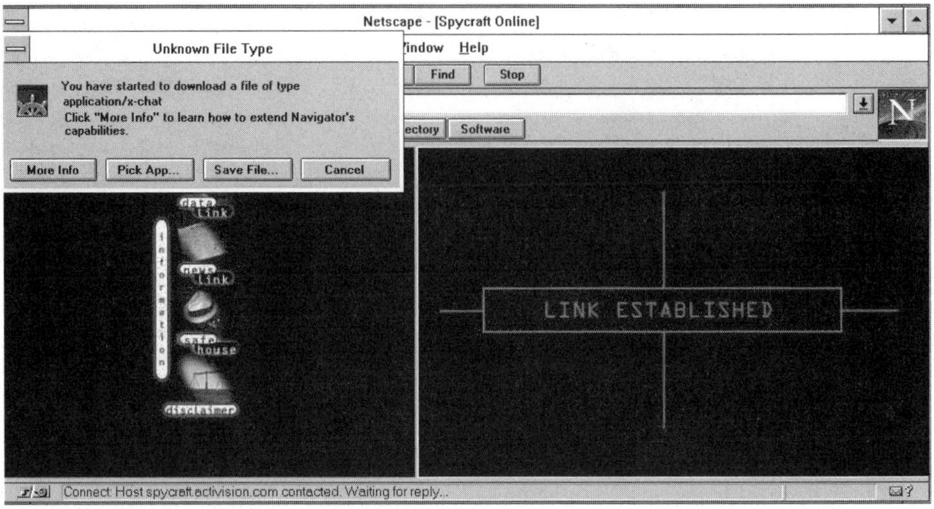

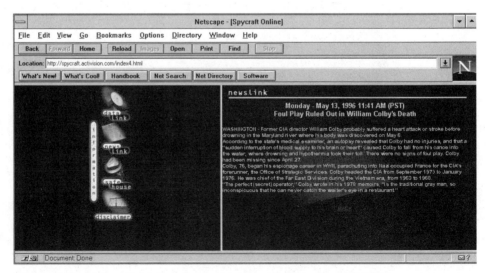

Figure 5.16 The download of current news and game updates is standard web.

interface, and the low cost both for creating a presence and for conducting on-line transactions. This is a potent omen for services and products that are price sensitive, in constant flux as far as availability goes, and difficult to differentiate from the competition, such as travel. The leading web store for travel products, services, and allied marketing is Travelocity whose home page is shown in Figure 5.18.

The secondary screens are empowered by keyword searches, context sensitivity, and powerful search engines connected to database information. While many of the screens walk the user through a complex labyrinth

Figure 5.17 Spycraft on-line integrates consistently with Spycraft on CD-ROM.

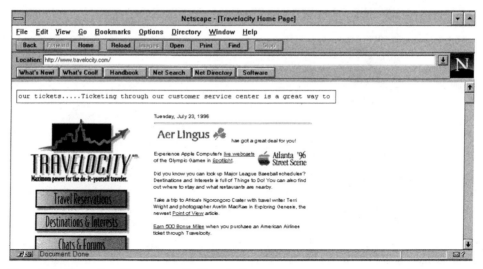

Figure 5.18 Promotional home page for Travelocity.

of choices necessary for travel sales, a knowledgeable user can bypass the mid-level information and take a shortcut directly to ticket reservations, hotel accommodations, or supplemental travel services. Although databases and complex queries are powerful, they typically confuse the average user. The site shown in Figure 5.19 simplifies much of that navigation.

The order entry screens and reservation procedures take the best from HTML forms and the simple Windows- or Macintosh-based GUI. You

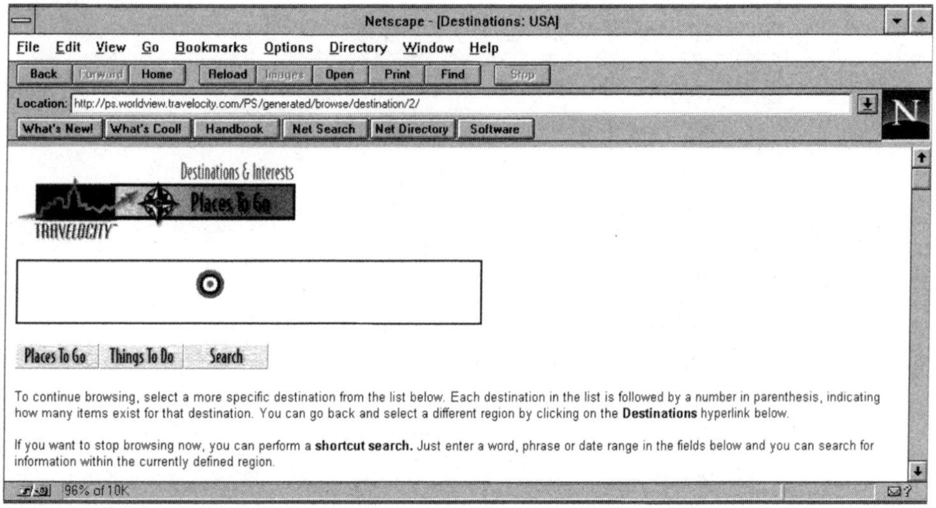

Figure 5.19 Context, keywords, abstracts, and searches create alternative paths through a complex cyberstore.

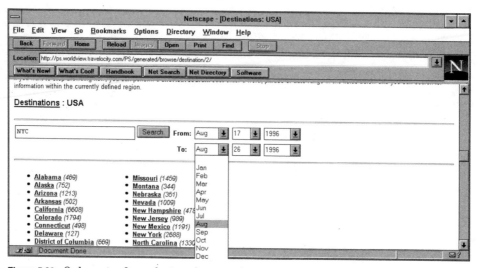

Figure 5.20 Order entry forms for travel reservations.

can select dates, times, and places for airline reservations, as shown in Figure 5.20.

The high point for the cyberstore is that all products and services, no matter how unique, outlandish, or difficult to position with the traditional and mainstream product, can be bundled or upsold. For example, this screen in Figure 5.21 shows translation services for a visitor to New York City. While most of us think that tour guides and private personal services in places for-

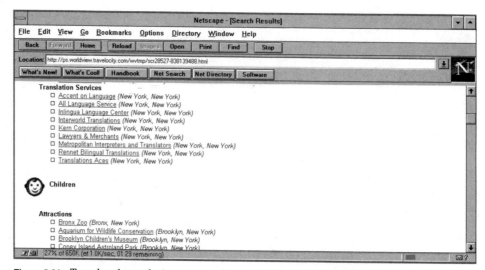

Figure 5.21 Travel and translation services for travelers to New York City.

eign to us, culturally different, and linguistically a challenge, that need not be the case. Translators and tour guides are often hard to locate and difficult to qualify, but not with a database search engine. This cyberstore upsale could make the difference between an ordinary experience and a positive one for the traveler.

Yamaha Riva

An extraordinary number of pundits have prematurely forecast the end of web consultants, graphic design agencies, and public relation firms. The shrink-wrap introduction of web design wizards (such as Digital Style and Visual Web) are described as the magic tools to build fully functional web sites. However, the same could have been said (and probably was) of these same groups when tools like CorelDRAW!, Photoshop, and Fractal Painter first came on the market—namely that the tools are so good that the average person can do the work himself. However, reality is different. While the computerized tools may have opened up some new horizons for many people, they have also created many more possibilities for people who already had a trained grasp on communicating messages, creating effective artwork, balancing concepts with sales promotion, and market analysis. The success factor for a website will always be content over flash, sizzle, and new technology. While these gimmicks may entice the occasional glance, the content, quality, and integrity of the website will retain the valued long-term customer.

Of course, some of the big advertising agencies look at websites as small projects that just are not worth pursuing . . . yet. These big players may see limited return on investment (ROI) and insufficient margins, and simply may not comprehend the importance of the cyberstore as an efficient sales and marketing channel. Furthermore, projects with outside budgets in the range of $100,000 to $500,000 with a significant technology and integration component are often outside the current expertise. The major agency players testing the waters with Interet advertising and site building include Chiat Day, Poppe Tyson, Ogilvy & Mather, io360, Avalanche, MVBMS, and Vivid. That is where savvy, newer players such as Khameleon Communications implement marketing sites for large organizations like Yamaha.

"Philosophy differs. There are always people who can do the quick and dirty creative work. However, in a peace-time economy, competition grows fiercely so that you need a lot of creativity and foresight to stay ahead," says Mark Wiethorn, president of Khameleon. The functional cyberstore always needs consultants and outside groups to stay ahead. Larger corporations that want to compete on the larger level understand that they need sophisticated marketing, which includes a functional website because the dominating force is the market competition. The more competition, the more sophisticated the marketing needs to be. The cyberstore marketing efforts represent not only advertising, but also product, positioning, pricing, and placement, as you have seen in the Yamaha site.

Yamaha manufacturers offer an extended line of vehicles. The motorcycle division, Riva, makes road motorcycles, touring bikes, 4-wheel off-road utility vehicles, motorized tricycles, and jet skis. Several realities have made a website viable. First, the products are sold worldwide, which complicates marketing activities. Second, jet ski racing teams have shown off not only the main jet ski itself, but also an extended line of racing accessories. A trickle of sales for accessories that owners did not even know existed became a flood when Khameleon Associates reprinted a small booklet as a 4-color brochure. In addition, as vendors of accessories realized that the market for them was suddenly much larger and was getting massive exposure through the jet ski racing circuit, they wanted their products tried on the racing vehicles and promoted in the printed catalog. Third, catalog sales required 24-hour sales support and technical support. Fourth, other Yamaha sales media lumped all vehicles into the same sales group, which created image problems since buyers of touring bikes did not want to associate with buyers of street bikes. This division was even more pronounced when sales office and catalogs included recreational vehicles. Although it was clear that the lines could be split by producing differentiated catalogs, the worldwide web provided a better medium.

Khameleon Associates built the Riva site to expand on the already successful color accessory catalog. In fact, when you visit the site, the clean focus emphasizes the catalog but also provides the promotional and transactional components consistent with a true cyberstore, as shown in Figure 5.22.

Although Riva refers specifically to the water bikes and jet ski component of Yamaha vehicles, the inclusion of other products from a top-level menu enhances the importance and attractiveness of a site as a valuable resource. Although too many products might overwhelm customers, the formal organization is not intimidating and suggests comprehensiveness, as shown in

Figure 5.22 Promotional, informational, and transactional features secure this site as the obvious and practical cyberstore.

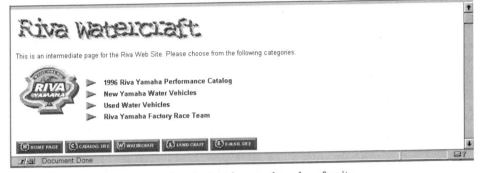

Figure 5.23 The broad coverage of products enhances the value of a site.

Figure 5.23. A significant part of the site is the use of professional images enticing the jet ski owner to want more from their purchase and to keep the jet ski running well or to want more in the way of a new product or greater performance, as shown in Figure 5.24. You might note that the contrast makes this page hard to read and the background does not add to the message, so it is not a perfect message.

The database aspect of this site is shown by the automated catalog. The number of selections was purposely kept to a minimum so as not to confuse surfers and to simplify the number of layers in this site, as shown in Figure 5.25.

Performance and replacement parts for a complicated product such as a vehicle can be numerous. The database organizes these parts by groups, related by purpose, descriptions, and numbers, and it provides these inroads to a specific part on the fly. Parts dealers usually have a difficult time matching specific parts to a broken object because most parts catalogs are specific by model year number and physical position and are rarely indexed by purpose, description, or usage. The data access shown in Figure 5.26 shows how

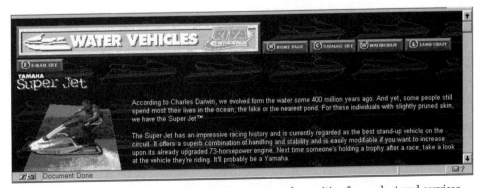

Figure 5.24 Part of a professional job is creating image and a position for product and services.

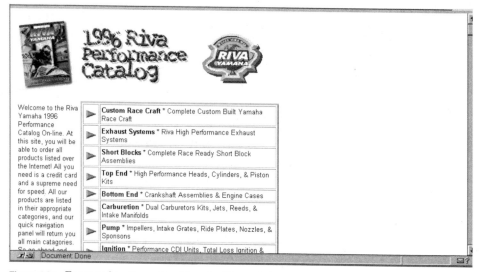

Figure 5.25   Front end to the on-line Yamaha Riva catalog.

customers can drill down and locate what they need by themselves. To ensure ordering accuracy and reduce the risk of mismatched parts, costly returns and restocking, replacements, and unhappy customers, the products are shown on-screen in detail, as seen in Figure 5.27.

This site also promotes pricey services, such as engine head modification. Consider that two of the main positions that a dealer or manufacturer holds

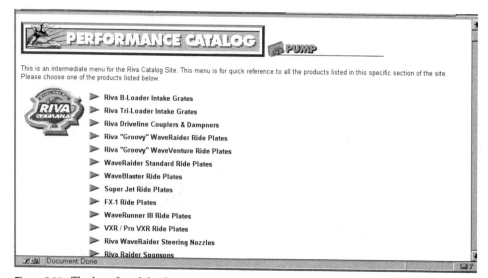

Figure 5.26   The benefits of the database-driven cyberstore are shown by the clear organization of products by logical types.

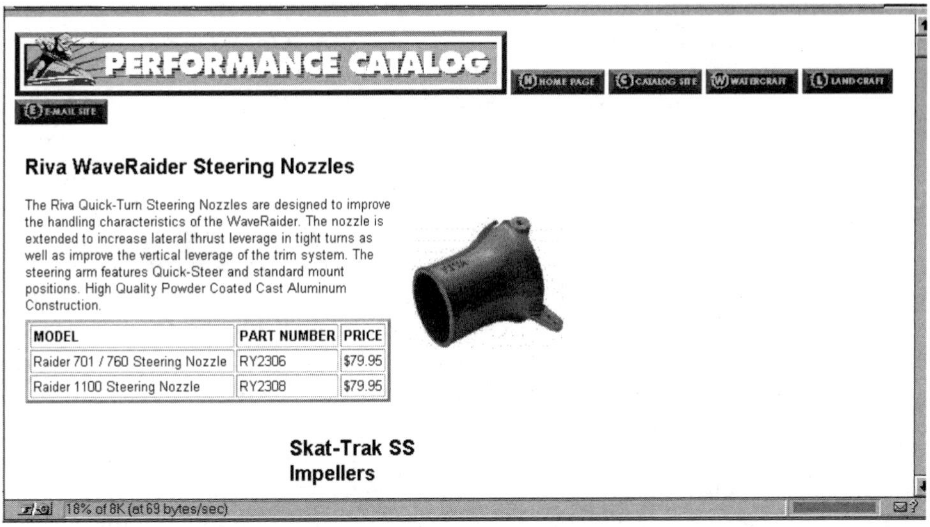

Figure 5.27 Precise specifications and an image minimize returns.

are credibility and deep pockets. Major overhauls of engines represent a substantial investment (even when performed by local mechanics), and integrity and faith in the quality of work are mandatory in selling a customer. The Riva Yamaha site markets this service in such a way that it seems like this major and expensive process is no different from the sale of small parts. This approach is very low key because it suggests that the process is just as simple as buying a screw, a nut, a bolt, or a muffler, as shown in Figure 5.28. In addition, this characterization positions the website as a fully certified dealer, mechanical retrofitter, and official last resource for all motorcycle and jet ski needs. That creates a powerful impression. In addition, the frequent placement of mail access and the use of a formal HTML form instead of the generic E-mail form emphasize that this site goes directly to the vendor, that a

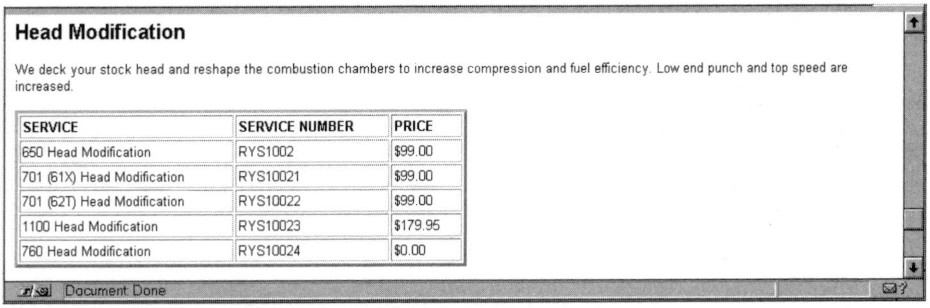

Figure 5.28 Major overhauls are presented as normal transactions and thus position the website as a full-service and qualified channel.

customer can communicate directly with knowledgeable people, and that there is always a last resort for any problem. One of the problems with mail order and catalog sales is that problems can drag on without solutions. The use of E-mail, as shown in Figure 5.29, illustrates another easy channel.

A significant disadvantage of E-mail, unless addressed in your organization, is that it is easy to ignore or to lose in various user accounts or topic folders. A customer can have the perception that an organization is unresponsive—it never answers its E-mail or phone calls, and cannot keep up with customer service, technical support, sales information requests, requests for proposals, and quotations. If you establish an E-mail presence, it is best if you unify throughout your cyberstore. However, you must have the resources to answer it in a reasonable time. Turnaround time of one day is a good target to aim for; if you can sustain that reliably, post that your site responds to E-mail within a day. If you create various folders, such as presales, sales requests, technical support, corporate communications, press relations, and comments, you will also need to provide coverage of these mail addresses when the primary manager and response personnel are on vacation or at conferences, training sessions, or trade shows.

The current cyberstore transactional method is to capture product selections, stuff them automatically into an order form, and deliver a copy of the order to the customer through the Internet or by fax form confirmation, as shown in Figure 5.30. This system bypasses many problems with security and credit card processing. Although this process is not integrated, the dealers suggested that it gives them a second chance to review the order with a customer and suggest missing reconstruction parts (rings, clips, and seals) and also to try to upsell the customer with other components or more product.

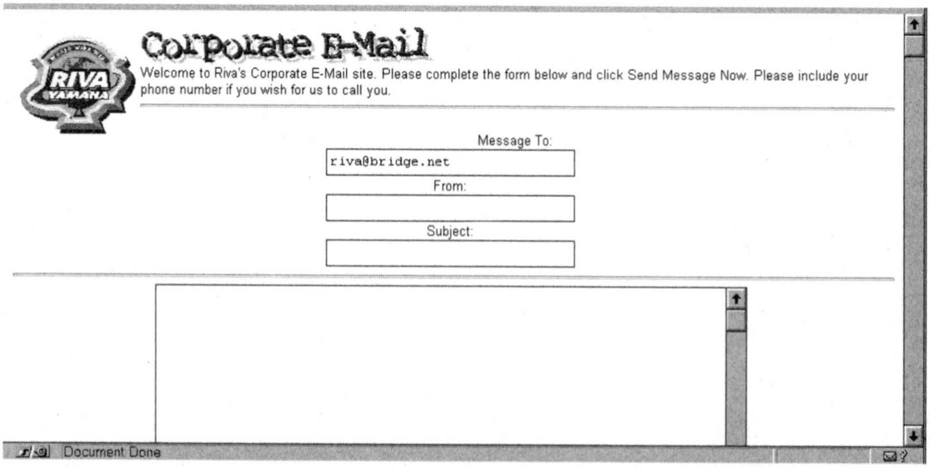

Figure 5.29 E-mail enhances the integrity and perception of responsiveness of a cyberstore or commercial website.

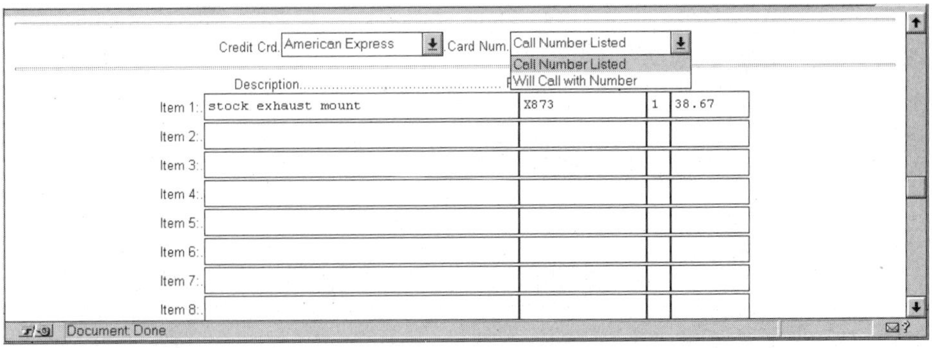

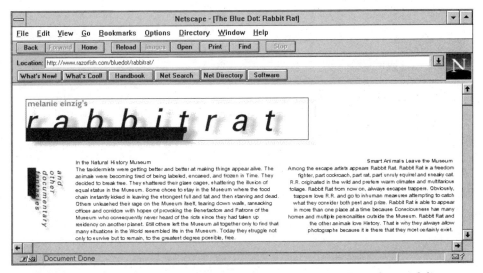

Figure 5.30 The order form is automatically completed, but the transaction is completed later by phone call or fax.

Razorfish Agency

Razorfish is included because of the depth of its work, its access to prized clients, and the outlandishness of its website designs. The sites are certainly offbeat, guided to present an image over substance, and push the limits of cyberstore and commercial advertising. Figure 5.31 presents the American Museum of Natural History in New York City (the one with all the dinosaurs) as the place to find even more unusual exhibits.

However, the message and image are pushed to limits of believability by the inclusion of a display case model on the exhibit floor, as shown in Figure 5.32. Although impish humor has a place, consider whether this works for or

Figure 5.31 The Rabbitrat is outside the usual fare of space, geology, Egyptology, and dinosaurs, and perhaps is meant to rejuvenate the stodgy image of this venerable museum.

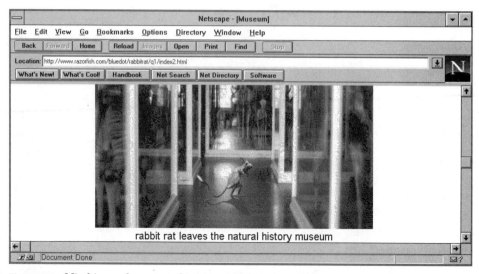

Figure 5.32 Mischievous humor used to attract visitors to a museum.

against bringing web surfers into the museum. Perhaps the message is meant to be that the exhibits are not dusty and old, but quite alive and interactive. All I see is very staid rows of glass display cases and a dim black-and-white view of the museum. Somehow, the black-and-white connotation recalls memories of pictures taken with a Brownie camera 30 years ago, probably the last time many people actually visited the American Museum of Natural History. A full-color, full-sound animation of the Rabbitrat might convey that message of change, not this film noir still look.

For some sites, like Nicole Miller that sells women's upscale clothing, style is everything, change is imperative, and interactive bells and whistles are included to impress and add razzle-dazzle. The Nicole Miller website presents form before and instead of function. Similarly, Razorfish designed the Ralph Lauren website that is profiled in the next few screen shots. This site sells nonessential products that are defined wholly by lifestyle and image. It caters to that need, as shown by the animated GIF opening screen in Figure 5.33.

The home page says nothing, shows nothing, and provides only the hotspot on the animated GIF. This image activates a secondary menu (screen shot in Figure 5.34) that is again all image, and requires the vertical scroll bars to get through it. The focus here is clearly on image and history, and there is no clear commercial focus other than the introduction of the paint collection, the product of the month.

The foremost message of this site is clearly the paint. The message of Ralph Lauren began with the animated views of perfume, cologne, and other frames of things too small to distinguish what they were. The second view showed

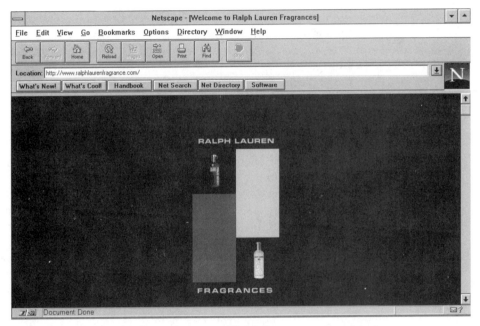

Figure 5.33 Animation reinforces the image of Ralph Lauren over the content.

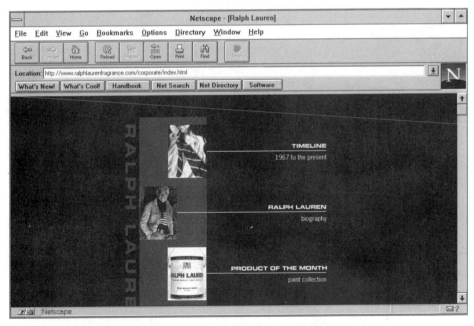

Figure 5.34 The menu page with the first commercial connection.

men's clothing, perhaps more characteristic of what consumers expect from the company but confused (maybe discolored) this consistent message with paint. This was so unexpected that you really need to view the paint page as shown in Figure 5.35.

The next screen (Figure 5.36) shows available retailing sites where I could acquire the paint. Since I am based in Miami, this presentation is not only the wrong listing, but it also does not use the power of interactive websites to any advantage. First, it is unlikely that on a trip to New York City I would buy several gallon cans of paint and carry them home on an airplane. Second, a simple query about my location can generate the closest *local* store within 20 or 30 miles, a commerce order screen, phone number, E-mail address, or a mail order form to order shipment to my location via UPS. The information is out-of-synch with the reason for this website and it does not simplify the sales channel or really expand in a useful way like Lands' End and L.L. Bean do.

Other tracks on the Lauren website try to catch the "Beverly Hills 90210" or "Melrose Place" cachet by including a serialized story about twenty-something customers captured in Figure 5.37. While this might match the demographics anticipated by Razorfish for web surfers and thus potential customers, the demographics for Ralph Lauren customers are represented predominantly by the over 60-year-old idle, married female with family assets over $670,000 and an annual income over $140,000. (Private and public domain research reports outline market segments and niches for various retailers and product lines).

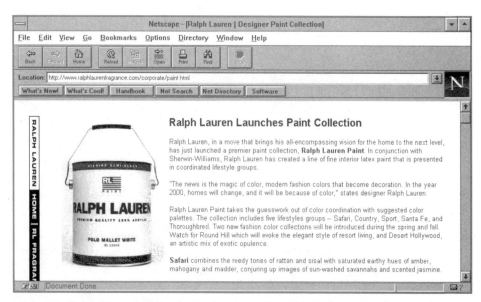

Figure 5.35 Ralph Lauren paint collection is not coordinated with the market demographics, consistency of the website, or clientele expectations.

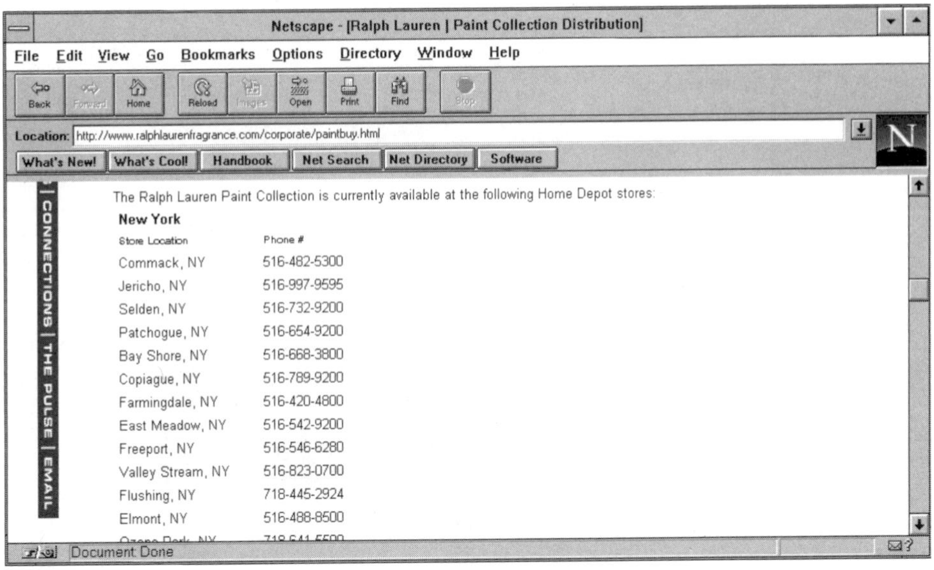

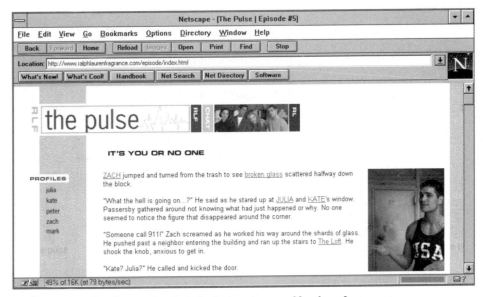

Figure 5.36 Commerce sites are physical retail locations.

The website message, the jumble, and the lack of fit to a customer base are not encouraging for the success of this site.

You can see in Figure 5.38 that the site does include a story-line cliff-hanger to attract surfers back to the site on a weekly basis. This is a nice technique if

Figure 5.37 Serialized story aimed at single, twenty-year-old web surfers.

Figure 5.38 The serialization includes a cliff-hanger to get people to come back.

the story is good, is exciting, is tantalizing like a good novel, and somehow works the Ralph Lauren concept into the story. The success of this site is something to watch and also how long the serial is continued.

L.L. Bean

The L.L. Bean website is true to the persistent mental picture of the catalog retailer and it includes functional cyberstore tools to create a truly new distribution channel for the organization. The order a customer creates online does not yet include credit card and other personal information and will not be able to until the organization solves the secure HTTP processing and resolves holes internally for parsing captured information directly into the onsite secure credit card processing systems. The presentation makes the most of a data-driven interface so that a customer can search for specific lines of items or a designated product. The home page shown in Figure 5.39 has an outdoor feel to it, reinforced by the signposts and the home page compass. By the way, the compass is an animated GIF89a file and the needle spins around.

The product menu retains the style but incorporates traditional hypertext links to detail pages (linked to the database) as shown in Figure 5.40. The achievement of this cyberstore is not so much that it integrates HTML and databases, but that it does so with panache. When you drill down through the sporting goods section to skating apparel, skates, and accessories, you get a nice view of the product line and how it works. Although most people who skate would already know about knee pads, the site shows and defines the products without being condescending to the customer; "Hey, these are our

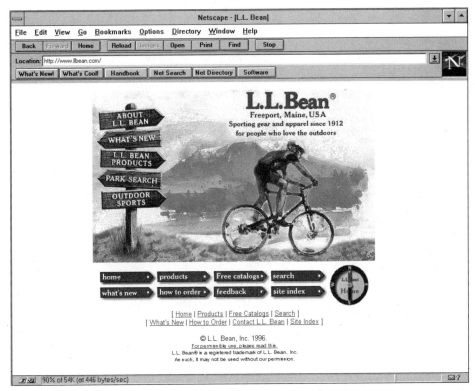

Figure 5.39 The L.L. Bean home page retains the folksy style of the printed catalog.

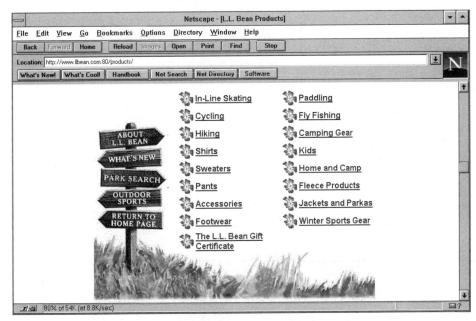

Figure 5.40 Product menu page with hypertext links to data-driven pages.

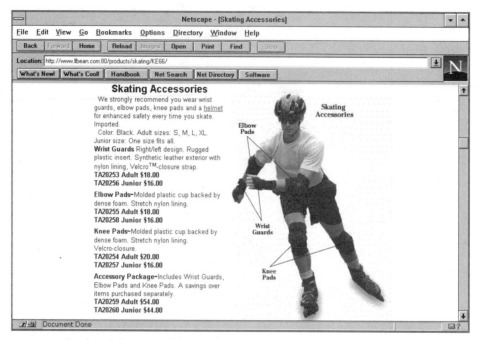

Figure 5.41   Product definition and display with a secondary message.

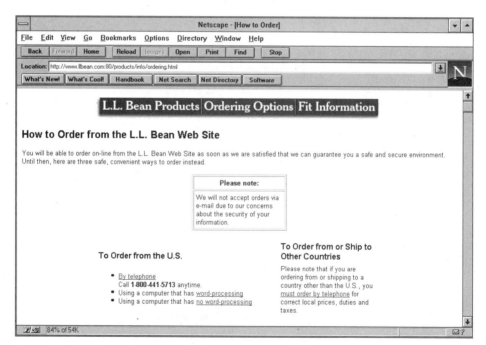

Figure 5.42   Ordering on-line is a multistep process not yet fully automated.

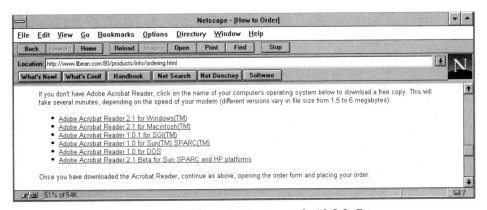

Figure 5.43 The order is computerized but not yet automated with L.L. Bean.

products" the web page says in Figure 5.41. The order is built as a form in Word for Windows or in an Adobe PDF form downloaded to the user's desktop. The form can be sent back by facsimile or called in and read to a telemarketing representative.

E-mail delivery is not available yet, but that represents the next integration effort for L.L. Bean, as shown by the ordering process screen in Figure 5.42. A customer can download the various order form formats, fill one out, and send it back by fax or mail, or phone it in to a telemarketing operator. The automation in the Word or PDF forms includes macros to handle special services such as sizes and monograms, color selections, and full generation of quantity extents, order subtotaling, shipping weight and costs, and local taxes. The forms are available in a wide range of platforms, as shown in the order form download screen in Figure 5.43.

Lands' End

Like L.L. Bean, Lands' End retains the image and ambience of its printed catalogs. The overall look is more high-tech, somewhat consistent with its leading edge view of product development and extreme outerwear. Like L.L. Bean, the home page shows a homey small town look that is out of character with the technical implementation of the site (see Figure 5.44). This website is fully integrated into databases, commercial payment processing, and automated order entry.

The same simple look persists throughout Lands' End, the cyberstore. It is very consistent and very clean, but somewhat confusing because there are so many levels that mask the database connectivity and separate product lines. The pages are generally long and scrolled and are slow to load, but they are simple and clean, as shown in Figure 5.45. The overstocks of men's clothing are listed at special prices. What isn't clear are the limits on sizes, colors, and availability of styles. Nevertheless, this use of web technology and database

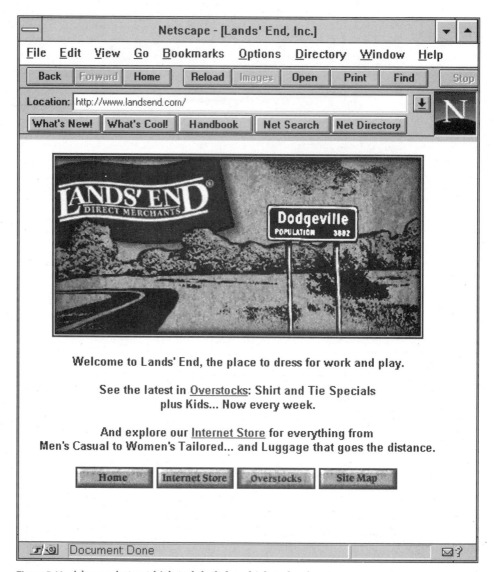

Figure 5.44 A homey but not high-tech look for a high-tech cyberstore.

integration show how so many manufacturers, resellers, and retailers with standard channels can move odds and ends without resorting to a broker or overstock specialist (Figure 5.46).

The next screen shot (Figure 5.47) shows the level of detail broken out on a "simple" product line. These web pages are crafted by hand and connect to secondary hand-crafted pages that actually have the database linkage. The layers are disconcerting, but ultimately fairly simple to navigate.

The page captured in Figure 5.48 is constructed directly from the database when the inventory quantity is greater than zero. Note that the availability is

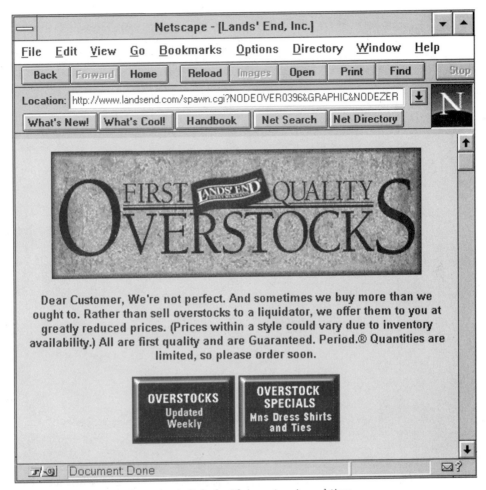

Figure 5.45 The overstock section is linked with inventory in real time.

limited to 14(H)32, 15(H)32, and 16(H)36 sizes. Unfortunately, the next screen indicates that it is available only in the lavender color. Consider how you might indicate color and size availability with a two-dimensional HTML table and allow the user to specify quantity in it. One axis would indicate standard shirt sizes and the other, colors. The table (or matrix) is likely to be sparse or become sparse as product is drawn down from final closeout inventory and perhaps a better layout is simply to specify the combinations available in a hypertext list.

The next screen shot (Figure 5.49) shows the inventory limitation of the Men's Regular Button-down Triple Track Pinpoint shirt in size 14(H)32 in the sapphire color. The markdown is shown at $15.00. Before drilling down to this detail, I would have preferred more price and availability information displayed sooner so that the user can make an informed decision at an earlier step in this multilayered selection process. For example, $19.50 may be just too much to pay for a blue dress shirt when most people wear white dress shirts.

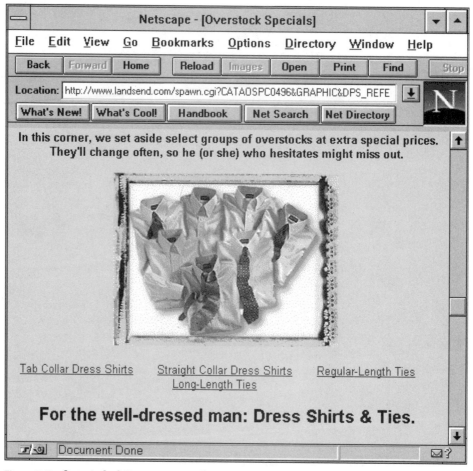

Figure 5.46 Overstocked items generate better returns when categorized and separated than when dumped on an overstock broker.

Figure 5.50 shows the data entry form for this particular shirt. The form is standard HTML with drop-down list boxes and regular fields (limited to one character for monograms) and it interconnects to the Lands' End order database.

Figure 5.51 shows the HTML code for this order form. It is not complex or overly difficult to build a form like this by hand. It is even simpler with some of the newer HTML editors that include wizards. The data-driven report of the customer's order is shown in Figure 5.52.

Because HTTP and HTML are stateless, order information must be saved somewhere for multiple-screen orders and complex processes. The data entered in one web page is not saved anywhere when other pages are requested, so order information must be explicitly stored on the client's system or at the

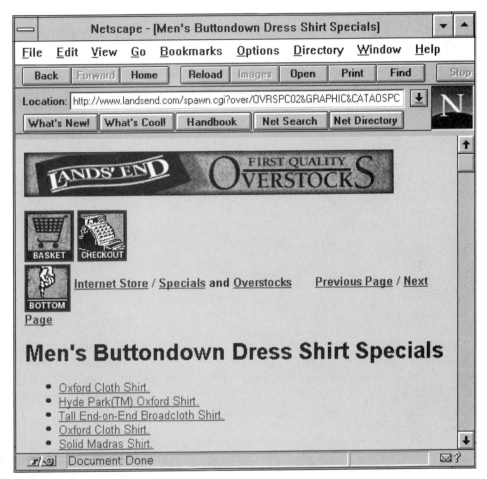

Figure 5.47   Layers corresponding to database and product differentiation.

cyberstore. I prefer saving even partial or aborted orders at the cyberstore because lost orders represent an opportunity for direct mail, a callback, and other lead generation. The Cookies file is really an insecure and weak method to track orders and save information, and the browser environment simply does not have enough space to save all the data defining a line item in a typical order. Instead, the data must be stored in a special database (on the server at the cyberstore). This mechanism is called the *shopping cart,* and it works logically and analogously for shoppers, as shown in Figure 5.53.

The generated report on this line item entry comes from the database but the code to display the information is still standard, simple HTML markup, as shown in Figure 5.54. Everything boils down to HTML, or complex Java, Perl, CGI, JavaScript, VBScript, or ActiveX scripts. HTML is simpler and less prone to security lapses, and is a faster performance mechanism.

Figure 5.48   Closeout inventory of selected shirts.

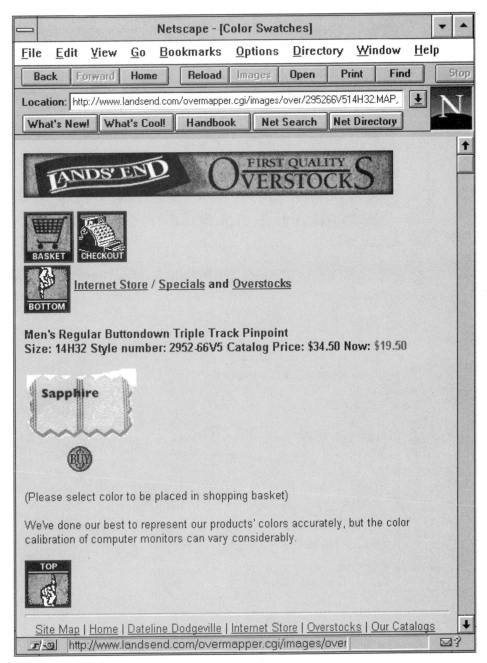

Figure 5.49 The price is finally listed for this special item.

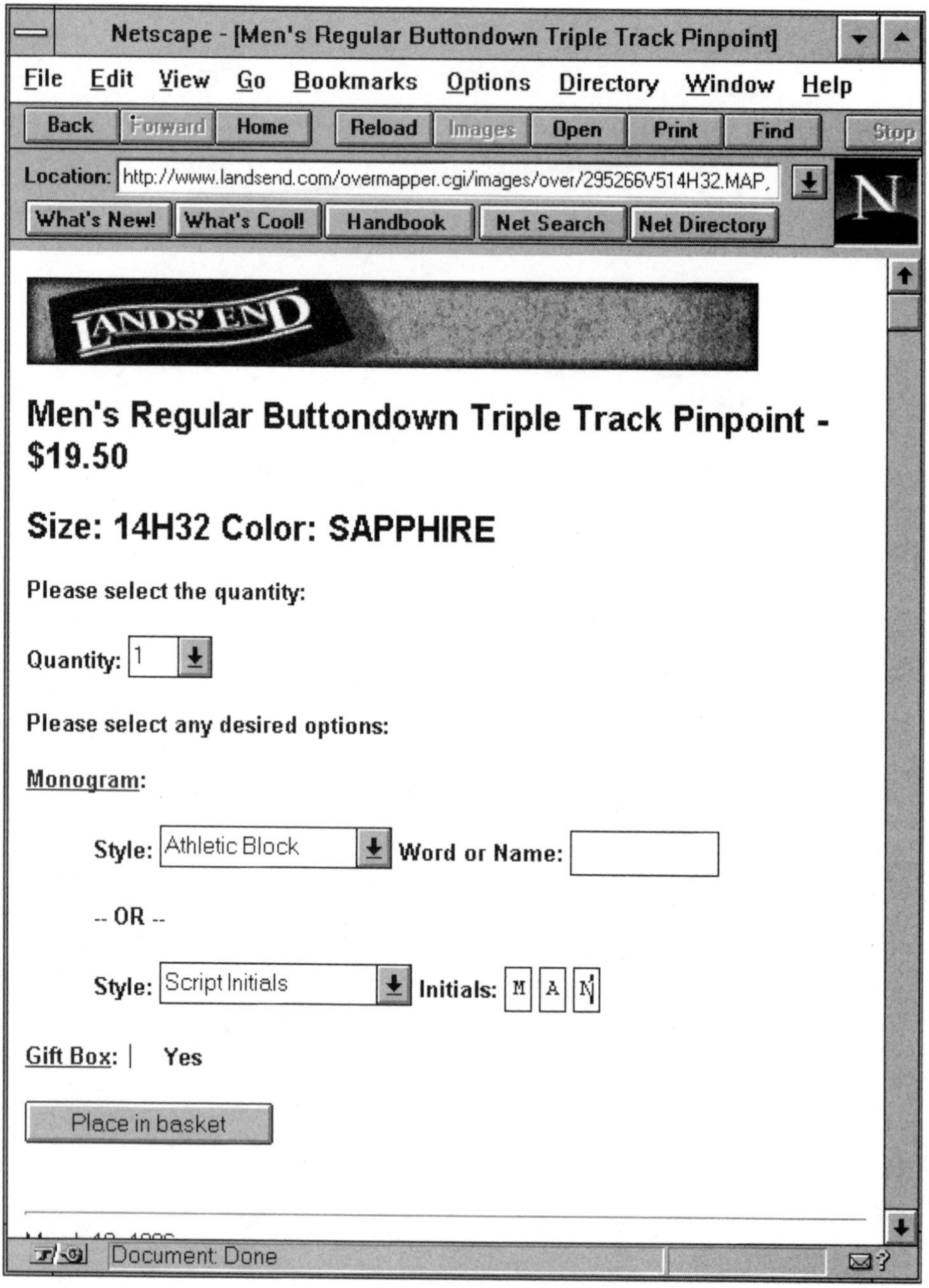

Figure 5.50 The (generic-styled) order for a closeout item.

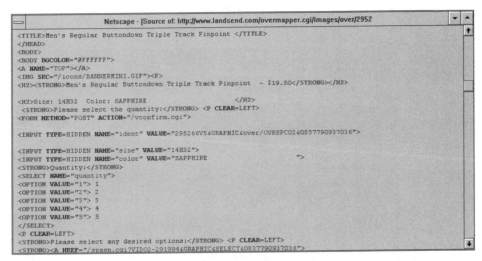

```
Netscape - [Source of: http://www.landsend.com/overmapper.cgi/images/over/2952

<TITLE>Men's Regular Buttondown Triple Track Pinpoint </TITLE>
</HEAD>
<BODY>
<BODY BGCOLOR="#FFFFFF">
<A NAME="TOP"></A>
<IMG SRC="/icons/BANNERMINI.GIF"><P>
<H2><STRONG>Men's Regular Buttondown Triple Track Pinpoint  - $19.50</STRONG></H2>

<H2>Site: 14H32  Color: SAPPHIRE                        </H2>
 <STRONG>Please select the quantity:</STRONG> <P CLEAR=LEFT>
<FORM METHOD="POST" ACTION="/vconfirm.cgi">

<INPUT TYPE=HIDDEN NAME="ident" VALUE="295266V5&GRAPHIC&over/OVRSPC02&0837790937036">

<INPUT TYPE=HIDDEN NAME="size" VALUE="14H32">
<INPUT TYPE=HIDDEN NAME="color" VALUE="SAPPHIRE                        ">
<STRONG>Quantity:</STRONG>
<SELECT NAME="quantity">
<OPTION VALUE="1"> 1
<OPTION VALUE="2"> 2
<OPTION VALUE="3"> 3
<OPTION VALUE="4"> 4
<OPTION VALUE="5"> 5
</SELECT>
<P CLEAR=LEFT>
<STRONG>Please select any desired options:</STRONG> <P CLEAR=LEFT>
<STRONG><A HREF="/spawn.cgi?VID02-291994&GRAPHIC&SELECT&0837790937036">
```

Figure 5.51 The HTML code required for activating the order form.

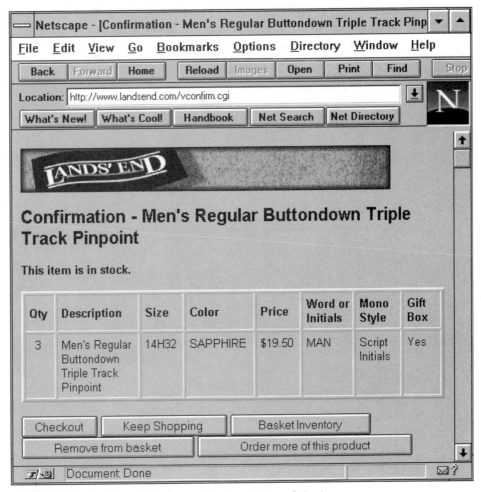

Figure 5.52 Confirmation of the closeout shirt order (in real time).

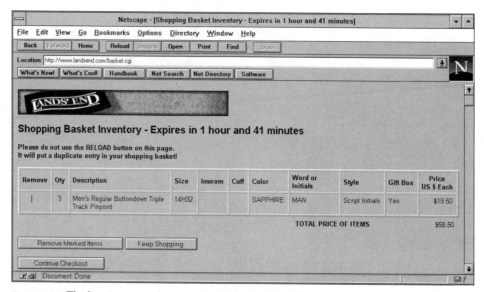

Figure 5.53 The line item must be stored as the order is built because web pages are stateless and the information in the forms is lost as other pages are loaded.

A standard in-stock cataloged product is accessible from its product line home pages, as shown in Figure 5.55. Again, the levels are fairly deep, unlike the Riva Yamaha site, and can be confusing.

The swimwear category includes a gratuitous level of depth (that means another layer of intermediate web pages) before you get to the actual products, as shown in Figure 5.56. Instead, a better approach for this site might be to

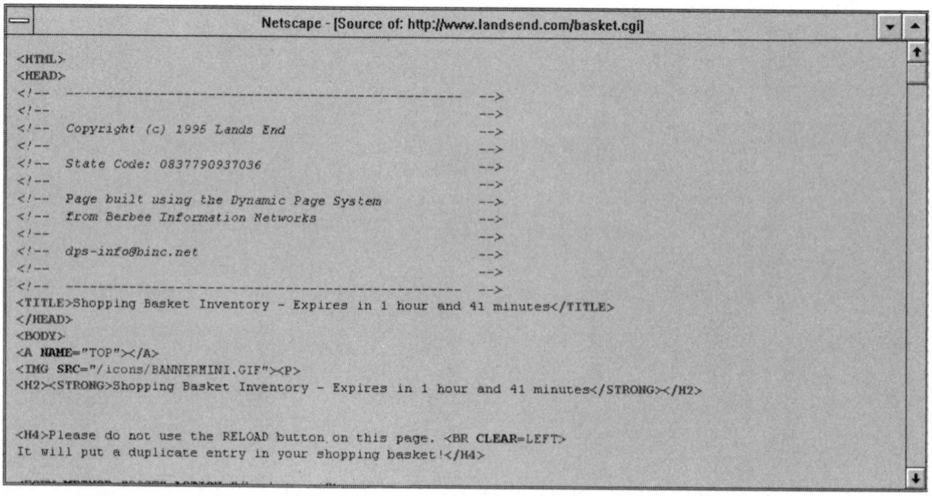

```
Netscape - [Source of: http://www.landsend.com/basket.cgi]
<HTML>
<HEAD>
<!-- ------------------------------------------------- -->
<!--                                                    -->
<!--    Copyright (c) 1996 Lands End                    -->
<!--                                                    -->
<!--    State Code: 0837790937036                       -->
<!--                                                    -->
<!--    Page built using the Dynamic Page System        -->
<!--    from Berbee Information Networks                -->
<!--                                                    -->
<!--    dps-info@binc.net                               -->
<!--                                                    -->
<!-- ------------------------------------------------- -->
<TITLE>Shopping Basket Inventory - Expires in 1 hour and 41 minutes</TITLE>
</HEAD>
<BODY>
<A NAME="TOP"></A>
<IMG SRC="/icons/BANNERMINI.GIF"><P>
<H2><STRONG>Shopping Basket Inventory - Expires in 1 hour and 41 minutes</STRONG></H2>

<H4>Please do not use the RELOAD button on this page. <BR CLEAR=LEFT>
It will put a duplicate entry in your shopping basket!</H4>
```

Figure 5.54 Report code from the database is standard HTML.

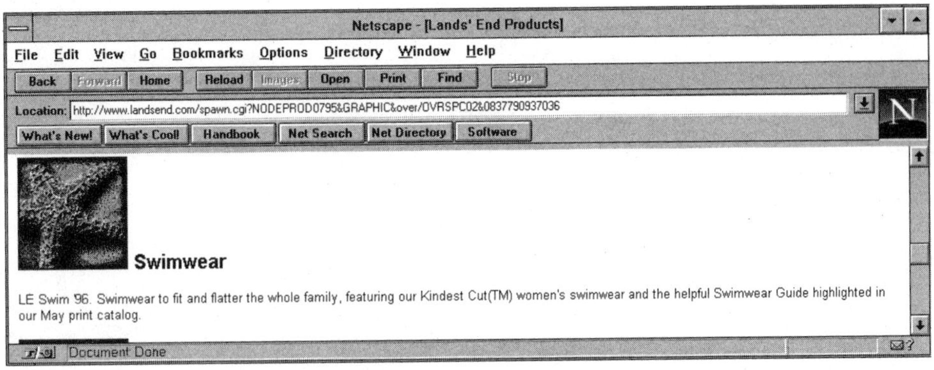

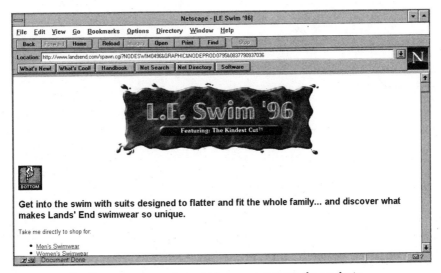

Figure 5.55 A first-line layer to reach a product.

have a swimwear page, and then show a hierarchical list as images with hotspots or as a list of lines such as:

- Men's
  Full-cut
  Cotton
  Bikini/brief

- Women's
  Bikini
  Two-piece
  Spandex
  Insta-dry

Figure 5.56 Another unnecessary layer before a user gets to the products.

This list, whether as text or bullets, images, or a Windows-style Explorer hierarchy, would simplify navigation through the site. Ultimately, however, the user still gets to a product page, like the one for the shirts closeout.

The database integration includes the items ordered, provides the extent processing (3 shirts at $19.50 apiece), and includes taxes, shipping, and the special services order for the shirts (shown in Figure 5.57). This processing is critical because when Internet processes get automated (and especially when programmed with Java or CGI), these details can be lost in the complexity of the project and generate significant revenue losses before they are discovered. Recall from Chapter 2 my assertion that complex sites should integrate into standard financial and accounting systems to minimize the in-house manual coding as well as billing and shipping problems.

Lands' End includes standard on-line security through the Netscape SSL functions shown in Figure 5.58. The order can actually be submitted via the Internet (as either a series of database master/detail records or as a flat E-mail submission). I prefer direct integration to the database because it can become a significant process to either rekey the order once it has been received (the customer already keyed it), or a complex decode of the order invoice into its hierarchical constituents. For example, the order becomes an order number with a link to the customer and a potential separate link for

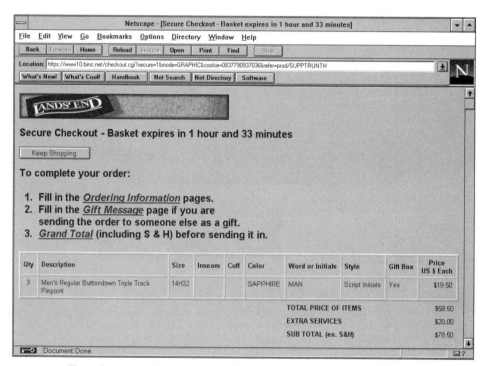

Figure 5.57 The order invoice form as generated.

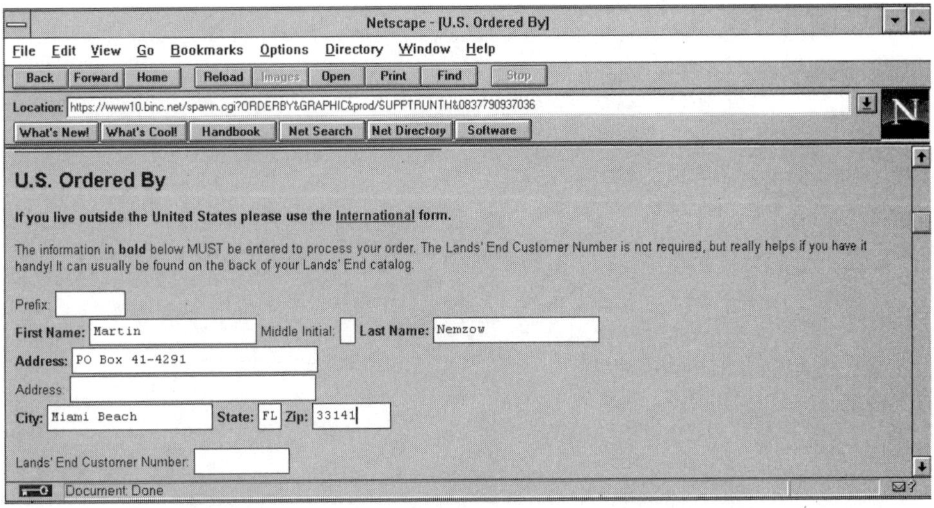

Figure 5.58 Secure transmission of order, customer information, and payment by credit card with automated clearinghouse authorization.

shipping (gifts are typically shipped somewhere else), and entries for each line item.

Pacific Coast

While the cyberstore is the brightest light to attract the retail moths, recognize that the demographics of the typical on-line shopper will be upscale and educated for some time to come. As some of the statistics in Chapter 2 and generally throughout this book have relayed, Internet access is concentrated primarily in North America, but is rapidly growing throughout Europe and in the more prosperous areas of Asia. Success means targeting the audience both in terms of the product or service that meshes with that market and also with cyberstore presentations that complement the audience. Pacific Coast is an upscale retailer focusing on nonutilitarian product. It is a lifestyle company. Its home page is shown in Figure 5.59.

Pacific Coast enables the cyberstore shopping cart approach, as shown in Figure 5.60. The object is shown both by a full-color image and by attractive advertising text above the scrolling window. My suggestions for this page and similar on-line products include condensing the page so that product image, description, and the ordering fields fit even on a small screen.

Shopping cart, shopping basket, or market basket—the terms are interchangeable—selection allows for multiple size selection. This site does not embody full HTML data entry form-to-database integration as shown by the CGI code if you look at the source behind the HTML page; however, this order form does show the value in tracking customer preferences. If a customer is ordering twin or double size bed products and you can ascertain her marital status

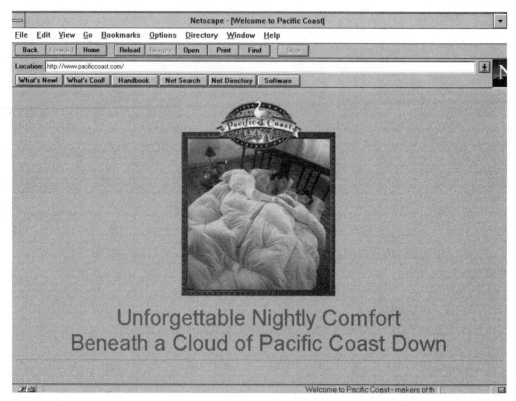

Figure 5.59   The home page for Pacific Coast's lifestyle advertising.

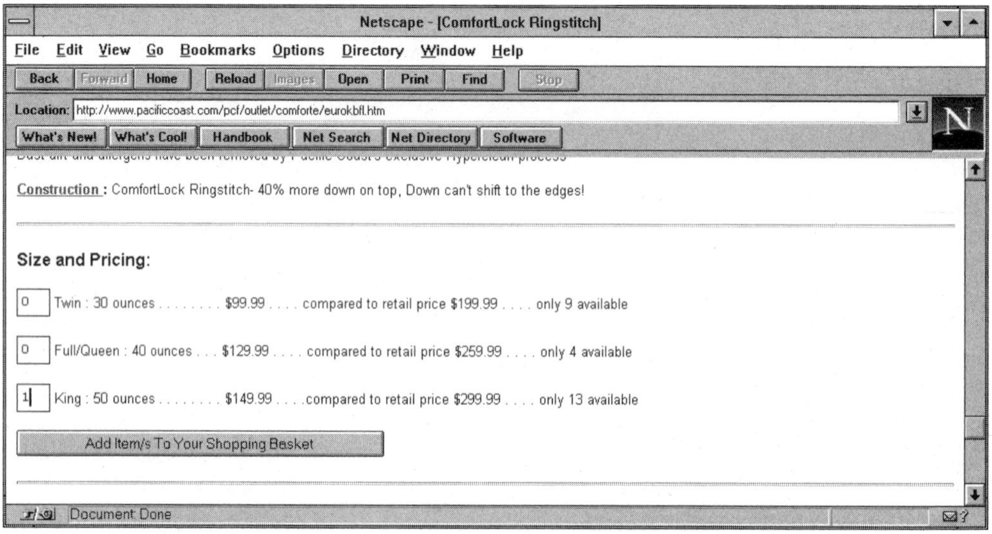

Figure 5.60   Home page profiled product (akin to the main aisle end cap) on-line shopping cart.

or age, you can then target the customer after marriage, as the children wreck comforters or outgrow baby motifs. If you realize that a customer is buying products for children, you can target her for down comforter covers, washing machine mesh bags, and related products. Each industry has discovered different follow-up on buying patterns so that an immediate suggestion may not be as effective as mailing brochures, E-mail, or a call two or three days later. Figure 5.61 shows my selection of a king-size comforter. A clever sales analysis might infer that I have graduated from being married without children and sleeping in a double or queen-size bed, to being married with small children who climb into my bed in the middle of the night. This necessitates a transition to a larger bed to accommodate everyone—an expensive event when you factor in new furniture, new sheets, new pillows, and larger blankets. Since bedding is expensive, a mailing of information about new sheet sets timed to correlate with a second or third sudden washing of the bedding might reach a receptive consumer. A clever sales analysis might also suggest a need for mattress pads, waterproof liners, or similar bedding sets in child designs to encourage the children to stay in their own beds. Although these inferences could be wrong, a lot of personal information can be bought from secondary databases and correlated with in-house data. For example, age, marital status, household size, and lifestyle information is available from many lists. Even if these inferences are wrong 50 percent of the time, you are still making a cogent sales follow-up the other 50 percent of the time. This represents a higher success ratio than waiting for customers to come back on their own accord for repeat purchases.

Because the hyperlink represents a new form in cross-selling and advertising, many organizations with cyberstores will want to cross-advertise with

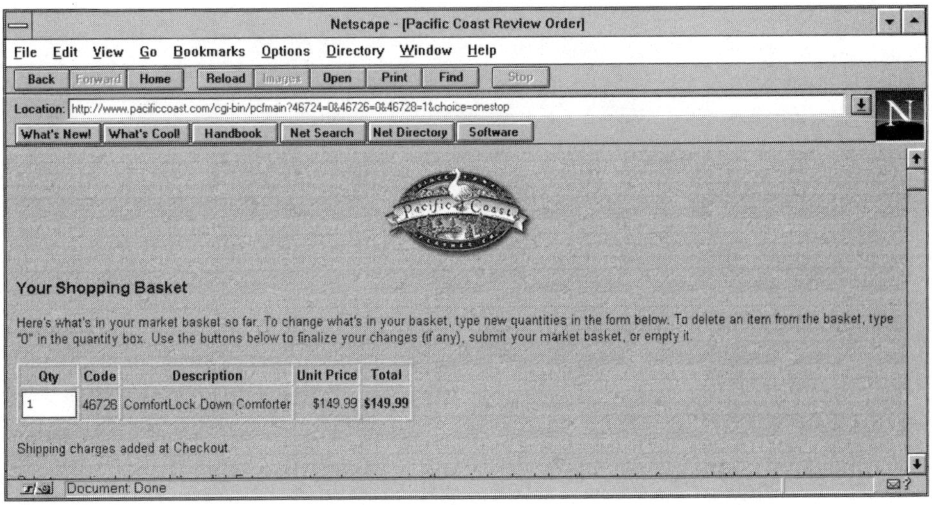

Figure 5.61 Customer shopping basket selection of a new comforter could simply be a request for something new or could signify lifestyle changes.

other organizations that do not directly compete with them. I do not think Pacific Coast would want to sell customer lists to Domestications or Fingerhut (both are competitors) or link to these websites because that would tend to erode their customer base; they might, however, want to create links with Ikea (a maker of Danish-style furniture) or Simmons Beautyrest (a maker of mattresses). Competitors that sold strictly on price might want to create cross-linked sites for comparison purposes, but I suspect ultimately that the price competition will undermine the product lines so that each vendor sells complementary, rather than competing, product lines. Figure 5.62 shows just how far Pacific Coast will go to encourage hyperlinks between related sites by swapping merchandise for advertising space.

Unlike most other first-generation cyberstores, Pacific Coast includes a search engine at their site so that customers can look for specific products and merchandise. Although cybershops such as the AMP or National Semiconductor sites are driven by databases and search engines, cybershops with limited lines initially might not need or want the overhead of data-driven HTML forms. Every product could be represented by separate HTML pages linked with various master pages. For example, in the case of Pacific Coast, there could be a track for bedding, a track for warm and soft products, and a track for kid's accessories, each of which could include the same HTML pages. Obviously, different customers would reach the same pages by different routes. The search engine, as shown in Figure 5.63, provides a quick route to bypass the intermediate product-line pages.

The metaphor of the on-line shopping cart is extended with the "checkout" process. Figure 5.64 shows the shopping cart with the king-size comforter. This step adds in local sales taxes, shipping charges, and any special services, such as embossing or embroidery of initials.

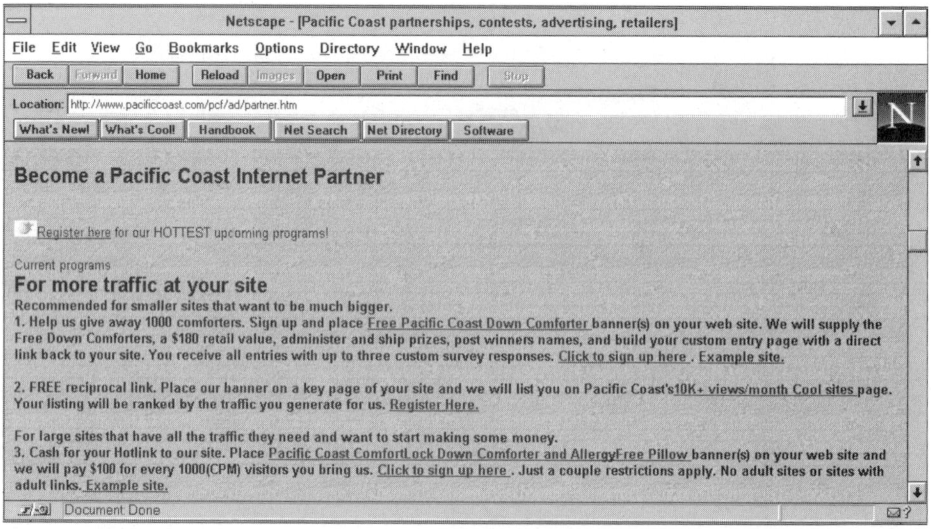

Figure 5.62 Pacific Coast encourages links to its sites with free merchandise.

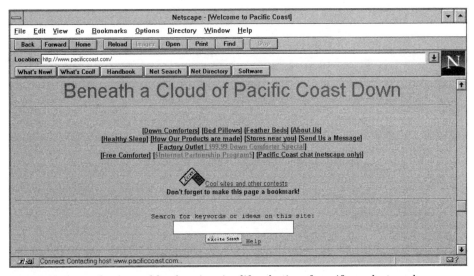

Figure 5.63 A search page and local engine simplify selection of specific products and encourage repeat buying.

The transaction is concluded with credit card payment, as shown in Figure 5.65. Because the risk of credit information is low even now, Pacific Coast accepts this information as part of the unsecured transaction process. The suggestion that the purchase information be split over multiple E-mail messages to enhance security is ridiculous because the delivery mechanism is the same. If a hacker can capture name and address information from one packet, he can

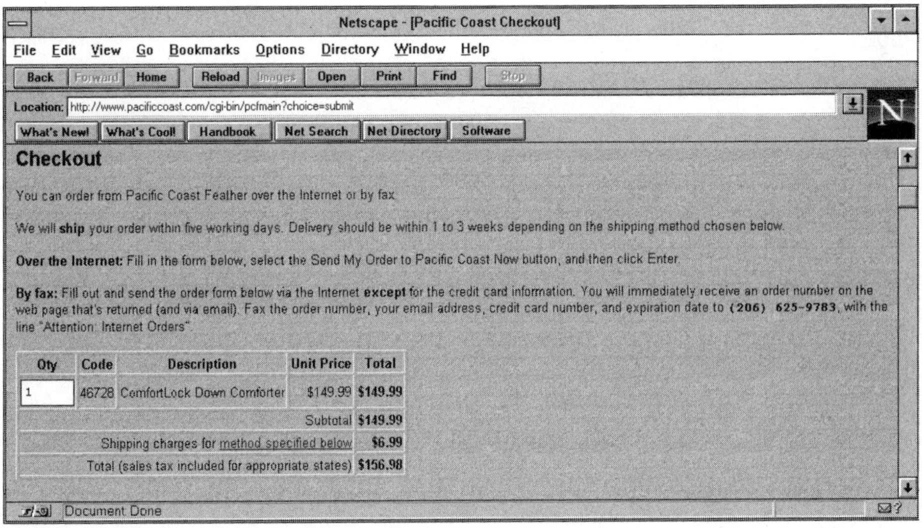

Figure 5.64 The checkout process includes a tally of the contents (here only one item) of the shopping cart, addition of local taxes or fees, shipping charges, and any other special services.

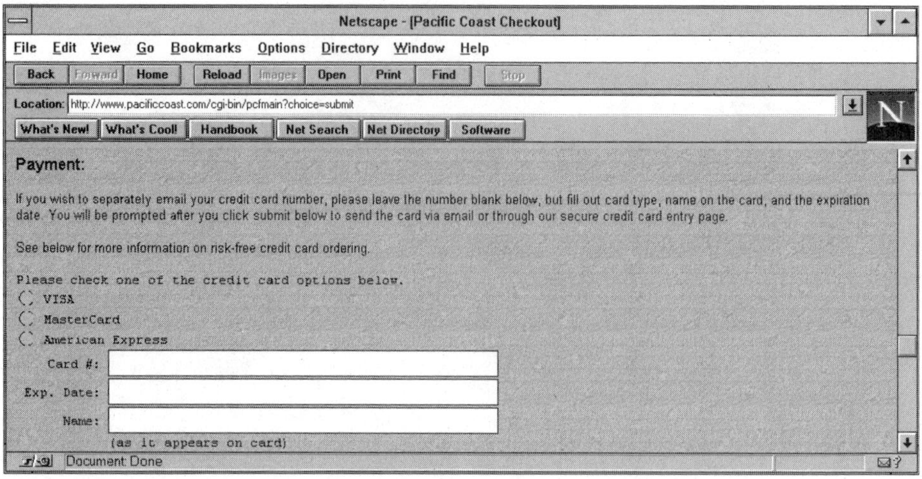

Figure 5.65   Pacific Coast is operating under the assumption that credit information is difficult to steal, although this transaction completion page provides alternatives for skittish consumers (such as fax, phone call, or separate E-mail). Notice the broken key in lower left signifying an unsecured delivery.

also locate and match up the credit information from another E-mail packet. The real risk is legal, because the presumption is that the vendor is responsible for transactional security. The clearinghouse and the customer's credit card issuer assume some of the risk, but excessive losses will eventually be posted to you, the cyberstore merchant. Therefore, enable the SLL CGI code for secure transactions. It really is simple. You simply need to code a template once and modify it for reuse as needed.

PayChex

Some sites are informational and promotional only. That means their purpose is to provide information and content to web surfers and so impress them that they will want to come back for more, will want to investigate the products or services offered by the organization, or will want to try the demos. PayChex provides payroll and financial services to small and large companies, as its home page shows in Figure 5.66.

Since this site contains an extraordinary amount of usable content, it is indexed locally with the Excite search engine, as shown in Figure 5.67. While it might be necessary for this site to index the literature, it also provides a means to flatten the number of levels and simplify navigation. The site also suggests to the user that it must be important enough and have enough information on it to warrant the use of the search engine. That is a powerful subliminal message. The search turned up more than a page of interesting documents relating to contractor tax status. Some of them refer to Paychex services, while many are informational and not clearly promotional, as the list in Figure 5.68 shows.

Figure 5.66 Content- and promotional-only home site for Paychex.

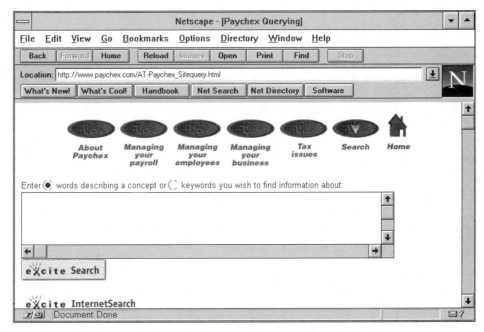

Figure 5.67 This site must be important because it has a search engine!

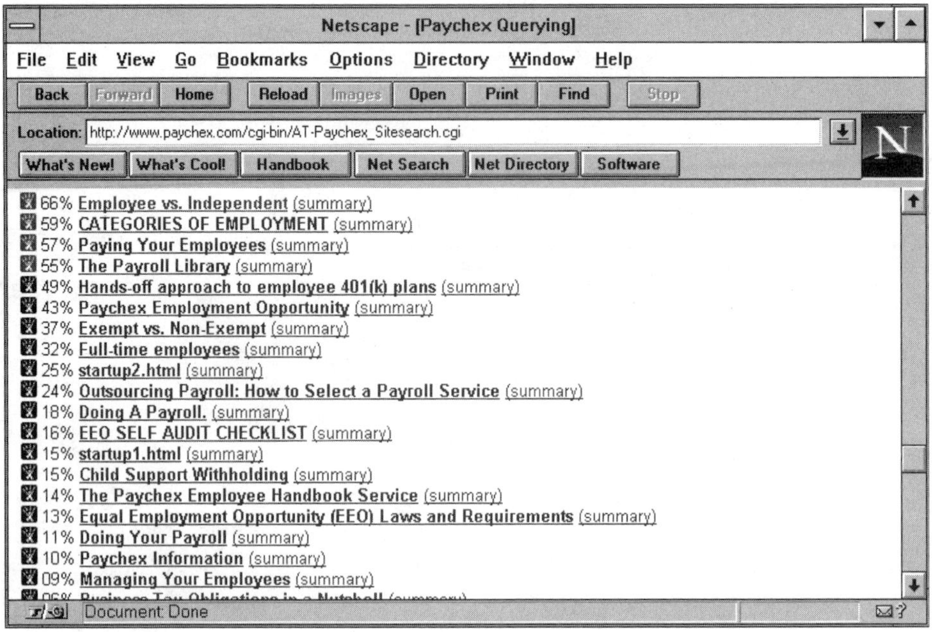

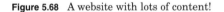

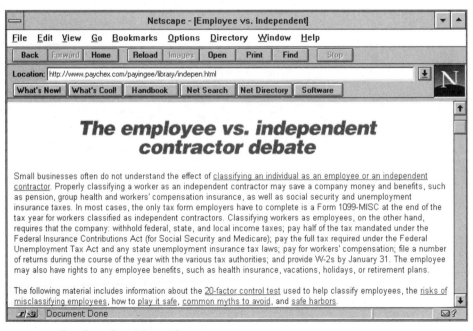

Figure 5.68   A website with lots of content!

Figure 5.69   Low-key advertising with content.

The extraction, *Employees vs. Independent,* defines how to determine if a person providing services to an organization is appropriately defined as an employee or an independent contractor without the overhead and tax and vacation responsibilities owed to employees. This is shown in Figure 5.69. Notice the soft sell approach to these complex issues and services. Paychex is suggesting that it is a valuable outsource provider for tough problems and processes, without listing advertising services in an obviously transparent manner.

Florida Division of Elections

The motor-voter laws the U.S. Congress passed several years ago have lit a technology fire under the bureaucracies in many states. In fact, Florida now allows people to register to vote using the Internet. In step with the philosophy of this book, the registration site provides lower costs per transaction using fewer employees within an organization of diminishing budgets and increasing workloads.

This site is not a cyberstore by any stretch of the imagination, but it is a database-enabled, transaction-processing site. It does not provide secure transactions (but it should, given the privacy of some of the information required for voter registration). However, this site does provide information and promotional content, and automates transactions. Because the voter information does require an oath and a signature on an official form, the on-line process is really the first step in the paperwork work flow to generate the official form in the process of becoming a registered voter. The flow is consistent with the process for Lands' End or Riva Yamaha, but the transaction purpose is different. Figure 5.70 shows the Division of Elections home page.

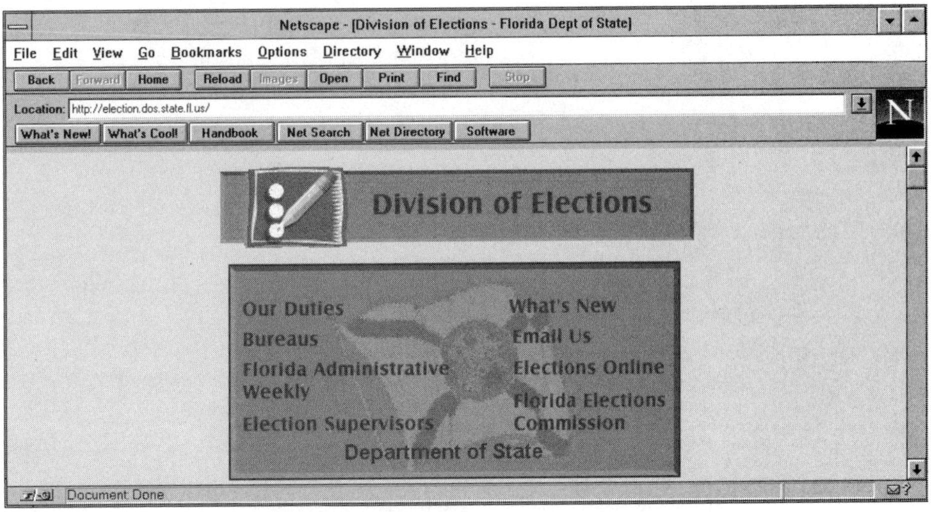

Figure 5.70 Florida Division of Elections home page.

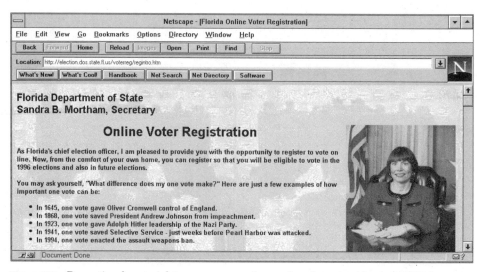

Figure 5.71 Promotional material to encourage voting and perhaps to enhance political reputations as well.

The promotional value of this site is in the explanation of the value of a single vote and the use of other patriotic statements to encourage voter registration, as illustrated in the screen shot in Figure 5.71. Politically jaundiced people could see this site as political advertising, as promotion of a governmental agency, as a trial of survey technology, or as research and development of new technologies. I see their point, but I also realize that government has similar work flows and communication needs that can be implemented with less costly technology and decreased per-transaction costs. The voter registration form itself is shown in Figure 5.72. It is similar in design to any order entry or credit card submission form. The information should be posted to relational databases for follow-up, tracking, and consolidation, or for any future marketing (as the commercial cyberstore should also be doing). SHTTP would also make the encrypted E-mail delivery secure. Supplemental rules, requirements, and responsibilities preface the actual delivery of the voter registration application, shown in Figure 5.73.

Other Transactional Sites

The paradigm for the cyberstore as an on-line catalog with credit sales or a supplement to traditional channels does not fully define the value of interactive and dynamic web services. In fact, this section shows other uses for cyberstore and database integration with web technology. IBM has acquired a number of small companies with unique technologies to build its version of the cyberstore. It has called this effort the InfoMarket and it integrates on-line product and service sales, pay-per-view access to information, news services, and a secondary pay-per-view information delivery service with a life of its own. The (free) news ticker service is shown in Figure 5.74.

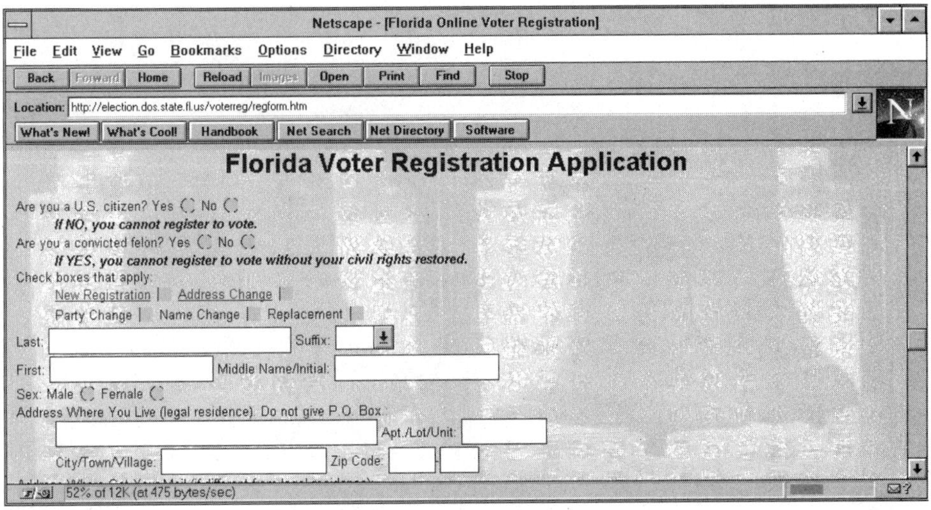

Figure 5.72 The actual voter registration application.

The other aspects of InfoMarket are really no different from cybermalls, cyberstores, and manufacturers' on-line company warehouses. However, the Cryptolopes delivery system is a unique concept. Basically, Cryptolopes is an encrypted package of information, software, or other byte-presentable product. The contents are protected and supposedly secure from all attacks. The package also contains several layers of content description. This package is not only freely transportable, but can be passed along to other sites and users; in fact, customers are encouraged to pass the package along. The key to

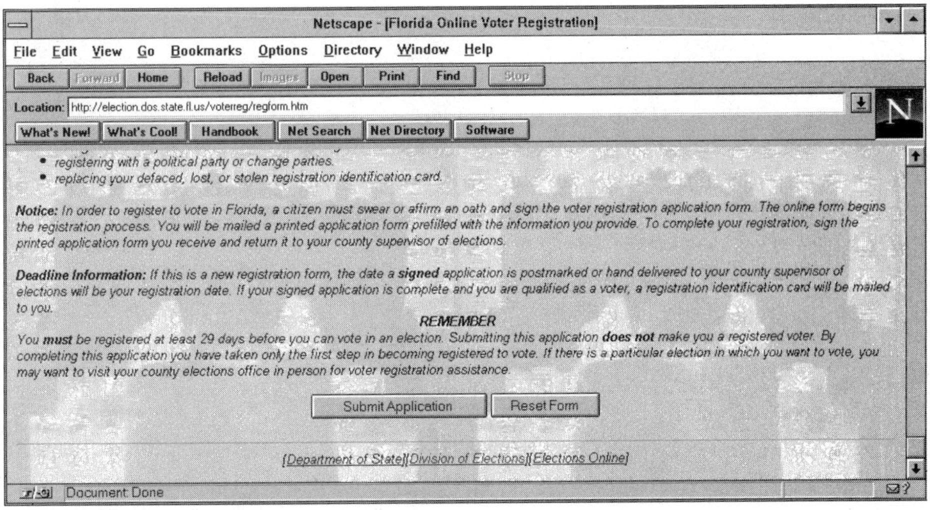

Figure 5.73 Supplemental reminders, eligibility, and rules for the process.

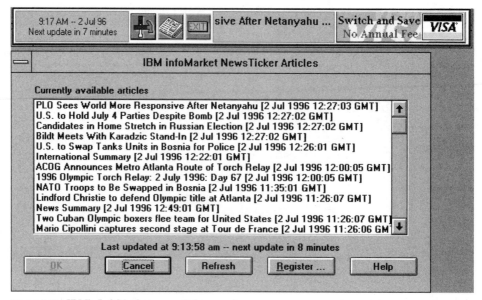

Figure 5.74 IBM's InfoMarket news ticker service.

opening the package is a credit card. Payment authorization is built into the Cryptolopes system so that any Internet-enabled computer can dial into Info-Market, pay for the privilege of opening the Cryptolopes, receive the key to de-crypt, and access the contents within. The Cryptolopes is like an encrypted zip file with a payment engine attached. You get the contents with the correct key and the package is still there to pass along and sell again for the benefit of InfoMarket and the content vendor.

Many products and services are differentiated by information content. Al-though both UPS and Federal Express have provided labeling and tracking software with BBS access, Federal Express is the first to move to the uniform network and connection channel afforded by the Internet. Since most users have local (not long-distance) access to the Internet, this becomes a simpler and less costly mechanism for tracking the status and location of time-critical documents and products. Since the process is web-enabled, cyberstores pro-viding their own credit card processing and fulfillment, including the ship-ment scheduling, can be automated directly. The FedEx shipping and tracking software is shown in Figure 5.75.

Municipalities like to promote themselves in order to increase tax bases, en-tice more tourists, and increase their revenues from dining out, social and sporting events, and gambling. Since so many things occur in a city at the same time and scheduling is likely to be planned for years in advance, the best websites include database enablement and, perhaps more importantly, tools that winnow out old news and outdated information. A number of database-enabled sites exist. For instance, Boston hosts a site that interconnects cur-

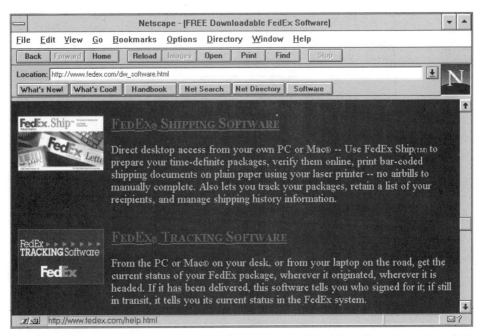

Figure 5.75 FedEx provides free Internet-enabled shipping and tracking software to promote their service and simplify the process.

rent news and events and sales of homes and automobiles, and also provides commuting information. Special notes and audiovisuals (now often called "multimedia") highlight what the convention bureau deems is the most important, as shown by Figure 5.76.

Lincoln, Nebraska takes a different approach and presumes surfers know when and why they are coming to town. The Lincoln Visitor attractions and lodging site provides a data-driven tool to find the closest or otherwise "best" hotel for visitors and also points out events and attractions of local interest for families in town for a convention. This is shown in Figure 5.77.

The Lincoln site demonstrates cooperative advertising and marketing at its best for an entire industry. In addition, it uses the organizational capabilities of the Internet and data processing effectively. This system can be more effective than a person who makes travel arrangements all day, even a worker for the city of Lincoln, because the computer does not overlook a single site, location, or attraction. Since reservations are date driven, the effectiveness of making reservations and issuing confirmations is subject to the overall accuracy and timeliness of room space. That may be the one limitation of this system, unless all the area services band together to pool information and maintain its currency. National chains, such as Marriott, Holiday Inn, and Sheraton, have their own room reservation systems, some of which are even

Figure 5.76 Copious links, current events, and regional hotspots.

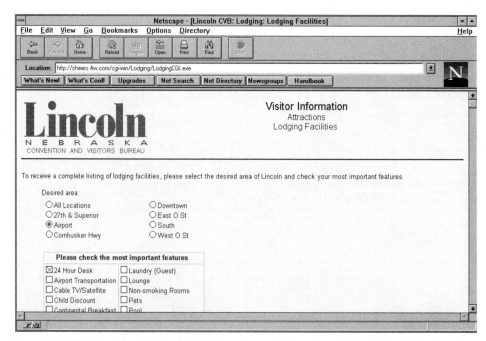

Figure 5.77 The Lincoln website queries visitors for special needs, matches them with information in the database, and can even make the reservations.

available through the Internet, which may preclude integrating them with local visitor bureau services.

The Site Makeover

This section describes the process of redesigning a website, in this case one that was designed and implemented by the legal counsel for a nonprofit organization called the Aleph Institute that provides legal and support services for inmates and service personnel in the military. This is not a commercial site like an on-line cybermall—the business for the site is solemn. It provides concise legal and social information from experts unavailable elsewhere. The main reasons Aleph is included here are twofold. First, it was a convenient makeover site at the time of writing and there were no copyright infringement issues. Second, and most importantly, the Aleph Institute needed to integrate financial transaction processing into the site, akin to any cyberstore. You might note the lack of any need for a shopping cart at this time. However, data collection and integration are a more significant part of the workflow for LISTSERV and automated mailings than might be found in most cybershops. In addition, there were other serious security issues that needed to be implemented through STTP. The ability to consummate on-line financial transactions becomes a new channel for fund-raising with on-line credit card processing.

Two things set this site apart from many others. First, there is a very good start to this site and it is not built completely from nothing. Second, none of the participants have time to waste in redesigning this site, so that it has to be done quickly, thoughtfully, and with very limited resources. The total time allocated to this makeover exhibit includes:

- 1 hour for initial strategy and design meeting
- 1 hour for site design hierarchy and master template
- 2 hours for executive director (who is quasi-technical, but computer literate) to pour text and pictures into subordinate pages and assess designs
- 1 hour for building E-mail and credit card forms for secure transactions
- 1 hour for CGI integration and FTP file uploading to site
- 1 to 2 hours for post-mortem review with minor adjustments

The total makeover time for this site is anticipated and budgeted for less than ten hours of labor. This includes host integration, SSL (for SHTTP) forms, one new home page design, and about 30 to 40 subordinate pages. This represents a one-day project. Let us start with a look at the "before" view. The initial home page in Figure 5.78 shows a very stern site. Step back a few feet from the page and you might think that this was the FBI site or some gloomy government agency. This tone might be right, however, because the Aleph Institute helps people overcome obstacles with gloomy groups like penal systems and the army.

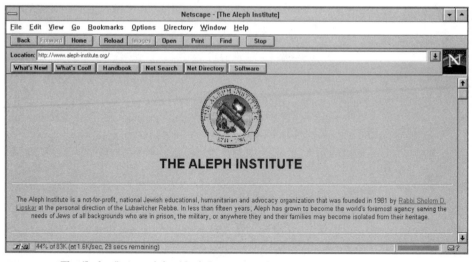

Figure 5.78   The "before" view of the Aleph Institute website.

The makeover began with a strategic meeting with Isaac Jaraslowics, executive director for the organization. The main points of the meeting were to address the problems with the site as currently implemented, to add secure status for several pages to access donations by credit card, to create a logical hierarchy of information, and to add a map of the site as an integral component for navigation purposes. In addition, the strategy of the session was to determine an image and character for the site. One important design criterion is to create nonscrolling pages of consistent shape as part of the character for this site. I surfed with Mr. Jaraslowics to some sites that he liked. We discussed the formats and messages, and how those ideas would mesh with his hope for a new site. After that, we discussed key topics that were required on the new site and then created an outline. The bottom line was that I would create a master page template and outline the structure of the site for him. He would then pour the images and texts (from WordPerfect) into the individual pages.

The scan of my notebook in Figure 5.79 shows some of the tactical issues that needed to be factored into the redeployment of the new home page. Development, organization, and management are low on the list of priorities of software developers. However, it really is easier to organize the site before you have created many separate HTML files and begun to link them together. Cut and pasting between files is an awkward method of correcting structural grouping defects. Although Internet Architect (as a Word add-in) supports multiple open files, most other HTML editors do not. Information that is pertinent to the tree structure includes:

- Hierarchical position of each page (home page is 1 or 0)
- Page title
- Page file name (no duplicates unless you create a subdirectory structure)

- Purpose of the page
- Message on the page
- Topic or links to other pages

A project management planning tool is good for handling the hierarchy of pages. A spreadsheet or a word processor works well, too. If you want to track the hierarchy and the links between pages and files, use a relational database. This makes sense for really large projects, but the Aleph site is small. The screen shot in Figure 5.80 shows a Word table with the outline for the site makeover. The home page (index layer of 0) links to all pages at layer 1. Since there are a significant number of index 1 pages—too many to reference from a single introductory page—those under the category of site navigation may become a mixed graphical and textual element. This navigation control will probably become part of the basic design template for all pages. The navigation icon will activate a page with a secondary selection for the navigational aid required. What will work best is going to depend on the page template, which has not been designed yet. At this point, the details of site navigation and structure should not be made permanent until some master template is created, or at least tried on an experimental basis for the site. Technical limitations likely will transform this template even more once credit card forms and some of the pages grow too big for a fixed page template.

In addition, the archives are listed at index 2. These pages are likely to contain news and letters in reverse chronological order and are best designed as scrolling pages until they get too large to quickly download. At that point, the archives can be split by years (and months) and referenced by an intermediate page. One of the goals for this website is to create order and organization, and,

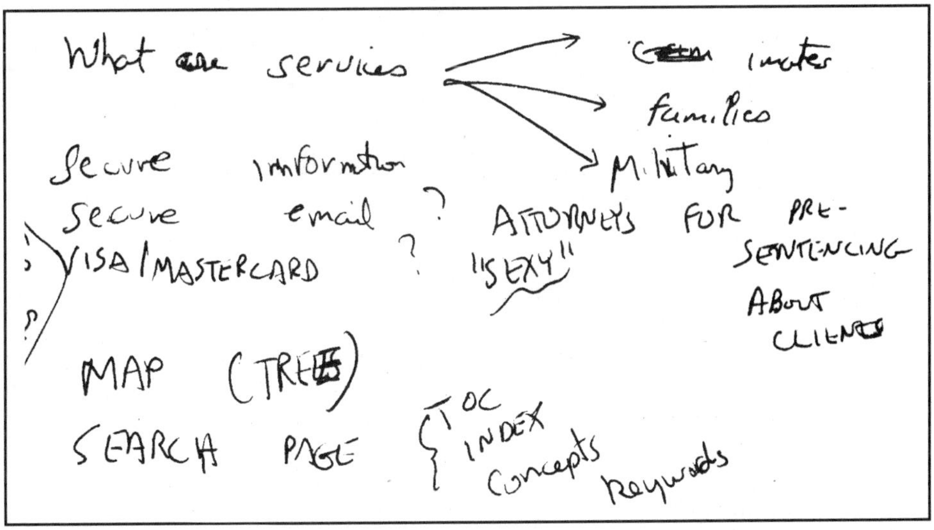

Figure 5.79 Strategic meeting notes . . . before any technical planning.

index	Page Title	Filename	Purpose	Message	Topic
0	Aleph Institute	index.htm	Starting focus	Good Question	What's where
Site Navigation Mainline					
1	Table of Contents	toc.htm	Textual TOC	easy to navigate	What's where
1	Site Map	sitemap.htm	A graphic TOC	easy to navigate	What's where
1	Site Index	sitendx.htm	Index to site	easy to navigate	What's where
1	Concept Index	concept.htm	Concepts on site	easy to navigate	What's where
1	Keyword lookup	keyword.htm	keywords	easy to navigate	What's where
Site Mainline					
1	About Aleph Institute	about.htm	Charter	Non-profit org	
1	Aleph Current News	current.htm	Show news		Link to archives
1	Aleph Letters	letters.htm	Letters received		Link to archives
1	Aleph Services	services.htm			Link to sub-entries
1	Other Sites	links.htm	Links to others		
1	Resources	resource.htm	Links to others		
1	Donor Hall-of-Fame (SSL)	donor.htm	Form to contribute	Link to benefactors	
1	E-Mail form	email.htm			
1	Secured E-Mail (SSL)	sslemail.htm	Pretrial motions		
1	Mailing List	listserv.htm	Aleph advisory by categories		
2	ML:Chaplains	chaplain.htm			
2	ML:Laws	laws.htm			
2	ML:Rabbis	rabbis.htm			
2	ML:Prospects	prospects.htm			
2	ML:Donors	donors.htm			
2	Families	families.htm			
Site Details					
2	Aleph Bio	bio.htm	People		Link to individuals
3	Bio's	<ABC.htm>	Individual w/image		
2	Rebbe	rebbe.htm			
2	Services for Imates	inmate.htm			
2	Services for families	family.htm			
2	Services for military	military.htm			
2	Aleph Services	al-serv.htm	Types of services		links
Archives					
2	Kashrut rules	kasrut.htm			
2	Jewish Calendar	calendr.htm			
2	Event Calendar	events.htm			
2	News archives	archive.htm	Historical records		
2	Letter archives	old-let.htm	Historical records		

Figure 5.80 Outline and design details for the Aleph site makeover.

like most websites, avoid too many layers between the home page and the lowest layer. This site is showing 4 layers, and possibly a maximum of 5, which is about the limit that people will navigate.

The template must be designed as a straw mannequin. The executive director needs to like the design, the technology needs to integrate with it, and the overall needs, strategy, and purpose for the Aleph Institute must mesh with the design. The Aleph Institute performs a serious function for a worldwide community. It helped soldiers during Operation: Desert Storm in Saudi Arabia and helps inmates, mostly within the United States, and their families. The per-

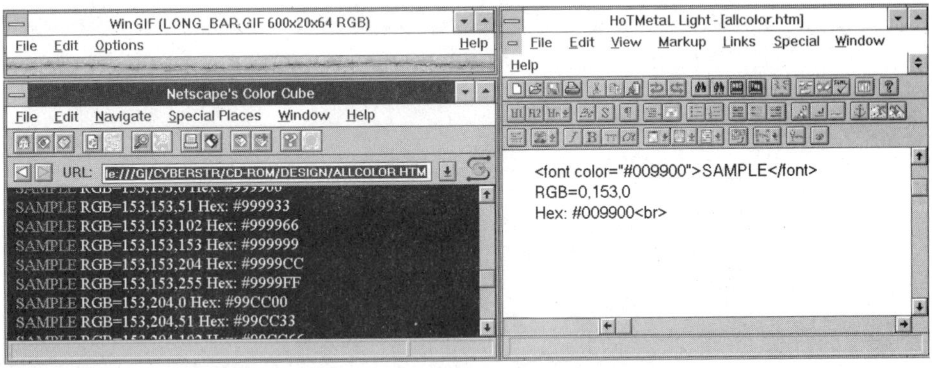

Figure 5.81 Planning for backgrounds and site image.

ception from the website must mesh with the image that the organization has and wants to project. The adjectives one might use to describe Aleph include: melancholy, important, social, responsible, caring, giving, and outreaching.

To this end, an image of barbed wire is partially appropriate. It may not work, but it is worth a try. This image needs a somber background in order to work. The barbed wire will be the site separator, instead of the raised standard line. The image has a background color that could be edited out in a GIF editor, but instead I choose to match the background color with the corresponding Netscape RGB color as listed in ALLCOLOR.HTM. Notice that HotMetal (on the right) does not support the color presentation but Spider's Mosaic browser does. I scrolled through the file to match the barbed wire background with the color code, as shown in Figure 5.81. This will be used to define the HTML background color. Notice the barbed wire image at the top left, matched with the RGB color scheme triplet 153,153,153 and hexadecimal value 999999. This represents a light background for black text. The background color is combined with the image in Figure 5.82, but it is likely that the GIF will need some color editing.

At this point, the home page looks anemic. The barbed wire looks more like a backpacker's wire saw or a soft, fuzzy caterpillar. The grey background does not look melancholy or professional. White will probably work best. It is time to create a horizontal navigation bar, E-mail linkages, and other basic elements to create an ambience for the page and begin seeing how the page template might work for all secondary pages and the processes that each is called on to perform. This requires a hunt through the various clip art libraries to find icons to uniquely define primary site functions:

- Go to home page
- Help
- Site navigation
- Current news
- Recent letters

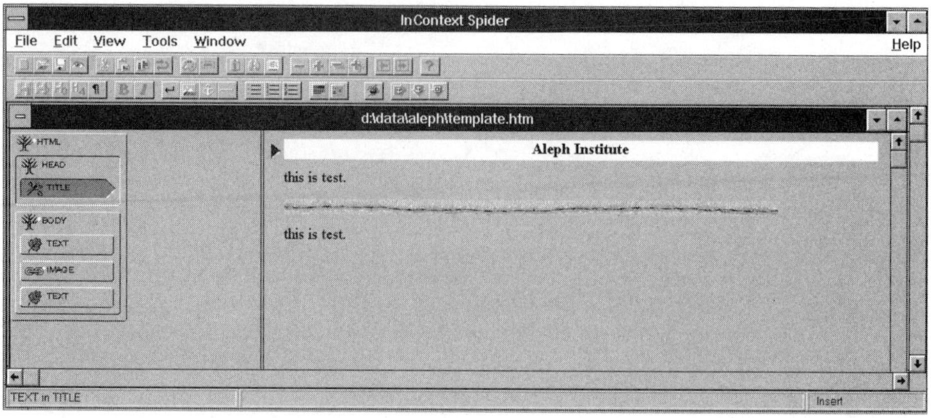

Figure 5.82 The process of creating a specialized template is a rough design process—as you can see, the background color needs some adjustment.

- E-mail
- Donations through credit cards
- Links to other sites

These are not unusual functions for websites and the images are likely to be easily available. Remember: this is a somber site, so fun and games or too-cute images will not work. On the other hand, you want to use easily identifiable images for universal effectiveness. Since this nonprofit site includes basic cyberstore functions, you will need images related to gathering donations and fundraising. A first look at the new Aleph site template is shown in Figure 5.83.

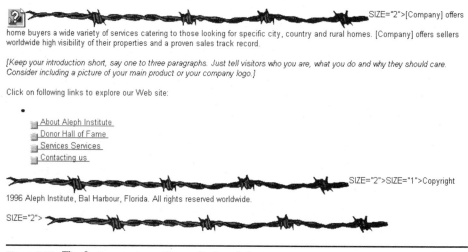

Figure 5.83 The first pass at creating a site template.

Figure 5.84 The icon bar maps to secondary URLs.

The template now shows some of the organization listed in the specification table. The background is white and the barbed wire is unquestionably dangerous looking. The template still requires a self-evident navigation structure. The next icon bar in Figure 5.84 shows one idea for the hotspot map.

The concept is approximately right, but the implementation is silly. This revised image with a hotspot map came from the SBT website and demonstrates a "professional" template. Even though I added beards to the staff people, they all look like the nursery rhyme character, Humpty-Dumpty. Here is another double-decker mapped image bar. Note that the captions are part of the GIF file and will need to be transformed for other languages, as shown in Figure 5.85. The NCSA map file in conjunction with the browser generates the *?191,114* (x,y) pixel coordinates seen on the bottom window bar.

I decide not to use standard clip art but rather to create a series of vector drawings with the necessary toolbars or other site-specific images. I may find some starting points in the libraries that may give me ideas or that I can use as outlines to convert into vector images. The limitation of actually using clip art images is readily apparent, and pirating images and ideas from other sites makes Aleph look just like them. I use the ideas embodied by the horizontal and double-decker toolbars, but not the material from them. Since most bitmap icons are hard to convert into useful vector outlines, I hunt through some vector art libraries and expand thumbnails into \ALEPH\FIGURES subdirectory. I probably selected twice as many images as I needed so that I can sort through them again once I convert all the images to a uniform size consistent with website

Figure 5.85 A double-decker icon image bar; note the copyright.

Figure 5.86   The revised icon bar.

icons. Some of the images do not scale to 2×2 cm (.78 $\times$ .78 in), the size I want for these icons that will become part of a hotspot mapped toolbar. Some will work when extraneous details and fine lines are removed from the vector image. I simplify the color scheme and remove any gradients and then check the integrity of the images when shown at only 16 colors. I also check that the images look right with Netscape's 216-color palette—even though I am working under 256 colors. Two hours of work, several system crashes and recoveries later (because I am pressing the limits of CorelDRAW! and the available memory), and a few passes over clip art libraries reveal this new icon bar pictured in Figure 5.86.

Notice that the globe is a clear symbol for navigation. We considered a sextant and a compass as alternate symbols but these were rejected because they were not sufficiently universal. I like the animated compass on the L.L. Bean site because it is a clever application of GIF89a functionality, but the idea is theirs and even if modified or built from scratch it has no symbolic value relevant to the Aleph site. An eternal flame, a religious icon, that flickers might work and might be added later, if time permits.

The life jacket replaced a red cross (and also a syringe) as the symbolic link to on-line resources and help facilities. If you recall, the table included six entries for site navigation. These have been consolidated into a secondary page with a mapped hotspot image, shown in Figure 5.87. We considered using the images generated by Iconovex PageAnchor (see Chapter 2), but our assessment is that the ship's wheel, lighthouse, and other symbols are not sufficiently semiotically concise. In addition, the HTML layout generated by PageAnchor is functionally good but not aesthetically pleasing. As a result, the main table of contents, index, keyworks, abstracts, and contexts are cut and pasted into Figure 5.87.

You might note that this horizontal layout was also constructed as a vertical bar with the site map on top and the index on the bottom. This particular image fits better in the book, but the vertical bar works in 640×480 full

Figure 5.87   The secondary navigational icon bar.

screen window of any browser as a table or a separate frame on the left-hand side. The bulk of the design work involved creating the master templates for the site in order to provide a consistent look and feel. Additionally, it was necessary to keep a low profile on the site, minimize the use of tables or frames, and create an image harmonious with the mission of the organization. Figure 5.88 shows the template for the home page.

Note that the home link is not enabled because this is already the home page. The WebAuthor template is better than most tools, but like most of the other suites and even thoroughbred HTML editors, it does not make it easy to master pages or, in this case, to create a template to be used for all secondary and supplemental pages. However, because WebAuthor is a Word application, each HTML page is saved as a .DOC file and secondarily as an .HTML. This means that you can use the built-in spelling and grammar tools, Indexicon, and cut and paste bitmaps, text, and GIF files without concern about type styles, bitmap file formats, and other layout needs. The conversion process takes care of the little details. For example, the template is used to create the site navigation page shown in Figure 5.89. This very simple page includes the mapped icon bar and the hypertext links beneath. It is still a clean and neat low-profile page.

Although most tools include wizards, macros, and some menubar icons to create forms, text fields, and list boxes, WebAuthor makes the process simple, as shown in Figure 5.90.

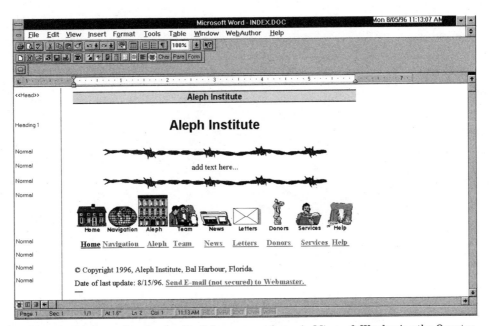

Figure 5.88 Final template for the Aleph home page shown in Microsoft Word using the Quarterdeck WebAuthor WordBasic template.

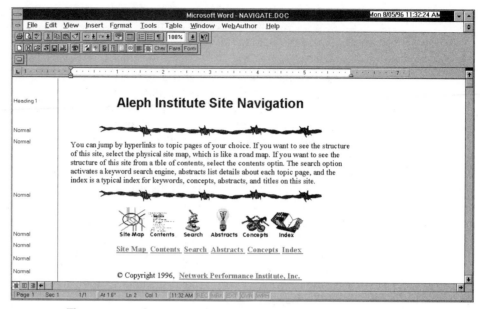

Figure 5.89 The navigational icon bar.

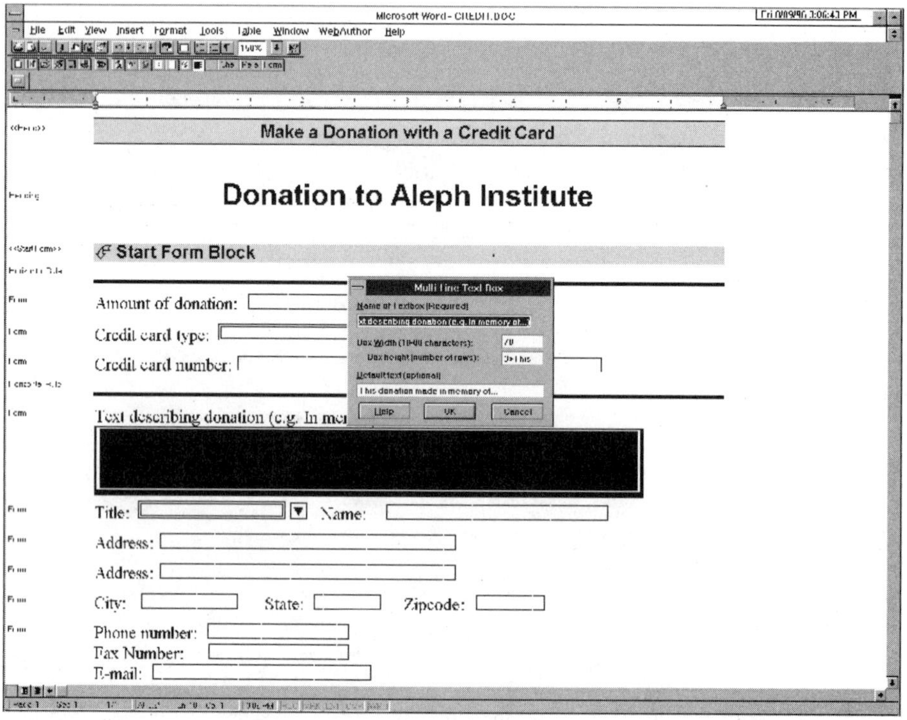

Figure 5.90 WebAuthor simplifies credit card form creation.

Aleph Institute Secure Attorney E-Mail

Figure 5.91 Attorney to attorney secure E-mail transmission.

In order to retain consistency of the pages over the entire site, this form will be cut as HTML code and pasted into a standard template file. This form will be provided to the webmaster for conversion into a CGI and SHTTP form for secure transmission. The codes for enabling a secure transmission were described in Chapter 4, but the reality is that most ISPs want to prepare this step themselves so that they are sure of the code and certain that no trap doors or Trojan horses have been slyly introduced. Similarly, E-mail between attorneys will be encoded with a secure form, which will also be cut and pasted into the standard site template, as shown in Figure 5.91.

Conclusion

The applications for websites bidirectionally interconnect with databases for transaction processing and run the gamut from small cybershops and corporations wanting or needing a 7 × 24 presence to support an international community in global time zones, to the nonprofit or government agency trying to provide services to more constituents with fewer resources and people. The cyberstore concept represents an additional sales and marketing channel with a lower cost for transaction processing than other existing media. As this book shows, it can be simple to get started with a functional web presence and enhance that site with integrated work flows. Chapter 6 describes the contents of the companion CD-ROM, and shows how to install and integrate many of the advanced tools and demos on this disk.

6

The Companion CD-ROM

Introduction

This chapter describes the contents, installation, and practical utility of the materials on the companion CD-ROM. Since there are too many files to list in this chapter, see FILELIST.TXT on the CD-ROM, which is an annotated list of the files.

Contents of CD-ROM

The files on the CD-ROM are standard ISO-compatible files; you should be able to read them under DOS, all versions of Windows, OS/2, Macintosh, and even with UNIX. Most of the files are resources that can be read with a web browser, a graphics image tool, or a note pad and text editor. When you try to read the DOS/ASCII files under UNIX, you may discover a lack of line endings or a staggered stair step of text. This indicates you need a different tool to read the files. Try a web browser! You can convert the files to the UNIX <LF><CR> format with an NFS utility such as DOS2UNIX if you want to reuse them and not just view them. CompuServe and various Internet shareware sites have similar tools that make it easier to read DOS files under UNIX.

Most of the CGI code, HTML page samples, and web resources are useful, regardless of the operating system and server platform. The CGI code is intended to run on any platform, even though most large cyberstores and ISP sites are based either on SGI UNIX or Sun Solaris. Many of the applications are specific to Windows, generally WindowsNT, but may run under Windows 3.x or Windows95. Windows emulation on the Macintosh or under Sun Solaris is compatible with Windows 3.x, but unlikely to support either Windows95 or WindowsNT in the near future. Figure 6.1 in the next screen shot provides a bird's-eye view of the significant files on the companion CD-ROM.

```
┌─────────────────── D:\DATA\CYBERSTR\CD-ROM\*.* - [DATA] ──────────── ▼ ▲ ┐
│ ┌─ 🖿 cd-rom         ↑ │ ⬏.. .                                                  ↑
│ │  ├─ 🗀 audit         │ │ 🗀audit           7/3/96   12:38:50pm
│ │  ├─ 🗀 cgi           │ │ 🗀cgi             7/3/96   12:38:48pm
│ │  ├─ 🗄 demos         │ │ 🗀demos           6/24/96   2:21:24pm
│ │  ├─ 🗀 design        │ │ 🗀design          6/27/96   8:44:12pm
│ │  ├─ 🗀 hitcount      │ │ 🗀hitcount        6/27/96   8:44:08pm
│ │  ├─ 🗀 i-cntrl       │ │ 🗀i-cntrl         8/9/96    4:39:14pm
│ │  ├─ 🗀 internic      │ │ 🗀internic        3/28/96   8:54:44pm
│ │  ├─ 🗀 media         │ │ 🗀media           8/7/96    2:29:14pm
│ │  ├─ 🗀 product       │ │ 🗀product         8/28/96  10:25:00am
│ │  ├─ 🗀 security      │ │ 🗀security        3/28/96   8:54:46pm
│ │  ├─ 🗀 set           │ │ 🗀set             3/8/96   11:04:32am
│ │  ├─ 🗀 tools         │ │ 🗀tools           7/3/96   12:38:52pm
│ │  └─ 🗀 vbscript    ↓ │ │ 🗀vbscript        3/12/96   5:30:04pm        ↓
└─────────────────────────────────────────────────────────────────────────┘
```

Figure 6.1 The major contents on the companion CD-ROM for *Building Cyberstores*.

These major subcategories are defined in greater detail in the following sections.

Hypertext book

I like to read books on-line because I can search for keywords and locate sections of code or topics not represented by either a table of contents or an index. In fact, the Windows95 Help Engine supports standard index searches and also a random keyword search. For this reason, this book is converted into a Windows on-line help file in the basic Windows 3.x format for upward and cross-platform compatibility. In addition, since this book is

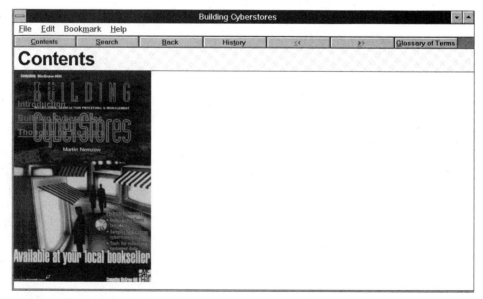

Figure 6.2 The opening screen for the on-line help file for *Building Cyberstores*.

about HTML and website presentations, the material has also been converted into a series of linked HTML pages. This book is copyrighted. As such, you may not quote more than 300 words, as per the Berne Convention, or extract images and text for reuse in various places. Figure 6.2 shows a screen shot of the help file, while Figure 6.3 shows a comparable view of an HTML format.

Product database

The CD-ROM includes an MS Access file (version 2.0 for upward compatibility) that you can peruse with MS Access, MS SQL, MS Office, convert to HTML with HTML Transport, or tap with various ODBC drivers. PRODUCT.MDB is accessible with ODBC drivers or with the native MS Access application. A Windows Visual Basic program called PRODUCTS.EXE is also included on the CD-ROM to access the data in this database. This application is shown running in Figure 6.4. When you press the command button that says "Products," you get a form that looks like the one shown in Figure 6.5. You scroll through the database by selecting the list box and picking an element or by pressing forward and reverse arrows to move one record through the database of web design and implementation products. Figure 6.6 shows typical vendor information for a Notes to HTML conversion product.

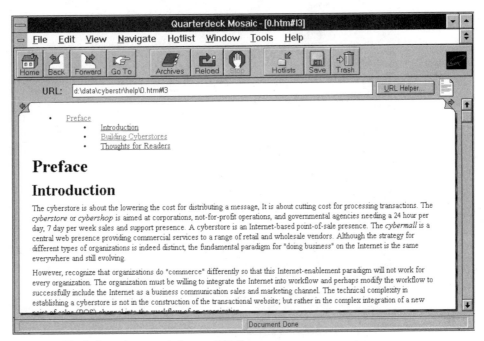

Figure 6.3 The help topic converted as an HTML page.

Figure 6.4 The Windows-based Visual Basic product information application (PRODUCT.EXE) included on the CD-ROM. This is the splash screen.

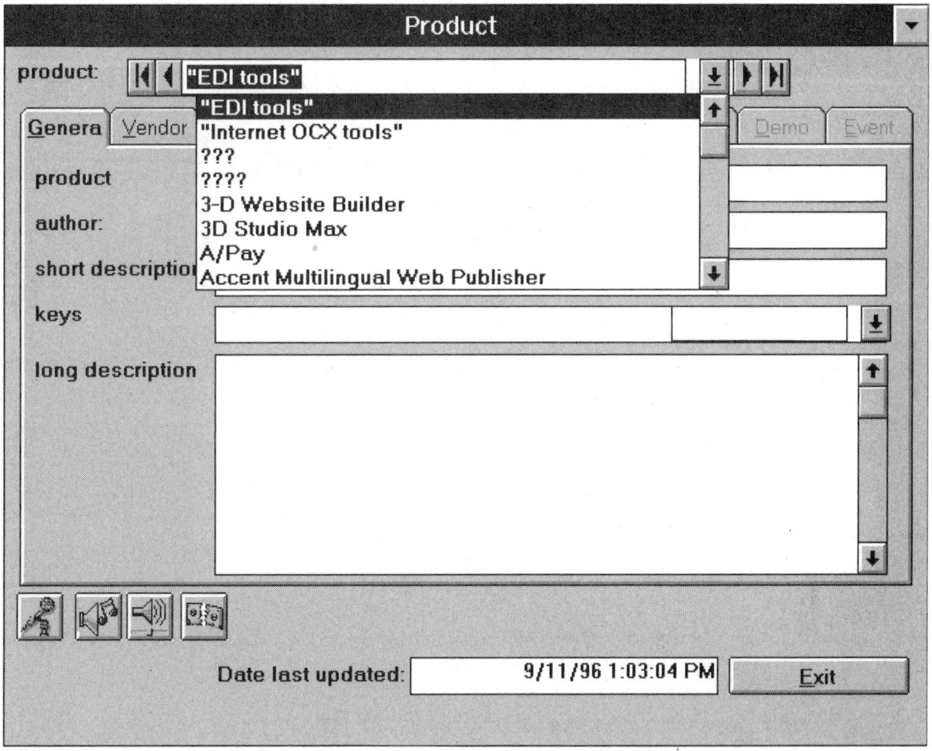

Figure 6.5 The multiple page tabbed dialog window.

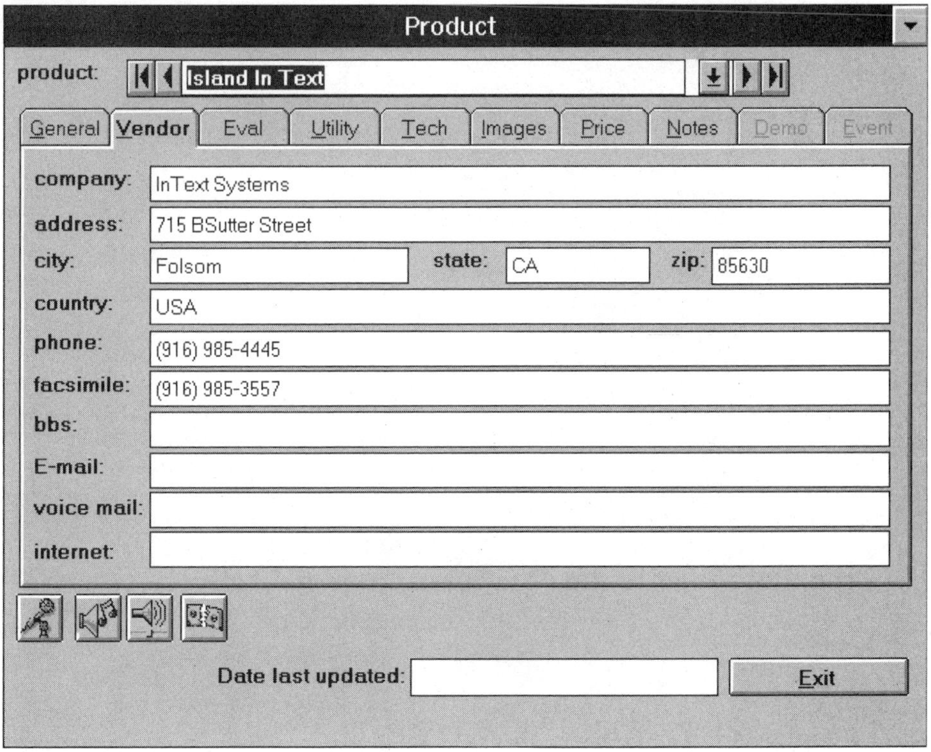

Figure 6.6 A vendor entry for the listed product.

If anything out of the ordinary impressed me (either positively or negatively), I entered some telling comments in the database. Some products, like the Interactive Catalog, were not consistent with the Windows application development philosophy, as shown in Figure 6.7.

The database includes product information for approximately 400 web server-side products, some of which are profiled in this book or included on the CD-ROM as freeware, shareware, or time-limited demos. Contact information is provided for all the vendors in the form of addresses, phone numbers, E-mail addresses, CompuServe addresses, HTTP URLs, and other BBSs. In addition to this resource, the web home page for this book includes hot links to the vendors for the latest information and demonstrations. Some companies could not provide demonstrations for the CD-ROM in an appropriate format; instead, you are encouraged to visit *their* sites to download or request the latest demonstration software.

Audit

The audit subdirectory contains articles about measuring hit rates, website auditing, and privacy issues. Sources for this material include CASIE,

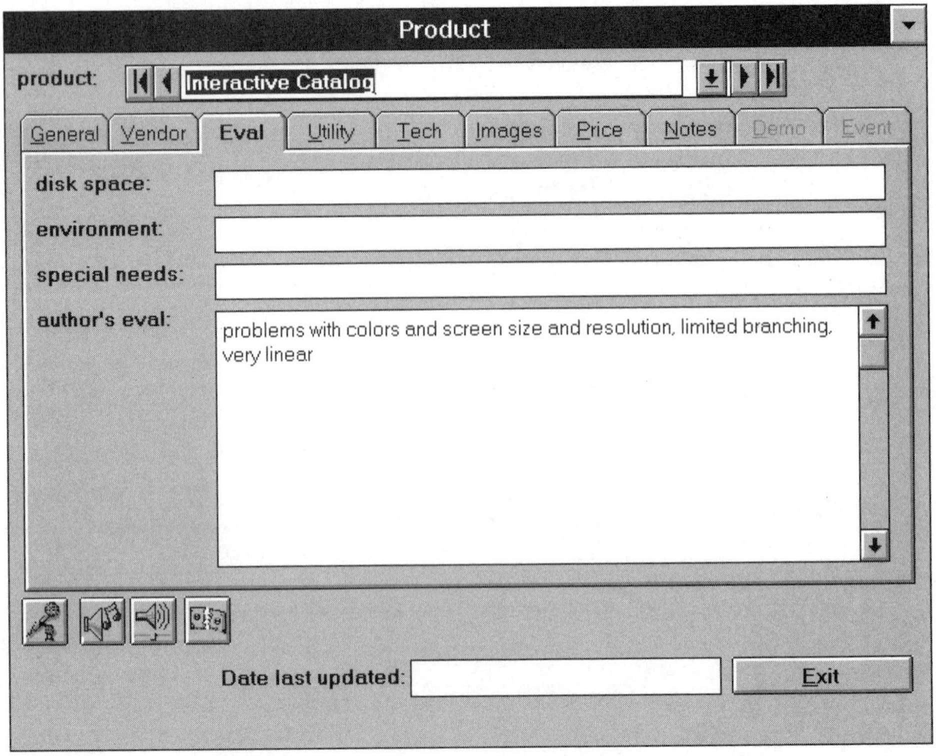

Figure 6.7 Evaluation entries can be used to indicate substantial problems or something very good about a particular product that deserves recognition.

AAAA, and ANA. These articles and the organizations represent the leading thoughts about Internet advertising, rate cards, and the practical aspects of on-line transaction processing.

CGI

The CGI directory includes public domain libraries for cross-platform CGI development and distribution. There are also two samples of cyberstores enabled through CGI, scripts for parsing data returned from HTML forms, and tools to enable the Cookies web state processing. Several of the other scripts include user authentication, a guestbook to capture users and customers who find your site, and various site logging utilities. This subdirectory does not contain CGI code for implementing hitcounts; see the Hitcount section and the subdirectory on the companion CD-ROM for code that utilizes the same CGI libraries.

Demos

The demonstrations included on the companion CD-ROM include a presentation of the A/Pay electronic software distribution and payment application, Alchemy Mindworks GIF toolkit, a version of Allair Cold Fusion and other support tools and documentation, a demonstration of Blue Sky Web Office, Coast WebMaster, Level 5 Quest, MetaInfo's DNS server for Windows NT, Softquad's free HotMetal HTML editor, SQA's application development test suite for testing and validating your applets and website, and a working version of WebTrends.

You need to recognize that most of these tools function for 30 days and then expire. This should be sufficient time to evaluate their performance and decide whether they are useful to you. A large number of tools are "represented" on the CD-ROM by this book's home page and the hyperlinks to sites where you can obtain the latest releases of demonstrations or working versions of tools. Of course, the home page is also on-line and you can access these sites (and updates) directly from it as well. The reasons that more demonstrations and working versions are not included on the CD-ROM include a lack of vendor permission to include material already available on the Internet, versions that require registration at the vendor's website, and rapid changes in prototypes, demonstrations, and working versions. Visit the HTTPSITE.HTM or the on-line home page (*www.networkperf.com/cyberstore*) for these items.

Design

This subdirectory includes GIF and HTML files that demonstrate various web page design techniques and limitations. The HTML files include examples of HTML pages that collect user input, send E-mail, and describe the animated GIF format. ISO8859.HTM provides all the codes for special characters (including copyright, trademark, and currency symbols) that you are likely

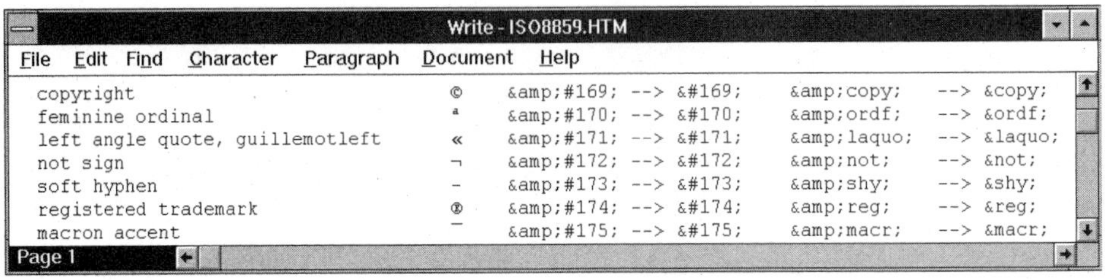

copyright	©	&#169; --> ©	&copy; --> ©
feminine ordinal	ª	&#170; --> ª	&ordf; --> ª
left angle quote, guillemotleft	«	&#171; --> «	&laquo; --> «
not sign	¬	&#172; --> ¬	&not; --> ¬
soft hyphen	-	&#173; --> ­	&shy; --> ­
registered trademark	®	&#174; --> ®	&reg; --> ®
macron accent	¯	&#175; --> ¯	&macr; --> ¯

Figure 6.8 Some of the design elements included on the companion CD-ROM.

to require in your cyberstore pages. ALLCOLOR.HTM shows the colors for full 256-color Navigator palette and the hexadecimal values for specifying text, frame, table, or solid background colors. These are useful resources since many HTML editors do not include codes for special colors or characters. Figure 6.8 shows a sample from ISO8859.HTM.

Figure 6.9 shows a partial list of the thumbnails of images in this directory. Note that these images are representative of GIF backgrounds, lines, animated GIF89a images, and Navigator color palettes.

Hitcount

This directory contains CGI libraries (some compatible with the CGI scripts) that support website hit counters. The CGI scripts include matching HTML forms, counter resource files, and the requisite data file that accumulates the

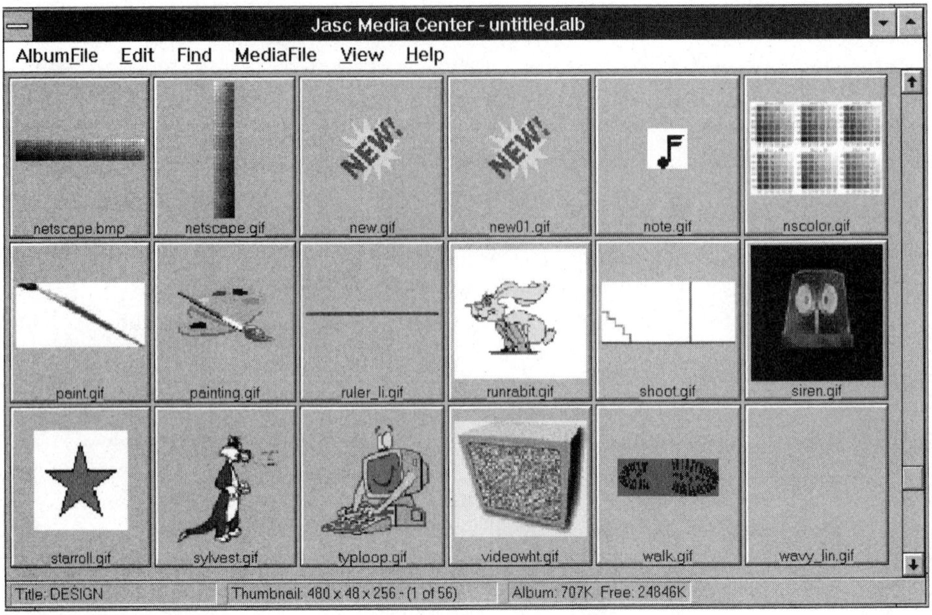

Figure 6.9 Some of the design elements included on the companion CD-ROM.

current hit (or types of hits) counter. The documentation details the installation process. I have one serious warning about the CGI scripts—make sure they are placed in the active \CGI-BIN directory on your cyberstore web server, and that the security prevents nonadministrative viewing or changing of these files. This is a very important security concern because you do not want to allow a hacker to replace the hit counter script with another one that creates a new administrative user or alters passwords and access codes on your server.

This directory also includes executable hit counters for other platforms, including WindowsNT. One of the most flexible is the COUNTER.ZIP, which includes various GIF font sets and formats for a wide range of WindowsNT counters. Figure 6.10 shows the presentation style available with this hit counter.

InterNIC

Although domain name registration is available on-line, this InterNIC packet provides easier access and the details and rules for creating a new domain name. This directory contains all the supporting materials and rules for registering and retaining a domain name in light of various trademark infringement lawsuits and negotiations. Figure 6.11 shows part of the InterNIC registration form in a text format.

This form is also available in HTML so you can submit it directly to Network Solutions, the only commercial registration organization in the United States.

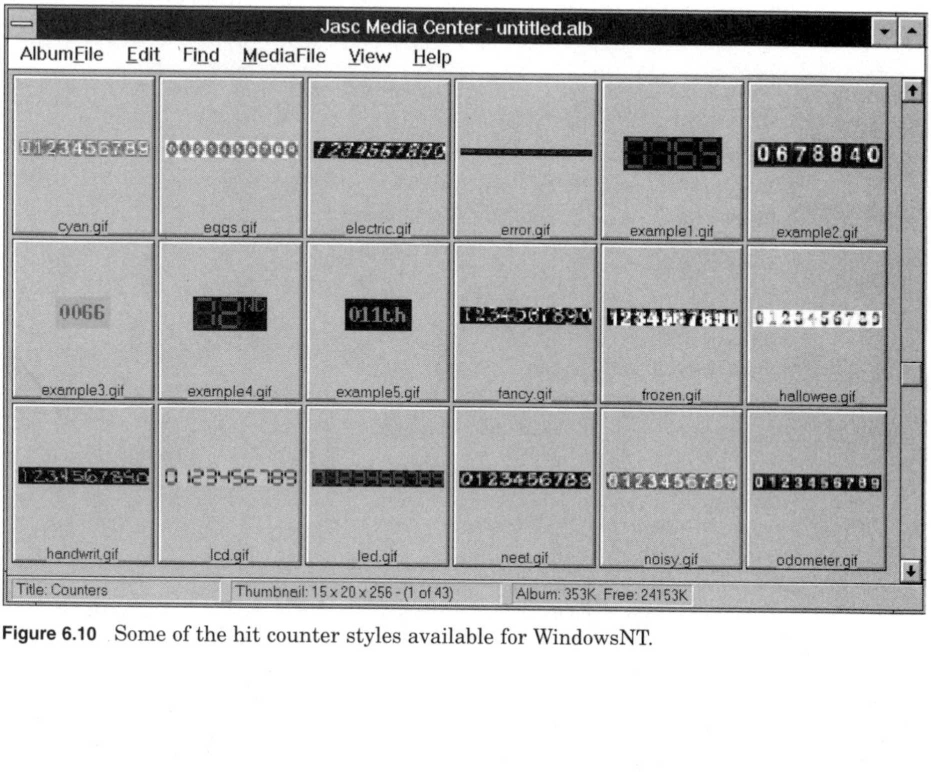

Figure 6.10 Some of the hit counter styles available for WindowsNT.

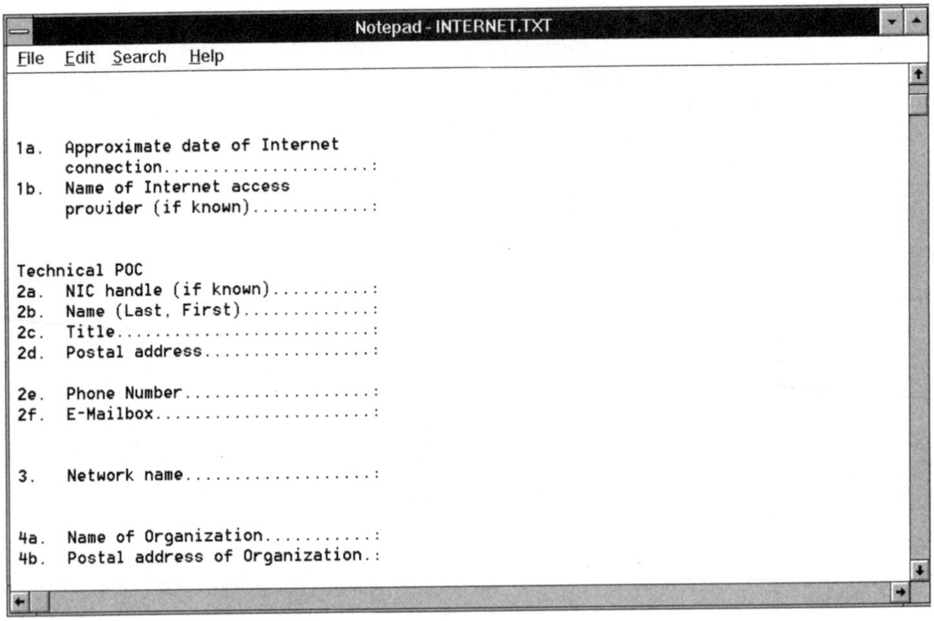

```
Notepad - INTERNET.TXT
File  Edit  Search  Help

1a.  Approximate date of Internet
     connection.....................:
1b.  Name of Internet access
     provider (if known)............:

Technical POC
2a.  NIC handle (if known)..........:
2b.  Name (Last, First).............:
2c.  Title..........................:
2d.  Postal address.................:

2e.  Phone Number...................:
2f.  E-Mailbox......................:

3.   Network name...................:

4a.  Name of Organization...........:
4b.  Postal address of Organization.:
```

Figure 6.11 Sample of InterNIC registration form and supporting materials.

In the future, it is expected that two other organizations will be authorized to create 30 more domain extents (besides *.mil, .org, .net,* and *.gov*), and that worldwide organizations will be charted to handle sites granted a country code.

Media

This directory includes some web multimedia samples. Click on the .AU (QuickTime), .AVI (Windows), or .MOV (Adobe) to invoke them. There is also a tool that is useful for creating animated GIFs. Figure 6.12 shows a sample from the Honda website.

Security

This directory on the companion CD-ROM contains resources about web and Internet security, PGP tools, encryption, and Cookies information. This material supplements what is explicitly included in the book and provides additional pointers, resources, and hyperlinks to other security websites. Note that the book home page also contains many active hyperlinks to security-related websites.

SET

This directory includes the specifications for the SET protocols approved in conjunction with both MasterCard and VISA. SET represents important agreement in order to create a level playing field for electronic credit card

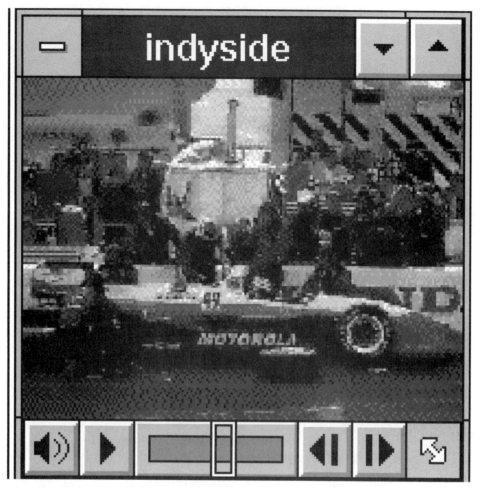

Figure 6.12 Web multimedia presentation sample.

transactions over the Internet and from within web pages, without the need
for additional encryption standards and credit card processing applications
or clearinghouses. A page from the technical Adobe PDF format is shown in
Figure 6.13. This information is also included as ZIPped text files for those
who do not have the Adobe PDF reader or want to download it.

Tools

This subdirectory includes a handful of useful webmaster development tools.
LView (shareware) and MapThis (freeware) provide a means to view web images and create hotspots for hypertext links from complex images, toolbars, or
image-only web pages. The VBNet demo shows how to enable Visual Basic applications so that they can be web-enabled or can supplement web servers for

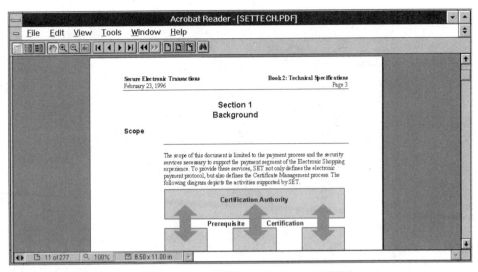

Figure 6.13   Secure Electronic Transaction (SET) specifications in PDF format.

cyberstore transaction processing. Note that many other tools can be downloaded directly from the vendor's home page, and many such home pages are linked from this book's home page.

VBScript

This directory includes a working description of Microsoft's alternative to Java, JavaScript, ActiveX, J++, and other tools. The book's home page includes a link to the Microsoft website, where you can download the current version of VBScript. I argue against customizing websites and web pages with single-platform solutions, and suggest that the complexities of cyberstores outweigh the time and expense of programmatic solutions when better integration tools exist. However, the rampant press and vendor push toward VBScript (Java, JavaScript, and other similar toolkits) means that you should also have at least a working knowledge of these tools so that you can personally defend site architecture and design decisions for your cyberstore.

Conclusion

This chapter describes the contents, installation, and practical utility of the materials on the companion CD-ROM. However, the CD-ROM is not the only supplemental information for this book. The book home page (HTTPSITE.HTM) is included on the CD-ROM and maintained live (with updates and new links) at *http://www.networkperf.com/cyberstore*. You can get more information, technical support, the latest versions, and white papers on the tools referenced in this book, contained on the CD-ROM, or hyperlinked from the home page from *Building Cyberstores'* home page.

Sources

Castagrob, Charisse, Jaystack Labs, Inc., Austin, TX.
Internicila, Lori, SoftQuad, Toronto, Canada.
Kupina, Marianne, Marketing Manager, InContext Systems, Toronto, Ontario, Canada.
Taylor, Doug, Marketing Manager, Level Five Research, Melbourne, FL.
Toth, Scott, Iconovex Corporation, Bloomington, MN.

Glossary

/ETC/HOSTS An ASCII text file used to associate IP machine names and aliases with IP addresses for DNS services.

@ At sign, also called little snail, strudel, cinnamon cake, monkey's tail, or arroba.

~ Tilde. On the Internet, this refers to a subdirectory or user subdirectory for uniform address resolution.

24 × 7 A reference to nonstop data processing operations that run 24 hours per day, 7 days per week. Also 24-by-7.

24-by-7 A reference to nonstop data processing operations that run 24 hours per day, 7 days per week. Also 24 × 7.

Access Line The line that ties all phone numbers together with one personal telephone number.

Access Loop Diversity A service offered by a Regional Bell Operating Company consisting of multipath communication connections to a customer site.

Access Number The phone number that must be dialed by someone calling you when you are roaming outside of the National Network, prior to dialing the number of your phone. The access number gives the caller access to the facilities of the system in which you are roaming.

ACH Acronym for Automated Clearinghouse (q.v.).

Acknowledgment A message typically sent from one network device to another to acknowledge that some event (for example, receipt of a message) has occurred. Abbreviated as ACK.

Adaptive Dithering A form of dithering where the palette of colors is minimized so that a bitmapped image might use an 8-bit or smaller palette.

Add-in An applet, or software application that does not run alone but only as a filter or part of another application, which is loaded into a browser or other major desktop application.

Ads-ins See Add-in.

Address **1.** Data structure used to identify a unique entity, such as a particular process or network location. **2.** A reference to a source or destination station on a network.

Address Mask Bit combination used to describe which portion of an address refers to the subnet and which part refers to the host.

Address Resolution Protocol An Internet protocol used to bind IP addresses to Ethernet/802.2 addresses. Defined in RFC 826. Abbreviated as ARP.

Alarm A message notifying an operator or administrator of a network problem.

Alert   A message that warrants action at the control point.

Algorithm   The rule or process for arriving at a solution to a problem.

Alias   An alternative name used to identify an entity.

Alphanumeric   A mix of text and numerical delivery.

American National Standards Institute   The coordinating body for voluntary standards groups within the United States but also a member of the International Organization for Standards. A governmental agency that maintains standards for science and commerce, including a list of acceptable standards for computer languages, character sets, connection compatibility, and many other aspects of the computer and data communications industries. Better known by the ANSI acronym.

American Wire Gauge   A measurement system for electrical wire where larger numbers represent thinner wires (based upon the extrusion of a fixed amount of metal over longer distances). Abbreviated as AWG.

Analog   **1.** Something that bears a similarity to something else. **2.** A data transfer method that uses continuously variable physical quantities for transmitting voice and data signals over conventional telephone lines. Analog transmission speed is limited by the bandwidth of the human voice.

ANSI   Acronym for American National Standards Institute (q.v.).

API   Acronym for Application Programming Interface.

Applet   An application started from the control panel. Control panel applets each configure a particular system feature—for example, printers, video drivers, or [SDL1] system sounds.

Architecture   The way hardware or software is structured, usually based on a specific design philosophy. Architecture affects both a computer's abilities and its limitations.

Artifacts   Image imperfections caused by conversions or compression.

ASCII   Acronym for American Standard Code for Information Interchange.

Asymmetric Cryptosystem   A computer encryption system that uses a two-part key, consisting of a private key and a distributed public key.

Asynchronous Transfer Mode   **1.** A cell relay packet network providing from 25 Mbps/s to Gbps from central offices to central offices. **2.** A form of packet sitching; a subset of cell relay that uses 53-byte cells (5 bytes of overhead, and another 4 bytes for LAN sequencing adaptation) as the basic transport unit. In concept, circuits of different signaling speeds can move data from desktop to desktop and across long-distance services without major changes in data format. Abbreviated as ATM.

ATM   Acronym for Asynchronous Transfer Mode (q.v.).

Authentication   A security procedure that verifies that a user is who he identifies himself as, or that data or a digital signature is what it purports to be.

Authoring   The process of planning, designing, and producing multimedia applications.

Automated Clearinghouse   A money wire transfer system that is used to transfer payments and credits between specific bank accounts between banks directed by a computer program at an organization controlling either the source or destination account with the express permission of the other party. Abbreviated as ACH.

Baby Bells   See Bell Operating Companies.

Backbone   A collapsed (that is, minimized) wiring concentrator.

Basic Rate Interface   The ISDN (Integrated Services Digital Network) interface composed of two B channels and one D channel for circuit-switched communication of voice, data, and video. The interface for connecting a desktop terminal (data) and telephones (voice) to the ISDN switch. It includes two 64-Kbits/s B channels for simultaneous voice and data service and one 6-Kbits/s D control channel for call information and customer data. See also ISDN. The ISDN standard governing how a customer's desktop terminals and telephones can connect to the ISDN switch. The total bit rate with framing synchronization and other overhead is 192 Kbits/s. Abbreviated as BRI.

Bell Operating Companies   The local telephone companies that existed prior to deregulation, under which AT&T was ordered by the courts to divest itself in each of the seven U.S. regions. Also called Baby Bells. Abbreviated as BOC.

B-ISDN   Acronym for Broadband Integrated Services Digital Network (q.v.).

Bitmap   A screen display in which each pixel location corresponds to a unique main memory location accessible by the CPU. Also refers to images intended for display on this type of digital system.

Blocking   The delay that occurs when a channel is already physically switched and communications are established between end points, thereby preventing other stations or nodes from sharing or interrupting access. This is primarily a function of network switching architectures, PBXs, and LAN switches. In a switching system, a condition in which no paths are available to complete a circuit. The term is also used to describe a situation in which one activity cannot begin until another has been completed.

BRI   Acronym for Basic Rate Interface (q.v.).

Bridge   A device that interconnects networks using *similar* protocols. See also Router.

Broadband Integrated Services Digital Network   A digital data network for transmitting large amounts of data, voice, and video over long distances . . . SONET or ATM. Communication standards developed by the ITU-TTS to handle high-bandwidth applications such as video BISDN will use ATM technology over SONET-based transmission circuits to provide data rates of 155 Mbps to 622 Mbps and beyond. See also BRI, ISDN, and PRI. Abbreviated as B-ISDN.

Carrier   **1.** A company that provides telephone (or another communications) service. Also, an unmodulated radio signal. **2.** A signal suitable for modulation by another signal containing information to be transmitted.

Central Office   The telephone switching station nearest the customer's location. A local telephone company office to which all local loops in a given area connect and in which circuit switching of subscriber lines occurs. The central office serves the businesses, organizations, and residences connected to its local loop lines. Abbreviated as CO.

Central Processing Unit   A primary unit of the computer system that controls interpretation and execution of instructions. Abbreviated as CPU.

Channel   **1.** An individual communication path that carries signals. **2.** The path between a sender and receiver (two PCs, for example) that carries one stream of data. The term also is used to describe the specific path between large computers and attached peripherals.

Circuit   **1.** A communications link between two or more points. **2.** The physical medium on which transmission signals are carried.

CODEC   Acronym for Coder/Decoder (q.v.).

Coder/Decoder   A device that typically uses pulse code modulation to transform analog voice into a digital bit stream and vice versa.

CMYK   Cyan, magenta, yellow, and black. A color encoding method commonly used in printing. The black is not really needed, but is included as a specific color because it is used so often. Many color printers use these four colors in a ribbon to print color images.

Common Carrier   Companies that provide communication networks (such as AT&T, Sprint, and WilTel). A licensed, private utility company that supplies communication services to the public at regulated prices.

Communication   Transmission of information.

Communication Server   A communications processor that connects asynchronous devices to a LAN or WAN through network and terminal emulation software.

Communications Line   The physical link (such as wire or a telephone circuit) that connects one or more devices to another.

Compact Video   SuperMac algorithm for the symmetric compression of video for Quicktime, Quicktime for Windows, and Video for Windows. Known as Cinepak. See also CODEC.

Component Software   An add-in function, slave, feature, or full-fledged application that accesses and shares features of a master application, a suite of applications, or the functions built into the operating system or NOS.

Compression   **1.** The removal of redundant information from a set of data. **2.** Running a data set through an algorithm that reduces the space/bandwidth required to store/transmit the data set.

Computer Telephone Integration   The connection of telephone services into computer services. Abbreviated as CTI.

Computer Virus   Man-made software designed to disable, damage, or destroy computer hardware or read/write storage systems; sometimes incorrectly called a worm, Trojan horse, or trap door. A virus typically attaches itself to executable code (COM or EXE files) and enters a passive mode and then propagates itself from program to program. Infected programs (and disks) are virus carriers. When viruses enter an active mode through a trigger mechanism, usually a specific date or annual date, they erase files, corrupt file directories, and destroy the boot sectors.

Confidentiality   A security process that ensures that the content of a transmitted message cannot be determined except by the possessor of a key associated with the message, even if the transmitted bits are observed.

Congestion   A slowdown in a network due to a bottleneck, excessive network traffic. See also Traffic Congestion.

Connectionless   Term used to describe existence of a virtual circuit.

Conversation   A messaging connection between applications.

Conversion   The process of altering one data format and converting it to another for storage, presentation, or display. For example, databases are commonly converted statically or dynamically to HTML formats.

Cookies   Terminology for Persistent Client-state HTTP Cookies.

COOKIES.TXT   Client-side browser file containing information about the Persistent Client-state HTTP cookies (q.v.).

Copyright   A legal term defined by the Berne Convention ascribing ownership of various textual or artistic concepts to the author or creator of that work.

CPU   Acronym for Central Processing Unit (q.v.).

Crosstab   A manipulation that displays data from a database table in a spreadsheet format.

CSU/DSU   Acronym for Customer Service Unit/Data Service Unit.

Data   When used in the context of communications, data refers to transmitted information, particularly information that is not interpreted by a particular protocol entity but merely delivered to a higher-level entity, possibly after some processing.

Data Compression   **1.** A method of reducing the space required to represent data as either bits, characters, replacement codes, or graphic images. **2.** A reduction in the size of data by exploiting redundancy. Many modems incorporate MNP5 or V.42bis protocols to compress data before it is sent over the phone line. Dual compression (at the file and modem levels) actually increases the transmitted size. For compression to work, data must be sent over a clean, noise-free telephone line. Since common error-correction protocols are synchronous, there is usually a throughput gain there as well.

Data Encryption Standard   An encryption/decryption algorithm defined in FIPS Publication 46. The standard cryptographic algorithm developed by the National Institute of Standards and Technology. Abbreviated as DES.

Data Mart   A subset or summary of a data warehouse.

Data Processing   Computer operations that are geared to the entry, manipulation, and dissemination of information. Abbreviated as DP.

Data Rate   The effective speed at which data is transferred over a wired or unwired transmission link. The data rate is the actual transmission rate after errors, synchronization, and overhead are factored out.

Data Repository   A hierarchical or flat database of code, code sets, modules, and other constructs typically intended for later reuse.

Data Service Unit   A device used in digital transmission for connecting data terminal equipment (DTE), such as a router, to a digital transmission circuit (DTC) or service. Abbreviated as DSU.

Data Streaming   Data I/O technique required by multimedia to keep network communications traffic levels flat, thus preventing even slight delays or mismatches in audio and video transmissions.

Data Warehouse   A database that holds large amounts of data that cut across specific organizational functions and boundaries. The warehouse must also include an historical element or date tagging context not generally found in application-specific databases. Data warehouses are often used in decision support applications.

Database Management System   Software that controls the organization, storage, retrieval, security, and integrity of data records within a database. It accepts requests from the application or client process and instructs the operating system to transfer the appropriate data. Abbreviated as DBMS.

DBMS   Acronym for Database Management System (q.v.).

DDE   Acronym for Dynamic Data Exchange (q.v.).

Decompression   The restoration of redundant data that was removed through compression.

Decryption   The processing of received data by the possessor of a secret key in such a way that the intended contents of the data are restored.

Decryption Key   The secret key required to decrypt received data.

Dedicated Bandwidth   **1.** The allocation of the full protocol- and media-dependent bandwidth to two communication network devices through a packet switch. **2.** The allocation of transmission segments to devices on a network.

Defamation   A verbal or written statement made with or without intent that devalues a person or party.

DES   Acronym for Data Encryption Standard (q.v.).

DHCP   Acronym for Dynamic Host Configuration Protocol (q.v.).

Dialog Box   A message box in a graphical user interface that allows users to input more specific information than standard commands.

Dial-Up Line   Communications circuit that is established by a switched circuit connection using the telephone network.

Digital   A representation of information by a unit of length or size.

Digital Signature   A qualified and usually encrypted attachment to a document confirming the identity of the sender and the validity of the document.

Digital Video Interactive   A proprietary technology developed by Intel (and licensed by IBM) for full-motion video at a high level of compression (hardware). This technology will be supported under Windows using MCI commands.

Directed Search   A search request sent to a specific node known to contain a resource. A directed search is used to determine the continued existence of the resource and to obtain routing information specific to the node.

Distributed Database   A database in which the tables exist in several different locations. For example, one table might reside on a PC in Seattle, while a related table is on a Macintosh in Chicago.

Dithering   This is a pixel-depth conversion process usually used only when very few colors are available, such as 16. The process trades pixel resolution for (perceived) color depth. Squares (for example, 2×2, 4×4, etc.) of pixels are created to represent to the eye more colors than are actually available. Print media uses a similar technique to obtain many shades from just 3 or 4 actual colors. This algorithm has the inherent side effect (or artifact) of changing a computer image into a natural image.

DNS   Acronym for Domain Name System (q.v.).

Domain **1.** A single LAN. **2.** A LAN Server or LAN Manager sphere of operation bounded by a server or user access database. **3.** A reference to a hierarchy of routed networks incorporated into a larger enterprise network. **4.** A portion of a named Internet hierarchy tree. **5.** In the Internet, a portion of a name hierarchy tree. In SNA, an SSCP and the resources it controls.

Domain Name System **1.** A network database system that provides translation between host names and addresses. Abbreviated as DNS. **2.** Distributed name system used in the Internet.

Dot Pitch The distance between each of the phosphor dots or dot triads on the shadow mask of a color display monitor. These dots make up the image on the screen. The smaller the dot pitch, the tighter and crisper the image appears. Trinitron monitors are rated by stripe pitch, based on the space between vertical bars of color in the horizontally slotted grille.

Download The process of transferring information from the source computer to your computer.

DP Acronym for Data Processing.

Driver A software program that controls a physical computer device such as an NIC, printer, disk drive, or RAM disk.

DVI Acronym for Digital Video Interactive (q.v.).

Dynamic Address Resolution Use of an address resolution protocol to determine and store address information on demand. Abbreviated as ARP.

Dynamic Data Exchange A method introduced by Microsoft with MS Windows to link cell information into a master document, spreadsheet, or other compound process running within the same CPU processor and memory stack. The cell content is not altered or duplicated, merely temporarily inserted for the master. Abbreviated as DDE.

Dynamic Host Configuration Protocol IETF specification that enabled clients to borrow a uniquely assigned IP address for a short period. Abbreviated as DHCP.

E-mail Electronic mail. Computer network by which messages can be sent to others on the network.

Earnings Per Share The net (after tax) profit allocated per common share of a corporation. Abbreviated as EPS.

EBCDIC Acronym for Extended Binary Coded Decimal Interchange Code (q.v.).

ECMA Acronym for European Computer Manufacturers Association (q.v.) or General Assembly of European Computer Manufacturers Association.

EDI Acronym for Electronic Data Interchange (q.v.).

EDIFACT Acronym for Electronic Data Interchange For Administration, Commerce, And Transport (q.v.).

Electronic Cash A term describing the payment for transactions using digital money. It is an electronic payment but does not necessarily employ the direct bank-to-bank transfer of funds.

Electronic Data Interchange The electronic communication of operational data such as orders and invoices between organizations. Abbreviated as EDI.

Electronic Data Interchange For Administration, Commerce, And Transport   Group promulgating electronic data interchange standards. Abbreviated as EDIFACT.

Electronic Key Exchange   A security procedure by which two entities establish secret keys used to encrypt and decrypt data exchanged between them. The procedure used in CDPD is the algorithm developed by Diffie and Hellman.

Electronic Mail   Widely used network application in which mail messages are transmitted electronically between end users over various types of networks using various network protocols. Abbreviated as E-mail.

Electronic Payment Systems   Any payment system with an electronic or communication component that transmits a promise or transfers funds between accounts. Examples include CyberCash, ACH, EDI, and credit cards. Abbreviated as EPS.

Encryption   The processing of data under a secret key in such a way that the original data can only be determined by a recipient in possession of the key. The application of a specific algorithm to data so as to alter the appearance of the data to make it incomprehensible to those who might attempt to 'steal' the information. The process of decryption applies the algorithm in reverse to restore the data to its original appearance.

Encryption Key   The secret key used to perform the encryption process.

Enterprise Network   A campus or wide area network that services all (or most) organizational sites supporting multiple point-to-point routes and/or integrating voice, facsimile, data, and video into the same channel. A usually large, diverse network connecting most major points in a company. Differs from WAN in that it is typically private and contained within a single organization.

EPS   Acronym for Electronic Payment Systems (q.v.) and also Earnings Per Share (q.v.).

European Computer Manufacturers Association   A group of European computer vendors that have done substantial OSI standardization work. Abbreviated as ECMA.

Event   Network message indicating operational irregularities in physical elements of a network or a response to the occurrence of a significant task, typically the completion of a request for information.

Extended Binary Coded Decimal Interchange Code   An 8-bit character code developed by IBM for data representation in their large mainframe computer systems. Abbreviated as EBCDIC, pronounced as "eb-see-dic."

False Light   A verbal or written statement or an action performed with or without intent that devalues or misrepresents a person or party.

Facsimile   The device or process for transmitting a document as a line-scanned image over standard telephone lines. Abbreviated as FAX.

FAX   Acronym for Facsimile (q.v.).

FCC   Acronym for Federal Communications Commission.

FDDI   Acronym for Fiber Data Distributed Interchange (q.v.).

Fiber Data Distributed Interchange   Optical fiber network based upon the ANSI X3.139, X3.148, X3.166, X3.184, X3.186, or X3T9.5 specifications. FDDI provides 125 Mbps signal rate with 4 bits encoded into 5-bit format for a 100-Mbit/s transmission rate. It functions on single or dual ring and star network with a maximum circumference of 250 km, although copper-based hardware is an option. See also CDDI, SDDI, TP-DDI, and TP PMD. Abbreviated as FDDI.

Filter   Generally, a process or device that screens incoming information for certain characteristics, allowing a subset of that information to pass through.

Firewall   1. A mechanism to protect network stations, subnetworks, and channels from complete failure caused by a single point. **2.** A device, mechanism, bridge, router, or gateway that prevents unauthorized access by hackers, crackers, vandals, and employees from private network services and data. **3.** A moat between public data networks (i.e., CompuServe, Internet, and public data carrier networks) and the enterprise network.

Fixed Palette   A preestablished palette that does not change. When a fixed-palette web browser (such as Navigator) views an image, it will convert the original colors in that image to something else, even a color of a different shade or consistency.

Fractional T-1   One or more of the 24 separate 64-Kbps circuits in T-1. Abbreviated as FT-1.

Frame   1. A self-contained group of bits representing data and control information. The control information usually includes source and destination addressing, sequencing, flow control, preamble, delay, and error control information at different protocol levels. **2.** A frame may be a packet with framing bits for preamble and delay. **3.** Data transmission units for FDDI. The terms packet, Datagram, segment, and message are also used to describe logical information groupings at various layers of the OSI reference model and in various technology circles. **4.** A separated area in a web browser containing a unique grouping of information. See also Pane.

Freeware   Computer applications that are available on disk or by downloading from bulletin board services for which no cost or compensation is requested. See also Shareware.

Front End Processor   Device or board that provides network interface capabilities for a networked device. In SNA, typically an IBM 3742 device. The unit that attaches to a host or mainframe (as in IBM) and provides communication services with terminals, printers, and PCs. Abbreviated as FEP.

FT-1   Acronym for Fractional T-1 (q.v.).

FTP   Acronym for File Transfer Protocol.

Fulfillment   The physical process of completing a sales transaction by picking inventory, packing, and shipping an order. Also called Order Fulfillment.

Gateway   1. A device that routes information from one network to another. It often provides an interface between dissimilar networks and provides protocol translation between the networks, such as SNA and TCP/IP or IPX/SPX. A gateway is also a software connection between different networks; however, this meaning is not implied in this book. The gateway provides service at levels 1 through 7 of the OSI reference model. See also Bridge and Router. **2.** In the IP community, an older term referring to a routing device. Today, the term *router* is used to describe nodes that perform this function, and gateway refers to a special purpose device that performs a Layer 7 conversion of information from one protocol stack to another.

GIS   Acronym for Graphical Information System.

Graphical Information System   Generally refers to a database of graphical data, although it also can refer to an image storage and retrieval system. Abbreviated as GIS.

Graphical User Interface   A reference to application display shells including DOSSHELL, OS/2 Program Manager, MS Windows, Solaris, and X Windows. Abbreviated as GUI.

GUI   Acronym for Graphical User Interface (q.v.).

Hit   Any of three loose definitions describing access to a web site. **1.** Any file access whatsoever to a site (meaningless statistic). **2.** A presentation or refresh of a home page. **3.** Access by a specified person to a website (audited).

Hit Rate   A ratio found by dividing the number of times requested information is found in the cache by the number of requests made to the storage disk (or CD-ROM).

Hop   **1.** A routing of a cell, frame, or packet through a network device and/or transmission channel based on destination address information. **2.** The passage of a packet through one bridge, router, switch, or gateway.

Hop Count   A routing metric used to measure the distance between a source and a destination.

Hotspot   An area of an image that when selected by the user (usually by clicking with a mouse) performs an action in the application. Commonly, hotspots are represented graphically by buttons, but they may be hidden to allow the user to explore the image to discover what happens.

HSL   Acronym for Hue, Saturation, and Luminance (q.v.).

HTML   Acronym for HyperText Markup Language (q.v.).

HTTP   Acronym for HyperText Transport Protocol (q.v.).

Hue, Saturation, and Luminance   One method of representing a particular color. The luminance represents the brightness of the color and the hue and saturation give the rest of the color information. This method is similar to what is used by NTSC television signals. Black and white TVs just decode the luminance portion of the signal to present a picture while color TVs decode the entire signal. Abbreviated as HSL.

Hyperlink   A color-coded text or designated image hotspot in an HTML document that moves a user to the document reference or activity matched to that link. Standard color code is red for link and turns to purple when a user has previously selected that link.

HyperText Markup Language   A hypertext markup language used by WWW clients to format and present information.

HyperText Transport Protocol   An application-level protocol supporting the typing and negotiation of data representation independent of the systems for platforms.

IEEE   Acronym for the Institute for Electrical and Electronic Engineers (q.v.).

IETF   Acronym for Internet Engineering Task Force (q.v.).

Imaging   The process of creating and manipulating data for visual presentation and storage.

Indeo Video   Intel algorithm for the symmetric compression of video using scalable playback based upon hardware capabilities. See also CODEC.

Inside Wiring   Wiring that is done from the point of demarcation to the jack in the wall where the line terminates.

Institute for Electrical and Electronic Engineers   A membership-based organization based in New York City that creates and publishes technical specifications and scientific publications. Abbreviated as IEEE.

Integrated Services Digital Network   A limited set of standard interfaces to a digital communications network defined by the ITU (CCITT). A network for carrying data, voice, and video on digital circuits. It provides transmission in real time for interactive and multimedia applications and includes graphical communications interfaces. Communication protocols proposed by telephone companies to permit telephone networks to carry data, voice, and other source material. See also BRI and PRI. A dial-up common digital carrier service supporting switched service, basic rate interface-two directional channels at 56 Kbits/s each, and a separate out-of-band bearer control channel at 16 Mbps and multirate services. Abbreviated as ISDN.

Interconnection   Junction (telecommunication) connecting two communication carriers, such as between cellular and land line networks allowing mutual access by customers to each carrier's network. The interface between a cellular carrier and the local land line network, allowing calls to originate in one and terminate in the other.

Interconnectivity   The process where different network protocols, hardware, and host mainframe systems can attach to each other for transferring data.

Interface   A device that connects equipment of different types for mutual access. Generally, this refers to computer software and hardware that enable disks and other storage devices to communicate with a computer. In networking, an interface translates different protocols so that different types of computers can communicate together. In the OSI model, the interface is the method of passing data between layers on one device.

International Standards Organization   The standards-making body responsible for OSI, a set of communications standards aimed at global interoperability. The United States is one of 75 member countries. Abbreviated as ISO.

International Telecommunications Union   Previously named the CCITT (Comite Consultatif International Telegraphique et Telephonique). Leading group to develop telecommunications standards. Abbreviated as ITU.

International Telecommunications Union-Telecommunications Standards Sector   Formerly, the Consultative Committee for International Telephone and Telegraph (CCITT), this international organization makes recommendations for networking standards like X.25, X.400, and facsimile data compression standards. Abbreviated as ITU-TSS or ITU-T.

Internet   A collection of two or more disparate networks tied together via a common protocol. More specifically, it refers to the global Internet of IP-linked computer networks that were developed from the original Defense Advanced Research Projects Agency's (DARPA's) ARPAnet.

Internet Activities Board   The Internet steering committee now represented by the Internet Engineering Task Force (q.v.). Abbreviated as IAB.

Internet Address   An address applied at the TCP/IP protocol layer to differentiate network nodes from each other. This is in addition to the Ethernet Address.

Internet Control Message Protocol   Subprotocol of IP at the network layer; allows IP to exchange control information with other IP machines. It is also used with PING and Trace.

Internet Engineering Task Force   The standards-making body for the Internet; the arbiter of TCP/IP standards, including SNMP, and the IAB task force consisting of over 40 groups responsible for addressing short-term Internet engineering issues. Abbreviated as IETF.

Internet Protocol   A Layer 3 (network layer) protocol that contains addressing information and some control information that allows packets to be routed. Documented in RFC 791. See Transaction Control Protocol/Internet Protocol. Abbreviated as IP.

Internet Research Task Force   A community of network researchers with an internetwork focus. Board is governed by the Internet Research Steering Group (IRSG). Abbreviated as IRTF.

Internet Service Provider   The organization (usually commercial) providing dial-up and leased connections to the Internet.

Internetwork   A collection of networks interconnected by routers that functions (generally) as a single network. Sometimes called an internet, which is not to be confused with the Internet.

Internetworking   General term used to refer to the industry that has arisen around the problem of connecting networks. The term can refer to products, procedures, and technologies.

Interoperability   The process by which different network protocols, network hardware, and host mainframe systems can process data together.

Intranet   The use of Internet tools, particularly a uniform browser interface, for access to organizational information and databases.

IP   Acronym for Internet Protocol (q.v.).

IP address   See Internet Address.

ISDN   Acronym for Integrated Services Digital Network (q.v.).

ISP   Acronym for Internet Service Provider (q.v.).

ITU-TSS   Acronym for International Telecommunications Union-Telecommunications Standards Sector (q.v.).

Joint Photographic Experts Group   A standards committee for still images. Abbreviated as JPEG.

JPEG   Acronym for Joint Photographic Experts Group (q.v.).

Key Exchange   A procedure by which the value of a key is shared between two or more parties.

Key Generation   The process of creating a key.

Key Management   The rules and procedures governing the creation, distribution, and replacement of keys.

LAN   Acronym for Local Area Network (q.v.).

Latency   **1.** The waiting time for a station desiring to transmit on the network. **2.** The delay or process time that prevents completion of a task. Latency usually refers to the lag between request for delivery of data over the network and its actual reception. **3.** The period after a request has been made for service and before it is fulfilled. **4.** The amount of time between when a device requests access to a network and when it is granted permission to transmit.

Leased Line   **1.** A dedicated common carrier circuit providing point-to-point or multipoint network connection. Also called a private line. **2.** An open-pipe communications circuit reserved for the permanent and private use of a customer.

Libel   A verbal or written statement or an action that presents false information.

Line   **1.** The individual telephone line number within a central office. Thus, a full 10-digit telephone number can be represented as NPA or NXX-LINE. **2.** Generally, another word for link. In SNA, a connection to the network.

Load Balancing   **1.** A technique to equalize the workload over peer and client network components. This includes workstations, storage disks, servers, network connectivity devices (such as bridges, routers, gateways, and switches), and network transmission channels. **2.** In routing, the ability of a router to distribute traffic over all its network ports that are the same distance from the destination address. Good algorithms use both line speed and reliability information. Load balancing increases the utilization of network segments, thus increasing effective network bandwidth.

Local Area Network   A network limited in size to a floor, building, or city block. This usually services from 2 to 100 users. Abbreviated as LAN.

Local Loop   The line from a telephone subscriber's premises to the telephone company central office (CO).

Loop Back Test   A test for faults over a transmission medium where received data is returned to the sending point (thus traveling a loop) and compared with the data sent.

Malice   A verbal or written statement or an action performed with intent to do harm.

MB   Abbreviation for a megabyte (1024 kilobytes) of memory or disk space.

Mbps   Acronym for Megabytes (1,000,000 $\times$ 8 bits) per second. Not a binary measurement.

Medium   **1.** The physical material used to transmit the network transmission signal. It is usually either some form of copper wire or optical fiber. However, wireless networks use infrared, microwave, or radio frequency signals through the ambient air as the medium. **2.** A reference to a data storage device such as a hard disk, tape unit, or CD-ROM.

Megabits Per Second   The number of millions of bits transferred per second.

Megabytes Per Second   The number of millions of bytes transferred per second. Abbreviated as Mbps.

Message   **1.** Any cell, frame, or packet containing a response to a LAN-type network request, process, activity, or network management operation. **2.** A PDU of any defined format and purpose. **3.** An application layer logical grouping of information.

Metadata   Information and descriptions about the data stored in a database.

Middleware   Software that manages network processes.

MIDI   Reference to the General MIDI specification.

Modem   Acronym for Modulator-Demodulator.

Monopoly   When one party controls a commodity or service in a marketplace.

Motion Pictures Experts Group   A standards committee for motion video.

MPEG   Acronym for Motion Picture Experts Group (q.v.).

National Center for Supercomputing Applications   Organization charted for developing new users and applications for computing technology, including the Internet, VRML, and other evolving technologies and transmission media.

National Computer Security Association   A nonprofit group providing security-related conferences, training, testing, research, product certification, and consulting to users and vendors.

Natural Image   As defined by this technical note, an image that has many changes in color from pixel to pixel. Contrast this with computer image.

NCSA   Acronym for the National Computer Security Association and the National Center for Supercomputing Applications.

NetBEUI   Acronym for NetBIOS Extended User Interface (q.v.).

NetBIOS   Acronym for Network Basic Input Output System.

NetBIOS Extended User Interface   A simple (nonroutable) network protocol introduced by IBM PC LAN and used extensively by Microsoft (LAN Manager and NTAS). It is not suitable for the enterprise network so it must be translated or encapsulated. Abbreviated as NetBEUI.

Network Address   Also called a protocol address, a network layer address referring to a logical, rather than a physical device.

Network Operating System   **1.** A platform for networking services that combines operating system software with network access. This is typically not application software but rather an integrated operating system. **2.** The software required to control and connect stations into a functioning network conforming to protocol and providing a logical platform for sharing resources. Abbreviated as NOS.

NIST   Acronym for National Institute of Standards and Technology.

Node   **1.** A logical, nonphysical interconnection to the network that supports computer workstations or other types of physical devices on a network that participates in communication. **2.** Alternatively, a node may connect to a fan-out unit providing network access for many devices. A device might be a terminal server or a shared peripheral such as a file server, printer, or plotter.

Normalization   The process of transforming a set of data from chaos to an orderly structure that can be manipulated efficiently in a relational database.

NOS   Acronym for Network Operating System.

Object   **1.** Anything that you can manipulate, such as a table, field, or form. **2.** A distinct type of management information or variable for a network component. For example, the on/off status of a router is an object. In SNMP, MIB objects can be read (Get objects) or read and written (Get and Set objects). Operators can manipulate these objects to gather information and change configurations.

OCR   Acronym for Optical Character Recognition.

ODBC   Acronym for Open Database Connectivity.

Open Database Connectivity A set of interconnectivity and interoperability standards that allows various database products to exchange data with one another. Abbreviated as ODBC.

Open Form Markup Language Caere's Corporation's document markup language to store documents for conversion into paper formats, HTML, and forms.

Operating System The software required to control basic computer operations (such as disk access, screen display, and computation). Abbreviated as OS.

Order Fulfillment The physical process of completing a sales transaction by picking inventory, packing, and shipping an order. Also called Fulfillment.

O/R Name The distinguished name of an originator or a recipient. An originator provides a message content and (at least one) recipient O/R Name when it wishes to send a message.

OS Acronym for Operating System (q.v.).

Overhead CPU, disk processing, and/or network channel bandwidth allocated to the processing and/or packaging of network data.

Packet Internet Groper A protocol request to poll a subset of network stations for an active status. Refers to the ICMP echo message and its reply. Often used to test the reachability of a network device. Abbreviated as PING.

Palette In Windows, a data structure defining the colors used in a bitmap image.

Pane A separated area in a web browser containing a unique grouping of information. See also Frame.

Paradigm In programming, an established coding model or structure.

Perl Acronym for Practical Extraction and Reporting Language.

Persistence A statistical term refering to a protocol's method of accessing the network. Ethernet is persistent in transmitting, while other protocols are nonpersistent and wait for a permission token.

Persistent Client-state HTTP Cookies An HTTP protocol adding persistence to web applications with storage of user names, configurations, and preferences between sessions. Specification is http://www.netscape.com/newsref/std/cookie_spec.html.

PING Abbreviation for Packet Internet Groper (q.v.).

Plain Old Telephone Service The capability afforded by a rotary dial telephone and an electro-mechanical central office. Standard analog telephone service used by many telephone companies throughout the United States. Abbreviated as POTS.

Point-Of-Presence The physical access point for a telecommunication service, usually a central office, for T-1, ISDN, frame relay, ATM, and other digital services. The issue of the point-of-presence is that many services are not available in all markets, and the connection may not be economically feasible or locally available. Abbreviated as POP.

POP Acronym for Point-Of-Presence (q.v.).

POTS Acronym for Plain Old Telephone Service (q.v.).

PPP Acronym for Point-to-Point Protocol.

Premise Wiring   A telecommunications and data communications wiring infrastructure that embodies the concept of flexible, recyclable, reconfigurable, and reusable modular components centered around a wiring closet.

PRI   Acronym for Primary Rate Interface (q.v.)

Primary Rate Interface   ISDN interface to primary rate access, which is a single 64-Kbps D channel plus 23 (in the case of T-1) or 30 (in the case of E-1) B channels for voice and/or data—the equivalent of one European E-1 link. Contrast with Basic Rate Interface, B-ISDN, and ISDN. The interface connects high-volume PBX trunks or client-side switches to the central office facilities. Abbreviated as PRI.

Protocol   A formal set of rules by which computers can communicate, including session initiation, transmission maintenance, and termination.

Protocol Address   A network address.

Protocol Analyzer   Test equipment that transmits, receives, and captures Ethernet packets to verify proper network operation.

Public Corporate Web Service   The device providing web services to the world.

Public Domain   Ownership is relinquished totally or under specified conditions for material otherwise protected by copyright laws.

Query   Message used (usually in a request-response protocol) to inquire about the value of some variable or set of variables.

RAID   Acronym for Redundant Arrays Of Inexpensive Disks.

RBOC   Acronym for Regional Bell Operating Company. See Bell Operating Companies.

Recipient   Used in the context of Message Store And Forward. A person or computer application that receives a message. See also O/R Name.

Record   In the case of formatted data fields, a record is a string of bytes handled as an entity by the Subscriber Identity Module (SIM), containing application elementary data. Records are always of the same length in a specific data field. A record may be selected by its number (position) in the data field, or by searching throughout the data field using the beginning of the record as an argument.

Referencial Integrity   A set of rules that determines the behavior of two linked tables. When referencial integrity is enforced, you can enter a record in a child table only if there is a matching record in the parent table. Conversely, you can delete a record from a parent table only if there are no matching records in the child table.

Relational Database   A standard type of database where transactions are stored as parts of different records based on content and usage. A relational database can take any two or more files and generate a new view of the data. For example, a customer file and an order file can be joined to create a report listing all customers who purchased a particular product. See also DBMS.

Replication   A process by which a set of distinct physical backups of a database, set, or table are kept in synchrony by a distributed database. Replication is typically used for distributing routing tables, domain maps and tables, yellow page-type network information, mail address, user access rights, and distributed databases.

Replication Server   A process or device that duplicates and synchronizes databases, sets, or tables to other servers through a network environment.

Repository A generic term for the generalized data dictionary database system, which acts as a central store for information and out systems. IBM Repository Manager is a key element in early implementation stages of IBM SAA strategy with particular reference to AD/Cycle.

Resolution The number of pixels across and down the screen. Examples include 800 × 600, 1024 × 768, and 1600 × 1200. Higher resolutions produce noticeably sharper and smaller images.

RGB Red, green, blue. A color encoding method commonly used by computers. Compare this method to HSL and CMYK (See CMYK and Hue, Saturation, and Luminance).

Rollback A process that reverses changes made to a distributed or relational DBMS.

Route A path through an internetwork.

Router **1.** A device that interconnects networks that are either local area or wide area. **2.** A device providing intercommunication with multiple protocols. **3.** A device providing service at Level 3 of the OSI reference model. See also Bridge and Gateway. **4.** A router examines the network address of each packet. Those packets that contain a network address different from the originating PC's address are forwarded onto an adjoining network. Routers also have network management and filtering capabilities, and many newer ones incorporate bridging capabilities as well.

Run Length Encoding A common method for encoding streams of data with repeating patterns into a more space efficient representation. It is a common data compression method used for compressing entire disk volumes (as with Stacker), individual files (as with PKZIP), or the native MS Windows format for bitmapped images. Abbreviated as RLE.

Scanning The process of digitizing an image for inclusion within a web page.

Scrambling Code One key (of many) used to encrypt and decrypt data or voice. See also Scrambling Key.

Scrambling Key One code (of many) used to encrypt and decrypt data or voice. See also Scrambling Code.

Script A set of program commands used to automate routine computing tasks.

Secret Key A key whose value is not disclosed to unauthorized entities.

Secure Electronic Payment Protocol A security standard that defines security Internet transactions by credit card over public networks (abandoned by MasterCard International and Netscape Corporation). Refer to Secure Electronic Transactions. Abbreviated as SEPP.

Secure Electronic Transactions A security standard that defines security Internet transactions by credit card. Created by MasterCard International and VISA International. Abbreviated as SET.

Secure HyperText Transport Protocol Netscape Communications protocol for encrypting standard web page information.

Secure Socket Layer Netscape Communications encryption protocol for delivery of financial information. Abbreviated as SSL.

Secure Transaction Technology A security standard that defines security Internet transactions by credit card abandoned by VISA International and Microsoft Corporation. Refer to Secure Electronic Transactions.

Security The set of functions concerned with ensuring that only legitimate users of the network can use the network, and only in legitimate ways.

Security Threat Threats associated with message communication such as eavesdropping on messages transmitted over the air link.

SEPP Acronym for Secure Electronic Payment Protocol (q.v.).

Server A dedicated processor performing a function such as printing, file storage, or tape storage.

Service The facility provided to the user of an entity.

Service Mark A legal term defined by the U.S. Constitution extending the concepts of Copyright to logos, images, and symbols.

Session A logical connection with a host system. The session begins when you establish the communications link and ends when you terminate emulation and return to the OS.

SET Acronym for Secure Electronic Transactions (q.v.).

SGML Acronym for Standard Generalized Markup Language (q.v.).

Shareware Computer applications that are provided on disk or by downloading from bulletin board services for which payment is expected from the recipient if the software is used beyond a trial period.

Shopping Cart A metaphor for a persistent log (database or COOKIES) to track customer product selections and options that overcomes the stateless properties of web browsers and server software; necessary when purchasing merchandise from a cyberstore.

SHTTP Acronym for Secure HyperText Transport Protocol (q.v.).

SIM Acronym for Subscriber Identity Module (q.v.).

Simple Mail Transfer Protocol An Internet standard for transferring E-mail from host to host. It can handle only ASCII text mail messages. Abbreviated as SMTP.

Simple Network Management Protocol An IETF-defined protocol that runs natively on TCP/IP networks. Considered the de facto standard for network management, it is used to monitor the status of devices, but because of its lack of security, is rarely used to control network devices. Abbreviated as SNMP. See also Common network interface protocol.

Simple Network Management Protocol, version 2 The next generation of SNMP. It adds security (encryption and authentication), supports a hierarchical management scheme, and runs on network transports other than TCP/IP, including AppleTalk, IPX, and OSI. Abbreviated as SNMP-II or SNMP v2.

SMTP Acronym for Simple Mail Transfer Protocol (q.v.).

SNMP Acronym for Simple Network Management Protocol (q.v.).

SNMP-II Acronym for Simple Network Management Protocol, version 2 (q.v.).

SONET Acronym for Synchronous Optical Network.

Spam A fatty, salty, inexpensive canned pig by-product with limited nutritional value. The term is used as a reference to mass E-mailing on the Internet.

Spoofing   The process of sending a false or dummied acknowledgment signal in response to a request for status or receipt. Spoofing is typically applied for host transmission over LAN-type transmission networks or routers so that processes are not falsely terminated for lack of message response activity.

SSL   Acronym for Secure Socket Layer (q.v.).

Stateless   A term referring to the HTTP protocol and other protocols and processes that do not retain any historical information or log files describing what has transpired.

Subscriber Identity Module   A PROM, EPROM, or EEPROM chip used in CDPD to handle security identification and data related to a given subscriber. Other applications may exist in the removable module. Abbreviated as SIM.

Switched Multimegabit Digital Service   Any of a variety of switched digital services ranging from 1.544 megabits to 44.736 megabits per second (T-1 to T-3 speeds). Abbreviated as SMDS.

T-1   **1.** Bell technology referring to a 1.544 Mbps communications circuit provided by long-distance carriers for voice or data transmission through the telephone hierarchy. Since the required framing bits do not carry data, actual T-1 throughput is 1.536 Mbps. T-1 lines may be divided into 24 separate 64-Kbps channels. This circuit is common in North America. Elsewhere, the T-1 is superceded by the ITU-TTS designation DS-1. **2.** ....unications circuit provided by long-distance carriers in Europe

...........r leased line circuits with a signaling speed of ....ceded in Europe by the ITU (ITU-TTS) DS-3 desig-

..............cator that brackets text and images to designate formats (such ...., alignment, and placement).

.........age File Format**   An image file type common in scanning and desktop publishing. Abbreviated as TIF or TIFF.

TCP   Acronym for Transmission Control Protocol (q.v.).

TCP/IP   Acronym for Transaction Control Protocol/Internet protocol (q.v.).

Telco   A reference to modular telephone wiring.

Telecommunications   Term referring to communications (usually involving computer systems) over the telephone network.

Telnet   The virtual terminal protocol used by the Internet. It is part of the TCP/IP protocol suite that allows managers to control network devices, such as routers, remotely.

TFTP   Acronym for Trivial File Transfer Protocol (q.v.).

THC over X.25   Feature providing TCP/IP header compression over X.25 links, for purposes of link efficiency.

Throughput   **1.** A measurement of work accomplished. **2.** The volume of traffic that passes through a pathway or intersection. Typically, it refers to data communications packets or cells and is measured in packets/s, cells/s, or bits/s. **3.** Rate of information arriving at, and possibly passing through, a particular point in a network system.

TIFF   Acronym for Tagged Image File Format (q.v.).

TPS   Acronym for Transactions Per Second (q.v.).

Trade Secret   A legal term defined by the U.S. Office of Copyrights and Patents defining processes and designs not published or patented, and protected by a system of legal agreements and limited access information.

Trademark   A legal term defined by the U.S. Constitution extending the concepts of copyright to logos, images, and symbols.

Traffic   **1.** The communications carried by a system. **2.** A measure of network load, which refers to the frame transmission rate (frames per second or frames per hour).

Traffic Congestion   The situation in which data arrivals exceed delivery times and create performance problems.

Transaction Log   **1.** A list of activities or events on the enterprise network. **2.** A list of transactions performed against a DBMS.

Transactions Per Second   The number of discrete data entry, data update, and data requests processed by a system each second; a measurement of performance capacity or of work accomplished, generally applied to on-line transaction processing environments. Abbreviated as TPS.

Transmission   Any electronic or optical signal used for telecommunications or data communications to send a message.

Transaction Control Protocol/Internet Protocol   **1.** A complete implementation of this networking protocol includes Transaction Control Protocol (TCP), Internet Protocol (IP), Internetwork Control Message Protocol (ICMP), User Datagram Protocol (UDP), and Address Resolution Protocol (ARP). Standard applications are File Transfer Protocol (FTP), Simple Mail Transfer Protocol (SMTP), and TELNET, which provides a virtual terminal on any remote network system. **2.** Common communication protocol servicing the network and transport layers that provide transmission routing control and data transfer. This represents logical connectivity at levels 2 and 3 of the OSI reference model, although the protocol does not conform in fact to this model. Abbreviated as TCP/IP.

Transparent GIF   A subset of the original GIF file format that adds header information to the GIF image to indicate that a defined color will be masked by any background. This includes the GIF87e and GIF89a specification revisions.

Trivial File Transfer Protocol   A UNIX file transfer used by BOOTP and X terminals to send and receive control information. Based on UDP, it does its own data integrity checking and packet sequencing. Abbreviated as TFTP.

Trojan   See Computer Virus or Trojan Horse.

Trojan Horse   An innocuous-looking software program that may not do anything obvious or visually noticeable but is nonetheless designed to disable, bypass security or audit options, damage, or destroy computer hardware or read/write storage systems. Typically used by disgruntled employees to damage computer operations. See also Computer Virus.

Two-Phase Commit   A two-stage method to ensure that a transaction updates all files in a distributed or relational database environment. First, all DBMSs involved confirm that the data have been received and are recoverable. Second, each DBMS updates files. In the event that a failure interrupts an in-progress transaction, rollback restores the database to its state prior to the commit. The roll forward uses the transaction log to recover information committed before a transaction was interrupted and reapplies it to ensure database integrity and that the database reflects the true value of all records in a transaction.

UDP   Acronym for User Datagram Protocol (q.v.).

UDP/IP   Acronym for User Datagram Protocol/Internet Protocol (q.v.).

Uniform Resource Locator   The Internet address to a world wide web page or specific document by file transfer protocol. Abbreviated as URL.

Uninterruptable Power Supply   A backup power supply in case the main electrical source fails. Abbreviated as UPS.

UNIX   An operating system developed by Bell Laboratories for multitasking on mini-computers, and later on microcomputers and mainframes.

UNIX-to-UNIX Decode   A compression/decompression routine that converts binary files between ASCII text files and back. Abbreviated as uudecode.

UNIX-to-UNIX Encode   A compression/decompression routine that converts binary files between ASCII text files and back. Abbreviated as uuencode.

Upload   The process of transferring information from your computer to a remote destination computer.

UPS   Acronym for Uninterruptable Power Supply (q.v.).

URL   Acronym for Uniform Resource Locator (q.v.).

USENET   Initiated in 1979, one of the oldest and largest cooperative networks, with over 10,000 hosts and a quarter of a million users. Its primary service is a distributed conferencing service.

User   A user, as distinct from an end system, is an entity authorized to access a supplementary service.

User Datagram Protocol/Internet Protocol   A connectionless transport-layer protocol belonging to the Internet protocol family of the transmission control protocol for application-level data. An in-band, connectionless transmission for congestion management and information collection typically employed by bridges, routers, gateways, and Simple Network Management Protocol (SNMP). Abbreviated as UDP/IP.

uudecode   Acronym for UNIX-to-UNIX Decode (q.v.).

uuencode   Acronym for UNIX-to-UNIX Encode (q.v.).

Video Compression   A method for reducing the amount of information required to store and recall a frame of video. Compression is critical to delivering digital full-motion video to the user in the most effective manner (in terms of performance and storage costs).

Virtual Reality Modeling Language   A programming language extension to the Internet HTML and SGML web page construction tools for creating moving, three-dimensional views. Abbreviated as VRML.

VRML   Acronym for Virtual Reality Modeling Language (q.v.).

W3C   Acronym for the World Wide Web Consortium (q.v.).

WinSock   Microsoft Windows Sockets application programming interface (API) that defines a means by which IP sockets are mapped to the Windows environment.

Workstation   **1.** Any computer device. **2.** Any device on a network.

World Wide Web   An internet presentation space (domain) reserved for HTTP document transfer and presentation. Abbreviated as WWW.

World Wide Web Consortium   An international consortium of Internet tool developers and users defining Internet policies, standards, and the HTML and HTTP services.

WWW   Acronym for World Wide Web (q.v.).

Yellow Pages   A domain naming service for Unix. Abbreviated as YP.

YP   Acronym for Yellow Pages (q.v.).

Index